TENSEGRUS

TENSEGRUS
TOUCHPOINTS OF RELATIONSHIPS
VICTOR WAYNE CARLSON
MATTHEW JAMES CARLSON

The Carlson Leadership Group

To Cathy. A nurturer to those in need and
the inspiration for this book.

Table of Contents

Table of Contents

Introduction

Tensegrus: Touchpoints of Relationships

The quality of our important relationships determines the quality of our life.

I have met with countless people to whom I asked the question, "What does the quality of the important relationships in your life have to do with the quality of your life?" Overwhelmingly, the most common answer has been, "Everything!" Virtually all have agreed that if their important relationships are wonderful, their life is wonderful, and if their important relationships are miserable, their life is miserable. Having agreed, I ask people, "If having quality relationships is so important, shouldn't education and training on how to develop and sustain quality relationships be a foundational subject taught in grade school, middle school, high school, and college?" Again, they all agree. Then I ask, "How many of you have received education and training in how to develop quality relationships in grade school, middle school, high school, or college?" The usual response shows that very few have had formal education or training about developing or sustaining quality relationships. When we ask the few where they received their education and training, almost all say they got it at home or church. Unfortunately, the people who educated and trained them at home or church probably didn't have formal relationship education and training. It suggests that nearly everyone's education and training about relationships comes from imitating what they see from others or an apprenticeship in a family. Imitation and apprenticeships may not be the best approach considering divorce rates and the number of dissatisfied people in our society.

Lack of education and training on having quality relationships is a vast educational vacuum that results in widespread relationship catastrophes in our society. One of the chief complaints I heard from graduate students at the Lake Forest Graduate School of Management in Illinois was: "Wayne, this relationship information is just common sense. How come we are in graduate school before being exposed to detailed relationship information that we should have had throughout all our previous education!?" My answer was, "I don't know why; you should have had this information early in your life." Hundreds of my graduate students asked me, "When are you going to write the book that makes this information available to everyone?" Well, this book is the answer to that last question. Sorry, it has taken me so long to write it.

Too many people don't have the kind of relationships they desire, and they don't know how to change things effectively to get what they need. People strive to meet their unfulfilled needs, either in healthy or unhealthy ways. Unfortunately, too many people choose unhealthy ways because they lack the know-how.

Harvard's Grant and Glueck studied the physical and emotional well-being of 456 poor men in Boston from 1939 to 2014 and 268 male Harvard grads between 1939 and 1944. The conclusion was that true happiness doesn't come from the quantity of the relationships you have, but the quality. Having deep, stable, and emotionally reciprocal relationships contributes to brain health and reduces stress, aiding overall emotional well-being and eliminating physical pain. Robert Waldinger, the director of the Harvard study, said, "The clearest message that we get from this 75-year study is this: Good relationships keep us happier and healthier. Period. It's not just the number of friends you have, and it's not whether or not you're in a committed relationship," says Waldinger. "It's the quality of your close relationships that matters."

What is Tensegrus?

Tensegrus is a name we created for the "Tensegrus Spectrum of Relationships," which defines our perspective of general categories of relationships and specific types of relationships within each category. Our relationship spectrum displays a wide range of relationships from Soulmate to Enemy. Relationships are the current status between people due to the interplay of six Relationship Touchpoints that connect and work together to determine the characteristics of each type of relationship in the spectrum. This clarity of relationship characteristics enables people to diagnose relationships and the places to focus when they need changing.

"Tensegrus" is a term we derived from tensegrity. Tensegrity is a noun used in architecture and medicine. In architecture, it describes the stability, balance, and integrity of a structure in terms of how of all its interconnected parts respond to one another under tension. It is a term usually used to describe the level of soundness of suspended structures, like a suspension bridge. An architect may say, "The tensegrity of this bridge is very high," meaning that the bridge, as a whole structure, will withstand stress on any of its parts. It encompasses the notion that the framework is interconnected and anything that happens to one part impacts all the other parts. Architectural tensegrity describes how effectively all of the interconnected parts support one another.

In medicine, it implies the same concept (only in terms of the human body). Tensegrity in medicine refers to the "homeostasis" of the human body (the status, or balance, of internal bodily functions). In other words, it is the physiological balance between the skeletal structure of the body and all of the other parts (fascia) that connect all of the body. In Human Physiology 101, the various body parts and functions are explained in terms of "human body systems," like the skeletal system, central nervous system, cardiovascular system, endocrine system, respiratory system, muscular system, reproductive system, etc. We learned that all of these systems are connected and operate as partners. Our body's systems work as a team, in conjunction with one another. If each system is doing what it is supposed to, we have a healthy, fully-functioning body. In medical terms, our body's tensegrity would be excellent.

A "Tensegrus Relationship" is the state of a relationship fashioned from the interplay of six relationship touchpoints: Emotional States, Operating Modes, Personal Boundaries, Power, Values, and Commitment Levels. These Tensegrus Relationship Touchpoints do for relationships what tensegrity elements do for architecture and medicine. These Tensegrus Relationship "Touchpoints" are the building blocks of relationships.

Just as in medicine, we can educate ourselves in the functions of the human body to better understand and manage our body's health and homeostatic status. So too, we can educate ourselves in the Touchpoints of relationships to better understand developing and sustaining quality relationships. We would love it if everyone understood the Relationship Touchpoints and knew how to apply them to form healthy relationships. We believe that becoming knowledgeable and skillful with the Relationship Touchpoints will make a meaningful difference in your life.

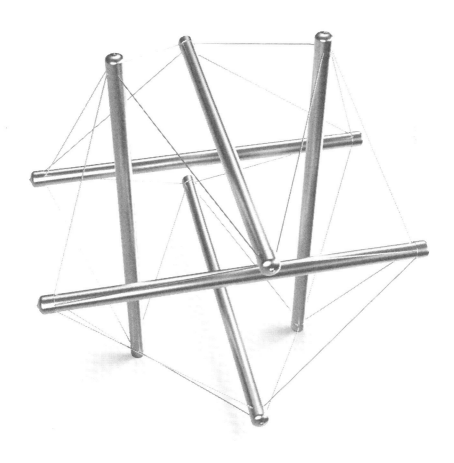

1

THE SPECTRUM

The Genesis of Relationships

When something brings people together, the potential for relationships exists. It could be school, a bar, social networks, a ball game, family, work, or a dance; virtually anything that causes people to meet can be the genesis for a relationship. Coming together puts people in contact with one another, which means an association has been made. All relationships begin as an association. Not all incidental associations will become relationships, but those that do, always start from a situation, cause, purpose, event, or anything that brought them together. Said another way, if we have no association, we will never have a relationship, but if we have come together for some reason and have established an association, a relationship is possible.

What happens after that first association determines the kind of relationships that develop. I say relationships rather than a relationship because relationships are dynamic; they change; a person can have many different types of relationships that emerge from initial associations. They can move in a positive direction and enhance your life or move in a negative direction and make your life miserable. The interaction of the Relationship Touchpoints determines the type of relationships that develop. While relationships that start positive tend to stay positive, they can shift course and move in a negative direction; it depends on how one is applying the Touchpoints.

In organisms, DNA contains the instructions needed to develop, survive, and reproduce. Relationship Touchpoints are like DNA elements for relationships. They determine how relationships develop, survive, and flourish or how they develop, struggle, and die. Each Touchpoint influences the type of relationship that develops, combining with all the other Touchpoints. They work together to determine our relationships – good or bad. There are six Relationship Touchpoints: Emotional States, Operating Modes, Personal Boundaries, Power, Values, and Levels of Commitment. Each Relationship Touchpoint has competencies we can use to operationalize them. We will explore each in detail, but first, we must understand the different Tensegrus relationships that the Touchpoints create.

We Determine Our Relationships

Relationships are the embodiment of how we connect and behave with others. The quality of our important relationships determines the quality of life. Important relationships are the ones from which we cannot walk away. If we can walk away, it indicates that they are no longer valuable enough to be considered important.

Think about it, when our most important relationships are fulfilling, we are fulfilled. When they are miserable, we are miserable. In New Market, Ontario, Canada, I counseled a 40-year-old man who was deeply dissatisfied. He explained that he had no relationship in his life that made him happy. His wife was a nagger, his kids were stupid and disobedient, his boss was an a** hole, and his co-workers were idiots. He was trying to find something (anything) that could change his life and make him happy. Religion frustrated him; doctors were stupid because they couldn't find anything wrong with him to explain his misery. Friends (he said he didn't have any) gave him dumb advice, which showed that they didn't understand what he was going through. They usually delivered useless platitudes like, "You need to start counting your blessings every time you feel miserable!"

After several sessions and a lot of listening, I asked him where he thought his misery came from and when it started. His answer came surprisingly quickly. "It all started with my dad. He's a f*****g a** hole. He destroyed my life." I asked what his dad did that destroyed his life, and he gave me a long list of offenses. I inquired when his dad had died to which he answered that he hadn't died but was still around messing with his life. He concluded that all his issues emanated from his father and that his troubles would vanish if his father changed.

I proposed his conclusion as a solution to his problems, "So, all we need to do is get your dad into counseling, fix him, and your life will become perfect? Right?" He offendedly queried, "How would that help me?" I summarized with, "Well, you told me that all your problems came from your dad and that if he changed, your issues would go away." He stated, "That's stupid!" Over time he finally came to accept that he blamed everyone, other than himself, for his misery and that looking to change everyone around him would not alter his unhappy perspective on life.

First, because people wouldn't change to make him happy, and second, if they did, it would benefit them, not him. His life began to change for the better when he examined his behavior, responses to situations, and interactions with others. Insight can be an excellent stepping stone for healing.

"We have met the enemy, and he is us."[1]

Taking personal responsibility for his feelings and circumstances provided a starting point for managing things he could control. He had a long journey ahead of him because he was learning an all-new set of principles and skills for living. His path was up and down, but his ability to connect, in healthy ways, with others improved. When we moved to England a couple of years later, he, at least, felt that his life was worth living and that his wife and kids were keepers.

I am a great fan of Dr. Viktor Frankl, an Austrian neurologist who wrote *Man's Search for Meaning* and the originator of Logotherapy.[2] Frankl founded his theory on the belief that humans are motivated by searching

---

1   Walt Kelly, cartoonist, *Pogo,* comic strip character.

2   Viktor Frankl, *Man's Search for Meaning* (Boston: Beacon Press, 1947).

for a life purpose; Logotherapy is the pursuit of that meaning for one's life. Frankl's theories were heavily influenced by his personal experiences of suffering and loss in Nazi concentration camps during World War II. He taught that three things give purpose (or meaning) to life:

1) Having someone you love or who loves you
2) Having a cause greater than yourself
3) How we deal with unavoidable tragedy

Loving and being loved is perhaps the greatest gift of life. Margaret Walkterhauser, a clinical psychologist on my staff at Janssen Pharmaceutica, once asked me if there was a moment in my life when I didn't feel loved. I, honestly, told her no, that I had felt loved every moment in my entire life. She said, "You are the richest person I have ever known!" I agree.

Having a cause greater than yourself brings light and energy to you and everyone around you. Self-sacrifice for the benefit of others is noble and engages the heads, hearts, and hands of all involved. Parents willing to give all they have to save a sick child gives purpose to their life. Soldiers dying on the battlefield to protect and save the lives of their brothers and sisters in arms provides meaning to life. Saving their comrades is more important than living.

How we deal with unavoidable tragedy highlights what is most important while still living. It's through the bad times that our purpose becomes clear. Caring for a dying loved one becomes so much more meaningful than the previous glory gained from business successes or trophies won in contests. Satisfying one another's needs, not with resentment, but with gratitude, fills the soul. Here, too, allowing our illness or personal tragedy to become a bridge for deeper and more personal connections gives purpose for tolerating the intolerable and enduring the unendurable. Sometimes we don't discover that until we face what appears to be an inevitable end. Maybe that's the test. Will we find courage, purpose, and meaning when facing impossible odds? Will that found meaning bring peace and resolution for all the suffering we had to endure?

As you can see, Dr. Frankl's theory, at its core, is about relationships. Our book is also about relationships. We want to define what they are, why they are important, and how to have wonderful, healthy, quality relationships that will bring joy to our life. Indeed, the quality of our important relationships determines the quality of our life. We want you to understand the different kinds of relationships in order to diagnose them and change them when a change would improve the quality of life.

The Tensegrus Relationship Spectrum

We will explore five categories of relationships and different kinds of relationships within each category.

Synergistic relationships are the most fulfilling relationships. Synergy means that the whole is greater than the sum of the parts. Here the focus is on the bonds developed from mutually beneficial relationships.

Associative relationships connect through common interests.

Command and Control relationships are all about power and control.

Mutually Destructive relationships are all about winning.

Indifference is the absence of relationships.

Categories of Relationships and Kinds of Relationships Within Each Category

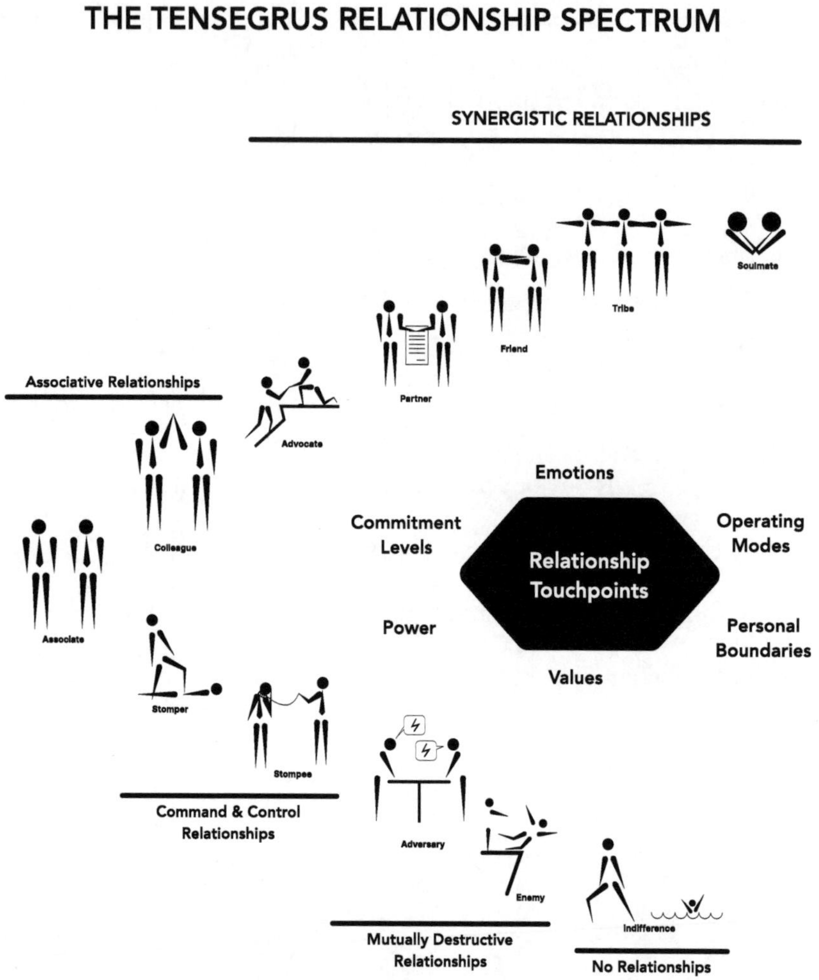

THE TENSEGRUS RELATIONSHIP SPECTRUM

SYNERGISTIC RELATIONSHIPS

Soulmate

Tribe

Friend

Partner

Advocate

Associative Relationships

Colleague

Associate

Stomper

Stompee

Command & Control
Relationships

Adversary

Enemy

Indifference

Mutually Destructive
Relationships

No Relationships

Emotions

Commitment
Levels

Relationship
Touchpoints

Operating
Modes

Power

Personal
Boundaries

Values

2

ASSOCIATIVE RELATIONSHIPS

THE TENSEGRUS RELATIONSHIP SPECTRUM

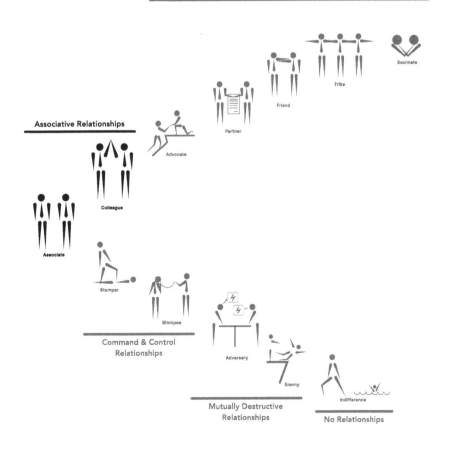

SYNERGISTIC RELATIONSHIPS

Associative Relationships

Soulmate

Tribe

Friend

Partner

Advocate

Colleague

Associate

Stomper

Stompee

Command & Control
Relationships

Adversary

Enemy

Indifference

Mutually Destructive
Relationships

No Relationships

Connected through a common purpose, interest, profession, system, society, or an association, these relationships tend to be inclusive.

All relationships begin due to an association of some kind. Think of middle school. The school (association) brought people together and, in a loose sense, we have an Associative Relationship with each other due to the school. However, as soon as we make a personal connection with someone, we embark on a possible deeper relationship. All associative relationships are casual until we find a common purpose.

Associative Relationships are linked through a common purpose and are usually members of organizations committed to advancing the interests of the same higher purpose. There are two categories within Associative Relationships: Colleagues and Associates. Colleagues tend to be more closely connected than do Associates. Being a Colleague is more intimate than being an Associate. The difference between the two may be in the eyes of the beholder. If someone considers us a Colleague, we are a Colleague. If they consider us an Associate, we are an Associate. We will attempt to clarify the nature of each.

Associate Relationships are generally inclusive.

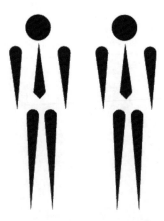

While Associate Relationships are still connected through a common purpose, interest, profession, system, society, or association, they tend to be more inclusive than exclusive. If we look at college basketball coaches, they would probably consider everyone who coaches college basketball as Colleagues, but everyone else who teaches other subjects at the college level as Associates. The Associate label suggests one as being an educator at the college level. In contrast, only those who coach basketball at the college level would be considered a Colleague. Collegial relationships suggest a degree of intimacy and a high level of commonality. Associate Relationships indicate a level of commonality, or uniformity, in purpose or interest but lack a sense of intimacy.

Business people consider other business people Associates. Union members consider other union members to be Associates. Members of the same union would consider themselves "Union Brothers and Sisters." People in the same industry working for different organizations would consider one another Associates. On the other hand, people working in the same professional specialty, albeit for different organizations, would probably be regarded as Colleagues. As the level of intimacy and personal association grows, a shift in the Associative Relationship can change; Associates can become Colleagues. It means that the degree of close or distant personal association becomes a significant factor in whether or not someone is considered a Colleague or an Associate.

For example, when I first started selling pharmaceuticals at McNeil Laboratories, they gave me a 100-page, self-starter, programmed learning book on anesthesia. (I didn't know shit from Shinola – a 1940s shoe polish. This was one of my dad's favorite expressions.) Yet, I was still expected to meet with anesthesiologists and sell them Sublimaze® (Fentanyl®, a tremendously powerful and short-acting narcotic) and Droperidol® (a long-acting antiemetic and anxiolytic medication – it minimized nausea and calmed patients' anxiety).

I went to Penrose Hospital in Colorado Springs. I ignored the no solicitation signs and went to the doctors' lounge near the operating suites and approached a doctor named Craig Wayne Larimer, Sr., and asked him if I could talk with him about our anesthesia products. He graciously accepted. After fumbling for about ten minutes in my attempts to sell him Sublimaze, I apologized for wasting his time, explaining that I didn't know enough about my products, or anesthesia, to sell him anything. He took pity on me and told me not to feel bad. Then he offered to teach me what I needed to know about anesthesia and how to talk with anesthesiologists logically that would cause them to look forward to seeing me. He called his chief resident and had him assign all of his cases to other doctors so he could spend the afternoon with me.

"Look," he said, "you can't teach anesthesiologists anything about your products. It will just piss them off; they know more about anesthesia products than you will ever know. Anesthesiologists are world-class pharmacologists. Nevertheless, I can teach you how your products can improve their anesthesia effectiveness in virtually all procedures." After a few hours of teaching me, he asked if I could join him at six a.m.

I arrived and watched him perform anesthesia on patients for eight hours and watched him fill out the anesthesia charts. He explained everything he was doing and why he was doing it. He explained the purpose of every drug he was using and its effect on the patient. At the end of the first day, he invited me to spend the next three days with him. I watched him perform anesthesia on many patients, and afterward, he would explain how my products could help in almost all anesthesia situations. He suggested that I take surgical charts to anesthesiologists and see how Fentanyl had improved the anesthesia. He further suggested that they provide me copies of their anesthesia charts (with the patient's name, doctor's name, and the hospital blacked out) to share their talents with other anesthesiologists. In his generosity, he offered to help me as much as I needed, for as long as I needed him. I am embarrassed to say that I probably called him three times a day for the next three weeks. He returned my call every time, in between anesthesia cases.

Fast forward six months, I was the leading anesthesia salesman in the country. All thanks to Dr. Larimer. I brought my sales manager to meet Dr. Larimer, and they both laughed at how this poor, sad young man was trying to sell something he knew nothing about. He told Fran, my manager, that he took pity and felt compelled to help me.

We continued to meet from time to time, and he would introduce me to his fellow practitioners as an anesthesia colleague. We became

Colleagues because he decided to help me as a teacher and mentor. He drew me close to him, and we developed an exclusive professional connection. In addition to being Colleagues (his label, not mine), we became one another's Advocate. He would connect me with other anesthesiologists and frequently invited me to attend anesthesia association events as his guest. In turn, I recommended him as a professional advisor to our company to benefit from his expertise. In return, the company could provide him opportunities for exposure to anesthesia associations from coast to coast. He did connect with the scientists from our company and became a pioneer in open-heart surgery using Fentanyl. Dr. Larimer was a remarkable, compassionate, and extraordinary man. He was the first board-certified anesthesiologist in Colorado. He served in the medical corps during World War II, part of which was administering aid to concentration camp survivors. His accomplishments are too numerous to mention, and his generous heart too large to explain. He died on May 20, 2015, at 96 years of age.

If Dr. Larimer hadn't taken pity and helped me that first day of selling anesthesia, my life and career would have been significantly different. My success as an anesthesia salesman was directly attributed to Dr. Larimer. His teachings became the prototype for all future anesthesia salespeople at J&J. I am forever grateful to a doctor, a great man, who rescheduled his entire afternoon to help support, an ignorant, inexperienced, young salesman and, in doing so, changed my life.

Colleague Relationships are generally exclusive.

Collegial relationships tend to be exclusive. Think of doctors who share the same medical specialty, like cardiovascular surgeons, anesthesiologists, etc. Being a Colleague suggests a commonality based on somewhat narrowly defined standards or qualifications. For example, members of the same Greek fraternity would consider themselves Colleagues but would likely view other fraternities' members as Associates. Teachers who teach in the same school may consider one another Colleagues while they would probably consider teachers from other schools to be Associates. Likewise, football players may see all players on their team as Colleagues and players on other teams as Associates. The same football player may see all quarterbacks, on any team, as Colleagues if they are also quarterbacks. Nuclear scientists who worked at the Manhattan Project (the project that built the first atomic bomb during World War II) considered all other nuclear scientists to be Colleagues.

In contrast, they considered other scientists to be Associates. The difference is the degree of connectedness and commonality felt toward the other party. If we say she is a Colleague, people will accept it. And, if we said she is an Associate, people would accept that, too. To some degree, we get to determine who are our Colleagues and who are our Associates. Still, the label we use may not be acceptable to them; particularly, if we consider them our Associates and they consider themselves our Colleagues.

Sometimes the differentiation between Collegial and Associative Relationships is determined by rank or status, such as presidents of organizations being Colleagues with other presidents and those of lesser stature being Associates, providing they are in the same field of endeavor. But there are exceptions.

When I was a young executive at Johnson & Johnson, I had the unique experience of interviewing Nautilus Submarine crew members. (They were all men; no women served on ships at the time.) Right off the bat, they made it clear to me that they considered everyone on their ship a Colleague, regardless of rank. It didn't take me too long to figure out why. You see, it takes a minimum of three people to bring a submarine home: one to steer, one to run the atomic reactor and engine, and one to navigate. (I am probably mistaken on the three roles, but not on the number required.) Every crew member is trained in all roles and functions of the ship. In theory, any three surviving members of the submarine crew would be able to bring the submarine home.

They were proud of being Submariners. Each had received countless hours of training that covered all the ship's functions at enormous educational costs. They would joke to me that they were million-dollar sailors. I found it amazing that if I had been blindfolded during the interviews, I would not have distinguished the officers from the enlisted men. Because they were all knowledgeable about every detail of engineering and operation of the submarine did not mean that rank didn't matter. The captain was still "The Captain," and he was king on board. Every sailor had assigned duties and functioned in their assigned role. Submariners followed the chain of command. Yet, anyone could perform in whatever capacity was required to bring the ship home if called upon. That is why they considered one another Colleagues.

3

SYNERGISTIC RELATIONSHIPS

THE TENSEGRUS RELATIONSHIP SPECTRUM

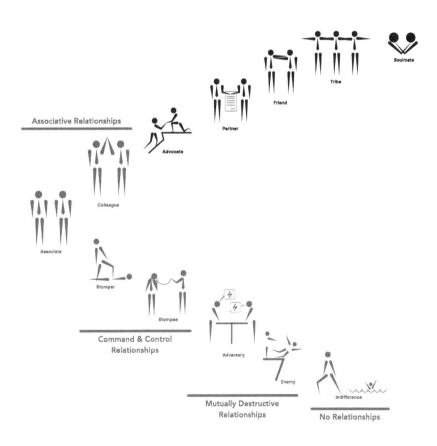

The focus is mutually beneficial relationship bonds.

Synergism: the interaction of elements that, when combined, produce a total effect that is greater than the sum of the individual parts.

It is fantastic to have Synergistic relationships; they are a source of self-validating, positive feelings. Each Synergistic relationship has unique benefits that differentiate it from other relationships. They encompass the people with whom we have close, positive interpersonal connections. The dimensions of Synergistic relationships can be singular, like business partners or friends. Still, they can also be multidimensional, like being a business partner, friend, advocate, and tribe member all at the same time.

Simply put, we can have multiple synergistic relationships with the same person. Our significant other can be our soulmate, tribe member, partner, friend, and advocate. However, we CANNOT be in different categories (Synergistic, Associative, Command and Control, Mutual Destructive, and Indifferent relationships) with the same person simultaneously. For example, Synergistic relationships cannot coexist with Associative, Command and Control, or Mutual Destructive relationships at the same time. However, we CAN be in different categories with the same person at other times. For example, we can have a Command and Control relationship at one moment, which shifts to a Mutually Destructive relationship later. Here, too, understand that relationships are not defined by intentions but by actions. We may want, desire, and intend to have a synergistic relationship, but we have a Command and Control relationship if we are controlling.

It seems to be a universal theme that we want to be judged for our intentions, but reality shows that others judge us for our actions. Even the courts judge us based on actions rather than intentions. As my dad used to say, "The road to hell is paved with good intentions." Bottom line, behavior trumps intentions. Likewise, relationships are defined by actions rather than intentions. Remember that we can simultaneously have multiple synergistic relationships with the same person. Still, we cannot have a Synergistic relationship with anyone when we have an Associative, Command and Control, or Mutual Destructive relationship with them.

Mary was a young, beautiful woman who said that she was going crazy because of her boyfriend. They had been dating seriously for a couple of years. She felt that she loved him and he loved her, but the relationship felt unstable and unpredictable. I asked her why? She explained that Jake, her boyfriend, made all the decisions told her how she was supposed to act and feel in virtually all situations. That generated mixed feelings in her and messed up her mind. The mixed feelings came from believing that he was protecting her because he loved her, which provided some security and a sense of personal worth. On the other hand, she didn't like the feeling of being controlled.

From what she told me, I observed that the relationship appeared to be very predictable and stable. She responded, "Exactly, so how come my mind is so messed up?" I asked if that was the stable and predictable relationship she wanted. She answered, "Yes, no, I don't know." I asked her to relax and forget about defending and explaining her current situation. "Just describe your fantasy relationship, your dream as it could be." She said that being in a loving relationship was most important and that marriage was part of that. She said that she was a smart, intelligent, and talented person and that she wanted the opportunity to achieve her potential. When asked to describe the ideal relationship she would hope to have with her future husband, she included the following characteristics: loving, caring, equal, sharing, partner, friend, respectful, and empathic. I found the empathic descriptor interesting and asked her to clarify that.

"Empathy means that he cares what I think and feel!" She came to her decision point, the moment of truth, when I asked, "Do you feel that that is the kind of future and relationship you are going to have with Jake?" "No, but I love him, and I know he loves me!" I observed that the kind of relationship she desired was in the Synergistic category but that her current one fit into the Command and Control category. When asked if she could be happy in a Command and Control relationship, she said she didn't think so. "But I don't want to leave him!" "What can I do?" Well, the obvious choice was to get Jake involved and see if what he wanted was aligned with what she wanted. They had to make some serious behavioral changes to have a synergistic soulmate relationship. If not, she would have to accept being controlled, or they would eventually slide toward a disconnection where both could act as they chose to. I agreed with Mary that it is tough to embrace our dreams or settle for the current relationship with mixed feelings and mind games. Incidentally, they broke up a few months later.

Advocate Relationships

Advocate: *a person who speaks or writes in support of a cause or a person, etc. People become advocates of people who meet or exceed their expectations. Advocates willingly recommend, promote, sponsor, or support a person, cause, or position.*

In the United Kingdom, the title "advocate" is the same as attorney in America. The English term makes more sense because it describes exactly what advocates do: support their clients. As a general rule, our willingness to advocate for someone depends on how effectively they are meeting or exceeding our positive expectations. When someone exceeds our high standards, it is easy to be an advocate for them. It is tough to advocate for someone who fails to meet our positive expectations. When we advocate for someone, we are willing to defend them, support them, testify for them, go to bat for them, etc. The advocate role is an honorable notion.

Think of advocates for civil rights, the poor, the needy; advocates are willing to utilize their talents and resources to benefit others. It becomes even more honorable if the support provided is because it is the right thing to do, rather than being based on the financial rewards they get from doing it.

When I was fourteen, I spent the summer working in the bean fields for Del Monte Canning Company. Because I was young and had the miserable job of stapling the upper and lower wires to the bean poles, I was the bottom man on the totem pole. Hence, a 16-year-old decided it was his job to make me miserable. His bullying was relentless. It reached my limit when he stapled my boot to the top of my foot as he was walking by. Besides the excruciating pain from pulling the inch-long staple from my foot, it also infuriated me! I was going to get even.

I found a piece of lumber broken into a shape similar to a baseball bat. As the bully was sitting against a tractor tire, eating a snack, I came at him with the full intent of knocking his head off with the broken board. Fortunately, or unfortunately, depending on your perspective, he saw me just as I swung the "bat," so it just glanced off his head. Well, that turned him into a raging bull. He chased me up and down the bean rows with a bump on his head and blood running down his cheek. If he had caught me, I don't think I would have survived. Providentially, as I turned the corner at the end of a bean row, with my pursuer close to catching me, Cleve Rodebush put out his arm and "clothes-lined" him. Cleve then kneeled beside him and told him that whatever he did to me, he would get ten times as much from him. Cleve watched him torment me and decided that he wouldn't let him do it again. He became my advocate and protector. That guy never bullied me again, although his looks continued to be terrifying. I was grateful for my advocate. Cleve Rodebush is still my hero. At the time, he was the quarterback for the football team at North Cache High School, so he was my double hero.

While we were living in the Chicago area, a young man and family friend named Chad became a hero and an advocate for a disabled young woman in their high school. Leslie walked with a limp due to one leg being shorter than the other, and she was shy and slow of speech. She was often the object of bullying and teasing from mean, insensitive jerks. One day, as Leslie was passing a group of guys in the hallway, they encircled and started taunting her and pushed her from one side of the circle to the other. She was a helpless victim. Within moments Chad, who, by the way, was a star football and basketball player, pushed his way through the circle and embraced Leslie. He turned to the persecutors and told them they should be ashamed of themselves. Chad informed them that Leslie was his friend and that whoever was unkind to her would have to answer to him.

He then walked her to her class. He, being her advocate, became her hero. Word spread quickly through the school and beyond. I heard about his chivalry by the end of the day. Chad's reputation as Leslie's advocate became legendary at the school. I asked him why he did it. He humbly said, "I simply did what anyone should have done." His advocacy changed Leslie's life too. Because she was now the acknowledged friend of Chad, she became an accepted person within the entire school.

Blessed are the advocates for the weak and disadvantaged; they are heroes. We can easily spot people who desperately need our advocacy if we look around. Be an advocate! Do it! Imagine the positive ripple effects!

Every synergistic relationship brings quality to our life. Our goal is to surround ourselves with Soulmate, Tribe, Friend, Partner, and Advocate Relationships.

Partner Relationships

Partner relationships are bound by common benefits, objectives, or obstacles.

They are characterized by agreement to work together for mutual gain.

Partners don't have to be friends, but it helps. A common reason a person seeks a partner (or partners) is that he can't do it alone, and the "partner" brings something to the table that is missing and essential. Likewise, multiple partners exist for the same reason – they each bring a missing element that is essential for success. Simply put, people become partners to capture opportunities, overcome obstacles, and receive expected benefits.

A partner relationship suggests a peer relationship while not necessarily an equal one. For example, one partner may have more equity in the organization and greater leverage in decision-making. It may be that an essential partner is not the majority partner. For example, in a partnership where the intellectual guru is subordinate to the person with the most stock, knowledge contributes more to the enterprise's success than the number of stock shares owned. Nevertheless, partnerships provide a means for combining talent, connections, and resources to capture opportunities otherwise unattainable. Great partnerships are rewarding, both economically and emotionally. When the right people come together, at the right time, in the right place, for the right opportunity, it is exhilarating!

I have been in great and bad partnerships; believe me; great partnerships are better! From personal experience, I have learned a few valuable lessons for me, although not necessarily for everyone. Lesson one: Never enter into a partnership where money is more important than relationships. Greed can bring disaster. Lesson two: Partner only with people who fill an essential need. I love partnering with Matt because he brings expertise to the table that I don't have. Lesson three: Value the people who see things from a different perspective than you do. They can see obstacles and challenges from another vantage point which may save your collective butts. But only if you listen to and respect the diverse perspectives. Lesson four: Dialogue-based communication is vital for successful partnerships; partnerships that lack open dialogue struggle.

I experienced a non-workable partnership with a partner who didn't like anyone to ask him questions. Questions made him defensive, and he put up barriers that made it nearly impossible to work through issues that required his expertise. Like too many others, he saw questions as accusatory; when partners get defensive, progress ceases. Partners should love questions; they are the means to deeper searches for understanding and truth. Questions and dialogue help us move from a level of understanding to ever greater levels of comprehension. I thank the Brazilians who taught me the wisdom contained in the phrase, "I understood, but I didn't comprehend." Levels of comprehension can expand endlessly. Lesson five: Partnerships founded on a higher purpose than self-interest provide the genesis for passion and internalized commitment. The energy and direction that serve a higher purpose make the seemingly impossible possible.

Great partnerships enrich experiences and relationships. As we write this book, my son and I refine my life's work that has focused on relationships. Diving into writing has caused a resurfacing of joyful and painful experiences that are being relived, analyzed, and captured to benefit our family and, I hope, for all readers. It is, for me, emancipating my history and life learnings. As a result of this partnership, we've experienced moments of Light, Energy, and Edification. It is indeed a marvelous bonding experience and a synergistic one where the total results are greater than the sum of our individual contributions.

Great Partnerships

In my life, when I think of great partnerships, first of all, I think of my wife, Lois; we complement one another. Our differences keep life exciting, but time seems to make the differences unimportant, or in some ways, charming. The other great partnership I have had in business is with Dale Karren. Together we founded Petrous, a consulting company. We are pretty different. He is an accounting major who started working for one of the "Big Five" accounting firms. I was a pre-law and social studies education major who began as a salesman for McNeil, a J&J company. He is an intuitive problem solver and decision-maker, whereas I am a deductive problem solver and decision-maker. He is an internal processor, whereas I am an external processor. What I mean by that is that he prefers to analyze information and data by himself to come to a conclusion before he discusses it with others. In contrast, I prefer to discuss it with others to arrive at a conclusion. You can imagine the frustration created in both of us until we learned how to use our differences for mutual advantage.

He loves the vision, mission, objectives, and action plans of consulting. I love the leadership, performance management, and relationship-building side of consulting. Thankfully, the companies we consulted with found value in both our loves. We partnered for approximately seventeen years, providing services to many great organizations, like KPMG, AstraZeneca, Abbott Laboratories, and Sears. Gratefully, we quickly became intimate friends as well as business partners. It was a great partnership because it aligned with all the lessons I shared above.

Bad Partnerships

I experienced a nightmare partnership experience with an organization I co-founded called MyGym. This horrible experience was the basis for the partnership lessons learned and listed here. MyGym was a home exercise product that combined a step platform with surgical tubing bands placed strategically around the platform. It allowed people to do virtually all the exercises that people could do on a full-size universal gym. The great part was that people could buy it for a price of approximately $150 rather than thousands of dollars. It was a great concept devised by a friend of my son Matt. He pitched Dale and me on the concept, and we decided to become partners with him and bring it to the marketplace. We built operating models to test the concept. Later, we found manufacturers in Kansas who had the blow molding machinery and capability to design and manufacture the molds. We developed a business plan and gathered investors to launch marketing efforts. We went to India and China to find suppliers for the tubing. While on a flight to Hong Kong, we serendipitously found a Nationalist Chinese manufacturer who could design, produce, and ship products to us for 60% of the price of our Kansas manufacturer. To make a long story short, we successfully launched the product on TV through telemarketing and were successful enough to attract Walmart's attention.

Walmart test-marketed the product and gave us a contract for 70,000 units, renewable semi-annually or quarterly if the product sold well. Once product success seemed in the bag, the originator of the MyGym concept, who had been a noncontributing partner, decided to sue us for all the product rights. We won the suit but lost our contract with Walmart, which dumped us when they discovered an internal company legal dispute. We worked for two years without pay, so Dale and I walked away. Greed destroyed a tremendous opportunity. Money, to the concept originator, was more important than relationships. He tried to continue without the investors and us, but after stiffing the Chinese manufacturer for tens of thousands of dollars he, and the company, disappeared. As you can see, he brought nothing to the partnership except the original concept, which was a lousy basis for a business partnership.

Friend Relationships

Friend: A person attached to another by feelings of affection or personal regard, who are bound by mutual trust, respect, and satisfying emotional connection.

Friend relationships are similar to tribe member relationships, although they may range from many to only one. I have friends who have very different perspectives on life than mine. Their lifestyle is vastly different, as well. But putting our differences aside, we like each other. Sometimes the friendship is enhanced by our differences. Friends provide satisfying emotional connections. One thing about friends is that there is always a bond of mutual trust and respect. Friends have each other's back. In my mind, friendship is more emotional than philosophical; I can't think of any close friendships that I can describe philosophically, but I can certainly see them emotionally. Mark is fun, funny, and entertaining. Margo is a fantastic artist who charms people with her flip chart story drawings. You get the point.

Friendship satisfies a very primal need within all of us. Everyone has a need from birth to connect with others. We get approbation from having friends. We get love, support, a community; it just feels good to get validation that we matter. Friends provide that validation; we are liked and loved and are OK just as we are.

My youngest brother, Moge (Morgan), had a knot-head friend named Mike, you know, really irresponsible. He didn't do well in school, but he was my youngest brother's best friend. He borrowed my brother's motorcycle and wrecked it. I asked Moge, "How can you put up with his crap?" He responded calmly, "He is my friend." Mike was wheel-less at one point in his life, so my parents gave him one of their old cars. True to form, Mike ran a blockade at a train crossing, and the train hit him. He died. To Moge, it didn't matter that he was a knot-head; he was his best friend.

Friendships encompass a wide range, from casual to intimate. Casual friends are lovely to have, but they are like the seasons; they come and go, they provide a change of climate and offer a span of freshness. I have many casual friends, high school classmates who I see at class reunions every five years. We golf a couple of times per year with some of the closer ones. We connect through the internet with others, which affords a 30,000-foot perspective into their lives. I don't want to diminish friendships of any sort; they provide an anchor to the past and churn up enjoyable memories, and maybe, a few embarrassing ones. I have neighbors who are friends. Their friendship is the basis of what might be called community. Good neighbors look out for one another and help when needed. Neighbor friends are great things to have. My neighbor friend, Don Clifford, got me playing golf a few years ago, and now we play a couple of times a week. I can blame him for becoming addicted to the game, which by the way, is going to keep me out of heaven.

Intimate friendship brings a deeper, richer, emotional, and spiritual connection. Boundaries become porous with intimate friends, allowing a free exchange of emotions and understanding. These friends are healers, applying salve to life's wounds. In a sense, they are often heroes, throwing out a lifeline when we are metaphorically drowning. Reed Taylor and Kasey Call are two friends who meet that standard with our family.

Reed Taylor was my mission companion in Santa Maria, Rio Grande do Sul, Brazil, for six months. After our missions, we attended Utah

State University, where our close association continued. In fact, for the last year and a half of schooling, Reed and his wife, Joselyn, and my wife, Lois, had adjoining apartments in a stately old house off-campus. Shortly after I returned from Brazil, I went to work in the oil fields of Alaska to earn funds for schooling, working for the summer then coming home. As it turned out, I got a job as a welder's Helper, which led to a painting supervisor position where I had painting crews on several oil rigs located offshore in the Cook Inlet by Kenai, Alaska. There I was making a mind-boggling salary of over $10.00 per hour compared to the $1.10 an hour I made working as a meat cutter near Utah State University. So, I decided to stay until I had saved enough money to pay for the next three years of college. However, before I ventured off to Alaska, I had fallen head-over-heels for a little beauty named Lois. I missed her too much to stay in Alaska by myself. So we got married in September of 1969, and I hauled her off to Kenai, Alaska. She became a bookkeeper for the same company I worked for, so we had double the salary with prospects of saving enough money to pay for the remainder of our undergraduate studies and possibly a big part of graduate school.

Here is where the story gets interesting. Bob, who worked for the same company, asked us to share his apartment. It reduced all of our living expenses, so we gladly accepted. As it turns out, he was a mover-and-a-shaker with all kinds of deals in the works. He drove a nice sports car and seemed to have the "Midas-touch" for business. He developed a deal to buy a grocery store in Kenai that would generate both cash and equity, and he invited us to partner with him. We shook hands and put all of our Alaska savings into the investment. The store did well, but the oil industry had entered hard times due to political battles, and work slowed down.

We decided it was time for Lois and me to head back to school. Bob said that he had a buyer for the store that would double the funds that we had invested and that he would handle the sale and send us our share of the profits. We went back to school at Utah State excited for the large sum of money that would pay for our education. Over the next six weeks, all communications with Bob ceased. I couldn't get in touch with him by any means that I could devise or afford. I called an uncle who lived in Kenai and asked him to find out what he could about the store. He reported that the store had been sold and was doing well with new management. At that moment, I realized Bob had betrayed our partnership and friendship. He had stolen our funds and moved on. Our dream to pay for higher education with our Alaska earnings vanished.

I was crushed, angry, and bitter. It affected all parts of my life. I stopped going to church, and although I kept going to school, I struggled to concentrate. My wife, family, and close friends, Reed and Joycelyn, were concerned about me. Reed came and talked with me. I told him, "I just want enough money to go back to Alaska and get my money and Bob!" He asked, "So it is all about the money?" I said, "Yes." He continued, "If you had the money, you would be OK and get your head on straight again?" "Yes."

The following Sunday evening, he and Jocelyn came to our apartment. When we sat down, he told me that he couldn't live with my pain and the thoughts of losing his special friend, me. Reed took out a folder that contained the deed to his family farm in Preston, Idaho. He said he was giving it to me to replace the funds I had lost in Alaska. We all cried. Of course, I wouldn't accept his farm, but his loving offer was a turning point in my life. He had tossed me a lifeline that enabled me to move on. I realized that I was a very rich man indeed!

Kasey Call was, and is, the best friend of my oldest son, Reed. They played high school volleyball and soccer together and are as connected as two friends can be. While Kasey's family lived only a mile away, he spent most of his time at our home in a suburb west of Chicago. He and the volleyball team ate lunch at our house every school day for four years. He slept at our house every Friday night, along with another twelve or so teenagers who were friends shared by Reed and his older sister Tiffany. We knew how many were staying over by counting the shoes at the front door. At midnight, the girls would go upstairs, and the boys would crash in the recreation area in the basement. They named themselves the "Posse." It was a fun and close group. They went to all the high school activities and dances as a group. It was interesting on prom night to take an individual picture of each girl, in her prom dress, one at a time, with every boy who was a Posse member. You might say that all the girls and boys had six to seven prom dates.

We came to regard Kasey as a member of our family, and he did likewise. Kasey graduated with honors and became a very successful oral surgeon. Reed's passion was always volleyball, and he focused his career on coaching volleyball and creating a nationally ranked volleyball club. Although living in different parts of the country, Kasey has remained close to Reed and our other kids, especially Matt, the tag-along younger brother. Matt and Reed became partners in the volleyball business. Kasey communicates several times a week with my boys, and they usually celebrate birthdays and holidays together, not to mention endless texting.

For years, all of our five of our children had kids, except Matt and Ashley (Matt's wife). Kasey and Jeanie (Kasey's wife) had three children as well. It was tough on Matt and Ashley to be the only childless couple, fifteen years and counting. They had tried the fertility specialist route a couple of times, resulting in nothing more than disappointment and exhausted resources. Kasey and Jeanie decided that Matt and Ashley needed the joy of parenthood as much as the rest of them, so they threw out a lifeline to fund a renewed effort with an expensive, highly-specialized fertility specialist. Because of Kasey and Jeanie, Matt and Ashley now have a baby girl, Isle. The willingness to provide tens of thousands of dollars to help friends have an opportunity for a baby sends a message of priceless love. Such is the nature of one special, intimate friendship.

Tribe Member Relationships

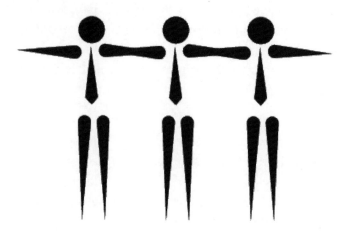

I like to think of tribe members as our dear sojourners in life's journey. They are important people with whom we link arms and share lives. Think of the people in our innermost circle; these are the people who have the same vision, values, and purpose in life. These are our loved ones, our best friends, the people we consider family (by blood or relationship). This inner circle seems united by a higher purpose. These people are an accepted, essential part of our life.

Most are loved ones and family members who share core perspectives passed generation to generation and passed family member to family member. They are the source of life philosophies drawn from shared stories and remembrances. Families tend to foster common goals, missions, and visions in life centered on shared values, standards, and operating principles. With people who we care deeply about and with whom we lived together, under the same roof, how could it be otherwise? Contrary to the family norms, even those who seem rebellious are making a back-handed validation of the same standards, which are the anchor points to which families adhere. Most families belong to the same political parties, aspire to the same educational standards, belong to the same church denominations, etc. Notice how frequently the children of professionals become professionals, and the union workers become union workers. Indeed, we tend to be "chips off the old block."

Interestingly, a new family couple becomes a combined culture derived from two different familial perspectives. If the perspectives are widely divergent, making a new cohesive unit may be turbulent and may take a long time, if ever, to accomplish. Indeed, the old saying that "opposites attract" is probably true, but it is also why the differences may ultimately doom the relationship. If the familial perspectives are similar, adjustments are easy, and the new family becomes simply a slightly modified extension of the families from which they came. In a general sense, it is accurate to say that your family is a tribe of which you are a member. Being a Tribe Member provides a foundation from which we gain identity and strength. Through the support of the tribe, during difficult times, people are nurtured and aided in overcoming adversity. I have come to believe that people, who love and are loved, can overcome virtually any relationship problem except incompatible, irreconcilable values. Hence, compatible values seem to be a vital element of all Tribe Member relationships.

In addition to families, there are other meaningful Tribe Member relationships. The potential exists in all walks of life and varieties of organizations. Think of sports, politics, religions, nations, businesses, medical associations, etc. Companies talk about establishing strong teams and aspire to do so. They recognize the supremacy of people with a common vision, purpose, values, standards, commitment, goals, and beliefs. And yet, developing extraordinary teams is challenging because organizations are the sum of countless people from innumerably different tribes with diverse perspectives and values. Even with such differences, Tribe Member relationships can and are developed. As the Apostle Paul said, "Many can become one." How does that happen? They must become one in purpose and standards. It happens with actions, not merely intentions. It requires time and effort to get buy-in from everyone who has the potential to become an intimate Tribe Member. A vision must be defined that encompasses all participants, along with the mission, goals, objectives, plans, processes, and especially absolute values. It is a refining process. It must permit each member to question, evaluate, and be a part of the consensus-building. People are converted and convert others.

Ideas and logic fly between participants until they start to congeal. When that congealing starts, the process becomes easier and faster because the consensus grows from areas of agreement rather than disagreement. As the areas of agreement increase, the areas of disagreement diminish. In processing the remaining areas of disagreement, people can discover additional areas of agreement if they discuss WHY they disagree rather than who is right and wrong.

When we accept people like intelligent, rational beings, we can accept their differing viewpoints as valid. It requires people to listen, hear, understand, and validate one another's perspectives. Many can become one.

At Johnson & Johnson, executives and management would convene every four or five years to have what we called a "J&J Credo Challenge." The Credo was crafted by General Robert Wood Johnson, the corporation's founder, as the core operating principles of the Johnson & Johnson companies. After he passed on, the company continued to grow and prosper, becoming, eventually, the largest health care company in the world. When I worked there, Jim Burke, the CEO, decided to either validate the J&J Credo, eliminate it, or change it. The challenges were two-day events, including hundreds of J&J leaders from all corners of the world. It was an expensive and talent-filled event, including many opinionated people. The Credo truly was challenged. But, in the end, after numerous Credo Challenges, the senior management changed only a few words and those for grammatical reasons. Leaders left the sessions committed to the Credo principles as the unconditional values and the basis for business decisions and actions. In the values section of the book, we will share an experience about J&J that exemplifies how seriously they believed in and adhered to the Credo, even in an existential crisis.

Our Credo (Johnson & Johnson)

We believe our first responsibility is to the patients, doctors and nurses, to mothers and fathers and all others who use our products and services. In meeting their needs everything we do must be of high quality. We must constantly strive to provide value, reduce our costs and maintain reasonable prices. Customers' orders must be serviced promptly and accurately. Our business partners must have an opportunity to make a fair profit.

We are responsible to our employees who work with us throughout the world. We must provide an inclusive work environment where each person must be considered as an individual. We must respect their diversity and dignity and recognize their merit. They must have a sense of security, fulfillment and purpose in their jobs. Compensation must be fair and adequate and working conditions clean, orderly and safe. We must support the health and well-being of our employees and help them fulfill their family and other personal responsibilities. Employees must feel free to make suggestions and complaints. There must be equal opportunity for employment, development and advancement for those qualified. We must provide highly capable leaders and their actions must be just and ethical.

We are responsible to the communities in which we live and work and to the world community as well. We must help people be healthier by supporting better access and care in more places around the world. We must be good citizens – support good works and charities, better health and education, and bear our fair share of taxes. We must maintain in good order the property we are privileged to use, protecting the environment and natural resources.

Our final responsibility is to our stockholders. Business must make a sound profit. We must experiment with new ideas. Research must be carried on, innovative programs developed, investments made for the future and mistakes paid for. New equipment must be purchased, new facilities provided and new products launched. Reserves must be created to provide for adverse times. When we operate according to these principles, the stockholders should realize a fair return.

As business consultants, my partners and I know how difficult it is to unify all the parts of an organization. We have helped organizations do it. When it happens, it is an extraordinary experience; people know when they are part of an intimate tribe. They feel a part of the higher purpose, and they feel valued. When we had finally helped our clients define their vision, mission, goals, objectives, core values, and action plans, we would ask the senior executives if they and their people could execute what had been developed. Sometimes the answer was yes, sometimes no, sometimes they didn't know. Every organizational strategy and operating plan is implemented best with synergy among its participants. Eventually, execution comes down to developing Synergistic Relationships with participants who can operate cohesively to get the jobs done. Organizations that develop Synergistic Relationships operationalize strategy and action plans more effectively. Synergistic Relationships provide untold benefits and strength to any organization.

Both of my sons are head coaches of volleyball at local high schools. They also coach nationally ranked club volleyball teams. I am immensely proud of them, not merely because of their winning records but because of how they can develop Synergistic Tribal Teams. I have been an assistant coach for my son Matt at Park City High School. I have seen him build Synergistic Tribal Teams of teenage girls who have a common vision, mission, goals, objectives, action plans, and unconditional values. It is a special experience for the girls, parents, and coaches. Being a part of something so distinct leaves a lasting and transferable legacy. My boys are fierce competitors who want to win, but the girls and boys who play on their volleyball teams always come first. When you think about it, it is not their skill in teaching volleyball that defines them; it is who they are that determines what and how they teach. What makes people great is how they impact other people's lives for the better. Great people are the nucleus of Synergistic Tribal Relationships.

I had a professor named Dr. Thaddeus Merrill. He had the ability to inspire people. He spat when he spoke. He taught political theory at Utah State University. At the beginning of every quarter, he would assign four very thick textbooks to be read (in those days, we didn't have semesters). If we came prepared, he gave us the most wonderful life perspectives. Humor was entwined in his being. But, if we didn't come prepared, if we didn't understand what he was talking about, then we certainly didn't catch the humor. I took every class he taught. He died of cancer during the last quarter of my senior year. While he was in the hospital, I visited him once or twice a week. He would give me a list and ask me to bring him academic books from the university library. I knew he was pleased to see me, but he would protest by saying that I certainly had better things to do as a young married man than to visit a sick, old man in the hospital. I cherished our visits; I knew a great man was nurturing me. Near the end, we had a dialog that changed my life.

During one visit, he lamented, "You know what I hate about dying?"

"You're not going to die; you'll be OK!"

He laughed and just patted me on the arm, "No, I am going to die, and soon."

And then he repeated his former sentence, "What I hate about dying is that there is so much I haven't read and learned yet." There was a slight pause, and then he said to me, "Mr. Carlson, I want you to make me a promise.

This is a deathbed promise, so it can't be taken lightly. I want you to read one book per month that pertains to your profession, or passion, for the rest of your life. Will you make me a solemn promise to do that?" I told him I would.

He was the most brilliant and wisest mentor I ever had. That was in 1972. Because of Dr. Merrill, I have dutifully read at least one book per month about my profession and passions for the past 50 years. I got heavily involved in studying the behavioral sciences, performance theory, leadership, management, and history.

He provided the door for me to find and to feed my passions. Dr. Thaddeus Merrill was a tribe member builder. His gift was pulling people into his inner circle of lifetime learning. He knew my name was Wayne, but he always insisted on calling me Mr. Carlson. The Thaddeus Merrill building on the campus at Utah State is a tribute testifying that I was not the only person whose life he touched deeply.

Soulmate Relationships

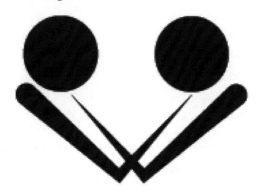

Soulmate Relationships complete us, make us whole, and bring joy in the process of living. Having Soulmate Relationships brings peace and personal authentication that we are loved unconditionally every second of our life. Soulmate interpersonal connections are, one might say, spiritual. We understand how profound the connections are if we are fortunate enough to have even one such relationship. The thing about soulful connections is that the bonds grow stronger through the good times and bad. When beautiful things happen, joy is shared. It strengthens the bond when horrible things occur, and the weight of disappointment and sorrow is borne jointly. In such relationships, identities become unified, and one doesn't consider oneself without including the other. I'm not suggesting a mutual dependence but rather a mutual enhancement. Soulmates aren't perfect people, but they are empathic, forgiving, and selfless. Differences don't divide but enhance. I think it fair to say that Soulmates couldn't imagine a heaven without one another.

My dad and mother had the most perfect Soulmate Relationship that I have ever witnessed. Their love and devotion to one another were tangible to all who knew them. Their lives defined one another. I learned of my father's unconditional love for my mother demonstrably when I was 12 years old. Being a cheeky tween, I argued with my mom and told her, "Oh shut up!" My dad, who witnessed my rudeness, grabbed me and threw me on the bed in another room and sent me a message I will never forget: "No man alive has spoken to my sweetheart that way, and you never will again... and live." I knew immediately that my mother was sacred to my dad. The last words we heard him say as they were taking him in the life flight helicopter before he passed away was "Donna P. Carlson" in answer to the question of what his wife's name was. He said it so proudly. We never heard him say another word.

My mother was kneeling by his bedside as he lay unconscious the night that he died. She said, "He was my knight in shining armor. I couldn't bear eternity without him." The year after my dad passed away, my mother said to me, "It's not that I miss him; I need him."

4

COMMAND AND CONTROL RELATIONSHIPS

THE TENSEGRUS RELATIONSHIP SPECTRUM

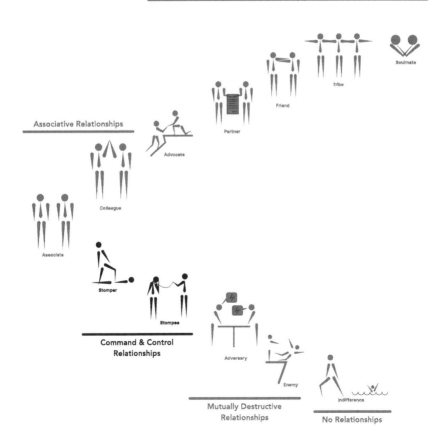

When people have power, they can force people to do their bidding. Those who use their ability to dominate and control others are Command and Control people. Commanders want to control their environment and everyone within it. Power and control divide people into two groups: those who dominate and control versus those who are dominated and controlled. Dominance results in a hierarchical culture where social standing and status depend upon where one fits on the hierarchy. Command and Control management is the most common approach used in our society. It is used in our homes, businesses, churches, government, in almost all types of organizations. Since it is the most common form of management style, we should understand the kind of relationships produced by using it.

The focus is all about Power and Control.

I watched the Jackie Gleason show when I was a young boy in the 1950s. I can still vividly remember one episode of *The Honeymooners* where Ralph (a New York bus driver) yells at his wife, "I'm the BOSS, Alice. I'm the BOSS!!" (Then he pounded his chest to show his dominance) and continued, "And you are NOTHING!"

His wife Alice smiled and calmly responded, "Big deal; so you're boss over nothing."

That still makes me laugh to this day. It shows the stereotyped mentality of relationships back in the 1950s in a little over-the-top depiction that the husband was the boss. It is typical of many Command and Control relationships that aim for compliant behavior. Obedience is the only acceptable behavior from underlings. The use of force and power makes that compliance or obedience "obedience by compulsion." It centralizes decision-making to the person at the top, the one with the power and the position to force compliance. It exemplifies expressions like: "It's my way or the highway!" or "As long as you live in my house, you will follow my rules!"

These may be the most common relationships in families and organizations worldwide; power fuels Command and Control relationships. A person with sufficient power can control circumstances to suit their will. On the other hand, a person without power must set aside their wants and focus on giving the person in charge what they desire or risk being punished, cast aside, or replaced by someone willing to meet power demands. Command and Control relationships' characteristics make them easy to identify.

Characteristics of Command and Control Relationships

They are hierarchical, separated by superior and inferior positions.

Those in high positions in such a culture control those below them and are submissive to those above them. It can be almost humorous to shadow a mid-level boss around and see the instantaneous transformations in his demeanor depending on whether he is in a superior or inferior position in the hierarchy. You can watch him make demands and threats with people lower on the scale and, in the next moment, witness him be fawning and obsequious with people he perceives to be above him.

My boss in Belgium, the worldwide marketing VP for Janssen Pharmaceutica, was a brilliant fellow; he spoke eight languages fluently, and his whole mannerism changed to align with the language's culture. He was confident and commanding to those of a lower level, and yet, in the presence of Paul Janssen (President of Janssen Pharmaceutica), he was submissive and fawning. It was entertaining to see him switch modes, mainly if Paul was in the same room with several of his subordinates. It was like watching Jekyll and Hyde transformations in fast-forward mode.

Command and Control environments are caste systems, a ladder of the privileged and powerful on top with the deprived and powerless on the bottom. In the U.S. Army, rank defines where one fits in the hierarchy. All commissioned officers outrank non-commissioned officers and enlisted men. But within the commissioned officer ranks, there is a well-defined hierarchy; Generals outrank Colonels, Colonels outrank Majors, Majors outrank Captains, Captains outrank 1st Lieutenants, and 1st Lieutenants outrank 2nd Lieutenants. And there is a hierarchy within the non-commissioned ranks as well. From top to bottom, it looks like this: Sergeant Major of the Army, Sergeant Major, Command Sergeant, Master or First Sergeant, Sergeant First Class, Staff Sergeant, Sergeant, Corporal, Specialist, Private First Class, Private, and Private Recruit. In this hierarchical system, the person with the senior rank makes the decisions, and the lower position must follow orders. We can imagine how insignificant a recruit, with no grade, feels looking from the bottom up. The sense of inferiority is moderated with tons of training, a loaded gun, and a growing sense of brotherhood as teams unify and relationships develop. And, unless you are a recruit, there is always somebody you can boss around.

Almost all business organizations operate as caste systems with a hierarchy of a CEO, a President, Vice Presidents, Directors, Managers, Supervisors, Team Leaders, functional Professionals, and non-exempts. Here too, decision-making is top-down.

Societies also have hierarchies with a definitive caste system.

South Africa was an Apartheid country where your skin color determined your position in the hierarchy. The white Africans at the top, the coloreds in the middle, and the blacks at the bottom. South Africa segregated people by color. Skin color determined where you could live and the kind of work you could do. Privileged whites enacted laws to maintain their status and disempower those of color, especially the blacks. Apartheid predetermined your fate based on your skin color.

India is also a caste society with strict boundaries between hundreds of caste classifications. Their complex caste system evolved over thousands of years, making it resistant to change. The class in which you were born predestines virtually all aspects of life, where you live, the kind of work you can do, the education opportunities available to you, those with whom you can associate, the clothes you wear, and even the food you eat. Americans visiting India are invariably shocked at the poverty of the masses, the disparity between the classes, and the helpless feeling that no one can change the situation. The system seems normal to Indians, with virtually everyone having accepted and justified their status.

The United States is a caste society, as well. The unresolved status of equality and opportunity between the races, genders, and sexual identity highlights the legacy of white dominance, power, and control. The current political polarization in our country testifies that the legacy lives on.

Many, if not most, families are hierarchical, with the parents exercising power, making decisions, and exerting control over their children. The parents are the generals in these family units, and the children are the privates. Ultimately, this is a temporary situation because children grow up. But the impact of a Command and Control environment lasts a lifetime. A fuller examination of this will occur in the section on Operating Modes.

Power and decision-making are from top-down.

In a Command and Control environment, those at the top can change things. When I was a new salesman at Johnson & Johnson, the Air Force Academy was part of my territory, so I visited the doctors who provided services there. Occasionally, I golfed with a few medical doctors and dentists. Once, on a return visit to the golf course, I noticed that a big tree was missing on the right side of the fairway on one particular par four. I asked my playing companions, "Didn't there use to be a big tree on the right side of the fairway?" They laughed and responded, "The general has a slice." If you are a general in the Air Force, you don't have to correct your slice because you can solve the problem by having the obstacle removed.

Centralized power and decision-making allow those at the top to maintain control.

Webster's Collegiate Dictionary defines control as: "…to exercise restraint or direction over; to hold in check; curb..." People at the top can maintain control by limiting the options available to those "below" them. "Only do what I tell you to do," exemplifies the spirit of top-down, centralized decision-making. These people aim at compliance and conformity to maintain their power and control. Forcing people to comply confirms their "right" to make the decisions and affirms their power. In Command and Control environments, deviation from the top-down direction is insubordination and is punishable. How often have parents declared: "As long as you live in my house, you will obey my rules!" People who aim at "obedience" as the cardinal standard for others maintain control by centralizing decision-making to themselves and using the power of their position on the hierarchy to do so.

The philosophy is: Remove other people's choices and control the outcomes.

The person in the superior position justifies their Command and Control under the guise of benefiting the person in the inferior position.

In counseling, there is a saying: "People can endure whatever they can justify." For example, people can put up with abuse if they can find reasons (or any reason) that explains why an abuser is abusing them. The justification concept can be applied in countless other ways: "We will pay what we can justify." Or "We will do what we can justify." People justify Command and Control behavior all the time. "I tell them what to do so they won't get hurt!" "Look, I have much more life experience, and doing what I say will help you avoid pain and heartache!" "I spank you because I love you!" "Spare the rod and spoil the child." Of course, this self-justification assumes that "the rod" means a stick rather than the Hebrew definition: "word of God." I wonder if they plugged in "word of God" in the quotation rather than "rod" if they would still feel justified in smacking the child.

Why Command and Control is the most common management approach

There are probably innumerable reasons why Command and Control are so common and popular, but we have listed some of the most prominent ones.

1) It gets results quickly.

Consensus takes time to get input and agreement on actions; the more people involved, the more time required. If I am the only decision-maker, making decisions takes only as long as it takes me to decide what to do. What could be better if I am always correct and don't make bad decisions? On the other hand, if I am prone to dumb decisions, bad outcomes come quickly.

2) It brings order from chaos.

We've all heard the adage, "Many hands make light work." That may be true, but "many" inputting can also create chaos. The inability to come to a decision can be paralyzing, so it makes sense that, in the absence of a well-established way to come to consensus and conclusions, centralizing and limiting the decision-making process to one person gets things done. On the other hand, if you are the sole decision-maker, you may become the bottleneck that paralyzes the entire organization. The most effective organizations push decision-making to the lowest practical level.

In preparation for the invasion of Western Europe during the World War II, the senior officers from the United States and Great Britain spent hundreds of thousands of hours planning the invasion. They had very different perspectives on what, when, and how it should occur. Without the Supreme Commander, Dwight D. Eisenhower, to make the ultimate decisions, it never would have happened. You may find it interesting to know that after he gave the go-ahead for the invasion, he drafted a letter personally taking full responsibility if the invasion was not successful. General Eisenhower made the ultimate decision in this situation, but his choices were based on input from countless wise and experienced experts. It would have been impossible for him to independently plan for and execute the largest sea-based invasion the world had ever seen.

3) It enables people who Command and Control to create concrete standards.

When we are in a Command and Control position, we set the standards. The more precise and clear we are, the more concrete the bar is. If our standards are vague, then interpretations cause variations. In short, as a sole decision-maker, the standards are what we decide them to be; they will only be as clear and as concrete as we define them to be. Nevertheless, clear or vague, it is still, "My way or the highway."

4) It satisfies the need for status described in Maslow's Hierarchy of Needs.[3]

In 1943, Abraham Maslow proposed a theory of human motivation wherein he identified a hierarchy of needs that drive human behavior. He explained that unfulfilled needs drive behavior and that as a lower-level need is satisfied, it ceases to motivate us. We are then motivated by the next higher unfulfilled need. He categorized these needs in a pyramid with two general classifications: "Dependency" needs and "Growth" needs. The Dependency needs are physiological, safety, belonging, and esteem needs from the lowest to the highest. The Growth needs in upward order are cognitive, aesthetic, self-actualization, and transcendence needs. People must satisfy Dependency needs before moving on to Growth needs. People who operate from Command and Control management behave in ways that meet their needs. Status needs are about being important. To Command and Control people, "being" important is having control and commanding others.

Examples are plentiful to illustrate Maslow's hierarchy of needs, showing how unfulfilled needs are met. For instance, during World War II in the Pacific, thousands of bombers crashed into the ocean. One crash experience, in particular, exemplifies how many of Maslow's hierarch of needs were satisfied by the airmen who survived the crash. In the Marshall Islands (in the Central Pacific), a B-24 bomber with eight crewmembers was lost while trying to return to their airbase. They all stayed with the plane rather than bailing out because they felt that was the best chance of survival. The airmen only had three life rafts on board, and they needed to stay near one another.

---

3   Abraham Maslow, "A Theory of Human Motivation" (The Journal of Psychological Review, 1943).

Being separated by miles and miles of empty ocean wasn't an acceptable option. When they crash-landed, everyone survived except the pilot and copilot. It was chaotic trying to gather the life rafts, food, water, and other things necessary for survival after the crash; the crash jumbled everything inside the plane. While trying to get essentials, all the survivors ended up underwater with a high probability of drowning. At that moment, gathering survival things no longer mattered. Immediately everyone's sole focus was to get to the surface and get air (physiological needs). Once they made it to the surface and filled their lungs with life-giving oxygen, getting air was no longer critical. But getting safely onshore, any shore, became paramount (safety needs). Fortunately, they found one raft and other floating pieces of cargo that became the means for making their way to a distant island. All the survivors were hurt in the crash but, thankfully, none with life-threatening injuries.

During the sea journey, night fell, and they became separated. As a result, they didn't know who had made it to shore and who didn't. Nor did they know if they would end up on the same island. But once safely on the beach, they looked for other survivors; the need to find others with whom they could unite drove all their attention and efforts (belonging needs). Thankfully, five of the surviving six made it to the same island, all making it ashore within a mile of one another. The radio operator, who was last seen just before dark, was never seen again. Once the five were united, everyone was elated that they had made it and had army brothers with them. Thankfully it was a relatively large island with the means of meeting their basic physiological needs (fresh water and ample food). The focus would have reverted to finding water and food as the primary driving need if it had not been.

But, since their physiological needs, safety needs, and belonging needs were are all being met, they needed to get organized. The senior non-commissioned sergeant took charge and assigned everyone unique roles to survive on the island (status needs). Fortunately, the U.S. Navy's exhaustive effort to find the lost airmen was successful; they found them before the Japanese did. All survivors made it home and attested that the experience had changed them. They were grateful to be alive, but fundamentally, they saw life in a new light. Common among them was the desire, deep within themselves, to make a difference and be all they could be for the rest of their lives as a tribute to their air mates who perished at sea (growth needs).

We hope that this story provides insight into the concept that unfulfilled needs drive behavior. Satisfying status or our ego needs can be challenging throughout much of life. Because life is dynamic, the status needs may be filled well for a time and then left unfilled due to changing circumstances. You may be flying high as the owner of a successful business, then a pandemic crushes the economy, and you have nothing. Most of our physiological needs rise and are satisfied each day quickly. If thirsty or hungry, we get something to drink and eat (physiological need gone). Our sense of belonging is reasonably stable for most of us; we are part of a family and, probably, part of organizations that evolve and change slowly; therefore, our need to belong feels secure. But status and ego seem to need constant gratification. Businesses constantly sell the idea that you are not good enough unless you use their product. Our society exalts the famous, sports heroes, and the exceptional. I guess that getting and keeping our esteem needs fulfilled has become, for many, a competitive and never-ending, ego-satisfying quest.

In short, being in Command and Control becomes, for many, a need that constantly requires fulfillment. The need for constant validation of status (esteem) becomes like heroin is to a heroin addict.

I was a meat cutter, part-time, during college. Most of the part-time workers were college students. Being a part-time meat cutter was a low-man-on-the-totem-pole job. Our floor manager was a middle-aged, heavy-set guy with a massive inferiority complex. Rumor had it that he quit high school his junior year. At the meat plant, his management position was his way of demonstrating his importance and superiority. He never let an opportunity slip by to berate anyone working for him, especially the part-time students. He constantly reminded us that he was the manager (like we needed reminding). I have a better understanding of his motivation now. Making us miserable was merely a means of satisfying his status and ego needs.

5) It is self-serving.

Those at the top of the Command and Control structure invariably can parlay that position and power for incredible personal benefits. One only needs to look at the CEO compensation packages compared to the average employee compensation to witness the self-serving nature and power of Command and Control. Their compensation is often thousands of times higher than the compensation of the employees who work for them. Bezos, the ex-CEO at Amazon, made billions per year while those producing the wealth made barely livable wages. I heard that part of Amazon's management philosophy is to keep turnover in the lower ranks high to keep employees fearful for their jobs and maintain a tension-based productivity culture. In the long run, it would appear that this approach will be self-limiting because as Amazon rises beyond being the world's largest employer, the ability to hire and maintain the number of employees needed will not tolerate high levels of turnover. The one constant thing will still be Bezos making thousands of times more than the average employee.

Dictators do and always have received unimaginable, self-serving recompenses derived from power and control. Hitler sought world domination and controlled virtually all of Western Europe before the Allies defeated his ego-mania, but not before over 50 million people died for his self-serving ambition. Putin reportedly is the wealthiest person in the world. Kim Jong-un, the dictator of North Korea, lives in splendor while his citizens are always on the edge of starvation. To garner personal benefits at the expense of others is the nature of dictatorships worldwide.

6) It's addictive.

I casually mentioned heroin addiction in Maslow's Hierarchy of Needs section review. But addictions play a considerable part in our daily interactions and behaviors. I learned a lot about addictions while be-ing a hospital pharmaceutical salesman in the Los Angeles area. My responsibilities focused solely on selling anesthesia and psychiatric products in the foremost hospitals and teaching institutions of South-ern California. I got to meet and interact extensively with the psychiat-ric community. Among them was a physician who successfully treated chronic burnt-out institutional psychotics and transformed them into "tax-paying, productive members of society." He loved my product, Haldol®, and helped me make it a mainstay in all of the psychiatric centers in Southern California. He was a recovering addict and told me that he used to eat a week's supply of prescription medications by lunchtime every day. He taught me much for which I will forever be grateful. One of the things he taught me about was addictions. He crit-icized my lack of personal understanding of the conditions my product treated, "How can you help treat psychosis if you have no clue about what it is and what it is like?" He said he would no longer meet me until I started attending Schizophrenics Anonymous sessions at the Los Angeles chapter. He said he would know if I was there because he was the chapter president and medical advisor. One of the most important things I learned at Schizophrenics Anonymous was that I was a behav-ioral addict and that most of us are. All addictions have three defining characteristics: 1. Compulsive behavior, 2. Short-term benefits, and 3. Long-term negative consequences.

Take alcoholism: 1) People drink compulsively. Drinking becomes an impulse they can't control. 2) Drinking provides a "buzz," the short-term benefit. 3) Addictive drinking damages your health and import-ant relationships (the long-term negative consequences). Of course, alcoholism is a chemical addiction. But behavioral addictions have the same addictive characteristics. Let's look at the addictive nature of Command and Control behaviors.

Ordering people about is an example of Command and Control behav-ior. It is compulsive behavior when it becomes "the way I get things done" mode. "I have to tell people what to do to get things done." The short-term benefits come in several ways:

- The rush of exerting power
- The immediate compliance from others
- The quick outcomes
- The ego gratification derived from dominance
- The release of pent-up emotions

The long-term negative consequences spawn from the resentment of control, namely, loss of respect and lousy relationships. As a negative consequence, we might also include the inability to manage in any other way. Commanding and controlling behavior is highly addicting. I know. I am a recovering criticizer who required the help of my sweetheart, family, and friends in the journey to overcome it.

My name is Wayne Carlson; I am a recovering criticizer. At this time, I have been criticism-free for two weeks and three days. My goal is to be criticism-free for the rest of my life.

7) Someone has to decide who is expendable.

One of the valid reasons for a chain of command is that someone has to make the hard, unavoidable decisions. In virtually all organizations, at some time, someone has to decide who is expendable. In war, someone has to decide who will live and die. Sergeants determine which soldiers are expendable, captains decide which platoons are expendable, and generals decide on expendable divisions. In business downturns and reorganizations, someone must decide who stays in the lifeboat and who goes over the side. Even in families, the situation arises where someone must decide where the highest priorities lie and whose needs are forfeited to benefit the rest. When the only option for survival is sacrifice, someone determines who is expendable.

Command and Control may be the most common way to manage in our society, but that doesn't justify it. I believe that Command and Control relationships are responsible for massive emotional, psychological, and physical damage passed on from generation to generation. And it is justified and acclaimed because it is so ubiquitous. Many see it as their duty to run a "tight ship" where they are the commander who controls everything.

Stomper/Stompee Relationships

Stomper

There are different Command and Control relationships, but perhaps, the most disturbing is what we call the "Stomper/Stompee" relationship. Just as it sounds, one person is stomping, and those underfoot are the Stompees. Stompers are BULLIES. They know who they can pick on and who won't allow it. While Stompers get fulfillment in taking control, their ultimate pleasure comes from dominance. Their buzz comes from intimidation and abrasiveness, as well as demanding, threatening, and belittling encounters. Resistance only makes them more assertive and threatening. Anyone seen as inferior, weak, helpless, or powerless is a target. Of course, Stompers avoid confrontations with those perceived as a more powerful or higher authority or rank. An odd thing often happens when high-ranking people have Stompers on their staff: They are entirely unaware that they have a Stomper stomping on people.

Our consulting company, Petrous, was helping a division of KPMG do a human resource audit of their organization. It became apparent to us that one of the Junior Partners was a terrible Stomper who was making the lives of those "beneath" him miserable. I mean, everyone lower on the pecking order was scared to death of this guy. When we reviewed the information gathered with the managing partners, they were aghast. They had no clue and, frankly, didn't believe it. They said that our descriptions of him were completely opposite of their experience with him. So, we set up interviews for managing partners with underlings, guaranteeing that there would be no negative repercussions for them telling the truth. Some were still reluctant, but many were honest and very graphic. Their honesty came as a real eye-opener to the managing partners.

As a consequence of the new information, they put the Stomper on probation and made frequent inquiries to see if further abuses occurred. There were, so he didn't last very long. The fact that the managing partners were oblivious to his stomping is not surprising. Stompers suck up to people perceived as superior while being dominant to those perceived as inferior.

There was a VP of marketing from one of the J&J companies. He was known as "Little Napoleon." He was full of himself. I remember him, five-foot-six-inches, poking his forefinger into the chest of his six-foot-three-inch national sales manager saying, "How come you are always on the wrong side of every issue?" At a speaking engagement for a J&J meeting, he proclaimed, "If I could have robots who say exactly what I want them to say and do exactly what I want them to do, I wouldn't need any of you salespeople." He didn't have many friends.

Little Napoleon was not well-liked by anyone. J&J leaders formed a new pharmaceutical division with a new leader. The new Vice-Chairman of the pharmaceutical division had one condition; he told the CEO, Jim Burke, that he didn't want Little Napoleon anywhere near the Pharmaceutical Division. Jim Burke found him a new position in a different part of J&J, much to the relief and joy of those who worked for him. When a Stomper's power is lost, those they abused on the way up cheer and facilitate their slide on the way down.

In the extreme, society knows Stompers as abusers. They are the wife beaters, the kid slammers, the violent sexual predators who stalk the vulnerable. There is a sadistic nature to their actions, which differentiates them from the super strict parent, or the overbearing boss. They get pleasure from making those they dominate fearful or submissive.

Hopefully, you don't have any Stompers in your life, which says something about you. But if you do, perhaps you have some "Stompee" in your nature.

My executive assistant for four years was Sharon. I can't say enough about how wonderful she was. She was beautiful, intelligent, sweet, talented, and dedicated to making my life better. My job as a VP at Janssen Pharmaceutica was a 24/7 assignment. She took burdens from me and made the job pleasant and fun. I mean, she could type, take dictation, edit and draft perfect correspondence. It was as though she could read my mind and anticipate what was needed. She would frequently prepare responses to letters sent to me and put "my response" on my desk for my signature. I rarely had to edit her answer; she made me appear better than I was. She managed my schedule, screened non-essential visitors and meetings, and was generally my gatekeeper and protector. I became dependent upon her abilities. I was so dependent that when we promoted her to a professional position within the company, I felt an enormous vacuum in my life. How do you replace the irreplaceable?

As talented and irreplaceable as she was at Janssen, her personal life was a disaster. She was a Stompee, a victim of spousal abuse, both physical and emotional. From time to time, she would come to work with bruises, walk with a limp, or favor a hurting portion of her body. When we asked about it, she always had some lame excuse. Our human resource and development team at Janssen became her support group. Work relationships validated her uniqueness and value.

She had gotten pregnant in high school, had a baby as a teenager, and married before she graduated. Her formal education was limited because of her circumstances. Still, our group convinced her to get a college degree while working part-time and take advantage of Janssen's educational support. She enrolled and excelled. But the more she excelled, the worse became the home abuse. At one point, she came to the office early and was there when I arrived. Her face was red and swollen. I was shocked at her injuries and asked her what had happened to cause such injuries. This time there was no evasion and no excuses; she let it all out, explaining that her husband beat her up. Because she didn't know where else to go, she came to the office and slept on the sofa in my office. She came to Janssen because she received unconditional love and support there. Betty Long and I took her to the Emergency Room and convinced her to press charges against her husband. She told us that he would kill her with one of the knives and guns kept in their house if she did. A lady police officer accompanied her home. Other officers took all the weapons out of her house. Her husband apologized, gave her flowers, and promised that he was a changed man who would never do anything to hurt her ever again. He was placed on probation but did not serve jail time.

That lasted for a few months, and again she came to the office battered. This time she required hospitalization. We were in her hospital room when she pressed charges against her husband a second time. This time they threw him in prison for three months. Again, he made promises, but she was finished with him. When she returned to work, Sharon told me that she needed to move out of her house because she was afraid to live there with her husband. Her grandparents had given her their house, so he needed to be the one leaving. She got an order of protection which prevented him from contacting her or coming near her. She filed for divorce and was soon single again. Her ex-husband sent her a letter that she read to us, in which he declared that he didn't need her fat ass. He moved in with another woman who promptly kicked him out.

Sharon finished her degree and married one of her professors, who truly appreciated her internal and external beauty. She later became a manager at Janssen. I lost contact with her and the rest of the group at Janssen, to my great shame. But she was a life changer who left an indelible mark on my life.

Stompee

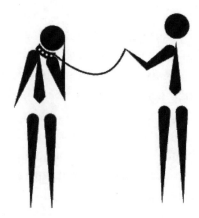

Stompees are the McFly's of the world. "Hello, McFly!" (Biff tapping McFly on the forehead.) In the movie *Back to the Future,*[4] Marty McFly goes back and sees his dad as the ultimate punching bag. Biff constantly harasses his dad. Dad McFly is a true Stompee. He takes all the emotional, physical, and mental abuses Biff dishes out. He is an excellent depiction of a Stompee: A person who just gets stomped on and submissively takes it. As you recall, Marty McFly is anything but a Stompee, and in the end, he helps his dad defend his (future) mom, which changes his dad's life trajectory from one of Stompee to super achiever. Fun, fun movie. I love it!!

Here is a list of typical descriptive Stompee characteristics:

- Expects others to take advantage
- Allows one's self to be used or be degraded
- Excuses inappropriate behavior toward self
- Minimizes or hides feelings
- Avoids confrontation except when exploding
- Manifests the explode cycle (represses the expression of emotions until they explode, feels guilty, apologizes, suppresses feelings again, etc.)

---

4   *Back to the Future*, starring Michael J. Fox and Christopher Lloyd, Directed by Robert Zemeckis (Universal Pictures Amblin Entertainment, 1985).

- Exhibits self-destructive behavior (drinking, overeating, cutting self, etc.)
- Goes overboard with efforts to please and ingratiate
- Withdraws or hides (emotionally and or physically)
- Is self-critical and self-blaming
- Uses emotions to get sympathy, manipulate others, and solve problems

I believe Stompees have a much higher acute and chronic illness rate than society's average: anxiety, phobia, depression, and self-destructive behavior link victims to Stompee behavior. In Dr. Harris's book, *I'm OK – You're OK,* he describes the people of the life position of "I'm Not OK – You're OK." These people see themselves as inadequate and insignificant in a world of the successful and powerful. He highlights the toddlers who see themselves as small and powerless surrounded by large and powerful people. Their progress to healthy self-image is through a process of achievement to achievement, never from failure to failure. He also highlights the teenager's awkward time determining self-identity who sees their body, personality, and popularity as less than acceptable. He describes the process they go through to gain self-identity and self-acceptance. But some never achieve an adequate level of self-identity and self-acceptance. Many of these, unfortunately, end up as Stompees. A joke someone told me while living in England exemplifies this self-perception.

"Excuse me, sir, do you have the time, or should I just piss off?"

Before starting my student teaching in 1972, a professor at USU shared this heart-rendering experience: "*Years ago, a sixth grade boy walked off the bus, collapsed, and died. The first time anyone really noticed him was when he collapsed. In class, at school, at home; no one noticed him, he was the 'invisible boy.'*

"*Not even his parents knew that he had a heart issue that had been causing him pain for months. He just kept to himself. Not ever creating an identity, not ever reaching out. At his funeral, as his teacher, I spoke.*

I explained that I didn't know him even though he said I was his fa-vorite teacher. He was in my class, but he had no identity or presence. I decided at that moment; there was never going to be another child without an identity that I ever taught. I will make a personal connec-tion with every kid."

My older brother is 11 months older than me. I thought my name was Dick and Wayne until I entered school because that's all I ever heard. Kids born less than a year apart are considered "Irish Twins." And that is what we were. We were about the same size, build, complexion, and even the same hair color. Personality-wise, we were vastly different. Dick was an artist and collector from the beginning. He was content to sit and draw for hours; I couldn't sit at all. If we went on a hike to Round Hill, about a mile east of our house, we had to walk across fields, an irrigation stream, and foothills covered with brush and scrub trees, with lots of ground squirrels, rabbits, and birds scattered along the way. It would usually take me 20 or 30 minutes to get to the top, where I could take in the vista and then head back. I usually found Dick less than a quarter of a mile from home on my return trip with his pockets filled with interesting rocks, bugs, and plants. The world to me was what I saw from the top of Round Hill. Dick could see the universe in the field next to our house.

We did everything together with our cousin Bob, who was almost a year older than I. Bob and Dick were a unit, and I was the spare wheel, which they took delight in teasing. When I got mad, I had a vein in my neck that would swell up like it was going to burst. They took every opportunity to see if they could make that vein burst. Except for the teasing, they were both pretty friendly and even-tempered, but I was a loving, sensitive child with a horrible temper. We lived a life of adven-ture. One time we watched a TV show called *Sky King* where there was an episode with parachuting. So we took one of my mother's sheets and tried jumping off of the front porch. That was not high enough to get the proper effect, so we climbed to the top of the barn roof. Standing at the edge of the barn roof, they convinced me to go first. As soon as they pushed me off, I let go of the sheet and landed in a manure pile where my head met squarely with my knee. When I woke up and got my bearings, I wanted to kill them. I wanted to kill them frequently. Another time we watched a hanging on a western TV program and decided to try it on the shade tree next to our house. Guess who the "hangee" was?

Dick and I probably had a fistfight several times a day until he turned 12 and I turned 11. He even broke his little finger in three places by hitting me on my head. After that, we never fought. We were skinny little guys, all bone, muscle, and ligaments with tremendous endurance. We could run forever. Dick was a sweet person who came across as a "soft touch" for bullies. He was submissive with bullies, not with me, mind you, but with other guys. In junior high and high school, we started calling one other "Brother Dear," which caught on with everyone. His friends would ask me where they could find Brother Dear as if that were his proper name. I couldn't stand being picked on or tolerate anyone picking on my brother. Most of my fights during those years were retribution for someone bullying Dick. The funny thing about him was he repressed his feelings until he exploded, then his tempest was hell on earth. But, shortly after that, he would apologize and appear calm and collected until the subsequent explosion of pent-up feelings.

My fighting days got a little more serious when I started boxing during my sophomore year. It began in a PE class when another fellow and I got into fisticuffs. The gym teacher, Coach Whitman, supposedly, was the middleweight boxing champion of the U.S. Army, at some point, during World War II. He intervened in our scuffle and told us that if we were going to fight, we should do it right. He determined that we would use Golden Glove rules, and he had the rest of the guys in the gym class hold hands and make a ring. He gave us each 16-ounce gloves and said we would proceed with three, three-minute rounds. By the end of the first round, neither could raise our arms. He met with me afterward and said, "You know, for about 30 seconds, you looked pretty good!" He started a boxing club at the school and was my boxing coach for the next year and a half. I thought I was pretty good until he took me to a Golden Gloves match where I boxed a little Hispanic guy who was my size. When I got to the corner after the first round, I told him that I must be fighting two people because the other guy hit me when I was ducking the first one. I hung up my gloves shortly after that, but no one seemed disposed to pick on me after my boxing phase.

From my perspective, getting back to Stomper/Stompee relationships, my Dear Brother still allows others to take advantage of him. He still avoids confrontation and still represses his feelings. I still want to protect him from people who would take advantage of his kindly nature. It never ends. If he is not the sweetest, most generous person in the world, he is undoubtedly a top ten contender.

What is the etiology of Stompees? It's a mindset people develop at a young age. From my research and observation, I believe people tend to be born with a disposition to either be more of a fighter or more compliant when faced with a Stomper. For a Stompee to exist, there has to be, or have been, dominance or power exerted over them. When faced with an authority Stomper parent, a young child has only two survival scenarios – comply or rebel. They are dependent upon the authority figure, so in their mind, a Stomper parent is good because believing otherwise is untenable for survival. Frequently, some children fight for self-identity, even though they come across as deserving of punishment. Preserved self-identity invariably includes physical, emotional, social, and intellectual scars. But the fighters are the lucky ones; they carve out an independent identity, albeit an angry one, or an "I'll prove you wrong" one.

Those who don't fight become submissive, passive, or become avoiders. They usually become super-focused on what allowed them to escape criticism or dominance. Through those escapes, they find some level of inner peace and tranquility. Being in a Stomper/Stompee environment at a young age imprints, models, and socializes that experience to be manifested in later life. As they mature, they adopt the hierarchical culture of being low on life's hierarchy. Their usual behavior is to comply or to avoid. If chronically stuck in the Stompee mode, Stompee becomes their overriding personality profile, taking on all the behavioral traits previously listed. An additional characteristic not listed above is a feeling of low self-esteem. Since their self-identity is not highly complementary, they often suffer from feelings of inferiority. Their self-identity gets caught up in what they do, how they see themselves, and how they expect others to treat them. These traits become part of how they manage their boundaries, which we will review in detail in the Personal Boundaries Touchpoint chapter.

Our mother was the most nurturing person in the world. From her, we learned to love and be loved. Dad was a loving, hyper-critical guy. Insecurity was what came with his criticism. My brother and I responded differently. I fought back and have spent my life trying to prove that I am OK. I believe my brother avoided confrontations and buried his life in his interests, art. Because he avoided confrontation, he came across as vulnerable, a "come and eat me signal" to predators.

Stanford Prison Experiment[5]

Nothing quite illustrates the tendency for people to gravitate toward Command and Control relationships and the disastrous effects it has on relationships quite like the Stanford Prison Experiment. In 1971, Stanford Psychology Professor Phillip Zimbardo, conducted an experiment where he wanted to see the power of "roles, rules, symbols, group identity, and situational validation of behavior that generally would repulse ordinary individuals." (1997 Stanford News Service)

The premise of the experiment was as follows: Zimbardo would create a mock prison in the basement of one of Stanford's Psychology buildings. He would find 24 psychologically stable and healthy male participants, and then, by coin flip, make half of the participants prisoners and the other half guards over those prisoners. The experiment would be conducted for a 14-day period and each participate would receive roughly $15 per day. Zimbardo himself would act as the Superintendent and his research assistant would be the Warden. What ensued, no one could have predicted.

---

5   "The Stanford Prison Experiment" was a role-play and simulation held at Stanford University in 1971 by Dr. Philip G Zimbardo. "A Simulation Study of the Psychology of Imprisonment" (PDF) (Stanford University, retrieved August 19, 2021).

On a Sunday morning in Northern California, a Palo Alto Police car, with sirens blaring, apprehended nine college students on violation of Penal Codes 211. The suspects were picked up at their homes, read their Miranda Rights, handcuffed, and placed into the back of the squad car. Such a scene produced frightened and surprised neighbors as they looked at the event from their homes. Just as fast as the squad car came in, it sped off to the police station. As the car arrived at the Palo Alto Police Station, the suspects were brought inside, fingerprinted, mug shots taken, and were blindfolded as they sat in a holding cell, waiting – waiting to be escorted to their new prison for the next 14 days.

Still blindfolded and mildly confused, the prisoners were then taken to the "Stanford County Jail" for further processing. They were brought into the jail one prisoner at a time. Their first interaction was greeted by the warden, who reminded them of the seriousness of their crimes and their new status as prisoners.

Zimbardo went to great lengths to make sure the entire experiment felt as real as possible. He completely transformed a 35-foot corridor of one of their psychology buildings into a fabricated prison. They converted offices into prison cells by replacing laboratory doors with customized doors with steel bars and converting a storage closet into a solitary confinement cell. The hallway was considered "The Yard," where prisoners were allowed to walk, eat, and exercise. At the entrance of "The Yard," there was a fabricated wall created to confine the prisoners to The Yard. Each cell was only six-by-nine feet and only contained a cot for each of the three prisoners who occupied the jail cell.

After being greeted by the warden, each prisoner was searched and stripped naked, head shaved, sprayed down to kill off any germs, and then issued a uniform that had their Prisoner ID Number on the front and a chain wrapped around their ankle. The guard's experience was vastly different. After being elected, they were given no specific training on how to be guards. They were reminded of the seriousness of their mission and were told that they were free, within limits, "to do whatever they thought was necessary to maintain law and order in the prison and to command respect of the prisoners." The guards made up their own set of rules under the supervision of the warden.

Of the 24 participants, 18 were used, which comprised nine prisoners and nine guards, with six in reserve. During the first night, the guards decided to do a "count" of the prisoners at 2:30 a.m. They blew their whistles and banged their batons to wake up the prisoners. The prisoners rebelled at this act of authority which angered the guards to the point where they sprayed the rebellious prisoners with fire extinguishers to regain control. Only after a day and a half, conditions at the prison declined rapidly.

The guards, armed with authority and position power, did whatever they could to maintain control. The prisoners, on the other hand, rebelled according to the level of authority or "command" that was used to govern them. Guards would only call prisoners by their assigned numbers, so the prisoners would rip off their numbered identity tags. Guards would do anything to maintain control, including taking away the prisoners' mattresses, forcing them to defecate in buckets in their cell, even forcing prisoners to lose their "clothing" privileges and having to sleep naked on the concrete floor. The more intense the punishment and control, the more rebellious the prisoners became.

The experiment was supposed to go on for 14 days. It only lasted six.

This is a perfect illustration of what happens with Command and Control relationships. This is the universal law of cause and effect which plainly states that every single action in the universe produces a resulting consequence. The more control exerted over another person, the more the controlee will retaliate – sometimes right away, sometimes it takes years – but the retaliation will happen; it is the natural law of the universe.

5

MUTUALLY DESTRUCTIVE RELATIONSHIPS

THE TENSEGRUS RELATIONSHIP SPECTRUM

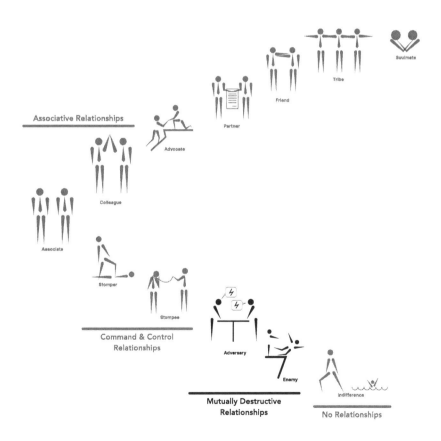

The focus is all about winning.

A man came to see me for counseling when I was a church bishop in Arlington Heights, Illinois. His story is a tale of mutual destruction between him and his ex-wife. He said they had a thriving business just four years prior with a beautiful house, two expensive cars, a boat, and money in the bank. They grew distant and angry with one another and argued constantly. Life became a contest about everything: who was good, who was bad, who was smarter, who had contributed most to their possessions, who was the best parent, etc. They became skilled in putting one another down. They accused each other of being insensitive and irresponsible. Both tried to prove that the other had made stupid decisions that were wrecking their marriage and lives. Both insisted that the other change and both started threatening each other with divorce. The threats became real when his ex-wife hired an attorney.

Consequently, he hired his attorney. As you can guess, devoted attorneys help their clients win at the expense of the other side. The contest exacerbated, and they ended up in divorce court. Both tried to garner as many of the assets as possible. He felt that she had a better attorney who helped her obtain most of the assets. They both spent so much money on attorneys that the cash flow from their business was inadequate to pay their bills. In short, they lost their home, their cars, their boat, and their business was in dire straits.

Somewhere around this time, the nature of the contest changed. Instead of striving for personal wins, the match became to make their ex lose worse. They stayed in the "game" despite huge personal losses so that they could continue to attack and injure the other more than they were injured. They ended up losing the business, and through child custody battles, she eventually got live-in custody of their two children. He became so angry that he violated the custody rulings, and then she got a "restraining order" against him that made it impossible for him to see his children. That is why he came to see me; he wanted more than anything to see and spend time with his two children. After we had spent a lot of time exploring their history and consequences, he asked me, "What should I do?" I told him to stop competing, stop attacking her, and cease this insane lose-lose contest. He looked rather shocked and said, "Then she will win everything!" I explained that there was nothing more for her to win except to create greater humiliation for him. I also explained that she would eventually find no pleasure in beating him up if he stopped fighting. He left that day pretty frustrated. I suppose he was looking for new angles from me to help him find victory in the ongoing battle.

He came back to see me a week or so later. He told me that he had been to see his attorney, who said I was crazy. I replied that he had to choose between his attorney's advice and mine. I also asked him if his attorney knew that he had no more money to pay him. The next day I received a call from his attorney. His attorney asked, "Who the hell are you?" I told him that I was a bishop at his client's church. He asked me to explain my advice, which I did. The attorney signed off, saying that his client was a lucky guy.

He stopped fighting. He accepted slings and arrows without complaint. Within a couple of months, his ex-wife let him have escorted visits with his kids. Within six months, she allowed them to come and stay at his apartment on occasional weekends. A year or so later, she was probably leaving the kids with him for a week or more so that she could go on vacation and take a break from the kids.

Their case is a pretty good example of a Mutually Destructive relationship. Mutually Destructive relationships are all about competition. In these relationships, people are drawn together despite being very hurtful. They are relationships that participants can't walk away from because there is an overpowering, negative emotional attraction. They are incredibly unhealthy. These are the type of relationships that have "clashing souls." They are opposition-based. Often, they start because one party becomes bent on changing the other party. Trying to change another person to make us happy is a losing formula. The more we try to change someone, the more they push back. It initiates contests.

In the early stages of the competition, it is all about personal wins; I win/you lose. Winning feels great for the winner but horrible for the loser. Winning occurs at the expense of the relationship. The more I win, the more you lose. Not a very good formula for building intimate relationships. Our mantra at the Lake Forest Graduate School of Management in the relationship course was: "If the relationship is important, don't compete!" Competing for personal wins is characteristic of "adversarial relationships." "I'm not trying to hurt you. I'm just trying to win." But with endless competition, there comes a tipping point where Adversarial relationships change to Enemy relationships.

The United States of America is rife with Adversarial relationships. America is a nation divided. Both sides try to prove that they are right and the other side is wrong. They look at one another as stupid because the opposition doesn't see or agree with their perspective. Facts are not persuasive because facts are insubordinate to deeply held feelings. The facts always seem to align with their emotions and beliefs. The more each side tries to prove their point and change their adversary, the greater the likelihood that the Adversarial relationship will become an Enemy relationship. American Politics is an excellent example of moving from Adversarial to Enemy relationships. Political positions are no longer about who is right and how to serve the American people best; they have become about making political enemies look horrible and causing them to lose elections. American politics has become an Enemy relationship contest about disempowering the opposition to control and win. This enemy approach to winning injures opponents and makes American citizens casualties of war.

Enemy relationships are still about winning, but the definition changes from, "I win, you lose," to "You will lose more than I will lose." Enemy relationships use behaviors that punish, hurt, get revenge, remove, disempower, eliminate, and ultimately, defeat the other party. Enemy relationships are self-destructive because all parties are willing to sacrifice and take damage to stay in the game and attempt to destroy the "bad guys." When we witness political parties passing laws to disempower their adversaries, it is no longer an adversarial contest but a war between enemies. Enemy relationships tend to amplify megalomania (obsession with personal power). The quest becomes to get and keep sufficient power to vanquish your enemy. It is pretty scary because genuine Enemy relationships are a form of warfare, and the ultimate aim of war is to defeat your enemy. The sad part is that ultimately no one wins because all parties are worse off at the end of the contest. I realize that victors would disagree.

Adversarial Relationships

Competition and the need for personal wins characterize Adversarial relationships. They often exemplify one party trying to change the other party to meet their expectations. Winning is getting the other party to change to make them happy. It happens when others comply with their wishes.

It's very common for loving relationships to become adversarial; it happens all the time. When we examine Command and Control parenting of teenagers, we frequently see teenagers who push back. The parents will tell themselves that they direct the teenager about what to do and how to do it is because they LOVE their child. (I agree that they love their child.) Parents believe that the child benefits (wins) if they do as commanded. Therefore, winning is now defined as having a compliant child from the parent's perspective. The teenager, feeling forced, wins by not following their parents' direction.

Unknowingly, from the parents' side, a contest has begun. The parents would be surprised to realize that their relationship with their teenager has become adversarial. Of course, they don't know that yet; but they will find out later on. Winning for the parent is a teenager who follows the rules; winning for the teenager is not complying. Winning becomes the most important thing for both the parent and the child. When parents start trying to force their way, it initiates a competition. The parents may believe that their child is complying, so they won the contest. What they don't realize is that the match is still in play.

The parents have the power to try and force compliance, but the teenager, realizing that they can't compete openly, will non-comply covertly. Hidden disobedience is the lifeline of the disempowered. From the teenager's perspective, "I win if I sneak out after curfew." The contest is ongoing, and both want to win. These contests are happening all across the country, and too few parents fail to recognize that it is happening until they move it from a covert competition to an open one. If the open contest becomes a win-at-all-costs standoff, the child will rebel. At that point, the parents lose their ability to force their child to do anything. The moral is: If the relationship is important, don't compete.

It is natural to compete when winning is more important than the relationship. When buying a car from a dealership, the relationship is seldom more important than getting the best price. While keeping us as an ongoing buyer is important to the dealership, reaching the highest price possible is job one, even more important than a possible future relationship. It is a game where many dealerships are well-versed in playing and winning.

Gamers think they are more intelligent than the other people playing the game. They also don't believe that other people see it. People are never as dumb as game players think they are. Have you noticed that a frequent ploy in dealerships is the "good guy, bad guy game"? The salesman tries to convince the car buyers that he is their advocate. The salesman would have us believe that he is "teaming up" with us against his management for our benefit. Really? Does anyone believe that car dealerships hire people who fight against their own company? Nope. It is a game. When we remove ourselves and think about it logically, it's a car dealership against the customer game. The play is that the salesman is your buddy, and he will be your advocate to get you the best price with the manager he portrays as the adversary. If you fall for that game, you are naïve; they both work for the dealership. The fastest way to expose the game is to call it; raise it to complete visibility. When we say, "Oh, I get it, you are the good guy advocating for me, and the manager is the bad guy advocating for the dealership. If you can't negotiate a deal with me, then hook me up with the person who can, or I will go to another dealership where I can work with the decision-maker." It is a covert game played by sneaky people. If we fall for their ploy, they win.

I taught a graduate class in negotiations and conflict management at the Lake Forest Graduate School of Management. There are three kinds of negotiations that everyone should be acquainted with: Creative negotiations (win/win), competitive (win/lose), and compromise (acceptable loss to maintain the relationship). Each negotiation method has principles, concepts, skills, and techniques, but this is not the time or place for that discussion. But for this book on relationships, just remember this: If a relationship is important, don't compete!

When I was coaching volleyball a few years ago, I filled in as a substitute coach for a young U12 team that included a team member named Meredith, who was born without her left forearm. She could not serve over the net, as her 11-year-old frame could not handle the coordination of tossing with one arm and then using the same arm to contact the ball with enough force to get it over the net. During the match, she missed serve after serve on her turn. Then amazingly, during the third set of the match, she made one, two, then seven serves in a row. On her final and eighth serve, she got an ace for the set win. Both sides, players and parents, stood up and gave her a standing ovation. During her celebration, she told me that someday she would play volleyball in the Para Olympics. She now plays varsity for her high school team and is on the Para Olympic beach volleyball team.

We are all touched and amazed when someone puts sportsmanship ahead of winning. It happens, even in the highest level of sports. For example, Abbey D'Agostino and Nikki Hamblin fell during the women's 5,000-meter event in the Rio Olympics. Around the 3,000-meter mark, Abbey slowed down to avoid contacting another runner; when she did so, Nikki bumped into her from behind, and they both tumbled onto the track. When Abbey got to her feet, she noticed that Nikki was injured and needed help. She put forth her hand and helped Nikki up, and together they finished the race. Abbey came in second to last, and Nikki finished in last place because of a twisted ankle. Because of their sportsmanship, they were both allowed to compete in the finals.

Sometimes contests become legacies passed from generation to generation.

My dad was one of 14 children raised during the depression; 12 made it to adulthood. He was the third oldest. His dad had trucks, and the government wouldn't give him aid because of that. As a result of the Great Depression, nobody had the funds needed to hire his trucks; his dad ended up losing his farm. The small town in Richmond, Utah, was very cliquish, and the starving were looked down upon by the affluent. Dad had the shabbiest of clothes.

Garr came from a very prosperous farm and looked down upon my dad. That social distinction between the two of them caused a great rift. Life was a contest between them. Until World War II, Garr had a distinct advantage. He had more money, a car, better clothes; in short, he was in a higher social class.

As a soldier in World War II, my dad quickly became the highest-ranking non-commissioned officer from Richmond. Garr did not enlist. Due to this, the competitive landscape between the two flipped. In Richmond, Dad now had a higher social status than did Garr. Dad was the war hero, and Garr was the farmer who stayed safely home.

This rivalry continued for the rest of their lives. Their rivalry passed to their children. Garr's kids were not allowed to associate with the Carlson kids. Although, to the disapproval of our parents, Ronnie, Garr's oldest son, and I became friends. The competition between the families continues as a well-known secret in Richmond. Although with each passing generation, it becomes much less pronounced. Members of both families still measure their successes compared to the achievements of the other. While the measurements for winning have become obscure, winning is still important. Perhaps, the Capulet-and-Montague-style feuds are more common than we think.

Relationships or winning is a choice.

When I was a Lake Forest Graduate School of Management professor, I had an NFL player in my relationship course. I had made the statement, "If the relationship is important, don't compete." After the class ended, he came to me and said, "That is absolute bulls**t. As an NFL player, my life is about competition. It is about beating other teams and people."

"OK. Is the relationship important with the other teams?"

"NO! Only proving that we are better."

"How about with competition with your players on your team?"

"Yeah! It's all about that too! You have to compete for your position. That is the life of football."

"Are you willing to forfeit the relationship to win your spot?"

"Absolutely."

"In football, winning is more important than relationships?"

"Yeah, absolutely! If I have to give up a relationship to win, that's what I'll do. My competitors on the team are doing the same thing."

"You are saying that the most important thing in your life is winning? For you, winning is more important than any relationships?"

"Correct."

"Does that same standard apply for your intimate relationships, like with your family?"

"I hadn't thought about it before."

"Well, your wife and kids would be disappointed to know that they are less important to you than winning. I suspect that they would be hurtful to them if they knew that. Maybe there are relationships in your life that matter more than winning."

He stood there for a moment. He gave me a nod.

People who see everything as a contest have difficulty establishing or maintaining long-term synergistic relationships. Where does the idea that "winning is everything" come from? Maybe it is a survival thing: We all fight for the last meatball on the plate to some degree. Whatever its etiology, we are ingrained with the importance of winning almost from our infancy. Life is the great shifter of winners and losers. Winners rise to the top, and losers languish at the bottom. Right? We are all programmed to get status and ego gratification from winning. We see life as a never-ending competition, and everyone is our competitor. Even high school reunions are where we get to compare our successes with those of our classmates. (After more than 50 years, it is just good to see who is still in the game and reconnect.) In our society, competing becomes part of us. We incorporate it into our role as parents when we problem solve. It becomes part of our management ethos. If I can get what I want, I win!!

How a Cincinnati mom competed with her son in an attempt to fix him

I taught a management course in Cincinnati, Ohio, and after the first day, a lady who had been in the class asked if she could meet with me. We found a nice isolated spot in the lobby. She shared her concerns about her 15-year-old son. She informed me that he had dropped out of school, moved out of her house, lived with his 14-year-old girlfriend, and was into smoking, drinking, and using pot. I asked her if the girlfriend's mother was OK with that arrangement, and she just shrugged her shoulders in response. I wondered what her relationship with her son was like, and she told me that they fought all the time. I asked if their relationship and interactions seemed to be a continuous contest, which she confirmed.

Me: "How will you know when you win?"

Mom: "He will come home, get back in school, and stop messing around with pot and his girlfriend!"

Me: "And, how will he win?"

Mom: "When he comes home, gets back in school, and stops messing around with pot and his girlfriend!"

Me: "If that is how he views winning, that is what he would be doing."

Mom: "He should; that is how he will win."

Me: "Let me put it to you from his perspective. 'I can come home and fight with my mom or sleep with my girlfriend; battle with mom, or have sex.' Which win do you think he will choose?"

Mom: "But if he keeps doing this s**t, it will destroy his future!!"

I told her that I agreed with her but that having this continual contest wouldn't get the results she wanted. She finally asked me, "What can I do?" I explained that we need to deal with him from where he is, not where we want him to be. I inquired if her son was a social fellow, which she said he was.

Me: "Why would a social fellow, your son, drop out of school, which is the social hub of teenagers?"

Mom: "I don't know."

Me: "Who does?"

Mom: "His teachers?"

Me: "They can guess, just like we can. Who really knows?"

Mom: "He does."

Me: "Have you asked him why he left school?"

Mom: "Yes."

Me: "What did he say?"

Mom: "He said, 'I don't know.'"

I asked if she would arrange a time to meet with her son after our class the next day. She said that she would, and she did. When I met with her son, I was impressed with his looks and manner; he was confident, although a little suspicious about our meeting. After having a small chat for a while, I asked him what he liked more than anything. He said he loved animals and hoped to become a veterinarian one day.

Me: "That is a grand vision to have, but you do realize that to become a vet, you will need to graduate from middle school, high school, college, and veterinarian school."
Mike: "Yeh, that is a problem."
Me: "Why did you drop out of school?"
Mike: "Because I couldn't fake it anymore."
Me: "I don't follow."
Mike: "I dropped out because I couldn't read. I didn't want the kids to think that I am stupid."
Me: "Clearly, you are very smart; how did you make it to ninth grade without being able to read?"
Mike: "It was easy!"

He explained his tricks and methods for getting his friends to help him and pulling the wool over his teachers' eyes. The same approach didn't work in ninth grade. I asked him if he was serious about becoming a vet, and he assured me that he was. Together, over a couple of evenings, we laid out a step-by-step plan of what he would need to do, beginning with becoming an excellent reader. When we parted, he was enthusiastic about his project and future.

I talked with his mother for a couple of years; then, she stopped calling. She stopped calling because I no longer filled a need for her or her son. By that time, he was reading well beyond his age group level and was doing well in school. Even though they no longer argued about school, home, girlfriend, pot, etc., I wonder if the contests continued on other fronts.

Conclusion: Competing is not an elegant way to problem solve, either in war or in our homes.

Being a winner still means: "I'm better than you, in our society." We tie our identities to winning. Winning has become so important that entire leagues ensure that every participant gets a trophy in children's events. "Everyone is a winner!" It begs the question: What is winning? People may not know the answer to that question, but they will conclude that, "My kid is a winner!" (even though no one kept score). Perhaps, competition without winning is less beneficial than we think it is. How does it benefit kids to receive trophies regardless of effort or excellence? Don't you think that people should be able to answer the question: "Why are you competing?"

When working with some competing couples, I sometimes ask the same question. "Why are you competing?" Far too many have no logical answer to that question. Many relationships would be better off if they had a logical answer. Fighting to win a contest with no purpose is senseless. It seems that some fight just to win. When asked, "What do you win?" There are seldom reasonable answers. Maybe it is a bad habit developed to fill an inadequate ego. If there were a practical purpose, then, perhaps, they would find a better way to get expectations met without having winners and losers. They may even find a way to get everyone's needs met and enhance the relationship at the same time.

If the relationship is important, don't compete! What are we supposed to do – lose?

I am saying that if the relationship is important, don't compete; I didn't say lose. I occasionally get invited to speak with coaches, players, and parents about building Synergistic relationships. Invariably, I bring up the concept that if the relationship is important, don't compete. That pretty much unnerves the coaches because they believe that their primary purpose is to create winning and competitive teams. It takes some time and explanation for them to understand that their job isn't to make their players "winners," "competitors," or "worthy adversaries." It is to help their players become excellent and to excel in their sport and life. Let me explain. Relationships are emotional states that exist between people. The emotional states between Synergistic relationships are very different from the emotional states that exist between dysfunctional relationships. You can't have a Tribe Member relationship and an Adversary relationship simultaneously. Below is a comparison of Tribe Member relationships with Adversary relationships:

Definitions of Tribe Member and Adversary Relationships

Tribe Member (the inner circle)	Bound by common vision, purpose, values, standards, and commitment; characterized by deeply shared goals, beliefs, and emotional commitment.
Adversary	Define winning as a personal victory against an adversary, characterized by competition (trying to get what I want at the expense of the opposition).

Do you see the dilemma that faces coaches who want both at the same time? While we can have Tribe Member relationships that focus on excellence and perfecting ourselves, we can't have two different kinds of relationships in the same moment with the same person. But we can have Tribe Member relationships that focus on personal excellence. Excelling is consistent with Synergistic Tribe Member relationships. Coaches who focus on excellence and excelling can have great per-forming teams who love, support, and nurture one another. Suppose they concentrate on developing competitors who only seek to win against their opposition, be it another school or a team member vying for the same position. In that case, they place winning superior to re-lationships. That is OK against competing teams. But team members can't compete and have Synergistic Tribe Member relationships on the same team because one will be a winner and the other a loser. "Birds of a feather flock together." Winners don't mesh with losers. Tribe Mem-bers who focus on excellence and excelling can accept and bond with others also focused on excellence. Varsity members who have a higher level of excellence can mentor and support the freshman who is also striving. The freshman is lifted and validated by their idol, which they acknowledge as a better player.

I frequently hear coaches yelling at their team to focus on a bad patch. Inwardly, I want to inform the coach that they **ARE** focusing on the wrong things. When we focus on competing, we focus on different things than when we focus on excellence.

The chart below compares the differences between focusing on excellence and excelling versus competing:

Excellence and Excelling	Excellence and Excelling
• Perfect execution • Building synergistic relationships (sisterhood/brotherhood) • Skills (technical, social, and emotional) • Processes rather than outcomes • Optimizing the potential of self and others • Creating synergy through a unified effort • Bringing light, energy, and enhancement to others and self • Commitment and diligence • Being pleased but never satisfied with improvement and successes • Individual and group excellence • Unconditional values • Being (character traits)	• Results or outcomes • Winning • Beating or dominating opponents • The opponent; not on execution • Self-comparison to others • Being better than • Ego gratification • Not losing • Status in a hierarchy (labels, position, or rank) • Symbols of success: awards, trophies, possessions, etc.

The Vince Lombardi Trophy is a Symbol of Excellence.

Coach Lombardi was the head coach of the Green Bay Packers from 1959 through 1967. They won five Super Bowl championships in his eight seasons as a Head Coach. Arguably, he is known as the greatest NFL football coach of all time. Interestingly, his focus was not on winning. It was on perfect execution. He was obsessed with excelling through excellence derived from perfect performance. To excel as a coach, player, and team, everyone needed to know their role and execute that role flawlessly. They focused fanatically on excelling through perfect execution. He told his players that it didn't matter if the other team knew what their plays would be because if they executed perfectly, the other team couldn't stop them. He derived great satisfaction from witnessing perfect execution from his team and his opponents. When the other team made a great play on televised games, the camera would immediately switch to Coach Lombardi to capture his reaction. They would find him standing there with a huge smile, admiring the excellence of the other team's execution.

When you became a Green Bay Packer, you became a brother in a family whose priorities were absolute: Unconditional commitment to God, to family, and the Green Bay Packers. Their quest to excel through perfect execution combined with fidelity to their core values connected them. The many players who became enshrined in the Football Hall of Fame always spoke of the challenges and honor of being a Green Bay Packer. They spoke reverently (sometimes irreverently) about their love for their team-mates. Their admiration for Coach Lombardi, who expected so much from them, was limitless. Virtually all of them said that being a Green Bay Packer instilled in them who they became for the rest of their lives.

Down to his toes, Vince Lombardi concentrated on excellence and brotherhood achieved through the quest for perfect execution. I'm sure he loved winning, not just to win but because winning was evidence of superior execution. In that sense, winning was merely the natural consequence of excellence. Experienced coaches know that winning is not always controllable; we can lose on our best day and win on our worst day. The perfect execution of those who play has a lot to say about the outcome. And, what we focus on is the determining factor.

Enemy Relationships

Divided by deep emotional and personal agendas; character-ized by a desire to punish, hurt, get revenge, remove, disem-power, and defeat the other party. Winning is making the other party lose more.

Adversarial relationships evolve into enemy relationships when the contest is not about personal wins anymore but is about conquering our opponent. Boxing is a pretty good example: "I may get hit, but if I stop, I can't hurt you, and I will stay in the contest until one of us is lying on the canvas." It is still about winning but winning changes to wanting the other person to lose more. Adversarial is about: "I have more, I am better than you, I am right – you are wrong." But in an enemy relationship, it is: "You will lose worse than I do."

Wars are supreme examples of enemy relationships. In World War II, over 50 million people died at the hand of their enemies. All the warring nations intended to defeat and destroy their enemies' ability to make war. The bombing of cities killed civilians in the tens of thousands and hundreds of thousands near the war's end. Armies fought, killed, and defeated opposing armies. Britain stood alone against the Nazis for over a year, willing to sacrifice, wait, and prepare to destroy their enemies. And, with the help of the allies, they were victorious. The United States dropped atomic bombs on two Japanese cities to clarify that they were willing to destroy Japan to stop the war. Finally, Japan got the message and surrendered. In enemy relationships winning is not a game. It is defeat or be defeated. It may mean survival or extinction.

I was a Vice President in a company where the CFO disliked me. He had been the President's chief advisor until I arrived. He started documenting everything that he thought could be interpreted as a mistake on my part and sending it to the President, our mutual boss. I confronted him and suggested that rather than sending documentation of all of these "offenses," we would be better off if he talked with me face-to-face so we could benefit from the discussion. He let me know that he intended to get me out of the company. I realized that, to him, I was an enemy. I explained that I did not want to be an enemy with him but was prepared for battle if he wanted to pursue that course. As we separated, I left him with the, not so subtle thought, "Never fight with a person who is not afraid to die." As it turned out, I saved his job when the corporate management found out that he was keeping two sets of books, one he sent to them and one we used to manage the company. I convinced them to keep him on as a Controller rather than CFO because he was a talented and essential accountant. I guess he never was my true enemy.

A very successful author, David Brooks, talks about the essential human skill to see others deeply relative to other people's need to be seen deeply. Enemy relationships will use that skill to find their enemies' weaknesses and defeat them. Enemies don't want to understand us unless that leads to them being able to whip us. Enemies always see themselves as right and their enemies as wrong. With enemy relationships, the lines of moral virtue get blurred. People find a way to justify their behavior, even if it is immoral. "My behavior is right because..." "What I am doing is not as bad as what they are doing." Enemies often develop the talent of justifying their immoral behavior by deflecting attention away from what they are doing toward something their enemy has done. "Don't talk about me; look at what Harold did!" To too many, vanquishing enemies justifies any means necessary. No one ever wins in an Enemy relationship.

Mutually Destructive relationships are the lowest form of relationships. Adversarial relationships have winners and losers, but always at the expense of a healthy relationship. In an Enemy relationship, there are only losers. If the relationship is important, don't compete!

6

INDIFFERENCE

THE TENSEGRUS RELATIONSHIP SPECTRUM

Indifference means there is no relationship.

Indifferent people lack emotion or don't care about what happens or doesn't happen to others.

We often hear that love and hate are opposite feelings. Not true; the opposite of both love and hate is indifference. Love and hate are similar in that they are manifestations of extreme emotions. Love is a positive feeling, whereas hate is a negative feeling. Both can fill every space of our emotional beings. Both are catalysts for action. Lovers behave in ways that express and display their love to validate and affirm the value of those they love. Haters behave in ways that express and show their hate to diminish and wound the identity of those they hate. Every relationship discussed up to this point is characterized by the feelings associated with that particular kind of relationship. Apathetic relationships lack feelings for others.

Apathetic relationships are not relationships at all because relationships require emotional connections. Apathy is indifference which is the absence of caring or concern. Apathy epitomizes the meaninglessness of others, generally or individually. Put in other words, if bad things happen to others, apathetic people don't care. If good things happen to others, apathetic people don't care. People learn of tragic events in distant places where thousands of people die, are injured, or are made homeless. Those who care take action to help them. The apathetic do nothing because they don't care or care sufficiently enough to act. Lack of action characterizes generalized indifference. If a neighbor is injured or killed and you don't care, that is individual indifference.

People can be a mixture of general or individual indifference and caring. For example, a person can care about starving children in Africa (general caring) and be indifferent about the well-being of their neighbor (individual indifference). Or they can care about the well-being of their neighbor (individual caring) and be apathetic toward the starving children in Africa (general indifference). During my childhood, my dad didn't care about the deplorable conditions and the discrimination against the black community. Still, he cared deeply and was concerned about the injustices directed at my dear, bullied friend Ernest. He was apathetic and did nothing to assist the black community, but he would defend and place himself in harm's way to protect Ernest.

Passion equates to action, and action indicates a relationship.

People who market products or seek donations understand that apathy is the enemy. They know that apathetic or indifferent people don't purchase their products or give money to their causes. They understand that without an emotional connection, there is no relationship, and without a relationship, there will be no purchases or donations. These people know that they need to generate emotions sufficient to emote action. Insurance companies use fear as the motivator to spur people to buy their coverage. They display scenes of accidents or injury to scare us into developing a relationship with them under the guise that they will protect our loved ones and us. They do it very successfully. Humanitarians show us pictures of cold and starving people and animals to stir sympathy and emotional guilt sufficient to cause us to open our checkbooks or send them our credit card numbers. Politicians fan the flames of emotions to get people to act. They use information and disinformation to motivate people to align with them and support them. Frequently, powerful politicians lie to make people's blood boil, so they will establish "commiseration clubs" where club members reinforce one another's misery and establish relationships based on shared suffering and injustice (perceived or actual). Anger is lucrative. Infuriated people give tons of money to people who successfully stir the hornets' nest. Could it be that politicians would be willing to lie and jeopardize our democracy to make lots of money or to hold on to power that appears to be waning?

Apathy and indifference suggest that there is no relationship. If we do not care about people or fail to experience joy in their successes or concern for their tragedies, there is no emotion or motive to help them.

Indifference can be fatal.

During World War II, many babies ended up in orphanages. Surprisingly, large numbers of infants died receiving adequate nourishment and cleanliness care. They just declined and died. An orphanage run by Catholic nuns was analyzed because it had evidence of high baby deaths and specific examples of thriving babies. When the researchers examined what was happening there, they found that the babies simply fed, changed, and bathed, eventually died. The babies that thrived were cared for by a nun who, in addition to feeding, changing, and bathing the infants, held them, hugged them, talked to them, nurtured them, and loved them. Touching and emotional connections are essential to early childhood development and even survival.[6]

In the U.S. and U.K., death rates of infants placed in orphanages, nurseries, and foundling hospitals were, in some cases, close to 100% (at the beginning of the 20th century). London's Foundling Museum documents these harsh realities in detail. In the 1940s, the work of psychoanalyst René Spitz[7] documented high infant death rates (one out of three) and reported that many of the babies who didn't die had high percentages of cognitive, behavioral, and psychological dysfunction. Most of these deaths were not due to starvation or disease, but to severe emotional and sensory deprivation, in other words, a lack of love. These babies were fed and medically treated but received no sensory stimulation, especially touch and affection.

---

6   R. D. Parke, P.A. Ornstein, J.J. Rieser, C. Zuhu-Waxler (Ed.) "A Century of Developmental Psychology" (American Physiological Association, 1946), 203-23.

7   R. N. Emde, "Individual meaning and increasing complexity: Contributions of Sigmund Freud and René Spitz to Developmental Psychology" (American Psychological Association, 1994).

The importance of touch

Human touch is fundamental for human development and survival. Research conducted by Ruth Feldman and Tiffany Field[8] has shown the positive effects of skin-to-skin touch in premature babies and that these effects remain for many years. Skin-to-skin stimulation triggers significant gains in neurological development, weight gain, and mental development of premature babies.

Infants in orphanages can be deprived of touch, individual attention, and love. It happens not because all orphanages are terrible places (although some are), but because there are usually too many babies for the staff to manage. The first half of the 20th century required nurses to cover their faces with surgical masks without interacting with babies. Medical staff believed that no contact would prevent infections from spreading and help keep babies healthy. Because of this thinking, parents and other family members were not allowed to visit and touch their babies. However, instead of getting better, the babies got worse.

Dr. Harry Bakwin[9] studied emotional deprivation in infants and published his findings in *The Journal of Pediatrics*. He stated that: "Failure of infants to thrive in institutions is due to emotional deprivation." The term "failure to thrive" is currently used as an umbrella term of conditions, ranging from growth delay, emotional misery, and death. It is a generalized health problem seen in high-income and low-income countries. However, it is more prevalent when poverty and a lack of human resources prevent the babies from receiving emotional and sensory stimulation (or love) daily.[10] If someone doesn't feel connected and loved throughout life, it spawns a myriad of physical, social, and emotional issues. We all need interpersonal connections and relationships to thrive.

---

8   "Mother-Infant-Skin-to-Skin Contact (Kangaroo Care): Theoretical, Clinical, and Empirical Aspects: Fruth Feldman, Infants and Young Children" (April 2004), 17(2): 145-161.

9   H. Bakwin, "Emotional Deprivation in Infants" (*Journal of Pediatrics*, 1949).

10   Ines Varela-Silva, Senior Lecturer in Human Biology Loughborough University (Printed in "The Conversation," the conversation.com/can-a-lack-of-love-be-deadly-58659, 2016).

7

How Our Capability to Have Relationships is Developed

Our formative years determine the relationships we have or are capable of having.

From birth to 16 or 17, our formative years essentially set the stage for relationships that will naturally come to us throughout our lives. During that formative time frame, we learn to see ourselves in terms of where and how we fit into the world.

Early Formative		Early Formative		Late Formative	
Birth 0 to 1	Infancy 1 to 3	Preschool 4 to 5	Grade School 6 to 11	Middle School 12 to 14	High School 15 to 18

The chart below generally depicts the level of dependency on our parents or primary caregivers as we age. They support our physical, emotional, and intellectual needs. Our dependency is 100% during our early formative years and declines as we age. By the time young people reach 18 or 19 years of age, how well their emotional needs will be satisfied has primarily been determined. By this time, they are a product of how well their physical, emotional, and intellectual needs were fulfilled during their formative years or weren't. How well those needs were, or were not, fulfilled has a dramatic impact on determining the kind of relationships we can have and probably, will have. From 18 or 19 years of age, people enter into the reformative years, where they can grow and change or languish with little change until they die.

100% Dependent   10% Dependent

The formative years determine our sense of self and how we connect with other people. We established our sense of safety and security during our earliest formative years (from birth to around two years of age). We were raised in a loving, nurturing, and supportive environment or a neglectful, hostile, or abusive environment in the extremes. The chart below will illustrate the impact of both environments on dependent children relative to how well their physical, emotional, and intellectual needs were satisfied.

Consequences of a Loving, nurturing, supportive Environment	The Early formative Years	Consequences of a Neglectful, hostile, or abusive Environment
Children survive and generally thrive physically when their physical needs are met.	Physical needs	Children don't survive or are compromised physically when their physical needs aren't met.
When the emotional needs are met, children are secure and feel **secure**. They are free to explore the world and find out where they fit into it. That is why we call them "Free Children." Free children are typically confident, social, empathic, caring, sensitive, and fun people to be around. Emotionally they can have synergistic relationships. They make many friends quickly learn the ground rules of being a good friend.	Emotional needs	When the emotional needs are unfulfilled, children feel **insecure** and **inferior**. They have learned not to trust people, so they focus on fulfilling the unfulfilled needs themselves. They feel secure when they have power, control, and status. These kids often manifest their security by dominating others. Or they accept their insecurity and inferiority by becoming submissive or avoiding other children. These kids have difficulty making friends. They will often be too shy or too aggressive.
When the intellectual needs are met, children feel secure and free to explore information and use it to become knowledgeable and decide where they want to fit into the world. They learn to love sharing information, developing and giving opinions, and disagreeing. They become confident in themselves intellectually. Intellectually they can have synergistic relationships.	Intellectual needs	When intellectual needs are not met, children feel insecure and inferior. They will either strive to satisfy those unfulfilled intellectual needs themselves and prove that they are intellectually OK, or they will accept their intellectual inferiority. In essence, this will be when they start to become young overachievers with a sense of inferiority or under-achievers who see themselves as "dumb." The overachievers will have an easier time making friends. However, they may see others as intellectual competitors (can't get too close to your competitors). The underachievers will have trouble relating to kids intellectually and making friends. They will come to be ever more isolated. Loneliness becomes a problem for many of these kids.

How well physical, emotional, and intellectual needs are met during the early formative years affects how children see themselves and how well they can relate to others. The later formative years follow a similar pattern but are much more heavily impacted by what happens outside their home. Kids raised in neglectful, hostile, and abusive environments may be safer and more secure outside the home. Away from home, a school may be the only place where the child is supported physically, emotionally, or intellectually. That may become the life raft that saves them from a life of insecurity and inferiority. I am always amazed and grateful to see those kids who rise above their circumstances to become confident, secure, and free children. I am surprised because they have done it despite circumstances rather than because of them. Thank heavens for those who throw needy children life rafts. Let's review the impact of fulfilled and unfulfilled physical, emotional, and intellectual needs on kids during the middle to the late stages of the formative years.

Consequences of a Loving, nurturing, supportive Environment	The Middle to Later Formative Years	Consequences of a Neglectful, hostile, or abusive Environment
When the physical needs are met, school-age children generally thrive physically. They have the energy and ability to do what they aspire to do physically. They start determining what happens to them physically.	Physical needs	School-age children with unmet needs show the effects of neglectful, hostile, or abusive environments. They typically fall into the lower percentiles of growth, physical health, social, and intellectual development. It almost always contributes to feelings of inferiority, making them vulnerable to predators or self-abusive behaviors like addictions or suicide.
When the emotional needs are met at home, school-age children feel **secure** at home. Their sense of safety and security will serve them well when others challenge them outside of the house. But because of their Free Child nature, they will be readily accepted by those who are also secure and confident. When challenged, they can go home to have their safety and security re-energized and restored. They will learn how to navigate successfully through life's emotional challenges. They will develop naturally and successfully through their formative years to reach maturity. Emotionally, they can have synergistic relationships and friends to share their lives fully. They will be willing to take emotional risks; it is part of their continued exploration of their fit in the world.	Emotional needs	When the emotional needs are unfulfilled at home, school-age children will feel only as safe and secure as they can provide for themselves. If they have been successful at overachieving, they may feel acceptance from others. If they have been really successful at finding ways to fill their emotional needs, they may even feel reasonably safe and secure emotionally. Still, they will seldom risk that emotional safety and security by putting it in the hands of others. Trust will not be their strong suit. They will emotionally struggle with making relationships where they have to be vulnerable with others. They may have many friends but few, or none, with whom they will be genuinely open and allow emotional vulnerability. The ones who were not successful in finding ways to fill their emotional needs may become true stompees or become emotional stompers (better to stomp than to be stomped on). Here too, additive and cumulative repressed anger may make them emotionally explosive.
When the intellectual needs continue to be met, school-age children feel even more secure and free to explore information and use it to become even more knowledgeable and decide where they want to fit into the world. The foundation laid in the early formative years becomes their launching pad during their later formative years. They learn to love sharing information, developing and giving opinions, and disagreeing. They become even more confident in themselves intellectually. Intellectually their ability to have synergistic relationships develops with their ongoing growth.	Intellectual needs	When intellectual needs continue not to be met, school-age children feel ever more insecure and inferior. Those who focus on intellectual overachievement to fill their emotional needs have a chance to fill their unfulfilled intellectual needs and beat the odds. Experience suggests that few rise above feelings of intellectual insecurity and inferiority. Most fall further behind in their intellectual ability to compete in a society that requires excellent intellectual capability. As they age, they drop down the intellectual power ladder and, if they are lucky, will find ways to survive and support themselves in non-intellectual pursuits as adults. As adults, we usually find them in the chronically unemployed or underemployed ranks. School-age children with intellectual needs that remain unfulfilled or under fulfilled have difficulty with relationships. Synergistic relationships won't happen unless a synergistic hero steps forth to connect with them.

There is a saying that the rich get richer and the poor get poorer. This saying could also apply to those with fulfilled and unfulfilled needs. We might say that those whose physical, emotional, and intellectual needs are satisfied in their formative years become safer and more secure as they move through life. During their formative years, those with unfulfilled physical, emotional, and intellectual needs become less safe and secure as they move through life. Of course, there are exceptions in both groups, but not many.

This section shows us a couple of important things about relationships. First, secure people likely will have Synergistic and Associative relationships. Second, insecure people will probably settle for Command and Control relationships or Mutually Destructive ones. Something else we should know: Secure people tend to connect with secure people, and they disconnect with insecure people over time. Insecure people connect with insecure people. For example, Stompers and Stompees are both manifestations of insecurity. The Stomper gets security through power, control, or status. The Stompee gets it by complying and being submissive to power, control, and status. That is a relationship. It can change. Relationships will become adversarial if Stompees decide to no longer be Stompees, and Stompers won't concede power, control, or status. That is a different relationship. An Adversarial relationship leads to a win, a loss, or a disconnection from one another. Both parties have to decide if the change in the relationship is worth the changes that will indeed happen. If we examine the chart that describes the different kinds of relationships, we can readily see where the secure reside and where the insecure people do. However, if they choose to change, insecure people can become secure.

After our formative years, we enter into our reformative years that last from the end of our formative years until we die. For most of us, that becomes a long time of status quo (stasis) or a time of change and growth. Most of us will no longer have mom, dad, or grandparents around to satisfy our unfulfilled needs. We may have other loved ones who can help do that. But the truth is: We will have to learn how to marshal the means for getting them satisfied for ourselves. It may mean that we have to nurture ourselves. The good thing about our reformative years is that we get to choose if we stay the same or change and grow. We all can change and grow. It will require that we engage our adult mode. We explain adult mode in the section about Operating Modes. It also requires that we implement the growth and change competencies in the last section of this book under competencies. We don't have to remain casualties of the unfulfilled needs of our formative years; we can choose to change and grow beyond our challenges.

A dear friend once told me that she was hesitant to get into an executive MBA program because it would take her five years at Rutgers to graduate. I asked her, "How old will you be when you graduate with an MBA?" She answered, "I will be 36." I then asked her, "And how old will you be in five years without an MBA?" She laughed and said, "36." My last question was, "Do you want to be 36 with an MBA or 36 without an MBA?" She got her MBA when she was 35.

To insecure people, I would ask, "How old will you be in ten years without addressing your insecurities and unfulfilled needs?" In ten years, you will be the same age with your insecurities and unfulfilled needs, or you will be the same age, having dealt with them and conquered them. Do you want to have them still or to get rid of them? That will be ten years of change and growth or ten years of status quo. That is a choice.

8

INTRODUCTION TO THE EMOTIONAL STATES

Feelings are the lens through which we perceive and experience life. They precipitate decisions and actions. Emotions are like the rails on which a train travels; how we feel determines our direction. Feelings govern the decisions we make and how we act. For example, depression is an emotion, but it is a poor foundation for a happy and fulfilling life or warm and loving relationships. If we have an important relationship and feel it is satisfying, life is good. If we find that a significant relationship is miserable, life is bleak.

On the other hand, when we feel it is beautiful and a blessing, then our life is beautiful and a blessing. As you can see, the adjectives that describe our feelings also describe our life. Emotions connect us or disconnect us from people; they draw us to others or repel us. They are a vital element of relationships. As our feelings change, relationships change accordingly, and, consequently, so does the direction of our life. Therefore, to the degree that we understand and manage emotions, we can manage interpersonal connections, influence relationships, and determine the direction of our lives.

I met Dr. Bob Carkhuff[11] at the University of Toronto, where he was teaching a course in counseling. He explained that understanding feelings, expressing them, and precisely interpreting them is a core life skill. It is also an essential component of counseling. To hear, understand, and validate people, we must interpret the feelings our eyes are seeing and the emotions our ears are hearing correctly. He taught us that people's feelings are precise, people feel what they feel and if we

---

11   Robert R. Carkhuff, "The Art of Helping: An Introduction to Life Skills" (Human Resource Development Press, Inc., 1973).

can't label their feelings accurately, they will not feel understood or validated. They may not be able to precisely explain what they are feeling, but they will know if we label their feelings correctly or incorrectly. These two types are what we call cognitive vs. functional vocabulary. He claimed that in America, most English-speaking people have a pretty good cognitive vocabulary (they understand well what they are feeling and if our authentication of their feelings is accurate). On the other hand, he believes that the functional vocabulary of those same people is minimal (the ability to state precisely how (or what) they feel).

Interestingly, he believes the Latino community generally has a much more significant cognitive and functional vocabulary because emotions play a much larger role in communicating and expressing themselves. He encouraged us emphatically to increase our active vocabulary to improve our ability to counsel effectively, advance our ability to manage our lives, and connect with others. He provided us with a feeling chart that we used as a counseling tool to better identify emotions accurately during our exercises. I have provided you with the same chart. His chart identifies seven categories of feelings, listed in alphabetical order. Each category has feelings that vary from mild to intense, but the level of intensity does not correspond with the alphabetical order.

Bob Carkhuff's Seven Categories of Feelings:

Notice that each descriptor is very specific within each category. And again, notice that the range of feelings in each category goes from mild to extreme. Identifying with people's emotions is a link for establishing interpersonal connections. To connect with people, we have to recognize that there is an issue, then hear, understand, and validate their feelings at the moment. Imagine talking with your daughter, she is visibly upset, and you are in a great mood. Your viewpoints are very different. The problem to her is a big deal. You, probably, aren't aware there is a problem. Both perspectives are off-beam when viewed from the other's point of view. And yet, each is reality. Each interprets life from their emotional state. Personal connection requires one to release a perspective and tune in to the emotions being expressed by the other.

Bob Carkbuffs 7 Categories of Feelings:

Happy	Sad	Angry	Confused	Scared	Weak	Strong
Alive	Angry	Aggravated	Anxious	Afraid	Ashamed	Active
Amused	Apathetic	Annoyed	Awkward	Anxious	Bored	Aggressive
Calm	Awful	Burned up	Baffled	Awed	Confused	Alert
Cheerful	Bad	Critical	Bothered	Chicken	Defenseless	Angry
Content	Blue	Disgusted	Crazy	Confused	Discouraged	Bold
Delighted	Crushed	Enraged	Dazed	Fearful	Embarrassed	Brave
Ecstatic	Depressed	Envious	Depressed	Frightened	Exhausted	Capable
Excited	Disappointed	Fed up	Disorganized	Horrified	Fragile	Confident
Fantastic	Dissatisfied	Frustrated	Disoriented	Insecure-	Frail	Determined
Fine	Disturbed	Furious	Distracted	Intimidated	Frustrated	Energetic
Fortunate	Down	Impatient	Disturbed	Jumpy	Guilty	Happy
Friendly	Embarrassed	Irritated	Embarrassed	Lonely	Helpless	Hateful
Glad	Gloomy	Mad	Frustrated	Nervous	Horrible	Healthy
Good	Glum	Mean	Helpless	Panicky	Ill	Intense
Great	Hateful	Outraged	Hopeless	Panicked	Impotent	Loud
Hopeful	Hopeless	Rage	Lost	Shaky	Inadequate	Love
Loving	Hurt	Resentful	Mixed up	Shy	Insecure	Mean
Motherly	Lonely	Sore	Panicky	Stunned	Lifeless	Open
Optimistic	Lost		Paralyzed	Tense	Lost	Positive
Peaceful	Low		Puzzled	Threatened	Overwhelmed	Potent
Pleased	Miserable		Struck	Timid	Powerless	Powerful
Proud	Painful		Surprised	Uneasy	Quiet	Quick
Relaxed	Sorry		Trapped	Unsure	Run-down	Rage
Relieved	Terrible		Troubles	Worried	Shaky	Secure
Satisfied	Turned off		Uncertain		Shy	Solid
Thankful	Uneasy		Uncomfortable		Sick	Super
Thrilled	Unhappy		Unsure		Timid	Tough
Turned on	Unloved		Upset		Tired	
UP	Upset		Weak		Unsure	
Warm					Useless	
Wonderful					Vulnerable	
					Wishy-washy	
					Worn out	

In this case, the daughter has the problem, so it would behoove the father to connect with the daughter's feelings. He must first recognize that she has a problem, then it is imperative to hear, understand, and validate her emotions and related unfulfilled needs.

You might wonder, how do I connect with someone who is in a different emotional state than myself? To make an interpersonal connection, *we must deal with people from where they are and not where we want them to be.* We can't problem-solve effectively or help them until we make an interpersonal connection, even if we have an ideal solution. An interpersonal connection begins when a person feels heard, understood, and validated. Note that validating feelings is not sympathizing. Sympathy is agreeing with the sentiments, whereas validating is understanding and authenticating the feelings. For example, you may despise a terrorist's violent acts, but you can confirm his feelings, which are the basis for his actions, and still despise the violent acts. Whether or not you would want to establish an interpersonal connection with a terrorist depends on your purpose for doing so. I guess I would if I were trying to negotiate a cease-fire.

People tend to reinforce one another's positive or negative feelings.
Have you ever been in such a great mood that you quickly find others who feel the same way? Emotional states create the ambiance in the "room" and, in particular, around ourselves. Notice that when people share a common emotion, the feelings are reinforced – for better or worse! When we feel similar positive emotions with others, Synergistic Relationships begin to form (or are reinforced).

Have you ever been in such a bad mood that you find all the happy people around you annoying? If a person feels outraged, they seek validation from others who are also outraged. They then validate one another's emotional state and, in a sense, justify their reasons for feeling the way they do. That is the source of "Commiseration Clubs."

Commiseration Clubs

Commiseration Clubs are a phenomenon common in virtually all organizations. There are three distinct roles in a Commiseration Club. One, the Chief Poop Stirrer; two, the Sympathizers; and three, the Martyr. The Chief Poop Stirrer is the guardian of the organizational "Poo Pot," where all the organizational poo is stored, both new deposits and ancient ones. The Chief Poop Stirrer is the receptionist for all new poop deposits. He gladly receives all contributions and can even inform the contributor how his deposit compares to previous contributions. The Chief Poop Stirrer is a leadership role, albeit a hidden one, for everyone who is not a club member. He is a central point for communication with the Sympathizers and validates everyone's misery.

The Sympathizers are members of the club who contribute poo to the pot and share their misery with other club members. They all have one standard message: "Ain't it awful!" Sympathizers reinforce and justify their common complaints. The magical thing about having one's misery justified is that the justification validates that "we are valid victims and someone else has the problem and needs to change!" A-ha! At this point, the Martyr enters the picture. The Martyr is an idealist who naturally feels that someone needs to tell the authority figures (management) that they have a problem and need to change. Of course, the Martyr volunteers to be the spokesperson for all the combined "Ain't it awful's." Before the Martyr exits the Commiseration Club, the Sympathizers help prepare him for the management confrontation. "When you are with management, make sure you tell them about…"

When the Martyr comes out of the Commiseration Club, he comes out spectacularly, with banners flying and waving. I picture him descending with a sky-diver parachute, colored smoke trailing behind. As he approaches the inner sanctum of management, I imagine double-wide swinging doors. He bursts through the doors and sees management sitting around a large board table. He says, "We believe that **you** have a lot of problems, and **you** need to change to make us happy!" Management leans back in their chairs and asks, "Who are we?" As the Martyr looks through the swinging doors, he sees Sympathizers scattering (like cockroaches when a light turns on). Not being a rat, he doesn't disclose their identities but testifies that they are real and that people in this very room cause their victimhood. Management thanks the Martyr for coming and providing valuable feedback, then a junior manager walks him to the exit. The Martyr instinctively knows that it didn't go too well. Next, we see two very different scenes: the Martyr reuniting with the Sympathizers and the management team discussing the Martyr.

When the Martyr, out of view from the management group, approaches the club, it looks like a group of six-year-olds surrounding a soccer ball, and he is the ball. "What did they say?' "What did you say….?" The Martyr hisses, "Where were you?!" He declares that he wants nothing more to do with these cowards. He revokes his membership from the Commiseration Club and decides that he will do whatever his supervisor asks him to do. His exit provides the Chief Poop Stirrer and Sympathizers with a new "Ain't it awful!" to add to the poo pot.

When the Martyr leaves the room, management has a conversation of its own. "John, isn't that guy one of your people? We just want you to know that whatever you need to do fix your problem, we are behind you." Their statement is a coded message to get rid of the Martyr.

When John meets with the Martyr, the Martyr immediately says, "Just tell me what you want me to do, boss." (Compliance is an insecure person's safety mode.) And the boss says, "About that...." (There is no easy way to say goodbye).

It is not easy to get out of a Commiseration Club. Eventually, people get tired of constant commiseration and want to distance themselves from people who are constantly in victim mode. But the Chief Poop Stirrer and Sympathizers have antidotes to keep people from moving on. We call the treatments "Little Green Stinkies." People cannot always congregate around the poo pot to pull out the best "Ain't It Awful!" So, they produce portable ones. They take poo from the pot and put it into tiny capsules that can be retrieved whenever needed. When encountering a person leaving the club, they can give him a "Little Green Stinky." If one dose proves insufficient, they keep giving them more until the person rejoins the club.

A word of caution about Commiseration Clubs: they institutionalize victimhood. Victimhood is a dependent state; if we solve victims' problems, the dependence remains. We should help them learn how to resolve their issues and be responsible for their solutions. Commiseration Clubs fulfill the need for belonging when people are emotionally wounded and feeling insecure. "Ain't it Awful's" are addictive; they become compulsive behaviors that provide an immediate buzz (it feels so good to release that emotional pressure), but they damage one's ability to be responsible for their feelings and actions. Secure people recognize victimhood and avoid associating with victims. Ultimately, the only associations remaining for victims are fellow victims. If you are in a position of authority and join a Commiseration Club, particularly with people who work for you, all the Sympathizers and the Chief Poop Stirrer will know you have been (or are) an active participant. You may be able to resolve your own "Ain't it Awful's," but you will always have the stigma of being a Commiseration Club member.

It is natural for children to commiserate from a position of powerlessness. As a parent, teach children early to take ownership of their expectations, problem solve, and give feedback (not criticism). Not a bad message for everyone. Best counsel: Don't commiserate.

Feelings are the lens through which we look at life. They are the source of our connections with others. People's feelings are specific, and to understand them, we need to develop our cognitive and functional vocabulary. We tend to connect with others who have similar feelings. People with similar negative feelings come together and form commiseration clubs. People with similar positive emotions tend to develop Synergistic Relationships.

9

THE ORIGIN OF FEELINGS

Why do we need to understand where feelings come from? First, if we know where feelings come from, it gives insight into how to govern them. Second, people who don't understand where their emotions come from may feel victimized by their negative feelings. It's like a beast inside of them that they can't control: it's the Mr. Hyde to their Dr. Jekyll. Depression, for many, is a beast that is devouring them. Learning to understand it and manage it is one of life's significant challenges. Oh, that we had the answer!

There are two places from which feelings originate:

1. Our subconscious brain (the limbic system)
2. Expectations (anticipated outcomes)

The Subconscious Feelings

Most people are running through life on autopilot. They let their subconscious make most of their everyday life decisions. From the moment they wake up, life is a series of habituated, preprogrammed decisions. It's like we are watching the movie *Click*, where Adam Sandler goes through life on autopilot because every decision was predetermined. Except we are living this movie. How is this possible?

One hundred billion brain cells comprise our brain that constantly make new connections based on our thoughts, sensory information, and feelings. Scientists call this action neuroplasticity, or the brain's ability to change or create new connections. Our repeated thoughts, behaviors, and emotions become hardwired in our brain, making these neural connections more permanent.

In his book *Evolve Your Brain*, Dr. Joe Dispenza wrote, "When we no longer learn new things, or we stop changing old habits, we are left only with living in routine. But the brain is not designed to stop learning. When we stop upgrading the brain with new information, it becomes hardwired, riddled with automatic programs of behavior that no longer support evolution."[12]

Unless we consciously create new experiences, we will, unconsciously and continuously, live our past life in the present. Our brain can only make new connections if we create unique experiences! Learning is a new experience, and thus our brain is changed forever. Feelings can become automatic and hardwired in our brain.

These emotions sit in our limbic system. For example, when we are sitting at work and the next thing we know, we become irritated without really knowing why, we can thank our limbic system for creating that emotion. We enable these subconscious feelings to be the scapegoat for all our behaviors and actions.

"Don't ever ask mom for something when she is grumpy."

"Watch out, kids – dad is in one of his moods."

"How's the boss today?"

It's as if we have never grown out of our toddler state, when throwing tantrums was our way of expressing our discontentedness. It's interesting to note that these feelings dictate how others perceive us, and it becomes an acceptable way of life as we grow older. Our emotions have become the standard justification of our behavior, and we accept it in our society. If you told a toddler, "No," their response would be to retaliate either by hitting back or throwing a fit.

I was at Costco when an employee politely asked a man, who was not wearing a mask, to please put one on. He looked at the employee and said in a booming voice, "No! You can't force me. I have my rights!" A

---

12   Joe Dispenza, *Evolve Your Brain: The Science of Changing Your Mind* (Health Communications Inc., Simon and Schuster, 2007).

few people applauded, a few gathered to watch, and the majority quickly avoided the scene. I don't mean for this to be a political statement. I am merely commenting that this gentleman was filled with rage and acted accordingly. A lady close to me commented to those around her, "At least he believes in something." I thought, "That poor employee, he didn't make the rules; he has to enforce them." I wonder how the relationship between those two will be when masks are no longer mandated."

The outraged fellow felt justified in his actions because he was offended. Justified actions based on negative emotions are of great concern for relationships. If we don't govern subconscious feelings when they arise within us, we can say and do things nearly impossible to repair.

Look at the husband who hits his wife in a moment of anger.
Look at the wife who says hurtful remarks to her husband in a moment of frustration.
Look at the upset kid who says he hates his parents and wishes he lived somewhere else.
Look at the friend who gossips behind the friend's back.
Look at the boss who yells at his employee for a mistake.
Look at the coach who berates his team after a loss.

How's the relationship after charged emotional events? Stephen Covey would say that a withdrawal was taken from the "emotional bank account." A single withdrawal may not have a profound and lasting impact, but frequent ones can doom relationships.

We have a fraction of a second to choose a better response in these moments. The moment of choice is where the conscious mind comes into play.

Our Conscious Mind – The Change Agent

We have a unique ability to change ourselves through our frontal lobe. The frontal lobe is where our consciousness resides, and our ability to make choices exists. It is the home to self-control, willpower, and decision-making. When feelings erupt, we can become automatic and react emotionally or engage our conscious mind and choose our response.

Our frontal lobe allows us to exercise executive functions and exhibit emotional control. It is a muscle. It takes fuel, training, and practice. One of the most significant ways to understand the conscious-governance side of emotions is to understand the connection between expectations and their fulfillment. Fulfilled and unfulfilled expectations determine our feelings and, therefore, our behavior (unless we consciously choose our actions).

Take golf, for instance. I love golf. I hate golf. People have to understand that when it comes to golf, "Hell! Shit! and Damn!" don't count as cuss words. I usually play with my good neighbor Don Clifford. He is an old jock. One morning, we were playing with his grandson-in-law, Tyler, and after a frustrating couple of holes, for me, I threw my golf club. Tyler looked at me, concerned. I told him that it was either throw the club or kill Don, and Don didn't know that he was the other option. Playing golf creates a constant clash between my subconscious mind (limbic system) and my expectations (frontal lobe).

I would love to play well in automatic, repeat mode. It would be wonderful to make perfect drives, approaches, pitches, and putts without thinking about it. Sometimes, it seems that my subconscious is in charge; I play, and, at times, I'm OK. Then my game goes south (I almost said "goes to shit"), and I wonder why I ever started playing this game. My handicap goes from ten to twenty, and I become miserable and frustrated. I become driven to change how I play this damn game. My frontal lobe becomes my "change partner." We analyze everything: my stand, grip, feet positioning, backswing, follow-through, golf hat, and chewing gum. And, eventually, I change, sometimes for the good and other times for the bad. Without my change partner, I would never change; I would play the game the same way, day after day (sounds like a bad Zombie movie). Maybe it shouldn't matter, but my frontal lobe can't tolerate such lousy play. Did I mention that I hate golf? That I love golf? Either way, golf is going to keep me out of heaven.

Expectations are the conscious fuel to feelings. The higher the expectation, the stronger the emotions. When I golf, I have high expectations despite my ability. Hence the pure bliss when I meet my expectations and pure frustration when I don't. Any unfulfilled expectation will elicit an array of negative feelings. I have a friend who golfs with me occasionally. He is a terrible golfer but enjoys every second. He has no expectations when it comes to his golf game. If a swing is good or bad, he appreciates both. His performance expectations are low, and his emotions are unaffected by his level of play. Using his example, one can assume that the key to happiness is to lower one's expectations.

In most of my seminars and classes, invariably, a recommendation is put forward from "helpers" trying to provide a solution for parents struggling with a troublesome teenager, "Why not just lower your expectations to improve the relationship?" I worked in psychiatric hospitals for years early in my career. I met with hundreds of psychiatrists and would talk with them about their philosophies.

Here too, many psychiatrists would recommend lowering expectations to resolve relationship issues. Their logic is that lowered expectations would allow people to avoid dealing with unfulfilled expectations. True. However, what kind of relationship would we have without expectations?

Indifferent. In the real world, **the more important the relationship, the greater the expectations**. **When we lower expectations, we change relationships**. I doubt that anyone would have meaningful relationships with minimal or no expectations. I recall the comments from a teenager who felt alone and abandoned by his parents, "My parents used to get mad at me when I messed up. Now they don't give a shit." It was sad to see how their son interpreted the parents' lowered expectations.

In short, we mustn't look at minimizing disappointment by simply lowering expectations but rather look at improving interpersonal connections by dealing with unfulfilled expectations in healthy ways. We need to look at unfulfilled positive expectations for what they are: opportunities. We can use such opportunities to make healthy connections rather than confrontations. We can use them to "trigger" our adult mode, control our feelings, and behave constructively rather than justify negative-feeling-based behavior.

To better understand the connection between expectations and relationships, let's examine a simple matrix that enables us to look at positive and negative expectations from a perspective of whether or are not they are met. We will understand the connection between the feelings generated, the behaviors caused by the emotions, and the predictable impact on interpersonal relations.

Introduction to Expectations Management

Fulfillment of our expectations has a significant impact on our feelings and, consequently, our relationships. As you recall, relationships are the emotional state that exists between people. Therefore, relationships reflect the emotions, and mindsets, derived from fulfilled or unfulfilled emotions.

The chart below shows four quadrants of potential mindsets related to having our expectations met or not met. Quadrant one is the **"Pleased"** feelings mindset resulting from having our positive expectations fulfilled. Quadrant two is the **"Dissatisfied"** feelings mindset when our positive expectations are not fulfilled. Quadrant three is the "**Validated**" feelings mindset occurring when we have fulfilled negative expectations. And quadrant four is the "**Mixed Feelings**" mindset that happens when our expectations are negative and unexpected positive things happen.

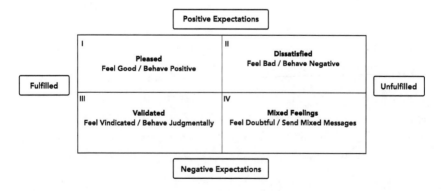

The "Pleased Feeling Mindset" is our natural emotional state when positive things happen when we have positive expectations. When we feel pleased, it is easy to have Synergistic relationships. The "Dissatisfied Feeling Mindset" is also a natural response when we have positive expectations and negative things happen. The negative feelings move us away from Synergistic relationships, at least, when we feel negatively toward the person who failed to meet our positive expectations. The "Validated Feelings Mindset" occurs when we have had a paradigm shift about someone and no longer have positive expectations but expect negative things to happen. For example, we validate our feelings and expectations when we expect people to be late, and they are late. With validated negative expectations, we feel justified in having negative feelings toward the people who "matched up" with our negative expectations of them. It is hard to have Synergistic relationships when we have justified our negative feelings about people. The "Mixed Feelings Mindset" happens when expecting negative things and positive things occur.

When that happens, people have a variety of emotional responses. Some are pleasantly surprised. Others may be skeptical or suspicious. Some may be cynical and feel that what happened is atypical of what will happen in the future. That is why we call this the Mixed Feelings Mindset. For example, suppose a family member who is an addict shows up at a family function sober and announces that he will never use addictive substances again. There will, undoubtedly, be a mixture of emotional responses to his sobriety and his announcement from family members. We might expect that the kinds of relationships that the addict has with individual family members, going forward, will align with the feelings they have toward him.

The linking of our expectations and feelings is a roadmap for our interpersonal connections. It would be ideal to learn how to deal with unfulfilled expectations in healthy ways rather than deal with the paradigm shift to a world of negative expectations. Prevention is so much better than living through a nightmare of managing negative expectations.

The above Expectations Management Matrix is an excellent visual tool to help explain what is driving our feelings. With fulfilled positive expectations, we feel pleased. With tongue in cheek, I tell people that the secret to life is to surround ourselves with people who meet all our positive expectations all of the time. That is not possible. Therefore, we need to learn to deal with unfulfilled expectations (the source of our displeased feelings) in healthy ways. Feelings are the starting point of our behaviors: We act how we feel. People use their feelings to explain (or justify) their actions. If we can learn to analyze and control our feelings, we can control our actions. Feelings and actions determine the kind of relationships we have.

10

Proactive verses Reactive Emotional States

People who simply respond to the feeling they have at the moment are reactive. They are like life's billiard balls; they go through life ricocheting off each interaction. Their contact with others and circumstances determines their direction. Each contact sets a new course. They are not anchored to a theme unless the theme is chaos. This reactive behavior is sometimes labeled "low impulse control." I have a nephew who is a marvelous fellow. An ordinary family discussion is: "What has Travis done to himself lately?" Some think he is accident-prone; others think he is unlucky. The truth is, he has moments of low impulse control. He acts impulsively. He does dumb things like shooting himself in the leg while doing quickdraws. If you ask him why he did the latest self-sacrifice, his response would be, "I didn't think about it." He is almost the perfect man: handsome, loving, caring, generous, out-going, and impulsive.

The power of being proactive comes from understanding why we are feeling the way we are. People who can look at their feelings and analyze them can have powerful internal dialogues and manage their emotions and actions. "I am feeling bored, and I don't like feeling bored. I am going to do something that is not boring." People who understand and validate their feelings become empathetic with themselves. People feel relieved and empowered when they understand themselves (metacognition). Through self-analysis of our feelings, we can become proactive in our actions. In the words of Dr. Morris Massey, "It's healthy to do a checkup, from the neck up."[13]

---

13 Morris Massey, *The People Puzzle: Understanding Yourself and Others* (Reston Publishing Company, 1979).

As a young man, I had been a pretty successful sales manager in a Fortune 100 company. I took pride in having everything in order, including my family. I wanted my family to be like the Von Trapp family from *Sound of Music*. As you remember, the Colonel controlled his children with whistles. I would be like Colonel Von Trapp, the authority figure, where no one would question my orders or commands.

After one of my longer business trips, I was anxious to get home. I was super-tired from traveling, and I called and left a message on the answering machine detailing how I would like to see the house when I got home. The list included having homework done, mowing the lawn, etc. Essentially, my demanding phone message was the icing on the cake for my sweetheart. I was greeted by her, not with wide-open loving arms, but with a punch in my chest and an intense look that made her five-foot-two frame seem more like she was six-foot-two.

"We don't work for you."

"What?"

"We... don't... work... for... you."

Her attitude and behavior stunned me. I had two feelings competing for attention: One was anger. I had been working 80+ hours each week for the past month. Can't my family recognize and appreciate that? The other was guilt. I realized that I was being judgmental and did not like how I felt and its impact on the relationship with my wife and kids. I quickly concluded that I needed to break that habit.

"I'm sorry... I didn't mean to be judgmental. Can we talk about this?"

After a great deal of hearing, understanding, and validating my wife and kids, we came up with the idea of having my family use a catch-phrase as a notification that I was being judgmental. I was looking for a trigger to bring my unconscious habituated behaviors to the conscious forefront.

My wife and kids would say, "Big J, Dad" or "Big J, Wayne."

It was a reminder to me that I had slipped over from being reasonable to acting judgmentally. The phrase was so jolting to me that I would quickly snap out of those behaviors that had become so second nature to me. Eventually, I became so sensitive to being judgmental that I became less self-centered and more others-centered at home and work. I wanted to understand other people's "why" before allowing myself to decide and act. My reactive self would have gone unglued and missed an opportunity to bond with my wife and kids. Being proactive requires the use of our frontal cortex for processing.

The Inevitable Consequences of Feelings

Two young fish were swimming in the ocean when an older fish swam by and said, "Morning, boys! How's the water?" The two young fish turned and looked at each other and asked, "What the hell is water?"

Our emotional states become an ocean of which we are blind and unaware; we don't know its existence. We live in these emotional states from day to day, not knowing that they are dictating our lives, even to the point that we use emotions to justify our decisions and behaviors. Our feelings paint our perception of the world, and our feelings become the basis for our truth. It is fair to say that feelings define our facts even more than the facts do. How do we know we are in the water?

Nobody knows they are in the water. Everyone creates their sense of reality based on their perceptions and feelings. Feelings determine truth more than facts determine truth. Another way of expressing the message is that our feelings determine our facts. As laid out below, turning feelings into realities is part of a logical, natural pattern. We call this the "My Truth Process."

The 'My Truth' Process
Feelings ➡ Beliefs (rationalized feelings) ➡ Behaviors ➡ Outcomes

Feelings are emotional states. Beliefs are rationalized feelings. Therefore, feelings become the basis for what we believe to be factual. Behaviors are the actions we take based on our beliefs. Outcomes are the resulting consequences or benefits of our actions. When we feel an emotion, it compels us to align our beliefs with our feelings to maintain our emotional balance. Internal chaos happens when beliefs and feelings don't match. Therefore, people make them correspond to resolve the internal conflict. We call that internal strife: Cognitive Dissonance.

In music, the dissonance (disharmony) occurs when our instrument is out of tune. Imagine playing the guitar that has one string out of tune. Playing that string in conjunction with any other note from the other strings creates disharmony. Musicians can hear the disharmonious sound waves and tune the instrument to cease the disharmony. Cognitive dissonance is an internal disharmony of our thoughts and beliefs in emotional states.

When I was a boy of eight or nine, my dad was racist toward blacks and people of color. One of my best friends, Ernest, had darker skin but wasn't African American. Still, the people in my town called him derogatory names and were prejudiced toward him. It was challenging living in Richmond, Utah, in the 1950s if people believed you to be a minority (even if you weren't). My dad told me that minorities (not the term he used) were lazy, good-for-nothing welfare addicts. He said they lived in shacks but drove Cadillacs and Lincolns (an obvious insinuation that their values were misplaced). He had other racist viewpoints, as well. I listened to his words and was deeply troubled.

I loved my dad and thought he was wise, and I believed what he taught me, yet I knew Ernest, his brother, and his family. They were nothing like dad said minorities were. They lived in a house like ours and drove a car similar to ours, only better. Ernest was taller than the rest of our class, and for several reasons, he was the most bullied kid in our class. He was intelligent, athletic, and willing to stand up for himself. He was not a member of our church which was a hanging offense in Richmond, unless you had a lot of money or were a dentist, store owner, or owned the liquor store. Ernest was my friend, making us both targets for our class bullies. We often defended one another when bullies picked on one of us. Dad's prejudices created emotional dissonance within me. How could I believe my dad while knowing Ernest and his family?

I had a gestalt! Dad was wrong!! My cognitive dissonance disappeared, the disharmony within me was gone. That day, the world changed for me; I disagreed with dad about minority people, and the universe didn't explode. I was at peace with my conclusion. And, I still loved my dad – and Ernest. It took years, but my dad's prejudiced beliefs about minorities diminished significantly. He knew that many of my friends and employees in New Jersey were minorities that I loved dearly. As he got to know them, his attitude changed. We had a gathering at our house one evening while my parents visited. The guest list included Whites, Blacks, Hispanics, and People of Jewish Faith; most worked with me at J&J. After the party, my dad made an unusual comment for him. "You love all these people, don't you?" "Yes, dad, I do."

While it doesn't relate to the topic at hand, I'd like you to know what happened to Ernest. When Ernest and I were in sixth grade, he and his family were in a horrible car accident. He was the only one who survived. He was severely injured. His spine was damaged, which left him partially paralyzed in his lower body. He was in the Primary Children's Hospital in Salt Lake for a long time. A wealthy white couple who lived in the east Salt Lake City area adopted him. Years later, I visited him and was grateful that he could walk (after a fashion). He told me that one day he would dance at a Junior Prom. I lost track of him and believed he became an attorney but later discovered that he developed and owned a successful dental technician company in California.

When we experience cognitive dissonance, we have two choices: we either have to change our feelings to match our conviction of truth, reality, and belief, or change our reality to fit our feelings. The natural inclination is to change reality to match our feelings. Ergo, Kellyanne Conway's statement of "alternative facts" when she justified Sean Spicer's statement that Trump's inauguration attendance was the largest, most-watched ever (when in fact it wasn't). The facts had to match up with her feelings and beliefs.

How do you know you are in the water? Feelings create the ocean in which we swim. One must analyze the root of the feelings to understand one's beliefs. If your feelings influence your beliefs, no matter what the facts say, you may be swimming in a "polluted ocean." Despite the overwhelming evidence of pollution, people swim in polluted oceans all around us. You can't clean up a polluted ocean with facts. We must go to the source of the pollution, which are feelings. Only by changing feelings can we change the ocean.

11

Truth

Jane and Doug have been married for 14 years. On the surface they seem extremely happy, both have sons and daughters from previous marriages and one child of their own. They had goals together, saving to buy a house, and plans for the future. For about ten years, if you asked them independently, they had a beautiful marriage. Then things began to change, not dramatically, but slowly. Jane felt that Doug was distancing himself, both physically and emotionally. She felt guilty about how she was feeling and asked Doug if they could talk. He constantly avoided the discussion. The more she pressed the topic, the more distant he became.

From Jane's perspective, she thought the marriage was based on love, honesty, and mutual respect. Doug would often leave on business trips for four or five days at a time without returning home with any money. When Jane asked where the money was, Doug would blow her off by saying, "I have expenses." Jane was dealing with so much cognitive dissonance because she kept questioning why she was doubting him. Something seemed off until one day, Jane's daughter found a picture of him with another woman on social media.

When Jane approached Doug with the evidence, he denied it. Finally, after tracking down the other woman, she informed Jane that Doug said that he was a widower; that his wife died months prior. Once the truth was revealed, both of Doug's relationships quickly became adversarial with Jane divorcing him and the other woman rejecting him.

Synergistic relationships are centered on truth and reality, while making allowances for empathy. In fact, falsehoods and misrepresentations are what often destroys relationships. Most "non-synergistic" relationships are centered on some type of falsehood or misrepresentation.

Synergistic relationships do not have elements of deceit. Synergistic relationships can endure the test of truth. Axiologist (philosophy dealing with values and ethics) Jeremy Boone says, "Strong relationships can bear the weight of any truth."

Let's make one thing clear; truth and honesty are not synonymous. You can have a perception of "truth," but it is not based on reality. That is what happened with Jane. Her truth was not based on reality, it was based on her perception of reality and that reality did not match up to her truth. So, what is truth? We see the truth in three categories: Verifiable truth, perceptive/relative truth, and inherent/self-evident truth. They may be separate but also inclusive of one another.

Verifiable Truth (Scientific Truth)

In science, truths are based on precise physical reality observations, validated through observation and experimentation. We can either validate or invalidate a truth hypothesis. As Richard Feynman, one of the great scientists in the 20th century, said, "The test of all knowledge is experiment. Experiment is the sole judge of scientific truth."

For scientific truth to be true, it must be tested through verification (in other words, it needs to be falsifiable). If it can't be verified with empirical data, observation, test, or experimentation, it cannot be classified as scientific truth. If the hypothesis is proven to be repeatable with the same inputs, we call this verifiable truth. A very simple example of this would be Sir Issac Newton and his discovery of gravity.

As a mathematician in England, Sir Issac Newton would often use observation to discover truth. One day, as he sat observing the world around him, he saw an apple fall from a tree. He asked why the apple fell straight down, instead of sideways or even upward. This event sparked years of experimentation to test his hypothesis. Because "gravity" can be tested and repeated, he was able to measure the "force" that makes objects fall, keeps us on the ground, and the moon and planets in their orbits. From these experiments of gravity and motion, Newton was able to create calculus, which was able to chart the constantly changing and variable state of nature.

As with all scientific truth, it is forever evolving with the discovery of new information and data. The year was 1846 and women were dying at staggering rates right after childbirth due to "childbed fever." Childbed fever was a horrible way to die. They would experience high fevers, infections in the uterus, birth canal, and extremely painful abscesses all over their body. After three days of horrible pain, the mothers would die. Doctors could not figure out what was causing their death and began performing autopsies on the deceased mothers.

A Hungarian doctor named Ignaz Phillip Semmelweis theorized that there were "cadaverous particles" that doctors were passing to the mothers during childbirth. During this outbreak, doctors would perform autopsies and then immediately deliver babies without any sort of sanitation process between procedures. Semmelweis hypothesized that doctors were passing invisible particles from the deceased to the mothers. He forced the doctors and medical staff at the Vienna General Hospital to wash their hands with a chlorine lime solution. Immediately, the cases for "childbed fever" dropped significantly. However, Semmelweis "germ theory" was widely criticized, especially among the medical staff, who were outraged at the thought that they were the cause of the outbreak. Semmelweis was fired from the hospital and sent to a mental asylum, where he died two weeks later.

It wasn't until 20 years later that Semmelweis "theory of invisible particles" would be embraced by the medical community. With the work of Louis Pasteur in the late 1860s, handwashing and hygiene became a standard medical practice. People's sense of truth may not be reality until it is proven. All scientific truths are verifiable, and all Synergistic Relationships are verifiable that can endure scrutiny. What happens when truth is verifiable from different perspectives? This brings us to Perceptive/Relative Truth.

Perceptive/Relative Truth

This is the individual viewpoint of fact. Truth is the facts as we perceive them (the interpretation of experiences from our perspective). People have different vantage points, life experiences, and emotional states that reflect their unique perceptions. Two people can participate in the same event and have vastly different experiences. That is "their" truth. It is essentially Einstein's thought experiment of people on a train.

Albert Einstein created a thought experiment to help understand the relativity of time, which helps explain the duality of truth. There are two people in this imagined scenario. A person is sitting on a train going 60 mph, and another person is standing on the train platform. Right as the person sitting on the train passes the bystander on the platform, lightning strikes the front of the train. Who saw it first? The person traveling on the train would see the lightning strike first, compared to the person standing on the platform. Why? Because the train would reach the bolt of lightning earlier than the bystander standing on the platform. The bystander would view the lightning bolt as hitting the back of the train. So, the same exact event would have two different recollections of what happened. Who is right? They both are. Duality of truth.

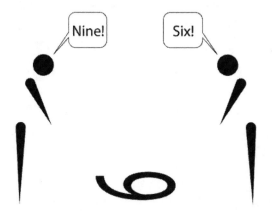

Look at this diagram of these two people. One person sees a 6. The other sees a 9. Who is right?

Again, they both are. To create healthy and meaningful relationships, one must empathize with the other's viewpoint, feelings, perceptions, etc. This is also very evident in "Mood Congruence Theory," which states that a person's mood will influence their perception of events. If you are in a great mood, things seem to be going better. If you bad mood, things appear to be a lot worse than they are.

Fundamental Attribution Errors – An Example of Perceptive Truth

A common response to perceptive truth is a Fundamental Attribution Error.[14] A Fundamental Attribution Error happens when a person experiences behavior they don't like, relative to their expectations. They take the behavior personally and assume negative intent from the person who failed to meet their expectations. This assumption leads to the creation of a negative-alternate-reality. It could be classified as a pandemic because it happens so often.

It is everywhere in our society and happens in everyday interactions. For example, imagine an employee walking down the hallway at work who says a pleasant, "Good morning," to her boss. The boss, looking straight ahead, doesn't acknowledge her. She immediately becomes uncomfortable and perceives his lack of response as a snub, takes it personally, and assumes negative intent. This fundamental attribution error grows into something more significant where the employee then begins to align her beliefs to match her feelings. Because he didn't respond to her greeting, she concludes that the boss doesn't like her. This negative feeling based on a false assumption creates a new belief. "The boss never talks to me." "The boss is a terrible person." "The boss hates me." "Did you hear what the boss said to the vendor?" Her interpretation of the boss's lack of response created a new reality.

Ironically, her false assumption about her boss was born from her insecurity. Insecure people see other people's behavior, somehow, as a reflection of themselves. Secure people see other people's behavior as a reflection of them. The truth is: Other people don't spend much time thinking about us unless there is a specific reason for doing so, despite the belief that insecure people have that everyone's thoughts and behaviors are in some way about them. In other words,

---

14   Lee Ross, The term "Fundamental Attribution Error" was created by social psychologist Lee Ross in 1977. Lee Ross, "The intuitive psychologist and his shortcomings: Distortions in the attribution process." In Berkowitz, L. (ed.). Advances in experimental social psychology. Vol. 10 (New York: Academic Press, 1977).

negative assumptions about other people come from our insecurity about ourselves.

For example, say you get a message from your boss that he needs to see you, right now. How many of us become anxious before we enter the room? "I wonder what I did wrong?" If the message was that he needs to see us first thing in the morning, how many of us would sleep well that evening? There is an old saying that our fears cause us to believe, or to expect, the worst. Insecure people have a lot of those worries.

With Fundamental Attribution Errors, three predictable things happen:

One, it causes a change in our thinking pattern to where we:

- See the world through a new lens and shift to a negative paradigm (*The boss hates me.*)
- Become self-centered – personalizes the incident (*It's all about me and my feeling, Poor me.*)
- Validate our feelings into a new reality (*I feel like the boss hates me and doesn't respect me. The boss is a terrible person.*)
- Transfer problem ownership **to be** the offender – the other person becomes the problem (*The boss didn't talk to me; the boss is now the problem.*)

Two, our thoughts and actions align with our new reality, we:

- Constantly defend our perspective (*Can you believe what the boss did?*)
- Make excuses and justify our feelings and behavior (*I don't think it's my fault. The boss is the bad person here.*)
- Blame others (*If the boss treated me with respect, I would be way more productive.*)
- Start to view all the other person's behavior as evidence of our new reality (*Did you see how the boss snubbed John the other day?*)
- Become convinced that our belief is the actual truth (*He doesn't care about us!*)

Three, ultimately, the outcome becomes a Self-Fulfilling Prophecy:

- Because the employee has aligned her thoughts, feelings, and behaviors toward the boss to match her reality, the boss now reacts differently. The new perspective and behaviors eventually lead to mutual disdain, and the once healthy relationship becomes toxic.

Here is an abbreviated sequence of a fundamental attribution error:

A Fundamental Attribution Error is an erroneous assumption about someone's intentions based on a faulty interpretation of their behavior.

The Behavior → The boss didn't say "Good morning" back.

The Feeling → The employee feels slighted for not being acknowledged.

The Belief → A belief based on our feelings. The boss hates me and is a terrible person. This becomes our alternate reality or perception of truth.

The Behavior → The employee starts acting consistently with her belief. She behaves in accordance to her beliefs (she snubs her boss).

The Outcome → The boss eventually dislikes her because of her behavior toward him and her belief becomes a Self-Fulfilling prophecy.

What the employee didn't realize was the real reason that her boss didn't respond to her. After meeting with the CFO, financial concerns pressed on his mind. Imagine how different the outcome would have been if the employee, at a later time, had merely asked the boss, "Are you doing OK? I was wondering because you didn't acknowledge me when I wished you a good morning."

We can avoid all fundamental attribution errors if we don't jump to negative conclusions and accept the notion that there are logical reasons why people are doing what they are doing instead. There could be logical reasons why people don't behave toward us as we expect them to. There are rational reasons why people are doing what they are doing, and it seldom has anything to do with us – unless we make it about us. All we need to do to avoid making a false assumption is to check out the behavior with the person who didn't meet our expectations. Of course, this requires that we verify its reality. When we make a fundamental attribution error, we make the self-centered, emotional, and incorrect assumption.

Tragically, there are endless stories about how a fundamental attribution error have led to generations of hate. A family has a wedding. Someone forgot to mail an invitation. The forgotten person concludes that the family doesn't like them.

He starts looking at the world through the lens of rejection. The overlooked person isolates himself from the family and starts shunning them. If that doesn't work, he starts being sarcastic toward them. He starts using his favorite behavioral addictions to gain short-term wins (gossiping, blaming, and criticizing). He views life through that negative lens and treats his family accordingly.

The family members he treats poorly respond in kind, and relationships become fractured.

It is credible how many times I counseled people about their fractured relationships with other members of their family and how often the core issues stemmed from some Fundamental Attribution Error that no one seemed able to recall where, how, or when it started. They recount their enemies' current and historic "Ain't it Awful's!," which now characterize their ruptured relationships.

Avoiding Fundamental Attribution Errors requires discovering the facts of the situation rather than operating from unvalidated assumptions. Road Rage usually flows from Fundamental Attribution Errors. "That person intentionally cut me off. How dare he do that? I'm not going to let that jerk do that to me. I'll show him how I deal with disrespect." Hopefully, the driver who was focused on picking up his daughter when he unconsciously cut off the fellow doesn't get shot.

Innate/Self-Evident Truth

Inherent truths are known to be true. We understand innate truth without proof and by ordinary human reasoning. Verification of innate truth comes from the inward or spiritual evidence flowing from conformity with, and inseparability from, self-evident truths. Inherent truths generate light, energy, and edification. In essence, these are eternal truths. The opposite of self-evident truth is anti-truth, which is like a black hole from which light and energy cannot escape. A black hole consumes everything which falls within its influence. We all know those people who bring light, energy, and feelings of self-enhancement when they enter a room. They brighten the place, and we feel better about ourselves because of their presence.

The opposite is true when a "black hole" person walks into a room. The ambiance changes to where light, energy, and edification dissipate. We feel the heaviness and darkness spread through the room. We must accept that, knowingly or not, our aura influences those around us. We have the opportunity to bring light, energy, and edification to those we encounter or to bring darkness.

At the USA Volleyball Nationals in Las Vegas in July 2021, our 15-year-old Club V team won the USA American National Championship. We met before each match to discuss how to draw light, energy, and enhancement from one another to aid us in our contests. The girls felt personal responsibility for finding that light and energy within themselves and sharing it with their team sisters. It was amazing how they lifted and supported one another despite errors. Their light and energy edified their teammates, their family members cheering them, and even the crowd who watched the matches. Light, energy, and enhancement spread like sunshine to all touched by it. It is magical when it happens; to be a part of it is remarkable – never to be forgotten.

We must search within ourselves for innate truths that will manifest with light, energy, and personal edification. Eternal principles and truth, when acted upon, bring those feelings of enlightenment and vitality. Inherent truths eventually become validated by scientific facts. In the end, we believe that all innate and scientific truths will merge.

Intrinsically, we know that love and kindness are better than hatred and meanness. Until recently, this was a self-evident truth that needed no proof to know its truth. Still, in 2019, a new book surfaced called "The Rabbit Effect" by Kelli Harding, whose scientific studies proved the profound impact that love, connections, and kindness have on our health and well-being. Being compassionate and lovingly giving of ourselves engenders personal vitality and provides a model for the world.

Conclusion

Synergistic Relationships are based on reality and lack misrepresentation and deceit. When Perceptive Truth is present (without the ability to verify actual events), we must listen with empathy and understand their version to maintain the relationship. Their perception is their truth and their reality. When it comes to building relationships, there are inherent truths that brighten and uplift. There are also other things that diminish and hurt others.

12

FEELINGS INFLUENCE RELATIONSHIPS

Emotions are manifest in every type relationship and determine the kind of relationships we have.

Feelings play a major part in every type of relationship. Each relationship type has emotions unique to that particular relationship (think of fingerprints). Consequently, we can use specific feelings to characterize each kind of relationship. Emotions are highly dynamic; they constantly change; so, in turn, do relationships change as well. To have the relationships we want, we must learn to manage and control our feelings. **By changing our emotions, we can change our relationships**. Understanding the previous principles in this section provides understanding of how feelings may surface and helps us recognize their impact on relationships. It also offers insight into managing our relationships through managing our emotions.

Whatever level of relationship we have, we associate particular feelings with it. The groupings below illustrate relationships from the perspective of descriptive feelings.

We and others feel the emotions associated with relationships surrounding us. Relationships and feelings are symbiotic; our relationships fluctuate as our emotional states fluctuate. If we don't learn how to control our feelings, we won't know how to manage relationships. Uncontrollable emotions result in unmanageable relationships. All people's feelings change with circumstances, but sustainable healthy relationships require a baseline of positive, synergistic feelings upon which to anchor. There are two types of emotions associated with relationships:

Emotions determine the kind of relationships we have.

1. Anchor Feelings: that define the relationship at its central core
2. Dynamic feelings: link changing relationships with changing emotions due to shifting circumstances

Anchor feelings are the sustainable emotions people feel toward one another in any given relationship over a prolonged time. It is the baseline of feelings people have toward one another. Baseline feelings apply to all types of relationships. How we feel when we are around a person constantly becomes our anchor feelings. It may begin with a first impression but is formed solidly through ongoing interactions. Our emotional baseline becomes the anchor that determines the more permanent relationships we have. How people experience themselves when they are around you is a huge determining factor of the associated emotions.

Our anchor or baseline emotional states will determine the kind of relationships we can sustain. Feelings will ALWAYS go above and below those anchor feelings. Hence, relationships will go up and down simultaneously in the extreme feeling moments. Even with these shifts, relationships can remain anchored to a baseline of feelings. Hedonic adaptation explains how people can experience highs and lows but remain anchored to their baseline emotional state. For example, hedonic adaptation happens when a person gets a huge pay increase and feels "over the moon" pleased about it for a time; but before long, it levels off to the same emotional state they had before the big raise. It explains how people can be anchored to a particular relationship while demonstrating various emotions and behaviors not aligned with their anchored emotional baseline.

Probably, most of us know a couple who have a fractious relationship, with rapidly changing high points and low points. We learn that it is just the way they are. Despite their tumultuous behavior toward one another, we know that they love each other and are committed to one another. They have an emotional baseline that anchors their relationship that could go on indefinitely. But if their emotional baseline shifts to an adversarial anchor, they will become adversaries.

In relationships, forgiving is part of the ability to maintain a synergistic emotional baseline anchor. We can love people but may not like them at the moment. Forgiveness enables us to sustain a healthy emotional anchor even through difficult times. Forgiveness assists hedonic adaptation. It allows us to realign with our emotional baseline anchor.

Of course, if no stable emotional baseline exists, our relationships become whatever our emotions are in the moment. If our feelings, and thus our relationships, are constantly changing without having time to establish a baseline emotional anchor, then we have no anchor. The matching of emotional states determines relationships.

Relationships have interconnected feelings. Relationships usually mirror feelings. Relationships fluctuate in tune with our emotions. If our feelings change, the relationship changes, and if the relationship changes, the feelings change. Relationships are not static; they are dynamic. We usually establish emotional baselines over time, but sometimes they are set with the first encounter. We hear of people falling in love at the first meeting. With some, those initial feelings become baseline feelings that last a lifetime. Occasionally, people don't like someone right off the bat, and those feelings never change. But with everyone, if the emotional baseline anchor changes, the relationship changes.

Recently, I was leading a discussion about relationships with a purchasing group. We reviewed the chart of Categories and Kinds of Relationships. Immediately after that, we examined the chart describing the feelings associated with each kind of relationship. They quickly pointed out that it was easy to change a Synergistic relationship to an Adversarial one. One person shared how her relationship with her daughter's basketball coach immediately changed from a Partnership relationship to an Adversarial one when the coach criticized her daughter. They also decided that it was much more challenging to change from a Command and Control, or a Dysfunctional relationship, to a Synergistic relationship.

After discussing relationships and the different types of relationships organizations can have, they decided they wanted their departmental emotional anchor to be Tribe Members. They realized that many had current adversarial feelings for each other. If they wanted to have Tribe Member relationships, they needed to behave in ways that engendered Tribe Member feelings. Tribe Membership requires constant, not occasional, Tribe Member behavior and feelings. They knew that they needed to establish a new emotional baseline anchor. Fast forward a few weeks, the department members worked incredibly hard to change their feelings and behaviors to match that of Tribe Members, and the results have been extraordinary.

Feelings connected to expectations influence relationships.

Feelings emerge as a reaction to whether or not our expectations are met. As mentioned earlier, relationships mirror feelings. Low expectations suggest unimportant relationships. A fact of life is the more important the relationship, the higher the expectations. Expectations are the highest in intimate relationships. Our expectations of one another directly determine the importance of the relationship. If we change expectations, we change the relationship. Raising expectations signifies that a relationship is becoming more important; declining expectations suggest that a relationship is becoming less important. Managing expectations becomes vital in managing relationships. We need to learn how to deal with unfulfilled expectations in healthy ways to sustain important relationships. Not knowing how to deal with unfulfilled expectations using healthy skills means that we CANNOT maintain Synergistic relationships, because lack of skill in dealing with unfulfilled expectations generates negative feelings. Negative feelings are inconsistent with synergistic relationships. Remember, relationships are dynamic; they change based on situations and emotions. Likewise, feelings are active; if we don't learn how to deal with feelings in healthy ways, we risk changing our anchor feelings and thus changing the health of our relationships. We will discuss how to manage emotions in the Competency section.

If we have no expectations, we have no relationship. Having no expectations indicates indifference, and indifference also signifies no ties. It is wise to remember that our most impactful relationships include intense emotions that define the relationship. Love and hate are both examples of powerful emotions, but they are not the opposite of one another; ironically, indifference is the opposite of both. Intimate soulmates and enemies are both relationships defined by intense emotions. Both come with high expectations. The passionate, intense feelings and associated expectations are why people are significantly impacted in both relationships.

Consequences of rejecting attempts to resolve unfulfilled expectations in healthy ways

Let's look again at the guy in Illinois who came to me for counseling because he and his wife were in an Enemy relationship causing him to lose everything that meant something to him, even his children. He was angry and bitter. He was feeling trapped victimized, and he thought it was all because of the actions of his horrible ex-wife. They indeed were in an Enemy relationship. Their objective became to try and hurt each other.

How did this once warm successful marriage become an enemy relationship? It was simply this: They didn't know how to deal with unfulfilled expectations in healthy ways. They blamed and competed with each other when they were each not getting what they wanted. They became adversarial, trying to win at the other's expense. They tried to take each other's resources. The only thing they had to barter with was the children, so they used them as fighting tools, which became the means for most hurting one another.

As you recall, when he asked, "What can I do?" I told him to stop fighting. He resisted my counsel because he felt that if he did so, she would win everything. I reminded him that he had nothing left to lose but his self-respect. Eventually, he decided to follow my counsel and, over time, was able to re-establish a relationship with his children. He, and she, learned that it is not very rewarding to beat on someone who doesn't fight back (sadists being the exception). They never reconciled, but they stopped being enemies. They both loved the kids and became respectful toward one another. Unfortunately, they got into a real-life, five-cent auction (explanation coming up).

We are competitive; it is one of the dynamics of our society. Winning appears to be the objective of life. We compete for our parents' attention during the imprinting stage and watch our parents compete for our attention. We were thrown into the deep end of competition – grades, sports, popularity during the modeling and socializing stage. Life is about winning – learning to be winners!!! People become convinced that they need to win and avoid losing at all costs.

I believe that every kid needs to think that they are the most popular, powerful, intelligent, hardworking kid in the world; this will provide a survival foundation for emotional identity when they become emotionally assaulted by other teenagers. Teenage competition tends to humble the secure kids and devastate the insecure ones. The bottom line, in life, is that we learn to compete or constantly lose. Debaters can debate whether people are motivated by the love of winning or the fear of losing. My guess is both. I guess, over the long run, the answer lies in the toll exacted by winning: Those motivated by the love of winning become refreshed with success, whereas those motivated by the fear of losing become exhausted and depleted.

The Five-Cent Auction

We have a bidding game we like to use to show how the need to win drives people from adversarial relationships (competing to win) to enemy relationships (hurting them more than they hurt us). It's a great simulation that I have done with hundreds and hundreds of groups. I would guess that 98% of the time, people want their opponent to lose much worse than they lose.

It is a simple simulation that doesn't require a genius to figure out, and yet, I have administered this game more than a thousand times, and only three times have the first two players made the maximum profit of ten cents. One of the three was the Management Board at Abbott Laboratories. They asked me if they could discuss it before beginning the bidding. Of course, I said that they could. They made the maximum amount with the first and only two players. They felt that the simulation was simple and obvious. And, yet they were the only group, in their entire organization, that got it right, out of the box.

The rules of the simulation are listed below.

Five-Cent Auction

The Simple Rules

- The objective of the game is to make as much money as possible bidding on five separate nickels
- There will be five different rounds, one for each nickel
- Each player must bid for the nickel in each round
- Players can choose who will bid first or decide that by flipping a coin

- There must be a minimum of three bids per round, but bids can continue for as many as desired
- The first bid must be for at least one cent, but can be any amount above that
- The second bid must be for at least one cent more than the first bid but can be any amount above that
- The third bid must be for at least one cent more than the second bid but can be any amount above that
- Players may pass after the third bid in each round but not before making a third bid
- Players earn (or lose) money by subtracting the amount bid for the nickel from the five-cent value of the nickel won

The simulation creates a situation where people have to cooperate to maximize their profit. To make the optimum amount of money, both participants need to be trusting when they are vulnerable and trustworthy when they have the power. You will notice that the objective is to make as much money as possible, alternately bidding a **minimum** of three bids per round for one nickel in each round. Both participants must bid the minimum amount possible in each round and pass after the third bid to make maximum profit. They can make two cents per round if the first bidder bids one cent, the second bidder bids two cents, the first bidder bids three cents, and the second bidder passes. If they stick to this routine, one will have made six cents and the other four cents. Together they can make ten cents in five rounds.

If they don't cooperate, they can cause their opponent to spend unlimited money to buy a nickel. What happens virtually every time is that people compete to win. They soon discover that they can bid any amount they choose in the second bid, and their competitor must bid at least one cent more. If they bid $100, their competitor has to bit at least $100.01. As soon as someone is forced to pay more than five cents to win the nickel, that person does the same thing back, only with an increased amount. Being compelled to pay more for the nickel than they can make by selling it is the moment when winning changes to making your opponent lose worse. It is when it shifts to being an Enemy relationship. In this simulation, it is not uncommon for people to require one another to pay billions or trillions of dollars for each nickel. Let me provide a quick example. The following is a typical flow of what happens during the simulation.

Administrator: "Let's do a coin flip to see who bids first. Jane, it looks like you go first."

Jane 1st bid, 1st round: "I bid one cent."
Bill 2nd bid, 1st round: "I bid five cents."
Jane 3rd bid, 1st round: "I pass."
Administrator: "You can't pass until after the third bid. You must bid at least one cent more than the second bid."
Jane 3rd bid, 1st round: "I guess I have to bid six cents."
Bill 4th bid, 1st round: "I pass."

Administrator: "In the first round, Jane has paid six cents for the first nickel. Jane, your profit is minus one cent. Bill will be the first bidder in the second round, and Jane will be the second."

Bill 1st bid, 2nd round: "I bid one cent."
Jane 2nd bid, 2nd round: "I bid one hundred dollars."
Bill 3rd bid, 2nd round: "I have to bid one hundred dollars and one cent."
Jane 4th bid, 2nd round: "I pass."

Administrator: "Bill, you have paid one hundred dollars and one cent for the second nickel. Your profit for this round is minus $99.96. Jane, you will be the first bidder in the third round."

Jane 1st bid, 3rd round: "I bid one cent."
Bill 2nd bid, 3rd round: "I bid one million dollars."
Jane 3rd bid, 3rd round: "I bid one million dollars and one cent."
Bill 4th bid, 3rd round: "I pass."

Administrator: "Jane, you have paid one million dollars and one cent for the third nickel. Your profit if we round it off is minus one million dollars. Bill, you will be the first bidder in the fourth round."

Bill 1st bid, 4th round: "I bid one cent."
Jane 2nd bid, 4th round: "I bid one billion dollars."
Bill 3rd bid, 4th round: "I bid one billion dollars and one cent."
Jane 4th bid, 4th round: "I pass."

Administrator: "Bill, you have paid one billion dollars and one cent for the fourth nickel. Your rounded profit is a minus one billion dollars. Jane, you will be the first bidder in the fifth round."

Jane 1st bid, 5th round: "I bid one cent."
Bill 2nd bid, 5th round: "I bid 20 trillion dollars."
Jane 3rd bid, 5th round: "I bid 20 trillion dollars and one cent."
Bill 4th bid, 5th round: "I pass."

Administrator: "Jane, you have bought the last nickel for 20 trillion dollars and one cent. Your rounded profit is a minus 20 trillion dollars."

Administrator: "Let's add up the profits that you both have individually and combined after five completed rounds.
Jane, you have a total of minus 20 trillion, one million dollars. Bill, you have a total of minus one billion, one hundred dollars. Combined, you have a rounded total of a minus 20 trillion, one billion, one hundred dollars."

Bill: "I won; you lost more than 20 trillion dollars. I just lost one billion dollars!"
Jane: "That is because I had to bid first on the last round. If you had been first, you'd have lost quadrillions."

Administrator: "Wow! The objective of this simulation was to make as much money as possible by bidding for five nickels. What happened?"

The typical answer is that the other person is a jerk (or something in that vein). It usually takes five or six couples doing the simulation before everyone watching catches on how to play the simulations cooperatively and make money. Some need help to catch on, but they realize that this is a game where they could lose trillions if they choose to play. These people will decline an offer to become a bidder. Usually, watchers don't catch on at the same time. It is interesting to watch the simulation when one knows how to make money and the other is still competing. If the one who understands is the second bidder, it is a moment of truth to see what happens in the fifth round. The people who catch on first usually discuss their strategy before starting the bidding. I always consent to that. The Abbott board did that before anyone started to bid.

Interestingly, people jump into the simulation with the unstated objective of "winning the game" despite the stated goal. Once they see that they are at the mercy of their opponent's unrestrained power to harm them, the game shifts to making their opponent lose worse than they do; that is the very definition of Enemy behavior. I have grown accustomed to seeing this simple game cause strong enemy feelings toward one another. When we debrief the simulation, we assuage the negative emotions, and people laugh about how the game and being victimized made them feel. They often state how omnipotent it made them feel to know that they could cause their opponent to lose unlimited amounts of money until they realized they would also be powerless in the next round.

The simulation does illustrate how competitive we are and how driven we are to win. It also shows that we define winning as making the enemy lose worse than we do. There are all kinds of takeaways from this simulation. One is: If the relationship is important, don't compete. Another might be that we will all be utterly vulnerable at specific points in the game of life, and at other times, we will have full situational power. Most people can't resist using absolute power absolutely for self-benefit. Just remember the old saying: "What goes around comes around." Mutual gain is preferable to having winners and losers, mainly if you are the loser. Maybe the biggest takeaway are the benefits derived from cooperation rather than competing.

Can you now see that the fellow's contest with his ex-wife was a five-cent auction? Five-cent auctions are happening around us all the time.

Summary Notes for the Feelings Touchpoint
Feelings are the lens through which we perceive and experience life.

There are seven general categories of feelings and the feelings within each category range from mild to intense.

Synergistic interpersonal connections require that we hear, understand, and validate one another's feelings.

People tend to sympathize with people who have common negative feelings and use them to justify their victimhood.

Feelings come from two places: our subconscious brain and as a result of our expectations.

We can learn to manage our feelings and improve our relationships through our frontal cortex (our analytical brain).

We can change from reactive behavior to proactive behavior.

Feelings determine our beliefs, which drive our behavior, which determines our outcomes.

There are three categories of truth: verifiable truth, perceptive or relative truth, and innate/self-evident truth.

Every kind of relationship has specific feelings that describe it.

As feelings change, relationships change.

We have baseline feelings that anchor our relationships and enable us to return to those anchor feelings.

There are negative consequences when people fail to use healthy ways to resolve unfulfilled expectations.

If the relationship is important, don't compete!

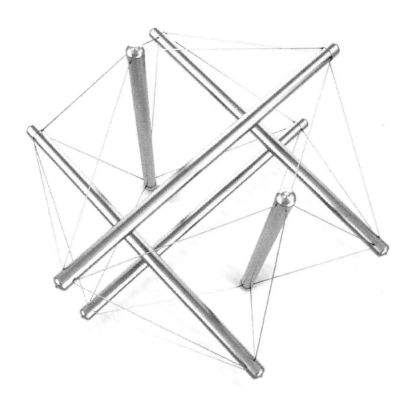

13

Introduction to Operating Modes

"Wilson!" I think every person who lived in the early 2000s gets that reference. In the movie *Castaway*, Tom Hanks plays a Fed Ex executive (Chuck Nolan) whose plane goes down in the middle of the Pacific. He ends up being the only survivor stranded on an island. A life that was all about personal connections and interpersonal transactions suddenly disappears. His only ties to his previous world were a picture of his fiancé and an unopened Fed Ex box. His need for human interaction is so intense that life becomes unbearable. The only option left was to commit suicide. After an unsuccessful suicide attempt, a volleyball washes up on shore, and Chuck Nolan decides to make a companion from an inanimate volleyball, which he names Wilson. He paints a face on the ball from the blood of his hand. During the remainder of the movie, Chuck dialogues with Wilson, which becomes a principal means of survival. Why?

Transaction and interpersonal connection are so vital to the human condition that Wilson saved his life. A big theme is about human interaction and what happens when removed. People crave connection. Without connection and interaction, what do we have? Connection gives meaning to life.

Connection is vital from the onset of life. Fifty years ago, medical doctors isolated and avoided unnecessary human contact with premature babies because they felt that contact endangered them. Too often, these isolated little ones died, which caused even greater isolation. Now, we know that human touch, nurturing sounds, and loving attention increases the chances of survival immeasurably.[15]

We also know that the kind of connection established between infants, toddlers, youngsters, and their parents largely determine the adult's personal identity. The sort of person we become reflects our parents' connection with each other and us. Healthy interactions are essential to well-being, happiness, and meaningful life. My parents' connection was so deep and soulful that a tremendous void and vacuum enveloped my mother when my father passed away. She was sustained for a while by memories of those connections until the memories could not satisfy the need for a real, physical, personal contact with dad. "Wayne, it's not that I miss him. It's that I need him." She longed to be with him, to the point that life was desperate without him. When she died six years later, we were comforted by the faith that they again were united – loving and nurturing one another.

As mentioned earlier, Viktor Frankl taught that three things give meaning to life:

---

15   Ruth Feldman, "Mother-Infant-Skin-to-Skin Contact (Kangaroo Care): Theoretical, Clinical, and Empirical Aspects: Infants and Young Children" (Dev Med Child Neurol. 2004) 274-81.

1. Loving and being loved
2. Being part of something greater than ourself
3. How we deal with unavoidable tragedy

Note that all three are about connections with others or providing direction and purpose. We cannot survive and live a healthy life without connecting with someone. The only way to connect is through interaction, verbal or nonverbal.

Life is all about interactions. Of course, we can have healthy interactions or harmful interactions. Dr. Eric Berne provided us with a framework for understanding human interactions. His framework is called "Transactional Analysis."[16] His book, *Games People Play,*[17] identifies three *ego states*[18] that are in play when people interact with one another. Transactional analysis enables us to understand where people are coming from by watching and analyzing their interactions with others. Berne explains that interactions occur between people within specific behavioral patterns that correspond with their state of mind. These states of mind he refers to as *ego states*. He describes the three ego states as Parent, Child, and Adult.

The Three Ego States		
Parent	**Adult**	**Child**
The ideas and beliefs we modeled and internalized from our parents when we were young.	The conscious reasoning and logical part of our mind that makes decisions based on reason, logic, and analysis.	The feelings we experienced and internalized in response to our parents and caregivers before we had language to label them.

Continued

---

16   Eric Berne, *Games People Play* (Ballantine Books, 1985).
17   *ibid.*
18   *ibid.*

The Three Ego States		
Parent	**Adult**	**Child**
We store them in our subconscious mind as our "parent recordings."	Our adult is our "personal change agent" who can make decisions by analyzing our parent and child recordings and new data gained from other sources.	We store them in our subconscious mind as our "child recordings."

People can shift from one ego state to another. When people interact, a person in one ego state sends a message to a person who receives it and responds from their ego state, which may or may not be the same. Transactional analysis is a way to understand human interactions or "transactions" and what is occurring between people as manifest from their *ego states*. Transactional analysis clarifies where they are coming from, why they behave the way they do, and what makes them act that way. It helps us understand interactions and provides us with a tool to manage interactions.

For purposes of this book about relationships, we have chosen to use the term *operating modes* rather than *ego states*. Using *operating modes* rather than *ego states* facilitates our ability to describe emotional states and behaviors from which people send and receive messages. Instead of the ego states of parent, child, and adult, we use *parent mode, child mode*, and *adult mode*. A person operating in parent mode would be operating from a parental ego state, a person in child mode operating from a child ego state, and a person operating in adult mode operating from an adult ego state. Using operating modes helps us illustrate the Touchpoint of Emotional States straightforwardly regarding the emotional state impact on relationships.

Interactions and connections are everywhere. When two people embrace and say they love each other, a significant connection occurs. Or when a parent gives some helpful feedback to a child who responds with an uninterested gaze. So too, when we say hello to the lady beside the cash register at the grocery store. Throughout life, we have innumerable interactions with people. Our interactions in life pretty much define what we call "living." We use them to tell stories that capture our past interactions' imageries. Interactions are the meat and potatoes of living.

Interactions differ in purpose and meaning. Some are pleasant, while others are miserable. Some lead to positive outcomes and others to adverse effects. One interaction seems to roll to the next and becomes like a snowball, getting bigger and weightier with each addition. Negative interactions add up. So do positive ones.

To some degree, they all leave an imprint on us, some in significant ways, others minutely. They make either emotional deposits or emotional withdrawals, according to Stephen Covey.[19] Some people are blessed with the aptitude to have positive interactions with almost everyone – all the time. Others seem cursed with the opposite talent. You may know someone who has the knack to have negative interactions with nearly everyone all the time.

Every kind of relationship manifests ego states during interactions. The interactions in Intimate Soulmate Relationships lift and feed one another's soul. In contrast, the interaction between enemies intends to suck the marrow from their enemy's bones, ultimately leaving only a vacuum of what could have been. In short, the kind of interactions we have and, therefore, the type of relationships we have are the embodiment of our interactions. Wouldn't it be marvelous if everyone understood the basis of interactions, the roles we play, and how to correct interactions when they are not working the way hoped? Fortunately, we don't have to become psychoanalysts to understand people's behavior – or our own. Using transactional analysis, we can analyze and understand why people behave the way they do and respond appropriately. We can choose to fill our lives with positive interactions rather than negative ones. In doing so, we can create positive relationships that enhance the quality of our lives and those around us.

---

19   Stephen Covey, *Seven Habits of Highly Effective People* (Free Press, 1989).

Analyzing the transactions between people, we can see which operating modes are present and which mode is primary, secondary, and tertiary (in terms of driving behavior). When we hear the terms parent and child, most people think of the "roles" of parent and child as in the traditional perspectives of father, mother, sons, and daughters. Parent mode, child mode, and adult mode are not titles within a family hierarchy with transactional analysis. They are the emotional operating modes that regulate our decisions and actions in interactions with others. They are present in every interaction with someone else. We can be in these modes with friends, employees, managers, parents, children, teammates, coaches, etc. Let's define each one.

14

Parent Mode

Parent Mode is the personal internalization of the thoughts, beliefs, and feelings derived, or modeled, from our parents or parent figures when we were young. Parent mode formed during a child's development in the early stages of life. Dr. Morris Massey explained the three stages of behavioral and value development during our first 20 years of life: imprinting, modeling, and socialization.[20] Infants are imprinted, just like baby ducklings. The imprinting stage of behavioral development happens from birth through age six or seven. During the imprinting stage, infants and young children absorb like sponges the behavior, teachings, and emotions they experience and observe. Infants are self-centered.

---

20   M. E. Massey, *The People Puzzle: Understanding Yourself and Others* (Reston Publishing Company, 1979).

They focus on their own needs. They are self-centered because it is necessary for survival; they take what they need from their parents' world. The child does what they need to do to get their needs met. If they are hungry, they cry or fuss, which is how the infant programs the parents to respond to their needs. The way the parent responds to their needs becomes an intricate part of the programmed parent mode later in life for their child.

Children then move into the modeling period of development (from around 7 through 13) – imprinting and modeling overlap. Modeling is the internal incorporation of the beliefs, behaviors, styles, and perspectives of our caregivers. As we get more intellectually advanced, we start adopting their beliefs, realities, views, and biases as reality. Children essentially become what they model. That doesn't mean that they always like it. Children of parents who smoke have a higher probability of smoking. Abused children have a higher chance of being abusive to their children. We write our subconscious parent mode programs during the imprinting and modeling stage. Imprinting and modeling are how our parent mode is established. It mirrors our caretakers' beliefs, behaviors, style, and life perspectives (aka their parent mode) unless we choose to change. (We will discuss how that change can occur later in the adult mode section.) In short, our parent mode models the parent mode of our caregivers.

The socialization period happens, usually, between ages 13 and 20. By this period, our parent mode has primarily been established and our peers begin to have greater influence over our attitudes, beliefs, and behaviors. During this period, we develop as individuals, looking for ways to distance ourselves from the modeling and imprinting stages. We still are drawn to people similar to us in character and interests.

Parent mode is a general operating mode subdivided into four distinct types of parent modes:

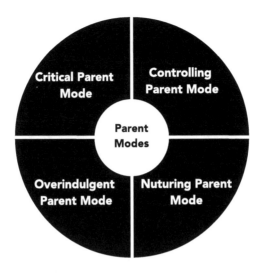

1. The Critical Parent Mode descriptions would include: moralistic, judgmental, authoritative, pessimistic, negative, never satisfied or pleased, and dominant. The overriding message is: "You are wrong." "You need to be fixed." "You are not OK." "You" messages are a pretty good signal that a person is operating from the Critical Parent Mode. They tend to be the devil's advocate in almost all situations (whatever anyone says, they will take the opposite position). Familiar phrases coming from them are: "I disagree!" "Let me tell you how it really is!" "I see the point you are trying to make, but…!" Someone is operating from Critical Parent Mode if they continuously find fault, diminish others, or point out the negative side of every situation.

2. The Controlling Parent Mode descriptions would include: being dominant, seeking compliance from others, being restrictive, commanding, demanding, micromanaging, taking absolute control, using absolute power, obedience is the only acceptable response, expecting obsequiousness from others. The overriding messages are: "I am in charge." "I have the power." "I" messages are a pretty good signal that a person is operating from the Controlling Parent Mode. "Don't question me, just do it!" Being correct or unquestionable is a good indicator that someone operates from Controlling Parent Mode. Open discussions end when their opinion is given. "When absolute authority speaks, discussion ceases." If they surround themselves with compliant and fawning people, they operate in Controlling Parent Mode.

3. The Overindulgent Parent Mode descriptions would include avoiding responsibility and accountability for unfulfilled expectations and transferring responsibility and accountability for undesirable outcomes from themselves or people within their care. They blame others for less than wanted results, make excuses for personal shortfalls, hover over those they indulge, intercede to solve other's issues or problems, and exaggerate achievements and successes. They make negative observations and comparisons about others perceived as competitors. They place an over important sense on winning or being the best. The overriding message is that, "It's always someone else's fault when we don't achieve what we want."

4. The Nurturing Parent Mode describes a person who is open, reassuring, caring, concerned, sensitive, supportive, understanding, empathetic, respectful, outgoing, and fun. The overriding message is: "I'm OK – You're OK."[21] The Nurturing Parent Mode strives for healthy relationships and interconnections. They protect their personal boundary and respect the boundaries of others. They prefer to lead from "why" rather than from "what" and "how." They aim for "buy-in" rather than compliance. If they have a lot of healthy interconnections and relationships, it is a pretty good indicator that they operate from the Nurturing Parent Mode. Nurturing Parent Mode people relieve tensions; they don't create them. They are comfortable to be with, and most people say they are friendly and fun.

---

21   T. A. Harris, *I'm OK – You're OK* (Harper & Row, 1967).

Critical Parent Mode

When we think of a critical parent mode, we think of a manager who always points out what is wrong. It's like a coach who only points out what a team is doing wrong during and after a match. They seldom, if ever, mention the things done right or well. The focus of attention is always about what is wrong, what is weak, inaccurate, or what needs to change. The message is constant along the lines of "Why can't you do anything right?" Figuratively speaking, there is always a pointing finger. "You are wrong." "You are the problem." "What is wrong with you?" Imagine what it would be like to live in an environment of constant criticism. Can you see the immediate and lasting impact it would have?

I had a father who operated from the Critical Parent Mode who brought his daughter to me for a "chat." As he dropped her off, he said, "Let's see what you can do to fix her; I give up!" I immediately thought, *She is right here and can hear everything you are saying. What in the hell is the matter with you?* The girl with whom I was meeting had zero self-esteem. She knew that her dad brought her to see me because she was damaged goods – a failure. It was hard to get her to talk. What could she say? She had no defenses for his constant criticisms, and she had "bought in" to his messages. Indeed, she didn't want to talk about herself, but I eventually found out that she loved dogs. Once she started talking about her dog, she was animated and expressive. She told me all about how much she loved her Golden Lab and how they were best friends. She talked of her loving attention to him and how much they adored one another. I observed that she knew a lot about dogs, caring for them, and bringing out the best in her dog. I asked her what else she was good at, and she responded, "Nothing, I'm not good at anything else." I gingerly asked her about her relationship with her parents. She said that her mother's health wasn't too good, but they had an OK relationship. She said that her mom didn't have much to say about anything. When I asked about her dad, she simply said she didn't talk with him because it wasn't pleasant to hear how disappointing she was.

I have to admit that she nearly broke my heart; she was a beautiful, sensitive, and, potentially, a very talented person who defined herself through the eyes of her critical father. Where she felt successful (her dog relationship), she emoted confidence. She just didn't have many positive experiences to see value in herself. She needed positive reinforcement; people develop from success to success, never from failure built upon failure. She needed success and positive reinforcement, but I could see that it would be difficult for her father to be a positive reinforcer. Yet, he needed to be; he was fundamental to her self-perception. I referred them to a competent family counselor. I advised that for his daughter to succeed in life, he needed counseling to help him change his parenting approach and create an environment where she could heal and see herself positively. The frightening thing is that he still thought that she was the problem.

People who operate in the Critical Parent Mode see the world from what's wrong with it. That applies to people, circumstances, situations, etc. The glass is half empty and disgusting. Some children raised in that environment learn to survive by adapting to it, being compliant and submissive, and behaving in ways that minimize criticism. Others will be inwardly offended by such critical accusations, become angry, and will fight to prove the criticizer incorrect. I feel the fighters are lucky because they never lose their identity, they may have an insecure one, but they still have one. In summary, parents who operate in Critical Parent Mode typically create two types of children: one, insecure, low self-esteem children, who lack confidence (his daughter is a prime example), and two, insecure, over-achievers who spend their life trying to prove that they are the opposite of the criticisms directed at them.

The concepts apply to ALL relationships, not just families. Whenever someone operates in Critical Parent Mode, the results will always produce two types of responses: insecure overachievement or insecure underachievement. Either way, the relationship cannot be synergistic.

Controlling Parent Mode

When trying to understand the Controlling Parent Mode, think of an orchestra conductor. The conductor is the master of the orchestra; he sets the tempo, interprets how the musical score should be played, and directs the musicians on how to do his bidding. He is the judge of performance for the group and each individual. His opinion is the only one that matters. To be a member of his orchestra, you follow his rules, direction, and opinion; doing otherwise is committing orchestral suicide. If he is a Master Conductor, the orchestra excels, with fame and fortune as a testimony to his talent. The conductor's success would seem to afford a convincing argument of the benefits of operating from Controlling Parent Mode. If it works for master conductors, it should work for us. Right? Not everyone is a Master Conductor, but most people think they are, which probably explains why Controlling Parent Mode is, overwhelmingly, the most common type of operating mode. In real life, it has advantages and disadvantages. As consultants, we have various ways to illustrate these advantages and disadvantages with our clients. One way was particularly enlightening.

We would occasionally do the "Airplane Game" exercise in some of our management sessions. We would organize the attendees into eight to ten people groups and either appoint or have each group select a group leader. We would tell the group members that they would get their game instructions from their group leader after we had met with their group leaders and provided them instructions. After that, the group leaders would return and provide game objectives and instructions. We separated the group leaders into two groups and met separately to provide game parameters. We instructed group leaders that the game's objective was to manufacture paper airplanes and throw as many as possible across the goal line, which was 20 feet from their throwing line. They would have four five-minute periods to manufacture and throw their paper planes. The planes needed to be aerodynamic, not merely paper sheets wadded into balls and thrown like rocks. Teams would be rated solely on the number of paper planes that landed beyond the goal line. After each five-minute throwing period, we, the administrators, would gather up their team's paper planes, count them and record their team score on a flip chart (each group had different colored paper). Those instructions were the same for all groups. But, the rest of the instructions for the two groups were very different.

We instructed one group of leaders to be **highly controlling**. They should make all the decisions for their group: the design of the paper planes, who would manufacture, who would throw, when they would throw, and even how they would throw. Their team members were there to follow instructions, not to give opinions. The group leader had the power; they could fire someone from their team if they wanted to. They could also promote someone. Changes to processes, design, incentives, or penalties were their prerogative. In short, they were in charge. The success of their team was in their hands.

We instructed the other group leaders to be **highly participative.** They should look at themselves as the facilitator and a supporter rather than as the decision-maker of the group. As a team, they could decide the design of the paper planes, how to manufacture them, who would manufacture them, who would throw them, etc. The team would decide how to make decisions and changes. Information and communications were to be free-flowing. In short, the group was in charge; the team's success was everyone's responsibility. In other words, everyone was accountable for the results.

It was interesting to witness how the group leaders shared the game objectives, guidelines, and roles. It is surprising how accepting and receptive group members were, **initially**, from their group leaders. Occasionally, an alpha male or alpha female in the highly controlling group objected to being in a compliance role, but that was exceptional rather than commonplace. But as the game played out, feelings and supportive attitudes changed dramatically, depending on how well the team was doing.

You might be surprised to learn that winning results between the highly controlled and the highly participative groups were virtually even. Overall, the highly participative groups won more often, but the huge, one-sided wins usually came from the highly controlled groups. Here, too, the sub-par performances usually came from the highly controlled groups. There are some explanations for this. If the highly controlling group leader knew how to design perfect airplanes, organize processes for maximum efficiency and effectiveness, and provide clear, precise directions, they invariably won – sometimes by a considerable margin. In this case, people are willing to sacrifice personal power and status to be part of a winning, highly-functional operation. On the other hand, if the group leader lacked these skills, they lost badly, and everyone in the group hated being in the group and resented the group leader. **Conclusion: If you are going to be a controlling leader, you better win cause if you don't, you will have hell to pay.**

The participative group often won because individual input ultimately produced better paper plane designs and processes for manufacturing and throwing, both in effectiveness and efficiency. It also created team spirit and relationships that fostered collaboration and genuine enjoyment of the exercise. So, why didn't they win big more often? Pretty simple, individual input into collective decisions takes time. It takes a group longer to make decisions than an individual; groups contribute and compare ideas and probabilities, analyze and postulate, disagree, and provide supportive evidence, or logic, for their input. Reasoning and consensus take time. In the long run, they end up with superior designs, processes, decisions, buy-in, outcomes, and potential, but it takes time to get there.

It was always enlightening to gather feedback from participants after the game. The feedback was pretty similar from exercise to exercise. Most people would prefer to be in a participative group; they like to have a voice and influence how things get accomplished. They could tolerate being in a highly controlled group if they were winning, but only short-term. But even these people said that they would not like, or probably stay, in an organization with a highly controlling boss. The participative groups were popular, although their biggest complaint was the time wasted making decisions and taking action. Most thought that there had to be a better way to get information and make decisions. Participants universally rejected the suggestion to centralize decision-making to one person. Everyone, except for controlling group leaders who won big, felt that in the long run, organizations who harness individual talent for collective benefit would be the most successful and far more pleasant places of which to be a part.

Of course, families are not professional organizations, but controlling or participative management principles apply. Too many times, families are governed, in my opinion, by parents who operate in Controlling Parent Mode. They make all the decisions and expect their children to comply happily. Unfortunately, most parents are not Master Conductors, and the results they get and the music they produce are not pleasant to see or hear. We will discuss later in this section the type of children generated from Controlling Parent Mode parenting.

By the way, people who have not imprinted, modeled, or socialized by growing up in a Controlling Parent Mode environment respond particularly poorly when placed in one. That point was seared into my soul while doing student teaching in 1972. Allow me to explain how I came to know that.

One of my majors in college was secondary education; I did my student teaching at Logan Junior High School. "Open Classrooms" was a popular trend at the time, so our student teaching involved combining four social studies classes into one big room. It was also when "Ping Pong" diplomacy was happening between the USA and Nationalist China. Through the vehicle of ping pong competitions, the United States and China opened communications with, and insight into, the communist behemoth hitherto hidden for decades. As luck would have it, our ninth-grade class was studying China at the time, and we had new information about China, specifically when I was doing my student teaching. I had a brainstorm and got approval to provide a didactic experience to learn about and feel what it was like to be a Chinese student. We turned our Utah classroom into a Chinese classroom.

We did textbook and news reviews of China for a couple of weeks to prepare the students for the next two weeks of the "real student life" Chinese style. The decorations in the class were Chinese motifs, and the five teachers all dressed in Chinese "Comrade" uniforms, including the cute little hats. Everyone in the room had red armbands with the Chinese symbol. Selected each day, from among the class was a "Party Representative" who stood in the front of the class, off to the right side, whose job was to observe the class members' conduct and report any subversive behavior. Each desk had paper, pencils, scissors, glue, and Chairman Mao's "Little Red Book" placed in the upper right-hand corner. Students were expected to sit straight, face forward, not speak unless asked. They were to be obedient, loyal members of the party. The sequence of each class period was pretty much the same each day. Each period included:

- A philosophical instruction focused on China's world superiority for five to ten minutes
- Five minutes standing and reciting, in unison, "truths" taken from Mao's Little Red Book

- Desk-centered assembly line manufacturing for ten minutes (the students could sell the products produced to anyone they pleased)
- Assembling the class several times per week, marching to the school's front lawn (think marching band), and then march behind a Chinese Flag, shouting anti-American slogans, popular among the students in China at the time

Many parents and the school principal did not look favorably at this Chinese classroom exercise. Some parents took their children out of the class. Nevertheless, the students simply had to go along with the simulation to get an A grade for the course. If they choose not to participate, they could still get an A grade by writing a research report about China, ten pages for each letter grade (40 pages for an A, 30 pages for a B, etc.) I think there were 14 or 15 students who chose research papers. Our project encountered obstacles from the outset. The principal would play the Star-Spangled Banner for several days at the beginning of each of my daily four class sessions. Some parents showed up in class to see what was going on and to protect, if necessary, their child from the clutches of the "Chinese Socialist Teacher."

Shortly after the first marches on the front lawn, the local news stations started sending reporters and cameras to our school and classroom. The principal wanted me fired. Through the support of my teacher supervisor, Dr. Dallas Holmes, I was allowed to continue the class. They had a condition that a school board member would evaluate my class daily and recommend it continue or stop. I repeatedly explained that I was not trying to convert the students to Chinese communism, and I assured them (the principal and the parents) that the students would learn a lot from the experience, especially the blessings of being raised in a democratic, free society. To accommodate interest and fears, we created a special section in the back of the classroom for parents and news people with the proviso that they could attend the classes if they made no interferences or contributions, in other words – be invisible.

It didn't take long for the principal to shift from naysayer to cheerleader for our Chinese experience. By the second week of the simulation, he took personal credit for everything. Within days you could hear students singing USA patriotic songs in the hallways. As students walked by our classroom, they slang slurs about China. One day I noticed that the young party representative at the front of the class was stretching his arms above his head a little too often to compensate for mere boredom or tiredness. I later learned that he had a small American Flag on the underside of his red armband. So, it turned out that the spotter for subversive behavior was himself a subversive. The burning of freedom and self-expression was so instilled in our kids that if we had wanted to teach the concept of how rebellions erupt, all we would have had to do was to continue the simulation for another week. No grade incentive would have stopped the universal covert disobedience from becoming open disobedience and rebellion.

After the simulation, we debriefed the students for another week. It was amazing to participate while sharing their feelings, observations, and conclusions. We all learned a great deal about acceptable and unacceptable interpersonal connections and relationships. Years later, students from the class would stop me on the sidewalk or elsewhere and explain that they had participated in our Chinese class and that it was one experience they would never forget.

Utah State University applauded the project and helped many other schools duplicate the experience. A note aside, the principal offered me a teaching position at the Junior High. Needless to say, I didn't take the job.

If your parenting mode suggests that perfection is considered zero deviation from your instruction, your way, or your perspective, then you are a Controlling Parent Mode parent. Controlling Parent Mode parents say and do things like this:
"You will be home by 10:00 pm on Saturday."
"No extracurricular activities until your homework is finished."
"You will be an A student."

Saying things like this does not make you a Master Conductor. It does indicate that you operate from Controlling Parent Mode. Realize that you may generate a compliant child or create a rebellious one in being controlling. We will discuss both possibilities in an upcoming section called: Controlling Parent Mode Spawns the Adaptive or Rebellious Child Mode Response.

Overindulgent Parent Mode

When trying to grasp Overindulgent Parent mode, think of the parent who blames you when their kid screws up while playing at your house. "If their kid hits a baseball into our big, plasma screen TV, how is it my fault?" From the Overindulgent Parent Mode parent, it's always someone else's fault when their "perfect" child does something un-acceptable. Overindulgent Parent mode continually defines me as the "good guys" and others as the "bad guys." They are the masters of transference of personal accountability and responsibility to others for things that should be theirs.

I have a dear friend who retired early from being a superior music teacher at a high school because it became the norm rather than the exception for parents to blame her for their child's lack of musical achievement. It didn't matter that the student didn't practice or put forth the effort necessary to improve, from the parents' perspective, even that was her fault. From their perspective, her students who excelled and moved on to college with acclaim and full-ride schol-arships did so because she pulled strings for them. "Those 'people' are no more deserving than my child." Their finger is always pointed at someone else when things don't turn out as well as they expect them to.

Their unfulfilled expectations turn them into the personification of victimhood; fulfilled expectations make them feel superior. They blame others for unwanted circumstances proclaiming that things would be different if others had done what they should have done. "I would work harder if the boss would give me more money." "If only the coach had given her more play-time, she would have caught the attention of top college scouts." Another is the constant sharing of "Ain't It Awful!" to justify their accusations and shift the blame for unfulfilled expectations to others. I can appreciate wanting the best things in life, but I have difficulty accepting that continuous shortfalls are always someone else's fault. Overindulgent Parent modes always shift the blame to others and do not take responsibility for their shortcomings.

Their superiority manifests in several ways: First, the tendency to project achievements as more significant than they are. It is buying that house you can't afford to make a statement about your accomplishments. Second is the practice of making unfavorable comparisons of others. No matter how accomplished, the object of the comparison is always inferior. "He may be rich but I bet that guy is a jerk." The third is the need to intercede when they believe their specialness is being questioned or threatened. I describe this as "parental hovering." They are quick to be the mouthpiece for their child's cause, issue, or for problem-solving. As you can guess, coaches love it when they have to deal with issues through the parent rather than directly with the player. (I am being sarcastic even though I should know better.) They remind me of a momma Killdeer bird who is ever-present to protect their chicks by pretending to have an injured wing when a predator approaches their nest. Momma tries to appear to be an easy meal causing the dangerous predator to chase after her, thus saving her babies.

I coached a 17-and-18-year-old girls volleyball team that certainly was incapable of competing nationally. Nevertheless, six girls on the team wanted to play college ball. We added two assistant coaches to the team to help them perform at a level that would get the attention of, at least, Junior College coaches. One of the players on the team, who really shouldn't have been, had a hovering mom who was always present to protect her chick. She would come and talk with her daughter during the game, standing with us coaches and the other players on the sideline. Her presence was always a reminder that, in her mind, her daughter should be on the court, playing. If her daughter didn't get "her fair share" of playing time, I had to explain why to her mom. She was constantly complaining, always sharing "Ain't It Awful's!" with anyone who would listen. She blamed me for ruining her daughter's love of the game and destroying her chances to play college ball.

If only I would recognize how special and talented her daughter was, she would get the opportunities due to her. The daughter sympathized with her mother to the detriment of her relationship with the other girls on the team. They didn't want to get in the middle of her complaints, so they avoided her. You guessed it – my fault. Five seniors on the team got full-ride scholarships, four of them to Junior Colleges and one to a prestigious private school in Denver. I was happy for their success, but that year was the most miserable coaching experience of my life. Now I think about interviewing players' parents before selecting a girl for my team.

Overindulgent parents will believe their child over the facts of any situation. Therefore, the overindulged children learn to tell their parents what they want their parents to believe. As a result, the child will learn to lie for personal benefits even if it damages the person they are lying about. For example, as a coach, I have had follow-up phone calls from parents within two minutes of a player finishing a conversation with me. The parent calls to express concern and frustration and demands that I do something about her daughter's report of my discussion with their child. With the child's emotions high and a "one-eyed" view of the discussion, they phone their parent with a version of the conversation that makes them out to be a victim and me out to be an insensitive persecutor. The parent reactively makes immediate demands of me. More often than not, their version of the "supposed" conversation is entirely inaccurate. With overindulgent parents, one thing is sure, their child is right, and I am wrong. Working through this kind of situation is especially difficult because for the parent to accept my explanation, they have to admit the possibility that their child has misinterpreted the conversation or lied. Not an easy thing for an indulgent parent to do. Overindulgent parents who have entitled kids are a coach's nightmare.

Coaches, teachers, any adult/child relationship hate dealing with parents about athlete/coach or student/teacher issues. Overindulgent parents never catch on to that concept. The Overindulgent Parent Mode is an operating mode that is becoming increasingly more prevalent in our society. This mode blames others and avoids responsibility for one's actions, feelings, and conditions in life. It is also taking accountability away from others and eliminating expectations of others in hopes to alleviate their life's challenges. This only handicaps the recipient and limits their ability to grow. It has the appearance of a Synergistic Relationship but truly only produces a dependency, Command and Control relationship. The dependent child actually becomes the Stomper, in the sense that the Overindulgent Parent becomes the Stompee driven to address all of their unfulfilled expectations.

Nurturing Parent Mode

People who operate in Nurturing Parent Mode are open, reassuring, caring, concerned, sensitive, supportive, understanding, empathetic, enthusiastic, respectful, outgoing, and fun. When interacting with someone in this mode, people feel validated, they feel uplifted, they feel empowered, and they feel special. If you do this and make people feel that way, then congratulations, you are operating in Nurturing Parent Mode. You probably have tons of people who want to spend time with you.

Nurturing Parent Mode does not mean to eliminate expectations (that is typical of an Overindulgent Parent Mode). It is having expectations and working with enthusiasm, empathy, and accountability to help others to meet their expectations, even with challenges.

Parents who operate in Nurturing Parent Mode do not "hover." They don't expect perfection. They allow for errors and mistakes as part of the natural evolution of development. They are curious while watching their children mature and develop. They let their kids play on the monkey bars (despite the risks) and enjoy watching their kids hang upside down on the horizontal ladder. They will empathize with their child who is hurting from not being invited to a birthday party – but they don't solve their problems for them. They discuss and teach their children how to solve their problems. They explain that there has to be a logical reason why something happened and discuss how to fix it.

When I was about ten-years-old, Ronnie Christensen didn't invite me to his birthday party. I believed myself to be the only boy in my class not invited. It hurt me a lot. My mother and I discussed it, and although she empathized deeply, she suggested that I treat him as if he were my best friend. It wasn't too long until we became friends.

People who operate in Nurturing Parent Modes are the kind of people who make us feel special, who buoy our self-image, who stamp our hearts and minds with the message that we are of immeasurable value – and loved. The outcomes of this mode mold us into something greater than we could ever accomplish on our own. This operating mode makes lifetime impressions.

Mrs. Leona McCarry was my fourth-grade teacher. She was tall, slender, and had dark hair. Mrs. McCarry inspired us to learn the "times tables" so well that we could do multiplication or division like tiny computers (not invented yet, the computers, not times tables). She brought new worlds and experiences into our lives through her hourly reading sessions, done daily. Our teacher transported us to that time and place when reading *The Box Car Children, Little House on the Prairie, Tom Sawyer,* and *Huckleberry Finn.* She was each of the characters in the books. Through her tone, voice, and manner, we realized who they were and what they sounded like; we visualized them through her. One day she came into class red-faced and upset. Earlier in the day, the boys in the class had chased the girls during recess. The boys were pulling up their skirts to see their panties. When she learned about this, she immediately decided to fix the problem.

When we were all back in the classroom, she dismissed the girls and gave the boys a memorable lesson. She said that she knew of our actions with the girls and understood our curiosity about panties and the need to explore the differences between boys and girls. She then lifted her dress in front of all the boys and showed us her undergarments. She told us to take a good look and that if ever in the future we felt the need to look at a girl's panties again, to just come to her, request politely, and she would, again, show us her panties. It was shocking, but, to my knowledge, none of the boys invaded the girls' privacy again.

Not so sure how that would play out in our society now, but in 1957, it was a pretty valuable lesson. Years later, after I had my kids in grade school, I felt the need to meet with Mrs. McCarry and tell her how wonderfully and demonstrably she had impacted my life. I went to her house, and her daughter greeted me at the door. She was now living in her mom's home. When I explained the purpose of my visit, she gasped and started to cry; in the months before her mother's death, her mother had expressed the sorrow she felt because she didn't believe that she had touched any of her students' lives in a meaningful way. To this day, I regret not telling Mrs. McCarry, while she was alive and years earlier, the crucial role she played in my life.

I wouldn't claim to operate in Nurturing Parent Mode as consistently as other people, but I have had a few memorable experiences. One, in particular, stands out. I was on a late-night flight from Newark to Los Angeles. Of course, most people on the flight were hoping to have a quiet, uneventful trip and perhaps, even catch a nap. It turned out a family was sitting in the row ahead of me. The parents were sitting in the aisle seats, the mother directly in front of me. Two school-age children were seated to his left. In the middle seat, a two-year-old toddler was to the mother's right, and on the right of the toddler was her six or seven-year-old sister in the window seat.

Probably within an hour after takeoff, the toddler started loudly crying. The mother tried holding her and walking with her to comfort her, to no avail. This situation became very annoying to many passengers within earshot, most of the plane. People began to sigh and complain, often loudly. Well, this embarrassed the parents, as you can imagine. The mom sat down with the baby and put her back into her baby seat with a bottle of apple juice. Within a few minutes, the baby threw up, spewing smelly, sour apple juice vomit all over her mother, her baby seat, the floor, and the back of the seat in front of her. Of course, the baby's clothes, face, and exposed skin were covered in vomit, as well. The good news is that after she purged her stomach, she stopped crying. The bad news is that the odor of the sour vomit permeated the whole aircraft, to the great displeasure of the passengers.

People were swearing and complaining to the flight attendants, which were also greatly exasperated. I could see that the parents were embarrassed and confused about what to do. The flight attendants amazingly disappeared, so I decided to manage the situation. I got up and asked the dad to go and get all the towels and paper towels he could get from the flight attendants. I focused my attention on the mother, who was distressed, and explained that I was a dad and a grandfather who had a lot of experience in such situations. I asked her to bring the baby with me to the lavatory to change her baby's clothes and clean her up, which we did. I then took the baby, who was now happy and pleasant, so her mother could do whatever she could to clean herself and her clothes. We then returned to their seating area and cleaned everything possible. Before we finished cleaning, the baby was sleeping peacefully, and so were the rest of their children. The rest of the passengers were relieved and grateful to put this episode behind them.

I spent the rest of the flight getting to know the parents and the purpose of their flight. As it turned out, they were moving to Los Angeles because he had a new management position with a new company. We had a pleasant conversation, and they dripped with an appreciation for the assistance and understanding afforded them. When we landed in Los Angeles and were taxiing toward our gate, the pilot came on the intercom system and asked that all the passengers remain seated until he permitted exiting. He wanted to introduce a special person on the plane. We all thought that unusual and wondered who the person could be. You can imagine my amazement when the crew asked me to come forward. The captain introduced me to everyone and expressed appreciation for my help with the baby and the family in distress. Then they presented me with a giant bottle of champagne. It had a ribbon tied on the neck of the bottle. I have no idea where they procured that bottle. Everyone on the plane gave me a standing ovation. I was a little embarrassed and pleased. On the way to and at the baggage claim area, I believe I shook hands with almost every passenger on the flight. I'm sure glad I decided to help instead of complaining. I don't drink, so I gave the bottle to our Director of Human Resources, who, I knew, would appreciate it.

As we conclude this portion of our discussion on Parent Modes, please remember that parent mode is not just describing a parenting style. It is an operating mode we can use in interactions with everyone. Each of these parent modes gives rise to specific sets of feelings, emotional states, and consequently, behaviors of their dependents. The parent mode we operate from becomes the basis for their children's parent modes. It is a cause-effect relationship. Every parent mode is a consequence of the environment created by the operating parent mode of our parents. Said another way, every parent mode is a distillation of the parent mode we imprinted and modeled.

If we are being critical with anyone, we are operating in a Critical Parent Mode. If we are forcing compliance on anyone, we are operating in a Controlling Parent Mode. When we avoid taking responsibility for our actions or the actions of someone close to us, we are probably operating in an Overindulgent Parent Mode and being self-centered. When we are considerate, caring, empathic, and supportive of others' feelings and circumstances, we operate in a Nurturing Parent Mode. Our operating mode is a state of mind manifest when interacting with others. Additionally, our identity becomes entwined with our dominate Parent Mode.

I had a friend who lent his neighbor $50,000 to help his family through some hard times. The neighbor agreed to pay it back within a month, when they sold their house. The house was sold within a few weeks and the neighbor disappeared. No money was repaid and no communication was able to be established. Finally, after two months after the note was due, contact was finally made. How would you respond?

The Critical Parent Mode would absolutely belittle, criticize, and attack this neighbor.

The Controlling Parent Mode would have already sued the neighbor.

The Overindulgent Parent Mode would have downplayed the severity of what happened, blamed the people who caused his hardship, and became a co-victim themselves.

The Nurturing Parent Mode would find out what happened, gather the facts, find out what is possible, and work with the neighbor to fulfill their obligation.

Interestingly enough, right before the house sold, the neighbor's wife was diagnosed with cancer, their son had a failed suicide attempt a week later, and the daughter was on suicide watch at the local hospital. When my friend was finally able to contact them, he decided to operate in Nurturing Parent Mode and discovered the aforementioned information. The neighbor had other priorities on his mind and promptly repaid his debt. There is only one mode that would produce a synergistic relationship. Choosing to operate in a Nurturing Parent Mode provides a solution and maintains the relationship.

Parents who do everything for their kids; listen closely. As you operate in the Overindulgent Parent Mode, you CANNOT have a Synergistic Relationship with your child. You are programmed to be the Stompee in the relationship whereas they are the Stomper because you are inheriting their problems and accountability for them. Overindulgent Parents are producing a generation of kids who cannot fight their own battles.

15

CHILD MODE

We recorded our child mode recordings during the same time as our parent mode recordings. Child mode is internal recordings of the feelings we experienced in response to our parents' parent mode behaviors and the behaviors of other essential caregivers. The child mode is the feelings and responses we replay, in maturity, due to the parent mode behaviors that impacted us during the imprinting and modeling stages of early life. When our child mode formed, we had limited verbal skills; consequently, our child modes are manifested almost exclusively through feelings and emotions. When we experience, as adults, a similar event that occurred in infancy, we feel and respond as we did then – emotionally. As Dr. Harris explains: "The evoked recollection is not the exact photographic or phonographic reproduction of past scenes or events. It is a reproduction of what [we] saw and heard and felt and understood."[22] The reasons for our child mode responses exist in our subconscious mind. Yet, when stimulated, our child mode is *hooked*. We know, for sure, what we are feeling, but we certainly have no clue why. "I don't know why I felt and acted that way. It makes me so disappointed with myself when I do that!" Well, now we know; it is our child mode (emotional) response to a similar experience that occurred when the only responses we were capable of making were emotional. That is why people who are into Transactional Analysis see the child mode as the feeling mode.

In the same way, our parent mode was passed to us during the imprinting and modeling stage by our caretakers; we also developed our child mode (*how we responded and felt* during our interactions with others during the imprinting and modeling stage) was passed to us as well. As adults, we model the parent mode of our caretakers AND we bring with us our emotional responses to those parenting modes via our child mode.

In short, when we experience a similar parent mode situation that we experienced as a child, we will have a child mode response that mimics the child mode response when we were young. As a child, we may have flopped down on the floor and kicked our feet when throwing a tantrum; we will have an updated version of that as an adult. As a toddler, we would kick our feet; as grade-schoolers, we would pout and sulk; as a teenager, we would get irate and say hurtful things or attack others; as an adult, we yell at the customer service worker who won't allow us to return our item. The current behavior manifests the same feelings we experienced before developing "rational or reasonable" responses to unpleasant stimuli.

The easy observation and conclusion are: when people are being emotional, we know they are operating in child mode. The emotions are, with few exceptions, the autonomic emotional responses we learned as a child in response to the parent mode environment from our infancy. The chief characteristic of child mode is a manifestation of emotions.

---

22   T. A. Harris, *I'm OK – You're OK* (Harper & Row, 1967), 26.

If we let emotions drive our decisions and behavior, we operate in child mode. However, not all subconscious child mode behaviors are the same.

The child modes that are spawned from the four parent modes

The child mode responses evoked in us are tied directly to our parents' specific parent mode environment. There is a cause-effect relationship between the four parent mode types and the child modes that flow from them. Each different parent mode environment spawns predictable child mode feelings and responses (from the early stages in life, teenagers, and even adults). Let's go through each one:

Child modes spawned from parent mode Parenting

Let's examine each of the typical child mode characteristics produced from parenting in the four parent modes:

The Critical Parent Mode Parenting which is moralistic, judgmental, authoritative, and dominant, spawns at least two predictable child mode feelings and responses:

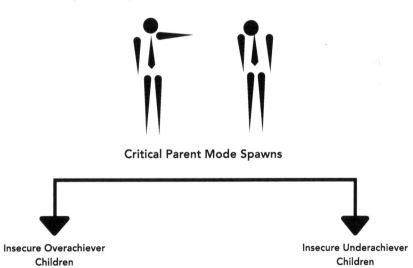

Critical Parent Mode Spawns

Insecure Overachiever
Children

Insecure Underachiever
Children

One child mode response manifests insecurity and low self-esteem, which projects a sense of inadequacy. It can also be manifest through sarcasm (latent hostility released through humor). Other times, it manifests in learned helplessness, where their sense of powerlessness caus-es them to give up quickly. We could call these child mode states Inse-cure Underachievers.

Another child mode response manifests through perfectionism and overachievement. A person with this child mode spends their life trying to prove that the "you" messages directed at them are wrong. Ironically, overachievers raised by critical parents are also insecure. In other words, their emotional state leads them to become insecure overachievers needing constant approbation.

While they may look different outwardly, they share similar underlying feelings that manifest differently. The general underlying self-depreca-tion causes a constant sense of resentment, anger, and self-doubt that generates anxiety (probably both emotionally and socially). Neither of these child modes offers a stress-free life. I know from personal experience.

My dad, raised in a Critical Parent Mode environment, was a master of sarcasm. People would tell me how funny my dad was for most of my life. I would respond, "Yeah, he's a hoot." At the same time, I was inwardly steaming from the resentment of being the target of many of his sarcastic "jokes." You see, sarcasm is a behavioral addiction. It is a compulsive behavior with short-term benefits and long-term destruc-tive consequences. He couldn't stop himself from being sarcastic, and he was good at it. It allowed him to release pent-up anger and hostility. Other people's laughter reinforced his behavior, and he came across as clever. Everyone thought he was funny except me and the other targets of his biting humor. Years later, as an adult, I discussed this with my dad. He felt terrible for hurting me, but he struggled for the rest of his life to find an acceptable alternative to sarcasm; he couldn't find any-thing that gave him a comparable buzz.

We anticipate that children raised in a critical parent mode environ-ment will become low-esteem underachievers or insecure, perfec-tionistic overachievers. That is a natural expectation when the over-riding critical parent mode message to them was: "You are damaged goods." Continual critical you, you, you, messages leave an indelible mark.

Discussing what I had just written about my dad, raised in a Critical Parent Mode environment, and his mode of being a Critical Parent with me, caused my son Matt to say to me, "Come on, dad, don't leave us hanging. Please share with us how that impacted you. You know you are an overachiever and have been your whole life. How did your dad influence you to become that way?"

OK, but understand that I am the spawn of two types of parent mode influences in the same household. My father operated from the Critical Parent mode, and my mother operated from the Nurturing Parent Mode. So, I became an insecure overachiever from my father, needing approval and affirmation. I became a caring, sensitive, empathic extrovert from my mother. Through her, I loved to be with people and have uplifting fun. I believe it was from her that I became a "ponderer" of people very early.

As a youngster, I couldn't stand to see people bullied, and I was deeply touched when I saw someone hurting or embarrassed. I was a contemplative child who analyzed current events and situations that impacted me and others. It is incredible how I can recall events that left an impression on me – even the feelings I felt at the time. It is a little surprising because when I share memories of distant experiences with people who were a part of it, they seldom remember it; or if they do, they have only a faint recall. I guess it didn't leave the same impression with them as it did with me.

I suppose tons of people like me grew up in different parent mode environments. My father was never critical of my mother; to this day, I can't imagine him being so with her. He saw her as the perfect woman. To friends, he often remarked, "People who spend time with Donna for 15 minutes know her as well as I do, and I have been married to her for over 50 years." His point was that she had no pretense and that her loving, nurturing nature genuinely drew people to her. All would agree that they had the same admirable impression of her when they first met her.

My dad had high expectations and was critical of me when I didn't measure up to his expectations. That pretty much changed during the middle of my sophomore year. During that year, my best friend of five years and I decided to go our separate ways. It was a life-altering decision but a necessary one for me.

While I was commercial fishing in Kenai, Alaska, with my family during the summer after my ninth-grade year, my friend discovered the joys of alcohol, smoking, and chasing girls. When we reconnected at the end of the summer, I joined him in the Friday night drinking sessions and activities. I couldn't stand smoking, and while profoundly attracted to girls, I didn't enjoy being around girls who liked smoking, drinking, and making out with someone they had just met.

Other fellows became our regular buddies for the Friday night activities. They were "Greasers," the guys with the oiled swept-back hairstyle who wore black leather jackets. Think of John Travolta's buddies in the movie *Grease*. I wasn't pleased to be associated with them, but that was part of the price to be paid to be with my friend.

As I mentioned earlier in this book, I was boxing and was pretty good at it during that time. Boxing skills came in handy for Friday drink nights, football games, and rock band challenges – all popular throughout our little valley. After one of these events, we would often find, or be found, by another group of greasers looking for a fight. My best friend should have been a boxing promoter because he was an expert at arranging fights for me with the other gang's chosen warriors. It was usually over quickly because I never encountered anyone who knew the first thing about boxing – this lifestyle required me to hide my activities from my parents. I didn't want to disappoint my dad or hurt my mother, and being open about what I was involved in would do both. It created tremendous cognitive dissonance within me. To resolve the inner disharmony, I either had to open up and tell my parents or change my lifestyle to one I could be comfortable with. I chose the latter.

I met with my friend, explained my discomfort, and requested that he join me on a different path. He declined. We hugged, expressed our love for one another, and went separate ways. It was a lonely, depressing time for me. If it weren't for my faithful dog Toby, I would have had no one with whom I could share my misery.

I came home from school and found my former best friend's parents sitting with my parents in our living room. When they saw me, they jumped to their feet, hugged me, and then started pleading with me to come back into their son's life. They were desperate. They said that they had lost him since he and I parted ways. They knew that he was involved with things that could influence his life in a bad way.

They wanted things to be how they perceived them when he and I were best friends. I tearfully responded, "I can't!" Then I departed quickly and didn't return until around midnight that evening. When I got home, my parents were waiting for me. I told them everything. I expressed my sorrow for disappointing them and explained why my best friend and I had parted company. We hugged and cried for a long time. The next day, my dad and I rode up the canyon on little Honda motorbikes to a camping spot beside High Creek, where we built a fire and just talked. He said he wanted to be alone to give me a "dad's" message. He stated that the choice I made few men would have made. He said that I was an emancipated man; I no longer needed their permission for anything unless I wanted to. He and my mother knew the kind of decisions I would make. I was proud that they would do that; at 16, I was entrusted with the autonomy to make my own decisions for my life. The wonderful thing is that I no longer wanted to do anything that would disappoint them or hurt my mother. The internal disharmony was gone. I don't recall my dad ever being critical of me after that. I became the one with whom he could share his life story, with all its challenges, sorrows, joys, and unresolved issues.

Still, the parent mode and child mode recordings remained a part of me, both my mother's nurturing and my father's criticism. I loved my dad; I adored him and spent most of my life seeking his approval. I recall helping him build a hay trailer when I was eight years old. He came over to inspect the section of welding that I had done on the trailer frame. I wanted him to tell me that I had welded it beautifully and that I had done an excellent job. He told me it looked like a chicken had pooped where I had welded and told me to grind it down and reweld it. That pissed me off, but I ground it down and made the new weld. It looked like a welded zipper, beautiful and uniform. He always loved having me work with him, but I was usually mad while we worked together. I wanted but never seemed to get his approval until after the High Creek emancipation chat.

One day while in high school, I went down to the machine shop at Utah State, where dad worked, to pay him a quick visit. I met a couple of new engineers who said to me when they learned who I was, "So you are the famous Wayne Carlson that your dad is always bragging about." My response was, "My dad is always bragging about me?" That surprised me; I wondered why he bragged about me with them but didn't express his pride about me, with me. Of course, that mostly changed while I was still 16. Years later, I talked with him one evening about what major I should take in college; he looked at me and said that I could be anything and do anything I chose to be or to do. He further stated that he didn't know anyone else about whom he could say that. After emancipating me, it seems that he was effusive in expressing how proud he was of me. That lasted for the rest of his life. I did indeed become the one person in his life with whom he could share his deepest thoughts, feelings, beliefs, and insecurities. Even though, as an adult, I could rationalize the child mode recordings of my infancy and youth and healthily control my responses, the old recordings remained. Underneath, I stayed the angry, insecure little boy seeking his father's approval, who was always trying to prove that "I'm OK." Such is the nature of child mode recordings, we can manage them, but we can't erase them.

That was later professionally confirmed for me through a Belgian psychologist. When we moved to Janssen Pharmaceutica's headquarters in Beerse, Belgium, management had me meet with a clinical psychologist to develop a psychological report about me. The information was for my boss and senior management of the company. Three things about that report stood out: One, I was a highly-driven person with boundless energy and determination. I also had an underlying anger level, which the psychologist believed was controlled by my religiously solid faith and upbringing. Three, I was unusually perceptive in seeing issues, analyzing them, and coming up with practical solutions, which would be very useful in my role as the Director of Organizational and Manpower Development. At the time, I didn't agree with the second point. Now, I can see that all three points were characteristics about me spawned due to my dad's critical operating mode and need to prove myself.

As I grew up, I always had something to prove. I couldn't be a loser in anything. During my sophomore year in high school, I tried out for the track team. As it turned out, my first race was a 440-yard sprint. I had never raced in an organized event before, so I didn't know how hard to run. We were running on cinder ashes gathered locally from the coal furnace ash deposits found near our high school; it was crunchy and crystalized, something you didn't want to fall on. All the other guys in the race had track shoes with metal spikes that provided traction to optimize their speed and stability. I wore canvas Converse tennis shoes that were pretty slick on the bottom and weighed three times as much as their fancy track shoes. When the gun went off, I ran as hard as I could for the whole quarter mile. When I came in second, the track coach was at the finish line waiting for me. He put his arms around me and said, "I didn't know you could run so fast, especially in those damn Converse tennis shoes!" I made the team and ran the 440 in the individual events, a 440 leg in the mile relay, and the individual mile. I later learned that I wasn't supposed to run as fast as I could for the whole quarter-mile but glide through the middle third of the race and then sprint the last 100 yards. When I tried out for the track team, I just wanted to make the team. I would have died before slowing down.

When I was boxing my sophomore year, the boxing coach told me, "You know you aren't the fastest guy around. But do you know why you win boxing matches? Because you would die before quitting." I knew he was right.

In my 70s, the insecurity and need for approval are manifest in my need to be relevant. That might be what is driving me to spend countless hours writing. It is the hope that our messages will positively impact the lives of others and, in some way, demonstrate that I am relevant. The child mode recordings remain.

Enough about my insecurity and over-achievement because of my Critical Parent Mode dad.

One 13-year-old young woman stands out in my mind as an example of a child with low self-esteem. I became acquainted with Emily due to a phone call from a mom who was a friend and neighbor of Emily's mom. She called me and asked if I would meet with Emily and assess her volleyball capabilities and potential. She explained that she had tried out for her junior high volleyball team was devastated when she didn't make it. She promised Emily's mom to call me and arrange for an independent assessment, which she did.

When I met with Emily and her mom, I could sense an anxious undercurrent within her mom. I had a fun assessment session with Emily and was happy to report that, in my opinion, Emily should try out for a club team. Her mom asked me if I was sure. She said, "If she doesn't make it, I can't tell you how devastating it will be to her. You have to be sure Emily will make a team before she tries out." I told her, "I am pretty sure she will make a team." Her mom said, "Pretty sure doesn't cut it, you have to promise me that she will make a team if she tries out!" I promised her that I would make sure that Emily made a team.

She tried out and ended up borderline for a club team. I was going to be coaching a 14-year-old club team, so my boys, who own the club, said, "Why don't you put her on your team?" I did and found out why her mother was so concerned about Emily. She was an extremely fragile child, emotionally and socially. She would fragment if she sensed criticism or a slight of any kind. Volleyball is a game of mistakes and recovery, so providing coaching direction always risks the perception of criticism. Fortunately, we had a natural-born leader on our team, Kiah Johnson, who was loving, nurturing, and inclusive. She was the de facto team captain before the girls elected her.

Kiah adopted Emily and all the other girls on the team, including another girl with diagnosed emotional control problems. Kiah's mother, Candice, informally became our team's assistant coach. We both knew that this team would be a challenge and that we had a couple of girls requiring sensitive coaching and support. When Emily's emotions overcame her, Candice would put her arms around her and gently talk her through the crisis. To this day, I am appreciative of the Johnson girls who provide a safe place for fragile girls to be vulnerable, accepted, and loved.

Somehow, we discovered the joy of seeing the humor in mistakes on that team. That took the pressure off and made it OK to flub up. Everyone laughed with each other, not at each other. Observing coaches and teams noticed that our group seemed to laugh a lot. It was not unusual to see our whole team and coaches lying on the floor crying with laughter. It turned out to be the perfect environment for fragile girls, the place where they belonged, were included, were valued, and where they fit in. Partway through the year, Emily's mom met with me and told me how grateful she was for this team, these girls, and Emily's newfound self-identity, confidence, and sisterhood. She also confided that when Emily tried out for our team, she was suicidal. She confessed that if she hadn't made the team, she was afraid that not doing so would have been the trigger for her last fatal cry for help. I knew then why she said that I had to promise her that she would make a team if she tried out. Volleyball is about so much more than just volleyball.

I have no idea why Emily had such a low self-image. I saw no evidence that either of her parents operated from Critical Parent Mode, but somehow her recordings said, "I'm not OK." Her experience on the volleyball club team gave her tons of "I'm OK" evidence. I hope it is foundational in providing her a base for feeling "OK" for the rest of her life.

Kiah Johnson is now a college volleyball player who had to sit out part of last year's volleyball season due to a knee injury. She is still centermost in nurturing her college sister teammates. Everyone loves her, and so they should. She just got engaged to be married, so she will be a married volleyball player by the time this book is published.

I worked with a young man who recently was hired by my son's company. His parents were both Olympic athletes, his brothers and sisters were All-American Division 1 athletes, his cousins were professional athletes. He went to California's most prestigious private school that provided a top-notch education. His school produced some of the best athletes out of high school who afterward moved to college or professional sports. Both parents came from long lines of professional athletes and Olympians. There was a lot of tremendous pressure on this young man to follow suit. The overly critical nature of this parenting style had produced generations of overachievers, and then there was Bob, the black sheep of the family. Bob dropped out of college with a $300K high school education, didn't play sports in college, and worked for Walmart as a cashier. To this family, that was unacceptable. When you pull back the curtains and reveal the true Oz of this family, there are as many overachievers as underachievers. On a car ride one day, I asked, "How is your relationship with your parents?" His response was, "What do you think?"

The Controlling Parent Mode Parenting seeks dominance over and compliance from children. It restricts their choices and options and pursues absolute governance, which will invariably spawn one of two child mode types:

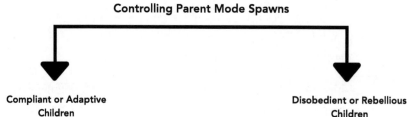

Controlling Parent Mode Spawns

Compliant or Adaptive
Children

Disobedient or Rebellious
Children

One: The compliant, submissive, or adaptive child mode

The dominant characteristic of this child mode is submission and obedience. The adaptive child goes with the flow and avoids disapproval. Adaptive children don't make waves. In some ways, they try to be invisible. Being invisible allows them to avoid conflict or being controlled. I also like to compare them to water which molds itself around objects. The adaptive child mode people learn how to mold themselves around the controlling people.

Two: The disobedient, rebellious, angry, defiant child mode

People with this type of child mode contest authority, rules, constraints, and restrictions. Life is a contest, a never-ending struggle for "personal freedom" or self-identity. I don't know anyone who loves rules, but the disobedient and rebellious child has an inward aversion to external constraints.

When the overriding message from others in their life is: "I am the boss, and your job is to be obedient to my direction," then we can expect to see either compliant or rebellious children.

Most of the teenagers I have helped came from controlling parent mode households. Generally, they were obedient, good kids until they weren't. Their fall from grace followed a familiar pattern. They were outwardly obedient but started being covertly disobedient when they found that the rules were too oppressive and overly restricted their ability for essential social connections or friendships. Covert disobedience becomes an escape hatch from unacceptable controls, particularly when parents get increasingly more controlling in the contest (that they are unaware is happening). Once they had justified their hidden disobedience, they became overtly disobedient. The parents soon find out that once a child is overtly disobedient, trying to force compliance doesn't work anymore; they realize that with openly defiant children, force generates counterforce. Aiming for compliance becomes an adversarial game where both parties try to win. Of course, adversarial relationships are, by their very nature, dysfunctional.

I recently asked a group of teenagers to raise their hands if they had ever sneaked out of the house at night. About half of them raised their hands. While that is not a "hanging offense," it is hidden disobedience. The fact that they felt the need to hide suggests a controlling parent mode environment. When people in charge decide to force things their way because they have the power to do so, it initiates a contest. Remember, when people with less power can't compete openly, they will compete covertly. Those in charge seldom know they are in a contest until covert disobedience becomes overt disobedience.

I was consulting with the City of Lake Forest, near Chicago, when a contest was going on between the police chief and the rest of the police force. I advised the city manager and the Chief of Police to sit down with the police force and have some serious discussions before the police force took some irretrievable actions. The Chief believed that he had everything under control; he had the power, and he felt that no one had the guts to take him on. The police force secretly organized and requested that a union organizer come to the city and administer a vote to unionize the police force. Of course, the city manager, the mayor, and the city council panicked.

At their request, I met with the managers and the employees in all city departments. After our departmental meetings, each department decided to have a separate unionization vote. The only department that voted to unionize was the Police Department. Afterward, the mayor and city manager asked my opinion about what had happened. I told them bluntly that they got a police force union because they deserved one. Once covert disobedience becomes overt disobedience, one cannot force someone to comply. The contest didn't cease after the police force unionized. It got worse because the power was now divided equally between the Chief and the unionized police force. Ultimately, the city manager fired the police chief and replaced him with the fire chief. He became the police chief and fire chief. He operated from a Nurturing Parent Mode, so the tensions eased quickly. Interestingly, a couple of years after the fire chief became the police chief; the police force decided they didn't want to pay union dues anymore; they didn't feel they were getting their money's worth.

Fortunately, or unfortunately, many kids never get to try out their wings until they head off to college. If they haven't had much experience making decisions, they don't know how to handle the "freedom" to make wise decisions. As a consequence, they make self-damaging decisions. When they don't know how to make good decisions, they too frequently connect with someone who senses their naivety and takes advantage of them. I see too many kids fail college or become hooked on drugs and alcohol because there was no one there to make wise decisions, and they didn't have the experience to do so independently.

I am not arguing for the benefits of keeping people in Controlling Parent Mode environments for their entire lives. I promote the concept that children make decisions as soon as they mature enough to choose wisely. Even being accountable, at a young age, for unwise decisions that have don't have serious consequences is a great training ground for making important decisions later on and throughout life.

One of the star volleyball players at Club V illustrates what can happen when a good kid leaves a Controlling Parent Mode environment and is thrust into decision-making unprepared. Arlene (not her real name) was a standout volleyball player in high school and club competitions nationally. As a result, she received a full-ride volleyball scholarship to a prestigious university. Her parents were very religious and super controlling. Before college, Arlene didn't have many opportunities to make many decisions because she didn't have to; her parents did it for her, and their choices served her well while she was under their control. She was intelligent, beautiful, talented, and highly recognized for her achievements. At the end of high school, she got what her parents had been praying for: an unparalleled educational opportunity being paid for at a top university through a full-ride volleyball scholarship.

Not long after she arrived on campus, her life changed. For the first time, she had the freedom to choose what, when, and how to spend her time and what she would do. She virtually had no prior experience with kids who partied and lived a "liberal" lifestyle. She certainly wanted to fit in and be a part of "real campus living." She connected with others willing to show her the "finer pleasures" of life. She experienced alcohol, pot, boys, and glorious fattening food. She also gained 80 pounds, making it impossible for her to play volleyball at a Division I level. She lost her volleyball scholarship. Her new lifestyle left little time for studying and class attendance. It wasn't long before she was placed on academic probation and then expelled from the university.

Her stunned parents decided to step in as they had always done and get her back on the "right" path. The trouble was, she didn't want her parents controlling her life anymore. The more they tried, the more she resisted. She eventually ceased all communication with her parents, moved, and didn't tell them where she went. You can imagine the panic and heartache her parents experienced and are still experiencing. They ask: "How could this be happening?" They are resentful of the "people" who took their daughter away from them. I'm not sure if they understand their part in their daughter's decisions and "disappointing" new life.

History shows us that the same principles apply in Controlling Parent Mode governments (dictatorships). Over time, they experience the same type of rebellious behavior Controlling Parent Mode families and organizations experience. As you know, Russia took over all the countries in Europe that the Russian armed forces occupied at the end of World War II. By centralizing the government in all these occupied countries, they established the Soviet Union, which comprised 21 nations. They established puppet communist governments in each occupied country. The countries all took direction from the Russian Kremlin. The Secretary-General of the Soviet Union was the dictator over all the countries within the Soviet Union. The Soviet government collectivized agriculture and nationalized industry. Decision-making was centralized, and those with political power controlled lives.

Covert disobedience rumbled within the previously independent countries – at first, within individual groups and with independent thinking societies. Then it spread throughout all the countries within the union, which eventually burst into overt civil disobedience between the republics and the central government. The Kremlin responded with threats, force, and violence, which only spawned greater levels of rebellion. The dissolution (collapse) of the Soviet Union took place from 1988 through 1991. The first Soviet republic to gain independence from the Soviet Union was Lithuania in 1990. The USSR (United Socialist Soviet Republic) ceased to exist when the three republics – Russia, Ukraine, and Byelorussia – declared that it didn't exist anymore. Once again, when open disobedience has been justified by the disobedient, force becomes ineffective – even in dictatorships (given sufficient time).

I am a fan of the people who rebelled against the dictatorship of the Soviet Union. They exemplify the second child mode spawned from Controlling Parent Mode – the disobedient, rebellious, angry, defiant child, who contests authority, rules, constraints, and restrictions. They are the fighters!

My nephew Mark is a fighter. His parents are two super-intelligent, super-religious, very structured people. They expected their children to be obedient and to follow the rules. Well, Mark didn't like rules, so he didn't obey them; he was smart and wanted to make his own decisions. As a result, he was short on obedience and long on covert, then overt disobedience. Mark spent most of his life pre-high school sitting in time-out or facing a wall as punishment for disobedience. The more he disobeyed, the more control his parents tried to exert over him, and the more control they wielded, the more he fought back. By the time Mark hit high school, he was a rebel. Whatever the rules were, he did the opposite. He moved out of his parents' home his junior year of high school and lived with friends. He had a "close" girlfriend. His parents knew that they could no longer control their son's decisions and behavior at this juncture. I'm sure they were confused, angry, disappointed, and at a loss regarding what action to take to save their son.

If it weren't for my parents, Mark's grandparents, I'm not sure what would have happened with him. Their home was a place of unconditional love and acceptance for him and other wrongdoers. My mother, concerned about the situation, asked me to provide our family, brothers, wives, and older children with a series of sessions on interpersonal connections and relationships (she knew that I taught courses on the subject at a graduate school). Mark participated in those sessions. The concepts hit him to his core. He later told me that it gave him insight into his life and relationship with his parents. It also gave him a language and a means to resolve his inner cognitive dissonance and manage the contests with his family. He applied his learnings well; he went on a mission for our church, married a wonderful woman, has a houseful of rambunctious, athletic boys, and is a successful attorney. He is an example of why I say that fighters are lucky and even luckier if they have the tools to manage relationships successfully.

The Overindulgent Parent Mode Parenting transfers responsibility and accountability away from themselves and their family, blaming others when expectations fall short. When blaming others is not plausible or possible, they make excuses, thus avoiding personal responsibility or accountability. The overriding message from them is: "It's always someone else's fault when we don't achieve what we want." They predictably spawn Self-Centered Child Mode Children who are either entitled, dependent, or narcissistic.

The people who operate from the Overindulgent Parent Mode are "hoverers" regarding their children. They would say they simply want what is best for their child, and they are ever-present to make sure it happens.

As mentioned earlier, they personify victimhood with unfulfilled expectations and are the quintessence of superiority when expectations are met. They are bearers of "Ain't It Awful's!" and throw fits when outcomes are less than desired. Another common characteristic is that they exaggerate their achievements and their children's.

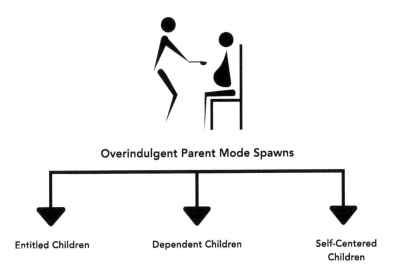

Overindulgent Parent Mode Spawns

| Entitled Children | Dependent Children | Self-Centered Children |

The Overindulgent Parent Mode parenting environment spawns child modes where people view themselves as the center of everything. Imagine a child who is never responsible or accountable for their actions. In that case, we discover a person with a spoiled, narcissistic, self-centered, accept-no-responsibility-or-accountability child mode who blames others for what they lack in life and who feels entitled to get everything they want. When life situations prove problematic, they are the perpetual victims who expect others to solve their problems. At the same time, they represent themselves as being extraordinary and deserving of everything they can get from others.

I have difficulty dealing with either the Overindulgent Parent or their narcissistic, self-centered, take-no-responsibility-or-accountability spawned child mode kids. It is not pleasant to work with these people because they come to me or someone else to solve their problems. Of course, the difficulty here is that they think it's someone else's problem. Unless they can realize that their unfulfilled expectations are their problem and that other people are not going to change, or fix the world, to make them happy, there is not a lot of hope for helping them cope with life, and its many complexities. Overindulgent Parent Mode people are transference-masters with built-in defense mechanisms that shield them from reality and workable solutions to their problems. It is hard to solve problems when it is always someone else's problem.

Remember the fellow from Toronto with a miserable life? He believed that his dad was the cause of his problems. If his dad changed, it would solve his issues. He is an example of a person who takes no responsibility for his happiness and situation. When presented with the obvious conclusion that the answer to his issues was to get his dad into therapy, he saw the suggestion as stupid. It was not until he started taking responsibility for his expectations and feelings that he started moving forward.

The common dilemma of dealing with the Child Mode children of indulgent parents is transference, the shifting of problem ownership, personal responsibility and accountability, and solutions to others for things they should own and fix. The ironic thing is that, over time, the Overindulgent Parent and their children all come to feel victimized by their created situations.

I have friends who have retired and are living on a fixed income with sufficient resources to cover their basic needs but not much beyond that. The problem is that they have a daughter with three kids, no job, no husband, and no income who has moved in with them and who expects her parents to provide her and her kids with the lifestyle that they think they deserve. They believe that they deserve a lot because they are "extraordinary." The parents feel like victims and want their daughter to change (be responsible and accountable for herself and her kids and find another residence). The daughter feels victimized by the situation and blames her parents (and many others) for her troubles. The parents told me that their daughter accused them of not preparing her to be successful in life; it was their fault that she and her kids lived with them. Because of their "shitty" parenting, they should provide a better lifestyle than they were currently providing. How do we resolve issues where both parties want the other party to change and solve their problem, particularly when they think others have the problem? Of course, nothing constructive will happen until the participants in the conundrum accept ownership of their problems and are willing to be responsible for the solutions. People in this situation have both an educational challenge and an it's-never-my-fault problem.

People in victim mode are fundamentally dependent on others and live in an alternate reality. When people fail to accept ownership of their expectations or transfer the problem to someone else to solve it, they fail to accept reality. The actual truth is: my unfulfilled expectations are my problems, not yours. A false reality makes it impossible to produce a reality-based solution. How can a reality-based solution happen within an alternate reality (a fantasy)? If we accept the responsibility for solving the problem based on their reality, it becomes our problem. If we inherit it, they remain dependent upon us, and we become the victims of their situation. Victimhood continues as long as people do not accept responsibility for and become engaged in solving their issues.

Too often, the Overindulgent Parent Mode parents spawn child modes who burden society and the parents who spawned them. In short, these people believe that they are entitled to anything they need or want. I had a cousin who was constantly needing help and resources from others. He routinely sought out financial assistance from my parents and other aunts and uncles within the family. He believed that he deserved their resources. When my aunt asked him why his wife wasn't working, he, offended, responded: "My wife is not going to work!" My aunt then pointed out that he was seeking funds from families where all the wives were working and that it was unreasonable for him to ask for money from the families of working women when he would not expect his wife to work. He retorted: "How can you watch us suffer while you go on vacations, buy lots of fancy stuff when you have so much, and we have so little?" He felt that he was a victim and others should solve his problems. Still, the family helped out, becoming enablers and kicking the can down the road. But they were never happy about it. My cousin never realized that the solution to his problems was within his and his wife's realm of controllability. Somehow, he thought that his resource deficiencies were his aunts' and uncles' problem, to be solved by them.

Unfortunately, he is not the only one who thinks that way. If only the President would solve all our problems. I am not suggesting that there aren't real victims. Acts of God victimize people: earthquakes, floods, hurricanes, and tsunamis. Through no fault of their own, some people find themselves victims of circumstances beyond their control. Slavery is a humongous example of that. In the USA, the black community is still negatively impacted by slavery. Slavery has left its scars from its beginning until the present. We need to recognize that fact and offer remedial action in virtually all aspects of life negatively impacted by slavery. While we can never erase slavery from our past, we can help those unfairly affected by it. Health catastrophes strike those who have done nothing to deserve it. I am grateful for the assistance provided to those who need it when they are the victims of circumstances. The Covid 19 pandemic has victimized all of us. The service provided by those who have personally sacrificed for our benefit deserves admiration and adoration. However, the child mode spawns of Overindulgent Parent Modes, the narcissistic, self-centered, entitled child modes are not so deserving; their victimhood results from parents operating in their Overindulgent Parent Mode. From that perspective, they are actual victims of parents who spoiled them and made them narcissistic.

Regrettably, the number of indulgent parents and narcissistic child mode kids with a sense of entitlement is growing as a percentage of society. Teachers and coaches evermore feel the burden and accusations of parents who blame the teacher, or the coach, when their child does not achieve as wanted. It is a reality at Club V Volleyball that an increasing number of parents, each year, hold the coaches responsible for everything relative to their child's progress and success. We are well aware of the commiseration club members. They broadcast "Ain't It Awful's!" in a perverted attempt to transfer responsibility and accountability for subpar performance, away from an undedicated player, who happens to be their daughter, to the shoulders of the coaches. If the child is genuinely undedicated, that is the coach's fault in the parents' mind. Amazingly, many teachers and coaches put up with this crap. They put up with it because they love the kids and teaching and coaching.

Effectively dealing with the aftermath of the Overindulgent Parent Mode parenting requires understanding some things in upcoming sections of this book. After the Nurturing Parent Mode review, we need to understand "Adult Mode," the next area for study. We need to understand problem ownership, expectations management, simple versus complex problems, primary and secondary needs of helpers and helpers, and how to coach in a way that helps people understand and define their solutions to the issues that challenge them. We will discuss these topics in the competencies section of this book.

The Nurturing Parent Mode Parenting spawn nurturing child mode feelings and responses.

Nurturing Parent Mode Spawns

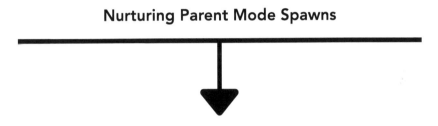

"Free Children" or Nurturing Children

The Nurturing Parent Mode is reassuring, caring, supportive, understanding, and empathetic. It epitomizes the "I'm OK. You're OK." life position as spoken of by Dr. Harris in his book of the same name. The people who operate from this mode make a positive difference in the lives of people with whom they connect – and they make a lot of positive connections. They can look beyond mistakes and shortfalls. They can see the beauty around them – in people, things, the environment, and circumstances. They also feel things deeply. They are leaders who see themselves as a support function for their team. They delight in the growth and accomplishment of others. For them, it is less about directing and more about supporting.

When Janssen Pharmaceutica launched in the United States, Jim Bodine was the first President. He was a bomber pilot who flew over Germany during WWII. He operated from a Nurturing Parent Mode. When someone was failing in their current position, he would look for ways to help them succeed. In discussing an employee with a performance problem, he would ask me, "So, where can we put (Tom) within the company where he can succeed?" He saw his job as building a company of successful people who would, in turn, make the company successful. He told me that he never wanted to contribute to a pattern of failure in anyone's life. He didn't give up on people; he sought to understand them and position them where they could flourish. The Nurturing Parent Mode is a source of development and growth in others. People who operate from this mode develop synergistic relationships and avoid command and control relationships or dysfunctional ones. They are a source of light, energy, and enhancement, and they spawn children (and adults) who do likewise.

Nurturing Parent Mode Parenting spawns the Free Child Mode.

Free Child Mode kids nurture others as their parents nurtured them. These kids are comfortable with others. They act naturally and with self-confidence. While every child develops an "I'm Not OK" part of themselves during the imprinting and modeling stages of infancy, the nurtured kids have had the benefit of a whole lot of loving and positive reinforcements that generate a plethora of positive child mode feelings. Because of the nurturing these child modes are secure and confident and feel "free" to explore the world around them. That is why we call them *free children*.

Consequently, as adults, they accept others and seem to intuitively understand that racial, social, and identity differences enrich us all and, in total, optimize society's potential. They would agree readily with the concept that the greatness of America is because it is a melting pot of diversity. These understanding, empathic, curious, energetic, fun-loving, caring, compassionate, spontaneous, and loving souls give those who need it meaning and purpose for living. There can never be enough nurturing parents and free child kids in the world.

Cathy Carlson Phillips is my youngest daughter. She went through a bad patch of depression and anxiety not long ago. She was hospitalized and eventually had electroshock therapy to help her survive and heal. Later she found that the source of her mental illness was post-partum depression. Her dear friends provided the lifeboat that she so desperately needed. They gave their time, support, and love. Why would they do that? Because she always had been there for them when they needed her. Cathy is the one who meets and gets to know the new people who move into the neighborhood or who are the new people in her church group. She is the one who invites them over for lunches or dinners and arranges for their kids to play together. Cathy is the emergency babysitter who her friends call when something comes up. She hears, understands, and validates when being listened to; she knows when understanding and validation is needed badly. She is everyone's best friend. She is so nurturing, loving, caring, accepting, and fun that people love being with her. I am so proud of her, and I am grateful that she is my daughter; she is a gift to the world.

Viktor Frankl undoubtedly understood the importance of nurturers in our lives. In his book, *Man's Search for Meaning*, the first thing he listed that gives meaning and purpose to life is to love or be loved by someone. People have loved and nurtured me my whole life, making me rich beyond measure. And, at opportune moments, I was blessed when nurturers stepped forward to help me. Their nurturing changed the direction of my life – for the better. All through my life, the nurturers have been there. I know that I am unbelievably fortunate. It would be wonderful if nurturers surrounded everyone in the world. Imagine a world where everyone cares for, loves one another, and nurtures others when they see needs. Fortunately, most people can think of one or more people in their lives who nurtured them when needed. These nurturers will always be the heroes in their life stories. The ones who had had no nurturers, or too few of them, seem to be the lost children, who have learned that they can only depend on themselves and no one else. As they heal from physical and emotional abuses, they acquire the life position of, "I'm OK, You Are Not OK."[23] When that happens, taking care of "number one" justifies every self-serving act; every win is at the expense of someone else. Our prisons are full of people abused or neglected who didn't get the nurturing they needed when they needed it.

---

23   T. A. Harris, *I'm OK – You're OK.* (Harper & Row, 1967), 50-52.

There are people around us who have had no one who nurtured them; these unfortunates often take the position of "I'm Not OK, You're Not OK."[24] They see no value in themselves or others. With zero self-esteem and a dismal self-image, just breathing is a chore. Sometimes they commit suicide. Some escape into fantasy worlds, where life is beautiful and exceptional. Millions seek validation or escape through drugs or alcohol, exacerbating their sense of worthlessness or nothingness. Others develop chronic illnesses so they won't be ignored and get the care of others paid to be nurturers. Thank heavens that such support is available. But for too many, the nurturers never show up. They are left to dangle, alone, hoping for, but never expecting life-affirming human connections – helplessness and hopelessness are their reality.

Everyone needs to be nurtured from time to time. If we are fortunate, someone is there to do it. If not, unfulfilled needs drive our thoughts and behavior. I am not sure how many people understand that unfulfilled needs drive behavior, especially unusual behavior. I am blessed far more than most; I have so many people I love and who love me. And yet, I need approbation in most of my endeavors. Even in writing this book, I need positive strokes to keep writing. Without it, I feel alone and like I'm dangling from the single strand of a spider web.

If you need nurturing, find someone who can nurture you. You can always pay for it, although not all paid nurturers are equally good at it. I believe that most great counselors help everyone who comes to them, while the bad ones help few. It is usually challenging to get an appointment with the good ones. Good nurturers are all around us; in society, there are a lot of them, and they are visible. We can spot them because they are usually part of a group where everyone nurtures one another. It is easier to become part of that group than we would imagine; their nurturing nature is inclusive, and they are pretty willing to wrap their empathy around us when they learn of our unfulfilled needs.

I want to remind you that when we talk about our child mode, we talk about our state of mind when emotions are in charge of our deci-

---

24   *ibid.*

sions and actions. Feelings are a wonderful part of us and sometimes a burdensome part. Some of us have emotional recordings from our infancy and youth that make life difficult to endure. The next chapter on adult modes will introduce how we can use our adult mode to analyze our feelings and manage them. Our child mode offers personal insight into emotional intelligence (a fantastic talent). Our emotions provide a bridge for people to connect with us. They're also a bridge for us to connect with others. We will explore some competencies for managing our emotions in the competency section in Emotional States Competencies.

16

ADULT MODE

The imprinting and modeling that occurred during the early stages (between birth and age 13) created our parent and child operating modes. The parent mode recordings are the things we were taught that form the basis for our subconscious "should's" and "ought-to's" throughout life. We recorded everything our parents said and did in our early life, and we absorbed them straight and unfiltered. These become "recordings" of unquestioned external events, by infants between birth and age five." (I'm OK – You're OK.)[25] Young people don't choose what happens to them; experiences happen to them and around them. These **external events** became the lessons they internalize, which determines their path. These external events define their perception of right, wrong,

25   T. A. Harris, *I'm OK – You're OK.* (Harper & Row, 1967), 22.

factual, and normal. Infants don't question the events around them and the lessons they learn from them. If our parents were racist, we became racist. If our parents were caring and generous, we became caring and generous. These external events became the basis for our internalized beliefs. They became our internal-rules-based parent mode.

At the same time, we recorded our parent mode; we also recorded all the emotions that we experienced from what we saw and heard as **internal events** became our child mode feelings. Since we were infants when we recorded them, we didn't have a vocabulary to catalog them; they exist simply as feelings. Both our parent and child modes reside in our subconscious mind. When current events happen that connect us to our early recordings, we replay the "taught" parent mode recordings and the "feeling" child mode recordings as reactions to the current experience.

Fortunately, the parent and child modes are not the only operating modes we have; otherwise, they would forever enslave us to believe, act, and feel as we did when we were infants. We are all blessed with an *adult mode*, which is the ability to reason and question our infant recordings, validate them, change them, or nullify them. The adult mode is not subconscious but operates from conscious thought, right out of our frontal lobe. Our adult mode is the computer in our brain that analyzes data and makes logical conclusions based on the data examined.

This data-processing computer makes decisions by analyzing the data from three sources: our parent mode recordings, our child mode recordings, and new data gained from observation, life experience, and new sources of information. Using our adult mode, we can do a "check-up from the neck up"[26] and decide if we still believe the "should's" and ought-to's" from our early childhood parent mode recordings.

It lets us determine if our emotions in certain situations are still valid or need to be modified or eliminated. It is our adult mode that asks, "Why do I feel this way?" It can then decide whether the feelings are appro-

---

26 Morris Massey, *The People Puzzle: Understanding Yourself and Others* (Reston Publishing Company, 1979).

priate or inappropriate and whether to accept them or change them. The adult mode enabled me to reject my dad's racist attitudes and still love him. Still, we need to understand that the adult mode allows us to manage obsolete parent mode recordings and inappropriate child mode recordings, but it cannot erase them. In my case, I understand that the over-achiever and insecurity manifestations that I still exhibit spawned from my dad's Critical Parent Mode parenting. My adult mode allows me to manage them. The adult mode will enable us to emancipate ourselves from old recordings that don't serve us well. It offers the agency to change responses to old recordings and replace them with new ones. It allows us to do what we reason to be correct, regardless of popular opinion or opposition.

The current beliefs of his day didn't limit Albert Einstein. He was willing to question with an open mind the laws of physics. He used his adult mode to examine his parent mode recordings and, in doing so, actually defined new realities of physics. His extraordinary intelligence enabled him to challenge his own and other people's unquestionable conclusions successfully. It is the adult mode of all of society's change-makers that allow them, and consequently us, to move beyond old paradigms, to discover new possibilities, and to make new realities.

We could say that our adult mode is our personal "change agent." It frees us to make decisions and take actions based on logical data analysis. Our adult mode enables us to be reasonable in complex circumstances, and it empowers us to change our minds and change ourselves – if we choose to do so. It enabled me to change my life course as a 16-year-old and align my decisions with better values. It justifies a new and current moral compass rather than one based on old biases, prejudices, and ill-founded mores. It is the basis for rational problem solving, based on facts and logic rather than archaic reasoning or strong feelings. The adult mode enables us to look forward and imagine the future as we hope it will be and as we want it to be. It then allows us to plan for it and make it happen.

Everyone will change given sufficient stimuli. People change when the pain and discomfort of the current path are no longer tolerable. For example, we know from observed experience that addicts often change when they hit "rock bottom" – assuming they don't die first. People also change from despair caused by unrelenting boredom.

In the movie *Groundhog Day,* a cynical TV weatherman, driven to despair by living the same day over and over again, searches for ways to escape his recycling misery. Each day he sought new methods for self-gratification until even that bored him. It created, in him, the hopelessness that motivated him to commit suicide, to no avail; he woke up and started the same day all over again. Things changed when he realized that he could use the situation to his advantage, and he started using each new day to grow and develop new talents (playing the piano) and gain new knowledge. He found his perfect love and moved beyond his selfish focus, which gave him meaning and purpose for living each day.

People also change because they realize that they can. Change made from the adult mode is a cognitive choice based on data analyzed by the frontal cortex. Notice that external stimuli stimulate the first two types of changes. In contrast, the adult mode drives changes internally. The adult mode reasons and concludes when change is a beneficial thing to do.

It is easy and obvious to see when people operate in the parent, child, or adult modes. People in parent mode are projecting their parent mode recordings and are looking for people who agree with them. We like to call that "stroking one another's prejudices." When they stroke each other's biases, the conversation goes on and on because they reinforce identical parent mode should's and ought to's. It is why conspiracy theories never die but continuously reinforce the current one and spawn new ones of the same vintage.

In the child mode, everyone can see, or sense, that emotions are front, center, and in charge. Sympathy is actually "stroking one another's feelings." Sympathy reinforces feelings; it does nothing to understand them or validate the person expressing them. Sympathy does nothing to help people control or change the negative emotions eating them alive.

People in adult mode empathize rather than sympathize. They are the ones who are actively listening, the ones trying to hear, understand, and validate the messages sent. I love transactional analysis because it teaches us how to see and understand interactions between people and to be able to analyze transactions to help people make sound, logical, and beneficial changes through personal choice. When people learn and understand the concepts of transactional analysis, they can see and understand the interactions of others. And more importantly, they can see and recognize their behaviors with others and utilize that understanding to change their life and repair damaged relationships.

17

TRANSACTIONAL INTERACTIONS

A transaction is sending and receiving messages between people. It is also called communication. Communication between two people consists of people who both have a parent mode, an adult mode, and a child mode. When people transact with one another, one person sends a message from one of his operating modes to a targeted operating mode of the person to whom they are sending their message. The person receiving the message receives it in an operating mode of their choosing and sends a response back to a targeted operating mode of the person they are responding to. If the sent message and the received message align as intended with one another's operating modes, we have a parallel transaction or communication. If the sent message and the received message do not align with one another's operating modes, we have a cross transaction or communication. Parallel transactions are received well. Cross transactions are received poorly. Remember that communication engages four operating modes, two from each party in the transaction.

To help us visualize what communication looks like between the various modes that people are operating from, let's imagine that a rope connects one person's operating mode to the operating mode of the other person. If the ropes connecting them are parallel, we say the communication (the transaction) is parallel or complementary. Parallel or complementary transactions are messages that are sent and received without conflict. The transactions can be adult to adult, parent to parent, child to child, parent to child, adult to parent, or adult to child, as long as the ropes remain parallel.[27] They are complementary because the message sent from the sender's operating mode to the receiver's

---

27 Eric Berne, *Games People Play* (Ballantine Books, 1985), 10-11.

targeted operating mode is received by the operating mode of the receiver as the sender intended. The receiver then sends a response to the same operating mode from which the sender sent the message. In the example below, notice the parallel lines between the sender and the receiver.

Example of a Parallel or Complimentary Transaction

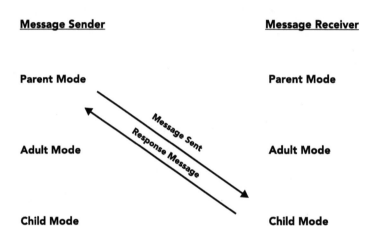

Parallel transactions or communications occur when the operating modes of the senders and receivers remain parallel with one another. Parent-to-parent communications are parallel when both parties are reinforcing each other's beliefs. Imagine a conversation between two people in 1920 discussing women's right to vote. People talking with someone who agreed with a women's right to vote would be a parallel transaction (women *should* have the right to vote). If two people agreed that women should not have the right to vote, that would also be complementary (because it reinforces their shared beliefs). Parent-to-parent mode complementary transactions happen when both parties agree on their should's and ought to's. They are stroking one another's beliefs.

Complementary transactions also occur child mode to child mode. We see this happen when two siblings are sent to bed early for fighting, and they sympathize with each other about how horrible mom and dad are.

They are stroking one another's feelings. A parent scolding a child can be a complementary transaction providing both accept the modes from which the other is operating.

Adult to adult would be complementary when two people have a reasonable, logical conversation based on fact or reality. For example, a husband and wife discuss the best way to raise their kids. It is people problem solving with reason and logic.

As long as the messages sent and received align with one another's operating mode, it is a parallel or complementary transaction or communication. If they aren't parallel, then we have a cross transaction. An important point to remember is that the kind of transactions we have impact our relationships.

Cross Transactional Interactions

One afternoon, I rode a bus in London and encountered a white gentleman right out of Mary Poppins. He obviously worked for the "City" (the English finance industry), as reflected by his bowler hat, dark suit, and umbrella on the arm. He entered the bus and sat beside me, directly behind the bus driver. Just as the bus door closed and the bus started to pull away, a black woman ran alongside the bus slapping its side to get the driver's attention so he would stop and let her on the bus. The driver saw her, stopped, and let her enter the bus. Bowler Hat leaned over during the excitement and said, "Don't you just hate sharing public transportation with Darkies?" I responded: "Not at all; my wife is black." He looked shocked, got up, and moved to a different bus section. Our transaction was non-complementary.[28] As you can guess, our ropes crossed. If I had agreed with him, we could have ridden together in perfect harmony, parent mode to parent mode, discussing the injustice of "Darkies" in society. Maybe I could have tried to hook his adult and ask why he hated sharing transportation with people of color. But considering his reaction after I responded to his question, I assumed he did not wish to have a logical, adult mode to adult mode discussion.

---

28   Eric Berne, *Games People Play* (Ballantine Books, 1985), 10-11.

That is typical of when a message is sent in one mode but received in a non-complementary mode. He sent a message from his parent mode, hoping for a sympathetic response from my parent mode. When I responded from my parent mode, it created a cross transaction or non-complementary communication. Cross transactions create cognitive dissonance. It happens when the message sent from one operating mode is not received well from the receiving operating mode of the other. Think of two rivers flowing parallel to one another versus one that enters the flow from the side. The parallel flowing rivers conjure an image of smooth waters, whereas the river entering from the side creates a picture of rough water and wild currents – it is similar, conceptually, with cross transactions.

Example of a cross transaction or non-complimentary communication

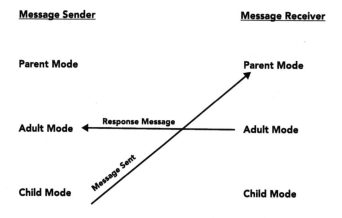

Example of a Cross Transaction between a husband and a wife

The husband is getting ready for work, turns to his wife, and says in parent mode, "Where did you put my socks?"

The wife responds in child mode, "I don't wear your socks."

The husband retorts in child mode, "Yeah… but what did you do with them?"

The wife responds in adult mode, "Have you looked where they are supposed to be? The same place as always?"

Husband's child mode response is, "They are not here!"

The wife's child mode jab, "Have you looked where they are not supposed to be?"

The husband's child mode blame, "I didn't wash the damn socks. It's your job to wash them!"

The wife's adult mode response, "I am not your maid!"

The husband's parent mode emotional criticism, "I work so much. Washing my clothes is only one of the jobs you are supposed to do!"

The wife's child mode put down, "You come home and throw your clothes on the floor. It drives me nuts."

The husband's child mode response, "Your mom always took care of your dad!"

The wife's child mode attack, "At least I'm sure who my father was."

The husband's child mode response, "What's that supposed to mean?"

This kind of cross transaction happens when a boss, operating from parent mode, approaches his employee, criticizing him for being late and expecting the employee to respond in compliant child mode, but the employee responds in adult mode. "I would have liked to be on time, but there are times when it is more important for me to hug my child who needed comforting." Rough water or wild currents? I guess the boss's response to the adult explanation would result in either an adult-to-adult conversation or a non-complementary argument.

We had a purchasing manager at Amersham who got under the skin of our USA company president. They couldn't have a complementary conversation. They came at one another in parent mode, but their parent modes had different should's and ought to's. It was always rough water and wild currents. The president just wanted her to shut up and do the job the way he wanted it done. In other words, he wanted her to respond to his demands in compliant child mode. That was the last thing she would do; she knew purchasing better than anyone in the company and wanted him to know it. Their cross transactions finally reached the point where the president wanted her gone. I asked him to let me talk to her before taking any irretrievable action.

When I met with her, I took the time to listen, hear, understand, and validate her beliefs about how to do purchasing well. During that conversation, I realized that her job, and Amersham, was her life. It was the core of her identity and self-esteem. Her attempt to make her points with our president was a means to try and validate her value and self-worth. She proved that we would all benefit if we let her do her job, as she wanted to do it. I went back to our president and shared my discoveries with him. He agreed to "Give her plenty of rope to hang herself." She took the opportunity and impressed everyone, including her peers in the purchasing community.

Later that year, she received an award from her purchasing association. After that, the president and all of us at Amersham looked at her differently. Amersham also recognized her contributions. She received a plaque for her contributions and a paid vacation to reward her excellent work. You would have thought she won the lottery; from that moment forward, she showed everyone who came through Amersham's doors the plaque given to her by our president.

By the way, effective problem solving, with mutual gain outcomes, only occurs in parallel transactions that are adult to adult. I just wanted to give you an advance peek about problem-solving that will address in our competencies section.

Hooking a Person's Adult Mode When They are Stuck in Parent Mode

When we see someone in parent mode, we can reasonably believe that something *hooked* their parent in the current situation. We can assume they are playing old parent mode recordings and living them in real time. We need to hook their adult mode to have an adult mode to adult mode conversation. Failing to hook their adult mode, we will have to stroke their prejudice and reinforce their old recordings or disagree and have an argument that will make everyone feel uncomfortable. Rather than argue, we can ask, "Why do you believe that?" As soon as they start explaining their beliefs, they are in adult mode. We hook the adult mode of someone who is *stuck* in parent mode by getting them to explain their position. They switch off their subconscious recordings and consciously use their frontal cortex to justify their belief when explaining their point of view. By the way, once a person has taken a strong position, they will often defend it with their life. Both parties need to be in adult mode to communicate adult mode to adult mode. Problem-solving or logical discussions are ineffective if only one discussant is rational, reasonable, fact-based, and seeking *truth*. When a person explains their beliefs (parent mode), the explanation occurs in adult mode. So, to hook the adult mode with someone stuck in parent mode, we ask them to explain why they believe what they are professing. If their rationale is reasonable, then they are likely in adult mode. They are still stuck in parent mode if their explanation is simply a strong rehash of the same message.

I had a manager who told me that she would never hire anyone who had worked in a bank. I asked her why. She said that everyone knows that people who work in banks can't make decisions. My manager was stuck in parent mode.

I attempted to hook her adult mode by requesting that she explain the belief that bank people can't make decisions. She eventually shared her experience that neither of the two people she once hired from the same bank could make decisions without getting confirmation from her on everything. It drove her nuts. Once she was in adult mode, we had a good conversation and agreed that the two probably didn't exemplify everyone who works in banks. We concluded that their reluctance to make decisions might reflect their previous bank manager's style. We agreed that in the future, we need to hire based on a candidate's capability and willingness to meet our performance expectations regardless of whether or not they had previously worked in a bank.

Hooking a Person's Adult Mode When They are Stuck in Child Mode

People get stuck in child mode just like people get stuck in parent mode. To problem solve effectively, both parties need to be in adult mode. Since child mode is manifest in feelings, we need to persuade emotional people to explain their feelings to transition to adult mode. It usually helps if we validate their feelings before requesting that they explain them. As they explain and justify their feelings, we connect with their adult mode. Once they are in adult mode, we can have logical discussions or problem solve. Please keep in mind that not everything needs a solution. Sometimes there are no solutions; people just need to feel validated.

My second child, Tiffany, is a five-foot beauty, dynamo, and go-getter. By the way, she married a fellow from Alberta who is six foot, six inches tall. She has always been an emotional person; it is part of her charm. As a teenager, her life was ecstasy or tragedy, with little in-between. After one emotional crash, she came to me with the lament, "Dad, why do these things always happen to me? What can I do?" I validated her exasperation and asked if that was a rhetorical question or if she wanted to discuss it. Hesitantly, she said she wanted to talk about it. The bottom line, her life was a roller coaster of emotions and drama. Emotions were a means for her to relieve emotional pressure, but they came with consequences regarding the impact on friends and family. We agreed that releasing the emotions was vital for her well-being.

She came to understand that there are two ways to release the pressure of pent-up emotions: live them or explain them. Living them, which was her way, placed her in child mode too frequently, becoming an obstacle to empathy. Explaining them centered her in adult mode and provided a means for family and friends to connect with her in loving and supportive ways. Her emotional perspective offers the world a profound, touching, and far-reaching panorama usually expressed with incomparable humor.

If we try, we can connect with the adult mode of young children. Lily was four years old and came to her grandma crying. Grandma Lois asked, "What's the matter, sweetheart?" Lily holds up a button in her hand and says, "Teddy lost his eye!" As soon as she explained why she was upset, she shifted from child mode to adult mode. She used reason and facts to help grandma understand her feelings and explain them. It astounds me to see adult mode demonstrated in very young children and how wise they are before we expect them to be.

Nelson Mandela was a marvel of adult mode responses to bigoted apartheid persecution. If anyone deserved to have justified child mode responses or the right to righteous parent mode indignation, one would think it would be he. He served 27 years in prison for conspiring to overthrow the state. He split his sentence between three prisons, where each prison had unique hardships and challenges. Later, while serving his prison sentence, he was also sentenced to life imprisonment for his anti-apartheid activities. After he was released, thanks to political pressures worldwide and within South Africa, he became the first black head of state. He was the first democratically-elected president in a fully representative democratic election in South Africa. He dedicated his life to establishing equality and opportunity for all South Africans. He never dwelled upon his injustices but instead focused on making the world a better place. I was always blown away by his ability to operate in adult mode with those who persecuted and hated him so fiercely. How could he do that?

A Quick Summary About How Operating Modes Influence Relationships

The Nurturing Parent Mode is the cornerstone of all Synergistic relationships. Nurturers spawn children who are, what we call, *Free Children* (secure children who feel free to explore the world and determine where they fit) and develop Synergistic relationships. They make society better. They use the power of adult mode to manage inappropriate parent mode and child mode behavior within themselves and with society.

I hope it is evident that people who operate from Controlling Parent Mode and Critical Parent Mode don't foster Synergistic relationships.

Controlling Parent Mode is the source of Command and Control relationships that are always hierarchy-based, with the power being on top. Someone once said, "Honey, I've been rich, and I've been poor. Rich is better." The Controlling Parent Mode people would parody her statement with: "I've been on top of the hierarchy, and I've been on the bottom of the hierarchy, and being on top is better."

Critical Parent Mode parenting spawns child mode responses that underachieve and overachieve. Both underachievers and overachievers share the trait of having some level of insecurity. In society, people in Critical Parent Mode rub people the wrong way and are the genesis of many conflicts, bruised egos, and dysfunctional relationships.

The Overindulgent Parent Mode parenting generates self-centered, entitled, or dependent child modes. They are an annoyance in society and a burden because they want to be seen as extraordinary while taking no responsibility or accountability for their own situation. They blame others for their misfortunes. The child mode response to the Overindulgent Parent mode plays the "victim" role expertly, expecting someone to save them, solve their problems, or inherit them. Since their approach to life mimics game playing, I would categorize them as members of Dysfunctional relationships.

We are in child mode when our emotions are in charge of our decisions and actions. And yet, emotions are not specific to one kind of relationship because they are an essential part of all relationships. Feelings define our emotional state and our emotional state determines the kind of relationships we have. The feelings in Synergistic relationships are very different from those in Command and Control, Adversary, or Enemy relationships. The kind of feelings we have determine the kind of relationships we have. To the degree that we can master our emotions, to the same degree, we can master our relationships. That means we need to learn how to proactively manage our feelings if we want to have Synergistic relationships.

Relationships are essential to our "being." We define who we are in the context of our important relationships. Our operating modes influence the kind of relationships we have and can have. Our adult mode can govern the parent and child modes and direct us away from Command and Control or Dysfunctional relationships toward Synergistic ones. Learning to use our adult mode optimally blesses ourselves and everyone around us.

18

Problem Ownership

The way we define problem ownership determines whether we operate in parent, child, or adult mode while problem-solving. Who we decide "has the problem" will determine our problem-solving approach.

Generally speaking, people are less effective with problem-solving than they could be because they have a distorted perception of problem ownership. As a result, they end up trying to solve the wrong problem. Understanding actual problem ownership can be a life-changing concept. When we understand and implement problem ownership correctly, it enables us to deal effectively with personal issues and the problems of others. When we don't know who owns the problem, we problem-solve ineffectively. And, most people don't understand who has (or owns) the problem. They end up transferring ownership of their problem to the person they are trying to fix. Transferring the ownership of our problems to others doesn't work!

Even if we have lots of power, people will not intentionally modify themselves to make us happy. They may project the appearance of change by being compliant or submissive, but they won't fundamentally change and they won't like us. All around us, people are trying to problem solve by trying to change people to meet their expectations. It is not an effective approach to problem-solving. Dr. Thomas Gordon taught the importance of problem ownership and relationships in his books about Teacher and Parent Effectiveness Training.[29]

---

29   Thomas Gordon, *Teacher Effectiveness Training* (Three Rivers Press, 1974).

Problem ownership exercise:

Let's take some time and see how you perceive problem ownership. In each of the eight scenarios, choose who you think "has the problem." You must select Parent or Child – you can't choose both – it has to be one or the other.

Who has the problem? Parent or Child?

1. Your daughter sleeps in, moves slowly, and is constantly late for school.

   Who has the problem? Parent or Child? Why?

2. The parent takes back permission for their son to go to a concert that he has planned for, saved for, and purchased tickets for because the son broke curfew by two hours.

   Who has the problem? Parent or Child? Why?

3. The parent uses intimidation and threats to get their son to do his chores.

   Who has the problem? Parent or Child? Why?

4. The parent has a drug issue that interferes with providing for his family.

   Who has the problem? Parent or Child? Why?

5. The daughter is constantly on her phone and doesn't finish her homework.

   Who has the problem? Parent or Child? Why?

6. The dad makes inappropriate jokes at the dinner table.

   Who has the problem? Parent or Child? Why?

7. The daughter doesn't feel that her parents appreciate the magnitude of her challenges.

   Who has the problem? Parent or Child? Why?

8. The son has a body odor that is offensive to everyone around him.

   Who has the problem? Parent or Child? Why?

How you answered the questions provides insight into how you view problem ownership. And, consequently, how you will problem solve. Typically, people have three general perspectives about who owns (or has) the problem with three complementary problem-solving approaches that align with their problem ownership perspective.

Three ways people decide problem ownership and their complementary problem-solving approaches

There are three prevalent ways people define who owns or has the problem: The first way is to decide who is wrong. If you are wrong, you have "the problem." Wrong people need fixing. The second way is the military definition of problem ownership: "If it happens on my watch, it is my problem." "IT IS MY PROBLEM when I am in charge, and I need to fix it." The third way is that the person with the unfulfilled expectation has the problem. "If I have an unfulfilled expectation, that is my problem, not yours. You have inappropriate behavior relative to my expectations."

The "You are wrong" problem ownership perspective

In this approach, whoever is perceived as "wrong" has the problem. If you do not meet my expectations, you are wrong, and you have the problem. With this approach, we problem solve by changing you. How do I do that? I fix you. "You are wrong people" love to provide "constructive criticism" and use negative consequences to change the wrongdoer. They transfer the ownership of their unfulfilled expectations to the person who is not meeting their expectations; if you are not meeting my expectation, you have the problem. When we define our unfulfilled expectations as somebody else's problem, problem-solving becomes a process of changing them to make us happy. Think about it, how many people are looking to change to make you happy? Probably fewer than you think. When we try to force others to change to make us happy, they would most assuredly like to make us miserable. Problem-solving with this approach happens in the parent mode.

So, let's get this straight with right and wrong problem ownership – if you are not meeting my expectation – YOU have the problem. With this approach, I can always effectively problem-solve (change you) if I have enough power to impose my will – or so I believe.

You fit in the "right and wrong" category of problem ownership if you selected:

Scenario 1 - Your daughter sleeps in, moves slowly, and is constantly late for school.
The Child – (if you think the daughter has the problem because she is lazy)

Scenario 2 - The parent takes back permission for their son to go to a concert that he has planned for, saved for, and purchased tickets for because the son broke curfew by two hours.
The Parent – (if you think the parent has the problem because they were unfair)
The Child – (if you think the son has the problem because he broke curfew)

Scenario 3 - The parent uses intimidation and threats to get their son to do his chores.
The Parent – (if you think the parent has the problem because they are being mean)

Scenario 4 - The parent has a drug issue that interferes with providing for his family.
The Parent – (if you think the parent has the problem because they are hurting their family)

Scenario 5 - The daughter is constantly on her phone and doesn't finish her homework.
The Child – (if you think the daughter is wrong because she is not doing what she is supposed to do)

Scenario 6 - The dad makes inappropriate jokes at the dinner table.
The Parent – (if you think the dad is wrong because he should know better)

Scenario 7 - The daughter doesn't feel that her parents appreciate the magnitude of her challenges.
The Child – (if you think the daughter is wrong because her problems are not that big of a deal)
The Parent – (if you think the parent is wrong because they are insensitive to her feelings)

Scenario 8 - The son has a body odor that is offensive to everyone around him.
The Child – (if you think the son is wrong because he doesn't wear deodorant or bathe regularly)

Notice that with this definition of problem ownership, the person will problem-solve by trying to change the person to satisfy their unfulfilled expectation. This problem-solving approach operates in parent mode.

This approach to problem-solving is the most common in our society. We live in a society where most people problem-solve by trying to change those who fail to meet their expectations. This approach creates adversarial relationships because no one likes to be changed. If people resisting the forced change can't openly compete because the person trying to change them has the power, they will compete covertly.

Problem-solving by trying to change people to satisfy our expectations is a power move that fosters disobedience and ultimately rebellion.

The military approach to problem-solving

The military concept for defining problem ownership and problem-solving fits under the philosophy: "If it happens under my watch, it's my problem." All responsibility and accountability for problems fall to the person in charge. With the military approach, people solve problems by analyzing the situation, making decisions, and expecting others to follow orders. Failure to follow orders is insubordination. Insubordination has "superimposed" consequences. **Superimposed Consequences** are punishments and penalties from the power broker.) "I may be responsible and accountable, but I can punish you for my problem."

Here are some examples of Superimposed Consequences:

"If you don't get up, I am taking your phone away. If you do it again, you are grounded."

"Your sentence is life imprisonment for malicious murder."

"You can't have dessert because you didn't eat your carrots."

"I am spanking you because you disobeyed me!"

"If you are late again, you will be fired!"

With this approach, people use a position of power to threaten or force someone to get what they demand. We might describe this approach to problem-solving as giving "marching orders." The way forward will be a well-marked path with plenty of orders, rules, and prescribed action plans. The problem is solved if you follow orders. If you don't, appropriate punishment follows. With this approach, the chain of command controls the actions to solve problems.

You are in this category if, in every scenario, you believe the person in charge has the problem and needs to fix it.

You would say the parent has the problem in all eight scenarios if you think the parent is in charge.

Notice that this approach also operates in parent mode. The military approach to problem-solving suggests that anything not up to standards is the problem of the person in charge. The solution is the action or steps chosen to punish or correct those not operating up to par. It is fixing things by bringing things up to a standard. It is an interesting way of looking at things: if I am in charge, any inappropriate behavior under my supervision is my problem. It certainly establishes clear responsibility and accountability – if there is a clear understanding of who is in charge. President Truman believed in this approach; he had a sign on his desk that said, "The Buck Stops Here!" Not too many presidents since then have lived by that decree. I, for one, would prefer not to live in a hierarchical world (although one could argue that we do).

"My Unfulfilled Expectation is My Problem" Approach to Problem-Solving.

With this approach, the person with the unfulfilled expectation has the problem. The behavior that fails to meet the expectation is never the problem; the unfulfilled expectation is always the problem. Behavior that does not meet the expectation is inappropriate relative to the expectation, but that is not the problem; the unfulfilled expectation is. If you are not meeting my expectations, your behavior is unacceptable because it is not meeting my expectations, but it is still my problem. Unfulfilled expectations are always the problem.

People who operate in adult mode own their expectations. When others fail to meet my expectations, that is a problem for me, not them. Their inappropriate behavior may be a good thing for them. For example, if someone is late for work, their lateness is a problem for me, who expected them to be at work on time. But for them, it is not a problem; they got to sleep in, have breakfast with the family and avoid rush-hour traffic.

People who accept ownership of their expectations and thereby ownership of the problem seldom, if ever, impose superimposed consequences. They know that inappropriate behavior has "natural consequences." (**Natural Consequences** – the outcomes, penalties, costs, and benefits derived from decisions and actions.)

Here are a few examples of Natural Consequences:

"If I don't get up in time, I will be late for school, get bad grades, repeat grades, etc."

"Eating sugar promotes cavities."

"Swearing out loud in church negatively impacts my reputation."

"If I lie frequently, people will stop believing me."

People who accept ownership of their unfulfilled expectations believe that the natural consequences for inappropriate behavior motivate people to alter behavior better than superimposed/forced consequences. As a result, they feel no need for superimposed punishments. However, they like to point out the natural benefits of meeting reasonable expectations. With this approach, people operate in adult mode.

You fit in the "unfulfilled expectation is the problem" category of problem ownership if you select:

Scenario 1 - Your daughter sleeps in, moves slow, and is constantly late for school.
The Parent – (if you think the parent has the unfulfilled expectation because they expect their daughter to be on time for school)

Scenario 2 - The parent takes back permission for their son to go to a concert that he has planned for, saved for, and purchased tickets for because the son broke curfew by two hours.
The Parent – (if you think the parent has the unfulfilled expectation because they expect their son to be home before curfew)
The Child – (if you think the child has the unfulfilled expectation because they were planning on going to the concert)

Scenario 3 - The parent uses intimidation and threats to get their son to do his chores.
The Child – (if you think the child has the unfulfilled expectation because they expect to be treated respectfully)

Scenario 4 - The parent has a drug issue that interferes with providing for his family.
The Child – (if you think the child has the unfulfilled expectation because they expect the parent to provide for the family)

Scenario 5 - The daughter is constantly on her phone and doesn't finish her homework.
The Parent – (if you think the parent has the unfulfilled expectation because they expect their daughter to be present and do her homework)

Scenario 6 - The dad makes inappropriate jokes at the dinner table.
The Child – (if you think the child has the unfulfilled expectation because they expect their dad to be an example of decorum)

Scenario 7 - The daughter doesn't feel that her parents appreciate the magnitude of her challenges.
The Child – (if you think the child has the unfulfilled expectation because she expect the parent to understand the overwhelming amount of pressure she feels)
The Parent – (if you think the parent has the unfulfilled expectation because they expect their child to be tougher and handle the stress that isn't as big as what they have to deal with)

Scenario 8 - The son has a body odor that is offensive to everyone around him.
The Parent – (if you think the parent has the unfulfilled expectation because they expect their son to wear deodorant and bathe regularly)

When we take ownership of our expectations (own the problem), we will be able to problem solve by discussing how the behavior is inappropriate relative to our expectations, how it negatively impacts our feelings, and results in natural consequences. It allows us to clarify our expectations and explain the benefits of meeting our expectations (without being preachy). It offers the person with inappropriate behavior a chance to understand how their behavior impacts others without being criticized. It also enables both parties to hear, understand, and validate one another's perspective in the problem-solving process.

Note: there is no power play involved here, merely adult to adult interaction.

When we accept ownership of our problem (unfulfilled expectations), we can give feedback from our adult mode and avoid hooking the child mode or the parent mode of the person we are providing feedback to.

With the "my unfulfilled expectation is my problem" approach, people problem solve in adult mode. People give feedback in adult mode.

With the "right-or-wrong" or "military" approaches, people solve problems in parent or child modes. They use force and criticism to change people to meet their expectations.

Remember! How we define problem ownership determines how we problem solve. Most people's problem-solving approaches are self-serving. Indeed, the right-or-wrong and the military approaches are self-serving. They both operate from the principle that the person with the power is in charge of the problem-solving process. And it is usually my way or else. "I determine the problem and the solution; your job is to comply." It happens with a command and control mentality. "If I can get my way, it validates my position, my power, and my omnipotence. It feels so good and reinforcing if I am controlling the solutions – at least it does to me." It doesn't feel great if you are being fixed or forced to change.

The natural response to force is counterforce or resistance, so you can imagine why these popular problem-solving approaches don't create lasting change or solutions. On the other hand, accepting unfulfilled expectations as our problem and others' behavior as inappropriate (because their behavior does not meet our expectations) allows discussing the situation logically and rationally without power moves and finding solutions that resolve the issue while enhancing the relationship. It is the only naturally win-win option available. But, of course, that assumes that quality relationships are an important consideration when choosing our problem-solving approach.

We will provide a template for giving feedback without criticism in the competency section. The feedback template embraces the "the unfulfilled expectation is the problem" approach and offers a rational, adult-to-adult way for problem-solving.

People who think others have "the problem" when their expectations are not met love "constructive criticism." In reality, there is no such thing as constructive criticism; it is just criticism. It is given in parent and child modes and is not constructive. The only one who feels good about constructive criticism is the person giving it. It transfers ownership of the unfulfilled expectation (my problem) to the one not meeting the expectation (inappropriate behavior relative to my expectation). People who use it convince themselves that the person who is not meeting their expectations has the problem. That is not reality, but they believe it is.

So, the solution, they believe, is to force people to change who are not meeting their expectations. They never consider the possibility that the person believed to have the problem doesn't think their behavior inappropriate. The chronically late person doesn't find it a problem; he gets to sleep longer, has breakfast with the family, and avoids traffic. If it were a problem for him, he wouldn't be late. If we think about it, the person using constructive criticism is actually in "victim mode" and uses their parent mode to force the other person to change to make them happy. It is a convoluted method, but it is very popular! It is power-based problem-solving; you can only do it if you have the power. If you are still not convinced, **try constructive criticism on your boss, and the truth will set you free.**

Transference of problem ownership happens all the time, all around us. For example, I remember a lady who worked at Amersham who had the worst body odor that you can imagine. It was so bad that it made people nauseous. No one wanted to work with her or be in her proximity. Everyone thought that she had a problem, but her, of course. She was oblivious about the issue (the olfactory nerves get used to smells constantly there), even when people gave her subtle hints like leaving deodorant, soap, or perfume on her desk. She just thought that she was popular and that her secret gift-giving friends liked her. People would draw straws to determine who would be the unlucky person to confront her. When someone did draw the short straw, they didn't approach her; they just dropped off another gift. It eventually ended up on my desk in the form of a signed petition with the stated objective of fixing her. She was such a sweet lady. I can imagine how she would have received devastatingly constructive criticism.

I asked her to meet with me for a picnic lunch outside, where we could meet alone, and the air could circulate freely. I shared with her my problem and explained how her body odor generated negative feelings with others and consequences for herself. Luckily, I didn't have to suggest what my expectations were. She was embarrassed, thanked me for the feedback, and asked if she could take the rest of the day off. Unsurprisingly, her inappropriate behavior relative to everyone's sensitive nose disappeared. She never exuded body odor again. Believe it or not, a few days later, a couple of people asked me if she had burned her clothes. I just shook my head in disbelief.

To clarify, she chose to change; she wasn't forced to. She looked at the natural consequences and they were unacceptable to her. If we used the "right and wrong" approach to problem solving, our conversation would have been very different and critical. Businesses do this all of the time with written warnings. Could you imagine how she would have felt to receive a written warning saying she needed to change her body odor? Synergistic relationships cannot exist with these types of problem solving approaches.

If we accept the premise that problems are unfulfilled expectations, it is logical that we should review the concept of expectations and how to manage them.

19

Expectations Management

So, let's quickly review some of the basics that we introduced in the Introduction to Expectations Management: People have two types of expectations in life: Positive expectations and negative expectations. Positive expectations are "good things" we expect to happen. Negative expectations are "bad things" we expect to happen. Expectations range from positive to negative. For example, let's pretend that you are a server at a restaurant, did a fantastic job, and are expecting a good tip. Expecting a good tip is an example of a positive expectation. Realize that the expectation will either be fulfilled (met) or unfulfilled (not met). We call these fulfilled or unfulfilled expectations. The meeting, or not meeting, of positive and negative expectations provides us a means of examining four types of situations:

1. Fulfilled positive expectations
2. Unfulfilled positive expectations
3. Fulfilled negative expectations
4. Unfulfilled negative expectations

Positive Expectations

	I	II	
Fulfilled	"Pleased" Feel Good/ Behave Positive	"Dissatisfied" Feel Bad Behave Negative	Unfulfilled
	III	IV	
	"Validated" Feel Vindicated/ Behave Judgmentally	"Mixed Feelings" Feel Doubtful/ Send mixed Messages	

Negative Expectations

1. Fulfilled Positive Expectations situations (Pleased Emotions and Behaviors)

It is fair to say that most situations begin with positive expectations. With fulfilled positive expectations, we feel great and behave great. Life is good. In that situation, everyone is a champion. Every supervisor is magnificent, every employee is top-notch, every parent is terrific, and every child is perfect. That would suggest that the secret to successful relationships is to surround ourselves with people who meet all of our expectations all the time! Ain't gonna happen.

Back to the server example, you feel great if you received a good tip! The tip matched the positive expectation. You are an excellent waitress, and the tipper is a great customer. The established relationship is such that you look forward to the subsequent encounter. In this situation, the positive expectation met validates the concept: **the degree to which positive expectations are met determines how life is rated on the "WONDERFUL!-to-the-TERRIBLE!" scale.** No one needs training or counseling to manage fulfilled positive expectations; there are no issues. But, having unfulfilled positive expectations is a cat of a different color!

2. Unfulfilled Positive Expectations situation (Dissatisfied Emotions and Behaviors)

As that server, now imagine that you received NO TIP. You had an unfulfilled positive expectation. Now, how do you feel? You feel cheated, right? How enthusiastically do you think you will serve those people the next time you see them?

If you saw the movie *Help*, you will undoubtedly remember how the maid got revenge for being accused and fired unjustly. She baked and delivered a beautiful chocolate "Poo Pie" to her tormentor. The point is that unfulfilled positive expectations generate negative feelings that become the basis for negative behaviors.

The level of emotion generated from an unfulfilled positive expectation depends on two factors: the importance of the expectation and how badly the behavior fell short of anticipated outcomes. For example, if you expected the whites and colored clothes to be washed separately, but they were washed together, you may feel annoyed. If you were a bride at the church with a thousand guests and the groom didn't show up, you would probably feel betrayed, crushed, violated, decimated, etc.

Revenge sells movies. Audiences love it when the good-guy victim gets the bad guys. There is a sense of justice and exhilaration in the film *Taken* when Bryan Mills kills the kidnappers and saves his daughter Kim. He justified his revenge because the bad guys violated his expectation that his daughter's virtue and well-being would be honored. I have to admit that I inwardly cheered his performance. Although, I don't believe he developed very healthy relationships with the bad guys, as manifested by the continuing series featuring ongoing battles.

Few people personify Bryan Mills' character, and yet, most people use unfulfilled expectations to justify their feelings and the associated behavior. Unfulfilled positive expectations spawn negative emotions and behaviors which negatively impact interpersonal connections and relationships.

My skin crawls when I see someone spank their child in anger and afterward tells the child, "Look what you made me do!" How about the good old saying, "You make me so mad!" Can you see how these behaviors and statements transfer problem-ownership to others and reject responsibility for the uncontrolled feelings and inappropriate behavior? While interviewing rapists and murders at Atascadero Prison in Atascadero, California, I witnessed such self-justification. I also see it with managers who justify their Stomper behavior toward less-than-perfect employees. I, unfortunately, see the consequences in too many of our homes, neighborhoods, cities, and with people in our country who use it to justify their decisions and actions.

Unfulfilled positive expectations are possibly the most common situation we encounter in life. Unfulfilled positive expectations happen all the time. Hence, we would think that learning to manage unfulfilled expectations would receive the attention and skill training it deserves. Sadly, that is not the case. Most approaches used to manage unfulfilled expectations are ineffective and unhealthy, primarily because people don't understand problem ownership. The **"you have the problem and you need to change"** system to manage unmet expectations passes from generation to generation. It is this approach that most strains and damages interpersonal connections and relationships. It is here we send irretrievable messages. It is here that "constructive criticism" rules. It is here that we problem-solve in Parent Mode and Child Mode. Here, child abusers and wife beaters transfer the responsibility for their actions to their victims. It is the source of innumerable behavioral addictions. It is the most used way to get unfulfilled needs met – unsuccessfully.

With repeated unfulfilled positive expectations, positive expectations change to negative expectations. We shift from a positive paradigm of expectations to a negative one. If our child is chronically late, we start expecting her to be late. If constant requests for a clean room are never delivered, we start expecting that it will always be messy. This "paradigm shift" signifies a permanent mental change of perspective and expectations. Once this happens, the world, relative to this person, will be viewed through a negative lens. Our negative lens will prejudice our interpretation of communications and taint our evaluation of their behaviors.

A volleyball coach at my sons' volleyball club had a stellar record of success and a reputation for excellence, built over a couple of decades of coaching. During the season, the expectations of the players on his team and their parents shifted from very high positive expectations to very high negative expectations. Once that shift occurred, his critics had negative expectations for everything he said and did. The girls "were never going to play for him again, and they would make sure that no one else did in the future." This sad situation jeopardized his current standing and future as a volleyball coach. Ironically, the problem needn't have happened. Feedback, discussion, and adult to adult problem-solving would have prevented the problem. The good news is that it was addressed, albeit late in the game, but there will always remain remnants of the paradigm shift.

The optimum opportunity to deal with positive unfulfilled expectations in healthy ways is to prevent the paradigm shift to negative expectations. Prevention is always better than operating from negative expectations where life, communication, and interpersonal connections become more complicated. It should be evident that negative expectations are hard things to manage. We want to avoid getting into situations where we have negative expectations. **The way to keep positive expectations from going negative is to deal with unfulfilled positive expectations healthily and quickly!**

Fundamental Attribution Errors Revisited

We are going to revisit Fundamental Attribution Errors from the lens of an unfulfilled positive expectation. As a reminder, a fundamental attribution error is a common phenomenon that occurs when a person is anticipating a positive response from someone and instead gets no response or a minimal one. They take the response personally (are offended) and assume negative intent in the person's response, or lack of it.

For example (using the same example in an earlier chapter), Anne sees her supervisor approaching her with his head down just before reaching her; she cheerily says, "Good morning, Sam!" But he doesn't acknowledge her and continues past unchanged in gait or appearance. She immediately assumes that he doesn't like her and purposely snubs her; her paradigm shifts from a positive to a negative. She now sees her boss's behavior as an indication that he doesn't like her and is a jerk. Once that paradigm shift happens, it affects her in three ways: her thinking, her actions, and the future outcome of their relationship.

Her assumption shifts her **thinking** from a positive to a negative paradigm. She now sees their relationship through that negative lens. She becomes self-centered. "Why doesn't my boss like me?" She needs to validate that new view, so she starts seeing everything he says or does as evidence of his dislike of her. In her mind, he becomes the problem. "Sam is such an inconsiderate jerk!"

Her **actions** align with her need to validate her thinking. She defends her perception of Sam as a jerk. She justifies her judgments with evidence that she interprets from his actions. No matter what he does is further evidence because she is looking for evidence to prove her perspective. Once she has justified her view, she feels OK in attacking him, blaming him, and having contests with him. She can justify moralizing about Sam because she believes that she is on the side of righteous indignation.

The **outcome** of her beliefs becomes a predictable self-fulfilling prophecy: He ends up disliking her very much. Her negative thinking and actions produce a reality aligned with her negative perspective.

The tragedy of this phenomenon is that it is an outcome based on a fantasy. It didn't have to happen. It shouldn't have happened. If Anne had known that when Sam didn't greet her in the hallway, it wasn't because he was trying to snub her; it was because he was thinking about other things, and so, he didn't even notice her. Before her negative actions toward him, he liked her.

Suppose she had taken the time and marshaled the courage to do something about it. In that case, she could have met her boss a short time later, when he wasn't so preoccupied and simply asked him something like: "Sam, yesterday we were passing by one another, and I said good morning to you, and you didn't even acknowledge me. Are you OK? Have I offended you in some way?" Sam would have probably have responded with something like, "Oh, I'm sorry, I don't recall seeing you yesterday. My mind was on other things. Sorry to have given you that impression. I feel like I'm in a fog most of the time. No, you haven't ever offended me. I appreciate all the support you have given me."

The antidote for avoiding fundamental attribution errors lies in three things:

One: Stay in adult mode, be objective, open-minded, and receptive to a reasonable explanation for unexpected behavior. Ask yourself: "Why would a rational, intelligent, caring, and committed supervisor treat me badly or not acknowledge me when I say good morning?"

Two: Check it out in adult mode: "I felt bad when you didn't respond to my greeting yesterday. I hope you are OK." Then listen, hear, understand, and validate his explanation.

Three: Focus on the unusual behavior, not the person.

Unfortunately, I have been a witness of far too many relationships bruised, damaged, or destroyed by fundamental attribution errors.

A friend of mine in high school had a crush on a beautiful but shy girl, a year younger than he, who attended a different high school. They didn't live too far from one another. He frequently talked about how much he wanted to take her on a date or a school dance. He always talked about it, but never did anything to try and secure a date. Finally, a couple of weeks before our junior prom, he buoyed his courage and decided to ask her to the dance. He saw her with a group of her friends on the lawn outside her school. He told me: "Now or never." Then he walked toward her with the full intent of asking her to go with him to the dance. As he approached the group, one of them looked up in his direction and then turned her attention back to her friends, and they started laughing. My friend froze in his tracks; he was immediately embarrassed and assumed that the group laughed at him. I witnessed what had happened and his reaction to it. As he walked away from the girls and past me, he said: "Come on, let's go!" As we walked back to our car, he told me that she (the girl he hoped would go to the prom with him) was such a "stuck-up" and that he didn't want to go to the dance with her anyway.

He saw her as a person who thought she was too good to go with him from that moment on. He didn't even have anything good to say about her or her friends. Everything they did or said proved in his mind that he was right. At first, he ignored her, but he started saying mean things about her to other kids later on. Those who knew her objected to his comments, but that didn't matter; to him, she was "Sheep's Ass" (that was a variation of her last name, Ramsbottom). Over time, they came to loathe one another. A year or so later, I attended a class with one of her friends at college, we somehow got on the subject of her friend and my friend. At one point, she said something along the lines of: "I don't know what happened between those two to make them dislike each other so much; when Janet and I were juniors, she was hoping that he would ask her out." This experience was a classical fundamental attribution error. (This time, I knew the source of it.)

I know a guy who didn't get personally invited to go on a rafting trip after a well-known whitewater rafter made a group invitation for everyone to go with him. Many people had gone on tremendously fun, whitewater rafting trips with him. All we have to do to make it happen is call him and set a date. The hopeful invitee never called the inviter but rather hoped he would call and personally invite him. He waited and stewed. I'm confident that the inviter would have been glad for him to join a group if he had called. Time passed without a phone call, and the disappointed wanna-be-rafter assumed that the whitewater guy didn't like him – he took it personally and believed that there was hostile intent. I noticed that at infrequent get-togethers, which seemed to include everyone, there was a frostiness from the offended non-invitee toward the neglectful inviter.

Being curious and not particularly reserved when seeing relationship issues, I cornered him and shared my observation regarding him and my whitewater friend. He said that he didn't care too much for him. He felt that our "friend" had pigeon-holed him into a lower, unacceptable class within the social group. I ask him why he would believe something so crazy. He gave me a few examples to prove his point (including not being invited on the whitewater trip). His negative interpretations validated his negative perspective. I asked if he would mind if I broached the issue with our friend, and he told me: "Stay out of my damn business!" Wish granted. I'm sure my generous whitewater rafting friend would feel horrible if he knew of our other friend's feelings toward him and that he would go to extreme ends to change the perception. But perhaps he doesn't approach him because he doesn't expect a warm reception. (It's tough to pet a porcupine.)

When I meet with people who have a negative paradigm, they can give me limitless evidence of why their perception is reality. I can rarely get to the source of what started it all. Interestingly, when I meet with the enemy, they seldom even resemble the picture the other side paints them to be.

I believe that people most vulnerable to fundamental attribution errors are insecure people. They are far more likely to embrace a negative interpretation of behavior, take it as a slight, and quickly have their child mode or parent mode hooked. They are less likely to check it out. Once the negative perception starts rolling, it doesn't stop until the self-fulfilling prophecy becomes a reality. My disappointed friend is a good example.

Let's summarize critical precepts about fulfilled and unfulfilled positive expectations. When we feel good, we behave well, and have excellent interpersonal connections with fulfilled positive expectations. If we have unfulfilled positive expectations, we feel negative emotions of a limitless variety. Our feelings become the road map of our behavior and the determining factor of our interpersonal connections. Since we cannot expect to have our positive expectations met all of the time, we must learn how to manage our emotional state when dealing with unfulfilled expectations. **How we deal with unfulfilled expectations determines the nature of relationships**.

We can deal with unfulfilled positive expectations in healthy ways or unhealthy ways. Don't worry; we will teach you how to do that in the competency section. Every touchpoint involves dealing with unfulfilled expectations, so we should become champs at this.

3. Fulfilled Negative Expectations Situations (Validated Conclusions)

Once our paradigm shifts from positive to negative expectations about someone's behavior, that becomes the lens through which we see and interpret their actions and intent. It becomes the way we perceive them, what we expect of them, and who we believe them to be. When the employee lies, as we expected him to, he is a liar. In our mind, he is a liar (or an unreliable person, a deceiving person, etc., whatever label we associate with lying). A shift from positive expectations of someone to negative expectations shifts not only our perception of his behavior it also shifts our view of his identity from a positive person to a negative one. How should a lying (behavior) deceiver (identity) be treated? Our behavior and feelings toward this person align with the negative label we pin on our negative expectations.

I once counseled a middle-aged couple who had been married for over thirty years. The wife said their marriage had an underlying tension for at least twenty years. She didn't understand the basis for the underlying tension, but she knew that her husband didn't trust her and was always critical. She had tried to be kind and respectful to him for their entire marriage. She said she had given up trying to resolve their issue by talking. In short, she felt like she was the accused in some crime but didn't know what the crime was. At this point, she felt that the marriage wasn't worth the price she was paying. She was emotionally spent and exhausted. The future seemed bleak.

When I met with the husband, he denied their marriage had big problems. He felt that he was a generous man who had been faithful to his marriage vows for the entire marriage. His emphasis on "his marriage vows" stirred me to explore that topic more thoroughly. Eventually, he shared with me that 20 years before, his wife had been unfaithful to him. Knowing his wife, I couldn't possibly imagine her doing so. I asked him to explain what had happened. He said he came home from work and found his wife and a furnace repairman leaving their bedroom together. He asked them, "What's going on?" His wife introduced the repairman and explained that he had checked the furnace and vents. I asked the husband where and when the unfaithfulness occurred.

He responded, "Isn't it obvious?" I said, "Not to me? Why would you assume that your wife had been unfaithful because a furnace repairman who was in your house to check your furnace and vents had exited the bedroom at the moment you came home?"

"Because they were coming from the bedroom!" he stated accusingly.

"Do you have a vent in your bedroom?" I queried.

"Well, yes," he responded.

"So did they exit fully dressed?"

"Yes."

"Did they seem embarrassed or flustered?"

"No."

"How did you conclude that they had messed around?"

"I don't know."

I asked, "What did she say when you discussed the situation?"

"We have never discussed it."

He sat there for a while, and then his whole demeanor changed; he looked like he had encountered a ghost.

He then asked hypothetically, "What if she didn't?"

"Didn't what?" I asked.

"What if she was never unfaithful to me?"

I said, "I guarantee that she wasn't."

His head dropped, his chin was in his chest, and he said, "I treated her like crap for 20 years for something she didn't do!"

It is sad to see the impact of 20-plus years of a negative paradigm, particularly an unjust one. Once the husband's image of his loving, faithful wife changed to a sinning cheat, it changed how he saw her and behaved toward her and not for the better.

He told me that we needed to meet with her and explain. I told him that his wife would never understand how he could believe such a thing of her. She wouldn't be able to rationalize, justify, or accept his explanation. I pointed out that his wife had borne the poison of his unverified belief and punitive actions for 20 years. For the rest of his life, it was his duty to make up for his secret obsession and negative perception by treating her as the beautiful and faithful wife that she was and always has been. His sense of guilt was overwhelming, and he desired a get-out-of-jail-free card.

Over the next couple of weeks, the wife reported that she didn't know what happened but that her husband seemed to be a changed man; he treated her like a queen. A few days later, she called me and asked if I could recommend a good divorce lawyer. She exclaimed, "Do you know what he accused me of?"

Their experience is a relatively extreme example of the dynamics and consequences of negative paradigms. It is better to prevent the paradigm shift from positive to negative than to operate from a negative paradigm. Can we fathom how different their life and relationship would have been had he simply had an open conversation with her about the furnace repairman on the day that he misinterpreted the events of that day 20 years before? He could have prevented all that misery and suffering.

We can be even more preventive by being clear about our expectations and enabling those who fulfill our expectations to participate in establishing them. If we agree on our expectations upfront and how to meet them, it will minimize the likelihood of positive expectations becoming negative ones. Open-minded dialogue is a good thing! In fact, dealing with unfulfilled needs in healthy ways actually strengthen and create long-lasting, strong relationships.

4. Unfulfilled Negative Expectations Situations (Mixed Feelings and Behaviors)

Unfulfilled negative expectations set up a crazy paradigm. When we are expecting negative things and positive things happen, it creates mixed feelings. For example, when people expect people to be late but arrive on time, they generate a genuinely mixed bag of feelings and responses. Some respond skeptically ("I don't believe this will last."). Some are pleased ("What a great surprise!"). Others may react with confusion ("What do you mean they are on time? They are never on time."). Some are pessimistic ("That is not who they really are. It won't last."). By the way, negative labels for behavior and identity mirror one another. They project a similar message if we say he is late or call him undependable.

In short, people receive mixed messages when they behave unexpectedly, especially if doing a good thing when others expect a bad thing. If we arrive on time when people assume we will be late, it creates a mixed bag of feelings for different people. People have different feelings and responses to our behavior because they develop stereotyped perceptions based on prior behavior. When someone has been stereotyped with a negative label, people expect behavior consistent with the label.

Unfulfilled negative expectations generate cognitive dissonance in people's minds; what they see is not what they expect to see. Bam! Instant internal disharmony.

If you are the one receiving the mixed messages, it isn't easy to know how to respond going forward. "How should I react if I'm on time and one person responds to my timeliness with skepticism, another with confusion, someone else with happiness, and still another with doubt?" Knowing how to respond appropriately in a world of mixed messages is difficult. Few people placed on performance probation successfully get off it because no matter how they perform, people still operate from the perception that they are a "sub-performer." They get confused because of the mixed messages. Once a person is labeled an "unacceptable performer," the paradigms of the decision-makers become negative. They expect negative results and character; that is what they look for, which is what they see; it validates their opinion. The negative label becomes their belief (validated feelings), and once that happens, reality aligns with their beliefs, which align with their negative emotions. All previous experiences of fulfilled negative expectations have validated their perspectives.

When we see the opposite of what we were expecting, cognitive dissonance happens within us. Our expectation governor becomes out of balance. Since everyone needs to reestablish balance when confronted with imbalance, we restore our balance by interpreting reality to align with our beliefs. If we believe a person on performance probation is a sub-performer, we will construe everything he does, good or bad, to align with our stereotyped label of him. Everyone has a method for resolving cognitive dissonance. It just happens that when we have labeled someone negatively, we fix our dissonance by pouring them into the mold that we have formed for them. It is tough to change people's minds once they have labeled us negatively and believe it.

In the case of experiencing behavior that fulfills positive expectations, there is no dissonance to resolve. But, when we have negative expectations that didn't happen, it screws up our validation of what we believed would happen. When that occurs, it initiates responses that can perplex the person doing the opposite of what the people with negative expectations anticipated.

I have witnessed the clashing perceptions between people placed on performance probation and their supervisor. I have seen the predictable dilemma that occurs in this situation. Here is how each participant views the situation. People placed on performance probation see performance correction in incremental improvement. In contrast, the supervisor considers performance as an absolute outcome.

Let's say that the manager establishes the acceptable performance at eight on a scale of ten. At the interim performance review, the performance has improved from two to six. The manager sees the performance as a failure and still sees it as unacceptable. In contrast, the person on probation sees a 300% improvement in his performance and expects recognition for dramatic improvement. Both feel justified in their perspective. The decision maker's perspective wins the day, and the fired employee feels unfairly treated. Perhaps this dilemma is the basis for many of the unfair-termination lawsuits.

We had a teenager in our house who lied a lot. Everyone assumed that she was lying, even when there was no apparent reason for lying. When she told the truth, she got all kinds of responses: doubt, skepticism, relief, challenge, etc. She once told us, "Why tell the truth? You don't believe me when I do tell the truth!" She became a reliable truth-teller somewhere along the line, but it was a heck of a journey for her and the family before family members trusted what she was saying.

Being negatively stereotyped is a pickle of a situation for both those being stereotyped and those doing the stereotyping. I know of only one way to work through the morass of unfulfilled negative expectations: everyone involved needs to operate in adult mode; only reason can establish logical perspectives and outcomes. And, only logic can reconcile cognitive dissonance and the imbalance it creates. Adult mode problem solving is vital to produce win-win solutions.

And, for sure, the least effective approach is avoidance. Unfortunately, when we don't deal with unfulfilled expectations, the people on the other end of the expectations see our avoidance as an approbation of our current beliefs. To deal with unfulfilled expectations, we need to do so in adult mode, and we need to have the skills to do so correctly.

We have looked at problem ownership and expectations management. So, one might expect that we would jump right into problem-solving. We will not do that now because the subject requires understanding other problem-solving skill sets. Problem-solving is all about healthily dealing with unfulfilled expectations. It is a core life skill. And yet, almost everyone is addicted to problem-solving without having the foundational concepts to be good at it. Too many try to problem solve before finding the core issues or before the person being helped is ready for it. Of course, it is nearly impossible to problem solve if we don't know who has the problem – our own or others. To learn how to problem solve correctly, we will get into the concepts and skills of problem-solving in the competency section.

Nevertheless, we won't leave you completely dangling until you get to the competency section. We have explored several things that can apply in managing expectations and solving problems before we get to the competency section. Some of the concepts listed below don't need to be justified because they are apparent.

- Reinforce fulfilled positive expectations. People repeat what is positively recognized.
- Address unfulfilled positive expectations before they shift to negative expectations. Don't allow yourself to slide into a fundamental attribution error.
- Own your expectations. If you have an unfulfilled expectation, it is your problem.
- Deal with unfulfilled expectations in the adult mode – only in the adult mode. Don't yell at the store clerk.
- If you are trying to problem-solve with someone stuck in parent mode or child mode and can't hook their adult, drop back, punt, and try again later when you believe you can hook their adult mode. To do otherwise only reinforces their parent mode or child mode position.
- Make your expectations clear upfront; people don't read minds.
- Get consensus of your expectations with others; people support what they help create.
- Be generous and open-minded with people who surprise you with positive behavior and outcomes when you have negative expectations. Maybe they have turned a leaf. Don't send mixed messages.
- Expect to have unfulfilled expectations with those close to you; the more important the relationship, the greater the expectations. Hence, the greater the probability of unfulfilled expectations. Their importance provides more reason to stay in adult mode and not give up. If the relationship is important, don't compete.
- Forgive those who don't meet your positive expectations. Forgiveness is not easy, but it frees you from the heavy burdens accompanying offenses. Forgive yourself; you are not perfect, but you are OK.

- Honor the agency of others to choose different paths than you have selected. That helps you to move beyond your differences and still accept one another. It adds diversity to our lives and depth to our perspectives.
- Be loving and accepting of others. They will know if they are special to you. Unconditional love is the most powerful force in life; it succeeds when everything else fails.

20

Socially Significant Events

Some events in our lives define us and change us the moment they happen; we are never the same after the event as we were before it. I learned about this concept in 1969 when I was in college. Somehow, I discovered a popular professor named Morris Massey. He had a fun lecture called: "What you are is what you were when."[30] He was entertaining and thought-provoking. The drift of this particular message was that each generation grows up with shared beliefs, social perspectives, and behavioral standards. For example, he said that people of the World War I generation were all very patriotic, loved the same music, and held similar political views for their whole lives. The World War II generation loved big bands and dancing the jitterbug. The young men of the WWII generation, en masse, volunteered to serve in the military and did so with great enthusiasm. After the war ended, they just wanted to come home, get married, get an education, have a family, and live a peaceful, successful life. They did and, in doing so, created the most outstanding public education system and economy the world has ever known. He taught that the "socially significant events" of their times define all generations.

The Great Depression, the bombing at Pearl Harbor, and World War II defined my parent's generation. Future socially significant events will define future generations. He predicted that my age group will still be "jiving" to the Beatles and loving rock-and-roll when we are seventy years old.

---

30 Morris Massey, "What You Are Is Where You Were When", value analysis theory video, (Enterprise Media, original 1976).

He explained that generational societies are defined and changed by socially significant events and individuals. Significant events imprinted into us are never forgotten. Whole generations of people can remember where they were when a socially significant event happened. For example, everyone near my age can tell you exactly where they were and what they were doing when they heard of President John F. Kennedy's assassination. My kids, and everyone older than they, can recall explicitly the moment they saw the space shuttle Challenger explode and what they were doing. Time freezes in the memory of those who witnessed the planes fly into the Twin Towers and who watched them burn and collapse. The world changed on that date, permanently. The Covid 19 pandemic has changed and has defined this generation.

Socially significant events don't need to be society-wide events. They can occur in small groups or even with one individual. The death of a loved one can be a socially significant event. Divorce can change us, never to be the same again. The birth of a child transforms us. Some of these events change us for the better, others for the worse. But they change us permanently. I guess they could also be called "Emotionally Significant Events" based on their impact on us emotionally and socially. I remember well two such events in my life that changed me.

The first was when I was eight years old. My mother had taken my older brother and me shopping for school clothes. When it came to buying jeans, I insisted that she buy me Wrangler Jeans. She insisted that I settle for another brand with built-in knee reinforcement because they would last longer and were a third of the price of the Wrangler Jeans. I didn't budge, so I went home with no jeans. That evening, while lying in my bed, I overheard a conversation between my mother and dad about the shopping experience. My mother told my dad that she was so angry with me that she could spit. She said that I was just a spoiled little shit who had to have those dang Wrangler Jeans or nothing. Then she started to cry. She told my dad that she was trying to save enough money to buy him a new pair of coveralls. She lamented that his coveralls had patches on patches and that he needed a new pair far more than I needed Wrangler Jeans. Having been raised poor during the Great Depression, my dad comforted her and told her to buy me the Wrangler Jeans. He said he knew what it was like not to have the popular jeans when everyone else had them. He told her that he didn't need new coveralls. Mother just sobbed and sobbed.

Their conversation was a socially significant event for me. Right then, I decided I would never cause my dad to have to wear coveralls with patches on patches ever again because of me. My mother tried to buy me some Wrangler Jeans, but I wouldn't accept them. I shoveled snow, picked chokecherries, or did anything that would provide me with funds so my parents wouldn't have to deprive themselves. I became quite the young entrepreneur; I acquired a paper route, mowed 15 lawns per week for people in town (primarily old widows that my mom committed me to), and spent any remaining free time working for farmers. They would pay me 50 cents an hour to drive their trucks to haul hay or sit on a tractor harrowing the fields in endless rotations. I learned to drive when I was eight.

The second emotionally significant event occurred when I was 19 years old. In 1967 I was a missionary in Southern Brazil assigned to Santa Maria. I had a horrible attitude. I didn't like Brazil, Brazilians, or anything related to the mission. I was negatively comparing everything about my life in Brazil to America. I had a mission companion named Reed Taylor; we were both raised in the same valley in Utah. He had lost his dad to cancer when he was 14. His mother was a nurse who worked for our family physician, but I had never met him before Santa Maria. I can only imagine how tired he grew of my complaining. One day, during study time, he asked me: "Can I tell you a story?" I agreed to listen. It went something like this:

Once upon a time, there lived an old blind man who had a special gift; he could speak the language of all animals. Because of his gift, he moved to the forest to be near his animal friends and enjoy their company. He lived there for many years and grew very old. He knew that he wouldn't live very much longer, but he needed to know what the world was like beyond his little space in the forest. He asked two of his special friends, the dove and the crow, to meet with him because he had a special request for them to do something for him that he could not do for himself. He told them that he had an overwhelming curiosity to know what the world was like; he wanted them to use their unique gift of flight to tour the world, explore its wonders, and then return and share everything with him had that they would see and experience. They agreed. Off they flew to the cheering of the other animals.

Months passed, but then, one day, he heard his friend, the crow, noisily pecking (crow kissing) everything in the chalet. He was delighted and overjoyed to greet his little boisterous and confident friend and a little surprised as well because he hadn't expected to see him so soon. He placed a plate of the crow's favorite food on the table and requested that he share his vast world tour experiences.

The crow explained that he took off heading east and flew to the east edge of the United States, where he rested before flying over the endless ocean in front of him.

The old man asked: "How did you make it across 3,000 miles of ocean?"

The crow said: "That may be easy for people to do in a plane or a ship, but you should try it by wing-power. I got so tired that I almost gave up and quit. Fortunately, below me, I saw the carcass of a dead whale floating on the surface, so I landed there for a bit of rest. I was hungry, and I thought, well, Eskimos eat whales, so I took a bite. It was sickening! Can you believe that anyone would eat a nasty whale? Not me, never again! Well, anyway, after that, I flew the rest of the way to Europe.

The old man asked excitedly: "Where did you enter Europe? What was it like?"

The crow responded: "I landed in the Netherlands, but it was flat, rainy, and boring; you wouldn't like it."

"Tell me about all the other places you visited!" pleaded the old man.

"Well," said the crow, "I went across Germany and over the Swiss Alps."

"What were they like?" asked the old man.

"They were high and cold. I nearly froze my beak off," said the crow.

"Where else did you go, and what else did you experience?" asked the old man.

The crow stated knowingly, "Oh, I went to the Middle East, which is, by the way, the most enormous sandpile you have ever seen. I didn't like it because everyone wore dresses, drove around in Cadillacs that churned up massive clouds of dust, and I couldn't understand a word they were speaking. Really disgusting! Then I went to Asia; you wouldn't believe what they eat. Everyone was running this way and that way; I couldn't get out of there fast enough. I came back by way of Russia, then to Alaska, and then through Canada. It was so good to hear people speaking English again. Did you know that Canada requires everything written in English and French? That is so dumb!

I came back into the states somewhere in the Midwest. The size of the grain fields would blow your mind. I thought, maybe I'll drop down and have a little grain snack. When I almost got to the ground, a guy jumped up with a shotgun and wham! I lost a tail feather. Not much else to tell; I made it back here, and I never want to go anywhere again."

The old man was grateful that his bold little friend had made it back in one piece. But he thought: "If the trip was so horrible for my tough little crow, what must it be like for my gentle and sensitive friend the dove?"

Weeks passed, and the old man despaired more about his lost dove with each passing week. After a time, he came to accept the probability that his gentle friend had perished in a cold, brutal, and cruel world, alone and away from those who loved him.

Then one sunny spring morning, he was lying in bed listening to his friends going about their activities and feeling the warmth of the sun on his legs when he heard gentle singing. It was his friend the dove! It excited him so that he jumped out of bed and scraped his shin on the bed frame. While jumping in pain and rejoicing simultaneously, he rushed to the window sill, where his little friend was singing.

The dove said: "Oh, I'm sorry, did my singing wake you? It is such a beautiful day that I just had to sing."

The old man said: "I can't believe that you are here and that you survived the ordeal I so stupidly sent you to do!"

The dove questionably asked: "What ordeal are you talking about?"

"The horrible world journeys!" cried the old man.

The dove said: "It wasn't horrible, it was beautiful. I have experienced many things and have seen millions of sights that filled me with wonder. If I were able to let you experience or see any one of them, it would enrich your life as it has done mine beyond measure."

He then shared his sights and experiences one by one. He told of his challenge flying across the great Atlantic Ocean and how in a moment of tired desperation, he looked at the waves below and realized that that is where his journey would likely end. Then, almost as an act of prayer, he looked up and saw far above him, giant birds gliding across the ocean, riding the trade winds. He garnered all of his remaining strength, climbed to where they were, and sailed to Europe, riding the trade winds with albatrosses. He entered Europe near Amsterdam, where fields of different colored poppies looked like patchwork quilts. He flew over the unbelievably beautiful Alps with majestic gray cliffs and snowcapped peaks, backed by the bluest of blue skies, accented by puffy white clouds. He went to the Middle East and Asia, where he observed people of all shapes, colors, and languages, and he realized that everyone was the same; everyone wanted what was best for them and their loved ones. They all laughed, cried, and made their way through life in a similar fashion. He, too, returned by way of Russia and Alaska, then entered the states in the Midwest. He observed wheat fields so large that the grain appeared as waves in the ocean when the wind *blew. Just before he finally returned to his beloved mountain home, he stopped in a Denver Park where an older woman with a young girl fed him tasty bits of bread.*

He told the old man: "I'm glad to be back with you and among my friends, but I do wish I could have taken you with me; you would have loved every second of it!"

Reed Taylor then gently asked me: "Do you get the point?" I got it; boy, did I get it! Not only did I realize that I was the crow in the story, I realized that I had chosen to see ugly rather than beauty. Choosing to see the world through a positive or a negative lens is a life choice available to all. The dove and the crow story was a significant emotional event for me; it changed my life.

After the story, I tried to see the world positively. I learned to love Brazil and the Brazilians. I no longer saw the Brazilian culture as inferior because it was not like the USA's culture, but I discovered its uniqueness and the charm of an emotional and ambitious people who lived life passionately. Reed was not only my mission companion; he became a dear, dear friend. He changed my experience in Brazil and my life.

Socially significant events will create a fundamental change in who we are. When they occur, we have an instantaneous paradigm shift. We see the world differently; our perception changes, so we change. And because we change, our relationships change.

A summary of a few concepts taught in the Operating Mode Touchpoints section

- Dr. Eric Berne Introduced us to "Transactional Analysis," which is a simple way to understand the interactions between people.
- He explained the different modes we operate from in our transactions: parent, adult, and child modes.
- We learned four parent modes: The critical parent mode, the controlling parent mode, the overindulgent parent mode, and the nurturing parent mode.

0 0 0 0 0 0 0 0 0 0 0 0 00 00 0 00 00 00 0 00 0 0 0 00 0 00000000000000000000000000000000000000000000000000000000000000000000000000000000000000000000000000000000000000000000000000000000000000000000000000000000000000

- We learned that the parent mode environment in which we were raised becomes the model for our parent mode when we become adults.
- We also learned that the parent mode of our parents has a determining influence on the kind of child modes engendered.
  - Critical parent modes produce insecure underachiever or overachiever child modes.
  - Controlling parent modes produce compliant and adaptive or rebellious child modes.
  - Overindulgent parent modes create self-centered, dependent, or entitled child modes.
  - And nurturing parent modes produce "free children" that are secure, confident, and able to explore the world and find where they fit child modes.
- Our child mode formed when we were infants, too young to have a way to describe our feelings, so our "adult child mode" is a recording of the emotions we felt during an experience when it was first recorded in our subconscious mind.
- Our adult mode is the logical and rational member of our operating modes. It is our "change agent" capable of reviewing our parent mode and child mode recordings and accepting them, replacing them, and managing them. Our adult mode allows us to grow, change, and develop. It frees us from being enslaved by old recordings, past events, and traumas. It allows us to choose our path and our future.
- Our operating modes when communicating with others determine whether we have parallel and complementary communications or cross transactions and non-complementary communications.
- Our operating modes largely determine our approach to problem-solving.
- There are three ways define problem ownership: "right or wrong" approach, the "military" approach, or the "my unfulfilled expectation is my problem" approach. Only the "my unfulfilled expectation is my problem approach" supports Synergistic relationships.

- Life is all about managing expectations. There are generally two types of expectations: positive and negative. Each one can either be fulfilled or unfulfilled. How we deal with unfulfilled expectations determines the kind of relationships we develop. Avoid having negative expectations by dealing with unfulfilled positive expectations before they become negative.
- Operating modes determine how we manage our expectations. Parent, child, and adult mode problem-solving are different and produce significantly different outcomes.
- Significant social or emotional events are life-changing events that impact our operating modes and set the stage for how we live after the event.

Operating modes is a relationship touchpoint connected to every other relationship touchpoint. Operating modes work in conjunction with all touchpoints to form relationships.

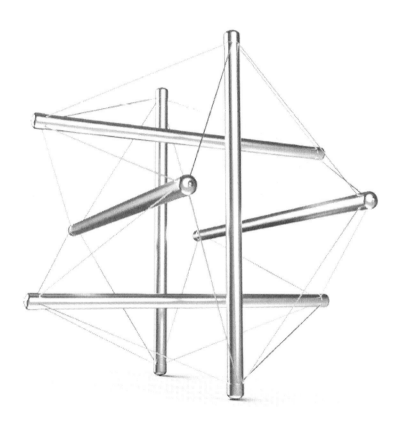

21

INTRODUCTION TO PERSONAL BOUNDARIES

After Sharon Smith was promoted, Leticia Lombardi became my administrative assistant at Janssen Pharmaceutica. She decided on a course of action with her family that vividly illustrates the personal boundaries concept.

Leticia was married to Vince Lombardi, a member of the Teamsters Union in New Jersey, not the Green Bay NFL football coach. She was the mother of four, three teenagers and one pre-teen. She was from the Bronx borough of New York City, and she just dripped with "Bronx-iness," including its accent, its in-your-face charms, and its manners of expression (I loved to hear her talk about anything). She was a "super-mom" who did everything and was expected to do everything for her family. She worked 40+ hours a week at Janssen and at home, cooked, cleaned, paid bills, helped with homework, and even kept the yard. She was overburdened and underappreciated; she felt used and abused. She talked about her issues regularly with her family and received verbal commitments for change, but nothing changed.

Consequently, she decided not to take it anymore. She completely separated herself from her family by moving into the guest bedroom and focused solely on herself. When she moved into the guest room, she did virtually nothing for her family. Her strike went on for five weeks, but her family was in chaos within hours. Everyone was dependent on her to do everything for them; no one in her family knew how to do anything previously done by Leticia.

Her self-removal generated all kinds of emotional responses: anger, resentment, accusations, finger-pointing at one another, and guilt trips, mainly aimed at her. Occasionally, she would receive a soft knock on her door (she just ignored the loud, angry knocks), and she would open it to find a sobbing child who would make emotional pleas and supplications. She told us (our HR department tuned in every day to get the latest update on this real-life soap-opera drama) that she would just gently place her child's head between her hands, kiss her on the forehead, tell her that she loved her, lead her to the door, close it, and ignore further attempts to get to her. The family battles raged and increased; necessary activities were not being accomplished. Not only was there no food in the house, no one paid the bills or washed the clothes. And kids didn't get to scheduled activities.

The situation reached panic proportions, with loud, angry arguments focused on roles, responsibilities, and accountabilities. Deciding who was responsible for what was not easy; before Letitia locked herself in the guest room, she was responsible for everything. Finally, the family, on their own, without Letitia's help, started to figure out how to get the necessary things accomplished. By the end of the five weeks, she could see that her family was functioning well, except for an occasional hissy-fit. With a sense of relief, she, at last, had a functioning family team where each family member contributed to the whole family's well-being.

Because of the positively changed environment, she decided to rejoin the family for a seven-day trial run to see if the changes, painfully made while she was isolated, would last once she returned. With glee and a little trepidation, the family opened their arms to receive the long-lost mom. As you probably anticipated, as soon as she returned, everyone, except her, decided to return to the good old days where mom did everything. Her intended seven-day trial lasted less than two. Almost immediately, the family expected her to be Supermom again. She quickly determined that the family was returning to the environment from which she had escaped. She returned to seclusion for another two weeks with the proviso that she would come back only if her family members would continue to do what they had been doing to be self-sufficient while she was incognito.

She explained that if the only way her family could function well as a team was if she was isolated from them; she would help them stay self-sufficient by returning permanently to the guest room. This time they knew that she was serious and would return to the guest room if they faltered in being a fully-functional family team. As it turned out, they changed, she changed, and their family's world seemed universally fair with a proper appreciation for favors rendered.

So, what happened in the context of personal boundaries? Simply put, they established appropriate personal boundaries. In other words, personal boundaries were established, protected, and respected. Leticia's experience is almost a perfect introduction to the discussion of boundaries. It illustrates how she felt her personal boundaries were disrespected and violated by the people she most loved. It demonstrates the challenge to her sense of identity and how she took active steps to clarify who she was and how she expected to be treated by her family.

So, what are boundaries? What do they have to do with relationships? Most people think of boundaries as their comfort zones, personal space, or cultural space. Well, they are, but they are much more than that. In many ways, they define our self-identity. Our self-identity is the foundation from which we express ourselves. We can't emote out from ourselves things we don't have. Dr. Melody Beattie, a widely read psychologist, uses the term "boundaries" to discuss healthy self-respect and how boundaries reflect, consciously, or sub-consciously, how a person believes they "deserve" to be treated and how they should treat others.[31] She says that the boundaries emerge from deep decisions about our belief in what we deserve and don't deserve. From her standpoint, it is essential to believe that what we want, need, like, and dislike is significant and worthy of respect. In this sense, boundaries are an integral part and a vital aspect of our self-image and self-identity.

For example, if a teenage girl sees herself as an ugly duckling, she will project that image to others. If she expects others to bully her, she will be bullied. And, when she is picked on, it reinforces the negative notion she has of herself. She will hate the bullying, but somewhere inside herself, she justifies it because she understands that bullying is what

---

31 Melody Beattie, *Codependent No More* (Hazelden Publishing, 1986).

happens to ugly ducklings. Her self-image is broadcast beyond herself and becomes a beacon for people who have an antenna for vulnerable people. When pounced on, it further reinforces her negative self-concept and fosters self-doubt, insecurity, and anxiety, both emotional and social. To survive, she develops defenses to protect herself from further injury. She may learn judo, and that would probably be a good thing.

Still, I'm referring to the subconscious defenses we place around ourselves to protect our most vulnerable selves. In this place, we are emotionally naked and exposed. Personal boundaries are the space or the barriers placed between ourselves and others to protect ourselves. These barriers determine what we allow others to do with our time, bodies, minds, emotions, possessions, information, and self-identity. Setting boundaries protects us from those who purposely or inadvertently take advantage of us. Boundaries protect us from being abused by others and keep us from accepting too much responsibility for others. Boundaries simplify life by allowing us to decide how far we will go ahead of time and how much we will permit others to impose on us. But personal boundaries can be, but need not be, like impenetrable walls which keep others out entirely, but can be more like movable fences. We can move the fences close enough to permit others to touch us when we choose to touch or push the fences back when we want protection and privacy. This flexibility allows us the benefits of close relationships and the security for individual freedom and dignity. Our fence may even have a gate made available to and opened for a very select few trustworthy of our emotional vulnerability and nakedness.

As you recall, people raised in Nurturing Parent Mode environments become Free Children. They are confident, sensitive, caring, friendly, fun, and relate well with others. They have fewer personal boundaries (barriers) than the kids raised in Critical Parent Mode or Controlling Parent Mode environments because they don't need them; their self-image is healthy. They have learned how to respect other people's boundaries and expect others to respect their boundaries. While it is true that everyone has some "I'm Not OK" parts of their self-image, the free child doesn't have many.

On the other hand, the rebellious, insecure, angry, underachievers, overachievers, and narcissists have tons. The children from critical, controlling, and over-indulgent parent modes, almost always, have skill deficiencies in either protecting their boundaries, respecting other people's boundaries, or both. As a result, they have a large and complex network of personal boundaries and barriers. They haven't learned healthy ways to protect themselves from social and emotional damage or to get respect for their boundaries so others won't hurt them. Quite the contrary, they have learned unhealthy ways to overcompensate for their self-image's "I'm Not OK" parts. And that is a shame for themselves and others.

One way of overcompensation for low self-esteem is to project oneself as extraordinary and exceptional. They compare themselves as always being superior to others. They compete, but they are different from people with healthy self-esteem who compete. They compete because they always have to be **winners**. If they don't win, they make excuses or blame the outcome on other people or circumstances beyond their control. Not every sore loser has low self-esteem, but every person with low self-esteem is a sore loser (or a fatalist: it was my destiny to fail, which also happens to be an excuse). Overcompensation is a manifestation of unfulfilled needs. It is another form of personal boundary.

Unfulfilled needs drive behavior; consequently, when we observe over-the-top or unusual behavior, it is evidence of unfulfilled needs: the more profound the unfulfilled need, the more extreme the behavior. A person talking about suicide, other than part of a social discussion, has unfulfilled needs requiring immediate attention. We may not see these extreme compensatory behaviors as barriers or defenses until we try to discuss and analyze with them their outward projections. For example, it will quickly become apparent that a braggart will defend his superiority to the death. He will do so because he has to compensate for his insecurity. One could say that the inability for a person to be provisional (open-minded) or objective about oneself might suggest a need for personal boundaries to prevent vulnerable personal exposure.

I had a dear friend named Scott Ryan (he died in Vietnam). He was labeled at that time "slow" (the 1950s). Scott was always trying to show how smart he was, and in doing so, he revealed just the opposite. Those of us who were his buddies confirmed his opinions because we knew it was vital for him to be appear to be wise. He may not have been smart, but he was stronger and more agile than any person I have ever met. He was like an ant; he could carry six ants on his back and run 25 yards. I know; I was one of the six ants.

Scott was a member of our friendship foursome. We were like the "Four Musketeers," only younger. We were a strange mix of misfits; Scott was slow, Ernest was colored in a small all-white community, Mark was big (his dad had been a lineman for the Los Angeles Rams), and I was little. We loved being with each other. Our connection started in kindergarten, but only Scott and I made it together through high school. Mark moved to Washington in sixth grade, and Ernest became an orphan from a horrible car accident around the same time frame. From the accident, he was partially paralyzed. After many months of recovery, he moved in with his step dad and away from a family that had adopted him.

I remember that in first grade, Scott excelled in tag; no one ever tagged him, even if we ganged up, he could elude everyone. One of the early defining moments when Scott stood out from the crowd was when some boys dared him to jump off the top of a two-story fire escape attached to the side of our school. He was in third grade. Scott jumped, and they dared him to do it again. Again, he climbed to the top of the stairs. But this time, his brother, who was in sixth grade, tried to talk him out of jumping. He wasn't successful but tried to catch Scott before landing on the ground. As a result, his brother was knocked unconscious and ended up in the hospital. Scott got up and limped around for a few weeks but seemed unfazed from his jump. He did enjoy the attention that his dare-devil act produced. We later found that he had broken the bones in the arches of both his feet from his fire escape jump (doctors discovered it during his army physical).

Scott moved up to the next class with us every year. He got "social promotions" that enabled him to stay with our age group. They didn't have special education classes for Scott at that time. Maybe they did have them, but Scott didn't attend them if they did. Nowadays, he would have been in classes suited to his abilities and interests – not then.

Scott's family was poor but not much more so than most of the families in Richmond. Nonetheless, he dressed the poor part. He used hay baling twine for a belt. His shoes, pants, and t-shirts looked like hobo garb—picture Huckleberry Finn. It is not that his parents couldn't afford better clothes; he just didn't care. In a way, he was a fashion statement—vagabond perfected. He worked at Guild Edge Flour Mill, walking or riding a bike for the 2-mile journey to work, six days a week. He started working there, after school, at age 14, stacking bags of grain and then loading them into big 18-wheel trailers driven across the country. He was tossing 100 sacks of grain around at a time when they weighed as much or more than he did. I don't know what they paid him, but I'm sure he was a bargain. He could make 50 cents an hour working for local farmers, and I'd bet they paid him less than that. I don't know if he worked there because he was strong or if he was strong because he worked there. Anyway, he worked there his entire youth until he entered the army at 18.

Scott was stubborn; no one could get him to do something he didn't want to do. During our ninth grade year, the state had its annual Junior High Pantheon, which featured many different athletic events. Our physical education instructor made us do the pantheon events at our Junior High school as part of our curriculum, first, to see if anyone could qualify for the meet and, second, to use our results as the basis for our PE grade. One of the events was the "softball throw." The PE teacher Mr. Swenson tried to get Scott to throw a softball to give him a passing grade for something. Scott would have no part of it. Finally, the frustrated coach asked me if I could get him to do it because he knew that Scott and I were friends and could sometimes persuade him. I tried to reason with Scott, and he told me: "No, I don't want to!" Finally, I just yelled at him, "Just throw the damn softball!" Scott standing flat-footed, threw the ball, I guess to get me off his back. Well, the coach had us measure the distance of his throw. It turned out to be 26 feet further than the throw that won the state pantheon. (He had such a good arm. When we were in grade school, no one wanted to play catch with him because he could knock you down with a football from 40 yards away.)

When we were sophomores, the assistant head coach of the football team had watched Scott's athletic prowess and had visions of turning Scott into a top-flight football player. He asked me to get Scott to try out for the football team, but I wasn't successful during the official tryouts. Later, I had Scott convinced that football was a fun game and he would enjoy playing it. So, "Soup" Jessop, the assistant football coach, and I took Scott into the dressing room and got him all attired in the football gear. We took him onto the field with the rest of the squad, and Soup explained that the quarterback would hand him the football, and his job was to run with the ball into the end zone. When the quarterback gave him the football, Scott took off running, but he didn't run for the endzone but instead dodged about just like he was in a game of tag. Both Soup and I were yelling at Scott, "Run, Scott, Run! Toward the end zone!" He didn't heed our advice and acted like a dog keeping a ball away from everyone.

He was dodging and running around the entire football field. The defense couldn't catch him, and, as it turned out, neither could the offense. You have never seen anything more hilarious than everyone on the field trying to catch Scott. Eventually, someone got hold of him and slowed him down enough that a half dozen guys piled on him. Scott just started screaming; he couldn't stand being physically constrained. When we returned to the dressing room to disrobe Scott, Soup looked at me and said, "If he could learn to play this game, he could be a pro." I just nodded my head. Scott couldn't grasp many things that everyone could naturally understand.

By our junior year in high school, Scott had saved up enough money to buy a new 310cc Honda motorcycle. He was proud of that bike! One afternoon he brought it to our place to show it to my dad, who also had a bike. Dad asked him if he wanted to race, and Scott excitedly agreed. They decided to race north to Webb's Corner, which had a 90-degree turn in the road. It was about one mile north of our house.

Halfway to Webb's Corner was an elevated part of the road that didn't allow people on either side to see something coming from the opposite direction. Off they raced, with dad 30 yards or so ahead of Scott when they reached the rise in the road. Just at the peak of the elevated road, dad zoomed past Tim Nelson, who was driving the opposite direction in a 1955 Chevy. When he looked back over his shoulder, he saw Scott flying over the car. Dad turned around, expecting to find Scott dead, or badly injured lying on the road. To his surprise, he saw no Scott. He stopped by the front of Tim's car, where Tim sat in shock in the driver's seat with a broken windshield and a motorcycle jammed in the middle of his grill up to the engine block. He found Scott hugging his bike and crying. I arrived on the scene moments later and watched Scott crying and heard him lament: "I saved for this motorcycle for seven years!" Someone called his parents and the police. His parents arrived first, and all they could think about was if he was OK. They kept asking him if he was OK until Scott ripped off his shirt and threw it to the ground, and said: "I'm OK! See?" No one could believe that he could have lived much less walk away from that accident.

Later, when the police examined his bike, they saw that he had squeezed the gas tank so tightly with his legs that both sides of the tank were touching one another. The handlebars were pulled together and bent forward, which explained how he hit the windshield with his butt. He did a forward roll over the handlebars in such a way that he hit the windshield with his butt and then flew over the car and landed on his feet behind the car and ran until he could stop. He never touched the road with anything except his feet until he kneeled next to his motor-cycle. He hobbled around for a month or more. A few days after the accident, he showed me his backside. He was black and blue from his shoulders to his knees. He was back at work at the Mill by then. He was indestructible, or so we thought.

We went to a new high school our junior year. Scott didn't disappear but became invisible. High school wasn't a place where he could shine. He didn't date or go to parties; I'm not sure he would have gone if invited. No one asked him that I know of. I didn't realize he was even interested in girls until he returned home on military leave before heading off to Viet Nam. After basic and infantry training, he came to see me in his fancy new uniform. He was proud to be a soldier, and I was proud of him. He told me on that visit that he wouldn't be coming home again. I told him that was crazy thinking and to be careful over there. He wondered if I would do him a favor before he left. His greatest desire was to go out with Barbara, a gorgeous girl from Lewiston, a small farming community near Richmond. He wanted me to line him up on a date with her. I talked with her and explained the situation, but she declined the invitation. He took the news like a soldier.

He was drafted into the army because he had failed to register with the draft board after turning 18 (Scott didn't know he had to). A few months later, they came and arrested him, put him in handcuffs, and the judge gave him the option of going immediately into the army or going to jail. His parents chose the military. I'm sure his drill sergeants were amazed at his strength and endurance. Probably not so much with his classroom acumen. He was in a machine-gun unit as an ammunition carrier. He wasn't in Vietnam very long before dying. I will always wonder if he didn't come back because his fellow soldiers thought him a liability. His parents resented his forced entry into the army. They were bitter about his death, and they were justified in their feelings. He should have never been an active-duty soldier; especially in combat. I can't imagine what went through this gentle soul's mind over there. I have never written about Scott before, but doing so brings him back to me. I hope that this is a fair representation and a tribute to him. I miss you, buddy!

Scott overcompensated for his mental deficiency through his athletic prowess. All unfulfilled needs drive behavior; Scott fulfilled his need to be clever by overcompensating with physical prowess. People protect their vulnerable selves with personal boundaries or by over-compensating. As it turned out, Scott's physical talents weren't enough.

I believe that we all try to protect our weaknesses and vulnerabilities with personal boundaries, barriers, or overcompensation of some kind. Everyone has some parts of themselves about which they are sensitive and a little defensive. Maybe an intended part of life's challenge is to see if we can overcome these "soft spots" in ourselves and find true acceptance of other people despite their "soft spots." Wouldn't it be wonderful if we could help others find self-acceptance while finding our own?

22

THE EVOLUTION OF BOUNDARIES

We all start life with our boundaries and our self-identity entwined with our parents. As babies, we don't have a separate identity from our parents, and the child becomes part of their identity. As children become older, parents have difficulty telling the difference between their children's emotions from their own. They feel their child's emotions. Their pain becomes the parents' pain; their joy becomes the parents' joy. It is a natural process of life. We need to be entwined with our parents as infants to survive. It is also essential to become unentwined to function in life as adults.

If you are a parent, you will, most likely, have shared the disappointment and hurt of one, or more, of your child's painful experiences. If your little boy comes home crying from kindergarten because he was the only kid in his class not invited to Ella's birthday party, you would have to be made of stone not to feel the disappointment and pain with him. You might be bitter and angry because your son was hurt. His hurt is your hurt. An offense to him is an offense to you. You may want to go out and chastise those who didn't invite him. (You certainly would like to solve the problem for him and prevent further occurrences or hurts.)

If you did reach out and confront the offenders, they would likely give you a halfhearted apology and wonder what in the world is the matter with you. The ironic part is that your actions won't solve the problem or help the child. Probably not the smartest thing to do. A good thing to do would be to teach your child how to problem solve and deal with their hurt and disappointments.

This example is quite personal to me as I have lived a similar experience. In the second grade, Ronnie didn't invite me to his birthday party. (A lifetime of bitter feelings existed between his dad and my dad, which they passed to their children.) He asked all the other boys in our class to his birthday party except me. I was crushed and went home crying to my mother for comfort. She was appropriately loving, but she didn't solve my problem. I am sure it hurt her as much as it did me. When I told her all of the bad things I should do to Ronnie, she gently corrected me.

"No… it would be best if you didn't do that. It will only make matters worse." I replied, "What can I do?" She suggested that I treat him like my best friend, maybe even bring him a birthday present. I missed the party, but I got him a birthday present a couple of days later. He looked pretty surprised and didn't know how to act. I continued to treat him like a good friend, even though he did not reciprocate my actions immediately; within a few months, we became good friends. Oh, how wise was my mother! She could look beyond our hurt to the bigger and long-term picture.

Most parents, who love their children, can't distinguish clearly between their children's boundaries and their own, at least during their early years. That is understandable because their identities are intertwined. I'm sure that is part of the overall survival plan for helpless infants and vulnerable youth devised by a higher power. It is a good and vital thing during this dependency stage in life.

However, there comes a time when children must separate their identity and boundaries from their parents. They will remain in a dependent state until they do. Intertwined boundaries can last a long time. But, becoming independent is a necessary step for becoming mature and self-sufficient. Usually, kids are ready for the separation before the parents are. Sometimes it is an easy process, and other times it isn't. Intertwined boundaries can sometimes last too long. If you are the parent of a 40-year-old dependent child, you understand what I mean.

The movie *Failure to Launch* is about a 35-year-old guy still living with his parents, the difficulty that situation becomes for his parents, and his inability to have healthy interdependent relations with other adults. It is funny in the movie but not so funny in real life. Even though his parents caused the problem by not helping him become independent at the appropriate time, it demonstrates that eventually, his dependence on them made their lives miserable. Children who grow up to be dependent adults can learn to love being dependent, so much so that they fight it until forced to become independent.

Tough love is a method designed to compel dependent people to take responsibility and accountability for their actions or lack of actions. An unacceptable or dangerous situation justifies the need for tough love. It operates from the philosophy that natural consequences are life's best teacher and change motivator. Tough love can be hard on the parents and the "tough loved" person.

A couple, who were our friends, had a 23-year-old daughter who was an alcoholic. They had been to a counselor who had her admitted to a treatment center for substance abuse twice. Both times the daughter quit the program and came home, where she continued excessive and frequent alcohol consumption. The family counselor explained that they were "enablers" for their daughter's addiction. Unless they changed their behavior, the daughter would never move beyond the addiction because she didn't have to; she knew her parents would throw her a "lifeline" whenever she needed one. The counselor further explained that they all needed to agree on the expectations to continue providing room and board. It was made clear that the daughter would have to be responsible and accountable for her decisions and behavior. The counselor cautioned the parents that they needed to show "tough love" and not intervene when their daughter messed up; if she drank, they needed to move her out of the house, not put her into a motel, or provide assistance of any kind. The counselor was clear that it was almost a certainty that their daughter would violate the agreement and expect them to do what they had always done previously – to continue making available a place to live, eat, and receive a little financial assistance. The counselor stressed that if they did not allow their daughter to be responsible and accountable for her decision to continue drinking, nothing would ever change except that the addiction would worsen and eventually lead to their daughter's demise.

She told them: "It will be harder to watch your daughter suffer the consequences for her decisions than to keep assisting her, but remember, by assisting her, you are not helping her but are enabling her to self-destruct! Your daughter may not survive on her own; she could die, but understand, she cannot continue the life you have enabled."

They enacted the contract with their daughter, and as predicted, she violated the agreement. The parents moved her out and, with utter anguish, let her be accountable for her decisions. They met with me to find an empathetic ear. They shared every detail of their daughter's suffering and their own. Once they nearly relented and allowed their daughter to move back into their home, when she appeared skin-and-bones, hungry, and desperate on their doorstep. While the father talked with the daughter on the front porch, the mother called the counselor for advice. The counselor empathized with their heartache and advised them to have a shelter professional come and pick up their daughter but not let her into the house. They called the shelter and then cried all night. That night was probably the turning point for their daughter. I guess she decided that she would die soon if she didn't change; she believed that her parents had given up on her and would let her die. She chose to live, really live, and not as an alcoholic. She got a job at the same shelter that picked her up from her parent's porch. She slowly created a new life for herself.

She and her parents reconnected later, on different terms. The parents told me that they were grateful that their daughter was alive and had moved on to a better life. Still, they said that they felt guilty for letting their daughter suffer. Logically, they understood it was something they had to do for their daughter's benefit, but emotionally they felt the scars deeply. Not every tough love situation turns out with a happy ending. The multitudes of homeless addicts on the streets so testify. Tough love is challenging, but it is still love, and love is the most powerful positive force in life.

The path to independence for a child need not be overly traumatic. Parents who foster decision-making and provide the authority to do so, with accountability for the results, aligned with the appropriate level of judgment and maturity for a child of that age, will have children who will move from dependence to independence successfully. One of the fun things to witness and be a part of is the passage of teenagers from wanting to be dependent sometimes and independent other times. (This phenomenon used to happen around ninth grade, but is probably happening at an earlier age now.) The independence gained one step at a time is a path of healthy progression. Kids who don't get the opportunity to become independent in a step-by-step advance, but rather in one fell swoop, often crash land because they don't know how to make wise decisions. Independence is dangerous if people don't know how to manage it.

Independence is an interim step rather than an endpoint. People must become independent before they can have healthy inter-dependent relationships. If a person is dependent on their parents when they enter a marriage relationship, they remain dependent in their marriage; he or she simply shifts the dependence from their parents to their spouse. Most spouses don't like or tolerate a dependent partner forever. A nightmare scenario occurs when both marriage partners are dependent on their parents, and both try to shift their dependency to their dependent spouse. If no one can be independent, how can they function interdependently? They can't!

Dependent partners are almost always the basis of dysfunctional families. And unfortunately, they pass that dependency onto their children. When entering such a household, one might reasonably ask: "Who is in charge here?" It is a rhetorical question because it is evident that no one is responsible or accountable within the household.

My cousin, who used to ask for financial help from all his aunts and uncles, was always dependent on his mother until she died. After his mother died, his first wife became the person he depended on until she couldn't take it anymore and divorced him. Unfortunately, his new wife was also a dependent person. Hence, their dependency search for relatives who would care for them continued until his death. Now his widow and her kids depend on the government to provide a meager existence. The crazy part is that as her kids became adults, they found partners on whom to place their dependence. Consequently, the reliance on others continues and will do so until someone in the line becomes independent and moves on to successful interdependent relationships.

LIFE BOUNDARY CONDITIONS

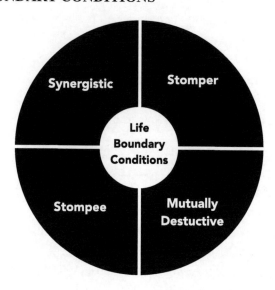

Let's examine what happens in life looking from four personal boundary perspectives:

Perspective One is when a person's boundaries are protected, and other people's boundaries are respected. We call this the *Synergistic Life Boundary condition.*

Perspective Two is when a person's boundaries are protected, and other people's boundaries are not respected. We call this the *Stomper Life Boundary condition.*

Perspective Three is when other people's boundaries are respected, but their own are not protected. We call this the *Stompee Life Boundary condition.*

Perspective Four happens when other people's boundaries are not respected, and neither are their own. We call this the *Mutually Destructive Life Boundary condition.*

Right up front, we want to clarify that only the Synergistic Life Boundary condition is healthy. All the other life boundary conditions are unhealthy. Let's provide a high-level perspective on each life boundary condition before we get into the details of each.

Synergistic Life Boundary condition

The boundary condition where people protect their boundaries and respect others is called Synergistic. It is a healthy condition. To be in this condition, people need to operate in adult mode and use Synergistic Power (which we will discuss in the next chapter). People who do this can establish synergistic interpersonal connections and relationships.

Stomper Life Boundary condition

The condition where people protect their boundaries but are disrespectful of other people's boundaries is called Stomper. It is an unhealthy condition. In this condition, people operate from parent mode and use Dominance Power (which we will discuss in the next chapter). People who do this create command and control relationships, which almost always leads to dysfunctional relationships.

Stompee Life Boundary condition

The condition where people respect other people's boundaries, or appear to, while not protecting their own is called Stompee. It is also an unhealthy condition. In this condition, people operate in child mode and allow others to use Dominance Power on them. People who do this permit themselves to be in Command and Control relationships. They are the ones being commanded and controlled. This condition frequently leads to destructive behavior directed at themselves or others.

Mutually Destructive Life Boundary condition

The condition where people do not protect their boundaries in healthy ways and disrespect others is called Mutually Destructive. It is also an unhealthy condition. In this condition, people operate in child mode and parent mode. Their interactions are cross-transactional, which leads to adversarial and enemy relationships.

Featured below is a model that lists behaviors typical of each life condition. Look through the lists and as you do so, check off any behaviors that you do.

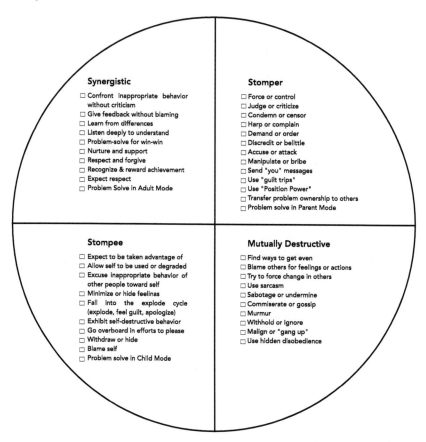

Synergistic
- ☐ Confront inappropriate behavior without criticism
- ☐ Give feedback without blaming
- ☐ Learn from differences
- ☐ Listen deeply to understand
- ☐ Problem-solve for win-win
- ☐ Nurture and support
- ☐ Respect and forgive
- ☐ Recognize & reward achievement
- ☐ Expect respect
- ☐ Problem Solve in Adult Mode

Stomper
- ☐ Force or control
- ☐ Judge or criticize
- ☐ Condemn or censor
- ☐ Harp or complain
- ☐ Demand or order
- ☐ Discredit or belittle
- ☐ Accuse or attack
- ☐ Manipulate or bribe
- ☐ Send "you" messages
- ☐ Use "guilt trips"
- ☐ Use "Position Power"
- ☐ Transfer problem ownership to others
- ☐ Problem solve in Parent Mode

Stompee
- ☐ Expect to be taken advantage of
- ☐ Allow self to be used or degraded
- ☐ Excuse inappropriate behavior of other people toward self
- ☐ Minimize or hide feelings
- ☐ Fall into the explode cycle (explode, feel guilt, apologize)
- ☐ Exhibit self-destructive behavior
- ☐ Go overboard in efforts to please
- ☐ Withdraw or hide
- ☐ Blame self
- ☐ Problem solve in Child Mode

Mutually Destructive
- ☐ Find ways to get even
- ☐ Blame others for feelings or actions
- ☐ Try to force change in others
- ☐ Use sarcasm
- ☐ Sabotage or undermine
- ☐ Commiserate or gossip
- ☐ Murmur
- ☐ Withhold or ignore
- ☐ Malign or "gang up"
- ☐ Use hidden disobedience

Now that you have finished checking your behaviors, examine your checkmarks and answer two questions:

1) In what circumstances do I behave that way?
2) With whom do I act that way?

Most people have checkmarks in all four quadrants. When I asked them why they have checkmarks in all four conditions, the most frequent response is: "Because I'm human."

However, the most self-revealing discoveries come from their answers regarding the circumstances when they demonstrate the behaviors and with whom they are displaying them. The area that seems to trouble people the most are checkmarks in the Stomper area. It troubles people because they realize that the people they stomp on the most are the people they love the most: their children. It really bothers them. And it should.

The answers to the questions apply to our families, work, and other activities in life. A dear friend was not surprised when his answers verified that he operates most of the time in the Stompee life condition at home, at work, and even while volunteering his time helping others. He shared with me how he had invested weeks preparing for a scouting activity that involved hundreds of scouts. He spent hundreds of dollars preparing the materials that the scouts would use. After the event, he went to the leaders of the scouting jamboree, requesting that they reimburse him for his expenses occurred at their request. They just told him to deduct his expenses from his taxes. When he reminded them that they had approved his efforts before he agreed to do the project, they said, "Sorry, we don't want to take the money from our scouting funds. But we really appreciative of what you did for our jamboree; it was the highlight of the event." Sadly, that kind of thing happens to him frequently. Stompers seem to know who they can take advantage of, people who will allow it.

Indeed, the reason for this chapter on personal boundaries is to help people recognize in which conditions they spend their life. If they discover that they spend too much time in unhealthy life conditions, and it is not where they want to be, awareness can become the starting point for change. Truthful self-awareness can motivate us to behave differently and permanently move to the synergistic life condition. So how did we end up in one of the Life Boundary Conditions we just defined?

23

THE SOURCE OF LIFE BOUNDARY CONDITIONS

Life conditions are reactions to, or manifestations of, our personal boundaries. So, where do these life conditions and personal boundaries come from? Are we born into these conditions, or do they develop over time? The first question answer is: They come from life experiences, starting in infancy and continuing throughout our lives. The second question answer is no and yes. When we are born, we are like a clean sheet of paper upon which nothing has been written. As soon as we leave our mother's womb, our sheet becomes the page upon which messages are written. We store some messages in our subconscious and others in our conscious minds. Everyone develops an "I'm Not OK"[32] life position during the imprinting stage of life (from birth through five), that is due to being small, helpless, and powerless in a world of big people. If we are in a loving home, we also get a lot of positive messages that make us feel good about ourselves. Through experimentation, nurtured children develop, progress, and realize that they are OK. Through positive reinforcement, they form a positive self-image. Our self-identity is an outcome of the process and is constantly evolving during this time.

As you recall, these experiences and imprinted feelings become our child mode. Any personal boundaries developed during this stage remain in our subconscious mind. More of our boundaries get put in place due to experiences occurring during our modeling stage (from five to twelve). When raised in a Nurturing Parent Mode environment, we naturally developed healthy personal boundaries and learned to respect other people's boundaries because we were secure and safe. On the other hand, if raised in a Controlling Parent Mode

---

32 T. A. Harris, *I'm OK – You're OK* (Harper & Row, 1967).

environment or a Critical Parent Mode environment, we develop a lot of unhealthy personal boundaries. Early experiences became an integral part of our self-identity. Our self-identity spawned from the parent mode environment in which we grew up. Most of the personal boundaries created from our home life occurred by six; our parents' messages about us happened by then. Ongoing parental messages after six years of age were pretty uniform and were not likely to change much, if at all. We likely adopted the Stomper life boundary condition if our child mode spawned from a Controlling Parent Mode. If raised in a Critical Parent Mode, we likely adopted the Stompee life boundary condition (or an insecure over-achiever life boundary condition). Children raised in an Overindulgent Parent Mode culture became self-centered, narcissistic, arrogant, and insensitive to other people's boundaries. Entitled children don't protect their boundaries; they expect others to do so. Therefore, they would fall into the Stomper life boundary condition and would eventually evolve to a mutually destructive life boundary condition.

The socialization stage (from eight to 18) has a significant impact on whether we remain in the life boundary condition we adopted during the modeling stage or shift to a different one based on the messages we receive from people with whom we socialize. Often the socialization stage merely reinforces the life position we developed in our early formative years. Other times the socialization stage dramatically changes how we perceive ourselves. We add additional personal boundaries to protect ourselves from others who would violate our boundaries. These teenage years are a tough time for many boys and girls. They can add many boundaries through the tough times, and their self-identity frequently changes. Sometimes people are fighters. They learn how to protect their boundaries. The non-fighters too often become Stompees.

The reformative years of our life (from 18 through the remainder of our life) only moderately modify our life boundary condition unless we want to change it. If we discover we are in an unhealthy life boundary condition and want to be healthy, we can change. If we engage our adult mode, we can shift to where we would rather be. Remember, our adult mode is our change agent.

Our life boundary condition and the life boundary condition of the people we interact with can determine the direction of our life and the kind of relationships we have if we allow it. We've reviewed a list of typical behaviors in each life boundary condition. Now we will examine the impact of those behaviors on people's lives in each life boundary condition. We will specifically look at their behavioral effect on people's time, bodies, minds, emotions, possessions, information, and self-identity. As you might expect, situations will have a different impact on people, depending on the life condition in which they live.

The various ways a person operating from a Synergistic Life Boundary condition would respond to other life boundary conditions

The reality is synergistic people are impacted very little by the behaviors of Stompers, Stompees, or Mutually Destructive people. They protect their personal boundaries and respect other people's boundaries. They don't initiate conflict, and they problem solve in adult mode when encountering problems. Unless there is a physical violation of their boundaries, like being assaulted or shot, they respond in adult mode and act rather than react. They don't let people control how they use their time because synergistic people know what is important to them, and that is where they focus their time. They can say no when they have a more important yes. They decide what happens to their bodies and who they will allow to get close or touch them. They control their mind by an active and present adult model that enables them to evaluate old parent mode and child mode recordings and decide if they are relevant or need to be changed. Their emotional state is based on verifiable facts, and they establish their beliefs on verifiable facts and innate truths instead of matching their beliefs to rationalized feelings. Possessions take third ranking in their focus. The hierarchy of important things is: Being, Doing, and Having. They love information because they never finish learning, and new information provides never-ending additions to what they know. Their self-identity consists of their adult mode discoveries and decisions made throughout life. They become what they choose to be.

Synergistic people love being with other synergistic people because their interconnectedness creates a relationship circle that is more than counting heads. They can be with Stompers, Stompees, and mutually destructive people because they can recognize the difference between who has the problem and who has inappropriate behavior. Therefore, they can let it slide when someone tells them they have a problem; they know differently. They don't like wasting time contesting dumb notions. When they see inappropriate behavior, they can problem-solve without criticism and use feedback to discuss situations rather than create polarization and contests. They can deal with people from where they are rather than where they want them to be. It is hard to offend synergistic people because when others criticize them, they accept the possibility that the criticism directed at them may have some validity. They are willing to discuss it with the criticizer to see if the criticism has merit. They are free and personally empowered by choosing their feelings and responses to life's ups and downs. As you can see, Synergistic people are pretty remarkable, and they have an advantage in life, and that is being synergistic. And, they would love it if everyone was synergistic as well. They will even help them get there.

One person stands out to me as an icon of the Synergistic Life Boundary Condition, Viktor Frankl. He spent his life helping to save lives, though he couldn't keep his loved ones from death at the hands of the Nazis during World War II. He survived unimaginable horrors and suffering during the war. He once said: "Those who have a 'why' to live can bear almost any 'how.'"

He had received a visa to go to the United States before the Nazis took over in Austria but chose to stay in Vienna because no other family member could have gone with him. He and his family decided to face the inevitable horrors coming at them together. He was, by that time, a renowned therapist known for treating suicidal patients and preventing suicides. He had a private practice and was on the staff of the major hospitals in Vienna. In 1938, the Germans invaded Austria. Being Jewish, he was not permitted to treat Aryan patients. The Rothschild Hospital in Vienna was the only place where he could treat Jewish patients, so he applied his gifts there as the head of the neurological department. Shortly later, he, his wife Tilly, his parents, and other family members were arrested and sent to a concentration camp in Czechoslovakia, Theresienstadt. He established a clinic there to help prisoners cope and prevent suicide. His family all survived that camp except his father, who died there. In 1944, he was ordered to go to Auschwitz. The Nazis sent his mother there also, but Tilly was not, so she volunteered to go there to stay near her husband. They separated them anyway; Tilly went to a camp named Bergen-Belsen, where she died. Viktor did not learn of her death until after the war. Still, thinking of her and about their future life together sustained him at Auschwitz. At first, the Nazis kept him and his mother in a shed with fifteen hundred others meant to hold only two hundred and fifty people. They had only one piece of bread per day.

To make room for new people arriving at their shed, the guards would take, from the shed, twice the number of the new prisoners arriving outside. They reduced the number returning to the hut to have the same number in the shed as before the new arrivals. When outdoors, they would order the prisoners to get into one of two lines; one line led back to the hut the other line led to the gas chamber. Viktor was ordered into the left line but defied the order and quickly jumped into the other line. The left line led to the gas chamber and death. He didn't know which line led to the gas chamber when he jumped.

One million one hundred thousand prisoners died at Auschwitz. Many died right away in the gas chambers, while the rest suffered deaths by starvation, disease, and exhaustion from forced labor. From his unspeakable experiences there, he found meaning in his suffering. He found comfort in the knowledge of love and started to crystalize his theory about what love means for human life. He captured his theory in his famous book *Man's Search for Meaning*. He wrote: "For the first time in my life, I saw the truth as it is set into song by so many poets, proclaimed as the final wisdom by so many thinkers. The truth – that love is the ultimate and highest goal to which man can aspire. Then I grasp the meaning of the greatest secret that human poetry and human thought and belief have to impart: The salvation of man is through love." He saw death and suffering up close; he was shoved into cattle cars, forced to march in freezing temperatures with insufficient food and clothes. He contracted typhoid fever; all the while separated from his loved ones. Why did he survive?

He explained: "I repeatedly tried to distance myself from the misery that surrounded me by externalizing it. I remember marching one morning from the camp to the worksite, hardly able to bear the hunger, the cold, and pain of my frozen and festering feet, so swollen. My situation seemed bleak, even hopeless. Then I imagined that I stood at a lectern in a large, beautiful, warm, and bright hall. I was about to give a lecture to an interested audience on 'Psychotherapeutic Experiences in a Concentration Camp'. In the imaginary lecture, I reported the things I am now living through. Believe me, ladies and gentlemen, at that moment, I could not dare to hope that someday it was to be my good fortune to actually give such a lecture."

He also found lessons in goodness and survival in the suffering he endured and witnessed. These lessons are manifest in his life's work. He taught: "We who lived in concentration camps can remember the men who walked through the huts comforting others, giving away their last piece of bread. They may have been few in number, but they offer sufficient proof that everything can be taken from a man but one thing: the last of the human freedoms – to choose one's attitude in any given set of circumstances, to choose one's own way."

I recall hearing him lecture (not in person) sometime during 1978 while living near Toronto. He explained the difference between liberty and freedom. He realized that the guards had more liberty than he did in the concentration camp but that he was freer than they were because he never relinquished his right to choose his feelings and responses to life's cruelty and unfairness. His psychological theory, called Logo Therapy, is a beacon for helping people find meaning in life and purpose for living. If you haven't read it, do yourself a favor and read *Man's Search for Meaning*.

The various ways a person operating from a Stomper Life Boundary condition would respond to other life boundary conditions

We need to keep in mind the five characteristics of Stompers when we analyze how they interact with other people. These characteristics play a part in all their dealings with others. They are:

One, they don't respect other people's boundaries.

Two, they live in a hierarchical world where they try to command and control (or bully) those lower than them in their perceived hierarchy and are submissive to those they perceive as above them.

Three, they seem to sense who they can bully and who they can't. Stompers avoid confrontations with people they know they can't bully and seek conflicts with those they can bully.

Four, at their very core, they are cowards. They won't participate in a fair fight and slink away from those who contest their bullying.

Five, Stompers with unlimited power are dangerous and destructive.

They **don't respect other people's boundaries**, making them insensitive toward others' pain, suffering, discomfort, misery, sorrow, or joy. In extreme cases, they are sociopathic (a personality disorder that manifests itself with antisocial attitudes and behavior and a lack of conscience). In mild cases, they are indifferent about other people's struggles, successes, highs, or lows; they don't care.

They live and operate in a hierarchical world. Stompers were likely raised in a Command and Control Parent Mode environment and developed an adaptive or submissive-child mode persona. As adults, they operate from a Command and Control Parent Mode the same as their parents with one variation: their command and control application adapts to the circumstances in which they find themselves. Hence, they control those who are lower on the pecking order and are submissive to those who are higher.

They seem to sense who they can bully and who they can't. Stompers avoid confrontations with people they know they can't bully and seek conflicts with those they can bully. People who won't accept bullying must have an aurora about them that the antenna of a Stomper sense and dissuades them from invading their space; while on the other hand, vulnerable people send out signals that attract bullies. Bullies become like sharks attracted to the smell of blood, and they stomp.

Four, at their very core, they are cowards. They won't participate in a fair fight and slink away from those who contest their bullying. Bullies can be found as active, shouting, fist-raising members of mobs. We see lots of them in cults like the KKK (why the masks?) and the White Supremacists. They vicariously feed on the mob's courage and power when surrounded by passionate people. If they become separated from the pack and stand-alone or need to defend their convictions courageously, they fall short. Particularly if those who challenge them rank high on the pecking order.

When I was about 10 or 11, a 13-year-old boy in town started bullying me. Whenever he saw me, he would run me down, punch me, throw me on the ground, and kick me. I didn't know why he did that, but he did. After he bullied me for a couple of weeks, I came home with a cut lip, and my dad asked me what had happened to my lip. Dad's question allowed me to explain the whole miserable situation to him. I said that I didn't know why he was picking on me; I hadn't done anything to him to cause him to be mean to me. My dad just looked at me and said that bullies don't need a reason; they do it because they can; they get their "jollies" from doing it. I asked him how I could get him to stop picking on me. He told me to fight him. He must have seen the concerned look on my face because he said: "I know you don't want to fight him, and you are afraid of him because he is bigger and stronger than you are. That is OK and natural, but you need to understand that bullies are cowards. If you overcome your fear and fight him, he will probably beat you up. But if you let him know that he was in a real fight, I guarantee that he won't pick on you again after you fight him. If I fight your battle for you, he will just find other ways to pick on you, and his bullying won't stop."

I dreaded my next encounter with him, but I had decided that I would fight him with everything I had if he came at me. I bumped into him a couple of days later on Erickson's corner, two blocks from my house. I didn't even try to run, he rushed me, and we had a real "round-house" fight. Of course, he beat me up and left me lying in the irrigation ditch that ran in front of Erickson's house. He never picked on me again, ever! My dad was right, he was a coward, and he didn't want to try his luck again with me. Upon reflection, I now recall that he was an outcast who older kids in town frequently bullied.

Five, Stompers with unlimited power are dangerous and destructive. When a Stomper is at the top of the hierarchy, everyone below them becomes Stompees. Chairman Mao Zedong was a Chinese communist revolutionary who was the founding father of the People's Republic of China. He ruled with an iron fist and initiated the Chinese Cultural Revolution, which cleansed the country of intellectuals, dissidents, or anyone who disagreed with him. During this revolution, he persecuted hundreds of millions of Chinese people. An untold number of deaths occurred, but we will never know for sure because no one recorded the deaths. In 1958, he launched the Great Leap Forward that aimed to rapidly transform China's economy from agrarian to industrial, leading to the greatest famine in history, resulting in the estimated deaths of over 50 million Chinese.

I went to China with a copy of his biography (Mao) in my luggage 15 years ago. Our manufacturing manager, Charles, who is Chinese and educated at NYU, came to my room and saw a copy of the book on my nightstand. He panicked and told me it was a death sentence if a Chinese citizen had that book. He secreted the book out of the hotel and burned it in one of his factory's furnaces. I never found out what the penalty would have been for me, an American Citizen – I didn't even ask.

Of course, we all know the atrocities and mass hardships on the North Korean people wrought by Kim Jong-un as the head of state. He is a totalitarian hereditary dictator who controls whether people live or die. He determines what happens to anyone lower on the totem pole than he—which is everyone. His uncle and brother garnered no sympathy before being executed for not being sufficiently submissive to him.

I knew a President of one of the Johnson & Johnson companies known as Little Napoleon by many of the people who worked for him. Everyone in his company was terrified of him and was fawning in his presence. When J&J reorganized the pharmaceutical divisions and placed them under a Pharmaceutical Vice-Chairman, his reign of terror ended. Everyone I knew was grateful that he was gone, and I might add, soon forgotten. The point is that he was a Stomper by nature and got his "jollies" from making people miserable. He indeed manifested sadistic tendencies and wasn't uncomfortable in the least when attacking or demeaning his employees. Yet, he was fawning and submissive in the presence of James Burke, Chairman of the Board at J&J.

Because I knew Jim Burke pretty well (I played tennis with him for a year and had many in-depth discussions) and because I loved my experience at J&J, I can't fathom how Little Napoleon ever became a president of one of the operating companies.

When Stompers interact with synergistic people

Stompers don't interact with synergistic people frequently, but when it happens, they are non-threatening. Adapting their demeanor is part of a Stomper's nature. They instinctively know that they can't bully secure people, so they seldom try. They probably would be described as indifferent or not involved with synergistic people. Synergistic people may be aware that bullying and bullies exist, but it is secondhand information because they seldom experience it.

Typical Stomper behavior like forcing, controlling, judging, criticizing, condemning, complaining, accusing, belittling, attacking, mocking, manipulating, ordering, etc., has little effect on synergistic people. It doesn't achieve the desired effect because synergistic people confront inappropriate behavior in adult mode. Stompers sense that their manipulative behavior won't work, so they seldom try. It pays to be a Synergistic person around Stompers.

When Stompers interact with Stompees, they are in their "sweet spot."

Interactions with Stompees provide the optimum environment for stomping: Stompees don't protect their boundaries, which matches with Stompers who don't respect boundaries anyway. Stompees are lower on the pecking order than almost everyone, so Stompers feel free to stomp. Stompees don't fight back, so courage is not a Stomper requirement. Stompers convince themselves that Stompees want Stompers to stomp them. The more they bully, the more submissive the Stompee becomes. This convoluted relationship creates the "perfect storm" for making victims and victimizers.

When Stompers interact with Mutually Destructive People (who tend to be passive-aggressive), they tread carefully.

The unpredictability of Mutually Destructive People makes Stompers wary of them. Stompers are ill-equipped to deal with the socially aggressive behavior that they sense accompanies Mutually Destructive People. The passive-aggressive behavior associated with Adversaries and Enemies requires sensitivity about other people's boundaries which Stompers don't have and can't navigate. They may gently attempt a Stomper move with an adversarial person but recognize a blunder immediately (picture a dog smelling a porcupine). Any counter force they experience will push their coward button and put them on the "Don't mess with them" list. They don't need Adversaries or Enemies because so many Stompees are available to harass.

Stompers' interactions with other Stompers are interesting.

Stomper to Stomper interaction creates unpredictable situations. On the one hand, Stompers don't like being stomped on but want to stomp. Because Stompers exhibit an adaptive command and control persona, they are hard to read on first encounters. They don't know if the other person is a Stomper unless they witness Stomper behavior used on someone else. If they do see it, then they avoid them.

On the other hand, they will carefully check out the new potential victim, barring such evidence. I picture this as two bull moose checking out their mating competition. When they determine who is higher in the pecking order during the sniffing contest, Stompers will stomp and expect the other person to respond submissively. If they are correct, the other person will cower appropriately. If they misread them, they will receive a stomping much greater than the one they gave, and they will obsequiously submit, thus becoming a Stompee.

You have heard the expression, "Birds of a feather flock together." Well, that is both true and false when it comes to Stompers. Stompers welcome becoming part of a stomping gang, as long as they don't have to pass a courage test. They still get the pleasure of the stomp even if they are not stomping personally. It can be lonely if they are not part of a stomping gang. The Somper mentality doesn't foster equality; people either have to be above them or below them on the hierarchy. If they are above them, then they will be submissive. If they are below them, then they will be dominating.

If they have absolute and unlimited power and meet resistance from others, they just eliminate them – as in making them dead. Voilà! No resistance.

The various ways a person operating from a Stompee Life Boundary condition would respond to other life boundary conditions

There are several characteristics of Stompees that we need to keep in mind when we analyze how they interact with other people.

One, they don't protect their personal boundaries effectively. Let me explain that. They may have personal boundaries for guarding or hiding their vulnerability or emotional nakedness, but not sufficient to stop or prevent Stompers from stomping. In fact, they send out signals that they are vulnerable, which attracts Stompers. I realize that I'm describing an emotional duality where it can't be both ways, but it is what it is. That may partially explain the problematic life of being a Stompee.

Picture what it must be like to know that Stompers are coming and not having the ability to prevent it. When we have nightmares, we can wake up and feel relieved that it was just a dream. Stompees can't wake up from the one they are living; it is not if they will be stomped on or taken advantage of; it is only a question of when and how bad will it be. That would make me anxious and depressed, how about you?

Two, they have a lot of complex personal boundaries, which makes them guarded about revealing themselves to others. As a result, they struggle to develop or maintain meaningful synergistic relationships. The personal boundaries they have created to protect their vulnerable self and naked emotions become the barriers that keep people from getting too close. A child of a Stompee that I know well told me: "We don't discuss issues in our family, we just avoid them, and it pisses me off because no problems ever get solved, and nothing ever changes!" She is now a clinical psychologist. Did I mention that not only are Stompees guarded about self-revelation, they are also avoiders? They are avoiders.

Three, they respect other people's boundaries or appear to do so. They never intentionally violate another person's boundary, and if they do, they feel guilty and are remorseful. Compared to most people, Stompees are sensitive to other people's boundaries. They approach other people, who have problems, as a soldier would approach a land mine, they avoid them, if possible; if not possible, then treat them with the utmost caution.

Four, their self-identity is manifested with low self-esteem. Stompees are generally seen as "nice" people and are generous with what little they do have. They live hoping that people will reciprocate their kindness and generosity but expect that they won't. Hence, they tend to be guarded and distrustful, often manifesting as fatalism, hoping for the best but expecting the worst. They are the child mode spawns of a Critical Parent Mode environment growing up. They got the message that they were inferior early on in life, and it stayed with them as teenagers and as adults. They are still operating from the "I'm Not OK" life position. As you might expect, a Stompee's low self-esteem makes them particularly susceptible to committing Fundamental Attribution Errors (when they see behavior they don't like, they take it personally and assume negative intent). We might expect that Stompees who didn't get the correct change from a cashier would conclude that the cashier did it as a personal slight and that she is a thief who intended to steal their money. And yet, as a Stompee, they wouldn't make a big deal about it, their perception of being cheated would be just one additional piece of evidence of their low position on life's totem pole.

Five, when attacked, they respond submissively but hate the attack. Stompees repress outward expressions of anger but internalize them where the repressed feelings grow and build extreme emotional and psychological pressures. That pressure eventually causes an explosion spewing emotional shrapnel in all directions. Afterward, they feel horrible about their actions. They apologize, withdraw, and repress their feelings even more than before.

Consequently, each time they explode, it is bigger than the last one. Imagine that Stompees' emotions as being compressed in a spherical metal ball that can only hold so much pressure before it detonates. When the explosion occurs, it disperses damaging pieces of emotions with the force of the blast being equal to the level of emotional propellent. Then imagine that in some way, all the emotions are captured and put back into another sphere with thicker metal walls which will require much more pressure to detonate. Then imagine what happens when passing that higher level of tolerance. Can you see how much bigger the blast will be? Then imagine this cycle repeating until the pent-up emotions are so enormous that the inevitable explosion kills everyone, including the Stompee.

Not every Stompee progresses to higher levels of explosiveness. Some continue to explode when they can't take it anymore emotionally, but the level of intensity doesn't change much. I am intimately acquainted with someone bullied in grade school and junior high. I didn't see much of it in high school, probably because he had a steady girlfriend that occupied most of his attention and prevented him from emanating signals of vulnerability. Also, she took on the role of protecting him from being bullied. After he graduated from college, he got a job that displayed his many talents. His talents were bountiful, but his Stomper employer sensed that he was a Stompee, so he exploited him. He never gave my acquaintance a pay raise in eight years. His pay was just barely sufficient to support his family's minimum needs. It was incredibly unfair because my Stompee acquaintance attracted most customers who utilized their business services and produced almost all of their profits. The owner drove an expensive sports car, lived in a nice neighborhood, and took frequent, costly vacations, but my acquaintance didn't share the benefits he created. I would ask him: "Why do you take this guff?" He would paraphrase the rationalization that his boss gave him when he didn't give him a pay raise: "He is taking all the risks, and there is only so much money to share." He had opportunities to take many higher-paying jobs in other locations, but his wife didn't want to leave an area where she felt safe, requiring a move to a place "where bad people live." People have taken advantage of him for as long as I have known him.

He fits in the ranks of the emotionally abused. From time to time, he explodes but then feels ashamed, apologizes, and goes back into his submissive shell. The intensity of his explosions has never varied a great deal. He seems to have accepted his fate in life. I believe that I'm the only person with whom he will share his feelings and life experiences and, sadly, even we talk less and less, partly because I feel inadequate to help him.

Six, over time, Stompees' unresolved feelings build to the point where they become mentally fatigued (unless they can find ways to categorize their life into boxes that allow them to continue by mentally escaping into a safe place when needed). If they don't have a safe place, this mental exhaustion may manifest as destructive tendencies directed at themselves or others. The self-damage may be subconscious, such as chronic illnesses or addictions to alcohol or drugs. Other manifestations might include mental and emotional imbalances like insomnia, anxiety, or depression. In extreme cases, they can go "postal," killing people who, in their minds, are representative of those who have continuously bullied them or who have mistreated them. They frequently include themselves in the killing. Too often, we witness on the news a story about a person recently dismissed from their job who returns with a gun and shoots fellow employees; some victims are specific targets like their boss, other times, their victims are chosen randomly. Stompees inability to protect their personal boundaries can have tragic results. Unresolved negative feelings have consequences, whether they are ours or others. Stompees can become a danger to themselves and others.

Stompee interactions with synergistic people

Stompees enjoy being with synergistic people; they feel safe physically and emotionally. They don't feel judged or inferior. Somehow, they know that they will not be taken advantage of, be used, or degraded. They do not need to go overboard to please because they are accepted as they are. They don't have to withdraw or hide because there is nothing from which to hide or retreat. It must feel a little bit like being on Fantasy Island when they are with synergistic people. So why don't they spend all their time with synergistic people? I don't know, and I wish they would; it would make their lives so much more pleasant. I have two theories why it doesn't happen as frequently as desired.

The first theory is that they have to take the initiative and their low self-esteem prevents them from doing so – "I'm too unworthy." Another part of the first theory is that their boundaries are barriers to proactive socialization. Here, too, is their sensitivity about infringing on other people's personal spaces.

The second theory is that Stompers find them, shifting their focus from healthy relationship choices to simply surviving. We can understand that they would focus on surviving when considering Maslow's Hierarchy of Needs. Safety and security needs supersede belonging and status needs. "When a bear is chasing me, I'm not thinking about making new friends."

It is a shame that they don't spend more time with synergistic people because they could hold the key to emancipating the Stompee from their unhealthy parent mode and child mode recordings. Close association with people who listen, hear, understand, and validate them would offer a safe way to move past the personal boundaries that protect their naked, vulnerable emotional self. It would empower their adult mode to examine their old recordings and determine if they are helpful or hurtful. It would enable them to replace unhealthy personal boundaries with healthy ones. It would offer a path for personal change, to move from a Stompee life to a synergistic one. Wouldn't it be wonderful if synergistic people looked for Stompees and established close relationships? It's a lot to hope for because so many need synergistic friends, and synergistic people are already happily associating with synergistic people. Maybe that is why we have psychologists, to help the rich Stompees. But what about the poor ones?

Stompee interactions with Stompers

We have already reviewed this relationship in the section of Stomper interactions with Stompees, only this time; we will look at it from the Stompee perspective. This view explains why Stompees allow abusive behavior toward them.

Stompees have learned that submissiveness is an essential trait for survival with Stompers. They understand that if they don't resist, the Stomper will eventually move on and that they have survived until the subsequent encounter. From the Stompees outlook, survival is day by day, experience by experience existence. Their association with Stompers validates every negative Critical Parent Mode recording in their subconscious mind. By validating the message, it self-justifies the personal abuse, and, as we know, we can endure what we can justify. This mindset leads to a fatalistic conclusion; a validation of oneself as inferior and deserving of abuse. It is a symbiotic relationship between victims and abusers.

It is this kind of relationship that creates feelings of despair and hopelessness. I believe it is the cause of most suicides committed by adults. It is prevalent among teenagers who can't cope with the persecution. Of course, there are other reasons like chronic pain, mental illness, and drug addiction. And nowadays, indeed, for young people, stomping is aided by a social network that allows people to stomp and persecute victims anonymously. The social web enables Stompers to attack people without personal accountability. The social network is a beautiful life tool when used responsibly. The social network is a cruel and sadistic instrument in the hands of Stompers.

In short, Stompers leverage every vulnerability of Stompees. If that is not sadistic behavior, I don't know what is. Few rational people can see the buzz derived from control and power over people as justification for the misery it causes, so they largely dismiss it or ignore it. Remember that unfulfilled needs drive behavior and that rational people are getting their most pressing needs filled. On the other hand, Stompers feel the buzz of victimizing people, and Stompees feel the stomping. When rational people dismiss the stomping or ignore it, no one saves the Stompees.

Stompee interactions with Mutually Destructive People

I don't see Mutually Destructive People and Stompees ever having much of a relationship. Mutually Destructive People are reactive rather than proactive. And since Stompees are extremely sensitive about offending people or invading their space, they have minimal opportunities to interact. I would expect it would mostly be circumstantial if they do have interactions. Stompees don't do many things that would trigger Mutually Destructive People's typical behavior. From the point of view of Mutually Destructive People, it is hard to blame someone if nothing worth condemning happens. Stompees avoid confrontation, so nothing exists to sabotage, undermine, or commiserate about. Besides, the Stompers are looking for someone to blame for not providing them what they believe they deserve as extraordinary people, and they instinctively know that Stompees can't do that. Adversaries or Enemies have very little interest in Stompees. (Why bother with someone on the bottom of the totem pole? Adversaries and Enemies are about winning and Stompees don't compete.)

For the most part, they are like ships passing in the night; except for incidental awareness of one another's presence, they influence one another's direction in life very little.

The various ways a person operating from a Mutually Destructive Boundary condition would respond to other life boundary conditions

(Remember, Mutually Destructive people don't protect their boundaries, and they don't respect other people's boundaries.)

An overview regarding the nature of Mutually Destructive people can provide us insight into their perspective on life, which explains their emotional states, how they interact with others, and their kinds of relationships. If we used one phrase to describe them, we would say they are passive-aggressive people. How can people be both passive and aggressive? That appears to be an oxymoron. The simple explanation is that they are passive about protecting their own boundaries and aggressive in disrespecting the boundaries of others. Hence, mutually destructive behavior.

Their passivity flows from the belief that they are not responsible for protecting their boundaries because that is someone else's responsibility. Their aggressiveness comes from feelings of resentment and anger directed toward those they hold responsible for not providing them with what they feel they are entitled to receive. To sum them up, they are the amalgamation of what happens when personal boundaries are not protected and the boundaries of others are not respected. This passivity about safeguarding their borders often results in personal injury by default, while the aggressiveness toward other people's boundaries causes damage to others and motivates aggressive reactions. When we realize that enemies – which is a Mutually Destructive relationship – are not focused on protecting their boundaries but are focused on hurting their Enemies, we can understand why they can be so destructive to one another.

Passive side characteristics of Mutually Destructive People

Arrogance, self-centeredness, and narcissism are characteristics of grown-up children of Overindulgent Parent Mode parenting. They have grown up with a feeling of entitlement. They take no responsibility or accountability for their situation in life. They become masterful in the transference of problem ownership, problem-solving, and shifting blame to others. They expect "someone" to overindulge them and change the world to make them happy when things are not as they believe they should be. As a result, they remain dependent on others.

As a consequence of their dependence, they tend to be in victim mode a lot, resentful that they have been betrayed by those who should have provided them with what they, as "special and deserving," should have received. They feel unjustly treated, which drives them to find and associate with people who also feel betrayed. They become sympathizers in commiseration clubs. Passivity, in this case, is simply not being responsible for protecting their boundaries. This passivity about safeguarding their boundaries becomes the justification for their aggressiveness toward others when their boundaries are violated. Crazy as it sounds, despite their continual dependency and victimhood, they really do believe that they are extraordinary.

This mindset is not entirely accurate for the overindulged children of the wealthy and idle rich who are spoiled and share all of the characteristics of their poor counterparts but miss out on the vagaries of having unfulfilled expectations because of their financial circumstances. They, too, believe that they are extraordinary, and their resources confirm that as long as they remain rich, with all its accompanying benefits. While it is true that their "being spoiled" may keep them continuously dissatisfied, they are never disadvantaged.

To the degree that the entitled kids are intelligent and talented, they may sense the variance between the reality that the overindulgent parent paints and the real one. Hopefully, they realize that they aren't as gifted and extraordinary as their parents would have everyone believe and move closer to reality. As they connect with reality, they will realize that the exaggerated painting ultimately won't serve them well. If they genuinely catch on to what is happening, they may start taking personal responsibility and accountability for their actions and become less dependent on others to fill their needs. When they are less dependent on others, they become more likely to respect the boundaries of others. Even with this greater connection to reality, they will still have to deal with their parents' overindulgence, which continuously removes responsibility and accountability. Being an overindulged child who becomes an adult is never an easy path, but it is tolerable as long as the wealth holds out.

Aggressive side characteristics of Mutually Destructive People

Mutually Destructive People don't respect other people's boundaries because they see themselves as superior to others (because their parents reinforced that belief). At the same time, they may feel victimized because their "specialness" is not recognized and rewarded as they expect it should. Therefore, they are justifiably angry and don't respect other people's boundaries. But it is more than that; if circumstances don't meet their expectations, it is always someone else's fault. If it is never their fault, they feel justified in being resentful, angry, accusatory, and vocal against those they blame. They are the masters of three skill sets that enable them to avoid l responsibility and accountability for unwanted circumstances: Blaming, excuse-making, and denying reality. In my mind, I can envision them meeting the devil at the gates of hell and him asking them: "Do you know why you are here?" And they answer him: "I am not here."

They are sympathizing members of commiseration clubs; they are not the type to stand alone for their ideals. They coalesce around a Chief Poop Stirrer, the spokesman for their victimhood. Ironically the Chief Poop Stirrer of mutually destructive commiseration clubs frequently takes advantage of them. He is usually a Stomper who sees their victimhood as an opportunity to exploit them for his benefit. Because of their dependence and victimhood, they readily accept someone famous or powerful to represent them and who they believe will be the catalyst to get the world to change for their benefit. At the same time, their spokesperson is not about to end his gravy train; he will invent conspiracies, supposedly about people or things that are out to get them, just to keep them engaged and united around him. Chief Poop Stirrers of mutually destructive commiseration clubs are skillful at reading the sympathizers and keeping emotions at a fever pitch. They operate out of self-interest and exploit those in victim mode without mercy.

Mutually Destructive People in commiseration clubs will believe virtually anything presented to them if it justifies their victimhood and affirms their sense of superiority. If told that all of the cows in all of the dairy herds in America were injected with a drug that makes "special people" miss out on opportunities, they would believe it. They would use that belief to justify their negative situation and attack others. "You see, it's not my fault; it's those damn cows!" Adverse situations are never their fault, and conspiracy theories that "prove it" are just as numerous as the negative situations and the unfulfilled needs of "special" people who feel victimized.

Sadly, we see Mutually Destructive People coming together in colossal commiseration clubs manipulated by politicians who use the victims' anger for political advantage – to get donations and get attention. Truth is set aside for self-interest. Ultimately democracy is damaged, which hurts us all, and the victims end up hurting themselves. Because Mutually Destructive People feel threatened by others seen as responsible for their victimhood, they seek to validate and strengthen their position by minimizing the power and influence of those seen as threats. And they support those they believe will remove their victimization – even though the ones they support are using them for selfish purposes and don't care what happens to them. To the people using them, they are merely pawns in a transactional relationship. (The users justify it by saying, "It's just politics.")

Passive and Aggressive Characteristics of Mutually Destructive People

A local school posted pictures of all the honor students on the bulletin board. The next day students returned to discover that someone had cut out the eyes of all the female honor students' pictures. That made a lot of people very nervous and paranoid. A high-performing track star went from an assembly to his car. The student body learned that he was awarded a full-ride scholarship. After the assembly, he went to his car and found that the tires on his vehicle were all slashed.

Both of these events occurred in the same school within the same week. Of course, the police got involved and solved who perpetrated the attacks. It turned out to be a young man who was angry and jealous of the recognition of others who, in his mind, were inferior to him. Obviously, he was aggressive but did it in a hidden way to avoid personal accountability.

Other times passive-aggressive behavior is shown by a delayed response to an offense. For example, suppose that a waitress in a restaurant is insulted by a rude customer. She doesn't respond immediately to the situation but seems to accept the inappropriate behavior meekly. She waits until his food is ready and then secretly blows her nose onto the contents of his plate. She delivers his order with a smile on her face and satisfied revenge in her heart. Passive-aggressive people may appear placid and demure, but they will try to get even.

I am concerned about the ability of Mutually Destructive People to use the social network as a tool for passive-aggressive attacks on others who are getting the kind of attention that they believe that they should be getting and aren't getting. Their identity can remain anonymous, while their attacks can be devastating. With their skills and access to social networking, teenagers have tremendous power to do immense harm anonymously. With Mutually Destructive People, access to the social network is like giving them a gun and lining up all the people who they blame for their unfulfilled expectations, while at the same time giving them a get-out-of-jail-free card before they start shooting.

Mutually Destructive People's interactions with Stompers

In the concentration camps run by the Nazis in western Europe during World War II, the internal workings of units within the concentration camps were managed by sadistic prisoners put in charge of the other prisoners. Survivors of the camps often described the sadistic prison guards as more brutal and vicious than the Nazi guards. The German guards were armed and were usually indifferent about the suffering of the prisoners, even when they murdered them. But the "Trusties" (a term used in our state and federal prisons that aptly describes the roles played by prisoners in charge of prisoners) were not indifferent; their sadism was personal and extreme. In the end, the Trusties suffered the same fate as the people they tortured – death. But while they were Trusties, they believed in the fantasy that their cruelty would ingratiate them with the Nazis and that it would save them. It didn't; the Nazis despised them and took particular glee in their demise. It is interesting to note that the Trusties played both the role of victim and persecutor, which was mutually destructive. Playing a mutually destructive role, they partnered with the Nazi Stompers.

Mutually Destructive People and Stompers have several things in common: neither respects other people's boundaries. Neither of them is a paragon of courage. Stompers tend to victimize people to fill an unfulfilled need for power and security, whereas Mutually Destructive People are indifferent about other people's boundaries. Their mentality is: "How does respecting other people's boundaries benefit me?" Mutually Destructive People don't respect others' boundaries, nor their own, and when partnering with Stompers, they become victims (as in the example with Trusties in partnership with the Nazis). If there exists an opportunity for Stompers to exploit Mutually Destructive People in victim mode, they will take advantage of the opportunity. Likewise, Mutually Destructive People are always looking for people to solve their problems. If Stompers convince them that they will represent their interests, they will connect with them, albeit a one-sided win for the Stomper. They make strange bedfellows but are bedfellows nonetheless. The nature of their bedfellow relationship will vary depending on the circumstances.

Mutually Destructive People's interactions with Stompees

Mutually destructive People look for people who will indulge their narcissism and solve their problems. Stompees can't do that, so they pretty much ignore Stompees unless the Stompee can serve as a valuable target for blame. Stompees are ideal for Mutually Destructive People who need a scapegoat because they don't fight back. Overall, they don't match up very well. Both operate in child mode, so there is no adult mode in the relationship when they are together. That means there is no one capable of problem-solving effectively. To expand this concept, realize that the Stompee has unfulfilled needs and operates from an inferiority perspective.

In contrast, the Mutually Destructive Person has unfulfilled needs and operates from a sense of superiority. Neither can solve either their own or the other's unfulfilled needs. Consequently, the needs of both go unfilled. When together, they do not have a very satisfying connection or relationship.

Mutually Destructive People sometimes gossip, belittle, or minimize Stompees to uplift their self-image. They seem to believe that belittling someone else somehow makes them better. They gossip passively, aggressively, and always to benefit themselves. Stompees are a perfect target for their personal enhanced, albeit shallow, self-image. Unfortunately, Stompees always remain on the bottom of the totem pole.

Mutually Destructive People's interactions with other Mutually Destructive People

Mutually Destructive People reinforce or stroke one another's victimhood as long as their situation appears similar when interacting with one another. If their biases are similar, they are "aligned." They can share "Ain't it Awful's!" and justify their common misery endlessly. On the other hand, if their victimhood is not aligned, they will get into contests. At first, both will try to justify their perspective and win; winning is defined as getting their adversary to agree with them. This adversarial positioning, "I'm right, you're wrong," will continue until one decides that the other is too obstinate or dumb to recognize a "well-explained reality." At that point, the contest continues, but the definition of winning changes from "I win, you lose," to "I'm going to make you lose worse than I do." The dynamics of a fair contest change to one of destroying the enemy. Mutually Destructive People in the Enemy group try to destroy one another.

The situation between the Proud Boys and Antifa exemplifies such a situation. At first, theirs was a contest of ideas between participants of differing points of view. Both tried to convince the other of the "truth" of their position. They failed to win. Now they see each other as enemies, with both groups' intending to damage or destroy the other. They are both hurting one another while contributing to self-mutualization. Yet they will both stay in the battle as long as they can inflict damage on their enemy. "Hurting you is worth the price of being hurt." That is the nature of the war between nations, between groups of people, and between individuals.

The sad thing is that we have a nation divided. There are people on both sides trying to win by convincing the other side of the "rightness" of their position. Neither seems to be capable of winning this way. Some have already shifted to the enemy approach and are trying to minimize or disempower their enemies. If everyone jumps into an enemy encampment, we will have a battle with the full intent to destroy one another, literally if not figuratively. That is a Mutually Destructive Relationship. Or said in another way, they are two mutually destructive groups in victim mode and they are problem-solving by trying to eliminate each other.

Mutually Destructive People's interactions with Synergistic People
As we have pointed out earlier, Mutually Destructive People look for people who will indulge them or solve their problems, and Synergistic People nurture people who need help. Therefore, we might assume that immediate bonding occurs between them at first glance. It is not quite like that; nurturing people empathize, they don't sympathize, and Mutually Destructive People want sympathy when they are in victim mode and affirmation when they feel good about themselves. Mutually Destructive People don't take responsibility or accountability for anything, including their negative feelings or adverse circumstances. Rather than doing so, they will blame others, make excuses, or deny that they have a problem. When a synergistic person listens, hears, understands, and validates their feelings, it feels good to a Mutually Destructive Person in victim mode. But, when the synergistic person tries to help them to help themselves, alarms start to go off in the victim's mind; they sense that the synergistic person is trying to get them to

assume responsibility for their condition and find their solution to their problems. The bonding process stops right there because the victim wants the synergistic person to inherit their problems and solve them. They get frustrated with the synergistic person because they won't sympathize, commiserate, or inherit their problems. Consequently, relationships between Mutually Destructive People and Synergistic People are disposed to be short-lived.

Mutually Destructive People often play the game of "Humpty Dumpty." The nursery rhyme goes like this: "Humpty Dumpty sat on a wall, Humpty Dumpty had a great fall. All the King's horses and all the King's men couldn't put Humpty together again." The Mutually Destructive Person's version goes like this: "Humpty Dumpty sat on a wall, Humpty Dumpty had a great fall. All the King's horses and all the King's men couldn't put **me** together again." A Mutually Destructive Person gets everyone around him to make suggestions to solve his problem. The Humpty Dumpty immediately shoots down each proposal until no more suggestions are forthcoming. He can then look at everyone with the justified conclusion: "You see, all of you together can't solve my problem." The game's payoff is that the victim has just justified his victimhood. Again, the conclusion confirms that it is never my fault. Not taking ownership of one's problems is self-destructive and a characteristic of self-victimhood. Self-justified victims want others to inherit their problems, but that won't happen with Synergistic helpers; they will help the victim help themselves – not what the victim is looking for.

Synergistic People operate in adult mode, and Mutually Destructive People operate in child mode. Consequently, their interactions are not aligned, so they end up as cross-transactional interactions. They don't work in a complementary way and constructive communications cease. Mutually Destructive People often look hopefully toward Synergistic People because they see them as successful and happy, everything they desire for themselves. They see them as people who can stroke them and solve their problems. Yet, the very nature of Synergistic People operating and staying in adult mode while analyzing problems and solving them rationally and logically doesn't work for Mutually Destructive People stuck in child mode. Mutually Destructive People often develop a pattern of moving from one Synergistic Person to another, hoping to find one who will save them (sympathize with them and inherit their problems). When Synergistic People don't inherit their problems or stroke their egos, the Mutually Destructive People often blame them for their adverse circumstances. "If you don't inherit my problem, then I'll blame you for it!"

If you are a parent, you have probably experienced the situation of children who go to dad to get something they want, and when dad doesn't give it to them, they go to mom. If mom also doesn't give it to them, they are mad at mom and dad and commiserate about their parents' being horrible people. That is what Mutually Destructive People often do with synergistic people.

If we make a side-by-side comparison of Synergistic people with Mutually Destructive people, in terms of life management skills, we see a dramatic difference. We will label the synergistic side as Achiever Mode and the mutually destructive side as Victim Mode.

Synergistic People		Mutually Destructive People
Achiever Mode	**Life Management Skills**	**Victim Mode**
Achievers have a clear and well-defined vision.	**Vision** The desired Future State	Victims have a vague or undefined vision.
Their mission aligns with the life vision	**Mission** The Ultimate Desired Outcome	Their mission is missing or misaligned with a life vision.
Their goals align with the life mission providing sequential steps for measuring progress and achieving the life mission.	**Goals** The Measurable Achievement Milestones to Achieve the mission	Victims' goals misalign with a life mission or is missing altogether. Victims focus on immediate wants, which are their only goals.
Achievers operate from well-defined unconditional standards used as the basis for decisions and actions in all situations.	**Values** The Standards for Personal Decisions and Actions	Victims operate from conditional values that change as circumstances change.
Achievers operate from internalized commitment and manage others to achieve internalized commitment.	**Commitment Level** The Operational Level of Commitment	Victims operate from compliance when seeking security. They display covert disobedience, overt disobedience, or rebellion when not getting what they want.
Achievers use synergistic power combined with circumstantial power to achieve mutually beneficial outcomes.	**Power** The Kind of Power Used with Others to Get Things Accomplished	Victims use dominant power combined with circumstantial power to achieve self-serving outcomes.
Achievers take personal accountability for making decisions and taking action. Seeks for the freedom to make more and bigger decisions.	**Responsibility** Where the Decision-Making Authority Resides	Victims avoid being responsible for decisions or actions that would result in personal accountability or involve a personal risk.
Achievers are personally answerable for decisions, actions, and outcomes originating from their own decisions and actions.	**Accountability** The Personal Ownership Taken for The Outcomes of Personal Actions and Decisions	Victims take personal credit for positive outcomes and transfer the blame to others for adverse outcomes.
Achievers are free to make decisions independently because of trustworthiness. Achievers are proactive.	**Decision Making Style** The Approach to Decision Making	Victims avoid making decisions but seek direction. They will be compliant to avoid risks. Victims are reactive.

24

BEHAVIORAL ADDICTIONS

Stompers, Stompees, and Mutually Destructive people frequently become behaviorally addicted to their actions in interactions with others. Just as an alcoholic becomes dependent on alcohol to function, they become dependent on behavioral addictions.

All addictions share three components:

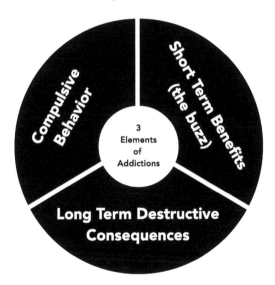

1) Compulsive behavior

Compulsive behavior is when a person is inwardly driven or compelled to do it. It is an action used so repeatedly that it becomes central to their methodology in interacting with people. Let's look at "nagging" as an example. Most of us know people in our life who are naggers. They persist in continuous faultfinding, complaining, or demanding to the point that it becomes very annoying to the people nagged.

2) Short-term benefit

A short-term benefit is what we like to call a "buzz." If you drink, then you recognize what an alcohol buzz is. If you are a nagger, you realize there can be several nagging buzzes (short-term benefits); nagging releases emotional tension (on the other hand, it creates it with the nagged people). Sometimes it provides a personal win; the nagged person does the nagger's bidding. It allows the nagger to project power and dominion over those they pester.

3) Long-term destructive consequences

The long-term negative consequences of chemical addictions like alcohol, heroin, or crack are well known. The adverse health ramifications are horrible, and the social and relationship costs are staggering. The long-term destructive consequences of nagging are sad. Naggers tend to drive people away from them. They lose their ability to influence people because the people they nag build up a tolerance to their nagging, so it does not affect them; when they try to nag more, it simply magnifies the negative consequences.

We have a concise definition of "Addiction" by putting all three components together. **Addiction is a compulsive behavior that provides short-term benefits and long-term destructive consequences.**

Behavioral addictions are part of the character and behaviors of the unhealthy life-boundary-conditions. Again, let's examine the typical behaviors that characterize Stompers, Stompees, and Mutually Destructive People. We can see how their compulsive behavior provides short-term buzzes and long-term negative consequences.

Below is the model listing the typical behavior of Synergistic People, Stompers, Stompees, and Mutually Destructive People. As you recall, we had you check the behaviors listed in each category that you have done recently. As you look at the behaviors, you might consider if you are behaviorally addicted to those checked behaviors in certain circumstances and situations.

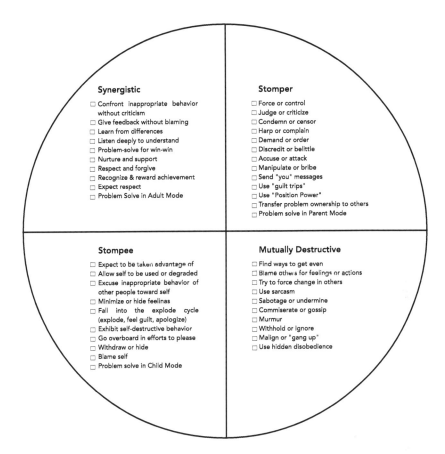

Synergistic
- ☐ Confront inappropriate behavior without criticism
- ☐ Give feedback without blaming
- ☐ Learn from differences
- ☐ Listen deeply to understand
- ☐ Problem-solve for win-win
- ☐ Nurture and support
- ☐ Respect and forgive
- ☐ Recognize & reward achievement
- ☐ Expect respect
- ☐ Problem Solve in Adult Mode

Stomper
- ☐ Force or control
- ☐ Judge or criticize
- ☐ Condemn or censor
- ☐ Harp or complain
- ☐ Demand or order
- ☐ Discredit or belittle
- ☐ Accuse or attack
- ☐ Manipulate or bribe
- ☐ Send "you" messages
- ☐ Use "guilt trips"
- ☐ Use "Position Power"
- ☐ Transfer problem ownership to others
- ☐ Problem solve in Parent Mode

Stompee
- ☐ Expect to be taken advantage of
- ☐ Allow self to be used or degraded
- ☐ Excuse inappropriate behavior of other people toward self
- ☐ Minimize or hide feelings
- ☐ Fall into the explode cycle (explode, feel guilt, apologize)
- ☐ Exhibit self-destructive behavior
- ☐ Go overboard in efforts to please
- ☐ Withdraw or hide
- ☐ Blame self
- ☐ Problem solve in Child Mode

Mutually Destructive
- ☐ Find ways to get even
- ☐ Blame others for feelings or actions
- ☐ Try to force change in others
- ☐ Use sarcasm
- ☐ Sabotage or undermine
- ☐ Commiserate or gossip
- ☐ Murmur
- ☐ Withhold or ignore
- ☐ Malign or "gang up"
- ☐ Use hidden disobedience

For all the checked items, we also asked you to identify the circumstances when you used them and with whom you use them. People are surprised when they examine themselves regarding behavioral addictions because everyone finds that they have them. People often realize that they use Stomper behavioral addictions to govern their children. Leaders in businesses or professional organizations usually recognize that they have grown dependent on Stomper's behaviors. More than once, I have had managers try and convince me that, in certain situations, Stomper behaviors are essential and are the only reasonable or practical approach to deal with "certain people." I usually just respond that, for them, that might be true. They just need to recognize that they don't know, or haven't yet developed, more effective synergistic ways to deal with those circumstances or "certain people."

Some people are not happy to see themselves as addicts to Stomper or Stompee behaviors. Others, only confidentially, admit to Mutually Destructive addictions. Despite our aversion to recognizing them or acknowledging that we have them, behavioral addictions exist all around us. They contribute significantly to defining our cultures. Of course, other things like traditions, values, and history also contribute. Still, organizations' operational and cultural low points are manifest in the behavioral addictions used to manage their organizations. If we recognize and remove our Stomper, Stompee, or Mutually Destructive behavioral addictions, we change our culture and become more synergistic.

Have you identified any behavioral addictions in your personal, people-manager toolbox? Before you wipe your brow and sigh in relief because you determined yourself to be sans-addiction, you need to test each checkmark against these four criteria that people use to refute their addiction or multiple addictions. See if you use these mind tricks to deny an addiction and justify the behavior.

The four ways people refute that they have an addiction:

1) Denial

The most actively enslaved dependent people deny their addiction or dependence. "I'm not an alcoholic." "I'm not a drug addict." "I'm not a Stomper; I can quit doing it anytime I want to. I just don't want to right now."

2) Justification

The reason for justification is: What I can justify, I can keep. When I justify my addictions, I don't need to change; I get to keep doing what I do. "Wayne, you have to admit that Stomper behavior is necessary for some situations with 'certain people!'" No, I don't! People justify their addictions, so they can keep doing them. By the way, their justifications don't need to make sense to anyone except themselves. I love the rationale that a four-pack-a-day smoker gave me to justify his smoking: "You have a greater chance of dying from a car accident than I do from smoking!" I know. There is no logic or connection between smoking and car accidents, and his statement seems ridiculous. It doesn't matter because it makes sense to him.

3) Projection, transference, and deflection

Projection, transference, and deflection are three ways people shift problem ownership or responsibility and accountability for their behaviors to others. In other words, "I don't have the problem; you have the problem." Or they have the problem. "You are aware that Jane is the real alcoholic here." Can you see the projection and transference taking place here? "Talking about stomping, did you see what the Cubs did to the White Sox?" In this quote, the person deflects the behavioral addiction (of stomping) by redirecting the issue to baseball. I'm amazed at politicians' projection, transference, and deflection skills. They are masters of shifting responsibility and accountability away from themselves to others and, in doing so, continue to do what they have been doing. Many should be awarded advanced degrees in projection, transference, and deflection.

4) Excuses, blaming, and rationalization

Excuse making, blaming, and rationalization are forms of justification; but then again, they are specific behaviors that people use to defend their behavior and protect their addictions; each deserves examination.

Excuses are the explanations offered by others to justify their actions or remove responsibility or accountability for their actions. I don't know about you, but excuses don't make me feel great about sub-standard performance. When I get excuses from someone who failed to deliver what they had promised me, I'm prone to say something like: "You know excuses don't make me feel better that you haven't delivered what was agreed, but an explanation might help." I don't feel terrific when people make excuses for their behavioral addictions, either.

Blaming is finding that the fault or the reason for the behavior lies with others, thus releasing me from the responsibility and accountability for the behaviors and consequences while, at the same time, enabling me to continue doing them. "Look at what you made me do!" I find it distasteful when an abuser blames others for justifying his abuse of his children or his wife.

Rationalizations ascribe the reasons for one's actions to causes or circumstances that justify the actions. "Given the circumstances, it seemed like the right thing to do." "I believe that if you were in my shoes, you would have knocked your wife unconscious just like I did mine." Of course, the intended message is: "Can't you see how reasonable my actions are?"

We are reviewing behavioral addictions in this book about interpersonal relations and relationships because behavioral addictions are all around us and inhibit Synergistic Relationships. We need to know what behavioral addictions are, how they negatively impact us, if we have any, and what we can do to get rid of them. We need to eliminate them from our families and organizations and replace them with healthy behavioral interactions.

We need to understand two concepts to make healthy changes:
First: **The Stages of Behavioral Change**
Second: **Treating Behavioral Addictions**

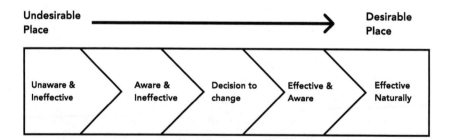

The stages of Behavioral Change

As with any change, we must go through various levels of awareness and success to eliminate behavioral addictions and replace them with synergistic behaviors. Understanding these stages can help us manage the difficulty of change. There are five stages of behavioral change:

First Stage: Unaware and ineffective

In this stage, people do not understand their behavioral addictions and the long-term negative impact on their lives. In this stage, people don't know what their behavioral addictions are, the ones that are causing them to be ineffective in their interpersonal interactions. They have no clue that they even have behavioral addictions. Most times, they look for the cause of inadequate interpersonal connections beyond themselves. At any rate, they are ignorant of how and why their behavior is causing problems.

Second Stage: Aware and ineffective

In this stage, a person has become knowledgeable about behavioral addictions, how they are used, who is using them, and the negative consequences they are producing. At least now, there is an awareness of the cause-and-effect impact of known behavioral addictions.

Third Stage: Decision to change

This is a critical stage because what happens here will determine if people move forward or stay where they are. It is an intimidating place because it requires that people face reality and truth. It is the stage where they will encounter all of the reasons and justifications for not changing – denial that they need to change and the rationale to keep doing what they are doing now. Here they will encounter the projection, transference, and deflection that will try and convince them that they aren't the ones needing change. Here, they have to face and reject the notion that other people have the problem and should change. "I don't have a problem; it is other people's problem; let them deal with it." In this stage, they will experience excuses, blaming, and rationalizations for not changing. In short, we will witness that people will do whatever they have to do to protect their behavioral addictions. It is not an easy stage, but it is essential. We will not progress or change until we decide and commit to do what we have to do to change. It is essential for becoming a synergistic person who can develop synergistic relationships. It requires courage, decisions, and a genuine commitment to decisions made.

Fourth Stage: Effective and aware

In this stage, we replace harmful behavioral addictions with healthy synergistic behaviors. Change decisions happen in the conscious mind, managed by our adult mode. Our adult mode is our change agent. Here, we behave effectively and synergistically by making ongoing conscious choices. In this stage, we are dependent on our conscious mind to control our behavior and decisions. We will stay in this stage as long as our adult mode is actively engaged in our choices. Suppose we disengage our conscious mind before it has formed new habits (internalized synergistic behaviors). In that case, our subconscious mind will take over and move us back to the old ineffective behavioral addictions.

Fifth Stage: Effective and natural (unconscious effectiveness)

In this stage, we have internalized the synergistic behaviors and can use them without conscious effort. Here the new behavior recordings have replaced the old behavior recordings in our subconscious mind. In short, we are no longer who we were before we changed.

The thing that excites me is that people can change. Stompees can transform from a Stompee existence to a Synergistic life. Stompees certainly have reasons to do so. Stompers can change, too. If they are successful Stompers, they may lack the motivation to do so, but change is possible if they choose to do so. The people on whom they stomp would undoubtedly wish they would.

The five stages of behavioral change could be called a change system or a process. Within the system or process of the five stages of change, another vital system is the Three Necessary Elements for Treating Behavioral Addictions.

As an analogy, think of the human body as a system comprised of other necessary and functional systems that enable the body to function and prosper. The human body is a system that includes the skeletal system, the endocrine system, the central nervous system, the gastrointestinal system, the cardiovascular system, etc. Each plays a vital part in the well-being of the human body. We can't live without all of them. The

Three Necessary Elements for Treating Behavioral Addictions are necessary to support the five stages of change.

The Three Necessary Elements for Treating Behavioral Addictions

The only person who can successfully overcome a behavioral addiction is the person with the addiction. We can't force change (the more significant the force, the greater the counterforce and resistance). Efforts by outside parties to change or to fix an addicted individual are minimally effective. For people to change, they must decide to change (Third Stage). They must personally manage three elements of addiction treatment. We can support their decisions for change, but we can never make the change happen.

Element One: Why I love the addiction

An addict must understand and have intimate knowledge of the addiction's power over them. They need awareness, understanding, and acceptance that the addiction provides them short-term benefits (real buzzes) that reinforce the addiction. It motivates them to keep coming back. I know that all addictions, including behavioral addictions, eventually become chemical addictions. At that point, the chemical makes the decisions and not the frontal cortex. And yet even here, when the chemical is in the driver's seat, there is the rational part of us that seeks help to survive. If we decide to change before it becomes a chemical dependency, we have better chances for successful changes. Fortunately, behavioral addictions do not frequently fit into the category of chemical dependencies, although they may lead to them. In short, **we must understand why we love the behavioral addictions that enslave us.**

Element Two: A better alternative

We won't change if we don't have a Synergistic replacement for the Stomper, Stompee, or Mutually Destructive addictions. Sometimes people don't have a better alternative, so they just repress the ones they don't want. That doesn't work, long-term. A law in physics describes the need for vacuums to be filled. That also applies to behavioral addiction vacuums created by repression. I read, or heard, somewhere in my psychology explorations that "repressed feelings eventually come out like a lion in the night to bite us in the butt." It sounds like something Bob Carkhuff would say, but I don't want to give him credit or blame. The point is that **repressing or stopping behavioral addictions "cold turkey" without replacing them with an appropriate alternative won't work long term**.

I had a couple of middle-aged parents who came to see me with their 40- ear-old son, who was addicted to cocaine. They wanted my assistance to help them, help him. Their son had a wife and two children who had kicked him out of their lives until he was "rehabilitated." When asked what steps he had taken toward rehabilitation, he didn't have much to share. That being the case, I wanted to know what his plan was going forward? He said that he had given all his money to his parents so that he wouldn't have the funds to buy cocaine. I concluded (correctly) that his plan and intent was to make his parents responsible and accountable to manage his addiction – if he got high again, they were responsible. Of course, he said that was not his intention but admitted it was true when he thought about it. I told them to give him his money back because his plan wouldn't work; he would find other ways to fund his addiction, and they would be the "fall guys" when he got high again.

His parents asked me tearfully what they could do. I told them to love him unconditionally but not enable his self-destructive behaviors. Then I told them: "Whether he lives or dies is not your decision. You cannot change the consequences of his poor decisions; you only speed up the pace at which they happen if you enable him." Then I said to him: "You have to decide whether you want to live or die, and you need to make that decision while it is still yours to make." Then I ask him:" What do you have to live for? What is the higher purpose that would motivate you to give up cocaine?" His eyes swelled up, and he said, "My kids."

We discussed the three elements for treating addiction in detail, and he left with the idea of coming and seeing me in a week or so. When he came back, he was excited to tell me that he had come to realize why he loved cocaine and the power it had over him. I congratulated him for giving up cocaine and asked him what he had chosen as the better alternative. He said: "Beer!" I asked him if he was sure that was a better alternative? He responded that it was a heck of a lot cheaper. I shook my head and explained that he had traded one addictive drug for another addictive drug and that he still got a drug buzz; while different from the cocaine buzz, it was still a chemical buzz and that beer was not a healthy alternative to cocaine. This story could go on and on. I just wanted to make the point about a "better alternative." You will be happy to know that he and his family reunited a year and a half later after he had not used addictive substances for a year. He was amazingly fit when I last saw him; he was now addicted to extreme physical exercise.

By the way, an acceptable alternative to Stomper, Stompee behavior, or Mutually Destructive behavior doesn't come from picking another activity in the same Life Boundary Condition list or one from another unhealthy condition; only from behaviors in the Synergistic area.

Element Three: Gotta Wanna
The motivation for change must be strong enough to endure the withdrawal symptoms (the loss of the benefits and the buzz) that happen

when the behavioral addiction is gone. Tony Robbins has a famous quote that says: "Change happens when the pain of staying the same is greater than the pain of change." If we don't have sufficient desire, we won't get past the Third Stage. Different people are motivated to change for various reasons. There is not a magic formula that inspires everyone to change. No one-size-fits-all motivation is available. Generally speaking, people will be motivated to change for four reasons: Sufficient pain and discomfort; extreme, unrelenting boredom; fear; or to fulfill a higher purpose. My 40-year-old cocaine addict friend's motivation was his kids, wife, parents, and a vision of unified, loving family life. I know people who changed because they knew they would die if they didn't change, and they decided to live. I have a highly educated and successful cousin who moved to Africa to help people he had grown to love there build profitable businesses for their families and community. I guess that fits into the higher purpose category. **The point is that the "Gotta Wanna" has to be strong enough to take us through all five stages of change.**

I have been following a consultant hired to help a manager change. The manager is highly intelligent and knowledgeable about his discipline. He has a lot of relationship issues with his employees and other colleagues with whom he interacts. His boss made an ultimatum to change his relationships or lose his position. I have watched him as he is going through the change process. He has moved into the Third Stage of the change process. He is deciding if he wants to change. He certainly wants to keep his position and improve his relationships, but it is uncertain if he wants to change himself.

He is a Stomper trying to act like a friend and partner. To some, his new behavior feels like an act. He admits that sometimes it is an act. He has shared his opinion with the consultant that, down deep, he doesn't believe that he has a problem. He knows that he is good at his specialty and believes that the people who work with him should learn to, "Suck it up." I suspect that he learned that his safety and security became his responsibility early in life because no one else provided it for him. As a result, he found that power and taking control provided the only way to feel safe and secure: "I am only secure when I have absolute control." The decision to change is a real problem because to change and to be able to have authentic Synergistic Relationships, he will have to rely on others for his safety and security. Change means he will have to let go of the way he learned to feel safe and secure – through dominance and by taking control.

He has been exploring alternative behaviors that would be more acceptable to those he interacts with. He is using some of these "better alternatives." He is trying to act more cooperatively. But since people have negative expectations of him, his behavior is met with mixed reactions. Some are pleased; others are skeptical; and others don't believe his behaviors are sincere and sustainable. Their reactions cause him some confusion and make it even more challenging to commit to personal change. He now better understands his behavioral addictions and their impact on others and himself. Still, it is not certain that his desire to change is significant enough to commit 100% to becoming a Synergistic person who can build and sustain Synergistic Relationships. He is in a challenging situation, and his choices are difficult. I hope he can hook his adult mode and find safety and security in becoming a person who can have and sustain Synergistic Relationships. Ironically, he could use his discipline expertise even more effectively as a Synergistic person.

Some Summary Points about Personal Boundaries
- Personal boundaries are the defenses, protections, or space we place around us to protect ourselves.
- They are an integral part of our self-identity; they define how we see ourselves and expect others to treat us.
- Personal boundaries formed when we were very young and continue to develop through life experiences as we age.
- Our personal boundaries are manifest in Life Mode Conditions, namely:
  - o The Synergistic Life Mode is where our boundaries are respected, and we respect the boundaries of others.
  - o The Stomper Life Mode is where our boundaries are respected but not the boundaries of others.

- o The Stompee Life Mode is where others' boundaries are respected but not our boundaries.
- o The Mutually Destructive Life Mode is where no one respects boundaries.
- The Life Boundary Condition from which people operate determines how they interact with others and the relationships developed.
- How Synergistic Life Mode People (Achievers) see the world and operate differs dramatically from Stomper, Stompee, and Mutually Destructive Life Mode People (Victims or Victimizers).
- People become addicted to Stomper, Stompee, and Mutually Destructive behaviors.
- Behavioral addictions have three characteristics: Compulsive behavior, short-term benefits (buzzes), and long-term negative consequences.
- People can treat and overcome addiction. People can change.
- Personal change has five Stages:
  - o The unaware and ineffective stage
  - o The aware and ineffective stage
  - o The decision to change or not change stage
  - o The aware and effective stage
  - o The unaware and effective stage
- Three elements must exist within the addict to enter the stages of change:
  - o The addict must understand and come to know why they love the addiction.
  - o They must have a healthy alternative to replace the behavioral addiction.
  - o They "gotta wanna" – they need to desire to change.
- By engaging their adult mode, they can internalize the three elements of behavioral addiction and enter into the stages of change. They can move from an unhealthy Life Boundary Condition to a healthy Synergistic Life Boundary Condition. It is a choice we make.

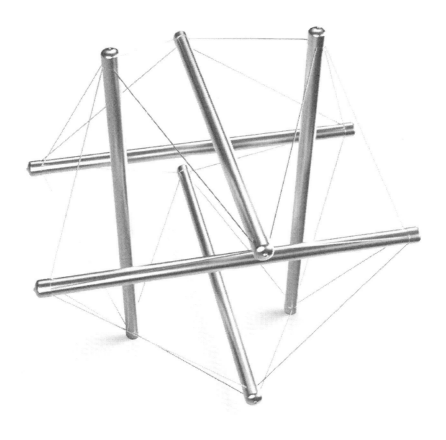

25

Introduction to Power

Power is the ability to act personally or to influence or to control the actions of others. Power has multiple aspects that make it worthwhile to study and to understand. People use power for self-interest and to benefit others. It may be used to achieve beautiful things or for destructive purposes. There are different kinds of power, and that is where we will begin our review.

The different kinds of power

There are two general categories of Power: Agency Power and Circumstantial Power. Agency Power is a choice we make, whereas Circumstantial Power comes to us from the conditions or situations we live in. When combined with agency power, circumstantial powers create many available power options. The combination of circumstantial and agency power magnifies the effect of the chosen agency power. This combined power is the catalyst for actions that deliver outcomes. The combined powers either support healthy relationships or produce unhealthy ones. This will become clearer as we understand what agency and circumstantial power are, how we can use them, and their impact.

Agency Power (Powers by Choice)

Two types of agency power sit on opposite ends of a spectrum. We get to choose which one we will use, hence the term: Agency Power. Imagine you are a parent of a 14-year-old daughter, and you realize how important it is for her to do well in school. Left to her own devices, she would spend most of her time on her phone and not do her homework. As a parent, what do you do?

Scenario One

You decide to implement strict school rules out of deep concern for your daughter's future: your daughter will do homework before any other activities, school attendance is mandatory, and there are penalties for not following the rules. No one would argue that you are doing this from a deep sense of love and concern.

Scenario Two

Out of deep concern for your daughter's future, you decide to sit down with your daughter and find out how she feels about school and homework and how it fits within her priorities of life. You trust her to use her adult mode to prioritize her most essential activities and what takes precedence in her decisions and actions. Then, you would guide her and help her understand other necessary things besides studying and homework. During the conversation, you work together to find time for these things.

The first scenario is an example of Dominance Power. It has some nice upsides: homework gets done, and she attends school. The issue of where she will focus her attention is quickly decided by the dad, and potential school problems will be avoided. The downside is this: although the parent may be feeling he is using love to help his daughter, the daughter does not feel loved or respected. She feels controlled. The natural response to being controlled is to push back against the control. If we use dominant power, we can expect covert or overt disobedience from those controlled.

The second scenario is an example of Synergistic Power. It has some nice upsides: homework gets done and school is attended, all by the daughter's choice rather than by the parent's compulsion. In the process, the child feels loved, valued, and respected. The downside is that this approach takes time, but loving parents spend time with their kids. Right? Parents who care, listen to their kids; and when they are hurting, they suffer with them. The child notices this and feels loved, valued, and respected.

In summary, Dominance Power is trying to get results through force which (unknowingly perhaps) trades desired results for expressions of love, value, and respect. While the intent may be to get positive outcomes from the other party, the recipient does not feel valued or respected. Synergistic power is hooking the adult mode of others to help them make wise decisions that benefit them while sending the message of love, value, and respect.

While the nature of Synergistic Power and Dominance power may be familiar to everyone because we see them used around us all the time, the consequence of their impact on people, relationships, organizations, and society may not be so obvious. Hopefully, you will sense what I mean when we add descriptive adjectives to each kind of power.

Synergistic Power Adjectives	Dominance Power Adjectives
Influencing	Controlling
Persuasive	Directing
Compassionate	Forcing
Empathic	Ordering
Understanding	Demanding
Supportive	Intimidating
Loving	Manipulating
Caring	Compulsory
Concerned	Self-serving
Kind	Leveraging
Sharing decision making	Advantage-taking
Being inclusive	Centralized decision making
Teaching	Being exclusive
Charismatic	Bossing
Patient	Stomping
Long-suffering	Blaming
Nurturing	Attacking
Focusing on internalized commitment	Focusing on compliance or obedience
Accepting personal responsibility and accountability	Taking authority
	Deflecting accountability away from self

As you can see, people can choose the type of agency power they use, with all its accompanying adjectives. Which kind of power would you choose to manage other people? If you had to choose to work for a manager who uses Synergistic or Dominance power, which would you choose? I suppose some would choose Dominance power, but if they did, I would have to ask them: "What in the hell is the matter with you?!"

But before we get into the impact each has on creating cultural climates, let's examine Circumstantial powers because environments are created by combining agency powers with Circumstantial powers. We want to understand what happens when we add Circumstantial powers to Synergistic powers and what happens when we add Circumstantial powers to Dominance power.

Circumstantial Powers are the dynamic powers derived by chance, providence, or preparation.

We derive circumstantial powers from various environmental conditions, like having the only freshwater spring in a desert. Others come to us from the situations we create, like getting a good education. Some we inherit, like wealth or position. Indeed, the Crown Princes and Princesses in England may be competent people, but royal status came from royal birth. Their position power was not a choice; it became theirs by circumstances of being the offspring of a queen. Whether they are good, bad, intelligent, dumb, capable, or incapable, it doesn't matter; they have position power. If their kingdom is overthrown or disbanded, circumstances will change, and so will their position power. Circumstantial power is dynamic; it changes as circumstances change. People can have tons of circumstantial power in one situation and zero in another.

I'm not sure that we can even list all the potential Circumstantial powers because so many different circumstances exist. Every situation has the potential of creating Circumstantial power. Circumstances give some power and take power away from others. For example, elections give one-party political power while taking it away from the other party. But let's list some of the more obvious Circumstantial powers that we would all recognize, like position power, information power, knowledge power, emotional intelligence power, ethical power, and relationship (connections) power. Let's examine each in a little more detail.

The Common Six Circumstantial Powers
Position Power
Information Power
Knowledge Power
Emotional Intelligence Power
Moral/Ethical Power
Connections Power

By the way, with few exceptions, everyone has some types and degrees of circumstantial power. Combining that power with synergy power or dominance power will determine the relationships surrounding them.

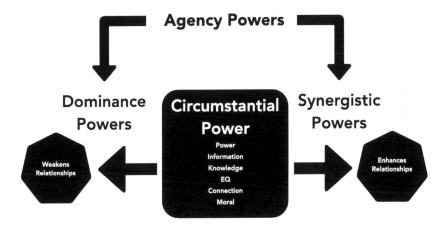

26

POSITION POWER

Position power could be described as hierarchical power, meaning the higher we are on the totem pole, the more power we have, and the lower we are on the totem pole, the less power we have. We also call it Authority power, as determined by the degree of freedom we have to make decisions without permission from others. Status within most organizations, or groups, is directly proportional to position power, although position power is not the only thing that determines organizational status. Status also comes from other situations we will review later. Generally speaking, the higher the position, the greater the power, and the greater the power, the greater the status.

A unique thing about position power is the ability to delegate decision-making power to others. People can delegate 100% of their decision-making power if they choose to, although most people delegate only a portion of it. Wise people who combine Position power with Synergistic power realize that they can multiply their influence by delegating it. They understand that the power they delegate does not diminish their power but multiplies it. Selfish people who combine their Position power with Dominance power see power as a limited resource. They see the power delegated as power taken from them, so they delegate only a tiny portion of their power. Let's look at two managers, one who sees power as something multiplied when delegated and the other who sees their power diminished when delegating. They both have four employees.

Helen, the power multiplier, gives the employee she trusts the most, Jack, 90% of her decision-making authority. She delegates 80% of her decision-making authority to Jane; she trusts her but not quite as much as she trusts Jack. Helen gives Alice 50% because Alice is pretty new has limited experience, and Helen wants to stretch her while still limiting her risk if Alice makes a poor decision. She delegates Rodrigues 40% because he is less secure about himself, and giving him too much decision-making power would make him anxious and insecure. Still, she wants to move him along without unnerving him. If you have been adding up the total percentage of decision-making authority that Helen has delegated, you see that it comes up to 260%. When added to her 100% decision-making authority, it totals 360%, 260% more than her starting point. She has increased her power from 100% to 360% by combining her Synergistic power with her Position power. Everyone wins in this situation (providing they all make good decisions).

On the other hand, Robert sees his decision-making authority as a limited resource. He thinks that when he delegates decision-making power to others, it takes it away from himself. Robert decides that delegation is a good thing but needs to be carefully managed, like stock ownership. He decides to keep, at minimum, 51% of his authority to maintain control. His most trusted employee, his backup, George, gets 25% of his decision-making power. He reasons that he still has 24% to delegate and still maintain 51% control, so with his remaining employees, he delegates 10% to Jay, 5% to Ellen, and 5% to Estelle. He feels pretty good because he has increased his decision-making power by 44% while maintaining control. He feels proud of himself because he still has 56% of his decision-making power. He delegated 4% less than he anticipated delegating, which increased his margin of control. The decision-making power delegated when combined with his totals 144% decision-making power. Combining his Dominance power with his Position power has increased his decision-making power from 100% to 144%. Not bad, he thinks to himself, with a little pat on his own back.

We have two managers with the same number of people and decision-making power. Both have an equal opportunity to impact the results of the company. But, Helen has multiplied her decision-making power to 360%, whereas Robert increased his to 144%. Who do you think will benefit the company, the employees, and themselves the most? I suspect that Helen's status will rise in the company faster and higher than Robert's will. I also believe that Helen will create more Synergistic Relationships than Robert will.

Position power also provides the ability to transfer accountability to others. Synergistic power managers combine Position power with their Synergistic power, as we have discussed above. Still, they never deflect or transfer accountability to others for the consequences of poor decisions made by themselves or by the people who report to them. They are quick to give credit and approbation to others for great results. Still, they never step aside from the accountability for poor consequences flowing from decisions made by people to whom they have delegated decision-making power. Can you see how this engenders Synergistic Relationships?

Dominance power managers who combine their Dominance power with Position power too frequently step out of the line of fire for accountability for poor outcomes. They tend to be quick to blame poor results on the people who report to them, whether or not they made the decision resulting in poor results. They do so because they can. "Better you be blamed and held accountable than me." Here, too, they, far too frequently, take credit for the good results flowing from wise decisions, whether or not their employee made the wise decision. The philosophy that "Glory rolls up and shit rolls down" indicates managers who combine Dominance power with Position power. As you can surmise, they tend to generate Stomper, Stompee, and Mutually Destructive Life Boundary Conditions. As you can recall, these three conditions do not align with Synergistic Relationships.

People can benefit themselves and others immensely by learning how to wrestle decision-making power away from those with Position power and Dominance decision-making power. Arlene met with me in my office shortly after earning her bachelor's degree in Marketing from Rutgers University in Piscataway, NJ. She was frustrated and wanted to let off some steam and air her complaint about the lack of opportunity at Janssen Pharmaceutica. In her early thirties, Arlene had sandy-colored hair was attractive, intelligent, and ambitious. She told me that she was pissed off because she had spent five years working full-time at Janssen and attending school part-time to get an education that would enable her to get a responsible position in marketing at a good company. "Why do I have to go to another company to get promoted after getting my degree?" She was an exempt professional in the clinical research department. The department director was a fellow named Don, who was in his early forties. He had bags under his eyes derived from long days of demanding deadlines to produce analyzed and vetted clinical research results used in FDA drug applications. I knew he was overextended; it was tough to get time with him, and his exhaustion was manifest physically.

I told Arlene that I was disappointed that she felt it necessary to seek an opportunity elsewhere, especially knowing that Don needed all the expertise and help that he could get. She explained that a big part of her frustration was that Don needed the help and didn't reach out to her. Before she sent out her resume, I suggested that she propose to Don to take some of the burdens from him and that doing so would benefit both of them. Amazingly, she asked me: "How do I do that?" I asked her: "How much of Don's job can you do as well as he can?" She said: "Half of it." I asked her: "Does he know that?" Her response: "He should; I have worked in his department for five years." I gently responded to her jab: "Well, he is probably focused on other things and hasn't taken the time to analyze all the options around him. But what would happen if you scheduled a meeting with him with the purpose being to suggest ways to improve his work life and departmental productivity?" She liked the suggestion. I advised that when she met with him, she did not accuse, attack, or blame him for her lack of opportunities but rather let him know that she noticed the pressure he was under and wanted to help. I recommended that she explain the parts of Don's job that she could do perfectly that would allow him to focus on other things. I cautioned her not to use the "trust me, I can do it" pitch but to explain how giving her the opportunity was zero risk because Don would be able to review and sign off on all her projects before they left his department. As a result, she, Don, the department, and Janssen would benefit from him giving her more responsibility.

As I explained, Arlene was intelligent and ambitious. She set up a meeting with Don a few days later. She went into the meeting well prepared. She came out of the meeting with responsibility for nearly everything she asked for. She marched directly into my office to announce her victory with Don and get a little praise. A few months later, she was promoted and became a new manager within the Clinical Research Department. She never forgot the lesson learned and continued to draw more responsibility from Don. She helped Don do a better job and expand his impact on Janssen and the industry. Approximately two years after her promotion to be a departmental manager, Don was spirited away by an executive recruiter to become the Vice President of Clinical Research for another pharmaceutical company. As you might have guessed, Arlene took his spot as Director of Clinical Research.

At the Janssen Pharmaceutica headquarters in New Jersey, we regularly met as a human resources management group to discuss how and to whom we could delegate more decision-making power. We found that people wanted as much authority as they could handle, and they sought opportunities to take on more responsibility. As they took on more, their ability to handle it grew as well. It became a process for personal development and for promoting capable people. People started asking for and getting more authority, and when they had shown that they could do the expanded job well, we promoted them. Within a couple of years, the rest of the Janssen departments adopted our take on more responsibility, do it well, and get promoted system. We had a compensation manager named Cathy Combs, who became the most knowledgeable person in our industry about job content, responsibilities, and compensation. She incorporated those three things plus performance to determine justified promotions and appropriate compensation packages. She had the decision-making power to review people's jobs and decide if their responsibilities and decision-making had grown to the level to justify promotion and an equivalent pay increase. Of course, she reviewed people's performance with their supervisors to ensure exceptional performance before she proposed and defended a promotion.

We would talk with individuals and groups within the company and explain how to optimize their opportunities and benefit themselves, their supervisor, their department, and the company by taking on more responsibility and accountability on the job – just as happened with Arlene. A typical discussion with someone would go kind of like this:

"So what parts of your supervisor's job can you do as well as she can?

Their responses varied, but it was usually a high percentage. "I can do this part of my supervisor's job well."

"OK, so why don't you go and talk with her? Tell her about how you can improve her life by giving you that part of her job. Be sure to point out that giving you that part of her job frees her to be able to do other things and expand her impact on the company."

It was magical for the employees, the managers, the departments, and the company. Our "take on more responsibility, do it well and get promoted system" produced dramatic results. Within three years, we had more people moving from non-exempt to exempt positions by more than three times the number (as a percentage of employee head-count) than any other company within Johnson & Johnson. Minorities at Janssen benefited greatly from this approach. They earned more significant promotions at Janssen than in any other well-established company within the tri-state area of New Jersey, New York, and Penn-sylvania. Of course, our success included people at all levels within Janssen.

At first, our system was criticized and bad-mouthed by human resource executives from other J&J companies. One VP of HR from a large sister company told me that I should be ashamed of myself for using people by expecting more from them without rewarding them upfront with a pay increase and a promotion. I responded by telling him that their standard practice of paying and promoting upfront placed people at risk because they were often promoted beyond their ability. When people can't demonstrate the ability to perform well in their new role, their careers stall, or they dismiss them for sub-performance. I stated the old saying that, "People rise to their level of incompetence," which is the situation they create by promoting people before they know they can perform well in the elevated position. As a result, while loving promotions, people become tentative about taking on additional duties or making higher-impact decisions. Our approach reduced the risk for them and the company while giving them the opportunity and incentives to expand, grow, and prosper. By the way, this approach, combined with Cathy's skills, kept us exactly where we wanted to be relative to our competitive pay levels. Once Janssen became known for opportunities and excellent pay, talent sought us out.

Combining Position power with Synergistic power and using them wisely can bless the lives of everyone involved.

You might find it interesting to learn how helpful Don was to me while taking calculus and statistics classes required to enroll into the Executive MBA programs at Columbia and Rutgers, where I had applied and was accepted. I was a VP at Janssen but felt that I needed an MBA, which my president thought was stupid regarding my career at J&J. Anyway, I signed up for summer classes in calculus and statistics at Rutgers. My statistics class had a brilliant Indian graduate student teaching it (I assume he was brilliant, but I couldn't understand what he was talking about). He lectured for three hours straight, two times each week. I left each class with a headache and feeling like the dumbest person alive. One day at lunch, I mentioned to Don my struggle with statistics. He said, "Will you let me help you? I am good at statistics, and I think that I can help you love it." I don't know where he found the time, but we met in the evenings after my statistics classes, and he would explain everything in 90 minutes that I was supposed to have learned in the three-hour statistics class but didn't. Even with his help, I struggled with statistics. (If you put lipstick on a pig, it is still a pig. I was still a statistics dummy.) I passed the course because on the day of the final, the graduate school professor, fearful that half the class would fail the course, walked silently among the test takers and provided tips on which formula to use with specific problems. He steered me to the right formula for several questions. I got a B in both calculus and statistics and immediately put both subjects out of my mind, never being used or approached again.

Making a case for "Trust" versus "Risk" proposals

You may find it helpful to get more detail about the concept that we taught to people who were looking to get authority from someone as to how they might present their case for getting more authority. We explained why giving a "trust me" pitch is unwise when trying to gain authority or resources from supervisors. Let me explain the concept.

Authority and resource seekers see the world from a personal perspective. From that viewpoint, they assume the supervisor's decision will ride on whether or not they are trusted. Well, that is not how authority and resource delegators see the world. Authority and resource givers see the world situationally. They decide to give, share, or delegate authority and resources from a "risk" perspective. Remember, seekers see the world as a personal trust issue, and that is how they usually try to sell their proposal: "You can trust me; I can do it!" They are mystified and confused when the boss rejects their proposal. They fail to understand that the giver of authority and resources sees themselves as guardians of resources, so they base their decisions on the level of risk involved in supporting proposals.

I realized this when I saw a VP of Marketing at Amersham make a proposal to the President of Amersham USA using the "trust me" pitch and hearing the president turn him down because he felt it was too risky. "If it doesn't work, corporate will have my head on a stake!" "But you can trust me!" cried the VP, to no avail. Thirty minutes later, the same VP who had presented the Trust Me proposal turned down a proposal from a manager who reported to him because he felt it was too risky. And, his manager cried to him: "But you can trust me; I can pull this off!" "Sorry, it's too risky; the president would nail me if it didn't work," retorted the VP.

Bottom line, if you seek resources, authority, or opportunities from someone who can give them, show them how providing them to you is risk-free or how it will minimize their risks. If it makes sense, why wouldn't they support it? Line up your proposal with what is most critical to them – personal benefits without undue risk. If you are an authority and resource giver and a person keeps giving you a "trust me" pitch, explain to them that your decision will be based on a risk assessment and ask them to show you how their proposal will be risk-free or will minimize risks. They will undoubtedly have to leave and prepare a new proposal because the thought of risk hadn't been the basis of their original proposal.

The same situation happens between parents and children. Let's pretend you are a parent of a 19-year-old daughter who is a freshman in college.

Daughter: "Hey, dad and mom, can I go with some friends to Florida for Spring Break?"

Dad and Mom: "Who are you going with, how will you get there, and where will you stay?"

Daughter: "Jenny is driving, and we'll stay in a motel in Ft. Lauderdale."

Dad and Mom: "Who else is going?"

Daughter: "Just some good friends."

Dad and Mom: "Who are these good friends?"

Daughter: "Just some friends from college."

Dad and Mom: "What are the names of these friends from college?"

Daughter: "Ugh, Brad and Blake, but they are terrific guys!"

Dad and Mom: "I don't think so!"

Daughter: "But, you can trust me!"

Dad and Mom: "We do trust you!"

Daughter: "Then why won't you let me go?"

Dad and Mom: "Because it's too risky."

Daughter: "But if you trust me, why is it risky?"

Dad and Mom: "Because you can't always control the actions of guys; raging hormones drive them."

Can you see that the daughter sees this as a trust issue, and the parents see this as a risk issue?

Having presented this scenario many times with groups of parents, at this point, I like to ask: "Under what conditions would you let her go?" The typical answers are: "If I went with them," or "If their grandmother could join them on vacation." Please look at the answers: Notice that they are all ways to minimize or eliminate risk; none address a solution from the trust perspective. We often teach teenagers how to make requests to their parents by showing what they want poses no risk. I love it when their eyes get big because they have just discovered a new way to get their parent's permission. If you are a parent, teach your kids this concept; if nothing else, they start thinking about the risks of what they are requesting.

Of course, in the big picture, both trust and risk play a part in delegation decisions. Let's look at four conditions that make it easy to determine if we should delegate or not delegate and when the decision will be easy or difficult.

In high-trust and low-risk situations, the decision is easy: Delegate.

In low-trust and high-risk situations, the decision is also easy: Don't delegate

In low-risk and low-trust situations, the decision is not too challenging: We don't have a lot to lose if we delegate, so take a chance.

In high-trust and high-risk situations: Decide based on the importance of the relationship relative to the risk you are willing to take that shows confidence in the person to whom you would delegate and decide accordingly.

High Trust

Smart to delegate	Choose relationship or security
Take a chance, not much to lose	Smart to not delegate

Low Risk (left)   High Risk (right)

Low Trust

In summary, position power is a beautiful thing to have, for everyone, if you combine it with synergistic power and use it for the benefit of everyone. It feels like a beautiful thing to have if you combine it with dominance power, for you at least, but it feels abusive to those on whom it is applied.

27

INFORMATION POWER

The British Royal Navy captured the German U-boat, U-110, on May 9, 1941, in the North Atlantic during World War II. With the capture of the U-boat, they recovered an Enigma machine (code machine), its cipher keys, and codebooks which allowed codebreakers to read German signal traffic in the Atlantic war zone. Capturing these tools enabled allied codebreakers to interpret German messages that had been pure gibberish before the capture. Once they had the machine, cipher keys, and codebooks, they had the tools to understand German messages and avoid the Submarine Wolf Packs that hunted and destroyed millions of tons of shipping vital to the survival of the United Kingdom. After a while, the Germans figured out that the allies had their coding tools. So, the Germans stopped using the current Enigma machine with three code wheels and replaced it with a device with four code wheels. At that moment, the Allies lost their information advantage and started losing enormous numbers of cargo ships again. The gloom lifted after the British seized another U-boat, U-599, with its codebooks and tools on October 30, 1942. This fortunate capture gave the Allies the ability to break German codes again. The ability of the Allies to understand German messages was instrumental in enabling the Allies to change the course of the war on the oceans. Information is power.[33]

Information power is about leverageable high value data and is used to obtain optimum benefit from the information. Information provides insight about people, situations, companies, conditions, statistics, etc. Information exists about virtually anything and everything, but it becomes power when it offers a benefit or an advantage when using it.

---

33   Hugh Sebag-Montefiore, *Enigma: The Battle for the Code* (Orion's Weidenfeld & Nicolson, 2017).

People can use information selfishly or altruistically. When they can use it to benefit themselves at the expense of others, it is self-serving and selfish. If used to help others, it is altruistic. Research companies and organizations exist to find useful information that will benefit someone and they make millions upon millions of dollars doing so. Doing a web search for marketing research companies will provide thousands of options for companies willing to find, analyze, and organize information into a useful format for their clients. If the information provided unearths unique facts that competitors don't have, it can produce enormous competitive advantages. By clicking on the website to find the top New York City marketing research companies, we are immediately overwhelmed by the number and variety of marketing research companies available, each promising unique value and returns for using their services. The point is that information is valuable.

Marketing companies use market research to define marketing strategies to spin their marketing message for specific buyers. They understand that strategies directed at everyone inspire no one. The old ploy of throwing spaghetti at a wall to see what sticks is too expensive and produces poor returns on investment. Therefore, they gather information to determine the high potential buyers of the products or services they are selling, and they develop marketing strategies that will connect directly with the needs and wants of those people. Our cell phones, iPads, and computers are prime sources of information about us and others that marketing companies pay dearly to obtain. Notice that if we look online for a particular product, shortly after that, ads for that type of product start showing up on our phones wherever and whenever we go online.

Because unique information is powerful and valuable, it is guarded and protected. Laws exist to protect intellectual property. Our online tools have products to protect our valuable data from falling into the hands of evil people. Not long ago, someone got access to our checking account through our debit card and stole $6,600 before we discovered the theft, and we were able to cancel the debit card. Whole industries within some countries exist to scam people. Other companies exist solely to protect us from being scammed. The information business is big business, and the returns from being part of it are massive.

I taught negotiation skills at Lake Forest Graduate School in Illinois. Information is one of the powerful tools when negotiating. There are three approaches to use when negotiating: The collaborative approach, the competitive approach, and the compromise approach. Each method has different motives, outcomes, critical drivers, core skills, and tactics. We will touch on each approach's motives and critical drivers, but we won't get into core skills or tactics; that is another book.

The collaborative approach motives are: to satisfy both party's needs, enhance relationships, build trust, and maximize mutual wins. The collaborative approach seeks the best possible outcome for everyone who is negotiating. The critical drivers of this approach are high expectations, mutual respect, commitment to mutual gain, mutual understanding, open-mindedness, commitment to uncompromised solutions, mutual sharing of information, and using tension as a creative catalyst. Finding mutually beneficial outcomes for everyone requires looking at all options from one another's vantage point. Anyone seeing a lopsided benefit for one party points out the disparity, and a new beneficial outcome replaces the unfair one. It is pretty fantastic to hear a party in collaborative negotiations ask: "I can certainly see how I benefit, but how do you benefit?" When everyone is acting in their own interests *and* everyone else's, outstanding outcomes are found or created. Collaborative negotiations for mutual benefit safely expand the boundaries of everyone's expectations and options. It reduces the risks because everyone is in the same boat. Everyone's boat rises with the same tide.

While working in Chicago for Amersham Health Care, I assisted our Canadian subsidiary in negotiating a new business agreement with their largest industrial customer. Their customer tested pipelines for cracks or weaknesses in the structure by sending a highly radioactive "pig" through the pipeline with an X-ray machine tracking it on the outside.

I decided to meet with our customer's management group a few days before our scheduled negotiations date to understand their feelings toward Amersham. I was shocked to find that they literally hated Amersham because they felt that Amersham was raising prices with no forewarning. When Amersham raised prices without notifying them, it damaged their relationships with their customers. They had to pass along the price increase with no ability to explain the higher prices except to blame Amersham. They felt that Amersham didn't value their business, and the customer intended to try and persuade their customers to go to another service provider if another were available.

Armed with this information, I reported to the Canadian Amersham management team the deep resentment their largest customer felt. I asked the management and negotiation team members from both organizations to spend two days with me going through a negotiations course that would benefit both companies. Both groups agreed to attend the class, but the customer group was decidedly more reluctant.

We reviewed all three approaches to negotiating with both teams and philosophically agreed that the collaborative approach was preferable in our upcoming negotiations. One participant disagreed. The VP of Marketing for the customer said the collaborative process would never work because Amersham was, and would always be, focused on making more profits at their expense. I threw his opinion out to the group to find a creative, mutually beneficial solution to the problem. The answer turned out to be pretty simple: They would combine the profits from the combined businesses and divide them equally in this business arena. That led to a discussion handling overhead from both companies in a way that would not penalize one company because of the overhead of the other. It was inspiring to watch and to participate in the discussions while they brought up one challenge after another and found creative, mutually beneficial solutions for each one. I fully expected the companies to merge as the final outcome, but they stopped just short of that. They remained separate companies but eliminated all duplication of technical services in both companies. As a result, both companies found ways to reduce their overheads, optimize technical expertise, and maximize revenue and shared profits. The agreements incentivized both companies to minimize operation expenditures and to optimize profits. Whatever helped one helped the other, and whatever hurt one hurt the other. What a fantastic partnership and unique creative collaboration! They quadrupled their profits the second year of their new business arrangement. Sadly, the Canadian Amersham subsidiary president died of a heart attack the third year into the new relationship; he was only 43 years old.

Collaborative solutions require trust and trustworthiness to achieve them and keep them going. Unfortunately, the Canadian president's replacement wanted to maximize Amersham's profits and was not committed to keeping their customer's profits equal to Amersham's. The win-win business partnership unwound, to the detriment of both.

In competitive negotiations, the motives are to: satisfy self-interest, win at others' expense, and maximize personal win. It is a "winner takes all" mentality and approach – winning matters, not relationships. The critical drivers of this approach are power (whoever has the most wins, including all varieties of circumstantial power combined with dominance power). Other drivers are high expectations, high need to win, indifference about the other party, controlling the process, getting information but not giving it, and knowing your B.T.N.A. (the best alternative to a negotiated agreement, which is the walk-away point). With this approach, information is power; the more information we can get without giving it, the more we have. In competitive negotiations, we release information at our own peril. In collaborative negotiations sharing information expands the speed, depth, and breadth of mutual gain outcomes. In contrast, competitive negotiations sharing information shifts the power to our negotiation adversary, curtailing our chances of success and limiting what we can win.

At Lake Forest Graduate School in Illinois, I gave extra credit to students who would write a personal report about successful competitive negotiations they had experienced during the semester. However, before they embarked upon these competitive negotiations, we would ensure that the relationships with people they would be negotiating with were not vital to them. I particularly loved teaching how and when to buy a car to get a "killer" deal. But the approach, motives, outcomes, critical drivers, core skills, and tactics applied to virtually all competitive negotiation situations. I recall marvelously entertaining reports: One fellow bragged about how he purchased $8,000 worth of photography equipment for $2800. Another reported buying a three-year-old car during a snowstorm on December 28. He explained how the dealer could minimize losses by selling it to him for $3500 even though the dealer had paid $4200 for the car from a widow.

When the salesman left the room to get a deal for him with the manager, he saw the car's information sheet on the desk with the name and phone number of the lady who had sold the car to the dealership. He called the lady and found out what they had paid her for the car and everything about the car, from her personal experience. With all this information and his insight about taxes the dealership would have to pay if the car were not sold before the end of the tax year, he convinced the dealer to sell it for $3500 – with an extended warranty. He said that afterward, he felt terrible for the salesman, so he dropped by the dealership and gave the salesman $300 to clear his conscience. I laughed myself sick when a female student told the class about buying a $600 tailored sheepskin coat for $200 that was on sale for $400. After she negotiated a price below the $400 sale price, she noticed that she could get another 25% discount on her purchases by signing up for the store's credit card. However, before she applied for the credit card, she negotiated a deal on a pair of costly Italian lambskin gloves and a Russian-looking furry hat. When she met the salesperson, who happened to be the department manager, she asked if it would be OK to apply for the store's credit card at the cash register. He said: "Of course." So, she filled out the paperwork and said she would like to apply the additional 25% discount for signing up for the credit card to all her purchases. When the manager handed her the receipt, she asked him if there were any other items on sale that he thought she would like. He just said: "Please, just leave the store!" She enjoyed giving our graduate class a fashion show featuring all the beautiful stuff she had negotiated at Nordstrom.

I would remind you: If the relationship is important, don't compete.

I will only briefly touch on the compromise approach to negotiations because this is a discussion about power. One motive for compromising is to minimize our losses because we don't have enough power to win competitively. Another reason for compromise is that the relationship is more important than winning. The motives for using the compromise approach to negotiating are: To sustain important relationships, to minimize losses (if it is all or nothing and nothing seems probable – make a deal to reduce losses), to achieve a marginal win (having both parties leave with something is often the better solution than one winning and the other losing), or to achieve an acceptable loss in return for something of more value. (Sometimes winning can't be measured in terms of money or material things. Love enables us to put our egos aside for the greater good.)

When we consider our motives for compromising, the desired outcomes should be pretty obvious:

- An acceptable win would be to give up something to benefit someone else.
- An acceptable loss would be to run slow enough so that your child could beat you in a race.
- Losing to sustain a meaningful relationship is a noble thing to do. We should ask ourselves before negotiating, "What is this relationship worth? Is it important enough for an acceptable loss or a lesser but acceptable win?

I genuinely appreciate my son-in-law Carl Purnell and how he deals with my small, passionate, emotional, fighter-spirit daughter Tiffany. They don't always agree, and his 6'6" and 250 lbs. could overpower her 5' height and 105 lbs., but he concedes to an acceptable loss or a minimized win with her because he loves her. To him, his relationship with her is more important than winning anything!

By the way, if you are negotiating from a collaborative approach and the other party is negotiating from a competitive approach, you will be taken to the cleaners. Decide and agree to collaborate before getting into negotiations. If you can't agree to cooperate, assume it is a competitive negotiation and marshal all the power, critical drivers, core skills, and tactics you can muster; it will be a winner-take-all contest.

28

KNOWLEDGE POWER

One of my dad's favorite sayings was: "I taught you everything I know, and you still don't know nothing."

Knowledge power is the first cousin to information power. Of course, knowledge is information, but information power is out there available to anyone clever enough to find it and turn it into knowledge. Knowledge power is refined information that serves a purpose. Knowledge is unique information that provides people opportunities and insight to accomplish things that others without the knowledge can't do. Knowledge power comes from being the only person or a select few with unique knowledge applied to situations to achieve notable feats. For example, during World War II, the Manhattan Project was a research and development undertaking that produced the first nuclear weapons. It was led by the United States and supported by the United Kingdom and Canada. It could only be successful by bringing together the best and brightest intellectuals in the fields of mathematics, physics, and nuclear science. It is the story of bringing together the most renowned scientists of that time to combine their knowledge and instincts to produce a theoretically possible atomic weapon. They combined their expertise and shared their knowledge. The scientists combined their individual information and knowledge to create new knowledge. That ever-growing and expanding knowledge had power; it changed the world. It led to weapons of mass destruction, but it enabled the creation of nuclear power to create electric power for mammoth ships and submarines. It spawned technology that we take for granted in our everyday lives, like our microwaves or the medical treatments based on nuclear technology. It created the need to manage enormous amounts of data leading to the development of computers. In a general sense, knowledge power harnesses information that moves humanity forward.

Formal or otherwise, the usual route to obtaining knowledge power is education. Everyone who goes to school captures some level of information that can translate into knowledge power for a little while. If you are the first to have that knowledge and show it off, it distinguishes you from others. If you are the only kid in kindergarten who knows how to tie your shoes, that unique knowledge makes you distinctive among your classmates. As soon as they can do it too, you lose that exclusiveness; even though you still have the knowledge, you lose its power; it is no longer exclusive to you – such is the fate of knowledge power. To maintain knowledge power, we need to continue our education to remain exclusive and obtain the benefits of having exclusive, valuable knowledge. We go on to high school, college, graduate school, and post-graduate studies to get more and more information about more specific subjects because knowledge power makes higher education worthwhile in terms of the opportunities it creates and the income it justifies. We learn that some areas of knowledge garner greater rewards than other areas of expertise. Hence, people choose to specialize in information areas that appeal to them. Some are rewarded handsomely for their knowledge while others aren't. The economic power of knowledge comes from people wanting to benefit from it and their willingness to pay to get it. I pay doctors for their medical knowledge to fix me or keep me functioning. I pay my accountant for his knowledge to do my tax returns, so I don't have to get the education that provides me with that knowledge. Their expertise, which I'm willing to pay for, is knowledge power. If we know a lot, but it is of no value to anyone, we may have knowledge, but it lacks power.

The story about a maintenance man from New York City exemplifies knowledge power. The building management fired him days before qualifying for his pension. He had been the maintenance man in this large and complex facility for 20 years and knew every detail about the ancient structure's heating, plumbing, and power systems. A few months after terminating him, a slight tremor in the area disrupted virtually all the building's heating, plumbing, and electrical systems. The building managers called in plumbing, heating, and power system experts who had to report to management that they had tried but failed to get their respective systems functioning again. One of the tenants suggested that management bring in "Old Joe" because everything worked fine when he maintained the building. Administration called Joe and asked him to come and see what he could do to get the systems functioning again.

Joe came and, to their surprise, had everything functioning within a few hours. They told Joe to send them a bill for his services. He did. It was an invoice for $1,800,000 (precisely the amount he would have received as a lifetime retirement benefit had they allowed him to stay in his job a few more days). They were shocked about the bill and asked him to come and justify the invoice. He came and explained. They mockingly asked him: "You mean to tell us that you charged us one point eight million dollars for a few hours of pushing buttons and turning valves?" "No, replied Joe, I charged you $1,800,000 for knowing what buttons to push and which valves to turn." His knowledge power came from the information he had harnessed from working in that facility for over 20 years. It was worth $1,800,000 to save the building and the property of everyone who lived and worked in the facility.

Knowledge power, to some degree, is a reflection of at least three things (and probably more): One, the exclusiveness of that knowledge. Two, if it can lead to new information that leads to new and exclusive, valuable knowledge. And three, how the knowledge is received and the benefits derived from it.

Knowledge exclusiveness

Kentucky Fried Chicken has built a worldwide franchise with secret knowledge about the herbs and spices that make their chicken "finger-lickin' good." One could suppose that sharing their secret knowledge would end their dominance in the marketplace. Likewise, Coca-Cola guards the secret of their unique taste. It emboldens them to willingly enter into taste competitions with their competitors to prove customer preference for their product. Knowledge can become intellectual property. It is valuable. It makes information exclusive and creates new value and opportunities in the marketplace. Lawyers specialize in practicing law that centers on intellectual property. Companies know that if they lose the exclusiveness of their product information, they lose the future of their company. That is why companies require employees and potential investors to sign confidentiality agreements.

New information that leads to new exclusive and valuable knowledge

We illustrated how new information led to new exclusive and valuable knowledge that changed the world with the example of the Manhattan Project. Steve Jobs changed the world when he harnessed information to create the Apple computer. From that fantastic feat, countless other products have reached us that enable us to communicate across the globe in real-time.

Knowledge improves our life and capabilities to do things that were previously undoable. I remember when my mother showed me a Xerox machine that could copy endless pages at the touch of a button. I remember when J&J purchased the first word-processing machines and how the VP secretaries who were the first to get them refused to use them. After we persuaded them to try them, they had a chance to use them and see that they could throw away the carbon papers and easily make changes on documents without having to white out errors or redo the entire document. Once they realized the benefits, they would have killed us if we tried to take away their word processors.

My wife and I knew that we couldn't operate our consulting business without the fax machine. Kids today would look at the miracles of our day as dinosaurs, extinct. Worldwide knowledge power creations put life-changing knowledge power capability into the hands of virtually anyone with access to it. Silicon Valley is an example of how knowledge power leads to more and greater knowledge power. At a point in time, exclusive knowledge power becomes public information. When that happens, the power of that knowledge is spread and made accessible to countless millions of people. Each person can take that old, used knowledge power and use it to find new and exclusive information that becomes the latest and life-changing knowledge power. Knowledge power is like a tree that grows and spreads through its roots and branches and spreads seeds that become new trees with spreading roots and branches that also spread seeds. Knowledge power grows exponentially. The more we have, the faster it occurs. It is all happening so quickly that it boggles the mind.

How the knowledge power is received and the benefits derived from it

Knowledge power is life-changing, but it does not affect all people to the same degree. Change is not received or welcomed in the same way by everyone. As business consultants, company executives hired us to help their organizations grow, develop, and become more "successful – in short, to change. We found that people received change efforts in organizations in five different ways. We categorized them because people in each category had to be dealt with differently:

Category One: Change Leaders

Change leaders are the people who see the need for change or who see the opportunities from making changes. They quickly find ways to harness knowledge power and use it to benefit themselves, their organization, and society. Seeing the benefits derived from it, they quickly become sponsors for change and the beneficiaries of the knowledge-power derived from change. They become the drivers to incorporate needed changes into their business, practices, and lives. These people are the tip of the spear for utilizing knowledge power to make beneficial changes happen. As consultants, we learned that no significant change would occur without change leaders who had position power and the commitment to make changes and harness the knowledge power. With change leaders, we developed synergistic relationships. Ideally, we became partners in the change process, leading to warm, valued friendships. In military parlance, they were the general officers, and we were executive staff advisors. They were the upfront and visible decision-makers; we were behind-the-scenes change experts, ensuring they had the information to make correct, decisive decisions that ensured success.

Category Two: Rapid adopters

Rapid adopters are the people who are pretty good at reading the "tea leaves" of change. They quickly absorb the reality that change is coming. They can either jump on board and benefit by supporting the change process or wait and just be swept up in the changes with unpredictable consequences for themselves. These people are the ones who choose to quickly engage with the change leaders and take a leadership role in making change happen. Rewards come for their rapid and wise decision to join the change leaders. They get additional position power and an elevation in personal and organizational status.

Category Three: Slow adopters

Slow adopters are those not as skillful in reading the "tea leaves" of change, or they are the people who are personally benefiting from the way things currently stand. These people approach change cautiously because they don't want to be caught on the wrong side of the change process. They are the "fence-sitters" who watch the battle from the sidelines until it becomes apparent what the outcome will be. When they see that the change efforts will succeed, they throw their support behind the change effort and the change leaders, trying to appear as if they had been supportive all along. If they determine that the change effort will fail, they join the naysayers, finding and expressing fault in the change-making actions. These fair-weather friends contribute little to change efforts; they can't be counted upon to take a definitive stand until the outcome is entirely predictable. Their approach to committing to the change would cause them to appear to fit into various relationship types. They would be a sort of a Stompee while sitting on the fence waiting to see the outcome before deciding their allegiance. Their passivity would feel like obsequiousness. They would appear to be Advocates when they finally decide to join the victors' camp after the hot part of the fray has been fought and the battle decided. They would appear to be an Enemy if the change effort was unsuccessful and they became part of the mob throwing spears and stones. Slow adopters are expendable; they are not proactive; they are reactive.

Category Four: Resisters

Resisters fight change. Their relationship with the change leaders and rapid adopters is adversarial and will probably become an Enemy if allowed to persist. They are deeply committed to keeping things just the way they are, perhaps because they are personally benefiting greatly from the current status of things. From their vantage point, any change would damage them and, therefore, damage the company. If they have a lot of position power, their resistance can doom change efforts, no matter how beneficial the changes could be for the organization. Change actions can never be successful if the "top dog" in the company doesn't support it. If the Board of Directors felt that change was imperative and that the needed changes couldn't happen if a Resister remained in control, they might remove him and find some Change Leader who would make the necessary changes. That happens infrequently, but it is not a rare occurrence. If the change leader is higher on the totem pole than the resister or resisters, the only viable option to move forward is to remove the resisters from the organization. To leave them in the organization while allowing them to continue to make decisions that would negatively impact the change efforts won't work. If they are allowed to remain, they will become chief poop stirrers within the organization, recruiting the fence-sitters and mobilizing the other resisters to stop the change process.

Category Five: The blissfully ignorant

These people are an enigma in my mind. I don't know how they can exist. They are the people who are unaware of the events going on around them. They have no "tea leaves," or they never use them if they do. Maybe they are so focused on their world that the events occurring outside their realm don't exist for them. They may be aware of the external world but have learned not to get involved (live and let live mentality). Maybe, their neutrality is a manifestation of personal boundaries put in place to protect themselves. I don't know why these people exist, but they do. In terms of supporting or rejecting change efforts, they are non-entities. They are not active players on any side. After the change efforts have succeeded or failed, just let them know what is expected of them in the organization in the future and let them focus on doing that. I am not sure what relationship category they would fit. It would probably be compliant Stompees.

When engaged as consultants in an organization's change process, we would meet with the change leaders early on and do a human resource audit of the people within the organization. We determined into which category everyone in the organization fit. Of course, we wanted to know who the rapid adopters would be (the change leaders were already in the room) to quickly get them engaged in helping to lead and support the change effort. We identified the resisters to get them out of the organization before it became public knowledge that change was afoot. Most times, the change leaders acted with compassion toward the resisters, recognizing that the changes would signify a personal loss. Usually, they would help them find a new position using executive recruiters or provide a severance package to act as a bridge until they could find new opportunities. The slow followers were given as much information as possible to let them know what was happening and that the change would be successful. The objective is to get them off the fence and start supporting the change process sooner rather than later. We supported the blissfully ignorant, so they could keep doing what they were doing before the change. If the company change required changes in their work, we informed them about their new duties.

New information always leads to new knowledge power. It changes the world for all of us. It is better to be a change leader or a rapid adopter to benefit from the inevitable changes. It is wise not to be a fence sitter for too long; if we sit and wait, we could have no choice to make. But, for heaven's sake, don't be a resister to predictable and inevitable change, no matter how much you benefit from the current circumstances. The outcome of resistance will be victimhood, and unfortunately, it will be self-inflicted because it could be avoided.

Knowledge power in combination with synergistic power

The cardiologist who put in my pacemaker is a perfect example of a person with knowledge power who uses it synergistically to bless the lives of his patients and, indirectly, all of their family, friends, and loved ones. Brian G. Crandall, MD, specialized in cardiology then went for further training to become a fellow in electrophysiology. When I entered the hospital, my resting heart rate was about 30 beats a minute, when it was beating. Then it started pausing for 3 to 15 seconds at a time. He told me: "I can't say this to everyone, but I can say this to you; I can fix you." He put the pacemaker in on Presidents Day in 2019, and since that time, I have lived an active life with a heartbeat that never drops below 60 beats per minute and goes as high as it needs to be when I am engaged in physical activities.

Countless people have knowledge power and use it to bless the lives of others. We should all be grateful for them.

Knowledge power in combination with dominance power

There are selfish and self-serving people who use their knowledge power to benefit only themselves, or maybe their stockholders, at the expense of everyone dependent on their knowledge or the products that are the fruits of their knowledge. I think of pharmaceutical companies who astronomically raise the prices on products they have exclusive rights to. Products and services that were once inexpensive and available to everyone have become so expensive that people die because they can't afford them. It is not because of product availability; it is still easily manufactured in unlimited quantities. It is because of greed. They do it because they can. They may make excuses by explaining the cost of research and drug approval processes but fail to mention that they have already recouped their investment hundreds or perhaps thousands of times over. I know people are dying because they can't afford insulin. Please explain to me how this product, once inexpensive and available to everyone, is now beyond the reach of modestly well-off people. I find it hard to accept that epinephrine pens have risen from single digits in cost to hundreds of dollars per unit. I understand that it is the nature of greedy people to put themselves first at the expense of those who benefit from their products. It demonstrated the power of exclusive knowledge.

29

EMOTIONAL INTELLIGENCE POWER

If you had to choose whether your child could have an extremely high IQ (intelligence quotient) or have an extremely high Emotional Intelligence, but not both, which would you choose? Which would allow your child to fare better in life? Logic might suggest that pure smarts would be the key to success in life; if you are smart enough, you can determine the correct answers to all of life's opportunities and avoid the consequences of all of life's pitfalls. As it turns out, Emotional Intelligence determines success in life and happiness more than pure intellectual smarts. While IQ may be a genetic gift, Emotional Intelligence may come with a genetic disposition. Still, it can be taught and learned, thereby giving all people of average smarts a better chance to use their emotional intelligence capacity to its full potential.

I see emotional intelligence as the ability to understand and apply our emotions in conjunction with our reasoning and intelligence to gain insight about ourselves and others to make wise decisions. To the degree that we can join our emotions with our intelligence to operate harmoniously, to that same degree, we can be extraordinary in our interpersonal connections and in developing synergistic relationships. Mastering the understanding and application of our own emotions enables us to understand the emotions and mindset of others better, allowing us to connect with them. In a sense, their emotional vibes connect with our emotional vibes. It will enable our reasoning ability to understand where they are coming from and empathize with what is going on between their ears. The world can be lonely and isolated for many people, even if people literally surround them. Feeling disconnected when longing to be connected is soulful torture. Too many think that no one understands them, cares about them, or loves them, so when they encounter someone who can understand and validate what they are feeling, it is a momentous experience. People who can relate to people have emotional intelligence, which can be tremendously powerful and influential.

Emotional intelligence certainly ranks as among the most influential powers available to humans, except for love, which is, in itself, an expression of Emotional Intelligence. I am grateful for Dr. Daniel Goleman and his life-changing book *Emotional Intelligence.*[34] He provides a scholarly and entertaining vision of emotional intelligence from a scientific and neurological perspective and offers practical applications useful for everyone. Dr. Goleman should get the credit for much of my scientific understanding of emotional intelligence. He brought my knowledge of it into focus. We will refer to his concepts to help our readers to, at least, grasp that this is a complex subject with loads of information that is hugely beneficial. I would recommend his books on emotional intelligence as sources of information and a key to knowledge that can be indeed life-changing. His insight has truly enhanced my life.

The power of emotional intelligence is manifest with people who have attained the ability to manage their thoughts and feelings. If they could do it perfectly, they would be masters of emotional intelligence. I don't know of anyone who is. Some are a lot better at it than others. People can learn it; people deficient in it can become good at it. But it is not just an intellectual process; if it were, the people with the highest IQ would be the best at emotional intelligence. They are not. Frequently those who have the most emotional intelligence are certainly not the smartest. But they are not the dumbest either. It requires the use of the adult mode to analyze the parent mode and the child mode recordings to direct our decisions and to contain, or limit, the behaviors driven by extreme emotions. People of high Emotional Intelligence are human; their feelings and emotional responses are controlled by the brain's emotional center (the amygdala and hippocampus), just like everyone else. They have the same emotional fight or flight reactions bestowed on all of us through generations of

34   Daniel Goleman, *Emotional Intelligence* (New York: Bantam Books, 1995).

evolution. Their prefrontal cortex, the brain's thinking and judgment sections operate as they do for others. The reasoning part of their brain governs their emotional reactions, except when the amygdala initiates a panic mode. They become driven solely by their emotions until their thinking brain intercedes and moderates their actions to match the reality of the situation, just like everyone else does. But in some ways, they are unique. They are not just emotionally oriented or intellectually oriented. They are both.

Emotional intelligence is not just being emotionally directed. It is a blending of our Adult, Child, and Parent modes to develop insights and abilities to maximize our ability to interact with other people and create a bond with them. A bond happens when others have insight and understand what others are feeling. Understanding yourself and controlling your emotions is a big part of emotional intelligence. That understanding and control become a foundation to understand and relate to other people and hear, understand, and validate them, creating bonds of trust. When we hear, understand, and validate people, they no longer feel alone. Connecting with them is like they're alone on an island and having someone come to shore to save them.

All of these things combined give people the ability to manage and create mutually beneficial and satisfying relationships. People who have developed these sensitivities and skills become very influential people. They are influential because people know that they understand them. People who use this power effectively don't use it judgmentally but try to understand people non-judgmentally. When people see that they are really trying to understand them, their barriers drop, and they feel a kinship to the other person. It makes them popular and leaders because people want to be around them.

I believe that people raised in a Nurturing Parent Mode environment have a great head start over those raised in a Controlling Parent Mode, a Critical Parent Mode, or an Overindulgent Parent Mode environment. In a Nurturing Parent Mode environment, people are loved and respected. Feelings are expressed, shared, and received between people who care and are concerned, especially when distressing emotions are displayed. In such environments, people experience empathy, and they, in turn, learn how to be empathetic with others.

Being an emotional child with a hot and uncontrollable temper, I appreciate my parents, who intervened when necessary and used those extreme emotional situations as teaching moments. My dad was hyper-critical frequently but understood when empathy and loving discussions were more critical. My mother was a nurturer 100% of the time. One situation stands out in my mind where incredible life lessons were given rather than an outcome of tragic proportions.

On Thursday, August 30, 1962, at 6:35 a.m., a magnitude 5.7 earthquake occurred in Richmond, Utah. The quake center was next to the town cemetery. It was a mile or so from the center of town and four blocks from our home. It was a pretty scary experience and a destructive one. It caused the condemnation of dozens of homes and our large town tabernacle. All of the houses and the tabernacle were demolished, and newly-built structures replaced them. One of the homes condemned belonged to Rulan (Bott) Thompson. He decided that while he was building a new house for him and his wife, he would also build a house for his parents. After the city knocked down the enormous old church, Bott had many dump truck loads of bricks brought to his property scavenged from the ruins of the tabernacle. He planned to use the old bricks to build new homes for himself and his parents. He hired my brother and me to prepare the old bricks to build his new houses. We chipped the mortar off the used bricks, stacked them onto pallets, and hauled them to the new home locations. Then we loaded the removed mortar onto a trailer where the refuse was taken to the local dump for disposal (which we would unload with scoop shovels).

Dick and I worked for several weeks, each of us putting in probably over 180 hours of labor to make the old bricks usable as new bricks for the houses. The usual wage for guys our age was about 50 cents an hour. We could earn that wage by doing farm work for the local farmers. We had put in approximately 180 hours, so we were both expecting about $90 for our labors. When we went to Bott for settlement, he gave us each $5.00 and a hearty thank you. I was shocked and angry, beyond belief angry, and Dick was shocked. Dick started ambling toward home, whereas I ran as hard as possible. I ran into the house and grabbed my .22 caliber, single-shot rifle and a handful of shells.

As I ran out of the house, heading back to Bott's house, I intended on shooting the bugger. I slammed the screen door at the back of the house. My dad heard the door bang and looked up from his welding job on a hay trailer to yell at me for slamming the screen door. He saw me running down the side of the house and onto the road, leading to Bott's place, carrying a rifle and looking wild and angry.

By the time I had made it a few blocks, dad had pulled up beside me on his Honda motorcycle and asked me to jump on. I declined at first, explaining that I needed to shoot Bott because he had cheated us. He persuaded me to get on the bike behind him, and we went home, just long enough to drop off the rifle, and then we rode the bike up to a campsite up High Creek, parked beside the stream, and there he built a fire. He sat close to me, and I let all my anger and frustrations fly. I remember telling him through tears that I should have just broken all the bricks. He listened until I was ready to listen, then he gave me some life lessons that reached into my head and touched my heart. He told me that, indeed, Dick and I were cheated, but it would have been wrong to ruin the bricks; doing so would have branded us as good-for-nothings, and that could leave us with a lasting lousy reputation for as long as we lived in Richmond.

He said that because we had done such a great job, we would be known as the boys who did a great job preparing the bricks that became the new houses for the Thompsons. He said that no matter how much someone pays us for a job, we should do our best because we will be known for the quality of our work and how hard we work. He told me that the best workers always rise just as cream rises to the top of the milk can. He said that if I lived by that principle, I would always receive less than I was worth but would always rise to the top. He said it is good to receive less than you are worth because it makes you rare and irreplaceable. He further explained that people paid more than they are worth don't have job security or many prospects for advancement.

A couple of days after our High Creek heart-to-heart, dad dropped off $100 checks for Dick and I signed by Bott. I can only imagine the discussion dad had with Bott before he wrote those checks. You might find it interesting to know that five years later, Bott became the bishop of our local church group, and he called me into his office just before my 19th birthday and asked my permission to send my name to the church headquarters to be called on a mission for our church. I agreed after some deep contemplation. I ended up serving in Southern Brazil.

That day beside High Creek, Dad added wisdom that extended beyond the Bott Thompson lesson. He advised me to learn everything about the organizations I would work for to understand the business better than anyone else in the organization. He said to look for unfulfilled needs in organizations and determine ways to fill those needs. Once you have the solution to the problem, then present the solution to the decision-makers within the organization; if you understand the problem and have an answer, it makes you the best person to be given the responsibility for managing it. The lessons from that day have stayed with me my whole life. I have always received less than the value I contributed to organizations I worked for but advanced sooner than I probably should have. The sales manager position in Vancouver, British Columbia, in 1975 was the last job where the position was pre-defined for me before I had it. Since then, all my posts came due to the needs I saw in organizations and the solutions I presented for filling them. True to form, at 33 years of age, I was the youngest and lowest-paid VP at Johnson & Johnson.

It has become a lifetime habit for me to seek unfulfilled needs and find solutions to fill those needs. That is why the behavioral sciences have always been so interesting to me. There are always unfulfilled needs looking for answers when it comes to people. I certainly don't have the solutions to people's unfulfilled needs, but I never tire of looking for the answers. I know that quality relationships fill many needs and prevent many unfulfilled needs. Emotional intelligence contributes immeasurably to developing synergistic relationships and healthy interpersonal connections. That is why it is something that everyone should explore, gain insight about, and incorporate into the process of living with other human beings.

Daniel Goleman[35] identifies four domains that make up emotional intelligence. 1) Self-awareness. 2) Self-management. 3) Empathy or social awareness. 4) Putting the first three together in skillfully managing relationships.

1) Self-awareness.

Self-insight becomes the basis of self-control. Knowing what we are feeling and why becomes the basis for sound decision-making and establishing our moral compass.

This reasoning seems pretty self-explanatory when relating it to the information about feelings in the first section of this book. Feelings are the basis of our beliefs (rationalized feelings). Our reality (our facts) aligns with our beliefs, regardless of actual truth; behaviors are based on our reality, and outcomes result from our behaviors. If we allow our feelings to determine our beliefs, detached from truth, our reality, behaviors, and outcomes determine our moral character. We become the slaves of our feelings in that condition, defining a moral compass at odds with true moral character. In other words, if our feelings misalign with truth and reality, then our decision-making and moral compass are also misaligned. We must align our self-awareness about our feelings with truth because it is the basis for our understanding, connections, and relationships with others. If we establish relationships based on false reality, everyone is bonded and operating from the same fantasy. That is the essence of moral corruption, individually and as a group. If it becomes too widespread, heaven help us all.

"To thine own self be true." (William Shakespeare, *Hamlet,* Act 1, Scene 3)

---

35   Daniel Goleman, "Big Think" (YouTube, April 2012).

2) Self-management

Much of self-management is about handling distressing emotions effectively that cripple us. This self-management includes: attuning to emotions to learn what we must learn to fit positively into society, marshaling positive emotions for getting ourselves involved and enthused about what we are doing, and finally, getting our actions aligned with our passions.

Self-management, to me, is mainly about applying what we discussed in the operating modes section about using our adult mode. We can use it to analyze our parent mode recordings (our should's and ought-to's) and our child mode recordings (our emotional responses learned before we had language to label them) and update them when needed. Old recordings that are outdated or out of touch with truth (reality) or developing and sustaining healthy relationships need to be examined and changed if required. When we are in a state of cognitive dissonance or unbalance, we need to re-establish that balance. If that is a state of imbalance about our moral values, then we have two choices, change our moral values or realign our behaviors to match our moral values. Just make sure to base the choice on truth; people who redefine reality to align with their behaviors become society rebels (people who have no beliefs other than their own to govern their actions).

If the unbalance comes from protecting our boundaries or respecting the boundaries of others, then again, the thinking part of the brain, our adult mode, needs to engage. Our adult mode can realign the parent mode recordings that justify disrespecting others' boundaries or allow our child mode recordings to invade our boundaries without invitation.

If the unbalance is because of negative feelings about ourselves or others, then we need our adult mode to help us change those emotions that mimic addictions. Remember, addictions always have three parts: 1) Compulsive behavior. 2) Short-term benefits (the buzz). 3) Long-term destructive consequences. To eliminate addictions (or, in this case, negative, destructive feelings), we need to do three things: 1) Use our adult mode (our thinking mind, the frontal cortex) to understand why we love or accept negative emotions. 2) Find a better alternative (or alternatives), in this case, positive and healthy emotions to replace the destructive ones. 3) Decide what we need to do and do it. Doing this ongoing will enable us to move through the change process steps, which are:

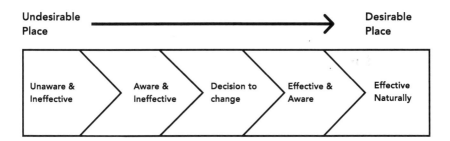

Step One: In-cognitive Ineffective to cognitive ineffective (We are messed up and don't know it.)

Step Two: Cognitive ineffective (We are messed up and know it.)

Step Three: The decision to change (This is a higher brain function: analyze, and decide what to do.)

Step Four: Cognitive effectiveness (We think and do healthy things when focused on it.)

Step Five: Naturally effective (We are thinking and doing healthy things without thinking about it. The new paradigm has replaced the old one.)

I believe that truth brings light, energy, and edification. If our passions align with truth, or if we align our passions with truth, it will light our souls, give us energy, and edify us to act with an internal motivation that is unbounded.

3) Empathy or Social Awareness
Knowing what someone else is feeling [and responding appropriately]

One afternoon I was shopping in an Arlington Heights, Illinois, grocery store near where we lived, and I happened to witness a four-year-old, beautiful girl throwing a temper tantrum in the store. She threw herself on the floor, screaming and crying. Her mother tried talking with her, but that only intensified the child's emotional fit. The mother would lift her, but the youngster would just collapse again. The mother tried dragging the screaming child, but that only increased the wails. The commotion started to draw people's attention and stares which caused the mother increasing embarrassment and anxiety. Her attempts to talk with the girl shifted from trying to reason with her to threatening her. I could see that the mother was frustrated to the point of losing it, and I was concerned that she would start spanking the youngster in the store, as she was threatening to do. I decided to jump into the fray, so I approached the mother and asked her if she would mind if I tried to talk with her daughter.

She said, "Be my guest." I was in a suit and tie, but I sat on the floor beside the out-of-control girl, just looking at her and waiting for her to notice me. It didn't take very long until she saw the strange guy sitting on the floor beside her. Her screaming changed into swallowed sobs as she got to her feet and moved to where she could hug her mother's leg, looking at me suspiciously. I scooted beside her and asked her if she was upset about something. She nodded her head, so I asked her what made her so upset. She replied that she wanted a toy that she saw but that her mother wouldn't let her stop and look at it. I just nodded my head and validated her message, "So, you're upset because your mother wouldn't let you look at the toy?" She said, "Yes, she never listens to what I want to do," while lifting her palms in a sign of exasperation. I responded to her, "Well, she is listening now. Do you think you could ask her again?" She just shrugged her shoulders and replied, "I don't think so."

I suggested, "Why don't you give it a try now? I think your mom will listen this time." She gave a four-year-old sigh and said, "Why don't you talk with her?" At that moment, she left her mom's side and came to me with her arms up, indicating that I should pick her up. I glanced at her mom, who nodded that it was OK. So, I picked her up, and together we faced her mother, encouraging her to tell her mother what she wanted. The little blonde beauty told her mom that she saw a toy she wanted "so much" and asked her mother to buy it. Her mother told her, "Honey, we don't have enough money to buy food and your toy today, I'm sorry!" Immediately, the little girl pointed at me and said, "Well, he does!" which caused her mother to winch and me to chuckle. I told the mother that it would give me great pleasure to buy the toy for her daughter. She tried to decline the offer politely, but I insisted that it would make her daughter and me happy and it would be a reward for her daughter's newly acquired emotional state. She agreed, and I put the girl on the floor so she could show us the toy she so badly wanted. We took it to the cash register and bought the toy.

The little girl's thank-you hug was one of the best I ever remember. As I was about to return to my shopping, the mother looked at me very earnestly and asked, "Who are you?!" I laughed and explained that I worked for Amersham, a healthcare company. She said that my connection with her daughter was a remarkable experience she would never forget; then, she thanked me and hugged me. We exchanged names and phone numbers then went our separate ways. I watched a very pleased little girl walk back to the shopping aisle with her mom, playing with her new toy. It was a good day.

You could arguably point out that what I did with the little girl and her mom was inappropriate and that I reinforced terrible behavior. You might be correct, but I would do it again; I just can't stand to see people hurting and ignore it. Hopefully, the mother gained some insight into dealing with a youngster stuck in child mode and finding a better alternative than spanking.

Emotional intelligence requires dealing with people from where they are rather than from where we want them to be.

In 1973, there was an internist and a family practitioner in southwest Kansas whose support I needed desperately. I needed his approval for my pharmaceutical products to be prescribed by physicians and stocked in pharmacies. He was the focal point for decision-making about medical services in southwest Kansas. His support could open doors, and his lack of support could doom my efforts in that part of the state. He was in charge of the formulary committee that determined which products would be stocked and used in hospitals and nursing homes. My product, Haldol® (a non-sedating major tranquilizer), was not on any formularies in western Kansas. I repeatedly tried to see him but was never successful.

On one visit to his town, I decided to wait in his office to see him no matter how long it took. I showed up just before his office hours closed, at around 4:00 p.m., and waited in his waiting room until 9:00 p.m. About 6:00 p.m., his staff left, so only he and I remained in the building; he was in his office and I in the waiting room. I knew he hadn't gone because I could occasionally hear movement in his office, and I could see his car in the parking lot. Finally, he poked his head from behind his office door and invited me in. He indifferently asked me, "What did you want to see me about?" As soon as I started my presentation, I could tell that he was emotionally burdened. He wasn't listening to my message, and he looked like he hurt all over. I stopped and asked him if he was OK, and he told me that he was fine and to continue.

I looked at him and said that I didn't think that he was fine and it would be OK if we needed to meet another time. He apologized and explained that his Godfather had just passed away the day before and that he was taking his death hard. His dad had passed away some 15 years earlier, and since his dad's passing, his Godfather had been like a father to him. He loved him so deeply and felt the vacuum caused by his passing more than any loss he had ever experienced before. I listened as he poured out his heart, relating memories and meaningful experiences about him and his Godfather. Sometimes he laughed, and sometimes he cried. He talked for two hours. When emotionally spent, he looked at his watch and said he was surprised at how much time had passed. He then said that he was ready to listen to my message. I told him that this was not the time for a sales pitch and that if he allowed me, I would see him again in three weeks. I thanked him for sharing the thoughts and feelings that were so precious to him and got up and shook his hand, ready to leave his office. He didn't let go of my hand; he held it firmly and said that I would never again have to wait to see him if I let his receptionist know what time I would be dropping by.

True to his word, the next time I dropped by, he whisked me into his office at the time scheduled with his receptionist. He asked, "So who are the patients that would benefit from Haldol, and how would they benefit?" We talked for quite a while and discussed some specific patients that were highly agitated and problems for the staff. He spoke with the nursing staff and decided to try Haldol to see if it would benefit them. I provided him with samples that he could prescribe and distribute. As it turned out, Haldol calmed one patient that had been highly agitated and disruptive with a small dose of Haldol without needing additional sedation. She became alert, communicative, and cooperative. Her family was grateful and thanked the doctor for his insightful care; previously, they had to knock her out with Thorazine® or other sedatives to control her aggressive behavior, leaving her unconscious and unable to interact with her family. With this new treatment, they felt that they had their grandmother back.

He almost single-handedly got Haldol approved on the formularies in all the nursing homes in western Kansas and the hospital. Until my family moved to Los Angeles, where I was a hospital specialist, we met regularly every three weeks for the next ten months. We even went to a couple of nursing homes together so that he could introduce me to staff members and I could meet patients who had positive transformations. It touched me that a 50-year-old physician would establish an emotional bond with a 24-year-old salesperson. It shows how much someone wants and needs to be heard, understood, and validated when carrying heavy emotional burdens and what can happen when listened to, understood, and validated.

Emotional intelligence enables us to connect with people and help them from where they are rather than changing them to be where we want them to be. Too many parents and bosses try to force people to change when they are not getting what they expect from them. Likewise, they are quick to provide advice or platitudes to "solve" problems before they understand the core issues which give rise to the problems exhibited. They deal with the outer manifestations of problems, usually displayed with anger about others or with excuses for themselves. They never get to the core issues. The core is the emotionally naked part protected by layers of defenses that prevent further injury. The layers were put there as a consequence of emotional trauma. The pre-mature problem solvers and advice-givers never get past the outer layers that mask the real underlying issues. Giving advice, solutions, or problem-solving at the outer layers is like providing prescriptions for disease symptoms rather than dealing with the disease itself. If we don't deal with the core issues, ongoing issues will continue to spew, appearing on an outer layer. These never-ending issues generate endless advice, solutions, and problem-solving. Skill with emotional intelligence enables us to listen, hear, understand, and validate each message which engenders trust and frees people to share the next issue closer to the core.

With the ongoing validation of each message, a fantastic thing happens: the messages stop being about others and start being about themselves. If we can stay emotionally and intellectually connected, without judgment, we can eventually arrive, layer by layer, at the emotionally naked, vulnerable core. That only happens when the person sharing information trusts the person they are sharing information with. We need to show trustworthiness with each message on the journey to the core. People want to be understood at their emotionally naked, vulnerable core. But that bonding experience will only happen with empathetic listening, hearing, understanding, and validating. Few people have the patience or the know-how to do it well.

The competencies section will carefully explore the skills of listening, hearing, understanding, validating, and problem-solving to peel the onion and get to core issues. Not surprisingly, when the core has been laid bare, and the person is ready to have us help them, we can genuinely help them get to a better place. The competencies section will show how to problem-solve by coaching rather than giving advice or providing platitudes.

Piggy in the Middle

Dr. Eric Berne, in his book *Games People Play*, gives many examples of how people play games to justify their victimhood. One of the games that I see victims frequently play is "Piggy in the Middle." It exemplifies well what happens when people try to solve outer layer problems put forth by victims seeking sympathy or justification for their victimhood. It goes like this:

The Piggy in the Middle is a person who has issues: "Lordy, Lordy, do I have issues! Help me, help me, help me please!" Piggy surrounds herself with all kinds of people who are eager to help solve her problems. Piggy throws out one problem after another, seeking advice or counsel to solve it. The eager helpers provide solutions and advice, hopeful to aid the victim. In turn, Piggy either explains why the advice wouldn't help her or accepts it and goes into compliance mode to show that their suggestions won't solve the problem. After a short period of compliance, she is sad (inwardly happy) to report that she did everything recommended and that it didn't solve the problem. The payoff is pleasing for Piggy! Because nothing anyone suggested helped alleviate her issues, she is truly a justified victim. "I don't have to change! But somebody has to do something because this situation is intolerable."

The next level of the game is to get someone to inherit her problems so she can enjoy the benefits of victimhood without putting forth effort. This transference of personal responsibility and accountability for one's problems to someone willing to accept them multiplies the problems: It may provide temporary relief to Piggy but creates additional problems for those receiving them. It creates a dependent relationship where none existed before. For example, if your brother-in-law is getting kicked out of his apartment because he isn't working and doesn't have the funds to pay his monthly rent and you inherit his problem, you are now responsible for the rent. Your brother-in-law is relieved that it is no longer a problem for him. It is now your problem until he gets a job or until you decide to stop paying the rent for him. Ironically, you paying the rent doesn't incentivize him to find work. His new problem is that he is dependent on you to pay his rent. As long as you continue to pay, that dependency is not a "real problem" for your brother-in-law. If you decide to stop paying the rent, he will see you as the problem and why he gets kicked out of the apartment. Sadly, inheriting other people's problems doesn't address the original issues.

As a bishop of our local church unit in Arlington Heights, Illinois, I frequently worked with people supported by governmental social services. They were usually pretty comfortable being taken care of by the state but were dissatisfied at the level of lifestyle provided by the state. Helping these people become self-sufficient was a difficult journey for many because they had gotten used to the dependent relationship and felt entitled to whatever help they were receiving. Most eventually caught the vision of the benefits of becoming independent and got engaged in becoming so. But these people who wanted to become self-sufficient and independent were the very people that the social services agents least wanted to lose from their client lists; they were the easiest to work with, and they seldom caused problems or extra work. You can guess the complexities of helping someone become self-sufficient while the social services agents tried to convince them to remain dependent. I would estimate about a 50% success rate in assisting people to become self-sufficient. Usually, we had to deal with a phase where the people we were helping saw that the help we were providing combined with the state's help could improve their standard of living. Of course, we wouldn't support that. They had to choose; if they decided on our help, to become independent and accept the standard of living that they could provide for themselves, which would rise as their self-sufficiency increased. If they chose the state, then they didn't have to work but would have to live the lifestyle provided by the state assistance, which usually, over time, declined due to inflation and rising costs year-to-year. Those who succeeded in becoming self-sufficient knew that we cared for them as people and strived to help them improve their lives.

Knowing, or finding out, what is going on in the hearts and minds of people establishes bonds of trust. It develops mutual respect and understanding that enables both to be conduits for healing and development for one another. Emotional intelligence helps create relationships that transform lives.

4) Combining emotional intelligence knowledge and skills to manage relationships

As we mentioned in the Touchpoint on feelings, "Relationships are emotional states that exist between people." The emotional states between synergistic relationships enable interpersonal connections that deliver enormous mutual benefits. These emotional states engender teamwork and unity in purpose and actions. They allow people to avoid many conflicts and work through conflict when it inevitably surfaces. It fosters mutual respect that enables people to influence and coach one another without defensiveness by the one being coached or influenced. It makes the meeting of the mind and hearts rewarding and straightforward. It minimizes the potential for tension, or force, that causes people to resist one another's gestures because it is not based on coercion or dominance but rather on mutual respect and acceptance. It reduces the possibility of fundamental attribution errors, which occur when people take something personally and assume negative intent when seeing abnormal or socially inappropriate behavior. It minimizes that misinterpretation because they innately know that the person they have a synergistic relationship with wouldn't purposely offend or harm them. And, they respond by finding out what happened based on their concern for the person who displayed the unexpected behavior.

People who have synergistic relationships can inspire one another. They find it stimulating to learn from one another and seek opportunities to meet. It is easy to be emotionally intelligent because of mutual respect and the emotional states in synergistic relationships. Each helps the other to be emotionally intelligent. It is easy to ask one another, "Why do you believe that?" Or to empathetically validate one another's feelings and messages without fear of push-back or rejection.

Emotional intelligence is virtually absent in Mutually Destructive Relationships, which are Adversarial or Enemy. In Adversarial Relationships, where the objective is to win, empathy does not exist. In Enemy

Relationships, where the aim is to make your rival lose worse than you do, there is no such thing as a positive emotional connection. In Mutually Destructive Relationships people experience extreme emotions, but they are not conducive to empathy. The emotional state that exists between these relationships is contrary to emotional intelligence. I am not sure that given a choice, Adversaries or Enemies would even accept it as a gift; in this arena, emotional intelligence has no value unless it would provide an advantage over the Adversary or the Enemy. If it did exist, it would be information coming from another source presented as a means to gain an edge in the contest. Essentially it would be the same as spies providing information about the enemy to their intelligence officers in the military to gain an advantage in future battles.

Still, not being emotionally intelligent need not be a permanent condition in life. Thankfully, I know many people who had a shortage of emotional intelligence who became very skillful in getting it and using it. I have seen the beginning of the change process. It frequently happens when people do a "check-up-from-the-neck-up" and realize that they are living as a Stompee or being a Stomper with the people they love and decide that they don't like it. Once they have this gestalt, they have moved from the arena of being unaware and ineffective (they didn't know that they were a Stompee or a Stomper) to being aware of their Stompee and Stomper behavior. When this happens, they gain much greater insight into their current condition's problems for themselves and others.

At this point, the people who choose to change from being Stompees and Stompers and to develop synergistic relationships have also decided to become more socially sensitive and develop emotional intelligence. Some require professional psychological or psychiatric help to do so. I have found that to be the case more frequently with Stompees than with Stompers. Some can do it pretty well on their own, using their adult mode to analyze the old recordings and messages that have previously governed their behaviors (and feelings) and replacing them with healthy and socially acceptable ones. Many get training through seminars or executive coaching to make the changes. They progress

when they replace Stompee and Stomper behavior with synergistic behavior, but to do so, they need to think about it and make it a conscious
act. If they keep doing it well, the synergistic behavior eventually becomes natural and requires no conscious effort. It should be comforting
to know that behavior change creates transformations in relationships.
Relationships that were once Stomper and Stompee relationships become synergistic: Soulmates, Tribe Members, Friends, Partners, and
Advocates. The change in relationships also creates change in feelings
(emotional states). The emotional states that exist in Synergistic relationships kindle emotional intelligence.

I have a dear friend who attended one of my Touchpoint seminars. He
said that it was a life-changing experience for him because he discovered that he operated in Command and Control parent mode most of
the time and in Critical Parent mode some of the time. He recognized
how his behavior, while intended to benefit his children, could be interpreted by them as disapproval or could send the message that they
were deficient. He saw one of his children as a rebellious child who
flaunted his and many societies' rules. He saw another as an Adaptive
child who was obedient and compliant with his every whim. She never
caused him any problems, but she seemed too removed from the social
interactions typical of teenage girls. One son is an overachiever who
acts as though he needs to prove that he is the best in everything he
does. My friend is very proud of him and tells him that, but his son
needs constant approval. My friend asked me, "How can he be so good
at everything and still seem insecure?" When he asked me that, he
didn't realize that insecure over-achieving children spawn from Critical Parent mode parenting. And, by the way, his over-achieving son is
pretty critical of his children.

My friend is like a sponge when it comes to relationship touchpoints.
He loves to talk about the subjects associated with relationships and
interpersonal connections. He wants to know everything possible
about the topics, not just information but skills, competencies, and
knowledge that can become part of his behavior, values, thinking, decisions, and behaviors. He desires that his children and posterity be-

come knowledgeable and skillful about the touchpoints so that they can avoid some of the hard lessons he experienced before he understood them. He shares his knowledge with everyone who wants it and others he sees who need it. He teaches touchpoints to his family, the people he works with, and even with strangers (if he can figure out a way to connect with them). He is one of the most loving, sensitive, and socially sensitive people I know. His emotional intelligence is impressive. How he could have been a Command and Control Parent and a Critical Parent seems foreign to who he is now, and it seems impossible that he ever was controlling and critical. He is grateful to have been exposed to the touchpoint principles, concepts, and competencies and for the differences they have made in his life. If you were ever to meet him, his emotional intelligence would embrace you. He is one of those remarkable people who live it better than I teach it.

Indeed, emotional intelligence has the power to transform lives for the better – our own and others.

30

ETHICAL OR MORAL POWER

I think it was Chairman Mao who said, "Honesty is nothing; the reputation of it is everything." His somewhat cynical view of honesty is pretty accurate. Honesty is a virtue that, in a perfect society, would be the core standard and behavior leading to success based on trust in all facets of society. But it is not honesty that motivates people's support; it is its reputation that motivates support. We have countless politicians broadcasting and testifying their honesty and trustworthiness, who lie and do precisely the opposite of what they tell us. For them, they have learned that being honest is nothing, but its reputation is everything.

A reputation of honesty and trustworthiness provides influence power over others. Sadly, there are way too many and numerous examples of dishonesty and deceit throughout time and societies that are well rewarded. We seem to accept much dishonesty, so it naturally becomes a tool in the bag of those who would use it for personal gain at the expense of others. People use the trust-me ploy to deceive people into giving them funds, only to betray that trust for personal benefit. Once they are known to be dishonest or untrustworthy, the ploy loses effectiveness if used again on the same people (if burnt once, shame on you; if burnt twice, shame on me). To continue using the ploy effectively, the untrustworthy need to find others who know nothing of their dishonesty. And yet, there seems to be an endless stream of people and organizations who prosper from deception. Organizations get rich from cheating their suppliers and customers. If one can maintain a reputation of honesty and trust while at the same time being dishonest and untrustworthy, returns can be beyond belief. But that is not an easy thing to do forever. E. F. Hutton ceased to exist because of fraud discovery.

Bernard L. Madoff was an American fraudster who amassed a $64.8 billion fortune before he was exposed. His reputation of skillful money management and trustworthiness led to his becoming the Chairman of the NASDAQ stock exchange for a time. Through his dishonesty and using a reputation of success and trustworthiness, he destroyed countless lives of those who trusted him financially and emotionally. He is one of the few white-collar criminals punished for his transgressions; he died in jail. Bernard would have never have lived long enough to get out of prison unless he lived over two hundred years.

William Shakespeare makes clear the importance of reputation in his play *Othello (No Fear)*, Act 3, Scene 3:

Iago: *"Nor for my manhood, honesty, and wisdom to let you know my thoughts."*

Othello: *"What dost thou mean?"*

Iago: *"Good name in man and woman, dear my Lord, is the immediate jewel of their souls.*

Who steals my purse steals trash.

'Tis something, nothing: 'Twas mine. 'Tis his, and has been slaves to thousands.

But he that filches from me my good name, robs me of that which not enriches him

And makes me poor indeed."

Power, of any sort, has the potential to do great good or great harm to those on whom exercised. That includes ethical or moral power. Economy theorists tell us that honesty and trust are rewarded in the marketplace because they create a positive reputation upon which customers can depend. In contrast, dishonesty produces a bad reputation that will cause a backlash of negative information that spreads exponentially by those treated dishonestly. I have experienced this personally, in a big way, while working for Janssen Pharmaceutica, a pharmaceutical division of Johnson & Johnson.

In 1982, seven people died from ingesting Tylenol capsules laced with potassium cyanide. It didn't take too long for the authorities to figure out the cause of the deaths. Unfortunately, none of the tainted capsules came from the same manufacturing batch or, in some cases, from the same manufacturing facility. That meant that a simple recall of the poisoned batches was out of the question because no one knew how widespread the tampering was. Fortunately, all of the deaths and reported cases happened within the greater Chicago metropolitan area, which suggested that a local criminal or criminals had caused these deaths. Hopefully, no further deaths would happen beyond the Chicago area.

Later, in 1988, I started playing tennis with Jim Burke, the Chairman of the Board at Johnson & Johnson, and some other executives, so I was able to personally get his account of how he, and they, decided to pull all the Tylenol off the shelves (and the supply chains) where Tylenol was sold and distributed. I will try and share this as an accurate narrative of what he told me.

When news of the Tylenol deaths reached Jim Burke, he immediately called his emergency board together to determine the appropriate actions to be taken. He said that when they were all gathered around the board table, he asked them first, "What accurate information do we have?" They told him of the deaths, where they occurred, and the cause of the deaths. They quickly found out from the police the batch numbers of the bottles from which the tainted capsules came. It became evident that more deaths could come from bottles with different batch numbers from the ones identified thus far. Jim asked each board member, "So given the information we have, what are our options?" He received different answers to the question from the various board members. One said that given the local nature of the deaths, J&J should immediately institute a regional recall of all Tylenol products. Another said that we should immediately do a total recall. Another explained that no product had ever recovered from a total recall in the market, so he suggested a recall but limited to the smallest area possible. There were other suggestions, but they are of little importance now.

After getting input from all of his advisors, he told me that he walked over to the wall, where the J&J Credo plaque was hanging on the wall, took it down and placed it in the middle of the board table, and asked them, "What does the first part of the first credo statement say?" It says: "*We believe our first responsibility is to the patients, doctors and nurses, to mothers and fathers and all others who use our products and services. In meeting their needs everything we do must be of high quality.*"

He stopped them at that point and asked, "Based on that, what are our options?" **One of the board members stated that if we use that as the basis of our decisions, there is only one option: a total recall of the product everywhere**. Jim said, "Now that has been decided, how do we do it?"

J&J recalled over 31 million bottles of Tylenol and promised to replace them with new bottles of Tylenol that would be secure and safe because of new manufacturing standards incorporated into every Tylenol product. First, J&J would no longer manufacture Tylenol capsules because of the ability for someone to mix poison into the contents. Caplets replaced capsules, tablets shaped like capsules but were solid throughout and unable to be tainted. Second, under the cap would be placed a seal indicating if someone had accessed the bottle's contents. Third, the cap would have a plastic seal placed around it and heat shrunk to fit tightly and show evidence if someone tried to access the bottle. Fourth, the box containing the bottle would have a seal placed on the opening flap showing that someone would have to break it to access the bottle. Jim explained that if any one of the three seals were broken or appeared to have been tampered with, to return the bottle to the place where they had purchased it, and the seller would immediately replace it.

Jim was straightforward and honest with the media and everyone; he pulled no punches and said it like it was. He got unbelievable exposure on TV demonstrating the new caplets and having the opportunity to explain the safety measures. His demonstrations and explanations created confidence in the Tylenol product lines. As a result, Tylenol returned, gaining the largest market share ever attained by a non-prescription analgesic, over 25%. Jim was considered a hero within the industry and with society in general. His decision to recall Tylenol and replace it has been taught in MBA programs across the country and worldwide as an example of ethical leadership and moral good business practice.

I remember him telling me, in person, and everyone, at a stockholder meeting that his decisions were not altruistic but were simply good business. He said that the only thing J&J sold that is enduring is trust and confidence in our products. Management's job is to ensure that trust and confidence.

Working at Janssen, and indirectly for J&J, during the Tylenol crisis provided proud memories. Everyone in every J&J company was on the phone helping to recall all the Tylenol sold or in the distribution line. It is memorable because we were part of something trustworthy and greater than ourselves.

By the way, the safety measures incorporated by J&J for Tylenol became the standard for all pharmaceutical non-prescription products. We can thank James Burke and J&J for the three layers of safety seals on our health care products sold over the counter.

Moral leadership can change the destiny of man and the world, as demonstrated by great moral leaders of antiquity like Jesus Christ, Mohammad, and Buddha. Great philosophers like Socrates, Plato, and Aristotle have provided ways of thinking and living that have influenced humankind for many hundreds of years. More recent philosophers like Immanuel Kant, Friedrich Nietzsche, Rene Descartes, John Locke, and David Hume still challenge our thoughts on life and living.

Recent vintage moral leaders have taught us who we are, who we should be, and how to become what we should be. Winston Churchill saved the world from unspeakable evil by uniting the United Kingdom and later the allies to fight and defeat Hitler and the Nazis. Nelson

Mandela led South Africans and eventually the world to throw out the racist apartheid government and replace it with the first fully representative government in that nation's history. Martin Luther King Jr. was an American Baptist minister. As a spokesman for American civil rights, he raised to high visibility the inequities and prejudice placed upon black people and minorities in the United States. Dr. King fought for equal civil rights for all Americans through nonviolent civil demonstrations. He was assassinated in 1965 by one of those prejudiced people whose mind and heart he failed to touch. But his moral power helped to pass critical civil rights legislation in the mid-1960s. His legacy carries the mission forward to the present time and will predictably continue until equal rights are available to everyone in this country. Dr. King learned his approach to nonviolent civil demonstrations to change society from Mahatma K. Gandhi.

Mahatma Karamchand Gandhi "…*was an Indian lawyer, anti-colonial nationalist, and political ethicist who employed nonviolent resistance to lead the successful campaign for India's independence from British rule and who, in turn, inspired the movement for civil rights and freedom across the world.*" (Internet Wikipedia). He never held an elected position, but he became the unquestioned moral leader of the Indian people who were governed by the British.

Gandhi[36] left India to go to law school in 1888 at the University College London, Faculty of Laws, as a quiet 18-year-old student. He graduated three years later in 1891, specializing in civil rights law. He returned to India in 1891 to practice in India but. in 1893. took a one-year contract to do legal work in Southern Africa, where many parts of the area were also governed by the British. As a result of the Boer War (1898-1900), Great Britain took the dominant governing role in the country, which became the country of South Africa. During the war, he was a medical assistant. He tried to claim his rights as a British subject during that time, but he was terribly abused for his efforts and saw that all the Indians in South Africa were treated in the same fashion. He stayed in

---

36 Biography.com Editors, *Mahatma Gandhi* (Biography.com website. https://www.biography.com/activist/mahatma-gandhi, February 2022).

South Africa for 21 years, trying to secure rights for the abused Indian British subjects there. In South Africa, he developed a method of fighting for civil rights based on principles of courage, nonviolence, and truth called Satyagraha, which promoted civil disobedience and nonviolence to achieve political and social goals. He returned to India in 1915, where he focused his experience and talents fighting for civil rights for Indians in India. Within 15 years, he became the leader of the Indian National Movement, which sought independence for India from Britain. He was arrested many times but felt it was honorable to go to prison for moral reasons. Gandhi became known as "Mahatma" by all Indians, and the rest of the world, an honorary name meaning Great Soul.

His fame grew, and his unquestionable moral leadership gave him virtually unlimited power to influence the actions of his fellow Indians. As his moral influence grew, so did the hatred of the British for him. He was a massive pain in the side of the British rulers, and they wanted him out of the way. Winston Churchill, an English nobleman who supported the English monarchy system and later became England's Prime Minister, hated him so much that he wanted him assassinated. He used his position in the House of Commons to try and find a way – any way – to dispose of this "anarchist" who would destroy nearly a hundred years of British rule in India. Churchill sensed that Mahatma was someone who would not go away unless he ceased to exist. He knew that Mahatma was an existential threat to the British rule in India and other British dominions. He was right to be concerned.

Mahatma knew that the British controlled the government in India and the economy. For example, they used India to grow the cotton sent to England, processed, and turned into linen and clothing. After becoming sellable merchandise, they sent the articles to India and sold them to Indians. The Indians would earn very little from growing the cotton, but the English who owned the plantations became immensely wealthy from the labor and cotton provided by the poor Indians. The English would get rich at the other end by manufacturing and selling Indian cotton back to India as finished products. They had a monopoly and knew how to keep it. Since they controlled the government, they made it illegal to manufacture cotton linen and clothing in India. Cotton was not the only area of monopoly. Virtually anything manufactured or processed fell under the control of England. England's economy and manufacturing grew while India remained poor, a supplier of wealth but not a beneficiary of the wealth. This arrangement provided Great Britain with cheap labor and resources that made Britain stronger and richer but kept India poor and dependent on the British.

Knowing that nothing would change as long as India remained dependent on Britain, Gandhi acted to eliminate British control by having the Indians produce their clothing and distill their salt. He knew that if India tried to create factories and industries to compete directly with Britain, England would crush them. He also knew that if all Indians grew their own cotton, made their own clothing, and produced their own salt, family by family, there was nothing the British could do to stop it. Both clothing and salt were staples for every family. The British monopoly entirely controlled them. Gandhi took off his suits, spun his cotton thread, and made his clothes. Here was a London-educated attorney wearing proudly, for the rest of his life, white homespun clothing. It became his trademark; it made him and his image an icon, known throughout the world as a symbol of freedom and independence. And hundreds of millions of Indians followed his example. Virtually every family obtained a spinning wheel and started wearing homespun clothing. That is why the icon of a spinning wheel is on the national flag of India. This single action took the wind out of the English clothing manufacturing and fanned the flames of even greater hatred toward Gandhi. They threw him in prison and threatened the Indian nation. Their reaction only caused millions more to start making their clothing.

Having proved his point with cotton production and clothing manufacturing, that India didn't need to depend on the British for clothing, he focused on the salt production and distribution industry. He decided to walk from his religious retreat near Ahmedabad to the Arabian Sea to distill his salt from the ocean waters. His "salt march" went from March through April in 1930. Tens of thousands of Indians joined the march. It was a march of over 240 miles, and along the way, over 60,000 Indians were arrested, including Mahatma. He organized a protest at a salt mine. Thousands of his followers met in front of the salt mine. They came unarmed and ready to sacrifice their lives, if need be, to protest the English monopoly of salt mining and production in India. Among their group were nurses and doctors there to treat the imminent casualties anticipated from the protest. The English had guards armed with clubs waiting for them at the mine entrance. The Indians lined up in rows of four slowly walked to the gates of the mine, where they were severely beaten with clubs by the guards. The medical volunteers gathered the injured and carried them back to the locations prepared to treat their injuries. From the clubbing, some died immediately; others did so later, after failing to heal. Large numbers were severely injured. But as those at the front of the lines were clubbed and hauled away, the following people in the queue stepped forward to be beaten., offering no resistance. Eventually, the guards, who were also Indian, threw down their clubs because they could no longer justify to themselves clubbing and injuring the defenseless men who faced them and courageously waited for injuries. In preparation for the protest, Gandhi told his followers that they were in a war and people would be injured and die. He said to them that there are many things that he would be willing to die for but nothing that he would be willing to kill for. An entire nation of Indians, hundreds of millions, untied behind his moral courage and an unbendable will.

Finally, the British knew that they could no longer govern India. The British Indian Governor said that to stay in power, they would have to kill all the Indians who supported Gandhi and Indian independence (that would have been hundreds of millions). But then he stated that we would have absolutely no one left to govern. India gained its independence in 1947. To me, Mahatma Gandhi is a supreme example of moral power. But the power of his moral character doesn't end with India's independence.

After India gained its independence, deciding who would govern the country instigated a huge civil contest between the Hindus and the

Muslims. Violence broke out between them neighborhood by neighborhood, community by community. Gandhi was more than troubled by the violence happening in his beloved India. He started a fast that he would only break when the violence ceased; he would rather have died than endure violence between his Indian brothers and sisters. Mahatma was loved by both the Hindus and the Muslims, even though they hated one another. Day by day, his health declined. Daily, the status of his declining health was broadcast throughout the nation, with leaders of both sects pleading with their followers to stop the fighting to save Gandhi's life. Just days before he would have died from his fasting, the nation was able to report to him that the violence had ceased. It is said that upon hearing the news, Mahatma weakly smiled and asked, "May I have a little milk?"

He was a peculiar little fellow. He loved testing himself and his commitments to self-sacrifice. The dietary restrictions and the commitment to live simply didn't seem much of a challenge for him. On the other hand, his vow of celibacy was another story. At his religious retreat, he used to sleep between two beautiful young women to test his commitment and willpower. His wife, who he married when they were 13-years-of-age and who was the mother of their four children, would just chuckle and shake her head when asked about this sleeping arrangement. She knew that celibacy was a true test for him. Mahatma died on January 30, 1948. I was 18 days old at the time. He was shot three times in the chest as he walked through a crowd by a Hindu fanatic.

Having gained some insight into him through the previous passages, we might gain insight into his influence and moral power from a few of his most famous quotes.

"An eye for an eye only ends up making the whole world blind."

"Happiness is when what you think, what you say, and what you do are in harmony."

"Where there is love, there is life."

"The weak can never forgive. Forgiveness is the attribute of the strong."

"Hate the sin, love the sinner."

"I am prepared to die, but there is no cause for which I am prepared to kill."

"Earth provides enough to satisfy every man's needs, but not every man's greed."

"In a gentle way, you can shake the world."

"Action expresses priorities."

"If you don't ask for it, you don't get it."

"The future depends on what we do in the present."

His book *The Story of My Experiences with Truth: An Autobiography*[37] is not a typical biography but rather is an explanation of his quest for truth. It explains his devotion to God and how he sought to become closer to His Devine Power by seeking purity through simple living, dietary practices, celibacy, and a life of respect for all living things. He was brilliant, was hated by the British, was imprisoned for his activities, and was relentless in his objective to gain India's independence from Britain. He was the architect of India's independence. His moral and ethical power came from his commitment to his unconditional values, which were the basis of all his decisions and actions regardless of the situation (we will review values in the Values Touchpoint of this book). We can all develop moral power when we have clearly defined unconditional values and use them as the basis for our decisions and actions in all situations.

If we think about it, we realize that America is an idea; its power and influence are based on moral and ethical principles. Its greatness lies in the mental, emotional, social, spiritual, and ethical ideas encompassed

---

37   M. K. Gandhi, *The Story of My Experiences with Truth: An Autobiography* (Published in his journal from 1925 to 1929. Reprinted by Penguin Random House, 2019).

in the moral principles it holds sacred. America is nothing more than how we live by our moral and ethical principles and standards. Our lives based on our moral standards ultimately determines who we are and what America is.

31

CONNECTION/RELATIONSHIP POWER

We derive another power from synergistic relationships. Who we know indeed creates opportunities for us. Unquestionably, graduates from Harvard become part of an inner circle. Those in the circle take special notice and give special attention to others in their circle. They may not know you personally, but you have a special relationship with everyone in the inner circle because you are a Harvard graduate. They have informal and formal networks that help Harvard graduates find and capture opportunities unavailable to non-Harvard graduates. I think it is great; it is one of the reasons for going to Harvard, in addition to getting a top-notch education.

In 1975, I left employment with J&J for one week and went to work for another company because I felt that McNeil had cheated me out of the majority of my year-end bonus. Allow me to explain. I was a hospital specialist in the Los Angeles area where I sold Haldol®, a non-sedating major tranquilizer used to treat psychosis and extreme agitation. I represented McNeil Laboratories in the 12 largest psychiatric hospitals in southern California. I also sold the anesthesia product Sublimaze® (Fentanyl), a powerful and short-acting narcotic used in anesthesia. I was the McNeil hospital representative for all the large teaching hospitals in southern California and the Kaiser Permanente hospitals.

In 1975, I was the first representative in the company's history to have more than a million dollars sales increase from those two products in one year. Before that year, the policy at McNeil was to give salespeople 5% of the yearly sales increase to sales representatives as a sales bonus. I expected to receive over $50,000 in bonus pay plus my base salary of approximately $15,000. As it turned out, just before payout, the company sent out a revised bonus plan that limited maximum bonus payouts to $5,000. I couldn't believe it, particularly since I was the only salesman in the entire company that the new bonus limits impacted. I was so upset that I called my dear friend, George, whose friendship began in Colorado when we were both pharmaceutical salesmen there. He worked for Flint Dialysis Corp., whose headquarters were in Chicago. I asked him if he would provide a reference for me with his company. He did and arranged for me to meet with the VP of Sales and Marketing in the home office. They flew me there, and I met with the VP of Sales and Marketing. He offered me a job on the spot. While there, we decided to enroll me in a two-week training program about dialysis treatments and about selling dialysis machines with their supporting products.

Within hours of being at their headquarters, I realized that almost all of the top management in the organization in Chicago were graduates from Notre Dame. Notre Dame is just like Harvard in that graduates from there are connected and look out for one another. The old saying that "If it looks like a duck, walks like a duck, and quacks like a duck, it is a duck," seemed to apply to the Flint Dialysis Corp. senior management group. It looked like a Notre Dame club, it moved like a Notre Dame club, and it spoke like a Notre Dame club; therefore, it was a Notre Dame club, and I was not a graduate of Notre Dame. I could see that I would never become a member of that special club. That was not the only consideration, but it was one of the reasons that I decided it was best if I stayed with Johnson & Johnson. While I was there, the VP of marketing for McNeil Laboratories flew back to Chicago to talk with me and convince me to return to Johnson & Johnson. By the time I got back to California, he had arranged four J&J international management opportunities. We moved to Vancouver, British Columbia, to become the sales manager for a J&J company in western Canada a couple of months later.

George's reference to Flint Dialysis Corp. and his support is a pretty good example of connection power.

If we take the time to notice, we are all surrounded by clubs that have inner circle memberships. They might exist because of religious affiliation, sexual orientation, food fetishes, or the kind of pets we have. There are an infinite number of reasons why they are there. The point is: they exist. We can't become a part of all of them, but we should become a part of one, or more, of them. They satisfy our basic need for belonging and to have status. Obviously, if it is reasonably healthy, our family should be a place where we are part of the club, the inner circle. In that intimate club, we should find protection, help to overcome obstacles and assistance in finding opportunities through our family connections. Not all families have equal prominence or influence power within our communities, our state, or the nation; the more significant the prominence and status, the greater the connection power. Heck, it even applies in our neighborhoods, not that I care much (wink, wink).

Some people think connection power is unfair. I guess that depends on where we sit concerning having the "right connections." It is reality. We don't have to isolate ourselves and be a lone wolf. Independence is a good thing, but so is belonging. Believe it or not, we can be independent people responsible and accountable for our emotions, decisions, and actions and still be part of a group. That is the best of both worlds, having a voice within a group that is accepting and supporting us. It may be ludicrous to say this because it is so obvious, but being independent doesn't mean we have to be anti-everything; we can independently agree or disagree with our inner circle. Usually, they will keep us if we disagree, but that depends on the group; agreeing may be part of the group charter. If you express an opinion contrary to the group-think in some groups, then you will no longer be welcome. The best response in that situation might be: "You can't fire me out because I have already quit!" Oh, what we do to preserve face.

One of the interesting characteristics of many groups is the appearance that they think and move as a single entity. If you are part of the group, the group's enemies are your enemies. Their causes are your causes, their biases are your biases, and their offenses are your offenses. It is a lot like being a core political party member. You must stick with the party line, no matter how crazy or illogical the party line may be. That is why I don't claim to be a political party member anymore. I want to choose my beliefs and causes and support things independently. I will not become a member of some clubs, no matter how they try to convince me. There are those select few that I will willingly join and support as long as we align in principles and morals.

When I was a senior in college in 1972, I took a political theory class from Professor Thaddeus Merrill. For my class project, another student and I decided to create the Conservative Student's Association, which was no association, just a fancy title for our project. There was no such thing as a home computer or even a thought of a social network or internet in those days. (You could tell who the computer science majors were because they carried punch cards around to feed information into the "so-called" computer. They differentiated themselves from the engineering students who always wore their slide rulers in their shirt pockets.) Anyway, the goal of our project was to gather the voting records for all the candidates running for office that year in Utah and Idaho and make them available to voters. We would invite local or statewide candidates to come to the student union building on the USU campus to talk with the students or anyone else who wanted to attend. We would make copies of their voting records available to everyone who participated in the candidate's presentation. (Thankfully, Dr. Merrill paid for the documents.) It was amazing how quickly a participating candidate found himself surrounded by foraging wolves when they claimed to have supported an issue contrary to their voting record. Once it became apparent to those invited to speak that their voting record would be visible to everyone, they made sure to avoid the issues where they had voted on both sides. If they couldn't avoid it, they had to explain why they voted the way they did.

Within a couple of weeks, politicians, or their representatives, started calling us to get scheduled at one of our union building gatherings. I was amazed when Senator Hansen called me and invited me to fly me to his Idaho office to have lunch with him. His motive became evident quickly; he was looking for an endorsement from the Conservative Students Association. I explained that we did not endorse any of the candidates but simply arranged for them to meet with the students and voters to share their messages while voters could see if their current positions aligned with their voting record. Senator Hansen told me that he understood but still wanted me to come and meet with him before he accepted an invitation to speak at one of our meetings. I gave him the excuse that I couldn't go because I couldn't miss work at my part-time job at Tri-Miller packing plant, where I was a meat cutter (which was true). My grandmother from Dayton, Idaho, wanted to shoot me when she found out that I turned down an invitation to meet and have lunch with Senator Hansen because she was a huge fan of his. (In 1984, he was convicted for violating the 1978 Ethics Act and was sentenced to six months in prison.)

Our project turned into something crazy; I had long lists of phone messages saved for me from local and state politicians wanting to talk with me and to schedule time to participate in our public venues.

I remember that Cal Rampton, a candidate running for the governor's office, wanted to speak at one of our sessions. But his expectations exceeded our ability to satisfy them, so we couldn't make it happen. We had a similar problem with his opposing candidate, Nicholas Strike, so we didn't get to put their voting records in front of the students. However, we gathered and summarized their voting records and made copies of that information available to anyone who would come to the Old Main building on campus and pick them up. Surprisingly, someone picked up all the copies. Dr. Merrill suspected that one of the candidates, or one of his representatives, picked them up to keep them out of the public's eye. Cal Rampton won the governorship easily, and my partner and I got an A on our project. I learned a lot about connection power and how important people wanted to use it and leverage it for their benefit.

We can choose to use connection power for good or bad, just like any other power. Some use connections to benefit others, and some use them for selfish purposes or for hurting their adversaries. There is a power that comes through relationships. Some power comes from being part of a mob where individual accountability is avoided because no one individual is responsible for the destructive behavior of everyone. The nature of mobs is that individuals lose their identity and simply become part of the flow of passions that quickly become out of control when strong passions unite with other strong emotions. By the same token, people who connect to fight hunger or treat those with no access to medical care join as members of an inner circle of goodness, compassion, and love. It would be wonderful if all connection power were tied together from synergistic relationships. Then the emotional connections would be positive and mutually supportive of good causes. Regrettably, Stompers and those seeking to dominate and control others harness too much connection power. We should be wise in the connections we make and the use of the power that comes from those connections. We do have choices in the alliances we make.

As a summary of circumstantial powers compared to the nature and characteristics of Dominance power used in combination with circumstantial powers.

Synergistic Power in combination with Circumstantial powers	Dominance Power in combination with Circumstantial powers
The Resulting Nature and Characteristics	The Resulting Nature and Characteristics
• Joins and builds synergistic relationships • Protects personal boundaries and respects the boundaries of other • Builds trust, if founded on respect • Engages the head, captures the heart, and mobilizes the hands of people • Aims for internalized commitment by explaining what needs to be done and why. How is only discussed when people don't know how to do something • Attracts good people • Strengthens and energizes people • Is influence based • Achieves results while enhancing relationships • Generates a high quality of life • Engenders high morale • Delivers short-term and long-term results • Others willingly give power to the leader • Is effortless when others are meeting expectations • Is receptive to other ideas, is provisional, and is open-minded • Defines a culture of an organization at its highest level or its best	• Distances and weakens relationships • Is disrespectful of others' boundaries • Creates distrust • Is founded on force and fear • Centralizes decision-making from the top down • Seeks only to mobilize the hands of people • Weakens, repels, and drains people • Aims at compliance or coerced obedience by focusing on telling people what to do and how to do it • Achieves results at the expense of relationships • Generates a low quality of life for those dominated • Engenders low morale • Focuses on and delivers short-term results with questionable long-term sustainability • Is imposed on others • Is used when others fail to meet expectations • Is close-minded to differing ideas • Defines the culture of an organization at its lowest worst point

Two questions:
One: Which kind of power would you choose for others to use with you?
Two: Which kind of power is the most commonly used in families, organizations, and society?

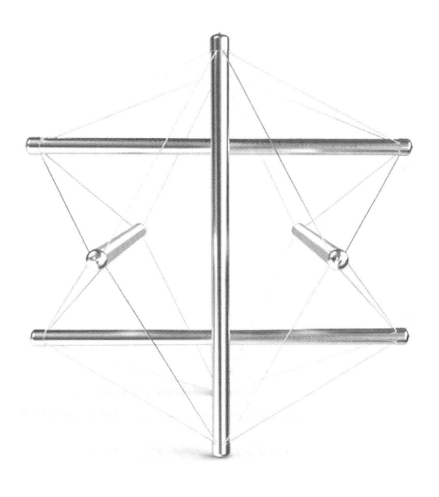

32

Introduction to Values

When our son, Reed was in second grade, he came home with an assignment to bring a list of our family rules to class. Well, we quickly realized that we didn't have a list of family rules for him to take to school. We did have a list of family values that we used as the basis for our decisions and actions, so we sent that list to school with Reed. That evening we received a call from his teacher, who explained that Reed was the only student in the class who didn't provide a list of family rules. She wasn't criticizing, which was our first reaction to her call, but she was intrigued by the concept of managing our family decisions and actions from values rather than rules. She invited our family to come to Reed's class and share our practice of leading by values rather than by rules with his classmates and parents.

Frankly, at the school presentation, all were intrigued by our message, although many were skeptical. We explained that rules, policies, and laws all aimed for compliance or obedience to standards that define the lowest acceptable level of behavior; any behavior below that is unacceptable. Rules set, metaphorically speaking, standards of behavior at sea level. Sea level behavior is mediocre. We explained that values inspire behavior that can reach 40,000 feet above sea level and beyond. People obey rules because they have to, whereas people live by values because they want to. With values, as our standards, the goal is not obedience but rather to internalize the values and use them as the basis of our decisions and actions. We explained that we didn't want our kids to obey our rules and be mediocre; we wanted them to think about their behavior within the context and meaning of the values as agreed upon by our family and use their conclusions from their analytical thoughts to guide their decisions and actions. Doing so would inspire extraordinary behavior, far above the minimum standard. It worked well with our family, not to say that our kids were perfect. Often, they acted selfishly or let their short-term desires drive them to foolish behaviors. It did, however, cause them to be responsible and accountable for the decisions they made. Sometimes our kids would ask us to decide for them, but we would usually tell them that they had to decide for themselves based on our values. Almost always, they would make the right decision, sometimes they didn't, which resulted in natural consequences that could be unpleasant; natural consequences for bad choices usually eliminate the need for parental punishments. They all turned out to be pretty good and responsible decision-makers. I'm not sure how many converts we made; we didn't hear from the school again about rules.

Each year my son Matt explains to his girls' volleyball teams why he doesn't set rules to govern the team's behavior. He uses the same rationale we used with Reed's second-grade class. The girls are amazed to discover that he didn't have a curfew when he was a teenager. It causes a buzz among the girls every year. The girls often take that information back to their parents, making them wonder if he is nuts. When asked how the no curfew situation came to be, he just points at me and says: "Papa Wayne" (my nickname in the volleyball community). Recently, at one of the volleyball matches at Park City High School, I was sitting and talking with the parent of one of our volleyball players when the mother turned to me with wide eyes and said, "You are him!" Bewildered, I asked, "I am him, what?" She said, "I just realized that you are the guy that didn't give Matt a curfew as a teenager and are the reason that Matt doesn't use rules to govern the volleyball team." I responded, "I'd like to think so." We spent 30 minutes or so after that discussing the values approach for governance and how wonderful her daughter is.

Because we have a whole section on Levels of Commitment after this section, I won't steal the thunder from that Touchpoint by going deeply into it now. I will share our family values used to govern our family's decisions and actions that Reed took to school.

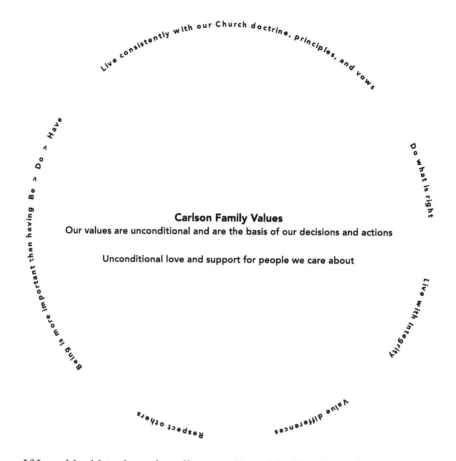

Live consistently with our Church doctrine, principles, and vows

Have
Do
Be
Being is more important than having

Do what is right

Carlson Family Values
Our values are unconditional and are the basis of our decisions and actions

Unconditional love and support for people we care about

Live with integrity

Respect others

Value differences

If I could add to the values list now, I would add at least these two: 1) Love learning 2) Identify unfulfilled needs and help people fill them passionately and compassionately.

If we were to look at the standards used to govern, we could make a list that includes: laws, statutes, regulations, rules, policies, guidelines, principles, natural laws, and eternal truths. Those most broadly used would define the minimum standards that people must adhere to be acceptable in society. These are standards like laws, statutes, rules, regulations, policies, and guidelines. They are necessary because society needs clearly defined minimum acceptable behavior because, without them, we would live in anarchy – a society based on individual rule. In a state of anarchy, everyone's rules would be self-serving and would likely be destructive to society as a whole. Therefore, to have a civilized society, we need standards defining minimally acceptable behavior. Anything below those standards would be considered illegal and grounds for punishment.

Still, everything that is not illegal is not necessarily moral and ethical. We are surrounded by unethical, amoral, and immoral people not considered criminals because they don't violate the minimum acceptable standard defined by society; they don't break the law. Consider, for example, Bobby (Robert Gene) Baker, an American political advisor to President Lyndon B. Johnson and a prominent organizer for the Democratic Party.[38] He became the Senate's Secretary to the Majority Leader. In 1963, he resigned during an investigation into his business and political activities. He was widely known to walk the edges between legal and illegal, but he galloped on the side of unethical. Some claimed that he went to law school to learn the laws so well that he could come close to being illegal but never completely cross that fine line.

But society, to be more than an authoritarian state, needs to be guided by standards of behavior and thought drawn from principles, moralities, and ethics that exceed the minimum acceptable standards.

Mahatma Gandhi's life was not defined by India's or Britain's laws but by his moral passion for creating a society with equal rights. India is independent of the United Kingdom and is self-governing. He was willing to die for his principles (and he did).

The need for standards in government that define minimum standards for society begs whether the same reasoning should be the basis for governing our organizations and our families. Most families manage by rules with the apparent implication that breaking the family rules will result in punishment. So do many, if not most, organizations. I can't help but wonder if how they are governing is getting them really what they want. I can't imagine they want and aim for the minimum acceptable behavior. But that is what they get if performance is based on standards that define the minimum expected behavior.

---

38 R. G. Baker, *Wheeling and Dealing: Confessions of a Capitol Hill Operator* (W. W. Norton & Company, 1980).

33

THE IMPACT OF USING RULES TO GOVERN BEHAVIOR

Let's examine a rule-based family compared to a value-based family. In many ways, it is **the difference between ruling a child and raising a child**. In both approaches, the parents love their children and want what is best for them. Governing a child with rules is similar to governing a monarchy. It is a hierarchy where the King and Queen rule and regulate their children through edicts. While the children may be royal, they are still subject to their Majesties' whims. Even the ranking among princesses and princes is prescribed from protocol or their majesties' favorable or unfavorable judgment. In most families, dad and mom play the roles of King and Queen. There is an appropriate formality when one rules over a kingdom, and everyone must maintain a proper distance between the King and Queen.

Decisions come from the top down. The protocol determines daily life. People must adhere to the protocols; because to do otherwise would place the offender in peril of losing his head or being imprisoned in the tower. The family equivalent of the tower is time-out in a bedroom. Protocol is passed down from generation to generation but can be changed or modified by the decree of the King or Queen. Subjects have the right to petition their Majesties, but only the King and Queen have the power to alter protocol or kingdom rules. The subjects serve at the pleasure of the majesties and are dependent upon them for favor, disfavor, rewards, or punishments. Monarchy reeks of superiority and inferiority and the Divine Right of Kings. They divvy responsibility and accountability at their pleasure to their subjects, but public accountability for their indiscretions would be improper. Subjects know the kingdom's protocols and rules and learn to align their lives to them strictly. Occasionally, there arise princes and princesses who cannot stand being ruled by autocracy, and they rebel and leave the kingdom, start their own, or try to overthrow it. In a rule-based family, children know that they are in a monarchy, know when they are ruled, and learn how to survive in the kingdom, reinforcing their majesties' sense of omnipotence. Not all princes and princesses are happy, and some never learn how to live successfully among others beyond the castle walls. Sometimes when they leave the castle, they encounter people who sense their vulnerability and lack of street-smarts who take advantage of them. Perhaps the disadvantages outweigh the benefits for those who have been dependent on the King and Queen their whole lives.

When people raise a child rather than rule one, it is like having a dance partner. The pace and rhythm of the music (values) determine the manner of dance. The one with the most experience usually leads, and the junior partner follows. Still, occasionally roles are switched to allow the novice the chance to see what it feels like to lead and to gain a broadened viewpoint about the art of dancing. There is a rhythm, cadence, and flow when dancing well. Partners touch one another and move in sync together. They share the experience, finding pleasure in the dance, the music, and just being together. It is a shared learning experience with each new and unique type of music introduced. Mistakes happen, with both partners, perhaps more with one than the other. Still, mistakes are accepted because that is the nature of learning to dance together, and it happens when introducing new music with a different pace, rhythm, or mood. Mistakes are seen merely as something that needs to be corrected, an opportunity to learn together, and something that makes both partners feel good about themselves when corrected. Dancing is not about rules; while principles of music govern the creation of excellent music, it is also about getting in the flow and feel of the piece so that the dancing becomes a personal interpretation of what the music is expressing. There are so many types of music and ways to express oneself that dancing becomes a demonstration of personal passion and identity. In dancing, both partners have standing and status; in fact, they become a unit, and the status of one becomes the status of both. The music and the synergy between the partners make dancing special. Dancing and raising a child in a value-based environment are both intimate and bonding experiences. To achieve the desired results takes a lot of time, effort, patience, and stick-to-it-ness. That is what it is like to raise a child in a value-based dance.

This week I was one of the coaches at a girls' volleyball match where our team played far below its potential and talent level. We lost in three straight sets. All three sets were close – 23-25, 21-25, and 23-25. Our team took the lead when the girls played according to the game plan. When they went rogue, they lost the lead and eventually the sets and the match. After the match, the varsity team met with the coaches for a feedback session. The girls didn't say much, other than that they tried hard and had a lot of fun. One of the coaches responded to their comments with 20 minutes of guilt-tripping, shaming, and criticism. He made it clear to everyone that he was the victim of the evening. Their lack of following his instructions caused them to lose the match and make him a victim. He felt righteous indignation about the loss, blaming them for it. He attacked them for their lack of sensitivity toward the coaches and felt justified in berating them; he wanted them to feel ashamed.

I was ashamed for sitting there, feeling uncomfortable, rather than interceding to stop the harangue. On the ride home after the match, I was asked for my thoughts on the coaches' feedback to the team. I said I was not a fan of guilt-tripping and shaming and regretted not stopping it. The coach who did it disagreed with my comments and defended his approach as the correct thing to do when dealing with crappy play. A couple of days later, I asked him if we were friends and that if we were, I would like him to permit me to provide him some feedback. He agreed that we were friends and that it was OK to give him some feedback.

I told him that I was ashamed of myself for sitting at the feedback session, feeling embarrassed and uncomfortable about his shaming message to the girls, and for sitting there doing nothing, feeling that it was wrong and yet not intervening. He said again that he thought it was the right message to give. "What gives you the right to do that?!" I asked. "I'm a coach!" was his response. His answer smacked of the

Divine Right of Kings. His position power, as a coach, in his mind justified his attacks. Because he is "the coach," it makes his decision to shame those not following protocol deserving of belittlement and emotional punishment. I responded with, "OK, you **can** do it because you are a coach, but **why** would you do it?" He explained that he was trying to protect Matt, the head coach and that he also saw it as motivating the players. I said that I didn't believe that it motivated anyone but did just the opposite and that it besmirched our character, making us guilty by association. Whether he knew it or not, he was trying to use emotional manipulation as a tool to control his subjects. The trouble is that his shaming cast a much wider net than for just those who played; it engulfed everyone present. He apparently does not realize that his speech motivated no one and benefited only himself. He didn't apologize but did admit that it was a selfish thing to do. I told him that I would apologize to the girls for my neglect of not protecting them from what I believed to be badly inappropriate behavior. I ended my part of the conversation with a statement that I would never again sit and watch anything like that happen without taking action.

This incident was, to me, a real-life example of ruling children rather than raising them. Coaching is about raising children to self-analyze, take responsibility, and be accountable for their performance. It is about helping them to learn and to stop making excuses. One of their favorite excuses is the one typical of almost everyone: "I intended to play well," as though intentions supersede results. We all know that people want to be judged on their good intentions while others judge us on the results we deliver. It is one of the lessons coaches should impart with their players, "Stop rating yourself from your intentions but rate yourself from your actual performance." Moving beyond intentions to doing is a gigantic leap toward maturity and success.

I met with the girls and apologized for my part in the shaming that they had endured. I explained that I was complicit because I sat there and did nothing while the coach shamed them. I ask for their forgiveness. They gave it. We all cried. I promised them that I would never again sit by and watch someone try to manipulate them emotionally or abuse them anyway.

Later, we will teach them the difference between feedback and criticism and how to use feedback to help people grow and change. We will help them know how to avoid giving criticism and how to counteract it when used on them or others. I am disappointed in myself and hurting because I did nothing when I knew I should have done something. (You may be asking yourself, "Does Wayne admitting this and apologizing to the girls absolve him from his dereliction of duty and assuage his hurt?" My answer is "no" to the dereliction of duty. My answer is "not yet, or maybe a little" concerning assuaging my hurt by admitting and apologizing to the girls.) Fortunately, I know that hurting and suffering are essential for personal growth, and I will grow from this experience. Ouch!

I had been the VP of Human Resources and Administration for Amersham International, and the General Manager of the Diagnostics division, in the USA for five years (the diagnostics division I led was sold to Kodak in Rochester, NY). After that, I was a contracted consultant for Amersham for the next eight years. One day the VP and general manager at one of the Amersham divisions called me to request that I help him write a tardiness policy. I agreed to help him but asked if I could come and meet with him before putting pen to paper. He agreed.

Now, remember, because I had worked at Amersham for years, I knew his part of the business and his people well. When we met, I asked him how extensive the tardiness problem was in his division. He said that it was only a problem with three people in his customer service area. I asked him how many people worked in his customer service area, which he informed me was ninety. I asked him how many of those ninety people were coming early and staying late, and he guessed maybe fifty of them. I asked him why he thought that they were doing that. He said they did so, "...because they wanted to, because it helps the company, and they are dedicated employees." I summarized the situation in this manner, "So you have three people who are chronically late in your diagnostic division, and fifty who are coming early and staying late. Right?" He confirmed that. I then asked, "To whom are you going to distribute this new tardiness policy?" He replied that he was sending it to everyone in his division, over two hundred people. I suggested that before we sent a policy to two hundred people, of which one hundred ninety-seven posed no problem, we should decide if this was the right action to get the type of results desired from everyone, not just the three chronically late people. He looked puzzled, so I explained it from a practical point of view.

My explanation and dialogue with him went something like this: "Let's suppose that we write the policy and send it to your two hundred people. What will happen with the three people who are tardy, the one hundred ninety-seven people who are coming on time, and particularly the fifty people who are coming early and staying late?" He said, "I'm not sure. What do you will think will happen?" Rather than answering, I asked, "Do you think that will cause the three latecomers to come on time?" He responded, "Not really, but then I would have grounds to fire them for being chronically late!" "True, I said, but how would it likely impact the rest of the people who are not coming late? You know you are telling everyone that you expect them to be on time, don't you?" He asked, "What do you mean?" I just asked another question rather than answering: "How many of the fifty who are coming early and staying late will continue to do so after you send this authoritarian policy out, best-case and worst-case guess?" He said that best-case maybe all fifty would keep coming early and worse-case maybe twenty would do so. I asked, "Do you do realize that you are providing a disincentive for coming early and staying late?" With frustration, he asked, "Then what should I do?!"

I then explained that we should have started with a solution for the three chronically late employees. In the end, I suggested that the customer service manager meet with the three late-arriving employees and explain why their tardiness was a problem. At that time, he should explain that if they couldn't come on time, they would be subject to a substandard-performance process. Their response to the substandard-performance situation would determine their future status with

Amersham; either way, that would solve the tardiness problem. We decided to go in a completely different direction for the rest of the group.

For the rest of his division, including the customer service group, we had them select a values leadership team to develop and get everyone's buy-in for the division's core values. The values developed and bought into by everyone became the basis used by everyone to govern their decisions and behavior. It was marvelous; it generated excitement, commitment to the company, and performance levels never achieved before. Turnover in the customer service group dropped from over 120% per year to 8%. Current employees loved to orient new employees regarding the division's values. It changed the culture of the entire division; people felt respected and valued. They changed the televised screen that reported the call holding time used to track and criticize people to measuring new levels of performance attainment and validating well-deserved recognition and rewards.

When the group achieved small improvements, management gave commensurate recognition, and when significant improvements happened, the whole department celebrated. The customer service group at Amersham USA became a fattening place to work because they celebrated every birthday with home cooking. Small performance improvement achievements resulted in the delivery of pizza or other calorie-laden catered foods to the customer service center. His division became the top division within all of Amersham. Senior management noticed Guy's leadership; he became Amersham International worldwide CEO.

Having used Guy and Amersham as an example of using values as the basis for decision making and the good things that result when that happens, we need to understand that values are just one of the standards used to govern behavior. While we briefly mentioned other standards for governance at the beginning of this chapter, we didn't discuss them in any detail. Let's look at these individual standards on a spectrum of standards. We will explain the uniqueness of each and how they are used in society and our families. The spectrum of standards is laws, statutes, rules, regulations, policies, guidelines, principles, and values.

34

Standards Used to Govern Behavior

At the core of all relationships is an element of governance. Governance is how you get others and yourself to do what you want them to do. Most people have a very limited arsenal of tools they use. We've gone out and asked hundreds of people how they govern themselves and others. Below are the most common responses based on the relationship type.

When asking families how they govern each other and themselves, the most common responses are rules, expectations, and family traditions. When we ask business managers what they use to govern their employees, the most common answers are rules, policies, and organizational objectives. Even when asking the police, they offer the most consistent answer: they just enforce the laws.

What this question illustrates is that people have a limited understanding of the available tools to use to govern themselves and others. There are so many more options available. We have identified the most common eight standards to govern behavior. They are depicted in this graph titled "Standards to Govern Behavior":

When you look at the above graph, you'll notice that there are two main groups of governance: the liberating and the controlling standards. The controlling standards have several characteristics in common. First, they define the minimum acceptable behavior. They define what you can and cannot do and, in that sense, they are aiming for compliant behavior. The lower you go on the pyramid; the more standards needed to define and govern the acceptable action. (This is why there are so many laws.) Keep in mind, for every standard that requires compliant behavior, you need resources to ensure compliance. Think of the IRS

Standards to Govern Behavior

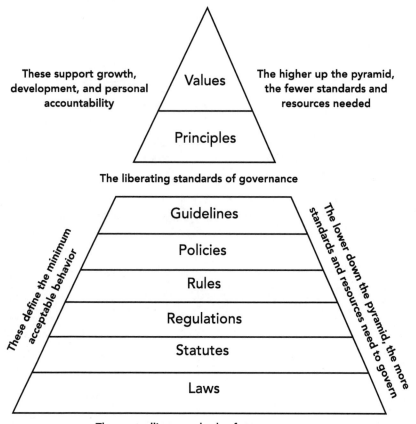

These support growth, development, and personal accountability

Values

The higher up the pyramid, the fewer standards and resources needed

Principles

The liberating standards of governance

Guidelines

Policies

Rules

Regulations

Statutes

Laws

These define the minimum acceptable behavior

The lower down the pyramid, the more standards and resources need to govern

The controlling standards of governance

tax code book. (Every year they add pages for new tax codes, which now totals over 74,000 pages.) It requires more laws and more IRS agents to enforce those laws.

The liberating standards reveals what is possible by choice. Personal agency goes far beyond the minimum standards of behavior. Liberating standards tap into our hearts and our minds and allow us to focus on achieving human potential (our own and others).

Now let's review these standards in detail and provide a more comprehensive explanation of what they are and why they are used.

Laws

In my mind, laws, in the simplest sense, are merely standards that govern behavior. They are probably the essential basic behavioral standards of all because they are a staple in the genesis of civilization. Think about it. Without laws, what kind of society would we have? If we have no laws, we have chaos; they bring order to disorderliness. They lift primal behavior to reasoned behavior. They enable civil behavior to supplant brutish behavior. Laws set and define the lowest acceptable behavior within society. By doing so, its people can become a nation, a community populated with citizens governed by standards that define, at least, the minimum level of behavior. With laws based on reason and compassion, people can live peaceably with one another. Laws are the pedestal upon which all other standards govern behavior, rest, and flow.

In 1965, I took a date to a film called *Lord of the Flies,* based on a 1954 book written by William Golding. His book was required reading in our social studies class, and I enjoyed it. But the movie made a deep impression on me. It was about boys from a British school who survived a crash landing next to an isolated Pacific Island. No adults survived the crash, so they were left alone on the island and had to find their way to survive and self-govern. At first, the social situation on the island was chaos, with small groups of boys banding together. A few compassionate older boys took the younger boys into their care and established a nurturing family environment. At the school, the compassionate older boys were intelligent, odd-boys-out kids who were not part of a clique as their family-type group formed; then another group formed, whose basis had been a choir at the English school. They had a leader and a hierarchy of rankings that carried over from the school to the island.

Early on, the boys tried to establish order and control, or so to speak, a government. One of the boys, Piggy, found a conch that Ralph used as a horn, the sound of which brought all the boys to a common site. The boys decided that whoever held the "conch" had the right to speak. It was the symbol of government, leadership, and authority. There was a debate to determine who would be the island's leader. Ralph was elected leader by all the boys, except for the choir boys. Ralph allowed the choir boys to establish a separate clique which became the Hunters, providing wild pig meat to everyone. The hunters, who were well organized and aggressive, became an independent society. They came to see Ralph and the others as enemies and eventual prey. The hunters stole the conch from Ralph and recruited or kidnapped the younger boys attached to Ralph and incorporated them into their tribe.

Their story is about civilized boys who revert to savagery. Only three of the older compassionate boys survive near the movie's end: Ralph, Piggy, and Simon. It becomes a story of good versus evil. The hunters kill Simon and Piggy, leaving only Ralph. He becomes the hunted, surviving by hiding and escaping from close death encounters with the hunters. At the conclusion of the movie, the hunters chase him to a beach where they intend to surround him and execute him. He hears them coming and collapses on the beach, waiting for the moment of his death. The sounds of their hunt cease, and Ralph glances up and sees the shadow of a man. He then looks up and sees a man dressed in a uniform standing in front of him, looking confused over the scene of a boy lying in front of him surrounded by boys, with painted faces and spears, intent on murdering the prostrate boy.

It moved me; it caused me to wonder what I would have done. I hoped that I would have been a part of Ralph's group, who understood the need for order and "doing things properly." The movie confirmed, in me, the need for a rule-based and value-based society and what can happen if a power-based one replaces it. It confirmed, for me, the need for "littl'uns" to be cared for and nurtured by "big'uns" who care for them and provide for them. The book and movie offer us a lot to ponder, especially as we consider standards for governing ourselves and others.

It is necessary to define the minimum acceptable standard of societal behavior in a society. Laws justify the establishment of government, whose job is to determine what laws should exist to establish a legal minimum acceptable standard of societal behavior. The government's job is to determine what level of behavior would be acceptable compared to the existing kind of current behavior considered unacceptable and draft laws that will purge the intolerable behavior and replace it with acceptable behavior. In this sense, governments are reactive rather than proactive to inappropriate behavior; they constantly chase and never get in front of unacceptable behavior. While laws don't define morality beyond the lowest acceptable legal level of behavior, they define the line, at which legal behavior becomes illegal behavior when crossed. Therefore, a significant part of their purpose is to regulate people's actions within a particular country, state, community, etc. The imposition of penalties allows them to punish people if their behavior violates the law (the minimum acceptable behavior).

We know that we are a society based on laws. That is true; insofar as we are a society that has decreed the lowest level of acceptable behavior allowed within our society. Truthfully, laws focus on telling us what not to do rather than telling us what we should be doing. They make clear the edge between what is legal and illegal. They do not inspire the highest moral character or behavior; that is not what they are designed to do. Frankly, governments can't keep up with drafting laws for conduct that should be illegal, let alone to engage in governing moral behavior. When I think of government in that context, I see them operating at sea level or below, and I should adjust my expectations. In other words, I should rate them according to their objectives, defining minimally acceptable behavior. Even so, I want politicians to operate from values rather than from just laws.

We have been looking at laws from a perspective of society rather than from an individual's viewpoint. Maybe that is because we make laws to govern society, and individuals are but grains of sand on the beach of society. And yet laws are written for a society to govern all individuals. Sometimes, governments draft societal laws because of the action of one person. The outrageous act of one person can create laws to rule everyone. For example, it is against the law to use a fake name to register for a hotel room in New Hampshire. Sometimes laws are nonsensical, like the anecdotal law in Vermont that says that,

"When two vehicles approach one another with insufficient room to pass, both vehicles must stop and wait until the other vehicle passes safely."

Still, for most people, laws only become visible to us when they directly impact us, like speed limits on the highway. We need a driver's license to drive legally or be twenty-one to buy alcohol. Many laws touch us directly, and those we are aware of, some we like and others we detest, such as laws centered on taxes that take money out of our pockets. But if we are living ethically and morally, most laws seem invisible to us because they never touch our lives.

As previously mentioned, laws are the cornerstone of civilized nations and societies, for, without them, society would be anarchy or a society of individual rule. In a lawless society, we would be like the "Wild West," where the fastest gun, the most ruthless, brazen, and powerful, would determine the fate of those residing within their domain. Therefore, in a sense, laws provide a means for protection and justice for those unable to protect themselves or unable to get justice for themselves. Of course, in lawless countries, those unable to protect themselves often band together to form vigilante groups to provide justice where no formal system for enforcing laws exists.

It happened in the Wild West, and even today, people band together to get justice when they feel that the formal system is failing them. It also provides an opportunity for the lawless to become the law. A 1972 film called *The Life and Times of Judge Roy Bean* entertainingly portrayed this concept. Judge Bean was saved from death by a young Mexican girl. He was formerly an outlaw who set himself up as the sole judge of the law in a small western town. The town prospers because he hangs anyone with money which comes through town, and in doing so, he brings a sense of law and order to the community. But his unchallenged haven of justice becomes insecure when his Mexican sidekick dies, and the townsfolk turn against him. Boy, that film certainly sounds like an illustration of multitudes of corrupt governments worldwide and some lawmakers within the United States.

For sure, laws don't guarantee a civilization with a uniform standard of behavior that never falls below an acceptable level for several reasons: One, there are not enough law officials to enforce the laws or hold people accountable for breaking laws. Second, there are far too many people in power who are supposed to pass laws to benefit society and protect the vulnerable who are corrupt. They do not adhere to the laws they have pledged to uphold, and they use their position power for self-benefit. The problem lies not in the laws themselves; we have more laws than we can imagine, but in the moral character of people who fail to abide by them. Third, laws tend to be static, designed to provide governance for specific situations, whereas society is dynamic, constantly changing. As a result, we have many laws that are out-of-date and no longer meet the needs of society. That is why government exists, to make sure that the laws align with the needs of the current state of society. Unfortunately, we create many new laws while the old, out-of-date laws remain, set aside in the corner of law libraries, gathering dust, until some attorney finds a further use for them as an obscure tool for prosecution or defense. And fourth, unethical people find ways to break laws without being caught or held accountable for their unlawful behavior.

As you know, we all have to be careful to prevent people who would scam us from invading our lives and stealing our precious funds or identity. For example, Nigeria has become one of the world's centers for scamming. Scamming is reported to be Nigeria's largest industry. A new study by the Techshielder website (pmnewsnigeria.com) recently revealed that Nigeria is the second-largest romance scammer in the world next to the Philippines. The dating scam centers around a scammer creating a profile that attracts people searching for friendship or romance online. Developing a relationship with sufficient credible information creates a climate where vulnerable, lonely people grow to trust them. This trust establishes a platform that enables scammers to take advantage of them.

When the level of romance and trust reaches a point where the people's personal boundaries are relaxed, the scammer explains that he finds himself in unavoidable circumstances where he desperately needs money. He uses this lie to request and, sometimes, demand money from people he has established a deep romantic relationship with (or so he claims). He usually includes in the romance lie a secondary lie that he has large sums of money that will become available to him once he has their money to work through the legal obstacles preventing him from obtaining the fortune. After getting their initial gift, he finds reason after reason for them to continue sending him money, e.g., he needs U.S. dollars to buy a plane ticket to come to see them, and he doesn't have access to U.S. dollars, etc. The ruse seems ridiculous to reasonable people, but they make millions upon millions from the scam, year after year. Scammers have years of experience to learn who is vulnerable and how to take advantage of that vulnerability. The different scams are limitless and come at us from all directions. I estimate that I have an average of ten to twelve potential scam calls to my cell phone every week. Sometimes the call appears to be local, and I actually get to chat with a scammer who claims to be a representative of Amazon, the Internal Revenue Service, or my credit card company, who is calling to report irregularities with my account and seeking to help me, all the while trying to get personal information to cheat me. We have laws that make most scams illegal, but scammers find loopholes to get around the laws and are experts in not getting caught and being prosecuted.

By the way, laws are virtually never the standards used by families to govern relationships and behavior. Since families are part of society, they are governed by the laws of society. Lawless families would, therefore, be society criminals. I don't personally know any families who have family laws. Maybe feuding families like the Hatfields and the McCoys do.

When recruited to be a professor for relationship, leadership, and conflict resolution classes at the Lake Forest Graduate School in Illinois, the school president gave me a syllabus for the conflict resolution class. I reviewed it quickly and told him that it looked like a labor attorney had prepared it. He said to me that, indeed, it had been. I told him that I would not teach a class based on that information because it was a summary of labor laws, deserving of a couple of hours for the entire semester. He asked me why? I told him that all laws did was define the minimum acceptable behavior, which would be lessons in mediocrity. I was not interested in teaching graduate students how to be mediocre. I wanted to help them operate far above the minimum standards defined by laws. I created and gave him my syllabus, which he loved. My syllabus focused on principles, values, and skills that would help and, hopefully, inspire people to operate at 40,000 feet above sea level and, hopefully, beyond that. My classes soon were enrolled beyond the standard numbers for graduate classes. We found ways to accommodate them. My relationship class had a two-year waiting list, and the dean told me that it was always the first course in the school to reach maximum enrollment. People don't want to be mediocre and operate at sea level; they want to soar above minimum standards.

Statutes

Statutes, to me, are basically agreements, principally between nations and governments (and departments within governments) to treat one another and behave toward one another in agreed ways that are legally binding. They are predominately long-lasting agreements (quasi-contracts) that document acceptable interactions that will exist between them. In short, they set the parameters for acceptable interactions and dealings that exist, or that are anticipated to exist, between them.

Sometimes some statutes exist between a government and its monarchy. I include monarchs because they are the only area where statues exist between a specific family and its government (that I know of).

Most of us don't know and don't care what statutes are; if they impact our lives, we probably aren't aware of how they do so. I see large protests for and against specific laws, but I don't recall any protest for or against statutes; but then again, I don't know much about statutes – not my area of interest.

A prime example of statutes is the treaties that exist between NATO Nations. In essence, the statutes constitute an agreement between participating nations of NATO that an attack on one member nation will be considered an attack on all member nations. Such an attack will initiate a response from all NATO nations as if personally attacked. A statute between countries is like a legalized, pinky promise between kids. In its simplest form, it is a legal commitment toward one another.

If your family does not have any statutes, don't feel bad; you are not an exception.

Regulations

Regulations are standards that flow from laws that clarify the intent and behavior of the laws. In a way, they are sub-laws. If a law is the tree trunk, regulations are the branches that grow and extend outward from which additional branches grow. The leaves from the branches would be like local ordinances flowing from the regulations.

Regulations serve a valuable function in society because they make laws, which tend to be legal standards, using legal jargon, understand-able and actionable. They take universal laws and tailor the laws to local or regional circumstances. Regulations take laws, or parts of a law, and make them operationally practical. They enable ordinary people not trained in law to understand and guide their actions following regulations, which automatically align us with the law upon which the regulations are founded.

We see regulations stated in fish and game manuals. They let us know where we can fish, what kinds of fish we can keep, and how many. We are guided by voting regulations when we go to vote. We must abide by the park regulations when visiting national parks or public locations. We are regulated by the regulations that flow from the laws. Departments or agencies responsible for enforcing the laws draft the regulations. They can be crafted locally by counties and communities so that the laws relate to and align with local conditions and situations. They enable flexibility within the law that accommodates, to a degree, to the unique requirements of locations or enforcing agencies. Society recognizes that legislators can't make laws to govern every actional item that requires some form of governance. Thus, they wisely delegate that power to those responsible for enforcing laws and making them enforceable for the public in various locations and circumstances.

Regulations govern families because all families within a regulation jurisdiction are expected to abide by existing regulations. But, families seldom draft family regulations; they don't need to because most families have other standards used to govern. Most use rules, some use values. Unfortunately, some use fear, intimidation, and other forms of control that don't fit as standards but are extreme control methods. Examples of this might be shaming, emotional manipulation, badgering, blackmailing, etc.

Rules

Rules are the most popular standards for governing families, organizations, teams, classrooms, companies, etc. Whenever we have more than two people together, rules of conduct seem to be the most common way to govern each other's behavior. We will use families as a basis for our discussion. However, all organizations use rules, so the illustrations regarding families will apply to all other organizations.

Rules are the top-down standards used by governments, management, and parents to manage and control behavior. Rules are the most common basis for teaching children and others how those in charge want the people under them to behave, treat, and respect other people. In short, rules are the most commonly used standard for behavioral control used by parents to govern, control, and teach their families. Why is that?

There are probably too many reasons to try and identify all of them, but let's list and review some of the more obvious ones.

Tradition

It seems that everyone was brought up in a rules-based family, and therefore, it is natural to be a rules-based parent. Certainly, we know that the parent mode of our parents becomes the parent mode of our adulthood unless we decide that we don't want the same parent mode as our parents, and we use our adult mode to change it. If our parents were controlling parents, we are likely to become controlling parents. If our parents were critical parents, we will likely become critical parents. If our parents were nurturing parents, we will likely become nurturing parents. If our parents were overindulging parents, we are likely to become narcissistic parents who basically can't see any relationships, including our children, as distinct from ourselves. I guess overindulging parents are the exception of parents who have children who mimic their parenting mode. Narcissistic parents don't serve the needs of their children; everything they do is self-serving. I don't particularly appreciate dealing with narcissistic kids, but they are the ones who need the most help. The difficulty I find dealing with them is that it is your fault if anything does not meet their expectations. To help them requires more time and commitment than I am willing to commit. It would be worse to try and help them and then stop short of success than to start. They need someone willing to help them for years if need be. And it should be a licensed therapist who knows how to deal with narcissism. Narcissists are a tough bunch.

Everyone does rules-based parenting; that is how parenting is done.

If you are a rules-based parent raised by a rules-based parent, that fact alone seems to justify it for themselves and everyone else who is a rules-based parent. You can certainly relate to what every other rules-based parent is doing and the experiences they are having; they are just like yours. You can get together and share stories and know that they understand what you are dealing with. You can share tips and ideas on dealing with your children doing the same things as their children and see them get the same responses you got. Perhaps two sayings apply to justify this commonality: "Birds of a feather flock together," and "Misery loves company."

Many of the shared stories are not happy ones. And yet, somehow, there is comfort in knowing that others have the same struggles you are having. Still, people carry on in the same fashion as always – rules and more rules. The more the children's behavior is contrary to the rules, the stiffer the rules; this continues until someone triumphs. As mentioned earlier in this book, rules no longer control behavior once the disobedience becomes open disobedience; additional rules only intensify disobedient behavior. You'd think that people would catch on and try something other than rules. They don't. But they do become frustrated and wonder what in the hell is going on. Is it my kid, or is it me?

Parents use rules to govern because they have position power; they are on top of the family totem pole.

It is natural to use position power when you can do so. When you are on the top of the family totem pole, the power mantel just seems to land on our shoulders and stays there. If you have it, why not use it? Note that it is the parents who write the rules in a rules-based family. The children seldom have any voice in the rules that govern them. I think that was the primary reason that America rebelled against British rule.

Interestingly, position power is addictive in that it becomes compulsive (used repeatedly); it gets short-term results (people do what you tell them to do) that could be called a power buzz. It causes long-term destructive consequences (it distances your relationship with your child and makes them dependent on you), which you won't experience until sometime in the future, but that doesn't matter now because, as parents, most of us live moment to moment.

The point is: rules-based parenting provides control, at least for a time. It establishes order from chaos and reinforces the power hierarchy for making decisions. It gets everyone marching in the same direction, a good thing in the military, not so sure about individuals in families. Central decision-making is the natural order of a rules-based family, and that makes sense because the parents have more life experience and can use it to benefit their children.

Rules aim at obedience, and rule-based parents believe that is good.

According to the Apostle Paul, obedience is the first principle of the gospel, and rules aim at obedience. Parents love having obedient children; it makes a fine impression on everyone when their children are obedient. Obedient children do the right things, say the right things, and are the right kind of people when their parents are there to make sure of it. Some kids love being obedient; others hate it and eventually aren't. Forcing children to be obedient carries risks, which we will discuss in detail in the section on commitment levels.

The skills associated with governing by rules come pretty naturally.

It doesn't take training, or much education, to govern by rules. The primary skills associated with rule-based governance are pretty straightforward. You can be an expert using them right out of the starting gate. The list of skills would include controlling, demanding, ordering, forcing, intimidating, threatening, bossing, punishing, and withholding things of value to the governed person who fails to behave as expected. All you need to use them is position power. Parents get position power as soon as they become parents.

All of the reasons listed above for using rules-based parenting appear to be self-justifying and come with many upsides. But some downsides should be considered and pondered deeply before choosing to become a rule-based family, or parent, especially when you become aware of other, and in my opinion, better alternatives (like value-based parenting).

Some downsides of rule-based parenting

Dependence

When parents use rules to govern their children's behavior, they direct their children to be obedient to their rules. They want compliant children. In a way, they are saying, "Don't think, just do as I say." Children are not expected to analyze situations that would require thought and reason and determine their actions based on their conclusions; they are merely expected to follow the rules. I will guess if children in families follow the same pattern as companies we consulted, who tried to manage with rules, they could expect compliance about 50% of the time. One or more children may comply virtually all of the time, while others would probably comply as little as possible. We will discuss this after a few more thoughts about dependence.

When children are removed from the responsibility to use their brain's cognitive function to analyze and make decisions, they respond to the power source upon whom they are dependent – they comply to survive. Whether they comply out of fear of punishment or simply not to disturb family dynamics, it doesn't matter because they learn to act habitually. After all, that is what they are compelled to do. It becomes the natural autonomic behavior regulated by the basal ganglia part of the brain (like brushing teeth or tying shoelaces, it doesn't require thought). After hearing the "As long as you live in my house, you will obey my rules!" message directed at them or another sibling, they catch on that obeying the rules is a survival measure. "As long as I obey the rules, I will be OK!"

Once they stop thinking, they lose the ability to self-govern and make wise decisions independently. In short, they become dependent on parents, or other authority figures, to think for them. They may still be great in math or other school subjects, but they have become relatively dysfunctional in independent life skills. They become deficient in protecting their boundaries or knowing how to respect others' boundaries. In some ways, it plays a major role in developing their personal identity. "Am I me or simply an extension of my parents' will or rules?" Children raised in dominant rule-based families who truly become adaptive to that environment are less able to leave home, go to college, or self-support successfully. That is one of the reasons I love fighters. The child who fails to submit to dominance has a much greater chance to maintain her identity and move successfully through life, albeit with a chip on their shoulder.

Rule-based management, or parenting, leads to covert disobedience, overt disobedience, and rebellion.

As I mentioned in the thoughts on dependence, as business consultants, we found that if a company had a 50% compliance rate with company rules, it was faring pretty well. Where does the rest of the behavior go? At first, we find that it manifests in covert disobedience (hidden disobedience). Invariably those who are covertly disobedient seek others who are also covertly disobedient. They need the validation that they are justified in their disobedience, and when connecting with fellow dissidents, they **will** validate their behavior as rational and appropriate. They **will** justify their feelings which will become their beliefs (rationalized feelings). Once their feelings become beliefs, their facts **will** align with their beliefs, and they **will** feel justified in becoming overtly disobedient (openly disobedient). Through this process, they develop an adversarial relationship with the power structure within their organization.

Believe it or not, the same thing happens with children in families. Kids get together and commiserate, and convince themselves that they are being unjustly treated and that mom and dad are horrible, mean people. Open disobedience in society is civil disobedience; companies call it an "oh shit situation." In families, it is called the "troubled child syndrome." Rule-based parents usually respond to troubled children by trying to take more control. They make more rules and intensify the punishments for breaking the rules. Once a child, or an employee, is openly disobedient because they have justified their behavior, the time for rules and discipline has passed, more rules won't get the desired compliance. They will get rebellious behavior, over which management and parents have no control. A parting of ways becomes the only logical alternative. The only other option that will work is for the parents to humble themselves and connect with their children from where they are rather than from trying to deal with them from where they want them to be. Unfortunately, few parents are willing to do so, and few know how to do it, even if they are willing.

We had a client company that brought in a new COO to manage the business in midtown Manhattan. He decided that he needed to tighten up the behavior at the midtown headquarters. Most of the staff were low-level professionals or non-exempt employees. He independently decided that his first official act was to institute a time clock check-in for all non-management employees to show that a new no-nonsense commander had arrived. No one was pleased with his decision, but he was insistent about the time clock. To show that he was serious, he declared that he would deduct an entire hour from the late arrival's paycheck for every minute a person was late. He further stated that anyone caught punching in for another employee would be fired. Everyone knew he was deadly serious.

Man, oh, man, did the time clock stir negative emotions within the organization! His managers tried to explain that the time clock hurt employee morale and company productivity. They explained that it was doing far more damage than it was worth. He turned a deaf ear and remained committed to showing his power and getting compliance or rid of those who resisted his mandates. It didn't take long for the employees to catch on to his style and intent. They decided to show him what real compliance was all about if he wanted compliance. Everyone below a management level stopped acting independently but went to their boss to get direction about what to do and about how to do it – for everything. They even started going to their bosses to obtain permission to go to the bathroom. If their boss was busy with someone, or something, they patiently waited until the boss could personally permit them to go. They waited (or held it) until permission was granted.

You would have thought that the COO would have realized his mistake and changed direction. He didn't; he felt that he would eventually win the, now covertly disobedient, contest between himself and all the non-management employees. Meanwhile, the non-management employees were not about to concede anything. They decided to make the time clock the focal point of their compliance movement. They agreed that they would show their determination by setting new records of the number of employees who could punch in during two minutes before start time until start time. The challenge was to get as many employees as feasible to punch in while not letting anyone punch in for anyone else. Part of the challenge was that there was only one time clock, and each check-in took time. Each time they inserted a card, the machine had a "cha-ching" cadence sound. The employees learned how to get each person clocked in a way that there was a steady cadence of "cha-chings" with no time in between each clock in. They spent coffee breaks, lunchtimes, and even some time after work planning how to execute just-in-time check-ins efficiently. They started coming to work

30 to 40 minutes early, assembling at the time clock area, and practicing how to optimize the number of people to check in during the two minutes. If you went to the clock-in site at 8:30 am, you would find over two hundred employees jammed together there. They practiced like a special forces team, learning to be fully synchronized and move like a finely tuned drill team. They learned how to hold their card in the best manner to insert and withdraw their card quickly. They practiced how to get in line, move in and punch, and then quickly move to the side to allow the next in line to do the same thing. They figured out how many could check-in at their current level of proficiency without anyone getting fined for being late. Everyone who was not part of the special squad of just-in-time check-ins would punch in early to provide practice and training time for the elite team who would be participants in that day's record-setting attempt. They were driven to learn how to check in as many employees as possible in the two minutes before penalties started. It was amazing to see the number of people who could do last-minute check-ins before the clock struck 9:00 a.m. They set a new record almost every day. As I recall, the top record was 118 employees. That is just under one every second. Can you envision just how precise their individual and collective movements had to be? They were literally in sync with the cadence of the time clock.

My business partner and I received invitations to come and witness their record-setting punch-ins. We were amazed at what we saw. We couldn't believe the artistry and mastery of their check-in process. We cheered with them when they set a new record. We noticed that one of the employees was filming the record-setting attempt. Later he made the film available for others to watch on his 8 mm camera in the break room and cafeteria. We reported to management that we had never seen such commitment, unity, passion, and drive to accomplish a shared objective. Wouldn't it be amazing if management could harness that same level of enthusiasm and commitment for company objectives? Our observation only made the COO angry. He asked us what we would do; he had hired us to solve the performance problems, not glorify them. Our recommendation was simple: get rid of the time clock, congratulate the employees on their accomplishments, and move to a value-based management approach. He wanted to fire us, but everyone, but him, could see that our recommendation was the only way forward. As soon as he stopped bullying the employees and started to work with them, they transferred their energy, commitment, and passion previously focused on the time clock to our client's business objectives. By the way, that business became the leader in performance for their industry. The COO never became popular with the non-management employees.

Position power too often leads the person to use their power excessively and inappropriately.

You've undoubtedly heard the expression that, "Power corrupts and absolute power corrupts absolutely." There is more than a bit of truth to the statement. Power and authority are dangerous in the hands of a narcissist. They tend to exaggerate controlling behavior. Position power probably generates a feeling of omnipotence (all-powerful) and omniscience (all-knowing) to those who have it. When people feel that way, they act that way; emotions precede actions. When they can act with unconstrained power, it validates their sense of unlimited power. They become more and more inclined to use that power for self-satisfaction and self-edification. It too often becomes an ever-expanding use of their position power. And unfortunately, that continues until something happens to stop it. But who is there to prevent a parent from misusing position power? It will continue until it becomes so over-the-top that someone feels compelled to stop it and calls the government to intercede? These calls usually come from a teacher or an emergency room doctor who sees unexplainable bruises or injuries on a child. The facts are that external intercession rarely occurs within families and is avoided whenever possible.

Adolf Hitler is a prime example of this ever-expanding use of position power for self-edification. His self-edification cost approximately 50 million lives. Only the victory by the allies over his Nazi regime stopped him.

While not as extreme, a similar phenomenon happens in families governed by rules. I see self-edification from controlling parents and a cycle of ever-expanding control. The difference is that rule-based parents, with few exceptions, genuinely love the children they are ruling and have their best interest at heart. It is just not the ideal way to help their children grow and progress to become successful and responsible adults.

Rule-based parenting creates a distance and formality that interferes with intimacy and bonding.

Rule-based parenting is a form of dominance, as mentioned in the metaphors earlier in this section about ruling children versus raising children. I restate that rule-based parenting creates an environment similar to a monarchy where, as parents, they are the king and queen (or king and king, queen and queen, etc.) who rule over their kingdom, giving edicts, and dispensing rewards and punishments according to their pleasure. This rule-based approach creates a formality and distance between their majesties and their subjects, as it also does between ruling parents and their children. Most ruling parents would suggest that distance and formality are just demonstrations of respect. OK, define it as you will and justify it as you want, but it is still distance. It results in lessening intimacy and personal bonding between parents and their children. Appropriate intimacy and bonding are essential to raising children, who when they become adults, are confident, competent, and nurturing to other people.

Rule-based governance replaces the intended message: Rule-based parents use rules as an expression of love, but children interpret rules as a message of dominance, force, and punishments.

While rule-based parents express love by punishing their child for a misdemeanor, the child doesn't feel loved; he feels punished. If the parent takes the time to explain why it is an expression of love, the child will probably understand and accept that explanation. I doubt that many rule-based parents take the time to make such an explanation; they are usually living in the moment and letting their anger, disappointment, frustration, etc., determine their actions. In short, they are acting in child mode and are stuck in child mode, which is an emotional reaction, not a well-reasoned one. If they, at a later moment, reconnect with their adult mode and use the conclusions from that thought process to follow-up and explain to their child their rationale and reasons, it will help their child feel more loved and less punished.

This concept brought to mind an experience when I was 11-years-old. I stayed at the city park and played baseball rather than coming home to milk my cow. On the way home, I remembered that my cow hadn't been milked and was probably suffering because of it. I ran home to milk my cow. When I got there, dad was just finishing milking my cow. He looked at me and said, "You know your cow is suffering because you didn't come home and milk her, right?" I hung my head and said I did and that I was sorry. Dad explained that he needed to give me a licking because of my negligence and told me to go to the plum tree and get a small branch that he would use to spank me. I went to the plumb tree and found an excellent spanking stick, appropriate, in my mind, to the level of negligence that I had committed; it was a pretty big stick. I returned to the barn and gave it to my dad. He told me he was sorry that he had to do this. I leaned against the window frame, and dad wacked me two times across my buttocks. I expected more and felt that I deserved more, but when I turned around, dad was crying, and he exclaimed, "Oh God!" It was the only time in my life that I heard him use the Lord's name in vain. It was an expression of soulful anguish. He used hell, shit, damn, and son-of-a-bitch in almost every sentence, but he never profaned.

When we got back to the house, he looked at my mother and said, "Donna, if there is any spanking that needs to be done in this family, you're going to have to be the one to do it; I can't do that again!" That was the only and last whipping I ever got.

Policies

Policies are statements of intent and implemented as procedures or protocols. They are designed to guide decisions and behavior to achieve organizational objectives within bounds acceptable to the organization. They define courses of action and act as the organizational conscience of conduct. I see them as akin to highway guard rails intended to keep people on the road, help them avoid dangerous circumstances, and provide a clearly defined roadway for operating safely and securely to the desired destinations without incident. But that is not how many organizations use them. Too often, and in too many places, they become the rulebook of an organization, defining the wrong things not to do and for which a person is punishable. Some places use policies like the Torah or books from the Old Testament, specifying the number of steps or actions people can take without inferring God's wrath. Or, in the case of organizations, the wrath of management.

They are similar to regulations but are not sub-laws that flow directly from laws but are closer to procedures that can be referred to as a reference to define unacceptable behavior. They always have laws in the background and ensure that no policy violates federal or state laws. But they do fit in the domain of those who have position power with an organization.

In many ways, they exemplify the arbitrary preferences and biases of those in charge. I see the value they can provide, but I see them as only one end of a rod for governance. One end of the rod should have policies, but the other should have defined unconditional values. The policy end should clarify the lowest acceptable behavior to those who design them. The other end should have the values that inspire behavior far above the minimum standards. Since most organizations list only policies in their policy manual, it stands to reason that the only people who they impact are the people who violate the policy, who then become subject to the discipline and punishments subscribed to them.

When we were consulting with a division of KPMG, the senior management of that division asked me to help them write a policy manual for their practice. I told them that it would be short and sweet if they left it entirely up to me to write the manual. They looked at me puzzled and waited for an explanation of my comment. I told them that my policy manual would have only one policy statement. It would say: "Stop doing all chicken shit behavior!" I explained that everyone recognizes chicken shit behavior when they see it and know it is chicken shit behavior when they do it. That policy statement should cover all situations. When they finished laughing, they agreed with me but stated that they needed more specific policies for managing specific situations within the practice. I agreed that I would help write the manual under one condition. The condition being that for every policy statement that defined unacceptable behavior, we would also reference a core value that would be a higher standard for inspiring personal behavior far above the policy. I further explained that for those who operated from core values, the policies would be invisible and, for all practical purposes, did not exist for them. They agreed, and so we developed a policy manual that included the set of core values that superseded the policies. That way clearly showed that values were more important than policies when guiding decisions and actions.

When Arthur Anderson shut down for unethical financial practices, many of their partners came to KPMG because it had a sterling reputation of being a value-based organization. In many situations, they accepted positions at KPMG that had over a million dollars less in base annual compensation than offered elsewhere. They chose KPMG because they wanted to be in a corporation that lived by unconditional core values. We will review unconditional values later in this section.

Guidelines

Guidelines are not rules or regulations in that they don't define the minimum acceptable behavior. They are more like strong suggestions or advice intended to guide us on our onward journey to reach the desired destination successfully. I picture guidelines to be like a rope leading us up perilous terrain so that we stay on course and reach our desired endpoint without injury or getting lost or side-tracked. They are like the page of a child's book, where the dots are connected to create a picture of something wonderful to emerge as the dots are connected. The child doesn't have to connect the dots correctly, but failing to do so creates a jumble of lines, and the magical picture doesn't emerge. Children connecting the dots soon learn the value of using the dots as guidelines for connecting their dots and being rewarded with a beautiful image they created.

At one end, guidelines are like instructions that show us how to put together a 1,000-piece toy for our children successfully. On the other end, they are like tips suggesting the best way to get somewhere or get something accomplished. For example, you may know a parent or a manager who says, "This is the way you need to do that. If you are smart, you will follow my instructions." The person offering the tips feels that he knows the best and most efficient way to get things done, and yet he still allows us the choice of doing otherwise. He may leave the room when we choose an alternate method because he anticipates the unsuccessful results we will achieve by doing it our way, and he can't stand being a witness to a train wreck.

At the other end are the people who give us tips or suggestions as guidelines for our efforts or journeys. "If you want to see the most beautiful mountain scenery in the Rocky Mountains on your way to Montrose, you may want to consider going over the Million Dollar Highway." They give us a choice to make, no pressure or arm twisting. Note that our friend provided a good reason for going that way, suggesting that the best guidelines also include reasons for following them.

Parents who use guidelines as a means for helping their children accomplish things that help their children in more ways than one. They support their child's ability to think, choose, and independently (quasi-independently) take action. They sponsor the child's ability to make mistakes and learn from them. They foster a sense of accomplishment when the child succeeds in her efforts – which is essential for their self-development and self-esteem. Giving people guidelines with good reasons for following them while allowing them to make decisions, regardless of our instructions or suggestions, is a gift we offer people that we love and respect that helps them grow and develop. I believe it is a valuable part of value-based parenting.

My dad frequently used the phrase, "You may want to consider...." I learned that it was wise to consider and utilize his suggestions. When I didn't, I learned first-hand why he suggested it.

Principles

Principles are parts of "truth" that are standards, or ideals, that enable us to live a life aligned with truth. What happens when we bond ourselves to truth, so it becomes our standard for decision making and actions? We recognize truth because it generates soulful light, energy, and edification. When we experience, encounter, or discover truth, it engulfs us, filling us with an internal awaking emotion that energizes us spiritually and physically and elevates us to a higher level of consciousness and a deeper comprehension of truth. Truth is reality. It exemplifies fact as it really is, not as we wish it or rationalize it to be. Many people's truth is based on their negative feelings because they are not experiencing what they want to experience, and they change truth to fit their feelings.

When we are not believing and acting aligned with truth, when we encounter it, truth causes us to feel guilty, defensive, angry, or confused because we have rationalized our beliefs and facts to align with our feelings rather than with reality. There are two ways to resolve this cognitive dissonance (mental and emotional disharmony). We can either recognize truth (reality) and align ourselves with it or create an alternate reality that aligns with our feelings. Many people choose the latter, leading to decisions and actions based on their truth and creating facts based on their feelings rather than actual reality and real facts.

We are living in an America that is currently "deeply divided." Both sides of the division operate from their definition of reality, claiming truth to be on their side. They accuse the other side of using "alternate facts" and creating a manufactured reality. Disappointment, fear, and desires for power, fame, and fortune generate their perspectives. That would suggest that both sides act purely out of self-interest and define reality and truth however needed to achieve their objectives. I think that is a relatively accurate description of our current political, and therefore social, environment. The division will cease when people attach themselves to actual truth and reality. What do you think is the likelihood of that happening?

Similar divisions happen in families. Divided family members operate from different realities and facts that conflict with one another's reality and facts. Both sides see themselves as the personification of truth and reality. Both sides feel righteous indignation and think that the other must concede their reality and adopt theirs. If neither does, the conflict becomes the justification to physically or emotionally part ways. We see too many parting ways, couples from couples, children from parents, siblings from siblings, etc. It needn't happen if divided parties would accept truth and reality. When operating from truth and reality, everyone involved would see and take responsibility for their contribution to the division. That would enable them to come together, united by a common understanding of truth and reality. Admittedly, bonding to truth and reality is difficult; it requires the ability to humble ourselves and accept the possibility that our perception of reality may be at odds with actual reality. But, doing so enables us to come into harmony with truth. When and if all parties align with truth, conflict and division ceases. One of the reasons therapists can provide valuable help is because they can help bring to consciousness the truth that we hide from ourselves.

We all face the challenge of finding truth; we are all subjected to misinformation projected as truth. Sometimes, to find truth, we need to look behind the information to the people's motivations for giving us the information they provide us. Information that is self-serving with political objectives is seldom yoked to truth.

Principles align perfectly with natural laws and eternal truths. It is not a valid principle if it doesn't. For example, gravity is a natural law. It aligns with absolute truth; "What goes up must come down."

While not all natural laws are observable (yet), the power and effects of gravity are evident and can be felt. If you were to shoot an arrow into the air in a perfect trajectory so that it would come down to the exact spot where you were standing when you shot it, you could see it rise and descend and would also feel it. We see and feel the long-term effects of gravity as we age; our height shortens, our breasts sag, our belly seems to change places with our chest as the focal point of our physique. Gravity is constant and dependable. We all have learned to use gravity as a tool for health, a tool for movement, a tool for growth, a tool for science, etc. We trust that it will continue to do its job. If it stopped doing its job, it would no longer be natural law, and we would be no more.

I see true love as an eternal truth. I also believe that all love is eternal, as long as it lasts. People with true love extend and express themselves physically, emotionally, socially, spiritually, and mentally. It can be felt and seen. Its impact on lives and living may be the most powerful thing available to us. It brings light to us, energizes us, and edifies us. When that happens to us, it results from an eternal truth or true love. According to Dr. M. Scott Peck, the absence of love, or the opposite of it, abuse and neglect at the early stages of life, is believed by many phycological therapists and psychiatrists as the primary source of mental illness. Lack of love, neglect, and abuse (physical and emotional) lay the foundation for illnesses such as psychosis, character disorders, neurosis, chronic anxiety, depression, etc. And the only effective way to treat the disorders is by filling the vacuum caused by the lack of love, neglect, and abuse with love. Later application of love will never replace the love provided at the appropriate time, but it can bring people back to high levels of functioning – "mental health."[39]

People talk about "falling in love." Authors write books about it, movies highlight it, and people yearn for it, truly believing that people fall in love and live happily ever after. That doesn't happen as much as we would like to think. What falling in love is really about is being captivated by another person, usually because of sexual attraction. It motivates us to extend ourselves emotionally, socially, mentally, and physically (especially sexually) for a time until we grow tired or bored of extending ourselves. Then we fall out of love because the source of our self-extension was actually self-serving actions intended to get what we wanted, or needed, from our love object at the time. That is why I said that all love is eternal, as long as it lasts. Self-serving love mimics true love only as long as we continue to extend ourselves.

---

39   M. Scott Peck, *The Road Less Traveled* (Simon and Schuster, 1978).

True love becomes eternal love when our extension never ceases but increases over time. It requires work, devotion, commitment, and discipline in extending ourselves to another. If we do, our effort intensifies and expands the light, energy, and edification within us and does the same for our eternal love. True love, just like gravity is constant and dependable, does its job. If it ceases to do its job, it ceases to be eternal love, and we are eternal lovers no more. True love is hard work that pays off handsomely; true lovers feel they are getting much more than giving. It generates a sense of gratitude for its gifts and motivates us to extend more and to give more, thus causing an ever-expanding source of light, energy, and edification.

My dad and mother were examples of eternal lovers. Their self-extension to one another was inspiring to see and feel; it engulfed them and all those around them. Near the end of his life, my dad told me that his love for my mother was deeper and grander than he ever imagined love could be. He said that it surprised him that his love was not dependent upon sexual activity because since sex wasn't a part of their life anymore, his passion for his love had grown and grown. I know now what he was trying to explain to me. Their profound, eternal love was based on the mutual extension to one another entirely and thoroughly. Their love extensions accentuated their individuality and personal identity rather than making them the same. Their extension from their own identity to another with a wholly distinct identity made the extensions all the more visible and miraculous. How could people who were very different love each other so much?

I came to understand what my dad was talking about when my sweetheart became an invalid for over six years. Our sexual connection ceased, but our extension of self was, and is, expressed in other ways providing light, energy, and edification. The new extensions of ourselves make us both grateful for one another. I thought that I would lose her within a year before we found a doctor who diagnosed the cause of her pain and inability to care for herself. She received two new hips and oral surgeries that significantly restored her health and have enabled her to care for herself. Our joy and gratitude are beyond measure. I don't know if sex will ever again be part of our self-extension to one another, but it doesn't matter; we have other ways of extending ourselves.

I believe that love is the most powerful force within the grasp of humanity. It lives beyond life; it blesses the lives of those who experience it by bringing light, energy, and edification that goes on and on. True love is an eternal truth.

We can sum up the spirit of principles by saying that principles are the distillation of natural laws and eternal truths. A principled person is a person whose decisions and actions align with truth and reality.

Go forth and be principled.

35

VALUE-BASED LEADERSHIP

Values are the personalized behavioral embodiment of principles used to govern our decisions and actions. They are standards that flow from principles. They are always in tune with principles; therefore, they align with natural laws and eternal principles. Values sit on top of the hierarchy, or spectrum, of standards, encompassing all laws, regulations, policies, and guidelines aligned with natural laws and eternal truths (which aren't very many).

You will notice that as we climb the ladder of standards, the number of standards in each category diminishes. There are millions of laws, statutes, and regulations written to govern individual decisions and behaviors within society. And they are attempting only to achieve minimally acceptable behavior (which they don't get with everyone). As we rise on the hierarchy, we can see far fewer policies than those lower on the standard spectrum. Guidelines are even far scarcer than policies. Principles become even more exclusive. Defining principles is like finding a freshwater spring in the Mojave Desert; they are more precious, and not so many are needed; a few principles will suffice. They, too, encompass all the standards below them that align with natural law and eternal truths.

Principles also bring into play standards that govern morality as well as legality. Values that reign over all other standards requires the fewest number to govern decisions and behaviors, both moral and legal. For example, Jesus Christ said only two are needed. (Matthew 22:36-40) *"36 Master, which is the great commandment in the law? 37 Jesus said unto him, Thou shalt love the Lord thy God with all they heart, and with all thy soul, and with all thy mind. 38 This is the first and great commandment. 39 And the second is like unto it, Thou shalt love thy neighbor as thyself. 40 On these two commandments hang all the law and the prophets"*. He makes the point clearly and distinctly. These two commandments are core values encompassing all other standards.

Understanding the nature and importance of values is critical for governing our lives aligned with truth. Therefore, we will review values in the context of their relative importance as governing standards. We will show why they should be the standards to govern behavior, ourselves, families, companies, and groups entrusted to us.

Interestingly, people see values from very different perspectives. To illustrate the point, we need to examine what people value as the basis for their values. When I meet new people, I ask them, "Who are you?" I get answers that always fall into three categories: What people have, what people do, or a description of their personal (or moral) characteristics.

"Have" People

For example, I interviewed a candidate in Belgium for the President of Janssen Pharmaceutica France. He responded to the question of "Who are you?" in the following way: He told me that he owned a grape vineyard and a winery near the southern coast of France. He had a lovely 48-foot yacht with personal dock space in a sailing club. He had two extraordinary and brilliant children who attended an exclusive private school. He humbly claimed an eight-bedroom mansion with six bathrooms and a guest house for visitors. I figured out that he saw himself in terms of what he owned or had.

When I turned the questioning over to him, you wouldn't be surprised to hear the object of his questions. He wanted to know how big his salary would be, what Janssen executives would base his bonus on, the nature and number of J&J stock options he would be eligible to receive, and when he would get them. He was a talented and intelligent guy, but he never explained how to start and lead a new Janssen company in France. I learned a lot about what was important to him. He valued possessions; things he owned or had reflected his identity. He was a "Have" person.

"Do" People

At a medical conference in Banff, British Columbia, I met a psychiatrist and said, "It is nice to meet you. Who are you?" He immediately told me that he was a board-certified psychiatrist who had earned his medical degree from McGill University. He specialized in psychiatry in Toronto, Ontario. He was currently the head of the department of psychiatry at a major teaching hospital that I recall as being located in Mississauga, Ontario. When I congratulated him on his achievements, he said that he heard that I was representing McNeil Labs at the conference. He told me that he wanted his hospital to become a clinical research center for testing psychiatric medications. He wanted me to get him in touch with Haldol® people in our company who could help him head up Haldol testing and do medical research using some of his patients. I did introduce him to our Clinical Research Director at McNeil Labs in Toronto. I don't remember if his hospital became a clinical testing center for Haldol. As you can see, what he does defines his identity. He is a "Do" person.

"Be" People

Occasionally, when I ask people, "Who are you?" they describe themselves in terms of their characteristics or the type of person they are. I met a kindly gentleman at our local golf course who belongs to our senior golf league. I had frequently seen him at the club, but we had never played together, so when we were assigned to the same golf cart to be playing partners, it allowed me to ask him, "Who are you?" and hear his way of identifying who he perceived himself to be.

He told me that he was just an older man trying the best he could to take care of a feeble wife. He said that most of his life, he tried to positively impact the lives of his family, his friends, and his neighbors. He told me that he was a handful for his parents as a teenager and caused them a lot of headaches and misery, but after getting married and having kids, he realized that he had been a jerk and decided to change his life. I asked him what he wanted to be and his goals. He responded that he just wanted people to remember him as a caring, concerned person who loved and served the people he loved. That short period of just two-and-one-half hours playing together started a friendship. We try to play together and get assigned to the same cart as often as possible. Being a person of noble character reflects his self-identity. He is a "Be" person.

We have provided examples of how people identify who they are and what they value: what they have, what they do, and who they are. We simply label these as "Have" people, "Do" people, and "Be" people. Understanding self-descriptions is essential because people value different things and choose different standards for self-identity. Their goals are different and how they measure success is vastly different.

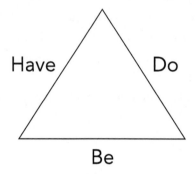

When we were living near Chicago, and I was consulting and teaching as a graduate school professor, the president of a large pharmaceutical company headquartered near Chicago asked me to do some career counseling for his VP of Marketing that he was replacing. He told me that he respected Jean greatly and loved her as a person but needed a change in leadership because he felt that being the VP of Marketing for their organization was not her calling. He wanted her heart as well as her head, and he was only getting her head. He wanted me to help her find a place to give both her head and heart with full passion. He offered to pay me for my services for up to four months if need be. He decided to give her a severance package that continued her base pay and a regular bonus, plus health benefits for twelve months. I thought, what a generous and caring person he was.

When I met with Jean (not her real name), she appeared a little embarrassed and guarded, as you would expect. But it didn't take long for her to relax and get fully engaged in our effort to kick-start her professional career in a new direction. She became very open once she realized that her ex-president intended to help her find her sweet spot in life. I asked her who she was, and she told me that she was a marketing professional. I listened to her dribble for a while and said she didn't sound enthusiastic about being a marketing professional. She defended her marketing identity for only a short time before I interrupted her and asked, "Who are you really?" She stopped, paused, looked at me square in the eyes, and said, "I'm a writer!" Immediately, her energy level went up, and she excitedly told me how much she loved to write. I listened to her excitement about the possibility of becoming a full-time writer.

I said that I believed that writing was what she wanted to do, but I wanted to know why. She again explained that she loved to write. I then explained that her answer was not specific enough, that it was too diffuse and would not give her a specific mission and goals to aim for and to which she could commit all her energy and passion. I asked her to think about it overnight and come to our session the next day to answer the kind of writing she wanted to do and the purpose of her writing.

When we met the next day, she came in excited to tell me that her mission was to help people, and her goal was to write Christian self-help books. Her enthusiasm was tremendous, and she wanted to start laying out the strategy and path to becoming a Christian writer immediately. She already knew what her first two books would be. I asked that if she knew what her mission was, knew her goals, and already had the primary content of the first two books in her mind, why didn't she start doing it full time right now? She said that she couldn't write full-time right now because she needed to find a full-time job. She explained that she needed a guaranteed income to pay her share of the bills and mortgage on their beautiful home in Barrington Hills, Illinois. I knew Barrington Hills to be an upper-class area with expensive homes, so I appreciated her dilemma. But I decided to see how big of an obstacle this house was.

Their house was a 5,500-square-foot beauty that they had designed and built with sub-contractors, who they personally managed. It was their dream house. They invited me to dinner at their house, where I met her husband, a Ph.D. pharmacologist who also worked for her old company in its quality testing laboratories. I met their lovely children, a boy and a girl; I guessed they were eight and ten years old. I got to meet their live-in maid, who also cooked, cleaned, and was a part-time nanny when they went out of town or went on trips as a couple.

At the next session with Jean, I asked her how much the house was worth. She said they could reasonably expect to get $1,200,000 if they sold it. To compare, we owned a 3,800-square-foot show-house in Arlington Heights located by an artificial lake, a mile in circumference. Our house was a high-end home that we sold for $300,000 when we moved to Utah. I just wanted to provide a frame of reference regarding the value of their home. I asked her how big their mortgage was. She said it was approximately $90,000. I asked in amazement, "So you have over $1,100,000 equity in your house right now?" Their monthly mortgage was something like $1200 a month. She confirmed the information. I then asked, "So you are not writing Christian books right now and looking for a full-time job that you don't want to do so that you can carry your share of the overhead on your house and overhead?" She sheepishly nodded her head. I asked her, "Do you know how crazy that sounds?" She reiterated that she needed to be fair with her husband and carry her share of the financial burdens. I noted that her husband's salary alone could carry all their financial obligations with plenty of income to spare.

We talked about putting the most important things before the less important things. I asked Jean what she would have left if the house had burnt down. She told me that she would still have the things that mattered most, her husband and children. I reasoned that if the house burned down, she would then be free to start her writing career and that maybe it would be a blessing if it disappeared. She agreed. I pointed out that she was putting having (the house) ahead of doing (writing Christian books) and being (helping people with her insight and skills to live better, more fulling lives). I pointed out that the dream house enslaved her and her whole family. She started to cry and asked, "What can I do? I'm beginning to hate that house!" I reminded her that her husband loved her and that he would probably be eager to help her get started on a new career path about which she could be passionate. I believed that he would support her because there was a minimum risk to their financial security.

Her husband met with Jean and me on her next session, and we laid out a plan and timetable for her to launch her writing career and still give her time to find another job if she couldn't make a go of it before her severance ran out. He agreed to give her six months to see if she could write and get her first book published. Meanwhile, they would save all her severance payments as a hedge against a possible time of becoming a single-income family.

I thought I had successfully completed my assignment as a carrier counselor for Jean. But, three months later, Jean called me and asked to meet because their family was in a crisis. When we met a few hours later, I found out that her writing was going exceptionally well, and she loved every minute of it. But the more successful she was, the more unhappy and depressed her husband became. I asked her if her husband would mind meeting together. She said that she would ask him. She did, and the three of us met the following evening.

The crux of the issue was: He felt trapped in a dead-end job that he found uninteresting, that was way below his intellectual talents, and he hated it. He was envious of Jean, who was "living her dream" while he was 'living a zombie existence." I asked him, "Who do you want to be?" He said, "I want to be a pharmaceutical research scientist and find new compounds to help humanity; that is what I went to graduate school to become." I asked him, "Why don't you do it?" He went into the same routine Jean did when I started with her. "We have our house, our dream house...." I exclaimed, "Sell the damn house and start doing what you would love to do and stop letting the 'dream house' be an obstacle for being what you want!" He asked me, "How can we do that?"

I called a friend in San Francisco who had become the president of a biopharmaceutical company and asked her if she would be willing to meet with Jean's husband and determine if he was qualified to work in their bio-research laboratories. She said that she couldn't do it but would talk to their VP of Research and see if he would. As it turned out, he went to San Francisco got a position in research there. They sold their house in Barrington Hills and bought a lovely home in the Bay area with almost no mortgage. Last I heard, Jean was a successful and popular Christian writer and public speaker and her husband was happy being a biopharmaceutical research scientist.

Their story is not unique; countless people put "having" ahead of "doing" and become enslaved by what they have or have to pay for. Too often, to fill their need for having, people get in debt to the degree that it curtails their ability to do what they want to do or be what they want to be. I visited a member of our church congregation who was incarcerated in the Cook County Department of Corrections because he found himself deeply in debt and turned to illegal behavior to find a solution. It didn't work; he compounded his debt with imprisonment, deeper debt, and horrible family damages due to his enslavement to having.

One of our core Carlson family values is Be, Do, and Have. Being is more important than having, and if we keep that priority front and center, we will be the kind of people we want to be, which will lead us to do the type of work we want to do, and have the rewards that our work will provide us. To not let our priorities get out of kilter, we need to learn how to live within our means and be grateful for what we have; being is more important than having.

If we are to be a values-based family, company, or nation, we have to govern ourselves by core values. As we mentioned at the beginning of this section, "Values are the personalized behavioral embodiment of principles used to govern our decisions and actions." They are standards that flow from principles. They are always in tune with principles; therefore, they align with natural laws and eternal principles. Values sit on top of the hierarchy, or spectrum, of standards, so they encompass all laws, regulations, policies, guidelines aligned with natural laws and eternal truths. Another way of describing values-based people is to say that they are people of moral character who live aligned with principles based on natural laws and eternal truths. OK, so what is moral character?

There are three kinds of moral character and behavior: moral, amoral, and immoral.

Moral character is virtuous, strives to do right, and is honest, trustworthy, brave, generous, loyal, etc. It develops and sustains synergistic relationships. It seeks synergistic power and applies it to all circumstantial power. Anything that alleviates suffering and does not cause suffering is moral behavior. Moral behavior aligns with truth; it generates light, energy, and edification. Moral character and behavior benefit people instead of harming them.

Amoral character is indifferent to right, wrong, honesty, trustworthiness, integrity, etc. Amoral characters have "transactional" relationships that are valued only as long as they benefit them. Amoral characters optimize the statement, "Honesty is nothing, the reputation of honesty is everything." (Chairman Mao) Amoralists do not care to be moral, virtuous, honest, trustworthy, etc.; they only seek the self-serving benefits derived from the appearance of being ethical. When it serves their purposes, they will use any circumstantial power combined with dominance power. Amoral character people are narcissistic in that everything they do serves themselves, whether or not it helps or hurts someone else. The impact of their decisions and actions on other people matters to them only to the extent that it will positively or negatively sway people's support of them. This self-serving behavior describes many politicians. Unfortunately, politics, for too many, is an amoral business.

Immoral character is not bound to moral or ethical principles. Immoral people do evil acts and create destructive relationships. Immoral people seek dominance power and combine it with any circumstantial power that will serve them well. Truth means nothing to them. Immoral people use emotions, deceit, lies, power, or virtually anything to get what they want. Sadism is a form of immoral behavior; sadists intentionally seek to hurt others.

Summary thoughts about character and choosing to be value-based

If we have moral character, we must be value-based individuals, families, and organizations. We must anchor ourselves to core values based on moral character. Rules, policies, guidelines, statutes, and laws fall below the mark. We can't be value-based on any standard other than value standards of moral character. Only value-based standards inspire lofty decisions and behavior. If we are value-based, we need to live by our core values unconditionally.

Unconditional Values

Being value-based is not easy; it requires absolute and total commitment to live by the moral standards we choose as our core values. Total commitment means that we will **unconditionally** abide by our core values. Unconditionally means that we will use our core values as the basis for all our decisions and actions in all situations. We create an elevated environment and expect higher behavior than operating from lesser standards. For example, rule-based families and organizations expect obedience and compliant behavior, to the rules dictated, based on the moral character of the rule maker. As Charles Dickens clearly showed in his book *Oliver Twist*, Fagan, who was the rule maker for his band of thieves, expected his kids to be expert pickpockets. Laudable behavior, for him, was immoral behavior by society's standards. We can see that while rules govern all rule-based families, each family has its own set of rules. What is proper in one family is wrong and improper in another.

Earlier in this book, I explained how James Burke, the CEO of J&J, operated unconditionally and absolutely to live by the credo values of J&J when the organization, and J&J customers, faced an existential threat because someone, or some people, laced Tylenol capsules with potassium cyanide. The first three sentences of the J&J Credo unconditionally determined the behavior and actions of Jim Burke. The first unconditional value includes the following message: *"In meeting the needs of patients, doctors, nurses, mothers, fathers and all others who use our products and services, everything we do must be of high quality. This commitment extends to everything we do to bring our products and services to the people who use them."*

To Jim Burke, unconditionally living the J&J credo values was not an option; it was the only way to move forward. Admittedly, some executives advising him wanted to use the credo standards as guidelines (or suggestions) for making decisions rather than as absolute standards of moral character. If he accepted their advice and followed it, the J&J credo standards would have become conditional standards, flexible and changeable according to the extremity of the situation. If the Credo statements were merely suggestions for making decisions and taking action, the total Tylenol recall wouldn't have happened, and we will never know how many more people would have died. Of course, he saw the J&J credo statements as the core values of J&J that would be the basis of all decisions and actions. At that moment, he and J&J were completely value-based, fully aligned with the highest standards of moral character. Value-based living is the personification of integrity.

Conditional Values

Conditional values are not absolute or unconditional; they change, adapt, and align themselves according to situations or conditions. In short, situations and circumstances determine what the values and standards are to be. Conditional standards are flexible and mold themselves to the problem at hand. With conditional values, different situations require different standards. Right? That is right only if you see and use standards conditionally as tips or suggestions to guide decisions and behavior. It is incorrect when seeing standards as unconditional and the basis for decisions and actions based on admirable moral character. The convenience of having conditional values is that they are like water which molds itself around any object, just as conditional values mold themselves around any situation.

If values and standards are conditional, they are not real standards. Conditional values align to standards other than principles and values of moral and ethical characteristics. Values defined by circumstances are nothing more than a way to present ourselves as something appearing to be more virtuous than we are or intend to be. Conditional values are false advertisements to gain personal benefits. They are deceptive to those who believe and depend on their integrity.

While I was the VP of Administration at Amersham in the USA, I was also the General Manager of the company's Diagnostics Division in the USA. As General Manager, I was invited to England to participate in a worldwide conference with all the other twenty-eight GMs of the Diagnostic divisions in companies worldwide. Also attending were six members of the corporate board of directors. Bill, the CEO of Amersham International, chaired the conference and led the group discussions.

As it turned out, one of the discussions concerned establishing a Worldwide Total Quality Program for the diagnostics divisions. It was a curious thing to do since all the diagnostic products were under the control and direction of the Diagnostic Production Director who resided in England. The quality of the diagnostic products depended on his production processes and quality standards, no matter where produced. We were all seated on a large circle with Bill and the rest of the board at the circle's power end. Bill ceremoniously stood and proposed that we establish a worldwide total-quality program that Amersham would announce to the markets in every country where Amersham Diagnostic divisions existed. He explained how marvelous it would be for our reputation and stature within the industry and how much it would help our marketing efforts. He then went around the room, asking each GM to vote on the proposal. Each GM sitting to my right and left voted a hearty Yea. I asked permission to vote last, and he granted my request. When he finally got to me, I explained that my vote depended on his answer to a straightforward question.

The question was: "If we know that our diagnostic products are clinically safe and effective but do not meet the specifications listed on the vials and boxes in which they are sold, would we still sell them?" His answer was, "It depends." I immediately voted "Nay." My no vote was like sticking a hot poker up his butt; he started jumping up and down and yelling at me. He screamed, "What in the hell is the matter with you?!" He demanded that I explain my "Nay" vote. I told him, and everyone there, that the question that I had asked him was, in fact, the reality in which we, who sold the diagnostic products, lived. I explained that every GM present, and probably he and the board, all knew that are our diagnostic products, while clinically safe and effective, did not match the specifications listed on their containers. If we want to have a credible total-quality program, everyone without deliberation would instantly know that we can't sell products whose specifications fail to match the products contained within the containers and still consider ourselves a total quality company.

He tried to rationalize his "it depends" comment from various rationale. Try as he could, his arguments still didn't constitute a commitment to total quality; each rationale argument presented made total quality conditional to the situation. He and everyone else tried to convince me that I should change my vote to Yea so Amersham would have a unanimous vote. I declined to change my vote. The resolution passed 32 Yeas to my one Nay.

After launching it, Amersham canceled the total-quality program a year or so later. Announcing such a program knowing that we were not living up to the standards of a total-quality program and having our customers confirm that fact nearly killed the diagnostic divisions worldwide. It certainly negatively impacted our reputation. I didn't have to worry about it in the USA because I had arranged a co-marketing relationship with Kodak Diagnostics, headquartered in Rochester, NY. Before consummating our marketing relationship, Bill took over the discussions sold the US diagnostics division to Kodak. He informed me after the fact.

As you can see, conditional values are mush. They are not standards that stand for anything. They are like chameleons changing colors constantly to fit their surroundings. It is the nature of most standards within most organizations. As consultants, we have helped many companies become unconditional value-based organizations. It is not easy for them to do or for us to get them there. Our consulting business reached a point where we would not commit to working with a company unless they agreed to become a value-based organization. Our decision-making anchors had to be moral principles, and so did theirs, if we were to work together successfully. If not mutually grounded to the same ethical principles and characteristics, we would have constant disharmony between us in virtually everything we attempted to do together; it simply wouldn't work. Helping them crystalize the core values that would become the basis for all their decisions and actions was work.

Some organizations wanted to develop a list of moral characteristics similar to the Boy Scout laws: "A scout is trustworthy, loyal, helpful, friendly, courteous, kind, obedient, cheerful, thrifty, brave, clean, and reverent." That approach usually ran out of gas when they found it impossible to use all of them or decide which one to use as the basis for a decision in specific situations. Other companies went to the other extreme: "Operate from integrity." As you can see, that covered the entire scope of moral character and provided no specific standards that dealt with the particular situations surfacing in their business. We recommended establishing four, five, or six-core values to guide all their business situations. We asked them to start with the complex problems in their organizations and work backward. We wanted them to use the problematic situations to answer, "What unconditional moral value would open our heads and hearts and would direct us to the right moral behavior in this situation?"

Most organizations found peace with around four or five core values that provided moral direction to virtually all predictable situations. With four or five core values, they could present hypothetical and real situations to their employees and find consistent answers to problems while remaining aligned with the moral character and behavior they aspired to exemplify. We have included some thoughts on crystalizing a list of core values in the competencies section.

You might ask, "What was this business about **have** people, **do** people, and **be** people, and what does that have to do with conditional and unconditional values?" Well, I'm glad you asked. The simple answers are that the labels indicate the basis upon which we identify ourselves. They offer insight into who we are or want to be. They signify what people see as valuable. The things we see as valuable become our valuables. Our valuables indicate what is important to us. What is important to us becomes the focus of our attention. It becomes the place where we extend ourselves physically, emotionally, socially, spiritually, and mentally. Where we have cathexis (a deep emotional investment) becomes who or what we "love."

"Have" people and moral character

When someone says, "I love this car, house, boat, toolbox, motorcycle, racehorse, etc.," they have cathexis for things – for having. Having becomes the highest priority. If we are a "Have" person and given a choice between having, doing, or being, we would choose to have. Easy choice. Of course, we would explain that having **is** also our being. If having is being, then our values are attached to what we have, what we want to have, or what we want to keep. Having will guide our decisions and actions; because having is our highest priority. If a value didn't support what we need to do to get what we want, we wouldn't choose it as one of our values. Thus, in a real sense, what we want to have determines what we need to do to get it and decides the values we adopt. Having people justify anything they must do to get what they need to have; therefore, their values must align with the actions necessary to get it. Hence values for have-people are conditional; they become whatever they need to be to get or have "valuables."

The typical relationships of have people are transactional. Transactional relationships are valued and endure only as long as the relationship helps them get what they want or is seen as being connected to something valuable to them. Synergistic relationships aren't in their bailiwick; having stuff is more important than relationships. We see people spending countless hours in the pursuit of gaining wealth and having things. Unfortunately, that dedication to having too often comes at the expense and well-being of people who should be important in their lives. We often see them give expensive gifts, assuming that it is a true expression of love (because things are what they love). Ralph Waldo Emerson said, "Rings and jewels are not gifts, but apologies for gifts. The only gift is a portion of thyself."

Some wealthy people are "Be" people. They are people grounded in a moral character. Their cathexis is to ethical principles. If given a choice between having or being, they would unhesitatingly choose to be. They don't center their identity on what they have but who they are. They are generous, kind, caring, empathic wealthy people. As a percentage of society, they are rare and unique, but they exist. For example, Gayle Miller, widow of the deceased Larry H. Miller, is a very wealthy woman. She is also a kind, generous woman who is a "Be" person from my experience, observation, and association. She doesn't flaunt the things she owns, but she puts her energy into good causes and loving people.

"Do" people and moral character

"Do" people emotionally invest in what they do. What they do is the basis of their self-identity. They focus on doing because doing is their being. Doing is what is important to them. It is their highest priority. "Do" people exist in all categories of morality. They may be morally, amorally, or immorally grounded. The point is that their primary focus is not on character but on what they do. Al Capone, "Pretty Boy" Floyd, John Dillinger, and Baby Face Nelson, notorious criminals from the 1930s, took great pride in their immoral behavior; it defined them and exemplified who they were and wanted to be. Robbing and stealing were what they did; murdering was collateral damage to the job. They chose that doing was more important than being. But, of course, their doing was perceived by them as being.

At the other end of the morality spectrum, we find Dr. David Livingstone[40], a Scottish physician, a missionary, an explorer, and a medical humanitarian of the late 19th century. He devoted his life to the care and keeping of Africans deep in Africa. He rose to fame when the journalist Henry Morgan Stanley led an expedition to find the "lost" Dr. Livingstone or prove his death. He found Dr. Livingstone living in a village near the shores of Lake Tanganyika, which is now in present-day Tanzania. When Stanley found him, he supposedly greeted him with the famous expression, "Dr. Livingstone, I presume?" Dr. Livingstone was a British hero. He saw himself as a missionary, explorer, and physician; that was who he was. He also happened to be morally grounded. He had loving and intimate relationships with the people he served.

---

40   M. Dugard, *Into Africa* (New York: Broadway Books, 2003).

He extended himself physically, emotionally, socially, spiritually, and mentally in the service of Africans. I remember reading of him telling Stanley, something of the sort, that black people are the most beautiful people in the world, who make white people look pale and feeble by comparison. He exemplified the expression that, "We learn to love those we serve."

Sometimes "Do" people get so focused on what they do that other matters become secondary and seem unimportant to them. We find the children of doers frequently neglected because caring for and nurturing is not on the priority list of what matters most. If given the choice of doing or being, they would undoubtedly say they are the same thing. They can also be very caring and nurturing if what they do, their job, is nurturing and caring for people. We just hope that the people they care for and nurture are their loved ones. Workaholics universally see what they do as the most important thing. Sometimes they rationalize that they are working endlessly to show love and support their loved ones, which may be true. But if it is true but not necessary, then it is just an excuse that justifies putting what they love to do (need to do) before the needs of others.

"Do" people can have relationships that fit into various relationship categories. The kind of relationships depends on the emotional states created between themselves and others by what they do. If what they do supports synergistic relationships, they will have them. If it supports domination, then they will have Command and Control relationships. If what they do is adversarial or contentious, they will have Mutually Destructive relationships. The point about "Do" people is that what they do is the most important thing to them and is the basis of their decisions and actions. What they choose to do may support principles and moral character or not. What they do is the basis of their self-identity and is the basis of their decisions and actions. Their values are secondary considerations as compared to what they do. Therefore, they operate from conditional values. I picture values to "Do" people as being like a cart attached to a workhorse which follows whichever direction the horse chooses to take.

"Be" people and moral character

While both "Have" people and "Do" people see themselves as being, only "Be" people see being as living synonymously with moral character based on principles aligned with natural law and eternal truths. "Be" people are the only people who operate from unconditional values inseparably connected with truth and reality. "Be" people make all decisions and take actions based on the core values to be their moral anchors for living. Decisions and actions unconditionally tied to their core values determine what they will do, not only for the basis for the jobs they take or the professions they pursue but also for their day-to-day and moment-to-moment decisions and actions associated with living. "Be" people are people of integrity. Integrity is living true to core values.

"Be" people have synergistic relationships. They do because they engender emotional states between themselves and others that develop Intimate Soulmates, Teammates (Inner circle), Friends, Partners, and Advocate relationships. They are trustworthy because being less than trustworthy is unacceptable because it would violate moral principles and character.

There are few 100% perfect "Be" people, probably true perfect ones don't exist, because even those who try and aspire to be perfect "Be" people come up short, simply because they are human, prone to human weaknesses, passions, and stupidity. But even though they are imperfect, they attach themselves, without excuse and unconditionally, to principles and moral standards based on natural law, eternal truths, truth, and reality. These standards are constant, unchanging, and dependable. As long as "Be" people remain unconditionally anchored to them, they may error and lose their way for a time, but will be able to return to a solid place that is always there to guide their decisions and actions toward light, energy, and edification.

I can think of only one person who exemplifies a 100% perfect be person: Jesus Christ. I'm not trying to convert anyone, only to point out that he alone lived unconditionally in tune with natural laws, eternal truths, truth, and reality from everything I have learned and studied. His perfectness didn't guarantee synergistic relationships with everyone; most Jewish leaders hated him, and the Roman rulers feared his influence would create social upheaval. Their combined hate and fear resulted in his crucifixion. Still, his teachings and example have become the ideal way to live and be for countless people worldwide. His truths bring light, energy, and edification.

If you haven't guessed, I'm firmly committed to a "Be" person approach as the best way to govern ourselves, our families, our companies, and society. It certainly optimizes our growth and development, socially, emotionally, physically, mentally, and spiritually. And, it offers the best way to optimize the same for others, especially the ones we are responsible for governing or raising, who we aspire to assure that they can become the best, healthiest, and happiest possible.

We list the "Be" priority for living as the best way to develop synergistic relationships. If we operate from being, do and have will take care of themselves, we have an excellent chance of having a life of loving and nurturing relationships.

As a summary of the values section, we conclude with these thoughts.

Life is a continuous stream of situations and circumstances that require decisions and actions. We can tie our choices and actions to conditional values, which means our values are subordinate to the situation. When we use conditional values as the basis for our decisions and actions, our values shift and align to circumstances and conditions. Values that change and adapt to the situation become situational values, not principle-based values. In short, situational values make principle-based values expendable. **While few people would admit to being amoral or immoral, choosing circumstances as the basis of decisions rather than moral or ethical principles suggests movement away from moral character toward amoral or immoral character.** The guiding principle of people who operate from conditional values might be: "the ends justify the means" or "values are subordinate to personal benefits." Who among us has not made a self-serving decision and justified the moral lapse if required? Accepting power while avoiding account-ability is a common characteristic within society.

People who operate from unconditional values make decisions and ac-tions based on moral and ethical principles in all situations. For these people, circumstances and situations are subordinate to moral and eth-ical principles and values. Moral character and principles do not shift, change, or align to the situation; they stay firmly attached to natural laws and eternal truths. Decisions and actions aligned with uncondi-tional ethical values lead to moral character and ethical behavior. To become a moral person, Aristotle would call it "virtue ethics" devel-oped by being good, honest, brave, just, generous, and so on.

A person operating from unconditional values will choose synergistic power and apply it to circumstantial power. Unconditional value people develop trust because they are trustworthy. They do not adjust values to suit the situation but apply moral principles and values to manage the circumstance. In doing so, they become "predictable" because people can anticipate that their behavior will be principle-based. Uncondition-al value people develop synergistic relationships. They have a highly functional adult mode which validates a nurturing parent mode and a free, natural child mode. Their boundaries are synergistic (protecting their own and respecting others). They experience emotional states across all categories of feelings. Still, they tend to be happy, positive, uplifting, grateful, sensitive, empathetic, and loving, thereby bringing light, energy, and edification to those around them. They accept respon-sibility and accountability for their decisions, actions, and outcomes. They readily admit mistakes; they do "checkups from the neck up" (Dr. Morris Massey), repent, and move on. They acknowledge the imper-fection in themselves and others but "are slow to judge and quick to forgive" (Donna Carlson, my mother). They see the value in diversity and differences that make the whole greater than the sum of its parts.

Living by unconditional values and being able to continue to do so requires three things:

1) Identifying and defining core guiding principles and values that become the basis of our decisions and actions

2) Validating, challenging, and correcting unconditional values when cognitive dissonance surfaces

3) Sustaining, reinforcing, and protecting our core principles and values

1) Identifying and defining core principles and values that become the basis of our decisions and actions

Taking the time and making an effort to define your principles and core values is essential. This action defines our moral "north stars" (Stephen Covey). It makes our north stars visible and available for life navigation. If we fail to do so, by default, it facilitates circumstances and situations to be the deciding factors for our decisions and actions. Proximate and stressful situations overwhelm and supersede ill-defined principles and values, particularly if the values are not understood or lack internalized commitment. This applies to individuals, couples, family units, organizations, and society.

2) Validating, challenging, and correcting unconditional values when cognitive dissonance surfaces

Moral principles and absolute values can stand scrutiny. In fact, scrutiny reinforces and validates them if they are sound. Applying an adult mode examination will validate them and raise our commitment toward them.

J&J would pull all the VPs and senior executives together to do a J&J Credo Challenge every few years. We would spend a day, or more, with everyone debating whether the Credo Statement should be the basis of decisions for all our business actions. Some felt that the profits should be the most prominent value. But in 25 years, the Credo was changed in only a few parts, and they were only grammatical corrections. After they did the challenges, it was clear to everyone that our J&J credo statements were the basis of our decisions and actions.

From time to time, it is natural to question. When doubt or questions surface, we experience cognitive dissonance, a state of intellectual, emotional, spiritual, social, or moral imbalance. We must address the dissonance to restore balance. It requires examination to regain balance. The examination will have one of several possible outcomes:

One, it will validate our principles and values (balance restored).

Two, it will update the principles and values (balance restored).

Three, it will correct a misunderstanding about the values (balance restored).

Four, it will discredit the current principle or value, resulting in changing the value to one better aligned with principles and moral character (balance restored).

3) Sustaining, reinforcing, and protecting our core principles and values

Unconditional values need protection from inappropriate behavior. One cannot surrender principles and core values from Stomper, Stompee, Adversarial, or Enemy behavior. The ability to protect our values suggests a need to know how to confront inappropriate behavior while maintaining our principles and values. We need to give feedback rather than criticism. We need to operate from logic, reality, facts, and reason rather than let others "hook" our dominant or critical parent or our emotional, rebellious, or submissive child. Protecting the boundaries and our principles and values will sustain them and reinforce them with ourselves and others with whom we share synergistic relationships.

While we were consulting with KPMG and had completed the laborious effort of defining and testing their chosen core values with KPMG employees, a situation arose that tested their commitment to living their unconditional core values. The top producing partner in their practice harassed an employee. Being warned twice that harassing anyone again would result in his expulsion as a partner in the firm didn't stop him from repeating the offense. The practice leader called my partner and me into his office and presented the situation. His head and heart were a mass of cognitive dissonance. Should he punish him in another fashion other than expulsion, thereby enabling KPMG to continue benefiting from his incredible income production? If he did, he knew that it would mean that their core values were, in fact, conditional values and weren't going to be the basis of decisions and actions within the firm; no one would take them seriously from the moment of reprieve moving forward.

If he fired him, it would send the message that the core values were absolute values that would be the basis for decisions and actions in their practice. But that would come at the price of losing the highest income producer in the company. The practice leader looked at us and asked, "What should I do?"

We simply asked him in return, "Do you want to be an unconditional value-based company, or not?" He fired him, which surprised the person fired, astonished everyone in KPMG, and sent the message to their industry, current customers, and potential customers that KPMG was a value-based company. That part of KPMG became the world performance leader.

.

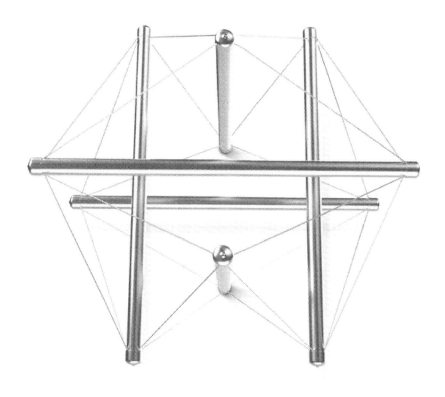

36

INTRODUCTION TO LEVELS OF COMMITMENT

In Cincinnati, Ohio, I taught a group of managers and directors who were part of the management team for one of the companies we consulted. I had just briefly introduced the concept of commitment levels when one of the managers, also a Southern Baptist minister, asked me, "Wayne, are you acquainted with the Apostle Paul?" I answered, "Not personally, but I have read his teachings in the Bible." He continued, "Then you know that he taught that the first principle of the gospel is obedience, right?" I agreed with him and then asked him, "What did Paul mean? Are you suggesting that Paul was saying that obedience is the highest level of commitment?" He looked a little puzzled and doubtfully answered, "Yes, I think so." I told him that I respectfully disagreed with him and that what Paul was saying was that obedience is the lowest level of support, not the highest. I reminded him that Paul later taught that when truly converted, we will have a change of heart and that after the change of heart, we would no longer be operating from blind obedience but willingly from our heart. Paul was teaching us the difference between being compliant and being internally committed. He taught that soulfully acting in concert with our beliefs and values is a much higher level of commitment than merely obeying. The minister said that it never occurred to him that obedience was the lowest level of support for Christ's teaching; he had always assumed that it was the highest.

I continued, "As long as we are having a scriptural discussion about commitment levels, let's look at the Book of Revelations in the Old Testament, where it says that God kicked Satan out of heaven for rebellion." I asked him, "What is rebellion, which was God's justification for kicking Satan out of Heaven?" He confidently answered that it is disobedience. I asked, "What kind of disobedience?" He asked back, "What do you mean?" I stated that are two kinds of disobedience: covert (hidden) disobedience and overt (open) disobedience. And then I asked him which kind of disobedience was the reason for Satan's removal? He said, with less certainty and almost questioningly, "Overt disobedience...?" I reminded him that all kinds of people were disobedient, both hidden and open, like Adam and Eve, and they only got kicked out of the Garden of Eden, not Heaven. I further reminded him that Satan was kicked out of Heaven for rebellion, not disobedience, according to the Book of Revelations. I asked him to explain the difference between disobedience and rebellion. He stated that he thought that they were the same thing.

The minister set the stage for an introductory discussion about commitment levels, starting with obedience and disobedience. Covert and overt disobedience are different from rebellion; disobedience is secretly or openly not complying with God's laws and commandments. Rebellion is anarchy. I explained that anarchy is self-rule. (In philosophy, the question might be asked: Is anarchy an absence of law or an over-abundance of law? If we have five billion people, with each person operating from his own set of laws, is that an absence of law or an over-abundance of law? I'll let you decide.)

Satan's case meant that Satan was governed by no law other than his own and that his laws were incompatible and irreconcilable with God's laws and values. They could not exist together with conflicting laws and values. Even today, relationships can endure virtually any problem between people except incompatible and irreconcilable values. The same principle applied to God and Satan. They could not coexist with one another. One-third of the hosts of heaven preferred Satan's laws and values to God's; they exited heaven with Satan to become his angels.

Whether the minister intended to do so or not, his opinion and the discussion that followed laid out a nearly perfect way to introduce the levels of commitment. There are eight levels of commitment:

Internalized commitment (personal ownership of our beliefs, decisions, and actions based on our values and standards)

Conversion (personalized justification leading to internalized commitment)

Validation (confirmation that obeying was correct)

Willing obedience (compliance based on personal agency, a choice)

Coerced obedience (forced compliance)

Covert disobedience (secretly not complying, hidden disobedience, pushing back against being forced)

Overt disobedience (openly and willingly being disobedient, principle-based open disobedience)

Rebellion (personal ownership of our beliefs, decisions, and actions based on our values and standards; unwillingness to accept other people's standards for oneself if they conflict with our own; to not submit oneself to any standard or value other than one's own)

Below is a depiction of the commitment levels laid out in step fashion. As you can see, if we look at obedience as a starting point, there are two paths available to us. One path starting with willing obedience leads toward internalized commitment, while the other starting with coerced obedience leads to rebellion. Each step on the upward path and the lower path mirrors one another. For example, **both willing and coerced obedience** are about compliance, albeit one aims at obedience by choice and the other by force. **Validation and covert disobedience** are both testing behaviors. **Validation** is testing whether or not obeying is correct. **Covert disobedience** tests whether or not a personal win is possible when pushing back against being forced. **Conversion and overt disobedience** are both forms of justified beliefs. **Conversion** is a justified belief born from validated evidence and experience. **Overt disobedience** is a justified belief about the moral rightness of our disobedience, so much so that we no longer hide our disobedience; we base our open disobedience on principle. **Internalized commitment**

and rebellion are soulful commitments to personal convictions. Both are unconditional commitments to our beliefs, values, and ways of living. Both are forms of internalized commitment that are incompatible and irreconcilable with each other.

Levels Of Commitment

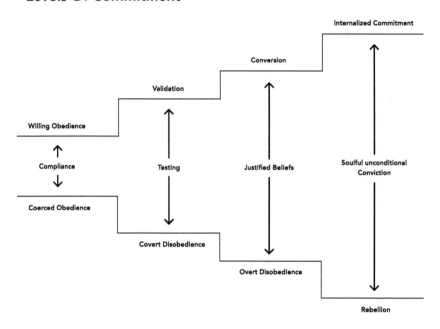

I hope you will notice that rebellion is essentially the same level of commitment as internalized commitment, although on opposite ends of the commitment spectrum. People have internalized commitment to beliefs, laws, values, or any standard that are incompatible or irreconcilable to one another. How can they have the same level of commitment and yet be in opposition with one another? Great question! Rebellious people have the same internalized commitment to their laws and standards as the people at the top of the hierarchy, but their beliefs, values, and standards oppose one another. The governing standards of one rule-maker or "establishment" are frequently incompatible with the desired governing standards of other rule-makers or establishment organizers. This opposition means that yours has to go if I have mine, or mine goes if yours remains. That, in short, was the situation described in Revelations that existed between God and Satan. If their laws and standards were identical and equally internalized, the commonality would have unified them. They would have been as one, rather than at opposite ends of the relationship spectrum and enemies.

We need to, and will, review each level of commitment in some detail. We will explain and demonstrate what each level is and how that commitment level influences relationships. However, we won't start with internalized commitment but rather with obedience. We will start with obedience because it is the lowest level of support we can demonstrate to lawmakers: society, organizational, and family standards (rules). We will start there because obedience, or compliance, is the level of commitment most used within almost all of society's organizations, including families.

The first thing we need to clarify about obedience is: There are two kinds of obedience.

Coerced obedience happens through force, dominance, control, and power. Coerced obedience focuses on compelling obedience to laws, statutes, regulations, rules, and policies. Coerced obedience is all about getting people to be submissive to forceful control – the most powerful people set and enforce the rules. **We also call this rule-based obedience**. With coerced obedience, people obey because they have to. If you were to ask a person governed in a rule-based environment, why do you obey, they would likely answer with something like this: "Because I have to so I don't get punished." Whether we call it coerced obedience or rule-based obedience, it doesn't matter; we are talking about the same thing.

The other kind is **willing obedience** which is about agency and choice, and the governance tools are reason and moral values. This obedience aligns behavior with principles based on logic, reason, and eternal truths. People who aim at this kind of obedience we call teachers. Teachers explain why compliance is essential; they help us understand things, so we willingly obey. **We also call willing obedience "value-based obedience."** With this kind of obedience, people comply because they want to. If you were to ask a person governed in a value-based environment why they obey, you would likely get a response like: "Because I think it is the right thing to do." Willing obedience and value-based obedience are both starting points of compliance that lead to dramatically different endpoints.

We will first review coerced obedience, or rule-based obedience, followed by examining covert disobedience, overt disobedience, and rebellion. We do this because these various commitment levels are linked together and form a pattern of behavior with outcomes that are predictable. After we review rebellion, we will come back and review willing obedience, followed by validation, conversion, and internalized commitment. We do this because value-based obedience, conversion, and internalized commitment also form a pattern of behavior and outcomes that are predictable. As you will see, rule-based obedience and value-based obedience are both starting points for paths delivering different results.

Levels Of Commitment

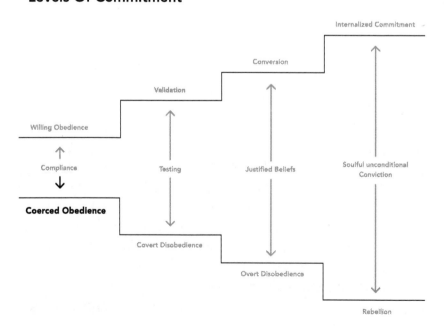

Coerced Obedience

It is possible to force people to obey. Our maximum and medium prison systems are good examples of forced compliance. Prisoners live in a controlled environment because they willingly violated society's minimum acceptable standards, and laws don't control them when they are free. But even in prisons, some people won't submit to a harsh rule-based environment; they require additional extreme measures to protect other inmates and correction officers from injury. If they violate the rules in the prison-controlled environment, prison officials place them in an even more strict environment within the prison – isolation. Isolation separates them from everyone in prison except the officers who feed them and supervise their allowed activities, like having a shower or taking a walk outside their cell. Being forced to comply is not fun, but it is sometimes necessary for the benefit of others.

Coerced obedience in families

I was having a phone conversation with a longtime friend who was a young member of our church group when I was the bishop in the area we both resided. During our conversation, I heard her yell at three of her four kids at least 20 to 30 times to stop doing what they were doing. She almost as often threatened them with time-out or being sent to their room if they didn't stop. Note that she didn't tell them what she would like them to do, but only what not to do. Why 20 to 30 times? Because they kept repeatedly doing what she told them to stop doing. Frankly, it wasn't working. I believe Einstein said that insanity is doing the same thing repeatedly and expecting different results. No one would suggest that she was insane, but some people might say that she needs to be tougher, even more demanding, and must follow through with her threats. That won't happen because it is not her nature; she is one of the most loving, compassionate, caring, empathetic people I know. Trying to be the commander, making her kids obey, was not working, and it was making her miserable. At wit's end, she and I started discussing what she could do to change the intolerable situation between herself and her children.

Friend: "Wayne, I am frustrated because my kids don't listen to me."

Me: "So this is kind of... pretty normal?"

Friend: "This is my life. But they listen to their dad."

Me: "Why?"

Friend: "Because they are afraid of him."

Me: "Hmmm...I have noticed that a couple of your kids are pretty independent-minded. Your kids are openly disobedient with you but not with their dad. Is it possible that they make their dad think they are compliant with him but covertly disobey? You know that kids understand that they can't win a direct power contest with their dad, but they still want to win, so frequently, they try to win by competing covertly. I notice that the kids with whom he has the most significant issues are the ones who are the most willing to push back. Are they are finding ways to appear compliant but are being purposely disobedient as a means of pushing back and sending a message that they don't like being controlled? I'll bet that your push back kids don't like being pushed around by anyone, including their father.

Friend: "I know that is happening, but what can I do? Wayne, I have to change this! I can't live like this; I don't want to live using fear and punishment. When I was growing up, I didn't live in a home ruled by fear and punishment, but that is what we have in our house. I hate it!"

I don't think she could use fear and punishment if she wanted to; it is just so foreign to her nurturing nature. That is why her kids feel free to disobey her openly and why, in part, her husband, seeing that they aren't respecting his wife, brings the hammer down on them.

Me: "Are you willing to explore a new way to manage your kids that will shift your family away from fear and punishment and toward self-governance, where your kids will do the right things because they choose to rather than from being compelled to do so?"

Friend: "Absolutely."

Me: "If you chose to change the culture of your family, then the goal is to change from being a rule-based family to becoming a value-based family. It is easy to say but much more difficult to do. Do you still want to proceed?"

Friend: "I do! Teach me what I need to do!"

Me: "This will be an ongoing journey. It will take us time and patience to implement. I'm ready to do whatever I can to assist you."

We started calling each other almost daily, making the journey step by step. After a few weeks, my young friend said to me, "Wayne, this is too much for me to remember; I need you to write it all down for me then we can discuss it, and I will have something in my hands that I can refer to and review when I get overwhelmed.

One of the reasons I decided to write this book is to help my friend and people like her. I want to provide her with the information and skill training she needs to help her change her family from a rule-based family to a value-based one. This book is for people who hate being in a rule-based household where they are required to play the roles of rule-maker, family cop, judge, and punisher. Some people still don't know that there are much better options. I send her unedited manuscripts to help her before completing the book. I will send her a complete edited book when it is published.

Based on my comments, you may believe that I am opposed to obedience and compliance. That is not true; I value obedience and compliance in society. Society wouldn't be civilized without it. Society has laws, statutes, regulations, etc., to ensure that we have minimum acceptable standards to govern behavior. Without them, we would have no minimum standard for managing society. These standards become the basis for legal and illegal behavior. If we fall below these standards, our conduct constitutes "breaking the law," where we can be held accountable and punished.

We classify behavior that fails to meet society's minimum standards by the level and degree of law-breaking seriousness. They may be classified as infractions, misdemeanors, or felonies, resulting in severe punishments, including fines, incarceration, or even death. Society has professions centered on law learning, law writing, and law enforcement. Branches of professional law people become skilled prosecutors of those who break the law, while others become skilled in defending people accused of breaking the law. Some people trained in law sit on the bench as judges tasked with presiding over trials and maintaining order in the prosecution and defense of alleged law-breakers. Judges make sure that even lawyers practice their profession within the boundaries of the law. Because laws are essential in society, that thinking might suggest a reason to use the same approach with families. Of course, families and family members are also members of society and are subject to society's standards. But families are also distinct elements of society and require different methods for governance. Law specialists are necessary for society because too many can't, or won't, abide by even society's minimum standards.

Societies are about law and order. Families are about relationships.

A healthy society requires laws. Healthy families need a governance approach that establishes healthy identity, self-confidence, life skills, and knowledge to become productive contributors within society. Families are where impressionable children are supposed to be loved and nurtured so that they, in turn, can be loving and nurturing to others. I don't believe that laws, statutes, regulations, and other social standards that aim for obedience and compliant behavior teach children how to have healthy relationships or be loving, empathic, and nurturing to others. They seem to do just the opposite; they become the standards that people learn to circumvent and covertly or overtly disobey. They help people become creative by finding ways not to get caught when they break the laws or rules. Often people feel gleeful when they violate laws or regulations without being caught or punished. I know many people who drive faster than the speed limit. They try to reach the limit of law enforcement patience without exceeding it, unless you are from Alberta, Canada (it takes forever to drive anywhere there because "everyone" goes the speed limit).

Rules do for families what laws do for society. They establish order and set the lowest standard of acceptable behavior. Family rules are about forcing obedience and compliant behavior that defines the minimum acceptable family behavior. But parents who believe that rules inspire lofty behavior above the minimum standards are fooling themselves. While rule-based parents may think they express love because they love their children when using rules to force them to be obedient and compliant, love is not what the children feel when being ruled. Rule-based parenting teaches obedience and compliance. Not much else. And rule-based parents are opening the door for their children to become skilled in covert disobedience. Hidden disobedience is natural when the drive for freedom and independence overrides the fear and consequences of being caught breaking the rules. In a way, rule-based parenting does a pretty good job of teaching and motivating high-spirited children to become good risk-takers. Oppressive ruling causes intelligent, high-spirited, independent-minded kids to engage the higher center of their brain that controls thinking into overdrive. Intelligent, independent-minded children will find ways to test parental rules. They start thinking more and more for themselves and less and less about complying with rules.

As we mentioned earlier in this book, once a child has justified covert disobedience, they become openly disobedient; they can't be controlled by rules any longer. Trying to use even greater controls will only hasten the speed at which separation will occur between the parents and the child, either physically, emotionally, or both. Looking back at my friend's experience with her kids who didn't listen to her commands and threats, we can see those very young children learn quickly if the parent follows through on her threats. They, of course, know that she won't and that her husband will. A couple of her children are highly independent-minded and are becoming experts in covert disobedience, with their dad, the one who follows through on his threats. In my mind, the unfortunate children are the ones who genuinely succumb to being ruled and lose the vision of having an independent identity or a free spirit.

Please let me clarify that when I talk about families or organizations whose management style aims for obedience or compliance, that is the same thing to me as rule-based management, they are interchangeable terms. You can interchangeably use obedience-based, compliance-based, or rule-based, and the meaning will be the same.

The main difference between a rule-based family and a value-based family is this: A rule-based family is about control from the top down. It is about asserting parental rules presented as family rules and enforcing obedience. Rules infer punishment for disobedience. Rule-based punishment is what we called earlier "super-imposed punishment," such as a spanking by the parent.

A value-based family is about individual choices for everyone. It is about establishing a rational, logical, moral-based value system that becomes the basis for everyone's decisions and actions. Value-based families spend a lot of time discussing **why**. If people understand why they don't need coercion to act, they will choose to do it. Becoming a value-based family requires family members to agree with the values and understand how they apply in making everyday decisions and determining behavior. Failure to live by values results in natural consequences that become object lessons about what naturally occurs when we set reason and values aside. But when they willingly live following family standards, they also experience the benefits derived by living them. The positive outcomes will validate the wisdom in living the standards. The sooner kids start experiencing the consequences of minor mistakes, the sooner they will avoid the consequences of making big mistakes. Rule-based parenting teaches children to fear the rule makers and to avoid punishment. Value-based parenting teaches children to be responsible and accountable for their decisions and actions.

With few exceptions, rule-based families, either the mother or the father, dominate. When the father is the rule-maker, the mother typically becomes the second in charge, not equal to him but higher in stature than the children. Sometimes, the mother is a nurturer. But if so, she has to nurture secretly, out of sight of the master of the house. She meets with the punished children, comforts them, and assures them that they are loved and valued. If she does not do so, a child is left only with the message of being a "bad person!" or unacceptable. The dad sits lower on the totem pole when the mother is the rule-maker. Frequently much lower. Then the responsibility of being the nurturer becomes his.

A domineering rule-based mother raised someone very near and dear to me. Her dad lived at home but in the background of the family. He never came to the children's rescue when the mom punished (which was very frequent) or met with them afterward to reassure them that they were unique, valued, and loved. Their mother had rules to govern every aspect of the home and their behavior. Weekly church attendance was an absolute requirement, so the church became a symbol of repression to them. Most left the church but came back later in life. The kids sometimes felt that their mother was harsh, critical, and brutal. **They felt her angry emotions, not her affection and love for them**. The children that were more independent-minded and who pushed back against their mother's parenting style were punished more severely than those who were compliant.

The five sisters banded together and provided one another the nurturing and support not given by either parent. They learned to depend on each other and avoid their mother and father. My special person left home at 16 and lived with friends until her high school music teacher saw her needs and invited her to live with her. Her music teacher virtually became her mom, advisor, and protector. From her music teacher, she felt loved, valued, and extraordinary. They are effectively mother and daughter and always will be. All five girls grew up resentful of their parents, particularly their father, because, in their minds, he should have done something to intervene or to mitigate their mother's abuse, but he did nothing. All the girls, as adults, have "issues" that they haven't resolved from their childhood. They still love, depend on, and protect one another. Their unfulfilled needs as children have become obsessions as adults. Since they grew up poor, having expensive things is tremendously important to them—too important. Because they didn't feel loved and respected as children, they are all unduly sensitive about perceived acts of disrespect toward them. They have excessive expectations of their husbands to demonstrate unconditional love to them and put them first over everything else, no matter how important everything else is.

In their mother's defense, she was a mother of eight children born within 12 years of one another. For all practical purposes, she was the sole breadwinner of the household. She was a full-time nurse who supervised the other nurses in the hospital. She had virtually no time for herself and had insufficient funds to support such a large family. She lived crisis to crisis. She didn't have time to spend one-on-one with each child, hence the rules. Of course, she loved her children, wholly and deeply, and she insisted that they do the "right" things. She had rules for everything to ensure that they did the right things. Because she loved them, she wanted them to do the right things, and she believed that her rules would make them do the right things. She punished them when they were disobedient or did the "wrong "things. She loved them, but they didn't feel loved. **And their mom didn't realize that when she demanded obedience, she also engendered covert disobedience, overt disobedience, and rebellion with the fighters and compliant adaptiveness with those not inclined to fight.**

In one sense, we could call her a hero; she did what she had to do to provide for her family under very adverse conditions. She provided life's necessities but little more than that. She gave them a home, clothing, food, and some transportation. They all survived and reached adulthood, albeit with baggage. The kids all have unpleasant childhood recordings that still play in their minds and greatly influence their current behavior. They haven't been fully able to empower their adult mode to examine those early recordings and to use their adult mode to explain why those things happened and to be able to move beyond them. When their mother died unexpectantly, I wrote an essay about their mother called "Who is a hero," which gave them another perspective of their mother. They all called me and thanked me because it gave them a different way to look at their mom and remember her more affectionately. After their mom died, some of them realized, maybe, for the first time how deeply their mother truly loved and valued them. She didn't express it with words; she did it with self-sacrifice, not realizing that loving words and behavior would have made all the difference.

Coercive obedience in organizations

Obedience and compliant behavior-centered businesses and organizations are little different than rule-based families. Aiming at obedience and compliant behavior is about establishing and maintaining control there. It has nothing to do with creating an environment of synergistic relationships. It has everything to do with establishing a Command and Control climate based on hierarchical position power that empowers high echelon people to control lower echelon people to get what they want. It creates demand for and urgency for people to get into the power echelon and get as high in the power echelon as possible.

The need for hierarchical positioning became apparent when I consulted for First Merchants, located near Chicago. It was a company that provided loans to people with less than stellar credit to buy cars (one of the first secondary credit companies). The President and CEO asked me to help him reorganize the work assignments within his organization. He said that it felt like he was doing everything in the company and that everyone was waiting for him to tell them what to do. That would mean that over 200 people were waiting for him to tell them what to do. When he provided me with an organization chart, per my request, I was flabbergasted at what I saw. First Merchants had as many layers of management as AT&T, maybe more. They had Senior VPs, VPs, Assistant VPs, Executive Directors, Directors, Assistant Directors, Managers, Assistant Managers, Supervisors, Assistant Supervisors, Team Leaders, and Assistant Team Leaders. Can you imagine that they had 14 layers to manage a company of approximately 200 people? Nuts, right!? Now imagine everyone in the 14 levels of management trying to direct the efforts of everyone lower on the totem pole. Fourteen layers of management, with each manager aiming at coerced obedience, exemplify dysfunctionality.

I asked the CEO how all these management layers happened; it was unlike anything I had ever seen before. He explained that he had to give employment candidates a management position to attract and keep the people he needed for this new company. Everyone wanted a management position, and, after a point, no one would consider joining his company without a title and subordinates because it would seem that they wouldn't be actual managers if they didn't supervise someone. Consequently, that is what he gave them. He had concluded that everyone, of consequence, in his company, needed to have someone to supervise. Sometimes a Senior VP would have only one direct report, a VP; an Executive Director would have only one direct report, a director. That pattern extended pretty much the same throughout all the levels in the company. It was 100% insane, stupid, illogical, etc.

How could you possibly manage a company this way? How could such an organization even establish rules, assuming it wanted them? They did. Often each manager had their own set of rules, independent of company rules and policies. Sometimes they aligned with the regulations in other departments; sometimes, they didn't. As you would expect, nobody knew who was responsible for what in an organization structured like this. Everyone was sensitive about stepping on someone else's toes or having someone step on their toes. But what became very apparent was that how high you sat on the totem pole determined your status, power, and ability to make people obey your orders. Everyone, except the CEO, knew that a person higher in the pecking order could change their orders. As a result, the Senior Vice Presidents were the only ones ultimately providing direction. As a result, the Senior VPs enmeshed themselves in decision-making at all company levels, including low-level activities that shouldn't have involved them.

I told the CEO that I had some good news and some bad news. The good news was that he could get rid of 12 layers of management and run the company as it was running currently; only the Senior VPs' direction mattered in the company's decision-making anyway. His eyes brightened as he thought about lowering his overhead by 85%. He asked me, "What is the bad news?" I explained the bad news was that he would be out of business in three months because the necessary functions for running a successful company didn't exist. I further stated that he was probably six months away from losing his company. Essential business functions were missing to support the company much beyond six months. He asked me what we needed to do. I suggested that we get the Four Roles of Organizational Leadership staffed and functioning as soon as possible, with no more or less than the correct number of qualified people needed to operate First Merchant's business.

Below is a model that depicts the four organizational functions necessary for successful organizations:

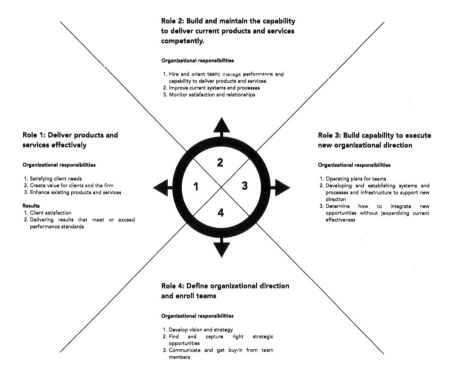

Role 2: Build and maintain the capability to deliver current products and services competently.

Organizational responsibilities

1. Hire and orient team; manage performance and capability to deliver products and services.
2. Improve current systems and processes
3. Monitor satisfaction and relationships

Role 1: Deliver products and services effectively

Organizational responsibilities

1. Satisfying client needs
2. Create value for clients and the firm
3. Enhance existing products and services

Results
1. Client satisfaction
2. Delivering results that meet or exceed performance standards

Role 3: Build capability to execute new organizational direction

Organizational responsibilities

1. Operating plans for teams
2. Developing and establishing systems and processes and infrastructure to support new direction
3. Determine how to integrate new opportunities without jeopardizing current effectiveness

Role 4: Define organizational direction and enroll teams

Organizational responsibilities

1. Develop vision and strategy
2. Find and capture right strategic opportunities
3. Communicate and get buy-in from team members

I explained that two management roles are essential for a company to be successful. The first management role centers on daily business operations: **To deliver products and services effectively**. Staffing for that role would be the most important for day-to-day business activities. People in that role would not need management titles or roles. They need to understand what to do, why to do it, and how. They need clear performance objectives, clearly defined work processes, knowledge (or education) about accomplishing their responsibilities, recognition for doing well, and accountability for doing poorly. They also needed to know the company mission and have a clearly defined set of values to govern their decisions and actions. They need policies only to define minimum acceptable behavior, which would be inconsequential if they lived according to their values. The people in this role constitute the most significant number of employees.

The second management role centers on daily business operations: **To manage the ability to do the first role well.** The people in this role would be responsible for hiring, educating, making work assignments, ensuring that the work processes are understood, teaching and exemplifying the company's core values, recognizing individuals and teams for laudable performance, and holding people accountable for poor performance. A big part of their responsibilities would be to develop synergistic relationships between themselves and the employees and between the employees and First Merchant's customers. People in this role would be the lower-level managers and supervisors. They need to understand that they are not to be "bosses." They are not to rule by fear and intimidation (aiming for obedient behavior), but to be supportive leaders leading with empathy, care, and concern for their employees. There would be no more managers or supervisors than required to support the people performing the first role. The success of the current business would largely depend on the abilities of the frontline managers and supervisors to perform First Merchant's second management function well.

The third function of organizational leadership is the first role of strategic leadership. It is: **To build capability to execute new organizational direction well, without negatively impacting day-to-day operations.**

People in this role would be responsible for developing operating plans for performance teams and developing and establishing systems, processes, and infrastructure to support new directions. They would determine how to integrate new opportunities without jeopardizing current operational effectiveness. These people would be senior managers, usually functional directors or VPs. They would be the **change lead-**

ers within the company. They would play a principal part in identifying company core values and getting them bought into and lived by everyone within the company. Usually, there would only be one VP for each primary function or department. If there were specialty functions within a department, that would justify a director position. Each specialty functional director would report to the overall functional VP. Nowadays, most major corporations only have eight or nine principal functions: Administration, finance, marketing, sales, manufacturing, research, communications, IT, HR, and legal. Smaller organizations frequently combine one or more principal functions.

The fourth role of organizational leadership is the second role of strategic leadership: defining organization direction and enrolling **teams**.

People in this role are responsible for developing an organizational vision, mission, strategy, and action plan. A big part of this job is finding and capturing the right strategic opportunities for their organization to ensure its future success. It is also to communicate and get buy-in from boards of directors, stockholders, and team members. This strategic function is where organizational culture is determined. It is where senior management decides whether or not to be a value-based or a rule-based organization. The CEOs, presidents, COOs, and engaged business owners reside here. James Burke, the CEO of Johnson & Johnson, sat here and influenced the direction, reputation, and future of J&J. This function plays a vital part in any long-enduring, successful company. And it can be the reason for the demise of an organization.

After determining the details of the four organizational leadership functions related to First Merchants, we had to decide how many people we needed for each role and who those people would be. That wasn't too hard to do. As you might guess, we trimmed the management and leadership group by about 70%, leaving no one-on-one reporting relationships. Then we needed to get everyone in those roles focusing on the right things. We call this "dialing people to the right place" or dialing to the right. Dialing to the right means each person should spend as much time as needed doing their prime responsibilities, such as deciding, determining, directing, executing, implementing, delivering, authorizing, or approving (direction or actions). They should spend the remainder of their time focused on fulfilling their second responsibilities, which are supportive. Examples of this would be advising, coaching, guiding, reviewing, justifying, selling, persuading, helping, assisting, participating, teaching, training, developing, measuring, evaluating, monitoring, recognizing, rewarding, reinforcing, clarifying, and providing resources and authority.

For example, the CEO and president of an organization should focus the time required on his primary role of defining organizational direction and enrolling teams, plus fulfilling the other responsibilities earlier described. The remainder of his time should be divided appropriately by supporting the different functions within the organization. He may see it wise to spend 30% of his focus on his primary role and 40% of his time supporting the strategic leadership of role three, building the capability to execute new organizational direction. With his remaining time, he may wish to focus 20% of his time supporting the second managerial role in the organization, building and maintaining the capability to deliver that current products and services competently. There he would be supporting the frontline managers and supervisors in their efforts. The remaining 10% of his focus would support the delivery of products and services. **You can see "dialing to the right" paints a picture of people who focus on helping others rather than ruling them.**

If companies implement the four essential functions well, VPs and departmental directors would have primary responsibilities on building capability to execute new organizational direction (deciding, directing, authorizing, approving, etc.) They would focus more time supporting other people's roles. They would help others define organization direction and enroll teams or support frontline managers and supervisors in building and maintaining the capability to deliver current products and services competently. They would help the people who deliver their products and services. They would have a lot more time to provide recognition and rewards for contributions in moving the organization forward.

Likewise, managers and supervisors would fulfill their primary responsibilities by deciding who to hire plus the training and development they would use for their people. They would determine how to instill the core organizational values with their employees and apply them as the unconditional basis for decisions and actions. The rest of their focus would be supportive, to help the CEO or president in organizational direction, or the Vice Presidents with building capability to execute new corporate direction. And finally, they would spend lots of time supporting their employees. The time spent supporting their employees sends the message that they are essential and valuable. It conveys that the company is grateful for them and appreciates their efforts and sacrifices.

Employees, of course, would spend most of their time and energy doing their jobs. But if they are empowered and supported, they will continually show the organization ways to improve current operations. If the layers above them are wise, they will keep the employees who deliver their products and services informed about the organization's direction, why that is the direction, and when to expect it. Frontline employees who are empowered to support all the organizational efforts can, and often do, present ideas that make the impossible, or improbable, doable, so it becomes a reality.

When we analyzed where First Merchant's management was spending their time and what they were doing at all levels, we found some, not so surprising, information. We found that virtually all levels of management were spending the majority of their time and focus on directing others about how to deliver products and services. First Merchants oversaturated organizational role number one (delivering products and services effectively). Of course, the directions given by one manager were inconsistent with previous orders; so it pretty much created a mess. And because everyone except the CEO was focused there, the other organizational leadership roles were severely neglected. That is why he felt like he had to do everything in the company. We got everyone dialed to the right place, performing their primary roles as they should be performed, spending the vast majority of their time and focus on supporting people in the other functions.

First Merchants took off. It quickly became a dominant player in the secondary loan market. It had changed from a rule-based (aimed at compliance), top-heavy organization to a value-based functional-oriented company where everyone knew their job and why they were important. I was so confident in the direction and future of the organization that I invested most of my savings in buying its stock. I became a board member of the company. Shortly after that, the company attorney informed me that the president and the CFO cooked the books. (They did that primarily to promote the value of the stock. The company's extraordinary performance was actual.) First Merchants shut down. Other companies bought parts of it (like the debt collections department). The collapse of the company hurt many people, including me. But the critical thing to take from this happy and sad event is that building an organization with clear primary and secondary responsibilities is good for everyone involved, as long as the core values are honored and lived.

Please note that supportive behaviors work in families as well as in organizations. Dads and moms (dads and dads, moms and moms) play roles three and four of organizational leadership in families. They determine the family direction and enroll family members to support that direction. They are responsible for establishing the capability to execute family direction and help family members be willing and supportive. In organizations, including families, where those on top play a dominant role in deciding, directing, and controlling all the activities and decisions, everyone below them becomes disempowered, devalued, and minimized. In organizations that "dial to the right place" and focus on supporting everything and everyone, people flourish, grow, develop, and learn to love themselves and others. That is why I believe in value-based organizations and families.

Think about it. If you had to choose, which would you choose? Membership in a family where the parents decide, direct, implement, control, authorize, and approve your every move and decision? Or would you choose membership in a family where parents support, advise, coach, guide, review, recommend, help, support, assist, participate, teach, train, develop, clarify, provide, recognize, reward, and reinforce you? The choice is between a Command and Control environment and a Synergistic one. It is the difference between a rule-based family and a value-based one. We could apply the same perspective to organizations. This comparison shows the difference between aiming for obedience and aiming for internalized commitment (we will review internalized commitment in Chapter 42).

37

COVERT DISOBEDIENCE

Levels Of Commitment

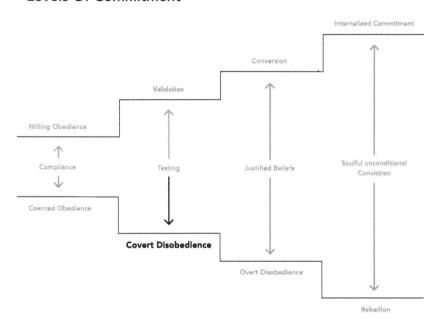

What causes people to break the rules secretly?

The simple answer is the rules. When parents or managers aim for compliant behavior and use rules to enforce it, they are at the same time setting themselves up for covertly disobedient children or employees who, after justifying their secret disobedience, will become openly disobedient. Rules are oppressive, and people do not like being oppressed. Rules tend to squelch people's individuality. An innate characteristic of people is that they are unique, different, and special and want other people to understand that.

Any behavior that diminishes innate characteristics will cause tension and pushback, either externally (through their behavior) or internally (through negative emotions). We realize that covert disobedience is a natural reaction when we think about it. Whenever rules are present and people are forced to obey rules, resentment rises in the subconscious mind. It will eventually rise to the conscious mind, which will become the basis for hidden disobedience.

We would hope, to expand this thought, that everyone sees that aiming for obedience or compliant behavior from others is pretty self-serving and narcissistic. Everyone seems to know and accept that narcissists are self-centered and everything is about them. But few people realize that true narcissists don't recognize any self-identity beyond their own identity; to them, other people's identities don't exist unless filtered as extensions of themselves. Narcissists subsume everyone else's identity into their own. Narcissistic parents don't recognize their children's identities as separate from their own. It is normal and natural to entwine the personal boundaries between parents and very young children. Their child's suffering becomes their suffering; their child's strong emotions are indistinguishable from their own. That is the way it should be, at that time; it is part of the maternal instinct to protect their offspring. It is there as a vital part of our species survivability. But separating identities and becoming a distinct person with a separate identity is also a natural progression between healthy parents and children.

Independence is a natural progression toward interdependence, where individuals can form synergistic relationships with other individuals. Narcissists don't support that healthy transition. They may prevent it from happening. In the narcissist's mind, their adaptive children's identity is an extension of themselves. You can imagine the impact that would have on their children. The lucky ones establish their own identities anyway. Somehow, they break away and become independent people. Once they do so, it is not without consequence. When they escape from their mother's or father's subsumption of their identity, they no longer become an active part of the narcissistic parent's identity; they become invisible, detached, and unimportant to the narcissist. They undoubtedly feel like an outsider with the narcissist and those still being actively and willingly subsumed.

Being an independent child of a narcissist is not an easy thing to be. They feel like orphans, cast aside by those they think should love them, support them, feel joy with them, sorrow with them, and nurture them. Instead, they mostly feel what they don't receive. It causes deep emotional pain and, too often, lifetime scars that never heal entirely. Fortunately, those who do escape and become independent also develop the ability to have loving interdependent relationships with others. These new interdependent relationships provide the means of feeling loved and valued. Yet, the vacuum created by the narcissistic parent never fills as one would wish because the person who made the vacuum is the only one who can fill it.

My son's sweetheart and wife is a child of a narcissist. She suffers from disconnection from her mother. She escaped from her mother's subsumption of her identity but is still profoundly impacted by her narcissism. Her mother cannot relate to her life. She and her mother don't share the things that bring joy, sorrow, happiness, and despair. The mother and other siblings, still subsumed by their mother, attack my daughter-in-law when she doesn't align entirely with her mother's views. She is the outsider, disconnected from her mother and subsumed siblings. She knows what is going on in her head and can rationalize it to make sense of her world, but her heart still aches. She is talented, beautiful, intelligent, and loved by all who know her and not subsumed by her mother's narcissism. She has a life full of everything that has meaningful value except her mother's love and appreciation for who she is.

As you may recognize, command and control people may not be true narcissists, but they mimic them very well. They may not subsume other people's identities but disregard them, making them invisible or irrelevant. People don't like their identities to become invisible or irrelevant, and most healthy people won't tolerate it. They will strive to make their identity, views, opinions, likes, and dislikes known. If they can do that, it proves that their identity exists and they feel validated as people. Typically, if they can't do that, the person they are trying to convince is not interested. Either because she is self-centered or because she has sufficient power to make the opinions and feelings of others irrelevant or to be unimportant to her. Not being recognized initiates a game where winning is doing what would be unacceptable to the person who fails to see their individuality and relevance. They know they can't compete openly in the game, so they do it covertly (secretly, surreptitiously). People successful in covert disobedience feel a sense of accomplishment. They almost always feel the need to share their successes with others and validate the righteousness of their behavior. Even if they are not successful, they still need to validate their feelings and the rightness of their discontentment.

I like to ask the teenage girls we coach at Park City High School and Club V Volleyball if they have ever sneaked out of their homes, purposely violating their parents' rules. Almost all seniors have, and most of the other high-school-age girls have. I ask them why they did that. The most common answer was that they had no other choice; they had to break the house rules to meet their friends to do what they wanted to do. They all had ways to justify their actions. When I asked them if they felt guilty about doing it, I got mixed reactions. Some said they felt a little guilty but would do it again if they had to. A few said they felt very guilty and wouldn't do it again. Most of them said they didn't feel guilty because their parents' rules were stupid (unreasonable) and that it was the right thing to do.

With many, I see their covert disobedience as evidence of children who are ready and eager to establish their independent self-identities and are acting on that inner compulsion. Virtually without exception, I learn that those who sneak out have Command and Control parents who run a rule-based family. Again, I will repeat that if you aim through rules to control behavior, you are, at the same time, setting yourself up for covertly disobedient children who, after justifying their secret disobedience, will become openly disobedient.

Covert disobedience is all around us. It thrives in our homes and our businesses, in our governments, and our churches. Why? Because people want to win, they will do whatever they have to do. Win what? You might ask. The simple answer is to win the right to be themselves, own their identity, have agency to control their own decisions and behaviors, and win from being oppressed or from being used or taken advantage of. When people adopt the role of commander and controller, rule-maker, and enforcer, to make the objects of their control and rules comply, it feels like oppression to the person tasked with being obedient. It doesn't matter how lovingly pure the intentions of the oppressor are; it still feels like and is oppression.

My friend, an ex-Chief Resident at a psychiatric hospital unit in California, said that everyone would lie to protect their ego. If he is right, I guess that is a sort of covert disobedience, hiding the truth for a personal win. And yet, I believe that much of the hidden disobedience in our families, businesses, and other organizations is because people feel unable to compete with people having greater power than they possess. If they can't compete openly, it doesn't diminish their desire to win. If they can't compete fairly and openly, they will do so covertly – winning is winning. If they can't win honestly, many will do so dishonestly. Sneaky winning has become very popular in our society. Our movies, books, and TV programs feature sneaky winning. They highlight the message that if you become good at cheating, you are successful.

One of my favorites, the *Pink Panther* movie series, glorifies Sir Charles Lytton, a fabulously wealthy jewel thief who never gets caught, as the epitome of success. Of course, they make the bumbling and ridiculous French Inspector Jacques Clouseau, the feature character of the movie series, which is beyond funny and, despite his naïveté and stupidness, he becomes a successful crime-solver despite himself. It is becoming more and more difficult to distinguish the good guys from the bad guys in films anymore since many popular movies feature and laud successful criminals.

I believe that most of us can relate to the bad guys; we know what it feels like to be the oppressed and disadvantaged, particularly if we grew up in a Command and Control environment or have worked in one. We have all been covertly disobedient as a kind of in-your-face response to oppression. My daughter, visiting from California, along with my son, my wife, and I discussed how people in our family tend to have attitudes and are good at protecting their boundaries. At one point in the conversation, my daughter pointed out how my wife was occasionally covertly disobedient when she felt oppressed. She said, "When mom got mad at dad, she would look at us kids and say, 'Let's go spend some of your dad's money!'" Everyone had a good laugh, including me; I can see my wife doing that. She doesn't take direction very well (at all). I learned to ask nicely or make suggestions early on rather than directing anything.

Might this sympathy for covert disobedience suggest relaxing our moral compass toward lawbreaking? Probably, but it does not diminish the expectations of Command and Control managers and parents to expect absolute obedience to their policies and rules. Despite all the evidence that Command and Control and rule-based environments foster disobedient feelings and behavior, people high on the totem pole still choose these approaches to govern their organizations and families. It feels to me that it is like handing someone a board with a nail poking through it and telling them to hit themselves in the head with it. And the crazy thing is: They do it! Why do people keep hitting themselves on the head with boards that have nails sticking out of them? Self-delusion, narcissism, a sense of power, or ego gratification? I don't know. It is not the wise thing to do, but somehow it makes sense to almost every parent and most bosses who aim for compliant behavior. Please understand I'm not justifying disobedience. I am just explaining why it happens so frequently in rule-based environments.

38

OVERT DISOBEDIENCE

Levels Of Commitment

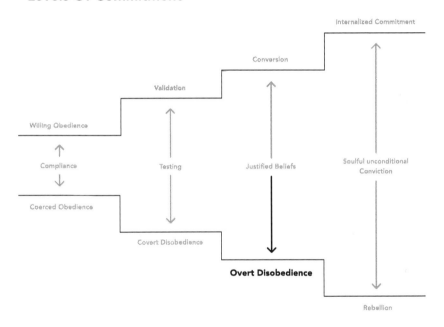

The 1960s was an era of social upheaval in America. We had a President and his brother assassinated. We also had a minister leading the movement for civil rights assassinated. I was a teenager during the 1960s and saw the horror of peaceful protestors attacked by police with clubs; white people hatefully shouting, jeering, and throwing things; and dogs who were unleashed to take down, bite, and injure innocent people who were simply marching for equal rights. I saw fire hoses knock black people down (men, women, and children) and send them sprawling and sliding across the road and into curbs, telephone poles, and buildings. I was shocked; it broke my heart to see those poor people abused. They were peacefully protesting to get the same rights and treatment I took for granted. Their bravery and sacrifices touched the conscience of good people throughout America and the world. They inspired changes to be made by those who had the power to make the changes. Their behavior changed society's hearts, except those whose hearts were stone and were insensitive to the sufferings of those they saw as less equal than they.

When any family or organization's standards, rules, and customs are unjust or unreasonable, people living in that environment will be disobedient, covertly when necessary, and then openly when possible. After the Civil War, despite emancipation, discrimination in the southern states continued unabated, with whites being at the top of the hierarchy and blacks being at the bottom.

Even though the U.S. constitution was amended to free the enslaved people, Jim Crow laws enabled the white population to oppress and discriminate against black people. Whites were adamantly opposed to allowing the blacks the right to vote, even though the constitution guaranteed that right for all males over 21 years of age.

They knew that the newly freed slaves could now vote and that through their votes, they could change the laws and distribute power to themselves, lessening or eliminating their own power. The whites would not allow that to happen. They would not allow the blacks to vote, no matter what the constitution of the United States said. The whites created ways to allow the white communities to maintain power and keep black people from getting it. Stopping the black vote was first and foremost on the white agenda. Their unfair and discriminatory tactics were endless. For example, white election officials developed tests to qualify people's right to vote in the Southern States. It was logical that people should be smart enough to vote wisely. A voting official might ask a white person to spell "cat" as a qualification of smartness to vote; the same official would ask a colored person to spell "chrysanthemum."

A white person might be required to name the current president of the United States. In contrast, a black person had to name all the justices on the Supreme Court (and their ages if necessary to show their ignorance to disqualify them from voting). At the time, black people had no recourse to contest the unfairness and the wrongness of what was happening to them. Another effective way was to implement poll taxes, which allowed only those with sufficient funds to vote. The Twenty-fourth Amendment outlawed the poll tax as a voting requirement for federal elections in 1962. Five southern states were still using poll taxes to stop African-American voters from voting until the Twenty-fourth Amendment passed.

Prejudiced whites denied African-American voting, but black resentment grew, and covert disobedience grew with it. Overt disobedience flowed from covert disobedience. Blacks sat at the counters of "whites only" diners waiting to be arrested. In 1955, Rosa Parks sat in a bus seat near the front of the bus and refused to give up her seat to a white man. Police arrested her, and her arrest became national news. She became a national hero to African-Americans and millions of people. Her arrest sparked a bus boycott in Montgomery, Alabama, that lasted 13 months. The mass protest ended when the Supreme Court ruled that segregation on public buses was unconstitutional. Non-violent civil disobedience, led by Dr. Martin Luther King, Jr., spread across the south and reverberated across the nation. Significant changes happened as a result of it. A white man murdered Dr. King because he became a symbol of African-American equal rights.

I wholly support overt disobedience if done for the right reasons. Civil disobedience is overt disobedience. Mahatma Gandhi used non-violent civil disobedience to gain independence for India from British rule and dominance (Mahatma means "Great Soul"). Dr. Martin Luther King used Gandhi's civil disobedience approach to gain equal rights for oppressed African-Americans and other minorities. The purpose of civil disobedience is to bring to light the injustice and inequity within our laws and within our societal customs and behaviors, to make them visible and show their obvious wrongness. It shows that changes for justice and equality must happen. It takes courage to do that because the people who are currently benefiting from the current laws, behaviors, and customs don't want the changes, and they will fight to stop them from happening.

There are examples of overt disobedience that we should admire, such as a soldier who refuses to obey an order from a superior officer because he perceives it to be unlawful, immoral, or unethical. In doing so, he places his military career in jeopardy and will possibly face a court-martial. It is a brave thing to do. Likewise, we have seen state attorney generals' resignation or threat of resignation from multiple states when ordered by federal officials to do unethical things that would benefit political party interests, themselves, or their boss. They repudiate the orders because it violates their professional ethics and oath of office. Their integrity defends democracy, but it also comes with burdensome personal and professional sacrifices. I appreciate such acts of moral character.

It should be apparent from our examples that overt disobedience manifests unhealthy relationships. If you are overtly disobedient or someone is overtly disobedient to you, rest assured that something is amiss in the relationship. The one feeling controlled is the one being overtly disobedient.

My superiors asked me to do something unethical or dishonest in my long career only a couple of times. They are so rare that I remember them distinctly; they are events that are lodged in my memory. One event happened while working as a VP for Janssen Pharmaceutica in New Jersey. The first president of Janssen in the USA was a man of impeccable integrity named James Bodine. He had been a bomber pilot During WWII and was dignified and completely anchored to moral character. I still feel privileged to have known him and worked under his exemplary leadership. Later came a man who was young, intelligent, and ambitious. He was very talented but detached from the core values that Jim Bodine had, or I had. He saw values as conditional standards, as mere suggestions or guidelines that could shift as circumstances required. For example, he chased officials at the FDA to try and get them to speed up approval on a couple of our products they were reviewing. He became known as the person FDA personnel should avoid or risk having their reputations marred. Eventually, an FDA attorney sent him a letter, with a copy to the CEO of J&J, demanding him to stop annoying them or they would ban him from FDA properties and push our products to the back of the review process. He didn't have the means for self-governing his behavior regarding conduct related to his aspirations and objectives.

As it turned out, he and I were invited to a special session with the other presidents and HR VPs of the J&J companies located in the Northeastern section of the United States. The invitation was to a meeting to discuss workers' compensation management and conditions in each of our companies because the workers' compensation situation in our area of the USA was not pretty. The executive hosting the session was the Executive VP of Administration for J&J corporate. He had a fearsome reputation. He told us that being invited to meet with him was never good and that there were never three invitations to meet with him (if you couldn't fix the problem in two times of meeting with him, you didn't get a third chance).

Our workers' compensation statistics at Janssen were not very good; not the worst, but, then again, they were far from the best. I reviewed our workers' compensation statistics and the reasons underlying them. From the analysis, I developed a plan of action to deal with our situation. A week or so before the session, my president met with me. He explained that he was very uncomfortable presenting our statistics at the joint session and asked me to change them so that we didn't look bad. I explained that I wouldn't do that and that we had to trust that our plan to deal with our workers' compensation problems would make sense to corporate management and that we would be OK. He left my office but returned the next day to make the same request but with an added condition; he told me that if I wouldn't make the changes that he wanted that he would take the responsibility out of my hands and give it to someone else who would grant his request. I told him that I still wouldn't do it and that it would look unusual to corporate officers if he were the only company president to show up at the session without his Human Resources VP in attendance. My response irritated him, and he left my office in a huff.

Two days before the corporate session, he again came into my office, this time with a personal threat. He stated that he was prepared to fire me and replace me with a new VP who would do what he asked him to do. I simply said, "That is your choice, but as long as I am here, I won't falsify our workers' compensation information. If you replace me, I will go but, on my way, out of the door, I will meet with the Executive VP of Administration at J&J and explain the situation." He left my office, furious with me, and we didn't speak again until after the corporate session. Under him, I assumed that my position wouldn't last too long.

At the corporate session, the Executive VP stood up and rebuked all of the J&J companies in the New Jersey area for our abysmal workers' compensation numbers. He then asked my president to join him on the speaker's platform. The Executive VP put his arm around the shoulders of my president and said something like, "Janssen Pharmaceutica doesn't have the best workers' compensation statistics in the company, but they are honest ones, and Janssen has a sensible plan to deal with the problem. Many of you have provided me with information that is b****s***. You have misrepresented your situation and have done unethical things like having employees on workers' compensation come to your workplaces in wheelchairs and other ridiculous things so that you could fudge your numbers. Shame on you. Harry Thompson (not my president's actual name) is an example for all of us, and you should follow his example." While the Executive VP shouted his praises, my president just looked at me, with longing and regretful eyes, seemingly to beg my forgiveness. As we left the conference room, my president asked me to meet with him at our Janssen headquarters; he then returned to accept the handshakes and back slaps as a moral example for the J&J companies.

It happened that as we were meeting in his Janssen office, a severe snowstorm settled on Piscataway; it was so bad that he and I had to spend the night in the headquarters. We talked most of the night. He thanked me for doing the right thing and expressed his appreciation for teaching him a valuable life lesson. His praise for me was effusive.

He promised that he would always be a man of integrity from this moment forward. He wasn't. He didn't change his ways or modify his adherence to core values; they remained conditional for him, merely suggestions to guide his behavior, not personal navigational anchors.

Another memorable unethical request came at the end of First Merchant's existence, caused by its president and CFO cooking the books. The CEO's replacement asked me to be the VP of Administration to help shut down the business. The person hired by the Board of Directors to head up the organizational closure was a snake. He wanted to capture all the funds possible for himself and the board members. How we did that was not important to him. Moral and ethical considerations were not important to him. I suggested the first thing we needed to do was put together incentive packages for remaining employees to keep them engaged until we shut the doors and give them a bridge to support them until they could find alternate employment. He felt that was a stupid thing to do because it would notify employees that we were shutting the business down. He didn't want them to know that. He wanted them to believe that their jobs were secure and essential to their futures. He simply wanted to optimize their collections as much and as fast as possible. He lied to them and wanted everyone managing the shutdown process to present a unified front. He wanted us to lie to them.

One of the first things he asked me to do was renew all the office leases for all the local branches of First Merchants. He intended to keep those offices functioning only as long as it took to rapidly collect all the outstanding debt from customers, then to walk away, to disappear. He had no intent to pay rent for the offices or pay anyone who worked in the offices beyond the point where they had collected as much money as possible. In short, he wanted to send the false message to the branch employees that First Merchants had new management and that their jobs were secure. They weren't. He wanted to cheat the landlords of the branch offices; he had "no intention of paying one more cent in rent." I refused to follow his orders. He offered me a six-month salary package if I would do as he asked. I again refused. He told me that I should do what he wanted me to do or get fired. I quit on the spot.

I spread the word as best I could to the branch people about what would happen to them. He countered my efforts by contacting them and telling them that I was a disgruntled loser fired for incompetence. He told them to trust that he would take care of them. I knew all of them and helped design their jobs and set up their work processes. I had personally trained most of them regarding compassionate and win-win approaches for loan collections and helped them improve their delinquent payment defaults by 60%. Still, they were afraid and wanted to believe whatever the new management told them. He cast most of them aside when their value was used up, without a severance package and with a warning not to call any of the other branch people. He warned them that he would sue them if they contacted anyone. When dismissed, some of them called me to tell me what had happened and explain how unfairly they were treated. They also asked if there was anything that I could do to help them. I had a pretty good idea of what they felt because I, too, had scary and sinking feelings caused by sudden unemployment without a predictable income. I felt sorry for them, apologized that I couldn't do anything to help them, and then focused my attention on finding and supporting other clients.

Usually, overt disobedience flows from covert disobedience rather than an in-the-moment stance against unethical or immoral behavior. Most commonly, it is a step on the way to rebellion. It happens when covert disobedience is justified, so hidden disobedience no longer seems the right thing to do. Almost always, overt disobedience follows covert disobedience. The mental state that develops after justifying covert behavior is very different from the mental state when hiding disobedience. Any guilt that people may have had by being covertly disobedient is replaced with a sense of justified open disobedience; they are disobeying openly and nobly based on principle. They will be resolute in their commitment to follow their new path; punishments be damned. It will be as if they are saying, "Put the blindfold on me; I am ready to be executed for my principles, and there is nothing you can do to change my mind!"

Parents are ill-equipped to deal with this new principle-based defiance. Force only intensifies their children's resoluteness. Parents who give in feel they have condoned behavior that they find objectionable. What can they do? That is the question that parents should have been asking themselves before the covert disobedience started. If they were attentive, they would have noticed the signs of hidden disobedience; then, they could have acted in a manner to prevent the covert disobedience. They would have had to change their parental management style from a controlling one to a supportive one.

We had some friends where it seemed that we followed one another from place to place. We became friends in Colorado Springs, Colorado, where Jack and I were pharmaceutical sales representatives working for different companies. His wife Jill was a registered nurse, and my wife Lois was a new mom of our oldest daughter. We loved being together, they were affectionate with our daughter, and we were thrilled when their oldest daughter was born and joined our friendship circle. A short time after their daughter arrived, we moved to California and later to Chicago. By the time we moved to Chicago, they had moved to South Bend, Indiana, because Jack and Jill were huge Notre Dame fans and wanted to live close to the university. They had hopes that both of their now-teenage daughters would attend college there. By the time we reconnected with them in the Midwest, we had five children, of whom two were teenage daughters of the approximate ages of their girls. We observed that Jack and Jill were both strict parents, especially Jack; he ruled with an iron fist, tolerating no backtalk or insubordination of any sort. Both of their girls were obedient, smart, and, what everyone would call, "good girls."

Before moving to Utah, Jack and Jill started sharing their problems with their oldest daughter. She was sneaking out of the house and came home with her clothes smelling like smoke. They suspected that she was becoming sexually involved. They were worried about the company she was keeping; she never brought her cronies home or even introduced them, even though they had requested that she do so many times. Their oldest daughter's grades tanked, and school officials suspended her for bringing beer to school and sharing it with her friends. Jack's response was to bring the hammer down. You might say that she was permanently grounded. She would just sneak out at night and sometimes fail to return home for a day or two. Jack changed the locks on her bedroom door. He put the lock on the outside of her door so that he could lock her in her bedroom. She just started climbing out the window. He threatened to put bars on her window, but before he could do that, she moved out of their home and started living with friends. They didn't know where she was or with whom she was staying. Their lives became an ongoing nightmare.

I don't know how Jack and Jill found her or how they talked her into coming home, but she came home. There was no apparent covert dis-obedience; she openly disregarded the family rules that guided her life previously. She started smoking in the house until Jill asked her to smoke outside if she had to smoke. Their daughter started openly buy-ing beer and storing it in the family refrigerator. She was considerate enough to offer her parents a beer when she had one. Jack stopped threatening to kick her out of the house if she broke the rules because he knew that she would leave if he threatened her. He told me that he, frankly, didn't know what to do or how to handle the situation with his daughter anymore. Jack hated her lifestyle and her open disobedience but loved her and felt that it was better if she lived at home where he and Jill could throw her a lifeline if required. He told me that all the ways he knew how to be a good father didn't work with his oldest child, so he just endured the unendurable, praying for a miracle.

Jack and Jill stayed in touch with Lois and me. We learned that his daughters remained living at home, even while attending college. The youngest daughter got into Notre Dame directly, but the oldest daugh-ter attended a less prestigious college until she could qualify to become a Notre Dame student. Jack and Jill were so proud that their daughters graduated from Notre Dame. The oldest daughter followed her moth-er's example and became a registered nurse. I don't recall the major of the youngest. The last we talked with Jack and Jill, we were pleased to find out that their oldest had married and had a little boy. (I'm sure Jack bought his grandson a small gold Notre Dame football helmet.) I asked him how his oldest daughter was doing. He said that she was just like Jill. She didn't smoke or drink. She was just the most caring and giving person that anyone could imagine. He told me that it was as if her rebellious teenage years never happened. I commented that it appears that his prayers were answered, and he got his miracle. He simply responded, "Yes, I did, thank God!"

Jack and Jill's experience with their oldest daughter is widespread in Command and Control households. I don't believe their youngest daughter followed in the disobedient steps of her older sister. She was an adaptive child who could adjust well to a highly controlled environment. I'm sure, being younger, seeing the conflict between her parents and her sister, and seeing the hurt happening in both her parents and her sister's lives, provided her lessons that she didn't want to experience firsthand in her own life. For sure, she felt the trauma and adjusted to it and fortunately, she learned a great deal. Her observations prevented her from the disfunction infecting her family. Most are not so fortunate or wise that they can learn and benefit from the traumatic experiences around them rather than being damaged permanently.

39

REBELLION

Levels Of Commitment

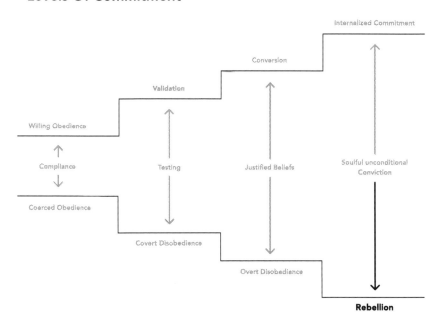

As you may recall earlier, I wrote of a Baptist Minister manager from Cincinnati who reminded me that the Apostle Paul had taught that obedience was the first principle of the gospel. According to the Book of Revelations, I also mentioned that God removed Satan out of heaven for rebellion. The example of Satan and God is a metaphor of what happens when someone becomes a rebel or a rebellious person. The rebellion concept applies fully to families or organizations of any type or ilk.

We will now review rebellion and clarify how it is different from covert or overt disobedience.

When asked to define rebellion, most people tell me that it is rule-breaking. If I explain that covert and overt disobedience covers rule-breaking, they will expand their definition by stating that it is firmly and openly breaking the rules. That, I explain, is firmly being overtly disobedient. Forceful overt disobedience doesn't qualify as rebellion. So, what does meet the standards of rebellion? What did Satan do to justify his removal from heaven?

He did much more than be disobedient. He was an anarchist. He would be governed by no law or value other than his own. And his laws and values were incompatible and irreconcilable with God's laws and values. We need to understand that disobedience is refuting, going against, or away from a set of standards or values. Rebellion is not only going away from and against a set of standards and values; it is also adopting or creating a different, incompatible set of standards and values for self-governance. It will also be the standards and values for those who embrace the conflicting norms and values. The new, different set of standards and values won't mesh with the standards and values of the organization they are replacing.

In 1978, I was a quorum president (priesthood leader of a men's group) in a small branch of our church group near Toronto, Canada. We had a relatively young fellow (early thirties) join our congregation. He was fun to be around. As it turned out, he also liked teenage girls. He was sexually inappropriate (primarily sexual innuendo comments) with several young ladies and mainly focused on one lovely lady. We confronted him and explained that what he was doing, and wanted to do, was unacceptable. If he misbehaved, in any way, again, with any young woman, we would expulse him from our church. He, once again, was suggestive with the girl to whom he was especially attracted. He was subsequently, through a church court, disfellowshipped from our church. Our church leader contacted the police and explained his offensive behavior to them. They said that technically he had not broken the law and that they could do nothing until he broke it. He actively started campaigning against our church, standards, and values almost immediately.

He started actively looking for another church that would accept him on his terms. A couple of churches readily accepted him but asked him to leave within a short time when they got to know him. He became pretty well known by many of our area's ministers, priests, and church congregation leaders. The leaders of local churches shared his unsavory reputation to sensitize others of potential difficulties if he showed up on their doorsteps.

In short, he would not willingly be governed by any standards or values other than his own. From my perspective, he was rebellious. From his perspective, he was a prophet, destined to start a new church with new standards and values that aligned with his desired lifestyle. He did launch his own church, and a few people joined his congregation until they found out what he was really like. He expected them to make themselves available to him sexually and support him financially. He married a lady with three daughters, two of which were teenagers. He molested them. He was convicted of statutory rape and sentenced to prison. After a bit of time, he started calling me collect from jail. I guess he was bored. At one point, he found an attorney who was willing to take him on as a client and who was ready to appeal his conviction. He called and asked me for a positive character reference to support his appeal, if you can believe it. That was the last time I accepted a collect call from him. He stopped calling, and I never talked with him again. He remained a self-anointed prophet governed by his standards and values, but the provincial corrections facility determined his lifestyle.

Another way to look at rebellion is to see it as apostasy combined with creating an organization whose beliefs, values, and standards are opposite, or anti, from the ones they have renounced. Apostasy happens when someone renounces, abandons, or repudiates the beliefs, norms, values, and organization they departed. Rebellion is apostasy plus, replacing the standards from the organization rejected with their own standards. People usually think of apostasy in a religious context. Still, while commonly used in the religious sense, it happens in families, in businesses, and all kinds and types of organizations.

For example, I know a man who used to be a good friend who abandoned his family, church, and old life because he didn't want to be governed by the expected standards in those organizations. He became a clinical psychologist whose practice specializes in helping other people who, like him, disregarded the beliefs, standards, and lifestyle from which he walked away. He has a congregation of sorts whose members rely on him to help them justify their new lifestyle and beliefs and establish connections with people who desire what he desires. He is doing more than being an apostate from the places and people he renounced; he is creating a following, an organization based on beliefs, standards, and values, which are incompatible and irreconcilable with the organizations and people from which he departed. That is rebellion.

Understand that people don't just wake up one day and become rebellious (unless they have a psychotic break with reality). It happens over time. It is a process that starts with covert disobedience that, when justified, becomes overt disobedience. When overt disobedience is based on beliefs, standards, and values that are incompatible or irreconcilable with the organization, and people, against which and against whom they are being overtly disobedient, they have only two choices before them. They can work through the cognitive dissonance (inner turmoil) that caused their covert and overt disobedience and reestablish themselves within the organization. Or second, they can establish or join an organization with beliefs, standards, and values that align with theirs.

As volleyball coaches, we see many young women living in Command and Control rule-based families who are covertly disobedient because they see it as a necessary thing to do. They become overtly disobedient when it becomes possible to do so. Alexis is an excellent example.

Alexis was a high-performance volleyball athlete and straight-A student living in a household governed by very strict parents. She wasn't able to do virtually anything not sanctioned and approved by one, or both, of her parents. She wasn't particularly happy, but she followed the family script. She was covertly disobedient in little forbidden acts, like using her iPhone during non-approved times or accessing internet sites that would not have been acceptable to her parents.

Her parents laid out her life like a well-written script. It had a prescribed and predictable plot with a happy ending. She seemed to be following the script perfectly until she left for college. At college, she could be covertly disobedient to the rules, beliefs, standards, and values left behind with her parents. Her parents didn't know the things in which she was getting involved. Had they known, they would have objected passionately. She did these things covertly, keeping them hidden from her parents until she felt justified in doing them openly. At that point, she didn't much care what her parents thought about her changed attitudes, beliefs, values, standards, and behaviors. She did want she wanted to do and found out that she liked it. Control by her parents ceased. They were no longer a consideration in her decisions and actions.

Her parents tried to connect with her and get her back on script. Alexis would have nothing to do with them; she had joined a new society that allowed her to be what she wanted to be. She only realized that this new person was the person she wanted to be, who could do what she wanted to do. This new person surfaced after having the freedom to make her own choices. From her parents' perspective, she threw her life away. From her viewpoint, she found it. Alexis is still young and nearly finished with college. Only she knows if she will return to the beliefs, values, standards, and organization that she renounced. Her parents are confused, angry, and looking for reasons why their perfect daughter has become what they tried to prevent her from becoming. Their Command and Control rule-based environment created to protect her didn't turn out as they hoped. It actually contributed to her becoming who she is now.

The thing that makes Alexis's future unpredictable is that dumb, or self-destructive, situations arrived at through personal choice are preferable to the person choosing them than are beneficial outcomes accomplished or obtained through coercion. Obedience achieved through force is distasteful to those dominated, even if the results are superior. They are distasteful because the "good outcomes" are tainted in the hearts and minds of those forced to comply because they were someone else's decision.

We need to understand that obedience driven by force or compulsion based on power, or the desire to control, creates an inner need to push back against being dominated or controlled. It stimulates the compulsion to do less than or the opposite of forced compliance. When people have insufficient power and authority to resist openly, they will push back covertly. They will find a way to avoid being controlled; they will not cooperate and let the person forcing them know what they are doing. When people convince themselves that their disobedience is proper, they will become openly disobedient. This disobedience is predictable if they have a lot of other people who believe as they do, especially if this "justified disobedience" is tied to some principle or value that provides the moral and ethical grounds to disobey. If they can't find an ethical or moral principle, they will create one. When people reach this point, they will not be governed or controlled by other people's rules or commands; only their standards will satisfy them. In essence, people become their own organization or social unit that is self-governing.

The birth of the United States of America is such an example. In the late 1700s, the British dominance of the American colony became increasingly more insufferable to many of the people living in America. England was at war with France and badly needed funds to support war efforts and the expenses of the British government. England found and implemented new and harsher ways to raise money through taxes. They did not ask, or get, input, or approval, for their ever more burdensome taxes. They simply expected those under the crown to pay up. Many people paid up. Others found ways to hide their resources or avoid paying the taxes, considered unfair. They met secretly to discuss and justify their disobedience. The British government placed taxes on the tea raised in one part of their dominion and sold it to people throughout their empire. The British made exorbitant profits from the plantations where the tea was grown. But by adding taxes on the sale of the tea, they took even more resources from their subjects' pockets. It caused outrage in those being squeezed dry. It prompted the Boston Tea Party, where men dressed up as American natives boarded English ships and threw the crated English tea into the harbor. This incident is possibly the most widely known American colonists' negative responses to English taxation without representation, but it was only one of many incidents. The English would not stand for such insubordination. They expected indemnity for the loss of their tea and reimbursement for the taxes they would have gained from the sale of the tea. American colonists refused to indemnify them for their losses or their taxes. In the British rulers' minds, American colonists were now openly and willfully disobedient masses, deserving punishment and stiff correction until they could learn how to be obedient and be loyal British subjects again. The British sent troops to force compliance and reimbursement for their losses. The American colonists contested their force and demands.

The British government, and the King, could see that the colonists were becoming an unruly bunch, and they wanted to nip their independent-mindedness in the bud. They sent more British troops and established martial law where the rebellion was rooted. Confrontations happened between the British soldiers and the American colonists, shots were fired, and people died. America became a colony divided between those loyal to British rule and those committed to self-governance. The contests escalated until there was no turning back for either side. The American Revolution became a war between the world's largest, most powerful military force and a people, who had had no military at all previous to this time, except some local militias; the British army and navy had been their military protectors. The British crown and government were determined to control the American colony and the people. Many people who lived in the American colonies wanted to remain subject to British rule. They banded together in America, or they sailed for Britain. Those not loyal to the crown became the American Revolutionists, who eventually won the American colonies' independence from Britain. These colonies later became the United States of America. A country born of covert disobedience, overt disobedience, and rebellion.

40

WILLING OBEDIENCE

Levels Of Commitment

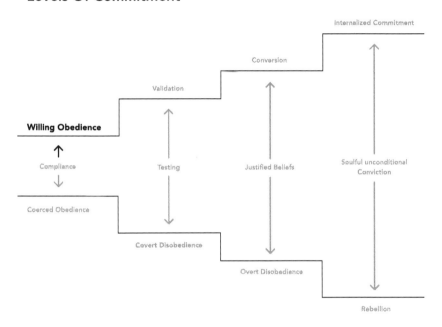

In the 1840s, a distinguished gentleman visited Nauvoo, Illinois, situated on the banks of the Mississippi River, upriver from St. Louis. He was amazed to discover a flourishing, orderly, progressive, and civilized city far more advanced than other communities in that area and era. It was growing faster than Chicago at the time. He asked Nauvoo's mayor and church leader, Joseph Smith (as best as I can recall), "How did you create such an amazing civilized city in this southern frontier of Illinois along the Mississippi?" Joseph simply replied, "I teach them correct principles, and they govern themselves." Such is the nature of willing obedience – it is a choice. When people's obedience aligns with their principles and values, they willingly choose to obey because they believe it is the right thing to do.

People will willingly comply if they know why complying is a good or wise thing to do. If the people aiming for compliance take the time to explain the whys, force and power aren't needed. People want to do the right things for the right reasons. It takes time and effort to justify something, so people willingly support it. But it is time well spent; when people believe in what they are doing, we get their head and heart, not merely their hands. "**Why**" people develop synergistic relationships; relationships develop while helping people understand why something is important or valuable. Nothing provides more pleasure than talking with a young child explaining something important. I enjoy children's wisdom; I know that behind that confident child is a parent (or parents) who takes the time to teach their child why. Children who understand the **why's** learn to engage their adult mode and become logical and reasonable in their perspectives about life. And they expect people to explain why rather than just giving orders. They don't make good Stompees.

If people think that obeying is the right thing to do, they will be obedient willingly, even if they don't know the principle their obedience is attached to. It is a kind of obedience that is very different from compliance derived from compulsion. These blind "observers" usually comply because they trust the person seeking their support. Their obedience is attached to their faith in the person they believe has their best interests at heart. If the person is tied to principles, they expect good things to happen by willingly obeying.

In short, when we choose to do the right thing, we feel good about ourselves and what we are doing. If we decide not to, we will not experience those positive emotions. Obedience by choice aligned with logic, reason, and principles obviates cognitive dissonance and inner turbulence. Conversely, compliance by coercion engenders negative feelings and urges push back or disobedience. Think about it: it is natural to push back if someone pushes you; unless someone is a masochist, no one wants to be dominated or forced to do anything.

The nature to push back starts very early in life. I remember my three-year-old granddaughter throwing a bowl of cereal on the floor because her mother insisted she finish eating it. Her mother decided to make her clean it up. The toddler wouldn't do it. So, her mother took her hands and made her clean up the mess. It was as if the toddler were a puppet controlled by her mother; nothing happened by choice, everything cleaned up was accomplished under the complete control of the mother. It did achieve another thing; her daughter burst into tears while being forced to clean. Her tears did not dissuade the determined mother from trying to teach her daughter to be obedient. What do you suppose that the toddler learned from that forced obedience? Did she learn to be obedient or to fear her mother's reprisals for not being compliant? They are different lessons.

When linked to reason, logic, and principles, willing obedience delivers benefits connected to principles. If we do the right things for the right reasons, we will benefit. We may grow morally, intellectually, socially, and spiritually. Even if we obey blindly, not knowing the principle upon which we base our decision, we will still receive the benefit attached to the principle. For example, in December, we won't get a plentiful harvest if we plant a garden in northern Utah. Even if we water and fertilize the plants, they will freeze and die. If we wait until after Memorial Day to do the planting in the same place and do the same things we did in December, we will likely get a bountiful harvest. Likewise, if we floss and brush our teeth twice a day, not knowing exactly why we are doing it, we will still benefit from doing so.

People in various parts of the world eat healthy, simple diets. They grow their food, consisting mainly of vegetables, nuts, and fruits. They drink milk from their cows, goats, or yaks. They generally eat meat sparingly because they have to raise and tend to the animals they eat. These poor people usually have limited land upon which the animals can obtain fodder. They don't eat this way because someone has told them to do it. They don't do it because scientists have said that eating this way is healthy. They do it because it is the only logical option that they have. They eat what they produce, or they die. They still receive the benefits of a simple and nutritious diet. Some of these "poor" people are the healthiest and longest-living people on our planet.

Of course, that is not the case for countless millions of poor people who have insufficient food or only have access to unhealthy food, with little or no choice of things to eat. They inherit the natural consequences of an unhealthy or inadequate diet; they become unhealthy and seldom live very long. The point is that there are benefits and consequences bequeathed by how well, or how poorly, we live following principles.

I have a granddaughter who is smart, beautiful, and very obedient. She is obedient because she chooses to be. If she were not compliant at home, her father would make her comply. Then she would do so because she has to. One day, her school classmates were being incredibly unruly, and the teacher decided to implement a new class rule to direct behavior and institute negative consequences for unruly behavior. She went around to every student and asked what they thought about the new rule. Some argued with the teacher about it; others hung their heads in disappointment about their added restrictions.

When she got to my granddaughter, she asked, "What are your thoughts?" She responded quickly and directly. "I won't have to think about it because I wouldn't be doing those things anyway." She does not need to be governed by the rules because she operates far above the rules from her values.

I don't know what type of person she would be or become if forced to obey. Her parents don't have to make her comply because she is never disobedient to their rules or societies' standards (rules are invisible to her because she operates so far above them). It is in her nature to be a value-based person; therefore, she is also a rule-abiding person. Rules and laws are irrelevant because she operates on a much higher plateau for making decisions. In the sense that she is operating far above the minimum acceptable behavior dictated by rules and laws, she isn't obedient; she is a "high flyer" who soars above and beyond obedience. She is a value-based young woman and has been as long as anyone has known her. How did she become that way? Maybe it is genetic, but I believe it is also because her mother is so loving, understanding, and value-based that she chose to model her mother's example very early. She is a fantastic person who, it seems, will glide gently and successfully through life using her intelligence, talents, extraordinary insights, and non-offensive nature as her vehicle for moving onward and upward.

Her younger sister spends a lot of time sitting in a room or, in time out. She gets punished a lot for disobeying. Her dad thinks she has an attitude, and he is determined to squelch that attitude by forcing her to obey. One Saturday afternoon, there was a mess in the back yard of their house (mud all over the exit door to the patio). Her dad ordered her to clean it up. "But I didn't do it!" she screamed. "I didn't ask if you did it. I told you to clean it up!" ordered her dad.

She proceeded to clean it up but "left her mark" on other windows. After cleaning the mud off the back door, she covered her hand with fresh mud and put handprints on the windows on each side of the door. You can force her to do something, but you can't get her to be what you want her to be.

She is smart, a "push-backer" who resists force and rules. She is constantly in a power struggle with people who try to dominate her. Life for her is a battle, and she is a fighter. It is not in her nature to blindly obey. If she feels any force, she responds with counterforce. She has a different approach to her destiny than her sister. In those places where she is appreciated and supported for her individuality, she is a super-star, a high achiever. In those situations, people can't say enough good things about her.

On the other hand, in those circumstances where she is expected to blend in, she does so until ordered to do something. If anyone uses a forceful manner with her, she pushes back so hard that the forcers soon brand her stubborn, obstinate, and a bit of a contrarian. Ironically, if someone were to ask her to do the same thing as a request rather than as a demand, she would bend over backward to accommodate the request. She doesn't usually need to be requested to do anything because when she sees a need, she spontaneously acts to fill it. If I could choose her circumstances, I would want her always surrounded by people who love her independent-mindedness and recognize her intelligence and logical reasoning. Since the world we live in is chock full of people who govern from rules and force, she is likely to have a lot of battles. Fortunately, she is tough and will fight as hard and often as required to maintain her self-identity. She is also well attached to values; she is tender, compassionate, and supportive of others, especially those picked on or mistreated. Like her older sister, she has fantastic insights into the world and the people who live in it. I love this girl partly because she is so independent-minded and fights hard for what she believes. It is good that she is well connected to values because if she weren't, she would be a daunting force with which to contend.

I am grateful for people who do the right things for the right reasons. They lift us all. They are beacons that help us see good things otherwise hidden in darkness. They enable us to believe in the goodness of others rightly. They are anchors of integrity, people we can attach ourselves to and feel secure that we won't be abandoned or set adrift. They offer us hope for the future and the courage to face difficult challenges in the present. I appreciate them because they are dependable and predictable; we know what they will do because their decisions and actions align with their core values. We have confidence in them because we know that challenging situations or circumstances won't cause their values to shift or to change. We can trust them because they are unconditionally value-based. These people exist; they are around us. My dad was hypercritical toward me when I was younger, but even then, I knew that he was a principled, value-based man who did what he believed was the right thing to do.

When I turned twelve, I became a Boy Scout. Dad was our scoutmaster. He believed in scouting and its benefits for boys and young men. He made sure that every scout in his troop achieved, at least, the First Class rank. That wasn't so easy because to qualify to become a First Class scout, a boy had to be able to send and receive messages by Morse Code. Some scouts found that requirement especially challenging. Dad would take the time to teach us one-on-one the Morse Code language and become so proficient at it that we could send and receive messages by sound or flashlight signals. It was gratifying to him to have scouts on camping trips, to be able to communicate with one another from long distances, like from one mountain peak to another.

One year he was given the assignment to collect funds for scouting to support our troop and the scouting council in our area. He went home to home, visiting virtually all the families in our community, of approximately 1400 people. He explained the purpose and benefits of scouting and encouraged people to give as much as they could, much if they had a lot and a little if they had little. His efforts exceeded the expectations of everyone at the council and those in leadership positions in our community. He raised so much that the town leaders decided to use the funds for other purposes. They chose not to use the funds for the areas he had promised the contributors.

When dad heard of their intentions, he objected passionately. He explained to the decision-makers that he had been very clear about why the people should contribute to scouting, and dad promised them that their contributions would be used as explained.

Based on his objections, the "city fathers" decided that it would be wise to have a town meeting and have all citizens who attended the meeting vote and approve their decision to use the donations for different purposes other than what dad had promised. Dad was among the 200 or so people who came to the town meeting. When they explained the intended usage of the funds, dad interrupted. He asked that they put in a provision that would allow anyone not wanting their funds applied to anything other than the scouting proposals to have their donations returned. The city leaders rejected his proposal without further consideration. Dad told them that he felt personally responsible for the solicited contributions. They held the vote and everyone, except dad, voted to redirect the funds.

After the town meeting, dad again visited all the families and told them that he would get their contributions back if they wanted their money returned. Surprisingly, quite a few families wanted their donations back, even some who voted to use them for different purposes at the town meeting. Dad recorded how much he would get back to them, asking for a bit of time to do so. Please understand that we were a poor family; what dad committed to doing caused a great sacrifice for our family. He returned all the money contributed to those who wanted their money returned. Sometimes, he welded their broken farm equipment and worked on their houses or property to pay his obligations. Some realized what he was doing and tried to forgive him for his promise to return their funds. He wouldn't do it; it was a matter of honor for him. It took him years to pay everyone back. In 1961, my parents bought a fishing site in Kenai, Alaska, where we spent the next two summers fishing for salmon. We had a couple of good years, and it finally provided the means to pay off his obligations. As we took every fish out of the net, he would say, "There's another fifty cents to pay off my debt." I am immensely proud of him; he was a man of absolute integrity. I cried while I wrote of this experience, remembering it still touches my soul and connects me to true honor.

Obedience by choice tied to core values is exemplified in business by the Toyota quality program implemented after World War II. After the war, the USA brought experts to Japan to help them rebuild their industries. Of particular note were statisticians, particularly W. Edwards Deming,[41] who taught statistical methods to show where they could make incremental improvements and track the progress as improvements were implemented. (Deming is revered in Japan and is recognized as the father of Japanese product quality and dependability.) They did not focus their quality approach on significant revolutionary changes. Their process was not like responding to an emergency, which would stir things up and create more confusion than progress, but rather in small steps called Kaizen. Kaizen centers on four core philosophies that contain 14 operational principles. Kaizen guides their decisions and actions like the credo statements do for Johnson &

---

41   W. E. Deming, *The New Economics for Industry, Government, Education* (MIT Press, 2000).

Johnson. Their first value is to have a long-term philosophy, even at the expense of short-term financial goals. The second value is that the proper process will produce the right results. The third value is to add value to the organization by developing people. And the fourth value is: Continuously solving root problems drives organizational learning. Around the four values are 14 principles used as the basis for everyone's decisions and actions.

One of the things that impress me the most about their commitment to product quality and dependability is the empowerment they give to every employee to stop production and bring it to a halt if they find a problem that needs fixing. Imagine how expensive it would be to have one person on the assembly line stop the entire production because they found a problem that needed to be fixed and prevent it from happening again. No one wants to be the one to stop production. Everyone does their best to see that problems are identified and fixed before they ever get to the production line to prevent that from happening. Toyota's quality management program focuses on preventing issues rather than catching them when they have become a fixture of the process; preventing them is preferred to catching them in the production process. A true game-changer is enabling people to get ahead of the problem rather than behind it. In 1960, W. Edwards Deming received the Order of the Sacred Treasure for his pioneering, introduction, and implementation of Kaizen in Japan. A short time later, the Union of Japanese Scientists and Engineers started awarding the annual and highly coveted Deming Prize to organizations that demonstrate exceptional process management and product quality.

The main lesson to be drawn from these concepts and examples is: If parents are wise and want to have children who are obedient for the right reasons, they should base their standards on principles and values. In addition, their children need to know and understand the principles and values upon which the standards are based. Once the children understand the principles and values, parents will find that rules are unnecessary and counterproductive. When values become the basis of decisions and actions, rules become redundant, at best, and insulting, at worst. Why do we have so many rules when values are better for making decisions and inspiring behavior?

The grand payoff is that when principles and values become the basis for decisions and actions, children (employees, members, people) become self-governing and willing to hold themselves responsible and accountable for their choices and behaviors. They will make sound ethical and moral decisions. The principles and lessons directed at parents and families in this section apply equally to managers, leaders, employees, and participants in businesses and organizations of all different kinds.

41

Validation

Levels Of Commitment

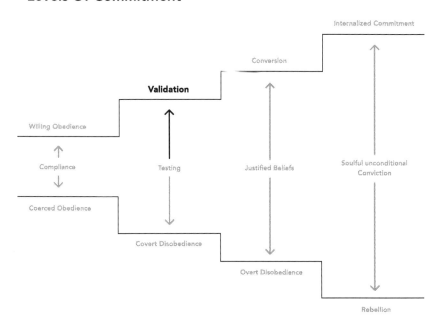

Validation is the next step upward after we willingly obey and receive confirmation that our decision was the right one. It is a test of our reason and logic. The verification of wise and thoughtful decisions and behaviors is validation. It comes to us seamlessly, without conscious effort. On the other hand, if we don't receive a confirmation, that lack of validation enables us to realize that perhaps we made a wrong decision. Validation, or lack of it, prompts us to take deliberate and logical approaches when faced with similar situations. Therefore, validation reinforces our ability to make correct decisions and become secure in our decisions and actions. It plays a connecting role between willing obedience and conversion.

There are two forms of validation. The first is **Instant Validation**, which happens almost immediately after acting. Instant validation frequently happens, like when we smile at someone, and they instantly smile back at us. It happens when we hug a loved one, and they hug us back a little longer than we expected them to. Instant positive validation reinforces our self-confidence and inspires us to be openly expressive with others. It engenders self-trust in our decision-making and actions. And when we are confident in ourselves, we tend to be more trusting with others. Instant validation between our actions and other people's reactions teaches us real-time social interaction skills. Instant validation reinforces positive decisions and behaviors and diminishes unhealthy ones.

It is joyous to watch infants and toddlers immediately validate their emotions from their loved ones. Little girls learn that a coy look melts the heart of loved ones, so they use coyness when needing validation. They also discover that their emotions become a form of language that their mothers understand. You may recall a mother saying when hearing their child cry, "Oh, that is a frustrated cry, not a hurt one." Emotionally and psychologically healthy children get instant validation to their emotional messages, which lays the foundation for their self-identity. It is a vital part of feeling safe and secure. Children who feel safe and secure can explore, unconsciously knowing that they have protectors. I love to watch confident little ones going about their discoveries of the world. It pains me to see other children afraid of venturing because of insecurity. Neglected or abused children are scared to explore.

The second form of validation is **Anticipated Validation**, which is what we expect to happen in the future. We could describe it as hopeful anticipation. An example could be the spectacular results we anticipate or hope to get from working out regularly. Another might be the weight loss we anticipate from a diet. In both these cases, people expect positive validation for their decisions and actions. However, their validation will largely depend on the nature of their expectations, such as when people set a time frame for their validation to occur. They won't feel validated if the validation doesn't happen within their expected time frame. If people don't get the spectacular body they anticipated getting from working out as soon as they expected, they often quit working out; or the people who don't get the anticipated weight loss as quickly as hoped stop dieting. Lack of validation probably has less to do with the correctness of their decisions and actions than with the reasonableness of their expectations. People with expectations of near-term or immediate validation have a hard time waiting to be validated.

I recall working with a couple who loved one another but had different love languages. Her love language was giving tokens that symbolized her affection toward him. His love language was doing things for her. Both expressed love in their way with extraordinary efforts. And yet, neither felt validated by the other. She hoped for gifts and tokens that would demonstrate his love for her. He hoped for acts of service to show him that she loved him enough to do those things for him.

When I met with them individually, it didn't take long to understand how deeply they cared for one another and how much they were trying to demonstrate their love. I was able to help them realize what was happening. Both were surprised at how they had undervalued the love messages sent by the other. The wife discovered that her husband's acts of service were expressions of his love toward her, and he realized that her constant gifts were her way of expressing love toward him. Problem solved, right? Nope.

As it turned out, they both now understood the love messages sent, but the wife mainly had difficulty expressing her love for her husband in the way he wanted it shown. He started giving her little unexpected gifts, which she adored (and he continued to do acts of service for her). He showed his love in two ways, using her love language and his. She felt loved and appreciated; her needs were being satisfied. She continued to give him tokens as expressions of her love. He became frustrated that she still wasn't providing acts of service for him, as much as he thought that she should. He didn't discuss his frustration with her, but she knew he wasn't feeling as loved as she wanted. As a result, she gave him more gifts and more expensive ones. That only frustrated him even more because he paid the credit card bills, which showed how much she was spending.

I discussed with her why her husband was troubled. She was perplexed. It was a bit of a revelation that her way of showing love was not enough since he understood that giving gifts was her love language. During the same period, I discussed with him that his wife was showing her love for him in her way. I explained that it would take her a little time to get used to showing him love using his love language. He said that he understood.

As it turned out, he wanted instant validation his way. It didn't happen immediately. We set a new time frame for his anticipated validation, with an action plan that included patiently teaching her how to show him love using his love language. At first, he had difficulty discussing his love language expectations with her because he felt that her acts of service should be spontaneous and not motivated by his feedback. I explained that his wife was not a mind-reader and that if he wanted his expectations met, he needed to make his expectations known. Over time, they demonstrated their love with two love languages: their love language and their spouse's love language. I see their postings on Facebook, and they seem happy and are still very loving toward one another.

Validation is crucial to children's self-identity; adults also need validation to feel secure in their self-identity and intimate relationships. Soulmates see themselves through the validation of their significant other. If a woman's lover sees her as classy and gracious, she will see herself as classy and gracious. The lesson to be learned here is to learn to see and express how we desire people to be because that is likely what they become.

Validation is an essential element that enables people to test and confirm their decisions and actions. When positive validation occurs consistently, it takes people to the point where they can justify their validations to become beliefs. Validation is the door to conversion, which is the next step up on the commitment level.

42

CONVERSION

Levels Of Commitment

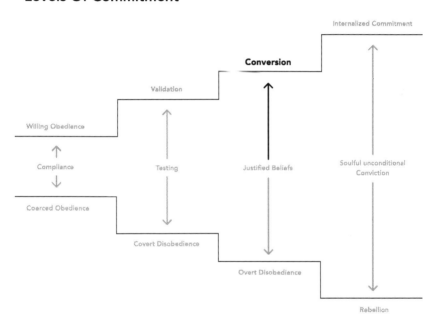

Conversion is the next higher level of commitment that flows from validation. It is the interim step between validation and internalized commitment. We can't get to the highest level of commitment without going through a conversion process.

Conversion is a process. It is not an event. It is a process that will never be fully complete because there is always more to learn and understand. The Brazilians have a saying that captures what I mean. It is: "I understood, but I didn't comprehend." They get it. While we may understand something or think we do, there are always more profound layers of comprehension that can be discovered, understood, and comprehended, only to find that more profound layers are before us. Even though we have learned much about natural laws and eternal truths, there is infinitesimally more to learn and apply to living our lives by exploring them. Our comprehension of what we understand or think we understand can go on and on, ever deeper and with more profundity.

People talk of being converted as having reached the final ideal destination. That is self-deluding because the state of being converted is only a photo shoot, one frame, in a never-ending film. If we think we are converted and there is no more truth to be found, we are not connected to the reality of natural laws and eternal truths. Conversion is multilayered; we replace the current conversion level with a deeper, more profound understanding and comprehension. That can only happen if we remain open and receptive to discovering and understanding other profound truths. The new truths that we find out will seem remarkable to us. Continuous conversion requires us to be humble, teachable, and open to new learnings and discoveries.

We believe in the current distillation of our conversion or justified beliefs. It is the state we have come to through the conclusions we have derived from the information that we have ingested and accepted at a point in time. If we search no further, we will forever be contained by what we believe to be the whole truth, with no other truth possible. From my point of view, that pretty much describes the conversion perspective of most converted people.

Conversion is a process that has moments of awakening, where we realize the reality of something that we didn't grasp before. That realization becomes the foundation of an expanded belief. If we base our beliefs on fact and truth, it will bring us internal light, energy, and edification. If we base our beliefs on negative feelings spawned from unwanted outcomes, not aligned with fact and truth, it will become the fuel that feeds the flames of our discontentment. Discontentment fosters an alternate reality, another version of the truth, which clashes with facts and reality.

I am a realist in that I appreciate that we are bound and limited by what we know, understand, and apply in our lives purposefully. And still, I am an idealist in the sense that I know that we know so little of what is yet to be discovered, learned, and brought into our lives. We all lack the means to skillfully and without error to dive deeper and move faster into the cosmos of natural laws and eternal truths. Part of the challenge for society is that so many of us are looking in different places to find and understand the truth. We see reality presented as being very different things by different people. Too often, the reality presented, by some, is self-serving, based on cherry-picked information drawn from sources that benefit themselves at the expense of others. Upon inspection, their truth fails to connect with what we know to be reality.

It has probably always been the case that reality is "spun" in ways that make winners heroes despite how ethically they won. The winners of wars are the ones who write history, and their version of history is always self-glorifying. It isn't easy to find a valid factual account of history within a country. It is always an interesting experience to see the same events recorded from the winners and losers who were combatants in the same war. We lived in England for a while, long enough to study an English historical version of the American Revolution. Their version does not present our revolutionary leaders as heroes but as traitors deserving to be condemned and hanged.

Part of the conversion process is the learnings and the insight we gain about principles from our life experience, good and bad. When I was nine years old, my mother, brother, and I went to Dayton, Idaho, to help my grandpa and grandma Phillips thin their sugar beet crop, a major and vital portion of their annual income. They had about three acres of sugar beets planted in rows approximately one block in length with three feet separating them. Farmers planted the sugar beets in the early spring after spring frosts ceased. When the new plants had grown to five or six inches in height, the extended family came together to "thin" the beets, which was hoeing out the excess beet plants and leaving a space of six inches between the remaining ones. Six inches of space would allow each beet to grow to an optimum size with the right texture for refining into high-quality sugar.

Grandpa explained how much he and grandma could make for each ton of sugar beets sold to the refinery. He told me to leave six inches between each plant. I wanted to help them make as much money as possible, so I figured that if I left only three inches between the sugar beets, they would get twice as many beets and make twice as much money. It took me two days to thin two rows. My mother could do a row in three hours, so she thinned 18 rows in two days compared to my two rows. My mother and grandparents told me how proud they were of me for working the whole two days without quitting and completing two entire rows.

I eagerly anticipated when the sugar beets would be harvested and see how much money my grandparents would earn from selling their sugar beet crop. At last, the day arrived when the harvest began. My grandpa used a team of workhorses, Clydesdales, to plow a ditch beside each row of sugar beets. The plowing broke up the soil and enabled us to use a sugar beet knife to extract each beet one at a time and prepare them for loading onto a trailer (a sugar beet knife is a machete-like sword with a claw on its end to hook a beet like a fish gaff and then to chop the green part of the sugar beet plant off, leaving only the meaty part of the beet). The trailer, when fully loaded, would carry a load of prepared sugar beets from the field to the trucks, which would haul them to the sugar refinery. The beets that were too small to be sold were left in the field to be gathered later and used for fodder for grandpa's pigs.

The completed harvest left a scattering of unsellable beets throughout the field, except for my two rows. Every sugar beet in my two rows was too small and fibrous to sell. In trying to make as much money as possible for my grandparents, I had cost them money. Grandpa told me how happy he was that we had so many sugar beets left to feed his hogs. I was not wholly dumb; I knew that he was trying to make me feel good about my efforts to help them. My intentions were pure, but the results aligned with natural law. The sugar beets needed room to grow to their full size and quality. I have wondered in the sixty-five plus years since that sugar beet harvest if my grandpa knowingly left my rows where the space between the thinned beets that I had thinned was too close so that I would learn a valuable life lesson. Whether he intended to do that or not, I learned the lesson.

If we think about it, grandpa's sugar beet lesson is also an excellent analogy for people. People, like sugar beets, need to be nurtured, and they need space, with sufficient room to grow, to realize their full potential.

The conversion process applies to virtually all parts of our life. For me, recently, it was necessary to lose weight and get my sugar levels back to normal. (I weighed 216 lbs.) In April, I went to our family doctor for routine blood tests. On May 4th, I met with Dr. Rodgers and received the blood test results. My sugar level had reached 120. The year before it was 105, and he had been warning me that I was a borderline diabetic. On May 4th, he informed me that I was now a diabetic. I told him that I didn't want to be a diabetic and asked him what I needed to do to no longer be one. His directions were simple. Eliminate all sugar products, no more processed flour, white rice, and drastically limit starchy food. Also, no more carbonated sodas, sugary or saccharine (that hurt). On the do-eat side of the ledger, I was to have five portions of vegetables every day, protein (the size of my palm), and a limited amount of fruit. Of course, several liters of water per day replaced the sodas and fruit drinks. Since May 4th, I've gone from 216 lbs. to 180 lbs. and back into a normal range for sugar, and I'm heading toward 175 lbs. (where I'm hoping to see my abs again).

Why do people decide to change, in other words, get into a conversion process? And how do we know if we or others are in the conversion process? Good questions. Looking at why we choose to change logically, from my logic anyway, I think that external and internal factors, either or both, stimulate us to seek to become different people than who we are or who we are becoming. Internal change factors come from within us and are manifest as a self-motivated desire to be different, including actions that achieve the change. External change factors act upon us; they are not born from us but come from beyond us. Factors cause us to change just like a billiard ball will travel in the direction it must go based on an impact from another billiard ball.

I believe that painful external motivators cause us to want to change, like watching a loved one get lung cancer from smoking and deciding to avoid that fate for ourselves. The catalyst for change came from external motivation. There are also pleasurable external motivators for changing, like cleaning ourselves up, so a loving person will want to spend time with us. Again, the motivation to change ourselves was external. Maybe we want to change (enter a conversion process) to escape something scary or dangerous, like learning how to stop offending people who can kick the snot out of us when we insult them. Perhaps it is to remove ourselves from situations or relationships that make us uncomfortable. It is like graciously changing the subject or removing ourselves from someone who tells ethnic jokes. Indeed, an event that shocks us can change who we are or want to be.

Dr. Morris Massy taught us about Significant Social (or emotional) events[42] that cause us to become a different person after the event than we were before the event. These events trigger an awakening in us, a gestalt that sets us immediately on a different path; it is as though the event, itself, made the change in us rather than our decision to do so. My dad told us brothers (four of us) that he knew that she was the lady he wanted to spend his life with when he met our mother. He also knew that he needed to knock off his rough edges, like smoking and crudity, to be good enough to win her affections and be with her. And he did. Indeed, external forces play a decisive role in our decisions to change or get into a conversion process to become a better version of ourselves. Desiring to have synergistic relationships would seem an apparent reason for changing ourselves.

Internal pain and pleasure are also powerful motivators for changing ourselves. For example, my decision to change my diet had both pain avoidance and pleasure. I knew that my weight was limiting my ability

---

42   Morris Massey, "What You Are Is What You Were When" (YouTube, Enterprise Media Video, 2014).

to do things well that I enjoy doing (I did it to myself, I can't blame the sugar); I couldn't move as quickly or control my balance as well as when I was thin. I had been a 125 lb. cross-country runner in high school who ran a four-minute, 22-second mile, by staying one step behind the high school national mile record holder at the Western States Invitational Track Meet in 1966. I hated how different I had become from whom I used to be. When I weighed 216 lbs., I couldn't run a mile in ten minutes, giving it everything I had. I didn't want the consequences of being a diabetic. Losing my eyesight, damaging my kidneys, ruining my vascular system, etc., weren't things I wanted.

I still want to avoid these things. Changing my diet was a simple decision. On the pleasure side of losing weight were several motivating factors. One of the most alluring was to improve my appearance. I didn't particularly appreciate having to wear suspenders to keep my pants up. I could envision how nice I would look if my belly weren't sticking out, making me look like I was trying to sneak a watermelon out of a grocery store. When swimming, I imagined how nice it would be to glide through the water like a fish rather than push the water in front of me like a hippopotamus. I anticipated, and now, love how losing weight has increased my endurance and enabled me to better cope with a chronic dizziness problem that is my new normal. Being able to do what I love doing is an internal pleasure motivator. I want to keep doing that for as long as I live. I miss fresh warm bread, especially when I smell its sweet aroma in a bakery, but you couldn't pay me or convince me to eat it. OK, I admit it, if you paid me enough, I would eat some bread again.

As we can see, there are reasons why people change and are willing to change. How do we know if people are genuinely in the conversion (the change) process? Well, the easiest way to know is to watch their current behavior. If they do the same things that they were doing before professing their conversion, they haven't changed; but have merely stated their intention to do so. If they are genuinely in the conversion process, their decisions and behaviors will reflect the version of themselves to which they are striving to become.

A simple example is how Matt and I have changed our Sunday morning breakfast since May 4th. I used to fix my special and famous, to those who have eaten them, waffles and Swedish pancakes. We would smother them in butter, apricot jam, real maple syrup and then top them with whipped cream. They were to-die-for, and they contained copious amounts of sugar and processed white flour, which is a no-no on my eating list. Now we enjoy some fruit, a small amount of bacon, eggs, and, maybe, some hashbrowns or a healthy bowl of what my dad used to call "mush," which is oatmeal or cream-of-wheat cereal. There are many examples, like, if a person is trying to be trustworthy and truthful, he does what he says he will do and tells the truth.

Another way to tell if a person is engaged fully in the conversion process is to see the changes in who they are and how they present themselves. One of the things I notice when people are genuinely changing is that they stop making excuses for what they are doing. If they are doing things that fall short of what they expect of themselves, they admit it and explain that they haven't arrived at being able to do and be what they wish to do and to be. I can readily accept their explanation and feel inclined to admire them for their honesty and erstwhile efforts. If possible, I would even like to help them. I don't think most people respond to their honesty and forthrightness differently than I do. In short, they are becoming a reflection of their decisions and actions. We can see it and feel it, as too can they.

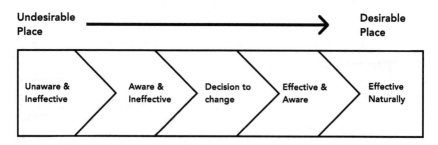

The change process follows a predictable pattern, with five definable stages of change:

1. Unaware and ineffective
2. Aware and ineffective

3. The decision to change
4. Aware and effective
5. Unaware and effective

Earlier in this book, we explained these as steps to deal with behavioral addictions. As you recall, there have to be three elements
present before people enter the change stages and can conquer an
addiction:

Element One: People need to understand why they are doing unacceptable behavior. (There are always reasons, maybe not good ones,
but there are reasons.) In my weight gain, I guess that overeating was
a means of self-comfort. My mother used food to express her love language, so did I. It was a way to love and to validate myself, albeit de-
structively. A part of people's motivation for their unwanted behavior
is the short-term benefits (the buzz) they get from doing it. The "buzz"
motivates addictive behavior (the kind of behavior we want to delete
from ourselves and move away from).

The buzz is the internal rewards we get from doing it. I liked feeling
full and having prepared something tasty upon which to feast. It was an
ego booster at the moment but an ego deflator after the buzz had worn
off. It also filled vacuums of boredom; it occupied unused space.

Element Two: We need to have a better and healthier option than our behavior. Simply not wanting to do it anymore won't keep the conversion process going; repressed feelings eventually emerge, usually more entrenched and powerful than before being repressed. Here too, we can always find, in a tempting moment, a sufficient rationalization to repeat what we told ourselves we wouldn't do anymore. In addition, if we haven't defined a better alternative, anything other than what we were doing will suffice. Unfortunately, unless we purposely and thoughtfully select a better option, we will probably engage in different behavior that gives us a similar buzz (motivation) as the one we attempt to escape. "A better alternative" given to me by a cocaine addict was beer. Beer was a much less expensive alternative, but it still had a similar buzz.

Element Three: "Gotta wanna." People have to want to change. Without the desire to change, change will not happen. Oh, maybe short-term and a minor change, but never long-lasting, worthwhile change. When the desire for change is greater than the resistance to change, then change is possible. When we have a great desire to change, the possibility and success for actual conversion increase dramatically.

If those three elements are present, we enter into the actual change process stages. We go from unaware and ineffective. (I didn't know that I had diabetes. I knew that I was doing things that would lead to it., but that didn't dissuade my dumb behavior.) We become aware and ineffective. (I learned that I had diabetes.) We decide to change. (It can take some time and usually has some starts and false starts, until the final decision to change happens. The diabetes diagnosis was a socially significant event for me; I decided to change immediately.) Next, we move on to the aware and effective stage, effective when we think about what we are doing (a conscious decision, in my case, the new diet). And finally, we reach the unaware and effective stage; we start doing things the way we desire to do things, without thinking about it. At that point, we have been successful in the change process because we are becoming what we want to be.

As you can see, making changes or being in the conversion process is the same process as overcoming addictions. Unwanted behaviors and things we don't like about ourselves are probably manifestations of behavioral addictions. Addictions surface to our conscious mind as things we wish to change and replace with things about ourselves that we would admire. Remember that behavioral addictions always have three components: Compulsive behavior, short-term benefits (the buzz), and long-term destructive consequences. I was a compulsive eater and drinker of sweet things. Overeating sweet things and snacking at night relieved my addiction cravings; it gave me momentary peace of mind (later replaced with guilt feelings). And over time, I gained a lot of weight, eventually resulting in diabetes. The conversion process has given me a new lease on life. My diabetes is completely diet controlled and will likely remain so long as I stick to my healthy diet and exercise regime.

Conversion is a process; it is not an endpoint. It takes us to a point where we achieve internalized commitment to the lessons and principles we have learned up to that moment. Internalized commitment comes from our conversion process. If we focus our conversion process on rules and regulations, then the lessons learned will be about the benefits and liabilities derived from aiming at obedience. Then our beliefs and behavioral standards will be rule-based, and we will believe that obedience is the highest level of commitment. If we focus our conversion process on principles and values, the lessons learned will help us better understand and comprehend natural laws and eternal truths. A logical value-based and principle-based conversion process will lead us to commit fully to live according to our current understanding of values and principles. Consequently, our beliefs and actions will align with values and principles. The focus of our conversion process will determine the kinds of lessons we learn that will form the basis of our beliefs and self-governing standards.

43

INTERNALIZED COMMITMENT

Levels Of Commitment

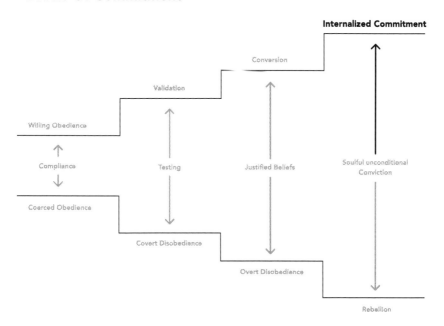

Internalized commitment is, in a sense, a destination, in that it is the distillation and application of the lessons we have learned, up to that point, from our conversion process. It forms the basis of our beliefs and defines our standards, whether they be rules or values, depending on whether the focus of our conversion process was rule-based or value-based. And yet, it is not a final destination, providing our conversion process continues beyond its current point. If the conversion process continues and, through that continuation we achieve new and greater understandings, then our level of internalized commitment will rise accordingly.

Note that people who share an internalized commitment to rules and obedience will establish a rule-based culture and organization. A rule-based culture is a top-down, power-based, and hierarchically based place. It is a Command and Control environment with Command and Control relationships. Individual growth and development will be a function of permission given from above. Someone trying to progress, develop insight, and make decisions without permission is perceived as covertly disobedient or even rebellious. It could be a punishable offense. It can only happen acceptably through the means prescribed by the powers that control decisions. This concept applies to organizations: Businesses, churches, societies, political organizations, or families.

The beliefs underlying our standards determine the kind of relationships we have. Our beliefs, and thus our standards, are the fruits of our conversion process. Our beliefs and standards become a reflection of who we are, our identity, how we treat others, and expect others to treat us. The beliefs of people who make decisions determine what is good and bad in a Command and Control environment.

For a little over two years, while I was in college, I worked as a meat cutter at Tri-Miller Packing. The job was especially tough physically later on when I became a "bull boner." The position of a bull boner is to take all the bones out of the front quarters or hindquarters of lean bulls and leave only meat hanging on a meat hook. I was pretty fast; I could debone a hindquarter in approximately 20 minutes and a front quarter in around 45 minutes. I needed to keep my knives sharp to do it that quickly. I can still sharpen knives like a pro. Another eight or nine college students also worked there (the number changed frequently). All of the college students were in the same boat; everyone was living paycheck to paycheck and doing whatever they could to pay for college and support a subsistence lifestyle. One of the good things about working there was buying meat at super-reduced prices. I could purchase prime rib steak at Tri-Miller Packing for less than the price of ground beef at the local grocery store. The bad thing about working there was the working environment. The manager who supervised the meat cutting area was flat-out mean and rude to all the college students working part-time.

He was friendly with the full-time employees; while they were working, they could share stories about their deer hunts, snowmobile trips, or debate which was the best pickup truck, the opinions always focused on Fords, Chevrolets, and Dodges. If a college student offered an opinion, the floor manager told them to shut up because they didn't know "nothing." If the college students tried to discuss something in the news or a subject that they were learning about at the university, the manager mocked them and told them that they had better focus on their work or he would give them so much more work to do that they wouldn't have time to discuss BS. The full-time employees had learned quickly never to challenge the boss's opinion about anything. The college students, being college students, could see opportunities to improve productivity or better ways of doing things. When they pointed out an opportunity for improvement, the boss would listen until they were finished and then say something like, "OK, Einstein, your smart-aleck, know-it-all comments are going to cost you one hour in the freezer!" Spending an hour in the freezer was considered terrible punishment because it was around 30 degrees Fahrenheit in there. The only coat and gloves available to wear in the freezer were old, stiff, and stinky (unless you brought your own because you were anticipating spending time there). Usually, in a day or two, the manager would come into the meat cutting area and announce that he had thought of a new way to improve our work performance. Then he would explain to all of us the very same thing that the college student had suggested, but this time taking all the credit as though it was his idea.

Some of the full-time employees discovered that they could get on the boss's good side by picking on the college students. If a college student pushed back against the harassment from a full-timer, the full-timer would tattle to the manager about the student's cheekiness. It resulted in freezer duty for the college student. Frequently, if the full-timers and college students were all working in the same room simultaneously, it became a criticizing and humiliation session by the boss, and the full-timers, against the powerless part-timers.

One college student who wouldn't suffer in silence was Gary Gustin. He was a 6'2", 210-pound ex-basketball player working part-time at Tri-Miller Packing because he had injured his knee, lost his scholarship, had three kids, and needed the $1.18 an hour job. He pushed back often enough that everyone just figured that he worked full time in the freezer. I was lucky because, as the bull-boner, I had my little workspace, and as long as I could debone bull quarters faster and cleaner than anyone else, it didn't pay to hassle me. They also didn't hassle me because the news had spread around the plant that I had been a boxer in high school who had boxed in the Golden Gloves. I didn't inform them that I had only one Golden Glove match and didn't box again after that because my opponent beat me badly.

The owner of Tri-Miller Packing was a nice enough fellow. He seldom spent much time on the cutting floor, and when he did come by, it was "everyone with heads down and elbows flying." He was like a plantation owner who hired a harsh field boss to get the most possible out of his slaves. Although, he did come to check on me one day after I cut the tip off my right thumb with a band saw while sawing off the bone of a ham hock. Immediately after I did it, I saw the end of my thumb sitting alongside the recycling band saw blade. When I tried to retrieve it, I accidentally pushed it, and it was sucked away by the saw blade, resulting in having no thumb tip for sewing back onto my thumb. When the owner saw my thumb, he said, "Well, there is nothing to sew back onto your thumb, so I guess you don't need to go to the doctor." The next day, I went to the doctor, where the doctor asked me, "Doesn't that hurt?" Of course, I told him that it did; I could painfully feel every heartbeat in my thumb all night long. He bandaged my thumb. Amazingly, most of my thumb grew back, but it was too tender to work with for weeks. As a part-timer, I didn't qualify for workers' compensation, so we ate pretty humbly until I could start working again. (Also, we dropped in to have dinner with our parents a lot more during that time.) From a hindsight perspective, I guess the owner didn't want to know the culture in the meat-cutting area. Nor did he care how management treated the students, as long as revenue and profits objectives were met or exceeded. Part-timers were considered expendable and easily replaced.

Tri-Miller Packing is the most Command and Control place I have ever worked. It wasn't fun, but it paid the bills, just barely. I learned that the supervisor's directions were considered laws to be obeyed without question or hesitation in that Stomper environment. The supervisor determined the standards for good or bad, acceptable or unacceptable. He did and no one else. Every college part-timer who worked there anticipated the day of their graduation anxiously. They looked forward to when management would appreciate their contributions and where their insights would help their companies. Getting out of this Stomper and Stompee company couldn't happen fast enough. I have spent time in a rule-based organization and several value-based organizations, and value-based places are infinitely better.

Internalized commitment by people to shared core values and principles creates a very different culture than a rule-based one. When our beliefs align with natural laws and eternal truths, the standards for our behavior are values and principles. In a value-based culture, we focus on obedience only to the point that it defines minimum standards of acceptable behavior. (Minimum standards don't define desirable or laudable behavior.) Compliance is seldom even considered. Desirable behavior is always reflected by how well we are in tune with our core values and principles.

Through a value-based culture, synergistic relations are possible and sustainable.

A value-based culture embraces expression, growth, and development. It does not restrict it; it expects it to happen and celebrates when it happens. Here, too, our beliefs and values become a reflection of who we are, our identity, how we treat others, and expect others to treat us. What we consider laudable is simply a measurement of how closely we align to values and principles aligned with logic, natural laws, and eternal truths. Others don't have to make a judgment of our good or bad behavior; we can make it ourselves based on our understanding and alignment with the values and principles to which we are committed.

Without exception, every organization we have contracted with for consultation to make needed changes has been rule-based companies willing to become value-based. Every couple and family I have counseled had issues related to power-based, Command and Control environments, except for mental illness issues. And, control struggles almost always exacerbated the mental illness issues. Why is that? That is a heck of a coincidence, if it is even possible. I know the problems are a consequence, and the ramifications, of rule-based and Command and Control environments. They engender relationship problems and performance issues; people push back when pushed. People fight, covertly or overtly, for their identity when dominated.

Rule-based organizations always have conflicting views about values. That happens, I suppose, because they seldom, if ever, focus on values, and if they do, it becomes a contest of differing points of view about what the values mean and when, or if, people should use them. Consequently, when people are separated, or disconnected, by incompatible and irreconcilable values, there is little hope, or none, for making relationships compatible, workable, synergistic, or sustainable. To make it work, someone would have to let go of his beliefs and values. They would have to align with the beliefs and values of the person with whom they disagree.

People seldom, if ever, let go of their deeply held beliefs and values. One would think it should be easy because everyone "should" have the same beliefs based on the same values. But that is not the case. We know that people base their beliefs on their feelings and the feelings people have when they disagree are not compatible. Beliefs are validated feelings, and facts align with their beliefs. Therefore, their reality aligns with their facts, and their values become conditional to their reality. That is why it is so difficult. The people in the United States of America disagree about reality and facts. Opposing sides have incompatible and irreconcilable beliefs and values. It is not easy to resolve;

using facts to prove reality is met with an alternate set of facts. Truth is hard to grab hold of these days. Everyone believes they have the truth. Everyone wants the other guy to let go of his reality and accept their reality. You figure out how likely it is that many people will let go of their perception of truth.

Being an employee at Janssen Pharmaceutica, headquartered in Piscataway, New Jersey, stands out as the epidemy of a value-based company. The biggest reason it was value-based was that our President, James Bodine, was a man of true integrity who wanted his company to operate from absolute values. He supported me because I brought systems and processes to help make that kind of culture happen. It also happened because we were a startup company in the United States. Janssen USA was a clean sheet of paper upon which we could write anything we chose to write. Fortunately, we decided to write a value-based script. We hired and staffed the entire company with people aligned with our core values. It was a liberating and progressive workplace; people respected one another, and their opinions and contributions mattered. It grew faster than Paul Janssen or the executives at J&J anticipated, which fostered even more support and freedom to make independent decisions.

My Human Resources, Manpower, and Organizational Development department was a joyous place to work; our team members loved and supported one another as teammates, friends, partners, and advocates. Our people grew, developed, and prospered. They became a source of growth, development, and prosperity for others throughout the company. Power to make decisions was delegated so that people continuously took on greater and greater responsibility and accountability and were recognized and rewarded for doing so. We were all like earthworms who ate our way forward, taking on new challenges in front of us and leaving behind us well-processed opportunities from which others could also richly profit. I was broken-hearted to leave Janssen after my eldest daughter had been abducted, raped, and consequently developed anorexia nervosa. Her illness motivated us to move to Chicago. Chicago had the best treatment center for eating disorders in the United

States. We moved there to get her admitted into their program. Fortunately, she survived, has five children, and lives happily in California.

Janssen USA became, in my mind, the business model and standard of what I believe value-based organizations can be. It provided the template for my consulting career. It provided the foundation for knowing how to build value-based organizations and families. It offered more than a philosophy; it provided experience about doing it. It provided validation as to why it is essential to do it. Since then, Dale Karren and I have helped many companies struggling in Command and Control, rule-based environments to become more successful value-based companies. They have greatly prospered and benefited from the change.

When we reach a point of internalized commitment, our parent mode (our should's and ought to's) and our child mode (our emotions) align with our adult mode (our reason center, our change agent, the operating mode that leads the conversion process). With internalized commitment, all operating modes come together and support one another; they enter a state of harmony. Cognitive dissonance ceases when we decide things and behave consistently with the standards upon which we base our internalized commitment. Cognitive dissonance only resurfaces when we stray from the standards of our internalized commitment.

For example, if a person's conversion process led them to internalized commitment based on rules and obedience and disobeyed "the rules" or allowed others to do so, they would feel uncomfortable. They would feel cognitive dissonance that would push them back into being obedient to the violated rules, and it would force others to do so if they were the ones who were out of bounds. This explanation may explain why it is difficult to change people who have internalized commitment to rules; they believe that rules and obedience are proper and that anything that does not support a rule-based philosophy is wrong. This mindset results in some unhealthy outcomes when it comes to relationships.

Charles was a man brought up in a highly stringent, rule-based family. His dad's whims were laws to be obeyed unless one was willing to be punished severely for non-obedience. Charles inherited wealth when his father died. He had attended private schools and an Ivy League college, earning a master's degree in finance. He became an investment banker. He modeled the company environment to be like his home life. He was the stringent dad; his rules were absolute. He set up a hierarchical structure, and he was on top.

Consequently, to him, people stacked in the management structure didn't matter much; they were of little importance; neither were relationships. When I examined the kinds of relationships in the company, all were Stomper and Stompee relationships and Mutually Destructive ones; people were either Adversaries or Enemies. I saw a consistent pattern in his organization: people were submissive to those above them and controlling to people below them. He wanted me to help him set up a performance management system in his company, where he could hold people accountable not only for obeying his rules but also for toeing the mark for meeting performance expectations. I worked with him for less than a week until I realized we operated from non-compatible management philosophies and values. I tried to reason with him, to explain why Synergistic relationships were necessary for the growth and success of his company. He believed that I didn't understand business and that I was the wrong guy to consult for him. I guess we both learned a good lesson; working with people who have different standards that guide their decisions and actions won't work.

That is why Dale and I reached a point in our consulting practice that we wouldn't consult for a company unless they were willing to become an unconditional value-based company. We knew before we started that if we weren't aiming to create a value-based organization, we wouldn't be successful working together.

Experience has confirmed my belief that people can move beyond almost any problem or issue in a relationship except incompatible and irreconcilable values. Working with Charles was just one of those experiences. I have confirmed the concept countless times when engaged in counseling and consulting.

Understanding the concept of Levels of Commitment is essential. It enables us to understand and predict the kind of relationships we can have, based on our connection to the various levels of commitment. Examining the commitment level model with internalized commitment being at the top and rebellion being at the bottom, we realize that they are both deeply held levels of commitment derived from different paths but whose beliefs and values are incompatible with one another. Both internalized commitment and rebellion are destinations in a conversion process that lead to an unconditional commitment to a set of beliefs and standards. The internalized commitment from one is incompatible with the other. Internalized commitment behavior by one group is rebellious behavior from the other's perspective. Looking at internalized commitment in this way helps us understand how two adamantly opposed groups develop beliefs and values, totally contrary to the other group's beliefs and values.

We mentioned that we arrive at internalized commitment or rebellion through different paths. Let's review both tracks.

The path to internalized commitment starts with willing obedience. It begins with proactive decision-making combined with decisive action. It is entirely something we choose to do. By making a proactive choice, we enter a conversion process that leads us to internalized commitment (or disassociation, depending on what we discover). Let's say that we contribute money to a charity because we heard that it does good things for needy people. We may not know how the charity uses our money with these "needy people." We assume that they use it wisely to help people. We are doing a good thing by choice (willing obedience) because we think it is correct. At this point, we are not obeying blindly by following our inner promptings and contributing, because we have a general understanding that we are contributing to something helpful to others. We proactively chose to donate, and we did so. Consequently, we garnered a sense of pleasure from doing it.

Later we see on a television report that the charity sent dozens of medical doctors and dentists to an impoverished part of Africa. The professionals apply their skills to serve people who otherwise have no medical or dental care. We suddenly become aware that our contribution makes a real difference in people's lives. The news validated our decision to contribute, and we feel grateful that we contributed and look for additional funds and other ways to support the charity. As we find more information, we get increasingly involved because we better understand what the charity is doing and how our involvement can help it achieve the good causes for which it exists. We want to support their efforts because we believe in what they strive to accomplish.

Our understanding and support of the charity and its admirable works lead us to an unshakable belief in the organization and faith that it is a worthy organization of which to be a part. We are converted. We contact the charity president and decide that we can magnify our support of the charity and its works by creating a local charity chapter. It dawns on us that what we did by making a small donation to a charity with a good reputation has now become a central and valuable part of our lives. And we are pleased to know that we connect to others who feel, believe, and act as we do. We have reached a level of internalized commitment to that charity; we have faith in it and believe in its purpose and values. We identify so seamlessly with what it stands for that it becomes a manifestation of who we are and how we wish to be known. When reaching this point of internalized commitment, our belief becomes a personification of our identity and self-concept.

On the other hand, the journey to rebellion starts with someone who uses compulsive obedience to make us comply with their demands. If lucky, maybe 50% of us, being commanded to do something, will do it. The rest of us start on the journey to rebellion by being disobedient. Because of their power, we know we can't be openly disobedient because we can't win that power contest. We still want to win, so we push back by being covertly disobedient. We are still in the competition to win, but they don't know of the competition, or if they suspect a contest has begun, they still don't know how we, their opponents, are playing the game. Usually, if the commanders think that people are pushing back, they intensify their controlling behavior to try and stop it. Not surprisingly, that only heightens the covert disobedience and provides more reasons for the covertly disobedient to disobey and recruit others who have begun to feel the same way. People who share a sense of oppression or injustice get together and discuss their feelings and why they feel that way. These discussions almost always push the process to justify covert disobedience in the minds of the disobedient. This justification process will continue until they feel justified in becoming overtly disobedient.

Overt (open) disobedience is a big step toward rebellion because it signifies that people feel justified in being disobedient. They now believe that it is appropriate and fitting to disobey oppression, and their disobedience is a righteous expression of what they have justified. From the viewpoint of the disobedient, it becomes an ideological stand for what is proper. When this happens, it becomes an open contest between the ideology of one and the ideology of the other. Open contests are power contests. But whether the commander knows it or not, the power base has shifted between them and the contestants. Their position (dominant) power still exists, albeit diminished due to their opponents' disobedience, but the disobedient have acquired synergistic power derived from their justified consensus. The disobedient people augment their synergistic power with situational power; they can negatively impact the organization's processes, productivity, and deliverables through their united commitment to hold fast to their position. The commander may also take a firm stand to hold fast to their position. The outcome will probably be decided by who has the most power or can best afford to lose the most.

As you can see, we have just described a classical labor strike between management and employees. Four outcomes become possible: One, the commander backs off and gives in to her adversaries. Two, the adversaries give in and comply with her demands. Three, both the commander and the adversaries compromise to find an acceptable win-win or lose-lose consensus (depending on your perspective). Or, fourth, rebellion by all, or part, of the dissenters. This rebellion will be against the commander and the organization's management philosophy, beliefs, and standards. Either the dissenters will leave the company and join an organization that aligns with their management philosophy, beliefs, and standards, or they will create their own organization.

Note that rebellion begins reactively rather than proactively. It starts like a billiard ball hit by another billiard ball. But unlike a billiard ball, the outcome happens by a series of choices initiated from forced compliance. Rebellion is a self-justified response to actions that violate people's beliefs and values. It doesn't happen all at once but occurs through a predictable, step-by-step process. When people are rebellious, it is always in opposition to something. People can be rebellious against any organization, institution, or family. It is the conclusion occurring from a person's adult mode analyzing a situation, circumstance, philosophy, etc., that they find unacceptable and concluding to adopt a different philosophy, belief, or set of values that more fully match their desired situation, circumstance, or lifestyle. We could say that one organization's "rebellious" is another's "internally-committed," and vice versa.

It is vital to understand that the level of commitment we aim for, for ourselves and others, will determine the kind of relationships we can have and do have. We can have Synergistic relationships if we aim for internalized commitment for ourselves and engage in the conversion process to get there. If we aim for obedience from others, we will develop a few mutually rewarding relationships with those who comply and enjoy doing so. We will also, predictably, create contentious relationships in which covert disobedience and rebellion will define the relationship. These will generally fall into the relationship spectrums of Stomper and Stompee, which become Adversary and Enemies relationships. Command and Control behavior will never produce Synergistic relationships, such as Intimate Soulmates, Teammates, Partners, Friends, or Advocates. I shouldn't say never because love is miraculous; some abused and oppressed people can look beyond the abuse and oppression and still feel loved and return it. I am amazed by these people; I wish everyone could do that. Unfortunately, few can. The knowledge that achieving internalized commitment is linked to principles and values and supporting the conversion process should incentivize people to choose that path.

Mike was a 14-year-old-young man from our church group who was incarcerated in a juvenile center because he was caught and convicted for committing several house burglaries. I was the leader of his church group and knew his family well. His stepfather was abusive with him and to his mother and seven-year-old sister. The stepfather was chronically unemployed and contributed little to support his family. Mike's mother was chronically depressed and coped by staying in bed for days on end. Our church was the family's primary source of income and food, so I got to know them by making regular visits to check on them.

Mike was clever with unlimited potential. But I was deeply concerned for him because he was running with a young gang of ruffians who participated in the burglaries. He was caught and convicted for several of them. Mike later told me that he committed many more crimes that remained unknown to the police. At first, when we met in the center, he wasn't too willing to talk with me and share his feelings or challenges. We had a break when I finally realized that his silence was a manifestation of his anger toward me for not intervening more to help his family's circumstances and prevent the abuse they were receiving. Once that was in the open, he became available and communicative.

When I expressed my concern about his affiliation with the youth gang, he laughed and explained that he was not a gang member; he was its leader. In graphic detail, he explained the abuses that he and his mother had suffered from his stepdad. He had physical evidence, scars on his back and buttocks, confirming the abuse. I contacted the authorities, and the police arrested his stepdad a few hours later. During the authorities' investigation, they found evidence of abuse on Mike's mother. They also saw that she was not currently capable of caring for her daughter, so they had child services take custody of her. I quickly got Mike's sister released from child services and placed with a family of licensed foster parents in our church group.

Mike's mother started divorce proceedings and kicked her abusive husband out of the house. I spent as much time with Mike as I could, and he shared with me that the reasons he robbed people's homes were to obtain food for his family and to support his little sister; Mike needed money to hire babysitters when he couldn't be there. He also said, rather proudly, that he got a lot of satisfaction from being the leader of his gang. I was able to help Mike get out of the corrections facility and became the responsible person for his behavior when back in the community. Our home became his crash pad and the escape place from the craziness at his house. He spent a lot of time at our house. Neighbors probably thought he lived with us (he sort of did). His mother improved after her husband was out of the picture, and she was able to bring her daughter home. Ladies from our church group set up a regular schedule to help her out at home and assist with caring for her daughter.

During Mike's sophomore year, he, his mother, and his little sister moved to Florida, where his mom had a sister. I heard from Mike regularly for a couple of years, then he disappeared. Before he disappeared, I learned that he was doing well in Florida. He was on the honor roll, and his mom remarried, this time to a widower accountant, who had a young daughter just a year older than Mike's sister. Mike was doing well; he had a stable family, two younger sisters driving him crazy, and looking forward to college. He no longer needed me and, as often happens, when Mike no longer needed me, he moved on, and we lost touch.

Even though disconnected, I always wondered what happened in his life and what he was doing. Maybe ten years later, he called me and said he was coming to Chicago and asked to meet. I was thrilled to hear from him and looked forward with anticipation to our luncheon reunion at a local restaurant. When he showed up, he came with a beautiful wife beside him and two lovely, very young daughters in tow. He proudly showed them to me with the additional announcement that he had graduated from law school and was now a successful practicing attorney. He wanted me to know about his new life. I told him how proud I was of him. His was an improbable success story. He was a victim of abuse and neglect, had been a rebel and a leader of a youth gang, and despite all of his life challenges, he was loving and kind, a father, a husband, and an officer of the court, specializing in family law. What are the chances? I am proud of him, not only for what he accomplished but also for who he became. While he was in the juvenile correction center, I repeatedly told him that I knew his heart and that he was a caring and fantastic leader who could be anything he chose. That day in Chicago, when we parted, he told me, "You told me that I could be anything that I wanted to be, and I did it!" Yes, he did.

A few thoughts on the Commitment Level Touchpoint

Using force or power to make people comply will produce covert and overt disobedience in the long run and lead to rebellious behavior.

Command and Control or rule-based approaches lead to Stomper, Stompee, Adversarial, and Enemy relationships. If you are a Command and Control or rule-based parent or manager, you should consider replacing that approach with a value-based one.

A value-based approach aligns with principles linked to natural laws and eternal truth. When our decisions and actions align with ethical and moral values, we receive light, energy, and personal edification. The world becomes joyous rather than burdensome.

"Be" people define themselves by moral character and have Synergistic Relationships, which are not attainable to "Have" people and "Do" people. "Be" people's lives are about relationships, not what they own or do for a living.

When we aim at internalized commitment for ourselves and others, that approach will change our paradigm from controlling to loving and supporting. Loving and supportive environments engender Synergistic Relationships.

Synergistic Relationships make life worth living. They are the quality relationships that determine the quality of our life. We can never have too many Synergistic relationships.

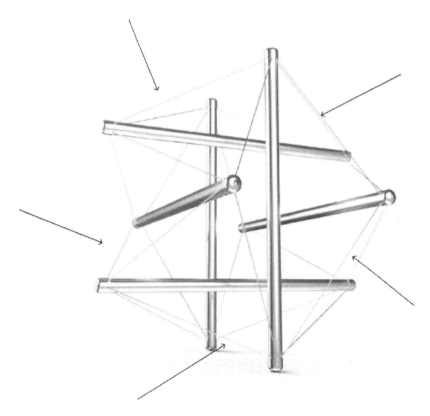

We have reviewed concepts explaining the six relationship touchpoints. We have profiled each touchpoint and described why each is an integral part of every kind of relationship we have, both good and bad, healthy and unhealthy. The seventh section of our relationship book focuses on the competencies needed to apply each touchpoint effectively. Competencies are connections between the Touchpoints. Touchpoint competencies are a combination of knowledge and skills associated with each touchpoint that harnesses the power of each one for creating Synergistic relationships. Learning the touchpoint competencies and applying them is what operationalizes them. We could say that the first six touchpoints are relationship swords, and the seventh section is about the competencies and skills needed to use the swords expertly. Each sword is only as good as the skill level of the person using it. The six touchpoints are the underpinnings of relationships; they are powerful relationship swords. Touchpoint competencies will make you a better swordsman.

44

EMOTIONAL STATES COMPETENCIES

The first emotional state competency is learning to manage and control our emotions.

"It was a hot August afternoon in 1963, the same day that the Rev. Martin Luther King, Jr. gave his "I Have a Dream" speech to a civil rights march on Washington. On that day, Richard Robles, a seasoned burglar who had just been paroled from a three-year sentence for more than one hundred break-ins he had pulled to support a heroin habit, decided to do one more. He wanted to renounce crime, Robles later claimed, but he desperately needed money for his girlfriend and their three-year-old daughter.

The apartment he broke into that day belonged to two young women, twenty-one-year-old Janice Wylie, a researcher at Newsweek magazine, and twenty-three-year-old Emily Hoffert, a grade-school teacher. Though Robles chose the apartment on New York's swanky Upper East Side to burglarize because he thought no one would be there, Wylie was home. Threatening her with a knife, Robles tied her up. As he was leaving, Hoffert came home. To make good his escape, Robles began to tie her up, too.

As Robles tells the tale years later, while he was tying up Hoffert, Janice Wylie warned him that he would not get away with his crime: She would remember his face and help the police track him down. Robles, who had promised himself this was to have been his last burglary, panicked at that, completely losing control. In a frenzy, he grabbed a soda bottle and clubbed the women until they were unconscious, then, awash in rage and fear, he slashed and stabbed them over and over with a kitchen knife. Looking back on that moment some twenty-five years later, Robles lamented, 'I just went bananas. My head just exploded.'

To this day, Robles has lots of time to regret those few minutes of rage unleashed. At the time of this writing, he is still in prison, some three decades later, for what became known as the 'Career Girl Murders.'

Such emotional explosions are neural hijackings. At those moments, evidence suggests, a center in the limbic brain proclaims an emergency, recruiting the rest of the brain to its urgent agenda. The hijacking occurs instantly, triggering this reaction crucial moments before the neocortex, the thinking brain, has had a chance to fully glimpse what is happening, let alone decide if it is a good idea. The hallmark of such a hijack is that once the moment passes, those so possessed have the sense of not knowing what came over them."[43]

While not everyone has neural hijackings that result in such a horrific tragedy, many of us have moments of powerful emotions that result in spur-of-the-moment actions about which we have remorse. Too many times, we hear of road rage resulting in severe injury or death. Far too often, people say things while hot-under-the-collar that shouldn't have been said, words that hurt and injure someone, comments that, immediately afterward, were regretted. Unfortunately, once spoken, we can't retrieve hurtful words. Yes, we can apologize and try to make amends, but that doesn't erase what was said; it only, hopefully, makes the injury less painful, less enduring, and, perhaps, hastens the forgiveness and healing process.

I had a bad temper as a youngster; I got into fistfights all the time. My brother and I constantly fought, which as we got older and were able to do some damage to one another, caused our mother to break us apart by whacking us with the wooden part of a broom. (She denied that she ever did that, but Dick and I know that she did.) Around the age of 12, he and I stopped fighting and never fought again, although I got into boxing which led me to even more fighting. Interestingly, when I was boxing, anger was no longer the motivation. Boxing actually helped

---

43   Goleman, Daniel. *Emotional Intelligence: Why It Can Matter More Than IQ* (New York: Random House, a division of Penguin Random House, LLC, 2020), 12.

me learn how to manage and control my emotions better. Boxing was a sport; it required skill, training, and practice. In fact, strong emotions lessened my ability to box effectively during a match. Emotions caused me to swing wildly and do stupid things, whereas remaining calm and focused allowed me to anticipate my opponent's actions and fight proactively rather than reactively. The more I stayed in control of my emotions, the better I could box. Of course, outstanding boxers also had ample talents, physical endowments, and abilities, which I didn't possess, that would have enabled me to compete beyond our local area.

The concept that "the more in control of my emotions I remained, the better I could box" also applies to living our lives well. The better we can control our emotions, the better we can live our lives (and have Synergistic relationships). Now I am not saying that feelings are wrong or that we shouldn't have emotions or express them. When we have little to no emotions, that is a symptom of psychological and emotional injury. For example, after the death of a loved one or the loss of a meaningful relationship, "Flat Affect" is a typical response. People lose the ability to feel emotions as they did before the trauma. They can't have fun or see the beautiful things around them. This emotional "numbness" makes life seem meaningless and without purpose. If they can't heal from the trauma, life often becomes a downward spiral.

Fortunately, most people heal from trauma, and they start to see beauty again; they can begin to have fun and enjoy living again. The ability to start seeing beauty again and having fun is a sign of healing. The ability to fully experience emotions appropriate to the situation is a sign of health. Regrettably, some have great difficulty healing, and they experience lasting emotional effects from the trauma they survived. This failure to heal from the trauma we diagnose as PTSD, Post Traumatic Stress Disorder. It handicaps people's ability to live full and happy lives. We usually associate PTSD with veterans, who have experienced horrific battle trauma, but it also happens in all parts of society where people are traumatized. It is especially sad for me to see adults traumatized when youngsters carry the burden of early traumatic experiences throughout their lives.

Learning to control our emotions, to a great extent, is a natural part of the maturation process. As people grow up, we learn to take things in stride and not overreact to situations. Some people learn to master their emotional responses even when viciously provoked. I was always impressed by how my dear friends in the Janssen HR department, who were African-Americans, could retain their composure and be dignified when confronted with a racial slight that would have sent me over the edge. Other people never gain mastery over their emotions and are enslaved by them, ever driven to react to life experiences rather than choose to live proactively. Some will never learn to master their feelings without psychological therapy, and even then, some will never do it. But for the vast majority of us, we can learn how to control and manage our emotions. We do that by engaging our adult mode.

Our adult mode is our change agent and our learning instructor. It enables us to learn and to progress. It helps us grow up and be wiser, with greater discernment, as we mature. It enables us to examine old recordings in our current parent and child modes and change what needs to be changed so we can move on, unencumbered by outdated recordings. It enables us to analyze our current beliefs, behaviors, and emotions and validate, to ourselves, whether they are correct or need to be modified, put aside, and/or replaced by those that make sense to us now, in our current reality. Indeed, our adult mode decides what our reality should be.

Our adult mode is the emancipator that frees us to choose our actions and emotional responses to circumstances and situations. It is the architect of our inner freedom. It helps us to become the master of ourselves. To the degree that we can engage our adult mode to manage our behavior and emotions, we become masters of ourselves. Mastery is freedom. For example, which musician is the freest: the person who has, through endless practice, personal sacrifice, and a life-long dedication to playing complex music, can play masterpieces exquisitely; or the person who sits down at the piano, for the first time, and expects to perform Mozart beautifully? One can choose to play Mozart's music with passion and skill; the other can't. One is free to do so, and the other is not. Mastery is freedom. So, too, is mastery of our emotions. If we master them, then we are free to express them exquisitely.

When we engage our adult mode to do a "check-up-from-the-neck-up," [44] we initiate self-development. If we ask ourselves to diagnose our feelings or why we are feeling something, we empower our frontal cortex to find reasonable answers. Through his book character, Huckleberry Finn, Mark Twain once wrote, "You can't pray a lie."[45] Our adult model won't lie to us, it will tell ourselves the truth, and then we can choose how to respond to it. At that point, our decisions are a matter of personal character. We can learn to manage and control our emotions through our adult mode. Mastery of our emotions frees us to choose our feelings and, consequently, our behaviors.

To some degree, I believe that I have provided sufficient information to know why it is important to control our emotions. On the other hand, I am aware that some people convinced of its importance are still looking for a more granular, step-by-step way to learn how to control them. The following is my attempt to provide that.

Four steps to manage our emotions

First step: Tune in to our emotions.

We all know that we have feelings, but we seldom focus on them as extensions that are a part of us and yet are not us. We certainly experience our emotions changing as circumstances change. Many of us experience them as though feelings are the horses we ride. The horses go where events lead them, and we are just along for the ride: **we adopt the idea that we are attached to our feelings rather than feelings being attached to us.** When we see our emotions as who we are, it suggests that our feelings control our decisions, actions, and identity (and for many, they do). However, we can have a life-changing paradigm shift when we realize that our feelings are attached to us, and it is

---

44 Morris Massey, "What You Are is What You Were When" (YouTube, Enterprise Media Video, 2014).

45 Mark Twain, *The Adventures of Huckleberry Finn* (Chatto & Windus/Charles L. Webster and Company, 1884), Chapter 31.

our choice to accept them, detach them, or change them. It is liberating to know that we can control our feelings rather than thinking that our feelings control us (or that we can direct the horses to take us where we want to go rather than the horses taking us where they choose to go).

But we can't realize that we can manage our feelings until we understand the nature and intent of our feelings. It helps when we can picture our feelings as personal guests to recognize them and know where they came from, when they will arrive, how long they will stay, and who the next guest is likely to be. When we see our feelings as temporary guests whom we can welcome or reject, then we come to understand that they can move in, stay with us, and become part of our lives, only if we want them, or allow them, to move in and allow them to stay. We need to get to know who wants to move in with us. We need to know if they will contribute positively and meaningfully to our life or if they will do just the opposite. We get acquainted with our feelings by stopping and taking the time to get to know them.

Recommendation:
1) Throughout days and weeks, stop and get to know your feelings during different situations.
2) Look them over, see their nature and characteristics.
3) Take the time to describe them in detail.

The better you describe them, the better you will understand and know them. You have many feelings, so know that it will take time, maybe lots of it, to know them all well. It will be pretty easy to understand your emotions as you get to know them. Once you know them, you can decide if you like them or dislike them and whether you want them to move in and become an influential part of your life. You can't get to know all of them at once, so recognize that it will happen one feeling at a time. It is a process, not an event. Be encouraged by knowing that you will better understand your emotions each time you analyze and describe one. It will probably be a process that lasts your whole life because new feelings enter our lives as we age and pass into new phases of living.

Here is an example of analyzing and describing a feeling.

"I don't know what to name you yet, but I know that you are a hole in my bucket that drains my life away, and what drains out can't be retrieved. I get nothing from you except pain and guilt. You keep me from enjoying and appreciating my life and make me live in a past from which I need to escape. You have enslaved me in a dark and lonely place. You are not a welcome guest, and I don't want you in my life anymore!"

What would you name this feeling? I call it "regret."

Second step: Analyze our emotions and give them a name (a label).
You can't provide feelings with a proper name until you analyze and understand them. Remember that each feeling is unique and has an exact *description* differentiating it from all other feelings. Each emotion has a one-of-a-kind personality and character. Once you have the correct, accurate label, you will understand its intentions (notice that we view feelings as an extension of ourselves). In doing this process regularly and frequently, we will become acquainted with many feelings that come to visit. Some emotions will want to come and stay. These willful feelings (intruders) will determine our decisions and actions if we allow them to stay. Other pleasant emotions we hope will remain. And some undesirable feelings, we won't be able to get rid of quickly enough.

We can learn to recognize the feelings that moved in on us uninvited, that we don't want to live with us anymore and need removal. We will meet the shy, elusive ones who need an invitation to come and stay. Over time, we will come to recognize each emotion and the part they play in our lives and if we want them to come, stay, move in, never come, or leave when they arrive.

Here is another example of labeling and describing an unpleasant feeling:

"**Prejudice**, there was a time when I believed in you and welcomed you into my heart. When I look at you now, I am disgusted because I realize that you spread lies and misinformation that convinced me to look down on people I should have loved and admired. I can't understand how I ever let you deceive me!"

Third Step: Find out where specific emotions come from and what purpose they serve.

Every feeling comes from somewhere, as do guests. And every feeling has a purpose in coming to visit us, as do guests. We already know who they are; we have even given them a name. But until we know where they are coming from and why they are coming, we won't know, for sure, how we should treat them. Once we know their embarkation point and why they are coming, we can determine the right thing to do with them. If they are coming to hurt us, then, of course, we would not like to see them and find a way to prevent that from happening. We can tell many feelings not to come because they will not be welcome. Some of them will come anyway. These obstinate guests, we must keep asking to leave until they get the message. Others may come looking innocent at first but reveal their true nature over time. We have to find a way to ask them to leave and not return. We discover others come from enchanting places and we look forward to seeing them often and having them stay as long as possible. Such is the nature of feelings, our invited and uninvited guests.

When we recognize a feeling, we can ask it questions to understand its purpose and point of origin.

"Well, anger, I see that you have come around again. Where did you come from this time, and what do you want with me?"

I realize that we are talking to ourselves. And yet we are not; we are talking to the feeling. We need to remember that our emotions are not us. But are merely guests coming to visit us, who have specific purposes for coming. We need to understand what will happen if we allow them to stay. Will you hurt me or others? Will you help me or others? The answer to your questions will let you decide if they will be a good part of your life or a destructive part.

For example:

"Anger, I have decided from previous experience that you are not welcome in this situation. I know that in other situations, you would be beneficial to me, and I would want you to stay but not today, not in this situation."

We can do this with every feeling, good or bad. We can look at love and say:

"Love, I haven't seen you in such a long time; where did you come from, and why are you here now? I am so happy you have come again."

We can look at remorse and ask:

"Remorse, I hoped never to see you again, but here you are. Where did you come from, and why me?"

We need to listen to our answers when we ask the questions because the answers teach us. We are, in reality, listening to our adult mode, which is our instructor. If we learn what we are supposed to learn, we will know what we should do with the feeling which came with a purpose. Questioning the emotion about its origin and purpose will lead us to the fourth step in controlling our emotions.

Fourth step: Decide what to do with the emotion (the guest) and do it.

Once we have tuned into our feelings, know who (or what) they are, have analyzed them to give them an exact label, have found out from where they came, why they are here, and have decided what we want to do with them, then we need to act on what we know and have decided to do. These four steps involve the same three elements for managing addictions. Namely, we need to understand why we have a negative emotion, what healthy emotion should replace the unhealthy one, and the desire and motivation to change so badly that we will make the change. We need to apply these elements for changing addictions with our unwanted emotions because unhealthy emotions are addictions.

They are harmful emotional addictions needing replacement with healthy emotions. We are not discussing the management of healthy emotions because desirable and beneficial emotions don't need to be managed; they just need to be nurtured.

The fourth step, deciding what to do with an undesirable emotion and doing it, is pretty simple. It requires six actions:

1. Decide what we will do with the emotion we don't want.
   "I'm feeling frustrated and don't want to feel that way!"
2. Decide on the healthy emotion to replace the one we don't want.
   "I want to feel motivated and determined to do better."
3. Determine the first thing we will do to make the change. (This is important because it initiates the actual change process.)
   "The first thing I am going to do is to stop being unreasonable with myself and be more patient about my mistakes."
4. Define the challenges we anticipate we will encounter when taking the first action.
   "The first challenge I will face is to convince myself not to quit when I am frustrated."
5. Decide how we will meet those challenges successfully.
   "When I am frustrated and want to quit, I will tell myself, 'I am not a quitter,' and to focus until I can do it right."
6. Decide on the following actions we need to take and then repeat steps 4, 5, and 6. When we have no more "next actions," we should be where we want to be.

Managing emotions is a pretty logical process when we look at it. It should be rational because it will happen under the leadership of our logical change agent, our adult mode. We need to remember that our emotions are an extension of us; we are not an extension of our emotions. We get to decide what emotions come, or stay and be part of our lives.

People who have the most difficulty managing their emotions have this turned around. They see themselves as an extension of their emotions.

Their emotions control them and define them. When we get it right, we choose which emotional guests we nurture, which we will accept, and the conditions to make them welcome. We also get to select the emotions that we remove from our life. Managing our emotions is a competency that gives us control over our feelings, a fundamental Touchpoint of Synergistic relationships.

In summary, the four steps for managing our emotions are:

1. **Tune into our emotions.**
2. **Analyze our emotions and give them a name (a label).**
3. **Determine where specific emotions come from and what purpose they serve.**
4. **Decide what to do with the emotion and do it.**

The second emotional state competency is acquiring an adequate and functional emotional vocabulary.

Humans are emotional beings. Emotions are entwined in our thoughts and actions. We could say people see us as our feelings project us to be. People who interact with us are interacting with our feelings; it is our feelings that they feel and see. If we are hysterical, people see us as hysterical (people see us through the lens of our projected emotions). If we are warm and genuine, people see us as warm and genuine. If we are joyous and happy, they see it and feel it. Of course, people can project feelings other than what they are feeling. People can have masks that allow them to appear as they wish, rather than as they are. Some people get very good at hiding their true feelings and pretending to have emotions other than what they feel. People who can do that are acting. Some actors become very successful, projecting themselves to play roles convincingly.

Most people use emotional masks to hide something about themselves from others that they don't want to reveal. Usually, what they are hiding is painful to them. When people present themselves as being and feeling one thing while being and feeling something entirely different, it creates a schizophrenic persona that doesn't seem somehow authentic unless they are great actors. People who interact with this two-person actor know that something is not valid. Kids know that their mom is not OK when she tells them that she is fine while trying to hide that she is definitely not OK. Emotions are kind of like the temperature gauges of our souls. They inform us about us, and they educate others about us. We need to listen to our feelings and fix ourselves when hurt or broken. And we need to know how to understand and validate other people's feelings to help fix them when they need a caring fixer-upper.

As mentioned earlier in our Emotional States touchstone, Dr. Bob Carkhuff taught us that understanding feelings, expressing them, and being able to interpret them precisely is a core life skill.[46] To connect with people, we need to connect with their emotions. To connect with us, they need to connect with our emotions. Feelings are bridges between people that we can choose to cross and meet or fail to cross and remain distant from one another. Feelings are manifest in our expressions that our eyes can see and interpret (if we know what to look for).

Relationships are the emotional states that exist between people. The emotional state between friends or lovers is very different from the emotional state between Adversaries or Enemies. The language and words used in various relationships are specific to those relationships. We can tell what kind of relationship we are in by tuning into the language, comments, and emotions expressed. The language used to validate feelings varies from the language and expressions we commonly use in our daily lives.

Consequently, most people don't have a sufficient functional vocabulary to express or interpret feelings well – our own or others. That is a problem because emotions and feelings have particular fingerprints. Each feeling is unique to all other feelings. Dr. Carkhuff listed seven separate categories of feelings: happy, sad, angry, confused, scared, weak, and strong.[47] Within each feeling category, hundreds, if not thou-

46   Robert Carkhuff, *The Art of Helping: An Introduction into Life Skills* (Human Resources Development Press, 1972).
47   Robert Carkhuff, *The Art of Helping: An Introduction into Life Skills* (Human Resources Development Press, 1972).

sands, of words exist that are unique expressions of feelings within that category. They range from mild feelings in each category to extreme emotions. To express our feelings well or validate other people's feelings well, we need to have an adequate emotional vocabulary to express and interpret the range of emotions in each category. Ironically, people have a much larger cognitive-emotional vocabulary than their functional-emotional vocabulary. This statement means that people know what they feel better than being able to describe what they feel. People may not use the correct descriptors to describe their feelings accurately. But, they will know and correct us if we are not using the right ones to describe the emotions they share with us because they know exactly how they feel. Having the correct label for feelings is essential because people will know if we are using the right emotional words to validate their feelings.

To the degree that we can understand and validate feelings accurately, we can connect with people.

People long to be understood and to be validated. If we can understand the feelings being expressed to us and validate them correctly, the people validated will have a rare and wonderful connecting experience with us, and we will connect with them. They will trust us because they know that we understand their feelings.

Please, expand your emotional vocabulary. Study Dr. Carkhuff's feeling vocabulary list. Talk to people and try to put the perfect label on the feelings they are sharing and you are seeing. Use a thesaurus to find similar words with slightly different meanings. Play "What kind of feeling am I sending to you?" games. Challenge them by choosing a feeling word you know others will have trouble identifying. Make them use just the correct word to capture your emotion (dictionaries or thesauruses are proper tools to use). Play the game with your young children and your older children; you can adjust the challenge to their level of maturity. By learning how to play the game well, they also learn how to use it in real life. Look for words that describe emotions in whatever you are reading. Please note them, write them down, and find a way to use them.

I have a group of varsity volleyball players at Park City High School who are excited each time we meet to share and receive new, previously unused emotional words. They love it, and as a result of our discussion, we soon see the word spreading among the other volleyball players. I'll hear the new word used during practice.

Learn to love words that emote or describe feelings accurately; as you learn to love them, you will use them more and more, both to express your feelings more clearly and explicitly and to validate the feelings of others. Maybe the most important thing you can do is become more aware of your emotions and analyze why you feel that way. This kind of "check-up-from-the-neck-up" [48] is always a good thing to do; we discover things that were previously unappreciated or unrecognized, and we grow from doing so.

Expanding our emotional vocabulary has practical benefits for ourselves and others. When we use explicit and exact words to express our feelings and emotions, we provide others with the planks and tiles that they can use to get across our emotional bridge and connect with us. When we use precisely the right words to validate the feelings that others share with us, we lay their planks and tiles and then use them to get across their emotional bridge to connect with them. It is such a high for both the validator and the validated. When someone is heard and validated, some for the first time, it is like they are no longer alone; someone has found them and is there with them!

Some Additional Essential Emotional State Competencies
The additional essential skills are to Hear, Listen, Understand, and Validate other people's emotional messages.

Dutch and Helen were a couple who had difficulty communicating with one another. They loved each other, but it usually became a heated argument when discussing family issues. Helen craved to be understood, but her approach to getting Dutch to understand her was highly emo-

---

48   Morris Massey, "What You Are Is What You Were When" (YouTube, Enterprise Media Video, 2014).

tional and directed an emotional barrage of accusations at him. Dutch responded defensively and then launched emotional missiles back at her. Over time, Dutch just started avoiding Helen, removing himself upon the first accusation. Dutch's avoidance made Helen even more passionate and created an even more profound need to be understood. Maybe it was intended as a shock treatment, but Helen put forward the dreaded term: "Divorce."

That is why they came to meet with me; I was their church leader from whom they sought counsel. It was immediately evident that neither of them wanted to get divorced. It was also apparent that they were hurting one another and wanted to find a way to stop doing that and solve their family issues. After a few pleasantries, I asked Helen to explain what she thought was causing their relationship struggles. A short phase of their conversation went something like this:

Helen: "I'm just so exhausted and frustrated. I want to deal with our problems, but Dutch just runs away when I try to talk about them."

Dutch: "That is not true, Helen, and you know it!"

Helen: "It is true! I wanted to talk with you two nights ago, and you got into your truck and just left me standing there with my mouth open!"

Dutch: "That was better than listening to you attack me and ending up in a big fight!"

Helen: "Wayne, you can see what I am dealing with. I used to love Dutch, but I'm not sure that I do anymore. Maybe we'd both be better off if we just separated and lived apart!"

Dutch: "Helen, you don't mean that!"

Helen: "I do mean that; we aren't living together right now! You don't love me enough to listen to me and to work through our issues!"

Dutch: "I used to try, but we don't work through our issues; we always end up fighting and hurting each other, and I don't want that to happen anymore!"

You catch the drift of the interaction. Both were sending messages, but neither were receiving messages sent to them and understanding the deeper meanings underlying the messages sent. I had them step back and describe the kind of relationship they would love to have with one another. It was enlightening; both wanted the same type of loving and nurturing relationship. They simply didn't know how to have it. They didn't know how to connect through the emotional bridges offered to one another. They failed to use the planks and the tiles (emotional words and messages) sent that they could have used to cross the emotional bridges and connect. They missed the opportunity to connect in a nurturing way but instead grew more removed from the kind of relationship that they both craved.

I continued to meet with them, and I arranged for them to meet with a clinical family psychologist who was very successful in helping couples develop practical and nurturing communication skills. I follow them on Facebook, and they just had their 50th wedding anniversary. They appear happy.

In my mind, there are five sets of core skills that enable us to connect with others effectively emotionally. The first is the skill to express our emotions clearly and accurately. We addressed that when we reviewed the need to acquire an adequate emotional vocabulary. That will also become vital when we explore how to validate other people's emotional messages. But getting to the point where we can validate messages requires four additional skill sets: hearing, listening, understanding messages, and then validating them. Each of these competencies has a unique set of skills. For example, hearing is not simply listening, and listening is much more than just hearing.

Hearing

"Hear" means to use our eyes and ears to receive and interpret the message sent. It is to engage our physical senses on the messages coming to us. "It is using our eyes and ears to full capacity."

Undoubtedly, we have all heard the snide comment: "We have two ears to hear with and one mouth to speak with; therefore, hearing is twice as important as speaking." Despite ending the first two phrases with a preposition, the statement has merit. The most important part of hearing is: well, hearing. We perceive a message through our auditory senses in a literal and narrow sense. It is to learn something from the messages we receive through our ears in a broader sense. We might call this hearing: Hearing with Intent. How do we hear with intent?

First of all, try not to miss anything said. Being deaf in my left ear and hard of hearing in my right, I know it takes effort to hear everything. The ears can decipher more than just sound; they become partners with the eyes to pick up on congruent and incongruent messages. Congruent messages are those where the message's content and feelings align. In other words, the messages received by the eyes and through the ears match one another. Incongruent messages are those where the messages seen and heard don't match up. Remember when we said that some people have masks to hide their true feelings? If we use just one of our senses to interpret messages sent to us, the actor is much more likely to fool us. But if we use both senses, hearing and seeing, in partnership with one another, it is difficult to be fooled. Bringing to light the incongruencies helps us gather a fuller picture of the messages being sent and opens doorways to dealing with them and helping us to face reality factually and courageously.

I believe that most people want to have their masks revealed (incongruencies surfaced) so that they can stop living a lie and move forward, centered in reality as one persona. They want the authentic self to be understood and validated, not the fake. It is the ears that perceive tone and inflections in verbal messages. The eyes interpret emotional expressions. The eyes interpret body language and compare it to the auditory message. Understanding people's messages are not likely to happen without the teamwork of both ears and eyes.

Listening

"Listen" means to be physically, emotionally, and intellectually receptive to the people sending the messages and to the messages sent. Oth-

er synonyms are to perceive, discern, pay attention, and take notice of what people are saying and feeling. We need to use all of our physical, emotional, and intellectual capabilities to receive the messages clearly and accurately.

Although listening suggests an auditory function, it is much more than that. Listening is the process of using our eyes, ears, and intellectual perception to interpret messages sent. The popular term for this type of listening is "Active Listening."[49] I prefer to use the term "Deep Listening." Deep listening requires us to focus all of our senses on the person sending us a message. They become the person in our spotlight. Just like an actor spotlighted for a scene where everything around her becomes unimportant, and she becomes the only thing that matters, so too does the person in the listening spotlight become the only thing relevant to us; nothing matters except them. This type of listening requires effort. Deep listening requires focus and discipline to stay centered on the person we deeply listen to. We can't let distractions remove us from the moment. We need to acknowledge the distraction and reconnect with the person sending us messages if we are distracted. To avoid situations where distractions can occur, we need to arrange for our conversation in a location where we won't have distractions. If we are already in discussion with distractions around us, we need to change locations.

The four characteristics of "Deep Listening" are: Spotlight, Now, Reference, and Validation

Spotlight	"Spotlight" means to keep our attention focused on the message senders and their messages at all times. Think of it as a spotlight focused on a performer during a stage performance. Once the spotlight is directed at the star everything and everyone, also on the stage, becomes irrelevant, unimportant, and, in essence, invisible. The only thing that captures our attention is what is happening with the star.
Now	"Now" means to stay focused on the present moment, the current message communicated.
Reference	"Reference" means to operate entirely within the message senders' point of reference, not our own or anyone else's.
Validate	"Validate" means to confirm our understanding of the sender's complete messages, both the emotional parts of it and the contextual parts of it. "Our understanding of the message sender's messages has been verified as being correctly understood."

49   C. Rogers, R. Farson, "Active Listening and counselor self-efficacy: Emphasis on one microskill in the beginning counselor training" (The Clinical Supervisor, reprinted in the volume Communicating in Business Today, 1980), 50-52.

We have already talked about the spotlight.

Now suggests that we need to stay in the moment, right here, right now, in the present. If we use the sender's message as a catalyst to take us to another time, place, or experience, we no longer listen deeply but have gone to another time, place, or experience. In short, we have disconnected from them and their message. The following is an example of what I mean.

Message sender: "When I lost my dad, I was devastated; his death nearly destroyed me. I can't seem to cope anymore!"

Listener: "I know what you mean; when I lost my dad, I cried for days. We were living in Buffalo at the time, and I couldn't spend as much time with my siblings as I wanted to. But time heals all wounds; you will feel better as time passes."

Can you see how the listener left the "now moment"? He left the present and ventured to another time that was meaningful to him and, although he was trying to show empathy, he was validating himself, his experience, at a different time and place. Although trying to help, he disconnected from the message sender.

Reference means that we need to stay inescapably connected to the message sender's frame of reference, not to ours or anyone else's. As you can see in the last example, not only did the listener move to a different time, he also changed the frame of reference from the message sender's frame of reference to his own. Changing the frame of reference in conversations frequently happens when people try to help others. Somehow, our society has developed the habit of shifting the spotlight, going to a different time and place, and changing the reference to ourselves or others when trying to show people that we care. The net result is that we are no longer with the message sender; we have taken the spotlight, gone to another time, and have replaced their frame of reference with one of our choosing.

Many people came to his viewing and funeral when my father-in-law passed away. He was greatly respected and loved by virtually everyone who knew him. His friends and loved ones wanted to let my wife and her family know how much they thought of him and how much they loved him. Dozens of people came to my wife with the message: "I know how you feel; when I lost my dad, I….." After receiving many of these heartfelt messages, Lois asked me to take a walk with her, and she told me tearfully, "I know they are trying to comfort me, I get that, but I'm the only one who lost **My Dad**; I am the only one who knows what I am feeling. I just can't stand to hear that they know how I feel about losing **My Dad** one more time. They don't!"

It would have been better if they had said something like, "I'm sorry. I loved him and will miss him so much; he meant the world to me."

Deep listening also requires that we use our body language to send the subliminal message that we are receptive to people's messages. We need to show an "open bosom" to the person we try to understand. An open bosom looks like what it sounds like. We need to square our body to their body so that if they fell forward, their head would bump into our chest or land on our lap. Our body needs to have a relaxed slight incline toward them. Our arms need to be receptive, as well. Crossing them while they speak will send them the message that we disagree or reject what they are saying. Keeping our fingers relaxed, with palms open and facing them, is a universal sigh of acceptance and sends the message that we will willingly receive whatever message they send us. People are incredibly sensitive to body language. If we cross our legs when they say something, it sends a message to them that will alter the message that they are sending. If we step back, it says, "I disagree with what you are saying." If you change your body angle while they are speaking, it will suggest to them that something they said didn't sit well with you. If you turn your head to the side, you send them a negative response to their message. If you turn and face away from them, it is a message of total rejection of what they are saying and actually of them.

To make the point to students learning deep listening skills, I like to sit in a chair or stand in front of a group and have them interpret the non-verbal messages I send them. I start out sitting in a chair display-ing an open bosom, with warm and attentive eye contact. I keep my hands open and relaxed, with my palms facing them. Then without anyone saying anything, I make small changes in my body language. If I close my hands, the students call out the change and interpret my message. Each shift from me elicits an interpretation from them. If I shift my head to the side or drop my chin, they immediately tell me that I am sending a non-accepting message. If I sigh and look toward the ceiling, they inform me that I am frustrated and running out of patience. If I turn my back on the group, it usually creates a loud reaction, and the students inform me that I have just totally rejected them. You should try this activity with friends or family members, you will have fun doing it, and you will all learn a lot about how people use body language to interpret messages.

The distance between the message sender and the active listener provides insight into the effectiveness of our emotional connection efforts. The sender should take the lead in determining the distance between you; if we take the lead and stand too far away, the message sender may interpret that as a message of non-acceptance. If we stand too close, they will feel uncomfortable. The message senders will stand at a distance that is comfortable to them. You will notice that as the message senders feel more comfortable with us and feel understood, they will move closer to us. When we make an emotional connection, the message sender usually ends up close enough to lean forward and touch our knee or forearm with their hand. That is a good sign.

Dr. Bob Carkhuff used to show us silent films of interactions between people. He had the sound shut off so that the only thing that we had to interpret what was happening, and decipher, was what we could decipher from what we could see. It was eye-opening to see both participants' body language and how they enhanced connections or diminished them. Time after time, we witnessed the message sender move closer toward the active listener until he could touch the active listener. It was apparent when the message sender felt that he was being listened to, understood, and validated.

When my kids were young, three or four, and they would get mad at me, I kneeled to get on their level and then asked them to explain why they were so mad at me. My oldest daughter, who was very smart and very emotional, used to stand about eight feet from me and scream at me, throwing her arms about and stomping her feet. As she vented her emotions and I validated what she was feeling and saying, the distance between us got closer and closer. She moved toward me in proportion to how well she thought I understood and accepted her messages. When she felt understood and validated, her messages were no longer angry but were tender and supplicative. When she put her arms were around my neck and snuggled up against me, I knew that we were OK and had reconnected.

Understanding

"Understand" means to comprehend the messages communicated. Complex messages have two parts – feeling and content. Understanding comprehends both the emotions and the context of the message. Understanding is a process of developing hypotheses of the messages being sent to us that we confirm with the person sending them to make sure that we genuinely understand their messages. We must comprehend all of the messages sent, both the ones expressed verbally and the ones expressed non-verbally.

Understanding is both a process and an endpoint. It is a process from the perspective that we establish a hypothesis that, hopefully, captures the true meaning of the message sent to us. It is only a correct understanding if our hypothesis is validated. If our hypothesis proves incorrect, we need to develop a better one and repeat the process until we have a correct one. When we arrive at an accurate understanding, it is no longer a process leading to an understanding but an endpoint.

In a counseling skill course, Dr. Bob Carkhuff used to teach us that saying "I understand" before we had validated our understanding of a message sender's message could destroy the sender's trust in us. He would tell us something along the lines of:

"If you say, 'I understand,' and later it comes to pass that you didn't understand, then the person you are counseling will not trust you because they accepted your word that you understood them and then you showed them that you didn't. Rather than saying 'I understand,' share with them what you think you understand. If you are correct, that will validate them, and they will confirm your understanding of their message. That will build trust. When you share your provisional understanding of their message and clarify that you are checking your understanding, they will work with you. If you are incorrect, they will correct you, as many times as they need to, until you understand. You can't lose doing that; because it leads you and the person you are trying to understand to a true mutual understanding."

His message was pretty straightforward; we never truly understand a message being sent to us until we confirm our understanding of the message with the person sending it. We confirm it by asking questions like: "Are you saying that you are ready to quit because you resent the way your boss is treating you?" If we don't have enough information or are confused about the information we are receiving, we can say things like: "I don't understand," or "I think I am missing the point you are making. Could you explain it again?" These requests for verification and clarification work because people want to be understood, and they will help us understand them if we ask for their help. Remember, everyone has an urgent need to be understood.

Validate

"Validate" means to confirm our understanding of the senders' complete messages, both the emotional parts of it and the contextual parts. Validation is where we confirm our hypothesis with the message sender. We have validated their message when our understanding of the senders' message is verified as correctly understood.

Emotional messages have two parts: the context (subject) of the message and the emotions connected to the context. Validation of a two-part emotional message requires that we validate three things:

1. We need to validate the message's subject.
2. We need to validate the feelings contained in the message.
3. And we need to know how the first two parts relate to one another.

When we have validated all three correctly, the message is validated. The following is a simple example:

"He is always late!"

This emotional message has two parts. The context (identified by the words used) is about being late. The emotion is expressed in the sender's inflection, tone, and body language (we hear by using our ears and eyes, as mentioned previously). To validate a message, we have to interpret both parts correctly. We might try using the word "exasperated" to validate the message sender's emotions. You could put it into a validating question, "Are you exasperated because he is often late?" This question is trying to validate the feeling and the relationship between the feeling and the context. If we are correct in our hypothesis, we may receive a response like, "Yes!" or "Absolutely!" If we are wrong in our hypothesis, they will correct us, at which point we will need to validate a new message based on the feedback just given us.

Let's use the example given in the listening review to illustrate how we validate both components of a message.

Message sender: "When I lost my dad, I was devastated; his death nearly destroyed me. I can't seem to cope anymore!"

Listener: "You feel overwhelmed with your dad's passing, and you are finding it tremendously difficult to adjust and live?"

If we have validated accurately, she will feel understood and validated because we have correctly connected the contextual message with the emotional one. If we miss the meanings of her message, she will correct us. Then we can try again. People want to be understood and validated.

When counseling others, we must understand that people will only give messages that are safe to share and, usually, they will provide only one message at a time. People who need counseling come to us constructed like an onion, with multilayers. The center of the onion is their emotionally naked and vulnerable self. The outer layers are "safe" messages almost always about others. When counseling someone who expresses anger and attacks others, we see only the outer layer issues that mask the real core issues hidden at the center of the onion. If we spend our time on the outer layers, we will never be truly helpful because the outer layer's issues don't address the real personal issues needing to be addressed. Focusing on outer layer problems with the intent of fixing others to make them happy is a loser's game. Finding others to blame for problems is easy; people can create an endless, never-ending list of the issues blamed on others and never address their issues at the core. The layers between the outer and inner issues are defenses established to protect the defenseless inner self. That's why we have to peel the onion. The messages at each layer need to be heard, listened to, understood, and validated one at a time. But the outer layer issues are never the issues needing to be problem-solved because addressing them doesn't address the real personal issues that lie at the core.

People want to be understood at the center. They want someone to understand their emotional nakedness, vulnerability, defenselessness, and loneliness. But they will not lead us to their vulnerable self unless they trust us. To get to the center to help them, we must demonstrate that we are trustworthy. We show trustworthiness by hearing, listening, understanding, and validating each message given to us, one at a time. Once a message is validated, they will provide us with the next one. Each validated message will bring us closer to the center, to their vulnerable, naked, defenseless self. As you move through the defensive layers and closer to the center, you will realize that the messages cease being about others and start being about themselves.

If, at any time during the process, to get to the center of their onion, we try to problem-solve, criticize, analyze or push for information not yet revealed, the process will cease. We will be left to problem-solve at the layer where they stopped sharing. That won't result in any lasting solutions; because we will address symptoms of the inner issues rather than the ones generating the symptoms. Realize that some people have many layers created over long periods. We can't be impatient or try to force the journey to the center of their onion. It won't happen that way. If we are patient and trustworthy, they will eventually take us to the center, where their core issues hide. They will let us see who they are and how vulnerable they are, and they will ask for our help – but only when they know we understand and they are ready to be helped.

Using this counseling process helps people with a few layers; the fewer the layers, the faster and easier the process is. If a person has no layers, it is simple to help; just give them what they need, or want. We will get into solving simple and complex problems later in the competencies section. But for now, understand that hearing, listening, understanding, and validating emotional messages is a core life skill that enables us to cross over people's emotional bridges and connect with them.

Peeling the Onion

Peeling the onion is a process to get to people's core issues to help them resolve their unfulfilled needs (problems). It requires us to use all four skills: hearing, listening, understanding, and validating.

This competency provides a way to validate people profoundly and intimately. It is a way to connect with them at a level that few other people ever achieve. It requires us to pass through the outer layers of the complex messages they send us to reach the inner layers where they are emotionally naked and vulnerable. **The core of their onion is always about themselves – always.** Getting to their core will not happen unless they trust us; therefore, we must be trustworthy with the information they share. As we approach the center of their onion, I feel that the information revealed is sacred. It needs to be kept confidential and locked in our hearts to be shared only with the person who shared it with us. **There are only two reasons to get to the center of their onion: The first is so that they will no longer be alone.** The core of their onion is a lonely, painful place. **The second reason is to bring to light the core issues they have been protecting and hiding to help them resolve these unresolved painful experiences and move**

forward. The journey from the outer layers of the messages to the inner ones may include many messages or only a few; it depends on the nature of their complex issues are and how many they have. One thing is sure; the journey will only move forward as we listen to, hear, understand, and validate each message given to us, one at a time. The journey will cease if we try to speed up the process by searching for more information, problem-solving, analyzing, judging, or criticizing after a message is revealed. Doing any of these things may even add additional layers.

Why the analogy of comparing people to an onion? And, what are the layers we are referring to?

People with complex problems are like onions because they have many layers, just as do onions. If they were hurt or damaged, that event creates a defensive layer in response to the experience. If they have many layers, it indicates the kind of life they have experienced. Damaged people have many layers and may require a lot of time, patience, listening, hearing, understanding, and validating to get to their core issues.

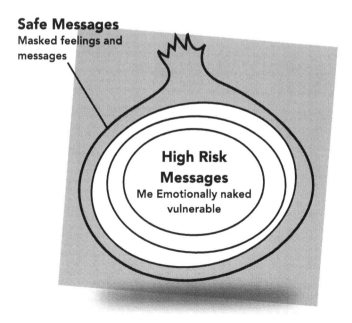

Understand that the outer layers are defenses and distractions from the core issues (with damaged people, the further away from their core, the better). The exterior issues (the complex problems) that people present to us, usually in the form of anger, blaming, resentment, hostility, judgment, criticism, personal attacks, etc., are rarely about themselves unless the playing victim is about themselves. They are about other people, events, and circumstances because they are safe messages to give; when judging, criticizing, or blaming others, they are not being judged, criticized, or blamed for their vulnerable issues. Can you see that their emotional focus on other people is just another layer of defense for themselves? Understanding that their attacks are defenses, you can choose not to take it personally when they attack you; because it is not about you. When they focus their negative jabs on others, they do so because it is their defense against their unresolved issues – those issues that are hidden from the world and maybe even from themselves.

The journey to the center of their onion we divide into four stages.
Reaching each new stage is an indication that we are making progress. The first stage is the outer layers of their onion; it contains messages focused on other people, events, or circumstances. "The people in my church are such hypocrites! They are so pious and self-righteous; it makes me sick!" The second stage is about themselves, which I labeled the "excuse stage." At this stage, they have moved from blaming others to exonerating or justifying their situation with excuses. "Look, I know that I was late, but traffic was so bad that anyone on the road at that time would have been just as late as I was." The third stage is a breakthrough stage where people start talking about themselves. They begin to share their feelings, situations, experiences, what is happening or had happened to them, and how those things impact them. At this stage, they don't want to talk about other people, nor do they want you to. "I am hurting so badly right now; I loved Harry so much, and I feel that it is my fault that he left me!" From this point until we reach their core, it is apparent they want to be understood and to be able to share to their core vulnerable self. But the closer to the center we get, the more fragile and vulnerable they will

feel. It is imperative that we remain 100% empathic and do nothing that we would suggest that we intend to do anything other than listening, hearing, understanding, and validating what they are saying, right now, in the present moment.

For many helpers, this is where the journey ends because the need to fix the problem just shared becomes more than they can bear, and they have to try and fix it. The fourth stage is the most magical state of all because this is where we have, together, reached and validated the core issues. At this stage, the person will ask for our help to help them resolve their unresolved core issues. The moment comes with an emotional release like an audible sigh, a look of relief, and a request for assistance (a dropping of the shoulders and a sigh followed by a relieved smile directed at us). Immediately they will ask for help. "What do you think I should do?"

At this point, they are ready for help, and because we have been trustworthy enough to be allowed to share their hidden and protected, emotional core issues, they will trust us and do anything that we suggest to them. We could start offering suggestions or advice, but that is the last thing we should do. They need to develop their own solutions to their own issues. We can help them by coaching them, not by giving them our solutions. Coaching is a process to help them help themselves. With quality coaching, they become independent rather than dependent on others to resolve their issues.

Listed in the chart below are some examples of Deep Listening skills that support the journey to the center of the onion, plus some that violate the characteristics of Deep Listening.

Peeling the onion and Deep Listening Skills that facilitate the process when peeling the onion		Common behavior that violates the characteristics of deep listening and interrupts or halts the process of peeling the onion	
Attend actively, verbally, and physically	Operate from the "open bosom" position (Body squared with the message sender and arms open with palms facing forward, standing and sitting)	**Non-caring, or rejective, body language**	Body language that sends an unreceptive message (crossed arms, facing at an angle [or away] from the message sender, or not looking at the message sender, etc.)
Give an invitation to share:	"Are you okay?" "Would you like to talk about it?" "I am available if you want someone to listen?"	**Use Imperatives** • Order, command, or demand	"Sit down and tell me what is going on!" "I want to know what is happening!" "Look at me when I am talking to you!"
Ask questions that: • Verify • Clarify • Confirm • Validate the message	"I'm not sure I understand." "I missed that." "Are you feeling...?" "If I hear you correctly, you are feeling" (label feeling) because (summarize reasons).	**Ask questions that:** • Interrogate • Probe • Seek new information in order to problem-solve	"What is going on?" "Why are you upset?" "Why don't you tell me what really happened?"
Validate the message: • Label feelings • Restate content • Confirm the connection between feelings and content	"Are you embarrassed?" "You're saying that..." "If I understand you correctly, you're feeling betrayed because your boss didn't keep his promise."	**Judge, evaluate, criticize or analyze the message sender**	"Why can't you ever consider someone else's point of view?" "Do you know what your problem is?" "If you would prepare, you wouldn't be in this mess."
Restate emotional and judgmental messages in calm and factual terms	"You're feeling helpless because you can't see a way out of this situation?"	**Assume understanding Argue** **Discount the message**	"I know just what you mean. "You don't really believe that." "You shouldn't feel that way. Just don't think about it."
Rephrase to validate the current message	"In other words, you're saying that..."		"Aren't you overstating the problem?"
Summarize to confirm your understanding of a collection of messages	"Let me see if I understand how all of this fits together.	**Ignore the message or change the subject**	"It doesn't do any good to dwell On it " "Lots of people have it worse than you do.

Use the independent conjunction "and" to make a different point or disagree. "And" accepts another point of view while offerin another	"I see why you might believe that **and** I see it differently." "You make a strong case **and** I disagree."	Use dependent conjunctions "but", "however", or "on-the-other-hand". They all are argumentative.	"OK, I see your point, **but**..." "You make a strong case, **however**..." "That is a great suggestion, **on-the-other-hand**..."
Be supportive **Accept as being valid what the other person sees, feels, or believes, whether or not you agree.** **Show respect for the other party's perspective.**	"I can appreciate that you are feeling angry because..." "From your perspective, I can see why you believe that." "I can accept that as being valid from your point of view." "I can see that you are frustrated and are looking for a way to resolve the issue."	Give unsolicited counsel or advice or start unsolicited problem-solving.	"What you should do is..." "Have you thought about ...?" "If I were you, I'd..." "Let me tell you what you should do..." "Would you like to know what would do?" "If that were my employee, I'd..."

Confront inappropriate behavior with feedback given in adult mode	"When you swear at me, I feel irritated because I am trying to help you." "What I would like to see is..." "This would provide the following benefits..." "What are your thoughts?"	Confront inappropriate behavior in parent-mode or child-mode 1. Command and control 2. Emotion-based 3. "Constructive criticism"	"This is the way it is going to be!" "After all I have done for you, how could you...!" "Here is some constructive criticism that is for your own good..."
Be empathetic • **Validate the feeling and the content of the message**	"So, you are angry because you believe that it was a stupid deal that never should have happened."	**Be sympathetic** **Be patronizing (minimize the problem)** **Ignore the problem**	"I know just how you feel." "I understand..." "It is OK; not everyone gets promoted." "Time heals all wounds. You'll feel better someday. "I know that you will find a way to overcome this."

Let me provide an abbreviated synopsis of a Peeling the Onion session I had with a woman who felt that some of her immediate family members were ostracizing her. She seemed pretty self-confident, so I didn't anticipate encountering many layers. Connie is not the actual person in this situation.

Outer layers focused on blaming others

Me: "Are you OK? You seem kind of out-of-sorts today."

Connie: "I'm fine, thank you."

Me: "Are you sure? You don't look fine."

Connie: "OK, I am upset with some of my family."

Me: "Some of your family members are getting to you?"

Connie: "Yeah, they are such jerks!"

Me: "Jerks?"

Connie: "They are inconsiderate and treat me like dirt sometimes."

Me: "You feel mistreated because they are insensitive about your feelings?"

Connie: "That's not really what I mean."

Me: "I'm not sure I understand what you are trying to tell me."

Connie: "I feel bad when they plan some fun event and fail to invite me or even let me know about it."

Me: "So, you feel bad that you don't get invited to the events they have?"

Connie: "Not all of their events. I just feel bad about the one planned for this weekend."

Me: "This one seems especially important to you. Why is that?"

Connie: "It is because this one is a small family reunion and some of my closest cousins are attending, and I would like to see them and get caught up."

The shift to self-focus. Connie is starting to focus on herself and her needs rather than others.

Me: "If I correctly hear what you are saying, you feel cheated because you will miss an opportunity to reconnect with some of your favorite cousins."

Connie: "Exactly!"

Me: "From your perspective, you do not feel valued enough to be invited to special events that would be important to you?"

Connie: "I don't know why they don't care about my feelings! I want them to care for me and to love me!"

Me: "You are not feeling very loved?"

Connie: "I don't know what is wrong with me. Why don't people I love and care about, care about and love me?"

Me: "Are you telling me that you doubt yourself and your self-doubts make you feel very conflicted?"

Connie: "Boy, am I ever!"

Breakthrough layers. Connie is sharing issues behind the defenses she created to protect her fragile and emotionally-naked self.

Me: "Let me summarize and see if I understand your feelings and why you feel that way. Are you saying that you feel rejected right now and are scared that people reject you because things about you cause others to push you away from them?"

Connie: "Doesn't that sound pathetic?"

Me: "Not at all. Probably most of us feel that way at some point in our life. You just happen to be feeling that way right now."

Connie: "I tend to feel that way most of the time."

Me: "Are you telling me that you think you may be unlovable?"

We are getting near to the core; she reveals things about herself that she didn't want people to know, things about herself for which she has no defenses, is vulnerable and emotionally-naked.

Connie: "Am I unlovable?"

Me: "No. You are one of the most lovable people that I know."

Connie: "I know that I am a pretty woman and a nice person and that everyone should love me. What can I do? How can I get rid of this stupid obsession that I am not good enough to be loved and cared for?"

We have arrived at the core, and she is ready to deal with her core issues.

Me: "I am glad you asked for help and that you are ready to put this self-doubt stuff behind you."

Connie: "Thank you! I feel so much better."

Now we move directly into the coaching model.

Step One: Define the place she wants to be.

Me: "Connie, take a few moments and paint a picture in your mind of the ideal place where you want to be in terms of how you want to see yourself and how you want others to value you, to care for you, and to love you."

As you can see, peeling the onion, if done well, leads to the opportunity to coach people and help find solutions for their unresolved issues. One of the reasons most of us have problems peeling the onion is because we are addicted to problem-solving and have a hard time waiting until we have reached the onion's core before we start problem-solving. As a result of our need to solve problems, we focus on solving the outer layer issues, which generally focus on other people. As a result, we seldom focus on the issues needing resolution. The table below illustrates some of the most common ways people stray from the four characteristics of Deep Listening.

The most frequent ways that onion peelers violate the four characteristics of "Deep Listening" are illustrated in the following table:

Common behavioral violations of Deep Listening Characteristics	Deep Listening characteristics that are violated by the behavior			
	Spotlight	Now	Reference	Validation of sent message sent
Telling personal experiences or "War stories" "When that happened to me, I...."	x	x	x	x
Trying to problem-solve "Here is the solution to your problem."	x	x	x	x
Trying to get more information in order to problem-solve "What else happened?"		x		x
Analyzing the message sender "Do you know what your problem is?"	x	x	x	x
Evaluating, judging, or criticizing "How can you expect anything else; you never are prepared, and you are just lazy!"	x	x	x	x
Showing sympathy "Oh, you poor dear! I know just how you feel!"	x	x	x	x
Giving unsolicited advice or suggestions "If I were you, I would..." "Do you know what you should do?" "You need to...."	x	x	x	x

As you can see, it is pretty easy, and in fact, it is hard not to violate the four characteristics of Deep Listening when peeling someone's onion.

Trying to solve the issues people throw at us in the outer layers is time and effort spent needlessly. Spending our time, and the time of the people we are trying to help, trying to change other people to make them happy is a waste of effort, time, and resources. Unfortunately, that is where too many people spend far too much time. If people took the time to listen, hear, understand, and validate the messages being sent to them until they reached the core of people's onions, we would be able to help them better resolve their own unfulfilled needs.

Most of us are addicted to problem-solving, and we try to problem-solve before we get to the center. Almost all of us are premature-problem-solvers, and as a result, we are not very effective in getting to core issues and resolving the ones that make a difference.

We will focus on problem-solving skills later in the competency section. We will provide an effective coaching process model. We will also explain and illustrate the difference between "Helpees" and "Helpers," plus the concept of primary and secondary needs. Before we go there, let's review skills associated with the Touchpoint of Operating Modes.

45

OPERATING MODE COMPETENCIES

As long as people are communicating adult mode to adult mode, there are seldom any competencies required other than having the ability to express and receive messages as well as is possible. When everyone is operating in reality and is being reasonable and logical, there is no cognitive dissonance generated, except differences of opinion. Even then, people can disagree, in adult mode, without being disagreeable. People in adult mode can discuss differing points of view without inflicting injury or causing offense. But as soon as someone leaves their adult mode, issues burst forth, and disagreements become personal. Parent mode positions will be manifest as unquestionable truths that will be defended with force, if necessary. Child mode responses will be emotional reactions that seem out-of-balance within the context of the situation. In the next area, we will focus on dealing with people stuck in their parent mode. We will also explore how to engage or reengage their adult mode.

Dealing with people stuck in Parent Mode

Upfront, please understand, if we can't engage someone's adult mode, who is stuck in parent mode, to discuss an issue or solve a problem, we are wasting our time; that's time better spent doing something else. People stuck in parent mode will only agree to discuss something with someone who has a parent mode position that aligns with their viewpoint. To believe otherwise is a waste of time and money (assuming your time is valuable). We see people stuck in their parent modes stroking each other's prejudices all around us; intolerant people fan the flames of their passionate beliefs with speeches, marches, protests, and attacks on those who are the objects of their biases. Trying to reason with a bigoted person is a hopeless adventure that will frustrate the person trying to be logical and intensify the bigot's feelings. The old saying, "Never argue with a fool because it is hard to tell the difference," would apply to arguing with a bigot. A person has to have an adult mode to hook for proper communication.

Through life experiences, I have come to believe a couple of things about people: The first is that **people can endure what they can justify**. If people can find a reason for what is happening to them, they find acceptance and the courage to cope. I have sat at the bedside of dying people who explained that the terrible thing killing them was OK because they had found a good enough reason to justify their suffering. My dad submitted to medical torture because my mother wanted him to try anything to save his life. His love for her, anything to make her happy or comfort her, was justification for enduring the unendurable.

The second is that **people will believe and act upon what they rationalize to be true**. If a person rationalizes something to be true, despite all other facts proving it to be otherwise, he will believe it and act in alignment with his belief. I introduced this section by stating that it is a waste of time trying to problem solve with a person stuck in parent mode. According to their rationalization, the truth is reality, and nothing we can do will change that. If their concept of truth and reality changes, it will come from within themselves, from their adult mode, rather than from any facts or proof offered by others who have a different sense of truth and reality than they do. As discussed previously, their reality is their rationalized feelings: rationalized feelings become their beliefs.

Happily, most people operating in parent mode have a "hookable" adult mode if not too far removed from reality. We can frequently hook their adult mode by simply asking them to explain why they believe what they believe or why they have that opinion. If they do explain, it is their adult mode that is explaining. We can continue to ask questions for further clarification. If they explain, in adult mode, we understand their logic and rationale about their beliefs and strong opinions. While we may disagree with their reasoning, we can accept their viewpoint as rational for them. In short, we can agree to disagree and still respect one another. The beauty of adult-to-adult communication is that it is mutually respectful of one another's boundaries whether or not we agree with one another. Sometimes when people have an adult-to-adult discussion, people can change their viewpoint and accept another perspective. When this happens, their adult mode took in the information, analyzed it, and adopted it as reasonable and acceptable. Here again, our adult mode is our change agent and our teacher. When our adult mode is engaged, we are open to hearing, analyzing, and taking in new ideas and concepts. Our adult mode is the starter motor that turns on our conversion engine. Hooking people's adult mode opens possibilities for them that they would never have had otherwise – certainly not if they had remained stuck in their parent mode.

I had a Director of Organizational Development at Janssen Pharmaceutica who was married, had no children, never wanted any, and believed it was wrong to bring children into this hateful, messed-up world. We talked quite often about the subject. He thought that Lois and I were nuts to have five children and felt that with so many kids, we would not be able to provide them with the education and the experiences necessary to give them a leg up in life. Barry was exceptionally clever; he had been a national merit scholar in high school and was an active member of Mensa International. Barry could paint a convincing picture for not having children. He would have been an excellent person to have on your debate team if your side of the topic was: Reasons for not having children.

We discussed our views, offering our perspectives and beliefs, but neither ever convinced the other until Barry and his wife found out she was pregnant. His deliberations about the subject were no longer theoretical; it was now a matter of life or death. They twisted and turned, this way and that way, trying to decide whether to keep this baby or terminate the pregnancy. He brought his wife to visit our family several times during that tumultuous period. They decided to let the pregnancy go full term; his sense of excitement about having a baby and his sense of guilt for allowing the pregnancy to happen created cognitive dissonance within him. We talked more frequently about having children and their impact on his and his wife's lives (and the joy the baby would bring to them). As the due date grew closer and closer, his feelings of excitement grew, and his reservations declined.

When they had their little boy, one would have thought he was the first and only baby boy born in this world. They were so proud of the baby and were beyond ecstatic about being parents. As one of the gals expressed to me at Janssen, after they had brought the baby to work to show us his latest achievement and to brag about how exceptional he was, "They kind of make you nauseated, don't they?" Well, they didn't make me nauseous because I could relate to their joy, and I was just thrilled for them to be proud parents of an "exceptional son."

When we left New Jersey, their son was about two years old. Barry and I recalled our earlier discussions when he felt it was wrong to bring children into the world. He just explained that before he had his son, he could never have comprehended how truly incorrect he had been. Our deeply held beliefs can change with sufficient evidence that presents itself in just the right way.

To make the obvious even more so, I want to clarify that our parent mode manifests our beliefs, values, and opinions upon which we center our decisions and actions. They guide us as though they are cast in cement until our adult mode examines them and decides whether to keep them, modify them, or replace them. While in parent mode, we are stuck in cement, immovable, until our adult mode frees us. That is why we need our adult mode and why we need to hook other people's adult mode. It enables us the freedom to move on from being stuck in cement laid down when we were very young. It may have been good cement then, and it may still be good cement now, but our adult mode empowers us to examine it for flaws and see if it is still excellent cement. Our adult mode is like a jackhammer that breaks up old cement and allows us to escape its bondage.

As you recall, in an earlier section in this book, I explained that as a child I had a "colored" friend and that my dad was prejudiced about minorities. Dad made critical comments about minorities that were belittling and offensive. He said things like: "They buy Cadillacs while living in shacks," obviously putting in question their values. His views about minorities could have laid the foundation for my perspectives of minorities if it weren't for my relationship with Earnest and his siblings. They were nothing like what my dad said. They were just the opposite, and I loved them.

I also witnessed prejudices, like my father's displayed on the TV. I could see minorities were discriminated against, beaten, and jailed for trying to obtain equal access to the protection of laws, equal educational opportunities, and equal access into public facilities or services that the rest of society took for granted. This discrepancy between what I knew personally and what I saw on TV caused an emotional disharmony within me too great to ignore or repress. My adult mode examined all the information I had gathered and concluded that my dad was wrong. It also convinced me that our society was unfair to allow unjust behaviors toward others because of biases and prejudices. My adult mode allowed me to develop a new understanding and reality. The adult mode will do for everyone what it did for me. All we have to do is engage it and then listen to the truths of its messages and accept them.

Dealing with people stuck in Child Mode

When stuck in child mode, feelings are in charge. People may have justifiable reasons for being very emotional; still, their feelings dominate their beliefs and reasoning when stuck in an extreme child mode state. Our child mode is a beautiful part of us; it provides pleasure, humor, joy, sadness, ecstasy, and despair. It carries us across the emotional spectrum from the highest of highs to the lowest of lows. Through our child mode, we emotionally connect with others. It provides an emotional bridge for people to cross from where they are and connect with us where we are. And yet, sometimes, we become so immersed in our emotions that they disconnect us from reality and isolate us from others.

Our child mode operates in the emotional center of our brain. The emotions recorded there happened before we had the verbal language or skill to label them. Our child mode is the library of all the feelings that we possess. Over time our feelings became connected to the thinking and the logical part of our brain, and they learned to work in tandem, both providing their valuable contribution to defining who we are. Together they make us unique and special. Jointly they make us human and distinct from all other humans. Some people are more emotional than other people. We could say that some people lead with their feelings and that their feelings define who they are more than their logic does. At times two highly emotional people get together, and they soar on one another's emotions flying in ecstasy, oblivious of others or anything else. Other highly passionate people find their feelings clashing, and that clash creates storms of destructive winds and waves that threaten to destroy one another and those around them. As we mentioned in the section on emotional state competencies, it is vital to learn how to manage and control our emotions. That is a good thing to know how to do. It is an excellent and marvelous skill to master. Unfortunately, not everyone becomes masters of their feelings, and they need help to understand and control their emotions.

One of the ways that we can help is by hearing and seeing their emotions and validating them. Particularly if we can validate the exact emotion they are feeling in that moment. If we can understand and validate their feelings, they are no longer alone and isolated from the world; someone has found them, understands what they are feeling, and becomes the means for rescuing them from the emotions overwhelming them. We described these skills in detail regarding hearing, listening, understanding, and validating.

Another thing that we can do to help people stuck in child mode is to validate their feeling and then ask them why they are feeling that way. When they explain their feelings, their adult mode is doing the explaining. Miraculously, their emotions immediately connect to their reasoning and logical self. As I explained to my lovely and emotional daughter when she was a teenager, "There are two ways to vent your feelings (which need expression): you can live them, or you can explain them." Up to that point, she mostly lived them, and, as a result, they controlled her life. As she gained skills in explaining them, it gave her adult mode more influence over her feelings, and she learned how to manage and control her emotions better.

As a volleyball coach, I get a lot of opportunities to try and hook the adult mode of teenage girl volleyball athletes who get stuck in child mode. A couple of months ago, I happened to see a player sitting in the bleachers with her mother, crying. I had watched her during a match and saw that she didn't execute very well. I also noticed that she pulled a sour face every time she made a mistake and yelled at someone else on the team. I joined her, and her mother introduced myself (she had just moved into the area) and mentioned that I had watched her during the match. She looked dismayed and said, "I stunk today!" I tried to validate her feelings by saying, "So you are pretty disappointed with yourself today?" Her response was, "Oh yeah!" I ask, "So why are you so disappointed with yourself?" She explained, "Because I am so much better than that!" I clarified her statement with, "What I think you are saying is that you have very high expectations of yourself, and when you don't measure up to your expectations, you beat yourself up and are generally really hard on yourself?" Her mother jumped in, "That is what she does, all the time!" Her daughter just nodded her head. I ask her, "How well is that working for you?" She responded, "Not well at all!"

I asked in response, "Do you think it is time to try a new approach?" She sat a little straighter and said, "Yes, what can I do?" She, her mother, and I spent the next 30 minutes or more discussing the options available to her and letting her decide what she felt would be best for her going forward. After she decided which was the best option, we focused on implementing it step-by-step. When I left, they were both happier people who were more confident in the progressive path that they had decided to take. From what I have observed since that session, she is doing much better in response to unforced personal errors committed during matches. She makes a point of talking with me after her games to see if I have noticed how much better she is handling herself.

By the way, her mother told Matt, my son, who is the program's head coach, that our connection was a fantastic experience, one for which she was grateful. She also told him that she thought that I was a remarkable person to have connected with her daughter when she needed someone so badly to connect with and help her. I am not remarkable; I am just a coach who saw a player who was hurting and enabled her to engage her adult mode when she was stuck in child mode and then worked with her adult mode to find preferable ways to deal with future personal shortfalls.

Often, I witness people trying to help people stuck in child mode by sympathizing with them. I know their intentions are pure but sympathizing with someone stuck in child mode doesn't help; it worsens things. It enables people to justify their uncontrollable emotions and to wallow in them. Sympathizing with people stuck in victim mode (a form of child mode) justifies their sense of victimhood and validates their routine to look to others to solve their problems. Sympathizing with people stuck in child mode encourages them to become dependent on others to solve their problems or manage their emotions. Feelings can only be controlled and managed by oneself.

Self-management happens when their adult mode engages and enables their reasoning mind to handle the storm. Sympathizing retards, or prevents that from happening. Sympathy and empathy are very different ways to try and support people who are suffering and stuck in child mode. Sympathy reinforces the pain and justifies it without providing a path out of the misery. Empathy validates the pain and provides a means to understand it and move through it. Hearing, listening, understanding, and validating the feeling of people stuck in child mode helps them engage their adult mode to find a way to save themselves.

Pain and suffering are miserable to experience. But they can also be a good thing that benefits us in the long run if we can push through it and learn from it. An important thing for us to remember if we want to help people is not to inherit their pain and suffering; it doesn't help them grow and develop, and we probably have our pain and suffering from which to learn. But instead, help them by validating their feelings so that they know that they are not alone and have someone to help them find ways to help themselves. If we ask a person who operates chronically in victim mode, "What can I do to help you?" they will take advantage of the opportunity and transfer their problems to our shoulders. Too many people end up asking themselves: "How did their problems become my problems?" The usual answer is: "We asked for it, and they gave it to us." We can't alleviate people's suffering in child mode by inheriting their pain and suffering; it only multiplies the pain and suffering by adding our pain and suffering to theirs. But we can lovingly help them engage their adult mode and find their best way to cope and move through it. When they get to the other side, they will also have earned the benefits learned during their journey.

I hope that I have made it pretty clear why it is essential to help people stuck in child mode to engage their adult mode to work through their emotional suffering and come out whole on the other side. And, again I hope, I have demonstrated how to do that to some helpful degree. Nevertheless, some may want a more concrete step-by-step process about providing that help. Keep in mind that the steps offered are not a "do this" script but rather an illustration of how you can do it. Your approach should align with your understanding of the person and your knowledge of the circumstances causing them problems.

The attached chart lists some "should do's" or things to consider when trying to help somebody stuck in child mode. We will use the feminine pronoun in these examples. The male pronoun would apply equally well.

I had you fill in Tracy's part of the conversation with this example. Still, I believe it provided enough information to interpret the gist of the conversation and see the hearing, listening, understanding, and validating skills that led to engaging Tracy's adult mode.

I'd recommend that you take the opportunity to practice these skills with loved ones when you encounter someone stuck in child mode. You will both feel enriched, providing that you don't criticize, judge, analyze, counsel, or try to problem-solve. Just wait to problem-solve until

What you might do	What you are seeing and examples of what you might say
Observe and develop a hypothesis about what you perceive the person is feeling	(Tracy is very emotional about something. She is crying, shaking her head, and looking skyward as if to say, "why?". Maybe she is disappointed about something).
Empathize with the feelings you are seeing and hearing	"It looks to me like you are terribly disappointed about something"
Invite the person to share	"If you would like to talk about it, I will try to understand." or "Would you like to talk about it?"
Validate the context and the feelings contained in her response message	Are you saying that you feel forgotten and feel like you are unimportant to your husband because he forgot your 25th anniversary and went to a football game instead?"
If necessary, validate any new information provided as a result of your last validation	"So, you are feeling a great deal more than just being unimportant; you feel betrayed?I"
If she makes a conclusion with which you disagree, Use the independent conduction "and" rather than "but" to offer a differing point of view (this accepts her perspective while allowing you to disagree, adult to adult)	"Because you feel so betrayed, you are not planning on not being here when he gets home. I appreciate why you might be considering that, and I doubt doing that would achieve the outcome you want. Have you considered that Paul might receive a different message than the one you intend him to get?"
Empathetically summarize all the information you have validated thus far	"Let me make sure I understand how all this fits together. You feel so betrayed by Paul's neglect of you, on your special day, that you should have spent together, that you are ready to make your point by stepping away from him for a sufficient period that he will get the message that he blew it? Is that correct?"
Invite her to engage her adult mode to work through the emotional trauma	"Tracy, let's take a step back and look at the situation logically and see if there might be a reason that Paul forgot your anniversary. Let's keep in mind that he has been married to you for 25 years and gives every appearance of loving you dearly, with this exception. Then let's talk about how you can help him see how much his decision hurt you. Then let's discuss things you might consider doing to avoid future disappointments and to put in place new ways to make things brighter for you in the future".
At this point, we would take the role of coach in trying to help her solve her problems. We will discuss this later as part of our problem-solving and coaching competencies reviews.	

they feel validated and ask for your help. You may be surprised that at that point, they won't want your advice, counsel, or problem-solving tips because, during the validation process, they formulated their own solutions.

46

PERSONAL BOUNDARIES COMPETENCIES

Andria was a kind of a shell of a person when I got acquainted with her. She was 24 years old and had dropped out of college twice. She acted lost in this big world. She had been an orphan for the last two years, having lost her mother when she was 19 and her dad at 22. She inherited her family's house and property and enough money to go to college without working. As a result of the losses of her parents, she was a very vulnerable and emotionally needy person. Her vulnerability attracted some sharks who sensed her neediness and took advantage of her. A young woman, whom she thought was a friend (they had met in college), moved in with her after her dad had died, with the supposed purpose of providing Andria companionship and comfort to help her through the grieving process. Her friend somehow ended up with Andria's car, her stereo, and TV when she moved out of Andria's place and in with her new boyfriend. Of course, her friend's actions hurt Andria, yet she was glad that her friend had found happiness.

She dropped out of school the second time because she didn't have a car anymore. Public transportation was too complicated, and it was too cold to cope without a car in Toronto. She dropped out the first time after her mother died unexpectedly. She got a job and eventually bought a used car that she paid far too much for because the car salesman quickly discerned that she didn't know anything about cars, and he sold her the one he most wanted to dump on a "sucker." As you would expect, the car started having mechanical problems, and the mechanic to whom she took the vehicle for repairs fixed the issues and overcharged her. People took advantage of her time after time until she felt that she wasn't worth very much.

She became a fatalist, believing that her life would be a continuous experience of bad people taking advantage of her. I felt terrible for her and wanted her to know that some people wouldn't take advantage of her. When she first met Lois (my wife), we only had one daughter, Nikki. Andria loved coming to our house, talking with us, and playing with Nikki. I had built a playhouse in the back yard, with a homemade slide from the top of the playhouse to the ground that had such a sharp angle that it made your knees buckle when you reached the bottom. Andria and Nikki would play for hours in the yard, both loving all the attention provided by the other. Afterward, when Nikki was in bed, we adults would spend the evening playing a board game and talking. We learned a lot about Andria's life. We convinced her to start seeing a therapist I helped her find from my contacts at Johnson & Johnson. I helped arrange her first therapy session.

As she reported to us, the therapist helped her see that she had issues with protecting her personal boundaries and spent the next two years helping her learn how to protect her boundaries better and become more assertive. The pendulum swung too far the other way for a while; she became pretty outspoken when it came to defending herself from "inappropriate behavior." At age 26, she went back to school and met an engineering student, who must have been heaven-sent. He was patient with her and seemed to know how to support her vulnerability while her self-confidence emerged. They were married before we moved to England. I was grateful that she had someone to love her and help protect her boundaries.

Learning how to protect our boundaries is a vital life skill. Without it, we are vulnerable like Andria, to those people who would violate our boundaries for their selfish purposes and who would leave us more injured and more vulnerable with each violation added on top of the last one. As we mentioned in our early discussion of personal boundaries, our boundaries become defining elements of our identity. They determine how we expect others to treat us and our treatment of others.

Here, too, they govern how we believe we can, and should, interact with others. Our identity tells us whether we can act as an equal with others, as a superior to them, or as an inferior. How we learn to protect our boundaries strongly influences how well we can operate in our adult mode instead of our parent or child modes. People who have healthy personal boundaries find it easy to engage their adult mode and to evaluate behavior from others directed at them and their behavior directed at others (in terms of appropriateness or inappropriateness). People who fail to protect their boundaries spend copious periods in child mode as a reaction to being constantly violated, or they get trapped in a parent mode that has taught them that they are inferior and deserve disrespect.

It is not surprising that bullies know who they can bully and who they can't. People who protect their boundaries have an aura that dissuades bullies from even trying to mess with them. On the other hand, people who don't defend their boundaries send a message to predators "come and eat me." I'm not sure how to achieve the "my boundaries are protected" message with everyone, but it would be nice if I could.

Still, the first personal boundary competency is accepting ourselves as worthy of having healthy personal boundaries. When we respect, love, or value ourselves, whatever self-caring term we wish to use, we will subconsciously project that other people need to respect us. I like the works of Dr. Melanie Beattie. If you are into self-help, she offers good information about developing healthy personal boundaries. Good therapists are invaluable for helping with self-identity issues and learning how to manage personal boundaries.

Let's look at how people typically manage their boundaries in various situations. Our **Personal Boundaries Behavioral Characteristics** model is shown below, which depicts personal boundary management behaviors in four different conditions. We will examine each and talk about the competencies associated with each quadrant.

Personal Boundaries Behavioral Characteristics

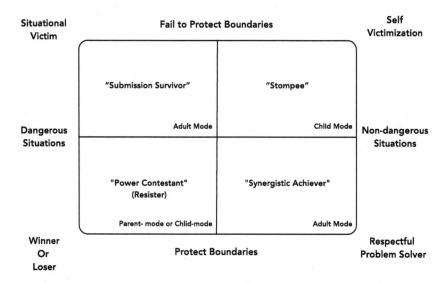

The upper-left quadrant is the **"Situational Victim"** that describes people who fail to protect their boundaries in dangerous situations because they choose survival over protecting their boundaries. It is an adult mode decision. Essentially, they say "Yes sir!" rather than defend their boundaries or possessions. We behave in this quadrant when we hand over our wallet, watch, and jewelry to an armed mugger. The essential competency in this situation is prioritizing what matters most, life over possessions or possessions over life, and deciding according to our logical conclusion. It goes without saying that if we choose possessions over life, we could surely lose both.

The upper-right **"Self-Victimization"** quadrant describes the behavior of people who fail to protect their personal boundaries in non-dangerous situations. We call it self-victimizing because people in non-dangerous situations could prevent others from violating their boundaries if they knew how to do it or chose to do so. It has two characteristics: One, a lack of skills in protecting personal boundaries. And two: A self-identity that, from somehow and somewhere, they came to believe that they were not worthy of protected personal boundaries.

Until they come to see themselves as valuable and worthy of respect, it is unlikely that they will ever master the skills of protecting their boundaries from external violation. This quadrant is where self-help, or therapy, to engage our adult mode to replace old unhealthy recordings with new healthy ones is priceless. That would suggest that the most valuable skill to master would be to engage our adult mode. "Check-ups from the neck up" are always beneficial if we are truthful with ourselves.

The lower-left **"Winner or Loser"** quadrant describes people who protect or try to protect their boundaries in dangerous situations. When confronted by armed robbers, they are the people who will refuse to hand over their possessions but instead choose to resist. If they are skilled enough in martial arts or have a fast draw, they may win the power contest. Then again, if they are not sufficiently qualified, they will likely be severely injured or killed. The motivation to behave in this manner can come from their parent mode or their child mode. If their ego is big enough, or their parent mode recordings are so dominant that they believe they are invincible, their actions will come from their parent mode, and they will resist. They are likely to say something like, "How dare you rob me! Do you know who you are dealing with?" Or their child mode causes powerful emotions that cause the "fight or flight" response that initiates a frontal battle or shots aimed at their rapidly retreating backside. It may be money well-invested in taking self-defense training if one plans to protect their boundaries in all situations – dangerous or not. Then again, maybe they should invest in changing their ego and parent mode recordings to one that will make decisions based on an engaged adult mode.

The lower-right **"Respectful Problem Solver"** quadrant describes people who use adult mode decisions to address the behavior of people who would compromise their boundaries. They have adult mode knowledge and skills to handle virtually any encroachment on their boundaries from people who have a hookable adult mode. They know when to walk away because they understand that the disrespectful person will not connect with reason and logic. They protect their boundaries, and they respect the personal boundaries of others. They give feedback to people who are insensitive to their boundaries in such a way as to avoid criticism and to engage the adult mode of the person to whom they are giving feedback so that they will choose to change the inappropriate behavior of their own volition. They understand and have the skills to effectively deal with people acting out of self-interest and who would take advantage of them. They also understand and know how to maximize mutual-gain outcomes with people willing to work creatively with them.

We will review a number of these competencies that will provide an overview of how to be a respectful problem-solver with people who can engage their adult mode when presented with logical personal boundary protection information. We will review the following skills:

- When to walk away
- How to give feedback rather than criticism
- How to deal with people who are competing with us out of self-interest
- How to collaborate with people who will appreciate mutually beneficial outcomes

When to walk away

Walking away is the simplest competency to learn and use effectively. Unfortunately, too many people don't know when to walk away. They end up not protecting their boundaries effectively and damage, to some degree, whatever relationship they have with the person with whom they are arguing or are trying to change.

Here is the competency: **If you can't hook the adult mode of a person stuck in their parent mode or child mode, walk away.** Of course, you can come back and try later and see if it is possible to hook their adult mode. Just like in football, if you can't make the necessary progress, this time, drop back, punt, and try again next time. You can keep trying until you succeed or until you give up. Don't problem-solve with a person stuck in parent or child mode; it is a waste of time and maybe more destructive than productive.

How to give feedback rather than criticism

First, let's compare the characteristics of feedback and criticism side by side.

Characteristics of Feedback	Characteristics of Criticism
Feedback is given in adult-mode	Criticism is given in parent-mode (sometimes in child-mode, if anger induced punishment is part of it)
The giver must accept ownership of the problem (the unfulfilled expectation)	The criticizer assumes that the person not meeting their expectations has the problem.
Feedback must be honest and reflect true feelings	Criticism is projected with judgmental emotions.
Feedback must objectively and factually describe the inappropriate behavior	Criticism is subjective with generalized disapproval of all associated behavior.
Feedback must explain why the behavior is inappropriate and the resulting natural consequences	Criticism threatens punishment or other super-imposed consequences from the criticizer.
Feedback must be given without blaming, attacking, or criticizing	Criticism blames, attacks, and is disparaging.
Feedback must provide clear expectations and lead to mutual gain outcomes	Criticism rarely provides clear expectations but only delivers "don't dos" with benefits to the criticizer.
Feedback provider must be willing to understand other points of view	Criticizers don't care about the point of view of the person being criticized.
Feedback focuses on capturing the head, heart, and hands of the person receiving it (developmental influence)	Criticism focuses on the dominance and power of the criticizer (compliant obedience)

When we look at them side by side, it demonstrates how different they are. People need to understand that no matter how much we love the person we criticize, love is not the message they receive; people connect with our actions, not our intentions. If we are spanking someone because we love them and want them to know that, then we are using the wrong methodology to show that and teach them. Criticism is a top-down, power-based action. There is no such thing as "constructive criticism" – criticism is criticism, and it is never constructive. Feedback is productive because it is influentially developmental and based on reason. If you don't believe it, **try criticism on your boss, and the truth will set you free.**

Let's get practical and show how adult mode feedback could be delivered. Let's assume we will have a feedback session with a person who has been late to work 30 minutes or more over the last five days.

Feedback Sequence	Feedback Tips or Reminders	Examples of Something You might Say
When you.....	• Describe the inappropriate behavior • Be factual and objective • Don't judge, criticize, evaluate, label, exaggerate or attack	"Tom, I have noticed that you have been late to arrive at work 30 or more minutes each of the last five days".
I'm Feeling..... Because.....	• Select the feeling that most accurately describes how you feel • Avoid the phrases "I feel that you..." "You made me feel.. (parent mode phrases) • Explain the connection between his or her behavior and your feelings	"I'm concerned that you might have issues that are making it impossible for you to arrive on time and I am worried about you".
As a consequence.....	• Explain the natural consequences of his or her behavior on relationships, outcomes, etc. • Don't threaten, preach, or moralize	"When you are late and I am not aware that you are going to be late, it messes up the schedule that I have prepared and we have to make last minute adjustments that inconveniences everyone. Not to mention that it irritates your fellow employees".
What I really want to see is.....	• Describe desired outcomes or behaviors	"What I would like to see is for you to be to work on time, but if that is not possible, I'd appreciate at least a 60-minute heads up".
Which benefits you by.....	• Explain the benefits he or she receives from meeting your expectations	"If you get to work on time, it will solve my scheduling problems and it will eliminate the negative feelings of your co-workers. But if you can't make it on time and let me know then I'll be able to adjust the schedule before it becomes an inconvenience for everyone in the department".
What is your thought about this?	• Sincerely ask for his comments and perspective • Avoid leading or loaded questions	"What are your thoughts, Tom?"
Listen deeply	• Physically focus on his message • Hear, understand, and validate • Identify points of agreement • On points of disagreement explore why there are different viewpoints rather than arguing about them	While hearing, understanding, validating Tom's response, we learn that his wife has had pneumonia for the last week and that he has two kids that need breakfast and a ride to school before he can get to work. Gratefully, she is on the mend and should be ok within another week.

Feedback, given in this manner, enables the recipient to logically and rationally decide whether to move from where he is to the place that will meet the feedback provider's expectations. The recipient's decision will rest on the validity of the content and how well it was delivered, providing the recipient understood the message and found it acceptable.

Caring people know when to give feedback and when it is wiser to hear, listen, understand, and validate. For example, if you intend to provide feedback to someone, but as they approach, you see they are having an emotional response to something traumatic that just happened in their life. It should be evident that providing feedback should be the second priority to validating what is going on in their lives. You are probably killing two birds with one stone since the traumatic experience is probably contributing to the reason that the feedback is needed.

I had a dear friend who asked me to listen to and provide her some feedback about the feedback she had prepared and was practicing giving to her husband of 25 years. The following is her feedback message to the best of my memory.

"Big Jim, you know that I love you and have loved you for nearly 27 years. But your drinking and drug use has disrupted our marriage and threatened to destroy everything that matters to me. Our daughter won't come over here anymore with our granddaughter because she doesn't know if you will be high when they arrive, so she has stopped coming. I have to go to her place to see them.

I feel betrayed and wounded because your addictions have made our lives unpredictable and unacceptable, especially my life. I won't live this way any longer. I have bought myself a townhouse, and I am moving there tomorrow. Here are my keys to this house. It is now your responsibility. You will need to pay the mortgage and the rest of the bills. You will have to keep the lights on.

I expect you to honor my wishes and not come to visit me while you are still addicted. You may call me, and we will talk every day if you wish because I care about you and want to know how you are doing. When you have been sober, alcohol and drug-free, for a minimum of six months and you promise never to use them again, then we can live as man and wife once more. I long for that day to come, but I will not accept anything less than that.

If you change your life and rid yourself of alcohol and drugs, then our life together can be better than ever because we have learned so much through these challenges and heartache. I will truly love living with you when the devils separating us are no longer there.

Oh, Jim, tell me what you are thinking. I need to know."

Through tears, I gave her an A+. You may be interested in knowing that ten months later, I found my feet four feet off the ground when Big Jim picked me up from behind and announced that he had been sober for seven months and that he was moving in with his sweetheart and was going to convince her to sell their house. She, her husband, and their family's lives were upgraded from anguish to cautious joy by protecting her boundaries and giving loving and clear feedback. By the way, she decided to rent their house, rather than to sell it, just in case.

How to deal with people who are violating our boundaries out of self-interest (Stompers)

Knowing how to deal with people trying to satisfy their needs at the expense of our needs requires understanding what we are dealing with. We need to look at them from their vantage point; then, we will see them in general terms and relate to their motives, desired outcomes, critical drivers, core skills, and tactics. Then we can look at the competencies that we can use to protect our boundaries from their efforts to take advantage of us.

The Nature of Stompers
(people who would violate our personal boundaries to serve their own self-interest)

	Descriptions and Characterizations of Stompers	Competencies we can use to protect our Personal Boundaries
Their motives	• To satisfy self-interest • To get what they want • To stroke their own ego • To solve their own problems • To fill their own unfulfilled needs	• Don't compete or argue. • **If you can't hook their adult mode, walk away.** (It is improbable that you will be able to, but if you can hook their adult mode, you have all the options usable with rational, logical people,) Then you could be able to do things like: - Peeling their onion and find out their deep, emotionally naked needs - Then coach them or refer them to a good therapist - Problem-solving* • Once they are in adult mode, focus on satisfying their unfulfilled needs rather than their unfulfilled wants.
Probable outcomes	They will probably: • Get what they want at the expense of other people's personal boundaries • Destroy any chance of Synergistic relationships • Initiate competition or submission • Cause someone to feel elated and the other to feel resentment • Force us to protect our boundaries or allow them to be violated (our choice)	• Stay in adult mode. • Don't compete. • Don't submit. • Provide feedback. • • If feedback doesn't hook their adult • mode, then walk away.

Their critical drivers (internal engines underlying their behavior)	They need:
	• To demonstrate their superiority in order to compensate for a deep sense of inferiority
	• Dominance and power
	• To have their expectations for what they want to be satisfied To win
	• Their ego stroked by making other people's personal boundaries irrelevant (I matter, you don't)
	• To control people, processes, and outcomes
	• Attention (to be in the center of the spotlight)
		• We need to establish beforehand what behavior is acceptable and not acceptable to us (otherwise, we are involved in the unacceptable behavior before we decide it is inappropriate).
		• We need to determine what is most important to us and say no to less important things.
		  - It is easy to say no when we have a more important yes.*
		  - We say "no way" and walk away from behavior that is unacceptable to us.
		(Ask yourself if you are willing to support any of the Stomper's critical drivers listed in the left column.)

The skills or means to achieve their desired outcomes	They will skillfully: • Modify their values to accommodate and to justify their self-serving decisions and actions • Leverage power to maximize the advantage • Be insensitive to other people's feelings or boundaries • Sense other people's vulnerabilities and weaknesses and use them as manipulation tools • Use dominant power combined with their circumstantial power to achieve their desired outcomes • Control and leverage people for self-serving purposes (relationships are transactional having value only as long as they serve the Stomper)	We need to skillfully: • Control and manage our emotions. (Once we lose control, we begin competing with Stompers or we will submit to them.) • Hook their adult mode (or failing that, walk away). • Offer alternative solutions (that will be conditional on whether or not we can hook their adult mode). • Find and help people whose personal boundaries are being violated by Stompers.
The tactics or methodologies that they use	They will use: • Fear, intimidation, and threats • Power moves and ploys • Rationalization to justify actions to get what they want • Narcissistic behavior as a means for self-gratification • Self-importance to make relationships expendable • They will use people to get what they want. • Parent mode or child mode behavior (whichever is necessary) to get desired results • Situations or circumstances as opportunities to determine what they will do or who they will be in order to get what they want	• We need to operate under the philosophy, "I don't know what you are going to do, but I know what I am going to do" • We need to disempower the game playing of Stompers. If someone is using power moves and plays (which is a game), raise the "game" to full visibility (by describing the game being played). Games cannot survive in full sunlight.* • If a relationship doesn't matter to them don't try and create a relationship. • If you can hook their adult mode, you will have to use your judgment to decide if you will be able to do so), then decide how you will proceed. Unless they can operate in adult mode, it is impossible to have a Synergistic relationship or to achieve mutually beneficial outcomes.

*The * signals a competency that we haven't reviewed and will now introduce before teaching the competency. It gives you a heads up.*

Problem Solving

We will delve into some vital problem-solving competencies later in the Power Touchpoint competencies section and in the Levels of Commitment competencies section.

It is easy to say *no* when we have a more important *yes*.

I picked this phrase up from Roger Merrill, who wrote the book *Connections: Quadrant II Time Management,*[50] which Franklin Covey later republished as *First Things First.*[51] I had the honor of spending an afternoon with Roger when Stephen Covey asked me to spend a day with his marketing VP to see if our leadership and relationship concepts were synergistic. When I was a VP with Janssen Pharmaceutica, I met with Roger. I was a Bishop for our church in New Jersey, a father of five children, and a husband of a beautiful wife, all of whom demanded my attention. I was operating in "Guilt Trip" time management. That meant that the area about which I felt the most guilt got priority attention. I shifted from one guilt trip priority to the next, never not feeling guilty about who or what I neglected.

I discussed my time challenges with Roger, and he said to me, "Wayne, it is easy to say 'no' when you have a more important 'yes.'" Boom, he changed my life! I just didn't know it yet, until I had time to absorb more of his messages. Then he explained the four quadrants of time management.

Quadrant II Time Management

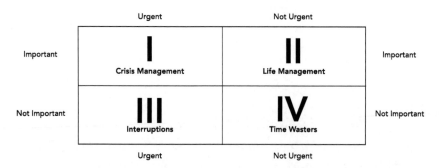

Quadrant I is centered on those things that are important and urgent. He explained that if we allow it to happen, we will live our lives in that

50   A. R. Merrill, R. R. Merrill, *Connections: Quadrant II Time Management* (Institute for Principle, 1989).

51   S. Covey, A. R. Merrill, R. R. Merrill, *First Things First* (Simon and Schuster, 1994).

quadrant. Life in that quadrant is crisis management because everything is important and urgent. That is the quadrant where I was living and was the reason I was always on a guilt trip; I simply couldn't handle all the crises simultaneously, no matter how much I wanted to or tried to do so.

He explained that Quadrant II centers on important but not urgent things. Doing Quadrant II things well is the key to managing our time and life. It includes prioritizing the most important things and focusing our time and efforts there. It incorporates planning, training, education, physical fitness, health maintenance, etc. It is the key to learning to manage our time well because if we don't take the time to focus on these things, they will become urgent (like failing health due to lack of proper nutrition and exercise). He further explained that to determine the most important, we need to look at our life from the big picture and long-term. We need to look at our life mission, life-long goals and objectives, life-guiding standards and decide what efforts and focus will achieve those essential things. He taught me that if we focus on anything else, it will distract us from achieving those things.

What we focus on is a choice, our choice. The most important lesson was that by focusing on managing Quadrant II, I could minimize the time I spent in Crisis Mode, which was almost all of my time. He helped me realize that most crises are preventable if we take time in Quadrant II to figure out how to prevent them. On the flight home and for the next couple of weeks, I took the time to figure out what the most important things were in my life and decided that I should prioritize my time and attention there. It changed my life and got me out of "guilt time management." I learned to say "no" to things of lesser importance.

Roger explained that Quadrant IV centered on things that were not important or urgent, like watching a rerun on TV again that we didn't like the first time we saw it. They are time wasters. Fortunately, I didn't spend much time in that quadrant.

Quadrant III centers on urgent but not important things, like a ringing telephone. I didn't have a cell phone at the time, so people answered a phone or it just continued ringing. Fortunately, I had an executive assistant who screened my work calls, but I still had to answer calls at home or get someone else to do so. The problem with Quadrant III things is that they are urgent and are pressing, and they take time away from Quadrant II and Quadrant I if we allow it to happen. A concept that Roger helped me recognize is that things that are urgent but not important to me are urgent and important to the person who is demanding my attention. An additional part of the lesson I learned was that bosses like to delegate to others the things that are unimportant to them. When they delegate something, it becomes important and urgent to the person they delegate it to. Bosses delegate the things they don't want to spend their time on down to their "people." It was unimportant to the boss, but it was suddenly a crisis to the employee he delegated it to. It is interesting how the importance of something changes depending on who delegates it.

I validated that concept when Jim Bodine, the president of Janssen USA, dropped by my office to delegate a new project. I asked him, "Jim, before you leave, would you please look at my list of priorities on my project board and tell me where this project fits on the importance scale? Wherever you place it will push the projects below it to a lower priority and will change the date upon which we can deliver them." He studied my priority list and said to me, "Keep your priority list as you currently have it. I will find someone else to handle this project."

Roger Merrill was a catalyst for me to look at my life, decide what was most important, and manage my time accordingly. He helped me become a better manager, father, and husband. In one short afternoon, he also motivated me to sit with my family and review our "Carlson Core Values" and to make them further the unconditional basis upon which we governed ourselves as members of the family. I'd recommend reading his book *Quadrant II Time Management* or Franklin Covey's book *First Things First.*

Calling Game Playing

Approximately 40 years ago, I read a book called *Games People Play* by Eric Berne, M.D. It was enlightening for me. It helped me understand that game players use games as manipulation tools to get what they want from others and reinforce and justify unsavory decisions and actions. I learned that game players think they are smarter than everyone else and believe that no one else will "catch on" to their game. And most importantly, to the game player, there is always a "payoff" to a game well played.

People play games all over the place. Salespeople play the "I can't help you because our policy won't allow me to help you game." They win when we admit defeat and accept their lame excuse. Keep in mind that someone decided on the policy to benefit their organization. It is logical to conclude that people within the organization can determine a dumb policy and make exceptions when it helps the company. I know that people hate it when they try that game with me when I know that the policy is ridiculous in the current situation because I won't let it lie. On principle, I call it a game and force someone to decide on actions that serve their organization better than their dumb policy does. I am usually successful, but occasionally someone sinks in their heels, and I have to drag them for a while before admitting defeat.

When I lose, I invariably get called by higher management who wants to discuss the issue and justify their dumb policy. If they are in adult mode, they will usually admit that the policy needs to be looked at again, especially if it is out of touch with their organization's best interests. Remember that policies define the minimally acceptable behavior and fall short of making decisions based on values that would better serve their organization. Ironically policies seldom are written for customers unless they don't care much for customers. Company officers usually write policies to prevent their employees from making dumb decisions. They use policies as the basis to fire someone who makes dumb decisions. In other words, if an employee behaves lower than the policy standard, they will remove them from the company. Company leadership doesn't fire people for operating above minimum standards; that would be nuts! If they take time to ponder it, no company leader wants their organization to operate from minimally acceptable behavior. If they have any sense, they will empower their people to make decisions and serve their customers from principles and values that inspire behavior far above policies. Mediocre organizations govern through policies. What does that say about families who do the same thing with rules?

If we find ourselves in a game, any game, like "good-guy-bad-guy" with salespeople in car dealerships, as soon as we explain the game to the people who are playing it, they will realize that we know that they are playing a self-serving game with us. They understand that they can't use it to manipulate us any longer. We can then move to an adult-to-adult conversation and find a mutually beneficial outcome. Bullies in management have tried to intimidate me until I call the game. Once we call the game, it no longer works. Games can't function when exposed. Games, like vampires, can't survive when brought into the light.

When Stompers try the "I'm in charge here" or "I am the star" game, we can stop it as soon as we recognize the game and explain to the Stomper how he is trying to use it to manipulate us. As soon as we do that, he loses the power derived from the game and can't continue successfully. Once Stompers realize that they can't manipulate us, they stop trying and move on to others with whom they can play the game effectively. The point is, they won't try and stomp on us anymore because they know we won't permit it.

If you have people in your family, or others with whom you associate, who are manipulators, watch them and figure out the games they are playing. If you want their game playing to stop, call them on their game. They will probably resent you for doing it, but the manipulated people will love you.

The internet has created an environment where unethical people play the game, "I'll steal everything you have." The crooked game players have become skillful in preying on our emotions to convince us to send them money or give them information that will enable them to steal our resources. They see our emotions as opportunities. If we are caring and generous, they will develop a game that takes advantage of our empathy and generosity. If we are lonely, they will play the part of being our dear friend or lover, who just happens to need our money desperately. They will make up any reason to get us to send them money. They may lie that they need our money to meet us face to face. If we are poor or greedy, they will use our desire for funds as a way to make us believe that they are the means for making us rich. As game players, they think they are clever while we are dumb and won't catch on to the fact that they are playing us. Unfortunately, too many times, they are right.

Every year unscrupulous game players steal billions of dollars from vulnerable people. When contacted by one of these people, the simple thing to do to protect ourselves is hang up the phone and delete their information. On the other hand, if you want to have a little fun with the game player and want to validate my conjecture that games can't continue when called, instead of hanging up, lead them along for a while and then call the game.

The conversation might go something like this:
You: "So, Jane, you tell me that you are an agent from the IRS and that you are calling to tell me that I am delinquent in my taxes. Let me get this straight, you want me to give you my credit card number to cover my unpaid taxes, and when I do so, you will cancel the order to have police officers come and arrest me, right?"

Jane: "Correct, your arrest is imminent. I'm the only chance you have to stop from being arrested! I can rescind the arrest order with a simple phone call, providing that you provide me a current credit card number immediately."

You: "Wow, you must be a very caring person. I can't believe you would do that for me."

Jane: "I hate to see anyone go to jail for a little mistake."

You: "You need to know how much I appreciate your help, particularly since you know that what you are doing is breaking the law and that you could be charged with a crime for doing it."

Jane: "What do you mean?"

You: "I mean you can't call me and represent yourself as an agent of the IRS; that is a fraud, which is, in itself, illegal, nor can you falsify information, about me, as a ruse to steal my money; that is racketeering and is a serious felony. I have a suggestion, why don't you meet me at the City Post Office this afternoon at 3:00 pm and I will give you a check."

Jane: *Click.*

It should be evident that games only serve to benefit the game player. Board games and sporting events are fun games that provide entertainment. Manipulative games, played by self-serving people who intend to manipulate or control us, violate our boundaries and leave scars in their wake. Don't play their game, call it, move on, and accept the personal satisfaction for having done so.

People who violate our personal boundaries out of concern for us

Not everyone who violates our boundaries is operating out of self-interest. Some people love us, care about us, and want to help us. They are willing to sacrifice their time and resources for our benefit. They would never intentionally do us harm or hurt us; in fact, they would do everything in their power to not do that. And yet, with the best of intentions, they violate our boundaries and hurt us.

I had an aunt who had passionate loving feelings for all her nieces and nephews (she had dozens of them). She regularly reached out to us to find out how we were faring. If we had a problem, it became her problem, and she was determined to fix it. In her efforts to help, she had a habit of doing three things that didn't help but hurt her relationships with many of us. First, she didn't keep her newfound knowledge of the loved one's problem to herself but shared it with all the rest of her loved ones (sometimes exaggerating the problem a lot). Sharing the confidential information embarrassed the loved one and created resentment toward my aunt. Over time, few people would share sensitive information with her.

Second, she was a chronic premature problem solver. She was constantly giving advice and counsel to help solve the problem. The advice and counsel she offered seldom addressed the central issue effectively because she only dealt with the symptoms of the core issue. She listened only long enough to define the first problem that surfaced, then immediately switched to being the problem solver. Trying to solve the superficial problem didn't resolve the problem's underlying issue. Her advice only addressed the symptomatic issue she discovered. And her advice wasn't too helpful. She compounded this problem-solving habit by sharing the problem with everyone who would listen, but she also shared the solutions that she was proposing to the loved one to deal with the problem, which led to the third hurtful habit.

Third, based on how well they implemented her counsel, she judged the person she was dispensing counsel as wise or foolish, right or wrong. And she shared her conclusions about them with everyone as if to show how smart she was and how foolish were those who failed to heed her advice (she had a tremendous need to be important). Her positive, or critical, judgment created (unknowingly, I'm sure) an emotional wedge between my aunt and the people with whom she was judgmental. When they emotionally created distance between themselves and my aunt to protect themselves, she noticed the distance and it made her feel horrible. The need to help and judge placed her in a schizophrenic position with her nieces and nephews; they viewed her as both an aunt who cared and loved them and an aunt with whom they couldn't share information. They knew she would share their information and the solutions that she was suggesting to them, and who would then be critical of them if they didn't follow her advice.

When I met with her in her senior years, she was always thrilled to meet me. I listened to her for as long as she needed me to listen. It was evident to her that I loved her and cared about her. She lamented that few of her nieces and nephews demonstrated that they loved her. She wanted to be important to them, and she desired to know all about them and what they were doing. She wanted to know about their successes (which they shared) and their challenges (which they didn't share). She never received enough information, or time, to feel that she was truly loved and valued. I loved my aunt and felt bad that she didn't think that she was as loved and was as important as she wanted to be with her beloved nieces and nephews. At her funeral, I overheard one of my cousins say, "Well, I loved her, but I won't miss her guilt trips."

If we graded life on intentions, she would receive an A+. If we graded it on how well we respect other people's boundaries, she would not receive too high of a mark. Her story is a little tragic because if she had known how to hear, listen, understand, and validate the sensitive messages shared with her by her loved ones (and kept them confidential), she would have been central to their lives. They would have looked forward to spending as much time with her as they could find. Here, too, if she had known how to help them find solutions to their problems and would have coached them in the process of solving their problems, she would have never been lonely and felt unappreciated. In hindsight, I wish that I had taken the time to teach her some of these essential competencies to help better connect and to stay connected with her loved ones. I'm not sure how receptive she would have been. Who am I to have taught her anything? Still, I wish that I had tried.

When we violate people's boundaries, even with the best intentions and lovingly, it becomes a catalyst for them to put up another personal boundary to protect themselves from us.

Listed below is a chart of seven personal boundaries that need to be respected by others and protected for ourselves. We have included some of the ways to do both.

Personal Boundary	Respect Others' Boundaries	Protect Our Boundaries
Time	• Recognize other peoples' time as precious, to be taken with the utmost consideration for them • Schedule time with others and stick to the schedule • Organize and plan meetings • Follow the plan • Start and end meetings as planned • Use time productively • Be on time • Ask permission for peoples' time • Give your undivided attention • Don't volunteer other peoples' time	• "Say no when you have a more important yes" • Call games to stop time-wasting • Give feedback when your time is not used effectively or efficiently • Avoid people or situations that are not productive • Walk away from time-wasting situations • Share your schedule with others who will use your time • Establish objectives when meeting with others • Warn others when available time is running out & leave when time is up • Reschedule important meetings that are not being productive or when not achieving intended objectives

Body	• Respect other peoples' bodies as private and sacred • Respect the autonomy of other people • Read the messages sent by others with your eyes and ears and respond appropriately • Stay in adult mode and avoid parent mode behaviors towards others; don't force anyone to do anything • Defend people who are mistreated • Help people get the help they need to protect themselves	• Stay in adult mode • Tell yourself how you expect to be treated • Set boundaries with various people: Intimate soulmates, family, friends, colleagues, strangers, etc. • Tell people how you expect to be treated when you suspect that they don't know • Give feedback when boundaries are violated • Say "no." Be assertive • Walk away, or ignore unwelcome encroachment • Take responsibility for your personal boundaries and protect them • Permit yourself self-nurturing and caring • Recognize that you are not responsible for making others happy • Fight to defend yourself if necessary
Mind	• Hear, listen, understand, and validate people struggling for personal understanding and control of themselves. • Peel their onion, and get to their emotionally naked, defenseless self. Then they will no longer be alone and defenseless • Provide coaching to help them to help themselves • Help people we care about to avoid these types of people who will negatively impact them: The arrogant, the gossips, the people who can't control their emotions, the people in self-inflicted victim mode, the self-centered or narcissists, the coveters, the manipulators, the "black hole" people who suck away light and energy, the sadistic or masochist people, and judgmental or critical people • Teach them how to operate in adult mode and to hook their adult made when needed	• Remember, your mind is your responsibility; no one can take it without your permission • Stay in adult mode, don't let people in parent mode or child mode hook your parent or child mode • Keep your power (don't allow others to take it or to diminish it • Stay positive • Ignore manipulative or narcissistic people; engaging them legitimizes them • Walk away; move to a different space • Choose your attitude and control your emotions • Be positive and stay productive • Avoid the destructive people listed and highlighted in the box to the left of this one • Surround yourself with positive people
Emotion	• Hear, listen, understand, and validate people who are struggling for personal understanding and control of their emotions • Peel their onion, and get to their emotionally naked, defenseless self. Then they will no longer be alone and defenseless • Offer them feedback so that they realize the impact of their actions, or lack of actions, on you and others and can use that to help them move forward in a proactive, positive way • Provide coaching to help them to help themselves - In the process of coaching, help them discover ways to protect their emotions listed in the column to the right	• Recognize that we have the right to feel what we feel: we shouldn't put moral judgments on feelings, ours or anyone else's • Manage our emotions - Tune into our emotions - Analyze our emotions and give them a name (a label) - Determine where specific emotions come from and what purpose they serve - Decide what to do with the emotion and do it - Stay in, or get into, adult mode • Give feedback to people who try to control our emotions • Walk away from people who attempt to control our emotions • Avoid the types of people who would negatively impact our emotions. They are listed and highlighted in the fourth bullet of the "respecting others' mind" box
Possessions	• Reverence other peoples' property and possessions • Avoid borrowing, unless necessary, and only if you are willing to replace what you damage or lose and return it in as good or better condition than when you borrowed it • Take good care of other peoples' possessions and property (that includes public assets)	• Keep important documents and valuables in a safe • Keep cash and credit cards on your person • Make copies of important documents • Lock up things people can steal • Be wary of scams • Make backups of electronic documents • Don't lend what you aren't willing to forsake • Take good care of things you value and want to keep • Get insurance to replace valuables

Information	• Keep other peoples' personal information confidential • Get permission to share confidential information before sharing it with anyone • Acknowledge and accept other peoples' opinions as valid for them • Be empathetic with others; empathy doesn't mean agreement with them • Stay in adult mode with people with whom you disagree • Provide feedback rather than criticism with points of view that don't align with yours • Explore the reasons for disagreements rather defending our perspective and attacking theirs • Value differences as learning opportunities	• Remember information is power. Don't share information that will remove your power, never in a competitive situation • Share information only when you are confident it will be used for achieving mutual benefits • Since we live in a digital world, remember the following: • Create strong passwords • Don't share on social media what you don't want to be known universally • Be cautious with Wi-Fi • Be aware of links and attachments • Check to make sure sites are secure • Consider getting additional protection • Have an expert validate the security of your digital information
Self-Identity	• Accept that others are unique and special, one-of-a-kind. No one can replace them • Accept that they have potential and qualities that make them valuable, acceptable, and worthwhile to others (maybe not to you) • Accept that they are not perfect, but they are on a life journey just as you are. They will make mistakes but can correct them and can become what they pay the price to become • Forgive and move past offenses they make towards you • Give others feedback to help them realize how they have negatively impacted you so that they can learn from your feedback and choose a different path going forward • Hear, listen, understand, and validate them so that you can understand who they are and why they are who they are; with that understanding comes some degree of acceptance	• Recognize that we are unique and special, one-of-a-kind in all of humanity. No one can replace us (People can only replace what we do or what we have) • Accept that we have potential and qualities that make us valuable, acceptable, and worthwhile • Accept that we are not perfect, nor are others, but that we are in a life journey filled with mistakes and corrections and that we can become what we pay the price to become • Be forgiving of personal short-sightedness and errors. Learn from them, rise above them, and move on wiser for the experiences • Learn to control your emotions • Engage your adult mode to act as your change agent to evaluate old parent or child mode recordings that need to be validated, modified, or replaced

Some summary thoughts about the Personal Boundaries Touchpoint

Our personal boundary competencies have focused on skills to live our lives synergistically with others. We have focused on ways to avoid becoming Stompers, Stompees, or involved in Mutually Destructive relationships, like Adversarial and Enemy relationships. We have examined seven areas of personal boundaries that need to be protected and respected and have listed specific ways to do so for each one. You will find many of the specific competencies discussed in this section to be valuable tools for living respectfully in society and being respected in return. We have profiled people who would purposely violate our personal boundaries (Stompers) to satisfy their self-interests and have provided ways to prevent ourselves from becoming their Stom-pees. We have reinforced the importance of operating in adult mode to protect our boundaries and to respect the boundaries of others. Being able to say "no" is important to protect our personal boundaries and manage our time effectively. Knowing when to walk away can save much heartache and regret. And maybe, one of the most valuable competencies is understanding the difference between feedback and criticism and knowing how to give feedback in adult mode rather than criticizing.

The following section that focuses on power competencies will get into problem-solving skills. I particularly love exploring problem-solving competencies because we live in a society addicted to problem-solving prematurely, thereby offsetting much of the help they could have provided if they better understood the real problem before trying to solve it.

47

POWER COMPETENCIES

Competencies Associated with Agency Power

Power is manifest in the impact that it has on people and things. We may have latent power, but that is only potential power. Until it is used and impacts someone or something, it is not yet power. As you recall, when we examine power competencies used by people, we are looking at a spectrum of power ranging from Synergistic power to Dominance power. We can combine both with circumstantial powers to create unique types of power that can enormously impact people and circumstances within their respective realms. For example, popular these days are films that depict superheroes and super bad guys with superpowers. Each superhero and super bad guy is unique, with special abilities to help, save, injure, or destroy. The films portray the good guys and the bad guys having epic battles, using their unique skills, which, depending on who wins, will determine the fate of people, nations, and the world. We can look at the competencies associated with Agency powers much in the same way. Let's make a side-by-side comparison of Synergistic powers and Dominant powers, and while doing so, let's examine their unique powers and the kind of impact each can have.

Below is a list of "power players" with labels signifying the nature of their power type:

People who use Synergistic power combined with Circumstantial power make the world a better place because they see the power they possess as opportunities to help others and improve everything around them. The good that people do with Synergistic power combined with Circumstantial power is beyond description. They use their powers and competencies to connect people, resolve issues, and help people devel-

Agency Powers			
Synergistic power combined with circumstantial powers		**Dominating power combined with circumstantial powers**	
• Synergistic position power	"Lifter Power"	"Big Boss Power"	Position dominance power
• Synergistic information power	"Tsunami Power"	"Manipulator Power"	Position dominance power
• Synergistic knowledge power	"Radiant Power"	"Blackhole Power"	Position dominance power
• Synergistic emotional intelligence power	"Radio Power"	"Receiver Power" or "Transmitter Power"	Emotional intelligence dominance power
• Synergistic ethical and moral power	"Righteous Power"	"Dictator Power" and "Criminal Power"	Ethical and moral dominance power
• Synergistic connections and relationships power	"Grid Power"	"Gang Leader Power"	Connections and Relationships dominance power

op and move forward in unimagined ways. When we combine Synergistic power with Circumstantial powers, we have virtually unlimited potential to help people change their lives for the better and improve the world.

On the other hand, Dominance power combined with Circumstantial power harnesses almost unlimited powers for self-benefit and for those with whom they decide to share those benefits. That is usually a tiny group of benefactors. Nowadays, people who combine Dominant power with Circumstantial power typically don't intend to hurt and destroy humanity and the world, as do the super bad guys in the movies portray. However, they will try to eliminate those people or things that can inhibit the achievement of their self-interests. They can be ruthless in how they do so. Still, history does have examples of people who have used Dominant powers combined Circumstantial powers to try and conquer the world. For instance, we can look at the Roman Empire's conquest of Western Europe, Greece, the Balkans, the Middle East, and North Africa between 200 BC and 14 AD.[52] Here, too, we see that Alexander the Great, in just 13 years, conquered the eastern Mediterranean, Egypt, the Middle East, and parts of Asia.[53] Some people still living witnessed Adolf Hitler and his Nazi empire conquer Poland, Norway, Denmark, Netherlands, Belgium, Luxembourg, France, Greece, Yugoslavia, Austria, and Italy between 1939 and 1941. Hitler's ambitions included the entire world, but the Allies defeated him and his regime in 1945. Over 50 million people died tragically due to his

52   Roman Empire Conquests (Wikipedia, https://en.m.wikipedia.org.wiki)
53   Q. C. Rufus, *The History of Alexander* (Penguin Classics, 1984).

Domination power combined with all the Circumstantial powers he could muster.

We can use each type of Circumstantial power with either Synergistic power or Domination power to achieve specific desired outcomes. Let's examine all of the power combinations and see their applications all around us.

Synergistic Position Power

"Lifter Power"

Synergistic Position Power people are the superheroes that I say have "Lifter Power" because they can lift everyone around them to better places. They are like elevators that lift us from lower floors to higher floors. Lifters seem extraordinary in their ability to be where they are needed when needed. They help people triumph over challenges. They have the capacity to support others that ordinary people seem to lack.

Betty Long, an African-American woman, raised in a tough project in New Jersey, was an honor student in high school and college. She put herself through college and became the Director of Human Resources at Janssen Pharmaceutica USA. She lifted everyone around her. Betty was tough, kind, caring, empathic, and a doer. What others talked about doing, she did. For example, I watched her organize and direct a scholarship program that provided hundreds of college scholarships for disadvantaged minorities from New Jersey who otherwise would not have been able to go to college. I saw her support virtually everyone she encountered who needed someone wise and strong to lean on and help them find a way forward. Somehow, she never seemed tired; she was always too engaged lifting others to get tired.

Lifting others is a competency. When we use our position power to benefit others, we develop that power. Lifting power grows more powerful each time we use it. It is just like developing muscles; the more repetitions we do and the greater the weight we press, the stronger we become and the longer we can continue to do so. If you want to develop your lifting competency, look for opportunities to lift others and then do it as often as you can.

But how do we get position power to lift people? Some people inherit it from influential parents who have lots of position power. The rest of us have to earn it. I don't know every way to get it, but I know of two sure ways that my dad taught me after he stopped me from shooting Bott Thompson. He taught me two powerful lessons that I have used throughout my life. The first lesson is: Learn everything you can about the organization for which you work and the business within which your organization operates. Knowledge translates into opportunities when you know more about your organization and business than anyone else. There is always a shortage of people who know the business and can run it more effectively, efficiently, and profitably.

The second way to create position power is to look for unfulfilled needs or problems within your organization. When you have identified one, or more, analyze them and study them until you understand the situation or the unfulfilled needs in every detail. When you have that level of understanding, define how to fill the unfulfilled needs or solve the problem. To make sure that you have thought of everything, write down everything you know. Think of your document as a "white paper" that will provide management with analysis and solutions for the problem, significantly benefiting the organization when resolved. The document will protect you from having someone else steal your analysis and use it as theirs, and it will also be evidence that you know what you are talking about. In short, you will be the best person to become responsible for managing that part of the organization. The bigger the problem and the better the solution, the greater its position. If it is a management-level problem, then it is a management-level position that it will support. If a systemic problem requires director-level management, then find a qualified director to promote you to the job.

Every parent has position power by the very fact of being a parent. Wise parents use their position power to lift and to support their children. Wise parents see their role as supportive rather than controlling. They want their children to make choices and decisions as early as possible so they will grow, develop, and learn lessons from the choices and decisions made. If their children make unwise decisions, they let their children suffer the consequences of their choices. They will suffer with them. They will not remove the suffering because they realize that suffering consequences is part of the development process. The consequences of unwise decisions made during youth are seldom grave. Still, the learnings and development that come from them are fundamental in making wise decisions when they become adults.

Position Dominance Power

"Big Boss Power"

I call position Dominance power "Big Boss Power" because people who use position Dominance power are bossy. Typically, Big Boss power people see the world from a hierarchical perspective. They figure out where they fit on the totem pole and are submissive to those higher on the totem pole and dominate those lower on the totem pole. They get little to no satisfaction from taking direction from above them, but they get a lot of pleasure, and ego gratification, from dominating and controlling people below them. To the people below them, they want to be known as the "Big Boss" – the person who determines their destiny. Going around them is considered a "hanging offense." The message is soon understood by everyone working for the "Big Boss" that everything goes through him (or her) when it comes to the job.

What are their competencies (if we want to call them that)? There is quite a list; it would include: intimidation, threats, orders, making demands, belittling, attacking, blaming, forcing, taking advantage of subordinates, taking credit for a positive outcome, deflecting accountability for unacceptable results, criticizing, putting people down, punishing, and taking ownership of other people's good ideas, etc. Of course, Big Bosses can also be very bright and capable which may explain how they gained that power.

In prisons throughout the United States, prisoners have developed a nickname for the particular guard who fits the Big Boss description; they call him "The Bull." He is the one no one pushes because he will make life miserable when provoked. He does so to make the point that he is the powerful "Big Boss."

How does one become the "Big Boss"? Not sure I know all of the reasons, but there are a few common routes. One of the ways is through seniority. If they last long enough, they will eventually move up the pecking order (providing they haven't offended someone higher on the pecking order). The funny thing about people disposed to being a "Big Boss" is that they don't offend people above them because they are submissive to a higher authority.

Another is by intimidating their competition. Sometimes Big Bosses rise to a power position because everyone around them is afraid of them. Management is left with little choice because management believes that none of the bully's peers could manage him. That is probably not accurate because the bully would become submissive as soon as someone is appointed superior.

It often happens that dominant people rise to power through organizational connections with higher position power. Keep in mind that those above them in the pecking order have a very different opinion of them than their peers and subordinates. They will invariably see the domineering person as cordial and accommodating rather than the scary person the peers and subordinates see.

Some get to a power position because they are good at doing their job. But that was the job before it entailed managing people. They may have shown dominating and controlling tendencies at home or in other situations away from work but didn't have the position power at work, enabling them to be dominating and controlling. The difference in the way people at different levels in the hierarchy view people should justify 360-degree reviews before promoting anyone up the totem pole.

When we become parents, we inherit the ability to choose whether we will be Synergistic position power "Lifter Power" parents or position Dominant "Big Boss Power" parents. The choice we make will have a life-long impact on our children. If we choose to be controlling parents, we have, in essence, determined to be powerful "Big Bosses." Lifter Power parents decide to raise their children while Big Boss Power parents rule their children. The competencies we use to parent will align with the power we have chosen to use. There may be little difference in the love that Big Boss Power parents and Lifter Power parents feel for their children, but how they express it and how children receive it is the difference between night and day. Nurturing and lifting skills like teaching, listening, and empathizing differ from ordering, enforcing rules, and providing punishments. And the outcome from our approach will largely determine how our children see themselves and how they treat others.

Lifter Power people versus Big Boss Power people (how each would likely handle different situations)

Situations	Synergistic Position Power "Lifter Power Response"	Position Dominance Power "Big Boss Power Response"
An employee/vendor/child make a mistake	In adult mode will seek to: • Understand what happened and why • Use the situation as an opportunity to support, teach, problem solve, and coach	In parent or child mode: • Blames, criticizes, threatens, and belittles • Tells them what to do next time • Demonstrates power and dominance
An unfulfilled need arises	In adult mode will seek to: • Understand the unfulfilled need • Understand why it is an unfulfilled need • Determine the best way to fulfill it	In parent or child mode will: • Order and demand an immediate solution • Tell people what to do and how to do it • Tells someone, "Go fix it, this way!"
Failure to deliver an agreed-opon objective	In adult mode will: • Provide feedback • Validate the other person's perspective • Problem-solve through coaching • Aim for internalized commitment	In parent or child mode will: • Belittle, intimidate, attack, shame, etc. • Demote the person • Reassign the objective to someone else • Terminate the person who failed
Extraordinary outcomes were achieved	In adult mode will: • Openly seek opportunities to recognize, praise, and reinforce extraordinary outcomes • Recognize individual achievement • Recognize group achievement • Never recognize individuals for group achievement	In parent or child mode will: • Take credit for others work or ideas • Fail to recognize, praise, or reinforce group or individual achievement • Make extraordinary achievement the new minimum standard (it becomes a reason to raise the bar) • Use it to reinforce and expand personal power and control
Personal expectations were not met	In adult mode will: • Understand what happened and why • Use an unfulfilled expectation as an opportunity to support and to teach • Use it as an opportunity to problem-solve and to coach	In parent or child mode will: • See it as a justification to exert power and dominance • Use behavior like: Intimidation, attacking, shaming, guilt trips, sarcasm, etc., to force expectations to be met

Personal boundaries were disrespected	In adult mode will: • Give feedback • Take action to prevent it from happening again • Use the situation as an opportunity to realign to establish a synergistic relationship through coaching	In parent or child mode will: • Attack the boundary violating the boundary • Punish people who made the violation • Label the violators as Adversaries and Enemies and treat them accordingly
Someone uses authority not given them	In adult mode will: • Address the situation with feedback • Manage the situation as a complex problem and will problem-solve accordingly • Coach to align behavior to be within acceptable bounds and to help the person get authority through the correct process	In parent or child mode will: • Use position power to make clear the limits of their authority • Use fear tactics to prevent it from happening again
Someone complains to someone in a higher position (bypasses the line of authority)	In adult mode will: • Understand what happened and why • Use it as an opportunity to support and to teach • Use it as an opportunity to problem-solve and coach	In parent or child mode will: • Use position power to threaten or to punish them for going around them • Use fear to get obsequious acceptance of the boss's position and power
The general operating mode each type of power uses when dealing with problems	Adult mode	Parent mode (often combined with child mode)

Synergistic Information Power

"Tsunami Power"

People generally think of tsunamis in terms of the destruction which they produce. For sure, they create destruction. But I want people to think of how a tsunami spreads its waters and power undeterred by objects or obstacles. A tsunami inundates everything in its path. It has power with incredible force and energy. It comes wave after wave, each one increasing the depth of its inundation and the breadth of its impact. In this day of cell phones, iPods, computers, and digitalized everything, information spreads like tsunamis that cover the whole world. Our society faces tsunamis of information constantly. It overwhelms us with the pure magnitude of the information that comes at us, ever deeper, broader, and spreading in all directions. This tsunami of information includes valuable things in its forward surge, but it has also picked up junk, garbage, and some dangerous stuff as well on its journey. Part of today's challenge with information is that there is so much of it that it can overwhelm us with the enormity of its quantity. Indeed, there is an enormous force associated with rushing water. But until it is harnessed and put to good use, it is just unchecked power. When channeled appropriately, it becomes valuable power. The trouble with harnessing the force of tsunamis is that they are unpredictable; we never know when they will arrive to overwhelm us.

On the other hand, the tsunamis of information are constantly flooding us and overwhelming us until we harness valuable data to become information power. It is pretty frustrating to be inundated with information while not knowing what to do with it. We may respond by trying to protect ourselves from it, just like we would if our house were flooded by a river overflowing its banks. We might try putting sandbags around our house, which would help until the water overflowed the sandbags. With surging information, we might try blocking information coming through our phone or digital devices, but somehow it gets to us and continues to annoy us. Ironically, we don't want to eliminate information; we need it; we just want to have the practical and valuable stuff and let the other information flow by us. Without information, we can gain no information power.

We need to understand three concepts associated with obtaining information power.

1. Information is unrefined knowledge (A mass of data and words all in a chaotic jumble. Unrefined information is not valuable to us.)

2. Information power starts by having access to information (The mass of data and words is the source of information power; it is like a spring of water that we can use for multiple purposes.)

3. Information power also comes from having the ability to control and refine it. (If we can't understand it and refine it, we can't develop it into knowledge. It is essential to understand that information power precedes knowledge power.) **Refined information is knowledge. Knowledge is vetted information.**

The relationship between information power and knowledge power is pretty simple: Information power is unrefined information capable of being refined into knowledge. Knowledge is information refined to the point that it becomes something valuable and powerful.

It was standard practice on the slave plantations in the south to prevent slave access to learning how to read. The enslavers understood that reading provided the power to refine information and gain knowledge. Knowledge, if not controlled, would inspire ideas not conducive to the enslavers' interests. Slave owners wanted to control the information made available to enslaved people. Of course, they wanted enslaved people to know about carpentry, housekeeping, growing cotton, or any other skills that supported plantation effectiveness and profits. But they wanted to control that knowledge for selfish purposes, only to benefit themselves. They couldn't control information flow entirely because, as in all societies, there were "rumor mills" (back channels of communication) that spread information among the slave plantations. But this information wasn't dangerous because it was limited to a pool of information that the enslaved people understood; they were just sharing something understood by all receiving it. Newly refined knowledge wasn't part of it. Still, the enslavers wanted to limit further the enslaved people's ability to refine information by denying them the information refiner's tool of reading. Reading was too dangerous to be made available to enslaved people; it could provide access to knowledge empowering people. One enslaved person who could read and was well-educated was a slave preacher named Nat Turner. He led a rebellion in August of 1831 called the Nat Turner Rebellion, also known as the Southampton Insurrection, which took place in Southampton County, Virginia.[54]

Nat was the personal slave of a wealthy plantation owner named Samuel Turner, who believed in educating his property. Nat learned to read and write. He also became a skilled carpenter. While he was young, his mother was brutally raped by an Irish overseer while his master was away, resulting in Nat's deep hatred for white people. Samuel Turner had promised Nat his freedom, but unfortunately, he sold Nat to an im-

---

54 P. H. Breen, *The Land Shall Be Deluged in Blood: A New History of the Nat Turner Revolt* (Oxford University Press, 2015).

poverished preacher named Reverend Eppes through a series of misunderstandings. The reverend was also a homosexual who tried to force Nat to provide him sexual pleasures. Nat avoided Eppes, who sold him to a pair of cruel redneck farmers, who brutally whipped and treated him like an animal. This brutal treatment further intensified his hostility toward whites. After that, he was sold to various masters for a few years until he became the property of a decent, hardworking farmer named Travis. Travis rented him out to do skilled carpentry for others, allowed him to read his Bible, and to preach to other enslaved people. He traveled to places where his owner hired him out as a carpenter. During those journeys, Nat fasted and slept in deserted woods. Around that time, he started having visions of black and white angels fighting in the sky, which led him to believe that he would lead the blacks in a holy war against the whites.

While the property of Travis, he met Margaret Whitehead, a beautiful, vivacious daughter of a wealthy widow who lived nearby. Though her family-owned many African-Americans, she opposed slavery and openly admired Nat's preaching. They became friends. The thought haunted Nat that Margaret would have to die if his holy war succeeded. He finally launched his rebellion, with recruited slaves, in August 1831. The rebellion began during the season when most wealthy whites were away on vacation, making it easier for the rebels to seize weapons and attack the local town of Jerusalem. The rebellion didn't go well from the very beginning because many of the insurgents quickly became drunk and brazenly killed men, women, and children. As it turns out, Margaret and her family didn't go on vacation, and the rebels killed all her family, except Margaret. When Nat arrived at her house, she taunted him to kill her to prove his manhood. He chased her into the woods, where he killed her. He lamented killing her, but that was part of the holy war, and she was white.

The rebelling slaves killed between 55 and 65 white people. The rebellion ceased within a few days, and in consequence, militias and mobs executed approximately 160 African-Americans. Not all executed African-Americans were part of the rebellion; whites killed many innocents to make the point that whites were in control. Nat survived in hiding for nearly two months before being caught, tried, and hanged. While he was in prison, awaiting his hanging, Nat said something profound. Nat said that reading provided him the means to see and understand everything in the world that was not available to him. Rather than being grateful for what he learned, it made him hate slavery and white people even more. Nat wanted the world to know that he was no man's Nigger.

After the rebellion, it became illegal in the southern states to allow blacks to read or learn how to read. After the Nat Turner rebellion, the Southerners knew that knowledge was power and that reading was a source for refining information to obtain knowledge power. Nat Turner was a supreme example of what could happen if blacks knew how to read. They wanted to control the information available to blacks and eliminate any possible way for enslaved people to refine information. Information power led to knowledge power, and the southerners wanted to deny both to their slaves.

Parents who use Synergistic information power as part of their child-rearing approach teach their children how to manage information to become selective about the information they allow to occupy their time and minds. They enable them to quickly screen helpful and valuable information from worthless or damaging information, thereby giving them the power to protect and improve themselves. The kind of information we expose to our children becomes the foundation of the information they will value and seek.

When our daughter Cathy was a sophomore in high school in Illinois, she had taken cello lessons since seventh grade. My wife was constantly nagging her to practice her cello. The more she nagged, the less Cathy practiced. My wife and I became concerned that she would grow to hate her cello. We decided to walk around the lake adjacent to our house and see if we could find a different way to get her to love practicing her cello.

As a result of our stroll, we decided to expose her to as much wonderful cello music as possible. We went to the local library and brought home CDs of cello masters playing fantastic music and had it playing on our eight-speaker stereo system when she got home from school. We took her to university concerts and bought season tickets to the Chicago Symphony. We surrounded her with uplifting music that featured cellos. Six months later, I had to laugh when I heard my wife tell my daughter, "Cathy, put down that cello and find something else to do."

Approximately a year later, Cathy came to me and asked if there was a way to earn some money for her and three friends. I asked her the purpose for making money, to which she replied that she and her three friends were forming a string quartet with her two violin-playing friends, her viola-playing friend, and herself as the cellist. I happily funded the purchase of music for their string quartet. Near the end of her junior year, they performed at the governor's ball in Urbana-Champaign at the University of Illinois. The governor provided a private flight for my wife and me to the university as his guests.

The point I wanted to make is that the type of valuable information we make available to our children encourages their passions for getting more of that kind of information. Exposing Cathy to beautiful music inspired her to make beautiful music.

Not all information is of equal value. Some information isn't beneficial, and some is extremely valuable. Being adrift in a tsunami of information is a problem that makes people who can throw us a lifeline especially valuable. Having that lifeline is power; those who have that lifeline can choose to save us, select someone else for saving, or let us all drown. Being able to save ourselves from drifting listlessly in endless information is incredible information power. To the degree that we can channel information to ourselves so that we have access to the kind of information that we want, to that same degree, we get a foothold for limiting the amount of information that we have to refine. That makes it easier to refine it to become useful and valuable information more quickly. That is part of the skills required to gain information power.

Information Dominance Power

"Manipulator Power"

Right now, we have a culture war in education in America between those who want to limit the kind of historical information available to students, particularly in the area of racial history. On one side, some want all the facts about our history to be made available and allow students to refine that information themselves to draw their conclusions about factual knowledge. On the other side, some want to restrict and tailor the information given to students so that the refined information aligns with the history they want the students to believe. These want "acceptable history." They don't want any information to come to light that would create any beliefs that our forefathers were anything other than virtuous, kind, and without biases or prejudices. They would have us believe that in 1492 when Columbus sailed the ocean blue and discovered America, he was a sinless saint. They want history to reflect that he was a kind, wise, and virtuous explorer hero, without guile or blemish. And they also demand that the grievous acts of genocide against native Americans, which he and his explorers committed, be removed from history. To me, history should be factual. It should give credit where credit is due and accountability where it should reside. Columbus made marvelous discoveries and was a fearless adventurer. He was also a product of his time, a person who believed in his moral superiority even at the expense of America's indigenous people. Why do we have to make him out to be a sinless explorer? What he did and why should be part of his history and our history.

Another reason people resist having accurate history, including racial atrocities and other injustices, is to avoid having descendants of those who committed those injustices feeling embarrassed or guilty about past sins. If we can deny them from the past, we can deny them in the present. People manipulate history for selfish purposes. Most reported history is partially true but not wholly accurate because the writers keep only the parts acceptable to those who never want the whole truth to be known. Most historical accounts produced under the guidance of those in power taint history to make them look ethical and hero personifications. Still, it would be wonderful if historical information was always factual and allowed us to feel guilty about the injustices that preceded us so that we might learn from them.

People who control information that others receive want to manipulate knowledge to be what they want it to be. Every politically biased major news network operates by doing this constantly and repeatedly. Conservative networks share refined information supporting the knowledge and beliefs they want to project. Liberal networks do the same thing. Right-wing Republicans refine information to create an entirely different reality than do the refined information of the liberal Democrats. The result is that we have a nation divided because of refined information that "spins information" to be what both sides want it to be. Those of us dependent upon the information as a basis for our knowledge are being manipulated. If we trust spun information and make it part of our current beliefs, we live in a manufactured reality; we are the victims of manipulation and misinformation.

Information Dominance Power is happening all around us more than we want to admit. When trying to sell us something, people who give only partial or misinformation manipulate us to accept their information as fact or truth. They know full well what they are doing. In the 1950s, cigarette advertisements were major sponsors of television shows when I was a youngster. They preached that smoking was good for us. They even had doctors testify about the positive health effects of smoking their brand of cigarettes. Cigarette companies had research information that proved the addictive power of tobacco and its disastrous impact on smokers' health. Yet, they hid the information, and when they couldn't hide it, they flat out lied about what they knew to be true.

Today, we see manipulators providing misinformation or misleading information to fool us into believing something to be fact or truth that is nothing of the sort. The vitamin supplement industry is notorious for doing that. Manipulators are people who give us partial information with the intent to mislead us and manipulate us into believing something false. When a manipulator has a lemon car for sale, he will manipulate us into believing what he wants us to believe. If asked if the vehicle is in excellent running condition, he will likely respond, "Oh, I had to change the spark plugs recently," failing to mention that he is selling the car because the transmission is on its last leg. He wants to dump it while it is still operational.

I call Information Dominance Power "Manipulator Power" because those who use this type of power use it to control or dominate the information we receive. It causes us to believe non-truth, and they hide the truth to benefit themselves.

In 2003 and 2004, I spent quite a bit of time in Nationalist China, mainly in Shanghai and the industrial areas of southeast China. I marveled at the growth and manufacturing capability of China. I came to believe that the religion of China was free enterprise. Unless someone criticized the government, it seemed that Chinese businesspeople could do pretty much what they pleased. At that time, I had real-time communications with our manufacturing liaison through our cell phones and computers. He was a Chinese citizen who had graduated in business from NYU. His dad was a famous Chinese General who had won great battles against the Japanese before being killed by Mao's military forces when the communists took over the country. While I was there, Charles (our manufacturer), his mother, and his brother were invited to Beijing as special guests to honor his deceased father. Frankly, at that time, I did not see much, if any, control over the internet within China. The internet seemed to be a tool that gave Chinese businesses worldwide access to conduct business.

Recently, Xi Jinping, the General Secretary of the Chinese Communist Party, was selected as a "Great Leader," which gives him absolute ruling power for life. The last one who had that title and power was Chairman Mao Zedong. Lately, I have been reading about how China has restricted all internet platforms not originating from and controlled by the Chinese government. They are making significant reforms about how business is conducted within and with China. From everything I can see, they are taking greater and greater control over the information available within China. By doing this, China is becoming the personification of Dominance information power. By controlling their people's access to information and the kind of information the Chinese people receive, the government will manipulate reality and truth to be whatever they choose it to be. Chairman Mao is believed to have killed over 50 million Chinese to establish his control of China.[55] Countless millions were sent to prison and concentration camps to be "re-educated." They could reenter Chinese society when they were submissive supporters of the Mao doctrine. I am curious how long it will take and how many victims there will be this time to establish the same level of control. One thing is for sure; the Chinese leaders will restrict information, provide misinformation, or offer partial information because they will demand their people to behave according to the narrative they create to serve their needs.

Tsunami Power People versus Manipulator Power People (how each would likely handle situations)

Situations	Synergistic Information Power "Tsunami Power People"	Information Dominance Power "Manipulator Power People"
The way Tsunami Power People and Manipulator Power People view information	They see valuable information as power - To be guarded in competitive situations - To be shared in creative and trustworthy situations - To be selectively traded in compromise situations • That validates information aligned with truth, facts, and reality • They manage information in adult mode • They use information legally and ethically	• They see valuable information as power to be used to control, dominate, or to manipulate people, circumstances, for personal benefit • They keep valuable information secret if keeping it secret would benefit themselves • They see information as a controlling or a manipulation tool • They use misinformation, lies, and half-truths to deceive and manipulate people - They will spin information to create a false reality, facts, or circumstances for self-benefit
Dealing with mass unvetted information	• They see mass information as being free and universaly owned by everyone which can be refined to gain knowledge which can be used as a valuable commodity, to be shared, bartered or sold • They see mass information as something needing to be sifted in order to separate valuable from unimportant information • They encourage everyone to participate in the information refining process and to share their findings • They see sifted information as something that needs refinement in order to become valuable knowledge • They teach people (especially their children) how to sift and refine information so that it becomes valuable knowledge that can benefit them	• They see mass information as an opportunity to use against vulnerable peoples' lack of information sifting and refining skills as a means of taking advantage of them • They use selected parts of mass information to create a sense of reality, or an opportunity, or as a means to convince vulnerable or unsuspecting people to believe in them enough that they can be taken advantage of or to be manipulated into parting with their resources • They tend to use mass information as a potter would use potting clay, as a creative tool to create whatever the want it to be

---

55   J. Chang, J. Halliday, *Mao: The Unknown Story* (Knopf Doubleday Publishing Group, 2006).

Dealing with valuable information	• They share valuable information with people they care about or those who would benefit from it • They teach others how to find valuable information • They teach others how to make valuable information into an applicable form of knowledge that can make them valuable to others • They support education which supports the refining of information to become knowledge, which can be used to support a healthy life and a healthy livelihood	• They use valuable information as means to create relationships and build trust in order to manipulate people by the illegal usage of that information • They use valuable information illegally (stock information manipulators or inside traders)
Dealing with false information, or misinformation	• They try to control the kind of information that comes to them • They try to limit or eliminate, all unimportant information from reaching them • They evaluate, shift, and refine information to determine if the information coming to them is accurate, true, and valuable • They call the game when people try to manipulate them or take advantage of them • They walk away from scammers and give them feedback • They report illegal information manipulators (scammers) to regulatory authorities	• They look to gain advantage through information management, either by controlling access to valuable information or by presenting misleading information to others as being valuable and true in order to manipulate them • They tailor information scamming and manipulation skills and use it on specific vulnerable people with unfulfilled needs (who are more easily manipulated or scammed) to manipulate them • They become masters of using false information for self-benefit; they use misinformation to create information that serves their selfish purposes • They learn from and try to emulate successful uses of information that scam or manipulate people • They create information scams • They team up with other scammers to augment their information management skills in order to manipulate or to take advantage of more people
The kind of information that is shared about others	• They look for positive performance and provide positive feedback to positive performers • They provide positive feedback to the people who can recognize and reward positive performers • They provide feedback when they see, or experience, unacceptable performance	• They provide positive or negative feedback about the performance of others only to the extent that it can be used to benefit themselves

The importance of providing positive feedback

I want to emphasize the importance of sharing positive information about the people who serve us well with those who recognize and reward them. Most of us are pretty good at giving negative feedback when we have been underserved, but great feedback is rarely given to the right people when people have far exceeded our positive expectations.

When my eldest child Nikki was to be married to her loving husband Adam, my wife and I wanted to send them to Hawaii to be married and spend their honeymoon (that was her dream wedding). We bought their plane tickets and hotel accommodations. We were expecting that everything would be just perfect and exciting for them. Then we found out that their plane ticket reservations had changed so that they were flying on different planes on different days to Hawaii.

I immediately started calling American Airlines customer service to get the mess straightened out. The first four agents I talked with put in a token effort and, in the end, explained that they couldn't correct the unfortunate situation. The fifth agent I connected with was Allison. I explained the situation to her and asked if she could help me. She explained that it would be challenging to make it happen the way I wanted it to happen due to unforeseen circumstances. She committed to giving it her best effort. She touched base with me every 30 minutes or so for the next five hours, giving me an update on the progress, or lack of it, that she was making. Finally, she called me with the news that she was able to get them on the same flight on the same day to arrive in Honolulu in time for their scheduled wedding ceremony. She then informed me that she had to upgrade them to First Class to make it happen. I was grateful and asked her how much more it would cost me for their flight. She said that she had to pull a few strings, but it wouldn't cost me any more than the original economy seat tickets. I couldn't believe it and asked her if there was anyone that I could write to about her to express my appreciation. She gave me the address of her airport supervisor and her employee number, explaining that there were several customer service agents with the same first name.

I was also able to get the address of the VP of Customer Relations for American Airlines. I sent a heartfelt letter of praise and gratitude to her supervisor and the VP. I explained in detail the efforts she performed to make it happen and the joy my daughter and her new husband experienced due to her hard work. I further expressed how much she had impressed me with her honesty, personal concern, and professionalism in projecting American Airlines as a customer-centered organization.

I expressed that, in my opinion, whatever they were paying her was a minuscule fraction of the value that she was creating for American Airlines. I sent the letters and expected to hear nothing more from American Airlines.

A couple of weeks later, to my surprise, while sitting in my office at Janssen Pharmaceutica, my assistant told me that I had a call from American Airlines. When I picked up the phone, the lady on the other end of the line introduced herself as the administrative assistant of the president of American Airlines and asked me if I could spare a few minutes to chat with him. "Of course," I said. "Sure, I'd love to!" When we were connected, he explained that he had received a copy of my letter praising Allison. He told me that it was unusual to receive such a detailed and remarkable thank you letter like the one I sent. He wanted to personally talk with me to validate that my praise was earnest and factual. We spoke for five to ten minutes, and then he thanked me for taking the time to write the letter of thanks and appreciation. His closing remarks to me were, "I think you just made Allison's day."

The following day, my assistant told me that I had a call from someone named Allison, who worked for American Airlines. When I answered the phone, she was emotional and in tears, so much so that I had difficulty understanding her. She composed herself and explained that she had just gotten off the phone with "The Man" (the president of American Airlines) and that he had become aware of her extraordinary efforts to help a dad send his kids to Hawaii to get married. He told her that what she did was exemplary of what customer service was supposed to be at American Airlines. To recognize her efforts, he would do the same thing for her and her husband that she had done for my daughter and son-in-law. She was blown away, and, frankly, so was I. She thanked me profusely. I just told her that she deserved whatever recognition she got and told her to contact me if she ever needed a job.

That one experience showed me the power of providing positive information to people who can recognize and reward extraordinary performance. I have had some other incidents where my feedback got people on the radar screen of important people and helped them get the recognition that jumpstarted their careers. I'm confident that how they served me indicated how they served everyone and that time would have brought them to the same place. And yet, it is not unusual to see people's careers take off more quickly when their senior management gets a well-crafted thank you letter about their exceptional employee.

When we can obtain information and channel it into being refined, we have gained the information power that can take us to knowledge power. Refined information is knowledge. And knowledge can be precious and powerful. Once we have valuable knowledge, it becomes a power that we get to choose how to use.

Synergistic Knowledge Power

"Radiant Power"

I call Synergistic knowledge power "Radiant Power" because people who share their knowledge are like the sunlight that brightens, enlightens, and energizes everyone it bathes. Albert Einstein changed science's perspective on physics by sharing his knowledge and insight. He was a leader who led harnessing the atom for both good and evil. He brought new energy to nuclear science, from which energy has become available to millions to whom it would not have been possible. Knowledge in this sense is information that has been vetted and is factual that we can use to solve problems, organize and manage things, and discover new facts and truths that take humanity to new, previously undiscovered knowledge.

I hope that we can all envision how people with valuable knowledge can use that knowledge as Synergistic power to bless the lives of others and to help us solve problems that lie beyond our current understanding. Likewise, we can visualize how teachers can share their knowledge and empower others to become teachers and problem solvers. Knowledge can be like a stone tossed into a lake that creates waves that spread from the entry point outward, in all directions, until they touch distant shores. Knowledge becomes synergistically powerful when it is shared in ways to benefit others. The more shared and passed on to others, the greater the knowledge power becomes. Perhaps some would say that when everyone has it, then it is no longer power. Maybe that is true from an advantaged perspective, and yet, once everyone has it, everyone benefits from it. Is that power lost or power realized?

How do we gain knowledge power? It is correct to simply ask how we gain knowledge because knowledge is intrinsic power. Knowledge leads to mastery, which is in itself a form of freedom. Freedom? Freedom to do or not to do. Without knowledge, both choices are not always available. Knowledge comes to us in the process of living. Knowledge depends to a certain degree on exposure to things during our life. We all gain extraordinary knowledge from life experiences; we benefit from learning from them and utilizing what we have learned.

How do we obtain knowledge? When we desire to acquire knowledge proactively, we can go to school or focus our studies on achieving that destination. In that case, we can expedite our obtaining knowledge in any specific area by studying, observing, researching, and problem-solving in that particular sphere of knowledge. We can connect with experts in the field to help us also become an expert. Such has been the approach in what we call the professions in our society. These include professions like law, medicine, science, and architecture. Also, the trade professions like plumbing, electricians, and heating and air conditioning technicians, for instance, requires academic preparation and apprenticeships.

Dr. Thaddeus Merrill from Utah State University was a sunlight (Radiant Power) giver to me and undoubtedly countless other students by sharing his incredible knowledge and insight. For me, he gave the added gift of having me make a promise to him on his death bed that I would read at least one book per month for the rest of my life on information about my profession or things for which I had developed a passion. Because of him, I have read probably over six hundred books focused primarily on the behavioral sciences, leadership, and history. He was a "Radiant Power Giver" that stands out to me from many Radiant Power givers who have brightened, enlightened, and energized my life. Perhaps this book will provide us the opportunity to Radiant Power givers for developing quality relationships.

How do we share knowledge power? First off, realize that no one has all knowledge. We only know what we know about natural laws and eternal truths. The knowledge before us is infinitesimal compared to that behind us. That makes it exciting and worthwhile to be part of the discovery process. But we should share what we know to be accurate; it will confirm or add to what others know to be accurate, and by sharing, we all leapfrog up the knowledge power climb. Likewise, sharing what we know is not valid, as if it were, will diminish our knowledge power. It will misdirect knowledge and truth-seekers because knowledge power reflects what people believe is true. Honesty is a vital part of helping others discover knowledge and truth.

Imagine yourself as a child raised by parents who are synergistic knowledge power people. Your parents will be like sunlight in your life. They will want you to learn everything, see everything, and experience everything as soon as you have the capability and maturity to grasp and understand its significance. They will help you love learning to become an integral part of your life, for your whole life. They will help you become a vessel for receiving knowledge and a conduit for sharing knowledge.

People who share valuable, vetted knowledge, and make it available to benefit everyone, willingly without being forced, are like a tsunami with a positive rather than a destructive force. Because of the internet, their valuable knowledge can spread over the whole civilized world in almost real time. Of course, some people believe that valuable knowledge should be shared as much as possible in the scientific, business, and academic world to solve global problems more quickly. For example, the USA biotechnology company Moderna shared its mRNA Covid 19 technology with the rest of the world without charge to save millions of lives. In doing so, they pretty much removed the exclusiveness of their knowledge and minimized the financial returns that could have been available to them by guarding that knowledge. And they have opened the door for others to compete with them by using their knowledge to compete against them.

Others believe that sharing valuable, exclusive knowledge is counter-productive. After all, it will stifle innovation and the willingness of people to get new valuable knowledge because it removes the monetary incentive to do so. Moderna is an example of synergistic knowledge power. They brought sunlight to the world. Those unwilling to share valuable knowledge to obtain personal benefits are examples of "Knowledge Dominance Power." How we get knowledge power is one thing. What we do with it, once we have it, is another.

Getting knowledge power requires the use of information power. Knowledge and expertise enable people to distinguish between worthless information and valuable information. Therefore, we need to do the things discussed in "How to obtain knowledge power" (contained in this section). Obtaining information power sets the stage for being able to harness knowledge power. Because the quantity of information is so enormous, people need to specialize in reducing data needing review and deciphering. Within their specialty, their value will be determined by how well they will distinguish between information that will be pertinent or valuable to them or people within their specialty field as opposed to worthless or less useful information.

Once we can decipher valuable information from worthless or less useful information, we get to choose how we want to use that information.

Knowledge Dominance Power

"Blackhole Power"

I call Knowledge Dominance power "Blackhole Power" because people use their knowledge only to benefit themselves or disadvantage others. They are like cosmic black holes that absorb all light and energy, letting nothing escape their power. Blackhole Power people do the same thing. They take in all the knowledge (light and valuable information) around them and use it for their benefit, not allowing any knowledge or valuable information to benefit others. This guarded approach is understandable because having unique and valuable knowledge makes it precious. For a person, or an organization, who are dependent upon knowledge as a source of income, we can see why they want that only themselves have that knowledge. Companies guard their unique knowledge lest it becomes common knowledge, making it less valuable for them in the marketplace.

When people have valuable and exclusive knowledge, they barter it like currency. People with knowledge dominance power gain the power to become commanding negotiators selling their knowledge for optimum returns. People who have knowledge and control can also become "Blackhole Power" knowledge people who can use their knowledge solely as a means for self-benefit. The difference between win-win negotiators and Blackhole people is that win-win negotiators want to spread their knowledge as widely as possible, as long as anyone who gets and uses their knowledge pays them for it (Microsoft software is such an example). Blackhole power negotiators want people to buy the products and services derived from their knowledge but never want their unique knowledge (the source of their products and services) shared with anyone (not part of their organization). It is customary with Blackhole power organizations to have their people sign non-disclosure and non-compete contracts to protect their knowledge and to keep it out of the hands of others who could, or would, compete with them.

Knowledge dominance power people are like regular business people who are marketing and selling any product or service; the only difference is that they sell a derivative of valuable vetted information. Once valuable knowledge is gained and shared, negotiators need to identify the market where the knowledge will be valued and sold. They need to do everything that marketing and salespeople do to sell their products successfully. They need a marketing plan, a sales plan, a distribution chain, and an organization to manage the knowledge they are selling.

How do we get Knowledge Dominance Power? First, we need to have valuable knowledge or access to it to find and obtain the rights to take advantage of it. After that, we need to learn how to be good business people who can package, market, and sell valuable knowledge effectively in the marketplace.

Governments recognize the value of protecting the right of knowledge ownership. People get patents for unique products and intellectual property protection for their special knowledge. Having this protection allows the knowledge owners to share it with others for a price without losing the bartering power of their unique knowledge. Knowledge protection enables valuable knowledge sharing without significant risk and forfeiture of potential earnings gained from selling their knowledge.

Copyrights for books and music are perfect examples. Authors can sell their books to millions of people and retain ownership of the information contained in the book. Music composers can enable millions of people to benefit from their masterful creations while keeping the rights to sell their music exclusively. Unfortunately, some dishonest people steal intellectual property and sell it as if they owned it.

Occasionally, we see people who lead extraordinary organizations that look beyond the monetary incentives. They share their knowledge because they believe that helping people is more important than making money from the knowledge. As mentioned earlier, the USA biotechnology company Moderna did that when sharing its mRNA Covid 19 technology with the rest of the world without charge to save millions of lives. That was a fantastic and selfless act. I would guess that gesture cost them billions of dollars in potential revenue but gained them much in gratitude and in creating an excellent reputation.

Pharmaceutical companies spend hundreds of millions of dollars funding research to find valuable products. Then they add to those expenses to prove the efficacy and safety of their products. The cost of finding and bringing a pharmaceutical product to the marketplace is staggering. And yet, we needn't feel sorry for them because they charge as much as the market will bear for their products after approval and during the time remaining within their intellectual property safety net.

Let's say that a pharmaceutical company spends two billion dollars a year to do pharmaceutical research and complete all the necessary steps required to get FDA approval to bring its product to market. Why would any company do that? The answer is simple math. What would you do if you could invest two billion dollars a year to make four billion dollars a year for years and years? Of course, the debate between pharmaceutical companies and the people who use their products is the level of reasonable profit that they should make from those investments. Customers believe that over a 100% return from investments each year is too much. Of course, business leaders and their stockholders see it as only a reasonable return for the risks they take. The government, or politicians, should protect both sides' interests. Those politicians heavily supported by pharmaceutical interests favor the pharmaceutical companies. Other politicians who feel it will best serve their interests to get votes by lowering pharmaceutical costs will pontificate about putting cost controls on pharmaceutical products. Unfortunately, the debate and outcomes have changed little in the last fifty years. I expect that it will continue unchanged for the foreseeable future. As you can see, politicians sell their support for personal benefits.

In industries whose success depends on a continuous supply of new and valuable knowledge that they can turn into products, we will see a lot of knowledge dominance power. Tech companies are all trying to create their Blackholes to gather and garner all the valuable information they can to become an unconquerable force in their universe. In short, it pays to be a significant knowledge person (and organization) in a knowledge-driven society.

In the mid-1980s, the CEO of J&J and the CEO of IBM became board members on one other's board. In doing so, the most decentralized large corporation in the world (J&J) and the most centralized large corporation (IBM) gained insight and access into the strengths and weaknesses of one another's approach to business. At the functional levels within the companies, management teams were able to meet and share information. I happened to be on the J&J Operating Committee for Recruiting and Hiring. Of course, we had 15 committee members (all company VPs) representing different J&J companies, each with different needs. Our committee's approach to hiring and recruiting improvement would be group members who met quarterly to share ideas, successes, and failures. There was no common philosophy or approach to recruiting and hiring within the operating companies at J&J (each of us did our own thing).

On the other hand, IBM had a corporate VP in charge of recruiting and hiring. He had a whole organization of directors, managers, and recruiting specialists working for him. Their recruiting and hiring processes made ours look amateurish. I was amazed when I met with IBM's corporate director of engineering recruitment and hiring; he showed me a catalog of every engineering student in engineering colleges across the USA, England, and parts of Western Europe. When I looked closely at their roster, he pointed out some of the names that had stars beside them. All of the names with stars represented students that they were looking to recruit and hire. Their goal was to hire 85% to 90% of the starred engineers. Their recruiting process started when the top engineering students were in their sophomore year of college. By starting their recruiting so early, they could influence the engineering students' courses and even affect whether they would go on to graduate engineering coursework. In essence, they were molding engineering students to meet the needs of IBM. IBM recruited and hired the top engineering students within the USA, the UK, and Western Europe. I immediately grasped why "Big Blue" was the Blackhole Power of technology at that time.

Even today, we see technology companies, who are such Blackhole Powers that they become monopolies in their industries, to the point that virtually no one can compete against them (Facebook would be one example). That is Blackhole Power!

Imagine that you are a child of knowledge dominance power parents. They will likely teach you how necessary knowledge is and help you get as much of it as possible. But you will also likely become a person who sees knowledge as a means to an end, to benefit yourself, rather than something intrinsically worthwhile to be shared to help multitudes. I suspect that you will become protective of your knowledge and keep it guarded and hidden from the view of others who would learn and benefit so much if shared with them. I expect that you will become a businessperson rather than a humanitarian.

All parents should consider a decision: If you had to choose, would you want your child to be a successful business person or a successful humanitarian? Parents, more than anyone, influence their children's choices.

Sunlight Power versus Blackhole Power (how each would likely handle situations)

Situations	Synergistic Knowledge Power "Radiant Power"	Knowledge Dominance Power "Blackhole Power"
They have valuable, but not exclusive knowledge, but knowledge that others need	They would: • Share it with those who need it • Teach it to those who need it or who want it • Sell it for a reasonable price to those willing to pay for it	They would: • Build walls around the current knowledge to make it as exclusive as possible (non-compete contracts with employees or with people who use their knowledge to produce products or services) • Modify the knowledge just enough to make it exclusive, then get intellectual property protection that will make it hard for anyone to use the knowledge without violating their intellectual property rights (example, brand name pharmaceutical products) • Share knowledge with those that help them profit from it but will not compete with them (sometimes they hire them) • Buy, or merge with everyone who also has the knowledge
Others have valuable knowledge that they need	They will: • Buy it for what it is worth • Join up with those who have it (work for them or with them) • Find a mutually beneficial way (and reason) for them to share	They will: • Buy it for a price as low as possible • Steal it from those who won't sell it below market value • Hire people who have the exclusive knowledge needed (usually from competitors who have it)
They have exclusive, valuable knowledge beneficial to others and society that no one else has	They will: • Use it for mutual benefit (trade or sell) • Exchange it for something beneficial • Share it as a gift to others and society	They will: • Keep the knowledge secret but create products and services based on that knowledge and sell the products and services (sell the golden eggs but not the goose that lays them)
They have knowledge that provides partial but not holistic solutions	They will: • Refine it further until it provides a holistic solution • Partner with those who have the other parts that provide a holistic solution (create mutually beneficial arrangements)	They will: • Refine it further until it provides a holistic solution • Partner with those who have the other parts that provide a holistic solution • Hire the key people from organizations that have the missing knowledge parts needed to have a holistic solution • Steal the information
They have knowledge that completes part of a puzzle but the other parts are not in their area of knowledge	They will: • Join up with people in every area of knowledge that completes the whole puzzle • Organize limited partnerships or alliances that make the puzzle complete • Make sure the arrangements are fair and equitable	They will: • Make sure they maintain total control of the knowledge. They may join up with others in a partnership but only if they have majority control • If they can't get the control they will try and sell their knowledge (if they have other options) Sometimes they create alliances with other groups and then try to squeeze out the weakest member until they have majority control

They have valuable knowledge in an area of dynamic change or evolution	They will: • Collect all of the knowledge available and continually add to it	They will: • Do whatever it takes to get as much knowledge as possible without sharing
General operating philosophies	Radiant Power People believe that: • Valuable knowledge should be shared with those who need it or who can benefit from it • People should get a fair and reasonable return by sharing valuable knowledge • Provide children as much of it as it is possible to provide	Blackhole Power People believe that: • People are either customers, adversaries, or enemies. - Customers are to be leveraged as much as possible. - Adversaries and enemies are to be defeated, by any means necessary • Valuable knowledge should be used to get as high a return as the market will bear for as long as possible

Radiant Power people will be taken advantage of unless they learn when to share knowledge and when to protect it.

Synergistic Emotional Intelligence Power

"Radio Power"

People with synergistic emotional intelligence power have "Radio Power" because of their ability to receive and transmit emotional messages very clearly. Relationships are the emotional states that exist between people. Therefore, people who can skillfully receive and send emotional messages can recognize relationships and manage them better than people with less emotional intelligence. Their power is manifest in the ability to establish synergistic connections with people.

The Great Depression was a worldwide economic depression that officially started in 1929, with the stock market crash lasting until the New Deal and World War II lifted the USA out of it. It was a time of great hardship and suffering. During this economic disaster, the entire country would gather around their radios to listen to President Franklin D. Roosevelt as he gave his "Fireside Chats." His messages comforted millions suffering and offered them real hope for the future. The radio connection provided a link to the most powerful man in the world and helped people hold on and believe they could overcome the depression. FDR had emotional intelligence power derived from receiving and appropriately interpreting the emotions and anguish of suffering people and then transmitting a clear and much-needed message of hope. He used synergistic emotional intelligence power in combination with his position power to marshal the resources of the United States government to create jobs for many of the unemployed and food for millions who were starving. This effort was called the New Deal. His Radio Power and position power lifted a nation until Japan attacked the United States at Pearl Harbor in Hawaii and brought the United States into the war as an active belligerent. The economic situation improved as everyone became engaged in producing the resources needed to wage World War II successfully against the Axis Powers. Without Radio Power combined with position power and applied where and when most needed, it is impossible to know if our society could have recovered and effectively prepared for and fought a worldwide war.

Emotional intelligence provides the power to impact success in life and relationships positively. When combined, knowledge and intelligence translate into competencies for synergistically connecting with people and resolving relationship issues. Human relationship competencies provide insight into the source of relationship issues and how to fix them and move on. *To the degree that we can use emotional intelligence to operate harmoniously with others, to that same degree, we can be extraordinary in our interpersonal connections and in developing synergistic relationships.*

How do we develop emotional intelligence and translate that into power?

Because emotional intelligence centers mostly on emotions, we need to harness the skill of understanding emotions – ours and others. I would refer you back to the skills for learning to control our emotions; we can't harness what we don't understand. As you recall, there are four steps in learning to control our own emotions. The first three steps help us understand our own emotions. The fourth step allows us to decide what to do with that understanding. The four steps are: 1) Tune into our emotions. 2) Analyze our emotions and give them a name (a label). 3) Determine where specific emotions come from and what purpose they serve. 4) Decide what to do with the emotion and do it. Understanding our emotions is a form of emotional intelligence. What we understand provides us insight into how to manage it. The emotional control we develop becomes a big part of our ability to connect with and influence others.

When we understand and control our own emotions, we gain insight into helping others understand and manage their emotions. Indeed, if we understand others' emotions and validate our understanding of them, they will trust us and allow us to assist them in helping themselves. There is a concept in counseling that I picked up from Dr. Bob Carkhuff; it is: "*To the degree that people feel understood, to that same degree people will be willing to understand.*" Said another way, if we want people to understand us, we must understand them first. There is tremendous emotional intelligence power contained in that concept. The more we understand people (their emotions) and validate them, the more they will trust us and be willing to open their minds to allow their adult mode to redirect their lives. Our validation of them provides insight for self-development, growth, and developing their emotional intelligence power. When we are good at both receiving and interpreting emotions and can validate them, we become like radios around which people gather for comfort and help. If you have a few minutes, go back and review the section on emotional power. I don't want to repeat everything, but I would like to share the following thoughts again.

The world can be lonely and isolated for many people, even if people literally surround them. Feeling disconnected when longing to be connected is soulful torture. Too many feel that no one understands them, cares about them, or loves them, so when they encounter someone who can understand and validate what they are feeling, it is a momentous experience. People who can relate to people have emotional intelligence, which can be tremendously powerful.

Parents who take the time to help their kids develop emotional intelligence give them the gift of connecting with people and developing synergistic relationships. Teach your children the four steps of learning to control their emotions. Walk them through the process as a personal coach. They will appreciate your help and insight, and it will be a bonding experience. Also, teach them to take their understanding of their own emotions and use it as a means for understanding and validating the emotions of others.

Take every opportunity to explore and analyze emotions with your kids. Please help them increase their emotional vocabulary to validate emotions accurately. As you watch movies together or witness experiences, good and bad, happy and sad, discuss the feelings that you are seeing. There are emotions available for analysis and discussion no matter where you turn. You will be pleased how quickly your children (and hopefully yourself) will become sensitive and insightful regarding emotions. With that insight comes emotional intelligence power.

While recently having a telephone chat with my daughter, her twelve-year-old daughter joined our conversation. We talked about how my daughter could connect with and help one of her friends having a difficult time. My granddaughter became engrossed in the conversation and brought up one of her friends that is also having a difficult time. We walked her through the process of tuning into her friend's feelings, labeling them, and guessing the source (reasons) for her friend's feelings. Then we asked her what she thought her friend could do to help herself if she understood her feelings well. She had some excellent suggestions. Then we asked her what she could do to help her friend understand her emotions. She became excited to try and help her friend. After more than two hours on the phone discussing this subject, my daughter and I decided it was time to hang up and do other things. My granddaughter objected strongly, "I am not ready to stop talking about this! Can't we keep discussing this for a little while longer?!" We set a time for the subsequent discussion. If your kids are like my daughter and granddaughter, they will love learning to better connect with and help others. Many people would want to have Radio Power if they understood how beneficial it is when used with compassion.

Emotional Intelligence Dominance Power

"Receiver Power" or "Transmitter Power"

I believe that people who use emotional intelligence Dominance power have "Receiver Power" or "Transmitter Power." They receive and understand the emotions of others, or they send emotional messages to others with the intent of exerting power over them. They are not a conduit of emotional intelligence that uses their competency for interpersonal connection and developing synergistic relationships. They use their gift of emotional intelligence for selfish purposes. Maybe that violates what emotional intelligence is if it requires connecting with people, empathizing with them, and helping them.

Emotional intelligence with dominant power people is not about helping people. It is to understand (read and correctly interpret people's emotions) and then use that understanding to control or manipulate them. There are a lot of people who are good at this. Many of them are con artists or scammers. In extreme cases, they are sadists, people who get a kick out of other people's pain and suffering, or pedophiles, who groom and use children as their sex objects. The difference between scammers (including con artists) and sadists is that scammers and con artists use their emotional intelligence to take advantage of people.

In contrast, sadists use their emotional intelligence power to intensify the pain and suffering of others. Scammers and con artists find pleasure in the win of cheating people successfully. Sadists find pleasure in maximizing pain and suffering and watching it. Pedophiles take advantage of children to gratify their sexual deviancy.

Con artists and scammers gain their emotional intelligence ability just like everyone else by becoming tuned to the emotions within themselves and the emotions emoted by others. Perhaps they gained their understanding of vulnerability, hurting, and painful emotions from personal experience. No matter how they gained that skill, somewhere along the line, they didn't develop empathy. Maybe, their moral gap is a manifestation of revenge or payback. I don't know why. For sure, I don't want to get into how to develop emotional intelligence to become a successful manipulator, con artist, or scammer. If any of these people want to learn how to use their gift to help people rather than to hurt them, I would think that finding a good therapist would be a good starting point. Maybe prison is even a better catalyst to motivate their desire to change.

Most of the things about how con artists and scammers gain their emotional intelligence power would also apply to sadists and pedophiles.

But with sadists and pedophiles, their emotional intelligence is directly wired to a mental disorder that makes them an extension of their emotions and drives them to do unspeakable things. We won't get into the etiology of sadism or pedophilia; doing so would require additional volumes focused solely on those subjects.

I would caution parents never to be examples of someone who would use emotional intelligence power for selfish purposes. Not long ago, I witnessed a relatively wealthy businessman justify his actions to a "friend" who trusted him that he had just taken advantage of by saying, "Don't take it personally; it is just business." How could his friend not take it personally? It was personal! Unfortunately, this self-justified moral decrepitude has become acceptable to many business people. It is spreading. Many kids adopt that value system because the ones teaching it are the very people they love who are raising them.

Help your children develop emotional intelligence to have incredible power to help others and never take advantage of them. Emotional intelligence power detached from integrity, empathy, and helping is dangerous.

Radio Power vs Receiver Power and Transmitter Power (how each would likely handle situations)

Synergistic Ethical and Moral Power

"Righteous Power"

Synergistic ethical and moral power I call "Righteous Power." Righteous Power has changed the world and will continue to change the world. When present and under the right conditions, righteous power grows until no one can contain it. The radiance of it changes the world and makes it better and fairer. Synergistic ethical and moral power is life-changing and requires tremendous courage and moral strength to make changes. Mahatma Gandhi, the man who led India to independence from British rule, had such ethical and moral power that he united a nation and most of the world to the idea that India should be independent and self-governing. His ethical and moral power gener-

Situations	Synergistic Emotional Intelligence Power "Radio Power"	Emotional Intelligence Dominance Power "Receiver Power" "Transmitter Power"
General application of emotional intelligence	They will use it: • To make interpersonal connections, to develop synergistic relationships, and to help people	They will use it: • To control, manipulate, or scam people
When others are **angry**, annoyed, enraged, impatient, irritated, resentful, envious, etc.	They will use it: • To connect with peoples' emotions, validate their emotions, and help them as needed, by doing the following: - Activity listen to the messages sent, both the content and the emotions, by using both our eyes and ears to listen - Hear the messages by keeping the spotlight on them, stay in the current moment, maintain their reference point, and validate each message - Understand what they are saying and what they are meaning to convey by developing hypothesizes about what their intended (real) messages are - Validate the hypothesizes by checking them out with the message sender. If correct, validation was achieved; if incorrect, they will correct us - Continue to validate each message until the center of their onion is reached (the emotionally naked core) - Validate the combined messages so that all their emotional messages are validated, and they feel understood and are ready to be helped - Help them by helping them to help themselves. Coach them to reach where they would rather be by using the REACH coaching model. (The REACH model will be reviewed later as part of our problem-solving + competencies) the acronym stands for Results, Evaluation, Alternatives, Choosing, and How Another thing we can do to show people we care about them and love them is to suffer with them when they are suffering and joy with them when they are joying (parents who do this send a clear message of love and support.)	• Receiver Power people use their skills of receiving and interpreting the emotions of others to make connections or to establish false synergistic relationships so that they can take advantage of people • They may utilize many of the same skills mentioned to the left of this column until they get to the part where they could help people, but at that point, they use the trust built to take advantage of the people who trust them. Moral and ethical standards are meaningless to them. • Transmitter Power people use their emotional intelligence primarily to understand the weaknesses and vulnerabilities of others to take advantage of them or manipulate them using their emotions against them. • Typically, they use their emotional transmitter power to exacerbate fear or insecurity to make vulnerable people give them what they ask for. • Their skill sets usually include: - Credible information - The representation of a power position that can harm the manipulated person - A threat of harmful consequences if demands are not met - Ability to avoid consequences for illegal or unethical behavior - Ability to make it difficult, if not, impossible to track or to retrieve money or resources stolen In short, Receiver Power people make fast direct connections to the fear center of our emotional brain and make us act before we can connect to our judgment part of the brain and stop ourselves from being manipulated (the greater the level of emotional panic they create, the greater their possibility to successfully manipulate us)
When others are **confused**, anxious, baffled, depressed, embarraessed, lost, mixed-up, uncomfortable, unsure, panicky, disoriented, etc.		
When others are **scared**, anxious, fearful, horrified, insecure, intimidated, lonely, stunned, timid, threatend, worried, etc.		
When others are feeling **weak**, ashamed, discouraged, exhausted, fragile, guilty, helpless, impotent, overwhelmed. useless, worn out, useless, irrelevant, powerless, etc.		
When others are feeling **sad**, bad, blue, crushed, depressed, disappointed, gloomy, lonely, lost, unhappy, unloved, etc.		
When others are feeling **strong**, bold, capable, confident, determined, positive, powerful, successful, secure, etc.		
When others are feeling **happy**, alive, cheerful, delighted, excited, fantastic, glad, joyful, loving, pleased, proud, thankful, wonderful, etc.		

ated such energy and commitment that English tradition and its Empire buckled under its relenting force. He was assassinated by a fanatic when I was born in 1948. He once said, "There are many things for which I am prepared to die, but there is no cause for which I am prepared to Kill."[56] His values were unconditional, tied to natural laws and eternal truths; nothing anyone did to him or could do to him ever changed the nature of his moral and ethical standards and the direction

---

56   Mahatma Gandhi Quotes (BrainyMedia, Inc.)

he headed. He was simply a force and had a power that the most powerful economic, military, and political power on the whole earth could not contain or control. Eventually, the only option left to them was to get out of its way.

My dad was a man of integrity. He had his flaws, but not having integrity was not one of them. I mentioned earlier in this book how he committed to personally returning any scouting donations that donators wanted to be returned after city leaders redirected the contributions to be used for purposes other than the ones they had donated. My father promised the contributors that their funds would be used as promised. Because of his promise, he took personal responsibility to get their donations back to them. He could have blamed the city leaders and used them as an excuse for diverting their donations. Instead, their donations became his personal debt. We were a poor family, so it took him over two years to get the money refunded. My pride and admiration for him make my resentment of the city leaders insignificant by comparison. What is the example of a parent's integrity worth in the life of his children? For me, it is a standard worthy of trying to emulate.

How do we develop the competencies associated with ethical and moral power? The straightforward answer is to operate within the standards of moral values. We don't need to develop moral competencies if we have unconditional values and use them as the basis for all of our decisions and actions. They happen naturally just by living true to our values. In the competencies section on values, we will discuss establishing unconditional values for ourselves and our families. The same process will apply to organizations. For people looking for immediate direction in developing ethical and moral power, I would offer one standard: Do the right thing and encourage your children to do the right things (based on moral values).

Parents, when we do the right thing, right makes might. Be an example of integrity. Focus on, teach, and discuss the difference between standards that focus on coerced obedience (like laws, rules, and policies) versus willing obedience (like values, principles, doing the right thing, etc.). Discuss decisions and behaviors in the context of moral and ethical values with your children. Children will seek light, energy, and personal enhancement if given the opportunity. With practice and encouragement, they will develop the capacity to make the right decisions, even in uncomfortable situations. Trying to force children to do the right thing doesn't work in the long run. Force will motivate them to push back and to do the wrong things. Be supportive and nurturing, not controlling and dominating.

Ethical and Moral Dominance Power

"Dictator Power"

People who use ethical and moral dominance power use "Dictator Power." Dictators get to define the ethical and moral standards for themselves and those they dominate. Not surprisingly, the standards are seldom the same for themselves as they are for others. Dictators justify and pardon personal actions that would be the grounds for execution or long, onerous prison terms if done by their subjects. We usually think of dictators in terms of people who govern countries, but dictators are all around us in organizations and families. Dictators use all their powers, dominance power combined with circumstantial power, to control and dominate others and circumstances. They create hierarchical cultures where they sit at the top. They permit no competition or pushback from anyone who would threaten their power and domination. They surround themselves with people who flatter them and reinforce their dominance. Their desires become the standards that govern behavior. Their desired ends justify any means to remove threats to their power. To people using dictator power, all values become conditional to their wants and unsatisfied needs. Dictators, by definition, are narcissists. Their behavior fits the label of narcissistic personality disorder. This type of person demonstrates the following characteristics: Arrogance, self-importance, grandiosity, insensitivity toward others, and the need for constant validation. May heaven help anyone who isn't subservient to them.

Dictators do not accept eternal truths as the standards for their decisions and actions but instead replace them with their standards. These standards protect their position and power and allow them to do un-encumbered what they want to do. They will expect their subjects to be honorable and trustworthy but have no such expectations for themselves. Hence, they have ethical and moral dominance power. Their end always justifies their means.

How does a person get ethical and moral dominance power? A fairly common way is to be born into it. Kim Jong-un is the first "great" North Korean dictator leader's dictator grandson. Another way is to conquer and eliminate all opposition, as Chairman Mao of Nationalist China. Many corporate dictators get dominance power by developing a unique and fantastic product (and subsequent product line) and building an organization around themselves, never relinquishing control, either decision making or financial, as did Apple's Steve Jobs.

The most common way, by far, to obtain dominance power is by becoming a parent. Soon after becoming one, we have helpless children with no power against our position and power. Parents get to choose whether to be nurturing and supportive parents or dominant ones. Nurturing parents focus on developing bright, independent, wise decision-making kids who accept responsibility and accountability for their decisions and actions. Dictator parents focus on making their children be what they want them to be or a dictator who defines right and wrong and acts as a policeman, judge, and consequences enforcer. There is no special training required to be a dictator parent; it is as easy as falling down. To be one, just remember to put your opinion, position, and power ahead of your children's needs and opinions. Why wouldn't we? We know far more than they do, and we have much more life experience to make wise decisions. I am not going to answer why. Take a little time and figure it out.

Amoral people are indifferent to ethical or moral standards. An amoral person would be someone who has no conscience. If he did something terrible, he would feel no guilt or remorse. Some would describe them as having no scruples.

An aged neighbor had her granddaughter living with her because her parents had booted her from their house. Her granddaughter's parents couldn't put up with her lying and stealing. They explained to my neighbor that she lied for no reason. When they asked her why she would lie when lying served no purpose, she would answer, "I don't know." Other times she simply denied lying. She started taking things from her parents' house and pawning them at a local pawn shop. When they figured out what was happening, the first place they would go when something came up missing was to the pawnshop. The missing items were usually there. They tried to convince the grandma not to let their daughter into her house, explaining that they had taken their daughter to therapy only to be informed that the daughter didn't want treatment. The therapist suggested that they allow her to suffer the consequences of her amoral actions to see if that might trigger a change in her behavior or open the door for her to be more willing to accept help.

The grandmother told me that she loved her granddaughter and couldn't stand the thought of not knowing where she would sleep or eat, and that is why she let her move into her house. Within a few weeks, things started missing around her home. She just couldn't find items. Some of her prescriptions came up missing. She became concerned and checked on some of her heirlooms in storage. Her husband's old army uniform jacket was gone, and some of his World War II memorabilia. She asked her granddaughter about missing items. Her granddaughter said she didn't know what had happened to any of the missing items (with a smile). The road ended when her granddaughter had a fender bender with her grandmother's car and then lied that it was the other person's fault. The insurance company canceled her grandmother's automobile insurance because it turned out that the granddaughter was responsible for the accident and had not responded to a summons to appear in court. My neighbor told her granddaughter that she needed to leave, and then she changed the locks on her doors. She told me that the whole situation with her granddaughter was driving her crazy. She couldn't imagine why her granddaughter would do such things. I suggested that my neighbor touch base with a therapist. Loving and caring people have difficulty understanding why someone they love would take advantage of them.

As long as people allow amoral people to use them or take advantage of them, it gives them a form of power to victimize them. The sooner we stop amoral people from harming us, the sooner we take their power away from them. Unfortunately, that doesn't change their moral character; it only provides self-defense.

"Criminal Power"

Immoral people do wicked things knowingly and willingly. Immoral people conscientiously reject moral and ethical standards; they scam, murder, steal, lie, or deceive to get something, or a lot of somethings, from us. They understand that they violate ethical and moral standards, and they skillfully plan to do so. That they purposely flaunt morality for personal benefit differentiates them from amoral people. Amoral implies an awareness of moral standards but a lack of concern for violating them. Immoral people are evil because they intend and plan to harm others to get something for themselves. Prisons are full of immoral people. Bernie Madoff is an excellent example of an immoral person. He was an American fraudster who developed and operated the largest Ponzi scheme in history (that we are aware of). Many corrupt people are brilliant and can avoid being caught. Bernie cheated people out of over $64 billion. He knowingly destroyed people's lives for selfish gain. He was so expert at being immoral skillfully that he became chairman of the New York stock exchange. His skillful immorality gave him tremendous power to dominate and take advantage of others. He lived like a king by stealing from the rich and poor without discrimination. We measure immoral people's ethical and moral dominance power by the willful destruction and harm inflicted on others.

Righteous Power versus Dictator Power and Criminal Power (How each would likely handle situations)

Synergistic Connections and Relationships Power

"Grid Power"

Synergistic Connections and Relationship Power derived from personal connections is "Grid Power." These personal connections benefit

Situations	Synergistic Ethical and Moral Power "Righteous Power"	Ethical and moral dominance power "Dictator Power" and "Criminal Power"
Dangerous circumstances where the lives and rights of others are threatened	They will: • Protect the lives and rights of others before consideration of their own	They will: • Willingly sacrifice others to save, or to benefit themselves • Exit the situation to escape accountability • Likely be the ones creating the dangerous situation and threatening others
Circumstances where lives or the lives of others are exposed unless lies are told (like being held at gunpoint)	They will: • Place the value of other peoples' lives above the truth until the immediate danger had passed then they would seek to correct the lies with truth • Lie to protect others but would die before violating their own core values	They will: • Likely be the ones who are manipulating people to lie for them • Require others to lie for them • In the situation needing to lie to protect themselves, they would lie (like crazy)
Circumstances where modifying, or aligning, standards to accommodate the situation would be beneficial	They will: • Stay true to their unconditional values and use them as the basis for their decisions and actions and accept the consequences	They will: • Operate from conditional values. Their moral and ethical values change to serve their interests • Dictators get to define the moral and ethical standards for themselves and for others, the standards they set are different for themselves as opposed to those set for others
Circumstances where everyone operates from standards incompatible with theirs		• Dictators change the standards to be compatible with their own or they punish or eliminate those who oppose their standards • Criminals align with whatever standard serves them best
Circumstances where their moral or ethical standards are being challenged		• Dictators punish or eliminate those who challenge their standards • Criminals accept any standard that benefits them and violate any standard that inhibits self-serving behavior
Situations where others are being unjustly treated or are being discriminated against	They will: • Step forward to support and protect those being discriminated against or who are being unjustly treated • Do everything within their power to help others with the exception of violating their own core values	• Dictators cause people to be unjustly treated or discriminated against. They will only change if it benefits them to do so. • Criminals unjustly treat others, that is what they do. • They may have their own standards about which they would punish people who violate their standard (like punishing pedophiles, or people who "rat" on other criminals)
Situations where the laws of the land are discriminatory and unjust	They will: • Use every synergistic power they possess to see that the laws of the land are changed to replace discrimination and injustice with equal treatment and rights under the law and justice • Vote, petition, write legislators, speak at public meetings, write editorials, contribute to groups supporting the change needed, etc.	• Dictators are responsible for laws of their land and practices that are discriminatory and unjust. They create them to maintain, demonstrate, and reinforce their power and control. • Criminals are basically indifferent to laws unless they are held accountable for violating them • Criminals often justify breaking laws because they feel that they have been discriminated against or have been unjustly treated. Ironically, they don't feel badly enough about unjustly treating others to stop doing it.

others. Imagine an electrical power grid that connects one area of the country with other parts. This massive grid also connects to communities and every household within communities. This power grid supports everyone connected to it. People's connections are like power grids. To become part of it, we need to apply, be accepted, or receive an invitation by someone already a part of the grid. The good news is that once we are part of the people connection grid, we have access to the whole grid.

One point of connection connects to all others. Grid Power combines all the power and influence of each member, and in that sense, each person adds, or subtracts, to the power of everyone else. Some offer tremendous energy, while others contribute nothing and drain energy. We all like connections to high-energy contributors. And if we are high-energy contributors, people want to be connected to us. When we are high-power contributors, we can use our connections to expand the power grid by adding valuable contributors to the grid.

For example, one of the measurement standards for leaders at Johnson & Johnson was the number of good leaders that a leader developed who could "move the business forward." When executives discussed a person's leadership ability, the question was always asked, "Who have they developed to be a leader who has moved their part of the business forward?" If there was no track record of leadership development, the person was considered a manager rather than a leader; leaders develop leaders.

In our human resources group at Janssen, we took the leadership development responsibility seriously. It was every person's responsibility to develop their backup and replacement. You couldn't move upwards or sideways until you had someone prepared to do your job as well, or better than you could do it. We kept track of those we were developing and where they were in the development process for every position in our HR department. J&J did the same thing for all its executives throughout the corporation. J&J ingrained the development of leaders into all of us.

One of the specific things we did was decide how much of our job we could safely give to our direct reports. The idea is that as we gave important responsibilities to one of our people, it would enable us to take on more responsibility from those we reported. It also helped us expand the breadth of our contributions into areas previously neglected or underserved. Janssen was a new startup company in the United States, and that growth created opportunities and provided for significant contributions. It may sound distasteful, but we referred to our leadership development approach in our HR department as "earthworm development," meaning that we would take in the opportunities in front of us and leave fertilized opportunities behind us to benefit those we were developing.

To make it work, we developed a compensation and recognition system where we recognized people with the appropriate title and salary commensurate with the duties they had accepted and performed well. It became a model throughout the Janssen company. People wanted to join Janssen because it became a company where talented people could progress and be recognized.

Helping people grow, developing synergistic relationships, and making them part of your connections, adds their talents and connections to the existing grid. The power grid grows and becomes even more powerful every time that happens with talented people.

To the degree that parents help their children develop synergistic relationships and expand their interpersonal connections, they are helping them establish power grids that can benefit them throughout their lives. Children who can do this successfully have a power grid that expands continuously. Their influence grows as their connections develop. The good part is that their ability to make a positive difference increases as their connections and influence expand.

Connections and Relationships Dominance Power

"Gang Leader Power"

A few years ago, a 16-year-old young woman was shot and killed while riding with friends in a car on the streets of Salt Lake City. It was a senseless act made even more senseless once we learned the reason for her murder. As it turned out, she was murdered by a "wannabe" gang member who killed her because the gang leader told him that to become a member of his gang, he had to murder someone, anyone, and that a gang member needed to witness the murder. He wanted to be a part of the gang so desperately that he jumped in a car with guys who were already gang members and drove the streets until he found his victim. His victim was his initiation test.

How could a gang leader garner such dominant power that people would kill if he asked for it? Abraham Maslow gave us some insight into how this happens in what has become known as the Maslow Hierarchy of Needs. Generally speaking, his hierarchy is a pyramid of needs that drive human behavior. The theory is that as each unfulfilled need is satisfied (or largely satisfied), starting at the bottom, it no longer drives behavior. The next unfulfilled need, higher on the hierarchy, then drives behavior. The point is: **Unfulfilled needs drive behavior**, and after we fill a need, we then strive to behave in ways that satisfy the next unfulfilled need, and thus we continue up the hierarchy that is one step higher on the hierarchy.

The pyramid's base is **physiological** needs, such as hunger, thirst, even the will to fight for air if deprived of it. The next level is the need to be **safe and secure**. This physiological need applies to many things that make us feel insecure, like our body, employment, and surroundings. Avoiding fearful stimuli and feeling safe is a basic human need. It explains why the fear of abandonment is universal among all infants and young children. The need at the next level explains why our murderer killed an innocent woman. It is the need to **belong and to be accepted**. As we can see, it was a strong enough unfulfilled need to motivate a young man to kill for acceptance into a gang. This ritual of doing crazy things to belong is not limited to gangs. We see initiation rites being done routinely by seemingly, ordinary people. People do dangerous or dumb things to prove they have the right stuff to belong to a particular group. At USU, I watched first-year students walk around with girls' pantyhose on their heads because that was part of an initiation they had to pass to join a specific fraternity (I won't mention which one). We see initiates die from alcohol poisoning, trying to prove that they were worthy of becoming a member. We see upper-level high school students go to jail for torturing first-year students to make them pay the price for admission to their team. The need to belong is powerful.

Once a person feels that he belongs and is accepted, it no longer drives his behavior. The next unfulfilled need gave the gang leader dominance power among his gang members. It is the need for **esteem and to be respected.** It is about ego gratification that is satisfied by controlling others. This unfulfilled need makes people desire the climb up the totem pole or the corporate ladder. It manifests itself in position power; the higher the ladder ranking and the greater the position power, the more the ego is fed. Ironically, this is a more challenging need to fill than those unfulfilled needs preceding it because the ego seems insatiable; as soon as we fill the ego at one level, it rises to a higher level. Maybe that explains why there are many positions on an organizational ladder. Remember that rank and position on society's totem pole determine those dominated and those obeyed.

A gang is like a pack of wolves where each pack member has a place, rank, and position. Every pack member behaves according to their status; submission to those higher in the pack and dominance to those lower is standard behavior. Stepping above rank results in immediate reprisals that quickly reinforce the hierarchical positions. The highest rank alpha leader gets all the other pack members' respect. All pack members must show respect. That respect continues until a weakness becomes apparent, motivating an aspiring wolf to challenge the alpha leader. The challenge usually is short and the consequences brutal. It is the same in gangs, as demonstrated by what we see and hear about drug cartels. They exemplify gang member connections, position status, and relationship dominance power.

The unfulfilled needs briefly examined thus far are what Maslow called Deficiency Needs.[57] It is these unfulfilled deficiency needs that drive

57 Abraham Maslow, "A Theory of Human Motivation" (Psychological Review, 1943) 370-96.

behavior. The need to fill unfulfilled needs motivates our behaviors to fill the vacuum. Deficiency needs are connected more to the limbic part of our brain, the emotional driver of behavior. The levels above the deficiency-needs Maslow called Growth Needs. They are needs we strive to fill that are driven by the frontal cortex, the thinking and conscious part of our brain. While they are not pertinent to our discussion of Gang Connection and Relationship Dominance power, we can't leave you hanging with no information about Growth Needs.

Maslow labeled Growth Needs as the upper part of his hierarchy of needs. They are, from the bottom of the growth needs to the top, labeled as follows: **Cognitive** needs, which refers to those connected with the need for creativity, foresight, curiosity, and finding meaning. Next, **Aesthetic** needs refer to needs for beauty and aesthetically pleasing experiences. **Self-actualization** is about the need for realizing one's own potential ("What a man can be, he must be." Abraham Maslow). And **Transcendence** is about giving oneself beyond oneself. It is about fulfilling one's spiritual needs (which is fundamentally different for all of us), which some describe as feeling a sense of personal integrity.

A thought for parents: I doubt that there are very many parents who want their children to become part of a gang. As much as we don't want that to happen, our children will do whatever they have to do to feel that they belong and are accepted. If they don't feel loved and accepted at home, they will look for it elsewhere. The problem is that immoral people in all parts of society look for and find people with unfilled needs for acceptance, belonging, and love. They offer acceptance, belonging, and love as a condition for serving them. They take advantage of them and victimize them unconscionably. And yet, many choose to stay. They prefer to be used and victimized because it is better than being unloved, lonely, or not part of something, even something sinister. Children who feel loved, cared for, safe, and a part of close family relationships seldom leave that safe, secure, and loving environment to be used and abused (unless there is mental illness involved). Children who feel loved and respected expect to be respected by everyone, and they seldom tolerate actions by others that would violate their boundaries. Love your children, respect their personal boundaries, and express that love openly and frequently with words and actions; if they hear it and experience it often enough, they will believe it.

Grid Power versus Gang Leader Power (how each would likely handle situations)

Situations	Synergistic connections and Synergistic power	Connections and Relationships dominance power "Gang Leader Power"
People with position power	Grid Power people: • Expand their power grid by delegating authority, with accountability, to people who report to them. They delegate according to the competency of their reports and their trust in them • Play a supportive role with their reports rather than a dominating or controlling one • Establish synergistic relationships with other people who have position power and find ways to connect people in their grid with the people of other grids	Gang Leader Power people: • Work only with people they can dominate and control. Their organizations are completely hierarchical, with the gang leader at the top dictating what members and officers of the gang are to do and not do • Direct and control people under them to ensure that there is no conflict or push back against them • Are incredibly territorial and see other peoples' grids (gangs) as threats. They treat them as enemies who need to be subjugated or to be defeated • Use intimidation, threats, and violence to maintain compliant behavior
People who have a lot of influential friends or contacts	Grid Power people: • Share their influential connections with people (make introductions, create opportunities to work together, etc.) • Invite new people into their grid of contacts	Gang Leader Power people: • Seek to gain control and influence over influential people to do gang business without fear of accountability. They will use fear, intimidation, and violence to gain control; they will make an example of some to send a message to others • Try to align with corrupt people with position power by "buying" their covert support (politicians, judges, policemen, etc.)
People who have few influential friends or contacts	People with few connections but who desire more connections will: • Expand their people grid by getting to know people and by taking the time to understand who they are and what they are interested in • Join clubs, associations, and groups of people with common interests • Volunteer their time and talents to help people or to support worthy causes • Move out of their comfort zone to connect with people	Gang Leader Power people: • Want no equal power relationships • Want to expand their power grid by increasing the number of people who are part of their gang who will be obedient and supportive of them • Use their power and reputation of power to recruit people who are powerless, vulnerable, and isolated to satisfy their unfulfilled needs for safety, security, and status

Some general thoughts on coping with unavoidable dominance power

Stay in adult mode. You may feel driven to move into parent mode, which is understandable. But in doing so, you will position yourself to enter a direct contest with power. If you have sufficient power to win the contest, be prepared for all the vagaries of a power battle. The battle will become an all-or-nothing situation because the person with the most power will win. If you have less power, you will lose.

This contest is the very situation happening when employees go on strike. They need total commitment despite the consequences of their defiance. They may win, lose, or compromise with a win that seems like an acceptable loss compared to what they wanted to achieve.

Neither contestant is willing to lose, but if both survive until the strike ends, one has to win, causing the other to lose, or both have to accept something less than what they defined as winning when the contest started. Still, the best way to wage the battle is to use adult mode rather than parent mode. Reason and logic need to be the foundation of how we proceed and what we accept; otherwise, pride and unrelinquishable positioning will doom both parties. If we can hook each other's adult mode, we can move forward. Then we can shift away from parent mode positions where both parties will defend their position to the death and operate from a place of reason with the outcome satisfying the best interests of both parties.

All of us will be in situations where someone will use domination and power to manage us. If all we do is focus on how victimized we are, we will drive ourselves crazy. If we stay there when we have other options, we are crazy, lazy, or too insecure to risk change; life will be miserable, and we will feel enslaved. We will go through the motions to survive. Rather than do that, we should look beyond surviving toward flourishing. To look beyond our misery, we need to understand why we choose to stay there. Remember: We can endure what we can justify. If we stay because we have no other alternative, we will feel like prisoners, incarcerated in an inescapable situation. But if we do so because it serves a higher purpose, we can find honor and dignity in doing it.

My friend who became the president of a biomedical company was incredibly proud of her parents because both of them worked for years in two jobs positioned at the bottom rung of society's totem pole to provide quality education for her and her brother. When she explained how her mother cleaned houses for wealthy people who saw her mother as an easily replaceable resource, not caring about her as a person, it made her mother's sacrifice all the more meaningful to her. Her gratitude made it all worthwhile to her mother. Her father worked two jobs, one as a janitor and a night-shift security guard. He focused on providing the means for his children to have opportunities unavailable to himself and his wife. I was honored to meet her father, who came to California from Puerto Rico, and her mother, who came to California through Hong Kong. Somehow these humble people seemed larger than life because I had learned about them from a daughter who described them as heroes. They are!

All of the USU students who were part-time meat cutters who submitted to the dominance and harassment of the bullying floor supervisor at the meat processing company did so because the miserable job provided a means to a better future. They stayed because, no matter how bleak the job was, it was the best alternative they had at the time. Of course, if they found a better option, they left.

Of course, we can always comply with the demands of a dominant person. That will enable us to survive but not flourish. We must change the culture or move ourselves to an amenable one to thrive. We can always attempt to change the culture by hooking the adult mode of a dominant person stuck in parent mode. It is not likely to happen, but if we are successful, we will be able to provide and receive feedback. That will free us to discuss the culture openly and, perhaps, agree on a mutually beneficial way forward. I don't believe that I am a pessimist, but I have found that the wisest course is to leave a dominant culture and join up with a synergistic one. No organization is perfect; still, there are many value-based places, and being there will seem like heaven compared to the Stomper environment you exited.

Nonetheless, some will fight until they have nothing left with which to fight. Fighters can move on when the battle finishes, knowing that they have fought the good fight and lost. Leaving having lost a well-fought struggle is preferable to many than just walking away without having tried.

If you are in an abusive, sadistic, or narcissistic relationship, separate yourself from them and get a good counselor; operating in adult mode won't work with them. They will mess up your mind and your life.

A quick summary of the Agency Power concepts and competencies

We have provided a perspective of power as a choice between Synergistic power to benefit others or a Controlling force to dominate others for personal benefit. We have also explained that we can combine Circumstantial powers with Synergistic or Controlling power, dramatically increasing those powers. We have given each power combination a label to make it easier to relate to the information. In addition, we have provided examples of the competencies used to optimize the power for each kind of combination power. We hope that readers will choose to use synergistic combinations of power when circumstances arise. We further hope that by including information about the controlling and dominating power combinations, people will recognize them and better protect themselves from being manipulated or controlled by people using them.

48

VALUES COMPETENCIES

There are two principal Values Competencies: The first is to define the moral and ethical standards that will be the basis for decisions and actions in all situations and circumstances. The second is to make the values we have defined unconditional, using them as the basis for our choices and actions. Fortunately, when we do a good job of defining and getting buy-in to our core values, it also accomplishes the second competency of getting people to use them as the basis of their decisions and actions.

As you recall in our values section, we defined our self-identity as how we define ourselves to be when asked the question: "Who are you?" The answer to that question provides insight into how people want to perceive themselves and be perceived by others. People answer that question in one of three ways: 1) They tell us what they do: "I'm an accountant." 2) They tell us what they have: "I'm a billionaire." Or 3) They describe characteristics about themselves: "I'm just a guy who is trying to make a difference in the world." We classify the people giving these three answers as: Do People, Have People, or Be People. It is essential to know the primary way people define themselves because how they define themselves determines how they behave and the kind of relationships they develop.

Let me explain. If we are Have People, we focus our identity and behavior on having things (wealth or possessions). If what we have is most important to us, what we do and who we are is secondary to what we need to have. If we need wealth or possessions, more than anything else, we will do whatever we need to do, or be whatever we need to be, to fulfill those have needs. Wealth and possessions will be the most important and necessary things in making decisions and taking action. Not having enough becomes the driving force. We often witness people willing to do illegal activities to fill the have needs. Not every wealthy person is dishonest. Jon Huntsman, the man who established the Huntsman Cancer Foundation in 1995, was a billionaire and was known to be an honest, kind, and generous man to all who knew him well. If asked, "Who are you?" he would have described himself as a man who was trying to help people with cancer get well and live happy, healthy lives. On the other hand, Bernie Madoff was a man willing to steal over $64 billion to satisfy his need for wealth and possessions.

By the same token, if we are Do People, we focus our identity on what we do (usually, the title is related to the kind of work we do or the kind of training we have). The "do" self-identity is understandable because the more we sacrifice to be able to do what we do, suggests how important that title and doing is to us. Do People plan their lives around what they want to do or be seen doing and be recognized for it. Do People place doing over having or being (from their perspective what they do and who they are the same thing). If we are Do People, what we do will determine what we have and who we are. Of course, some Do people get many things because of what they do. Still, the things they have are merely evidence of the value of what they do. In short, doing becomes the priority in life; having or being become secondary considerations. I used to work with hundreds of psychiatrists; most of them made it clear that their identity was their profession. The outstanding ones were in psychiatry to help people rather than be known for their title. It didn't take long to find out their motivations; they either talked about how to help people or about how important they were.

Be Peoples base their identity on the kind of person they are or hope to be. They see themselves as the moral characteristics that would describe them or the values that guide their decisions and behavior in life. Be people plan, and live their lives according to ethical and moral standards they have chosen as a way for living. What they do and have will be determined by their moral standards. They may have a lot and do a lot, but it will always be within the boundaries of their moral and ethical standards. Be people are "value-based" people. They base their decisions and actions on their core values.

We will focus our values competencies discussion on skills associated with becoming a Be person, a Be family, and a Be organization. The most critical and challenging task that Be People have to accomplish is deciding which ethical and moral standards they will use as their core values. These core values will become their "unconditional values," forming the foundation of all their decisions and actions in all situations. We want to achieve similar core standards for individuals, families, and organizations that the founding fathers did for America with the Declaration of Independence. The standards they set were: *"We hold these truths to be self-evident, that all men are created equal, that their Creator endows them with certain unalienable Rights, that among these are **Life, Liberty,** and the **pursuit of Happiness**."* We may argue whether or not these standards have been achieved, but these standards define the identity of what America is or is striving to be.

Defining our core values

Listed below are a few **guidelines** to keep in mind **in defining core values**. They are:

- Not too many and not too few
- Base them on the situations where decisions and actions will be needed
- Choose a value that is a symbol and is representative of many similar values
- Make sure the chosen values align with principles of natural laws and eternal truths
- For families and organizations, involve everyone and get their buy-in and commitment
- Take your time; this should be a process, not an event

Not too many and not too few

"Not too many" means that we shouldn't just make a long list of moral standards; a long list makes it too difficult and impractical to connect a specific value to a particular situation. It could become like choosing which snowflakes to make a snowman, if we have too many values. We need to quickly and logically link a situation to a core value that will be the basis for our decision.

Think of core values like strings on a string instrument. Guitars have six strings, banjoes have five strings, and violins, cellos, and basses have four strings, yet each instrument has the capability of being played with innumerable notes that create beautiful music. Of course, a pedal harp has 47 strings and seven pedals that raise or lower each pitch-class of strings. That may explain why so few people can play the harp; knowing which string to pluck, how to pluck it, and when to pluck it overwhelms all but the most dedicated musicians. We should create values more akin to guitars and violins rather than pedal harps.

Not too few

"Not too few" suggests that we need enough core values to be able to connect a specific value to a particular situation. If having as few as possible were our objective, then we could simply list "Integrity," Honesty," or "Morality" as our core value or values. I see nothing wrong with using any one of these as a centerpiece in our list of core values; they apply to every moral and ethical person. And yet, if we list other core values around them that describe the values that would deem us worthy of being honest, moral, or a person of integrity in specific situations, then we have the kind of value specificity that we are looking for. Again, choosing the number of core values we need should have more strings (values) than a one-string Canjo or a two-string Chinese violin. We may play these two string instruments beautifully to produce lovely music, their musical range and utility are limited. We are looking for maximum utility and minimum complexity in the core values that we choose.

Base them on the situations where decisions and actions will be needed.

Every individual, family, and organization has situations where decisions are needed to address them. For example, every person has conditions common to every other person and unique situations. Common situations may include how to treat loved ones and friends or treat people who disagree with them or dislike them. They may have situations regarding payment obligations or supporting others struggling financially. They may have situations regarding expectations of them at work or from their neighbors. They may have situations that are unique to themselves, such as serious health issues. Whatever their situations, they can use values as the basis for their decisions and actions. They need to tailor their core values to their personal situations.

Likewise, families have situations where decisions are needed. Families, too, have everyday situations similar to every other family and others unique to them. Family situations may include things like: How to treat other family members or family friends, especially regarding family disputes. Situations may entail dealing with a family member struggling financially, emotionally, intellectually, spiritually, or how to manage finances. Circumstances may involve prioritizing work and family time. It may center on ways the family should support neighbors, the community, and the country or how the family should view and participate in religious observances. Whatever the situations families encounter, core values can be the basis for family members' decisions. If they are united in their core values, then every family member can pretty much predict how every other member will act in response to the situation. Common family core values remove the need for Command and Control parenting. And, of course, family core values should be tailored to individual family situations.

Organizations have situations where decisions are needed, and organizational core values can be the basis for the decisions and actions that address those situations (if we have core values connected to the organization's issues). Some universal situations that organizations face are:

- How to treat the people who use our products and services.
- How to treat our suppliers and distributors.
- How to treat our employees.
- How we should treat one another as fellow employees.

- How we should treat the stakeholders in the organization.
- How we should look at and respond to government standards, laws, regulations, and directions.

Some situations are unique to the organization, such as a pricing philosophy or the organization's perspective on organizational debt. Unique viewpoints might include the philosophy is on market share or acceptable returns on investments. They may focus on the philosophy regarding salaries, employee education, development, etc. Here too, the core organizational values should be tailored to the organization's situations. To the degree that organizations have unconditional core values internalized by all members of the organization and aligned with organizational issues, to that same degree, the organization will be able to empower its members to make value-based situational decisions. In other words, the company can decentralize its decision-making to the people who deal directly with the situations and be confident in their employees' decisions.

Make sure the chosen core values align with principles of natural laws and eternal truths.

If we can't explain how a core value connects to principles of natural law or eternal truth, it is probably not an acceptable core value. If it is a self-evident truth, then it is OK.

For families and organizations, involve everyone and get their buy-in and commitment.

Core values are only as unifying as they are understood, accepted, and internalized by the people expected to use them as the basis for their decisions and actions. Ideally, everyone expected to live by the core values should develop, vet, and adopt them. Unfortunately, it rarely happens that way. In most organizations, senior management develops them and dictates them. I suppose that mandatory organizational values are better than nothing, but not much. When dictated from the top-down, people receiving them see them as an example of Command and Control management, which kind of defeats the purpose for establishing them. But there are things that management can do to get buy-in and internalized commitment to the core values. Management must foster and support a way that everyone can go through a process for achieving internalized commitment. They can't force buy-in or mandate it; they have to provide the means and support for people to go through a conversion process.

The process to get internalized commitment requires that people have the opportunity to participate in a personal justification process. That means that everyone gets the values explained and illustrated until they understand them and accept them. It also means that management must be ready to receive challenges, push back with open minds, and explain the values as thoroughly as the people in the organization require them to be explained and illustrated. This process takes time, effort, and resources. There is no way to shortcut the process of conversion. It takes as much time as it takes and as much effort as needed for people to accept and internalize the core values. When management provides clear and complete definitions, realistic illustrations, and real-life examples, it facilitates the conversion process.

With core values, organization members expect that they equally apply to senior management as they do to themselves. If they sense that management has a different set of core values, they will never accept them as their core values. Any examples that they see, or hear about, where a member of management didn't operate within the spirit of core values will invalidate them in the minds of organization members. Implementing core values in an organization is serious business and must universally apply to everyone, from top to bottom.

The process for getting everyone to have internalized commitment to the core values happens quickly if a visible test of the core values occurs. If management passes the test or supports people who pass the test, then the core values are validated and accepted. It happened at Johnson & Johnson during the Tylenol poisoning crisis in Chicago. Jim Burke, the CEO of J&J, got to show all the employees how committed he was to the J&J credo commitment to providing quality and safe products to everyone who used their products. He passed the test, and every employee knew that our J&J credo statements were our core values and that everyone was to use them as the basis for their decisions and actions. Not only did J&J employees know that, almost everyone in the civilized world knew that also. Jim Burke's decision to withdraw Tylenol enhanced J&J's reputation more than can be imagined.

It also happened at KPMG when a practice leader fired the top producing partner in a KPMG practice for violating one of their core values. Immediately, everyone in that practice knew that their core values were core values. That decision on that day made the newly drafted core values real, tangible, and applicable to everyone in the practice. It was why so many of the top partners from Arthur Andersen came to KPMG when Arthur Andersen shut down in 2001 after being indicted for having approved Enron's financial books.

There are other things that management can do to get buy-in for core values. One of them is to give everyone in the organization the opportunity to review, challenge, and provide their input into the core values. J&J did that regularly with all senior management at J&J, which validated core values at the senior management levels. Senior managers did the same process within their departments to ensure everyone had the opportunity to review, vet, and buy into the J&J core values.

Another thing that organizations can do to make the core values real and applicable is to discuss them at departmental meetings. If discussions center on real situations that have occurred or are likely to occur and everyone discusses how they would deal with those situations using the core values as the basis for their decisions and actions, they will internalize the values as standards for decisions and actions.

All family members should participate in defining, selecting, and implementing the core values at the family level. If the children are too young to contribute, allow them to participate anyway; even very young children appreciate being part of family discussions. If they get bored, they can focus on other things while still connected to the family activity. When core values are developed by a couple, before they had children, or before the children were old enough to grasp what is happening, they should consider doing the process again when the children are old enough to participate. It should be a pretty straightforward affair if the parents have been living by their core values; the kids will likely have already innately accepted the values in the process of being raised and growing up in a value-based environment.

Take your time; establishing core values should be a process, not an event.

Core values need not be created in one day and implemented in the next. It should be a process that takes as much time as required and involves as many people as possible. My experience has taught me that the combination of a top-down and a bottom-up approach for establishing core values is the best way to get insight and buy-in from everyone. When starting at the top, go ahead and develop the list of core values and their definitions and then send them to everyone in the organization for input. Ensure that everyone that the values are sent to understands that they are a preliminary list and not the final version. They will appreciate knowing that their information will be valued and considered and that the definitive list of core values will not look the same after everyone provides their input. If the organization has a history of top-down decisions, there may not be much information coming back because people already know that when authority speaks, the discussion is over. However, if the people in the organization are used to seeing input from many people, it will likely be an excellent place to start.

If the organization chooses to start from a bottom-up approach, send out communications explaining that the organization is looking to establish core values that will be the basis for decisions and actions for managing all situations. Ask for everyone's ideas for core values with an explanation of the values that they put forth. Make this as open a communication process as possible. Make everyone's thoughts available to everyone. People will get ideas from one another, and the suggestions will get better and more cogent. Usually, within a few weeks, publish all the recommendations and ask people to give their input again. It is generally wise, at this point, to establish a core values committee with representatives from all levels of the organization to become the vetting and communication vehicle for gathering and disseminating information throughout the organization.

If the committee members are active and communicative with the people in their part of the organization, the buy-in process occurs through interactions with their people. They will continue to get feedback and input from the people with whom they are interacting, and the core values list will become more refined and relevant with the passage of time and participation. Eventually, it becomes necessary to make a final decision. The parliamentary procedure is a great way to get the final core values vetted and approved. Someone on the committee should put forward a motion for a final list of the core values, and then someone on the committee should second it. Then all the committee members should vote either yea or nay (no abstentions). If the committee vote is unanimous, then the core values are available for everyone to approve. If the committee vote is not unanimous, the committee reviews the reasons for the nay votes and tries to reach a new consensus of thinking. If they can't agree, the motion and seconding process and committee vote get repeated until the committee vote is unanimous.

I have supported this bottom-up approach in two organizations. In both, the core values were accepted and became the basis for the decision and actions within the company. Working in those value-based organizations was a life-enhancing experience for everyone who worked there. It took time and effort, but it was well worth it.

After an organization has established core values, new people entering the organization need to go through the buy-in process for the core values. Management can usually accomplish that with the departmental manager and with a member of the organization at the same level or position as the oriented person. Together they walk through the justification (conversion) process. During the hiring process, it should determine, as much as possible, if the people hired align with the organizational core values. Never hire, under any conditions, people who have values that are incompatible with the organization's core values. That can't be fixed short of termination or a change of core values.

If we do a good job of establishing and getting buy-in for our core values, people will make decisions and take actions aligned with the core values. Organizations that operate from unconditional core values are wonderful places to work and contribute. Once we have been part of an unconditional value-based organization, we will never be satisfied with being a part of any other kind. It is the same for families.

49

COMMITMENT LEVEL COMPETENCIES

The commitment level competencies are about the skills of taking ourselves from a place where we are (and don't want to be) to a place
where we want to be. At the beginning of the process, we may not
know where we want to be; we just know that "**here**" is not the desired
place. I am not talking about the physical location but our status psychologically, emotionally, socially, or intellectually. In other words, the
skills required to facilitate change and growth.

**There are four symbiotic processes and competencies for personal
development.**

We can gauge change and development status from four perspectives,
or interconnected processes, that overlap one another (they are happening simultaneously).

The first process is the **five stages of change**.

The second process is the **state of mind** that people experience as they
move through the change process. We haven't discussed the state of
mind concept before, but you will recognize the various state of mind
changes that happen as people go through a change and growth process. We can see them listed in the second group down.

The third is where they are in terms of their **level of commitment** to
the change.

And the fourth is the **skills (competencies) used to facilitate the
changes** needed (or wanted) that incorporate all three interconnected
processes. First, let's provide a high-level model for each of the three
change processes, with brief explanations for each. Finally, we will

add the competencies to work through the processes to accomplish the needed changes and growth.

While reviewing these concepts, you can scan up and down the page to see how each part of a process aligns with the other processes.

The five stages of change and growth:

Stage 1 Unaware and ineffective	Stage 2 Aware and ineffective	Stage 3 Decision, planning and execution	Stage 4 Aware and Effective	Stage 5 Unconsciously Effective
• Unknowingly making poor decisions and acting in ways that put us where we don't like being. • We may not know where we would like to be, just not here.	• Knowing why we are ineffective and what it takes to be effective.	• Making the decision to make the changes needed. • Developing the plan to achieve the changes. • Executing the actions to implement the plan effectively.	• Actions are being executed to implement the changes effectively. • A conscious effort is required to be act effectively. • "We are effective when we think about it."	• Living congruently with what is required to be where we want to be. • We are acting unconsciously, or in a habituated way, to be effective and be where we want to be.

The five mindsets aligning with the five stages of change:

"Dissatisfaction" or "Confusion" The mindset with stage 1 of change	"Exploration" The mindset with stage 2 of change	"Take Action" The mindset with stage 3 of change	"Determination" The mindset with stage 4 of change	"Self-actualization" The mindset with Stage 5 of change
• Dissatisfaction or confusion with current status and wanting to be somewhere better.	• Willingly explore ideas about where we would rather be and come to a definitive conclusion. • Willingly determine what needs to change and what will need to happen to get there	• The decision to take action to make a change • Deciding the action to be taken (This is what I am going to do to get where I want to be). • Beginning the actions to make the change	• Unconditional commitment to making the change and following the plan. (I am resolute and will do whatever I have to do to get to where I want to be).	• Achievement of the desired changes • Actions are habituated, so they do not need conscious effort.

The commitment levels of positive change:

Willing Compliance	Validation	Conversion	Internalized Commitment
• It is engaging in a search to find a better place and determine what it will entail to get us to where we would rather be. • It is willingly using the information, ideas, or direction we find that takes us from where we don't want to what we have to do to get to the better place.	• It is testing and authenticating the ideas we found and the conclusions we made as being correct.	• It is accepting our validated decisions as the right thing to do. • It is developing an action plan to implement our justified decisions. • It makes sure our plans, decisions, and actions take us where we want to go.	• We own our decisions and conclusions, so we naturally act in tune with our validated decisions. • It is being where we want to be and living in a way to stay there.

You will shortly see how as people progress through the stages of change, they are also changing their mindsets and moving into higher levels of commitment.

COMPETENCIES THAT SUPPORT SELF-DEVELOPMENT AND GROWTH DURING THE CHANGE PROCESS

Below is an overview of how the four levels of commitment align with the five mindsets and the five stages of change. Listed above the stages of change, shifting mindsets, and rising commitment levels are the competencies used to support each phase of <u>self-development and growth.</u>

Stage 1 Change Competencies	Stage 2 Change Competencies	Stage 3 Change Competencies	Stage 4 Change Competencies	Stage 5 Change Competencies
The ability to: • Operate in adult mode to make needed changes. • Be humble - the willingness to learn. • Do an honest "Check up from the neck up." • Accept the truth in what we find. • Use our feelings to motivate change. • Search for the truth about ourselves and make needed changes based on what we find.	The ability to: • Operate in adult mode • Gather and refine information and understand "why" things are the way they are to solicit and accept information from others. • Explore, find, and accept truthful information about ourselves. develop courses of action and to choose the best alternative.	The ability to: • Operate in adult mode. • Understand why change is necessary & beneficial. • Decide to take action for change and growth. • Plan a course of action that will get the desired results. • Anticipate obstacles and figure out how to resolve them.	The ability to: • Operate in adult mode. • Refine information into actionable knowledge. • Align decisions and actions with the decided. course of action • Work through the challenges associated with personal change and growth.	The ability to: • Operate in adult mode. • Live the values and beliefs that are the basis of where we want to be. • Believe that the effort is worth the price to get where we want to be. • fight to stay where we want to be. • Internalize our commitment to be who we want to be.
Unaware and ineffective	Aware and effective	Decision, planning and execution	Aware and effective	Unconsciously Effective
Dissatisfaction	Exploration	Action	Determination	Self-actualization
Willing Compliance	Validation		Conversion	Internalized Commitment

Notice that the levels of commitment overlap and extend into more than one phase of the stages of change and changing mindsets. The boxes are not intended to align but to show that each level of commitment is included in more than one phase of the change stage or mindset.

COMPETENCIES WE USE TO HELP OTHERS GROW AND DEVELOP DURING THE CHANGE PROCESS

Below is a chart with the same change phases and processes as listed above but the competencies are directed toward <u>helping others grow and develop</u>.

Stage 1 Change Competencies	Stage 2 Change Competencies	Stage 3 Change Competencies	Stage 4 Change Competencies	Stage 5 Change Competencies
The ability to:	The ability to:	The ability to:	The ability to:	The ability to:
• Listen, hear, understand. and validate the messages coming from people who need help to change and grow. • Accept their reality without judgment. • Peel their onion to get to the core issues where they are vulnerable and emotionally naked, • Avoid problem-solving until the core issues are revealed and they are ready for help and ask for it.	• Hook the adult mode of the person being helped. • Empathize with them so that they trust us and feel secure enough to explore where they are and why. • Enable them to see reality and to accept the truth (without feeling judged). • Help them accept responsibility for the part they played in being where they are. • Help them envision where they would like to be • Help them realize that they can get what they envision. • Initiate action.	• Help them to decide what to do in adult mode. • Coach the change process using the REACH process (or something similar). REACH stands for: • Desired RESULTS. • EVALUATION of where they are and why. • Identifying the ALTERNATIVES for getting where they want to be. • CHOOSING the best alternative/s. • Developing a plan of HOW to get there(REACH is detailed in the next section on problem-solving	• Help them execute their plan in adult mode. • Help them stay motivated and implement their plan. • Utilize the correct problem-solving approach as problems arise. • Follow-up and track progress. • Reinforce, recognize, and reward forward progress. • Give adult-based feedback when needed.	• Support them in adult mode • Stay connected and supportive as long as needed. • Let go when they no longer need us.
Unware and ineffective	Aware and ineffective	Decision, planning and execution	Aware and effective	Unconsciously Effective
Dissatisfaction	Exploration	Action	Determination	Self-actualization
Willing Compilance	Validation		Conversion	Internalized Commitment

The importance of "Why" in the growth process

We have demonstrated the competencies used to help ourselves, or others, go through a needed growth process. We included many kinds of competencies illustrating, to some limited degree, the complexity and benefits of human change and growth. But if we wanted to get to the heart skill for moving up the levels of commitment to internalized commitment, it would be the skills associated with "why." If people understand the why of something and agree with it, they will support it. In other words, if we could boil the competencies associated with attaining high levels of commitment down to one competency, it would be the ability to explain **why** so well that others would understand **why**. Understanding **why** is necessary if we want people to get to an internalized level of commitment.

If we only care about others being obedient, then **what, how,** and **when** would be the magic words. Of course, then we wouldn't care if they understood why; we only want them to do what we want them to do, and if they don't know why to do it, we don't care. ("Just do what I tell you to do, how I tell you to do it, and when I tell you to do it!") As you can see, the **what-how-when** approach is a Command and Control method, whereas **why** is a supportive and influential one.

Most people want to know why they are doing something; if they understand why, they see the bigger picture and how everything fits together. It gives them a sense of completeness, wholeness, purposefulness, and personal mastery. The process to understand **why** hooks the adult mode and engages the frontal cortex. It makes understanding what, how, and when a logical mental process and justifies the willingness to do what is understood. When people understand why and justify it, they become partners with us and commit to getting it done. When they understand and commit to what, how, when, and why, they combine their thought process with ours. We become partners and advocates. As partners and advocates, we better accomplish the what, why, and how. And the great part is that they will do it because they want to, not because we want them to.

'Why people'" can be annoying to people who don't want to take the time to explain why. My youngest brother, Moge (Morgan), is a brilliant guy who always wants to understand the why of everything. As a boy in grade school, his teachers limited the number of questions he could ask in class. He just didn't want to know what, how, and when; he also wanted to know why. It is central to who he is and how he learns. In college, he studied to be an engineer but became a chiropractor. His unrelenting questions became a source of friction between himself and the professor in one of his engineering classes. Eventually, they met together and understood how the professor wanted to teach and what Morgan needed to understand. They ultimately agreed that Moge would write down all of his questions and that he and the professor would meet after class, where the professor would provide him all the whys he so badly needed. My son, Matt, and I share the same need to know why. Maybe that is a big part of why we enjoy working together and learning from one another.

People in charge can get desired results in basically two ways, looking at it from a level of commitment perspective. The first way is to direct people to get the desired result. The second way is to teach people why, what, how, and when. In the first instance, they aim for obedience. People who aim at obedience expect their people to perform like programmed robots, to do everything as programmed to do. If they don't, the programmer figures that people need reprogramming until they follow directions perfectly. These programmers believe that people who aren't programable aren't the right people.

Leaders who use the **why** approach to leadership aim for internalized commitment to ensure that their people understand what, how, when, and why. They want people to own and know what they are doing and why they are doing it.

Volleyball coaching provides us with excellent examples of both approaches to coaching. The strict coaches are what, how, and when programmers. They try to program their players to execute every part of volleyball as a well-programmed robot. They don't take the time to explain why; they just want players to do what they direct them to do.

Some programmer coaches get good results (with novice players), but it is not a very satisfying experience. Despite the coaches' preferred approach for robot coaching, players, needing to understand, usually find other ways to know why they are supposed to do the programmed behavior. We see them talking amongst themselves, discussing the whys. If we watch closely, we can see when cognition occurs. We see their eyes light up when they come to an understanding, and we can see internalized commitment flow into them. Frequently, we see the players asking other coaches why. These player-centered coaches help players to understand the whys and, in doing so, help players become less dependent upon their coach.

There is so much to learn about volleyball, like the fundamental technical skills of serving, passing, setting, blocking, and hitting, not to mention the tactical skills related to offensive and defensive positioning. Volleyball has demanding physical and mental aspects to play the game well. It isn't easy to fathom how overwhelming it is to become a good volleyball player. Robots wouldn't play at the highest levels; it takes intelligence and reasoning to play expertly. When we realize how much learning is needed, we can imagine how difficult it is to learn all those things without explaining why – knowing why connects all the parts and makes them understandable. When we can see how all the pieces fit together, we can use our understanding for self-improvement and explain to the coach how to better help us. Command and Control coaches knowingly or unknowingly create dependency relationships between themselves and their players. Maybe that is part of the reason they use that approach; it certainly does a lot for their ego; "I am the most important person on the team; they can't function without me!" Maybe that partly explains the scarcity of top volleyball programs among those that rely on the what, how, and when coaching.

"Why" coaches are just a joy to watch and be with. They develop synergistic relationships with their players because they focus on making sure that players understand all parts of volleyball. They want their players to program themselves rather than to program them. They realize that, as a coach, they have far more knowledge and experience with volleyball than the players. But they want their players to come to the highest possible understanding of volleyball and how to play it well. They want players to understand the why of every part of volleyball. That includes what to do, how to do it, and when to do it. They realize that a considerable part of their coaching job is to develop players who are not dependent upon them to know what, how, and when to do something. That level of player independence comes as players understand why they need to do those things.

How much players understand the game changes the role and interactions between the players and the coach. Influential coaches coach players according to their level of understanding of the game. Coaching then becomes individualized to the needs and knowledge of the players, as individuals, and as members of a team. It focuses on helping players understand what, how, and when they are doing something to understand better why what they are doing is effective or ineffective. "Why" coaches empower players, enabling them to coach themselves to expedite and optimize their self-development. To the degree that players understand what, how, when, and why, they can internalize their commitment and optimize their potential to get where they want to be.

Some additional competencies to help others solve their problems

We have not included, but need to include, several competencies that people need to know and use to help other people solve their problems. There are three of them: First is learning the difference between **simple and complex problems** and applying the right skills to address them. The second is clearly understanding the **primary and secondary needs** of people needing help to solve their problems (Helpees) versus the primary and secondary needs of those trying to help them solve their problems (Helpers). And the third is **coaching,** a five-step process used to help people solve their problems.

We would have included **Peeling the Onion** as part of this problem-solving section except that we included it in the section on the Four Characteristics of Deep Listening, which was a sub-section of the Emotional State Competencies.

Simple versus Complex Problems

I was lost in NYC and saw a couple of NYPD officers standing on the corner. I went up to them and asked for directions. One officer turned his back on me. The other officer looked at me and said, "Do I look like a map to you?" I was stunned. It was one of those moments where I didn't have the perfect response. I responded, "Oh… sorry…" and walked off sheepishly. If I had been on my game, I would have responded, "No, you don't look like a map, but you do look like an arrogant bugger." Probably good I didn't notice how the simple problem turned into a complex one. They definitely left an impression about New York City's finest.

All problems are not the same; some are simple, and others are complex. The approaches we use to deal with them should match the type of problem we face. This area will help people understand the differences so they can use the correct problem-solving approach.

A model showing the difference between Simple and Complex Problems

Simple Problem	Complex Problem
A simple unfulfilled need or issue without emotions	An unfulfilled need (context) combined with feelings or emotions
How to deal with each	
Provide a simple answer to the unfulfilled need or issue	Turn the complex problem into a simple problem by: • Dealing with the emotions first by validating and empathizing with the emotions being emoted • Once the emotions are validated and deflated then provide the simple answer to the unfulfilled need or issue
Examples	
Simple Problem owner: "Can you tell me where I can find the 3 hole punch?" Helper: "Sure, it is in the supply room equipment cabinet."	Complex Problem owner: "I am ready to burn this store down, this is the third time I have had to come into this junk hole to get a correct part! And, when I get here, I have to stand in line waiting for all the other people to get their messed-up problems fixed! I can't stand this!" Helper: "I see that you are really frustrated about not getting the right part the first time and for having to come back repeatedly for the same part. I am sorry for the errors and for the inconvenience that it has caused you. Shall we make sure that we get you the right part this time?" Complex Problem owner: "I hope so." But I doubt that this store can do anything right!" Helper: "I can see that you are still upset and are doubtful that we can get you the right part?" Problem Owner: "I guess I am, sorry for being a jerk with you." Helper: "You were just releasing your pent-up feelings. Shall we go get the right part and double-check that it is the right one?" Problem Owner: "I would really appreciate that and thank you for being so helpful." Helper: "And thank you for giving us one more chance to serve you, better."

We classify problems into two categories: simple and complex. **Simple problems are merely unfulfilled needs requiring simple solutions**. For example, if a person wants to know where the paper stapler is, that is a simple problem. He just needs to be told where to find the paper stapler to solve the problem. It is simple because there are no emotions involved.

On the other hand, if he were to ask, "Where in the heck did you hide the damn paper stapler, you idiot?" that would be a complex problem because strong emotions are involved. With complex problems, two issues need attention: the unfulfilled need and the feelings associated with the unfulfilled need. In short, **complex problems always have two parts; unfulfilled needs and strong emotions**. Simply telling a person with a complex problem where he could find the paper stapler would answer the location of the paper stapler, but it wouldn't resolve the emotional issue. To solve complex problems, we must deal with emotions and unfulfilled needs. And we must address the emotions before addressing the unfulfilled needs.

Effective problem-solving is about responding appropriately to the problem messages sent to us. With simple problems, the appropriate response is to provide an accurate answer. It is easy and effective to tell the person looking for a paper stapler where to find it. "It is in the top drawer in the upper left-hand corner of the desk." We meet the unfulfilled need and solve the problem. Simple solutions provide a straightforward solution to the unfulfilled need, nothing more, nothing less. The vast majority of problems we face every day don't seem like problems at all; they are just questions and answers that get asked and answered routinely. But if we fail to answer the questions or answer correctly, the simple problem transforms into a complex problem. This transformation happens because failure to satisfy *unfilled needs provokes emotions*.

Responding appropriately to complex problems requires addressing the emotion first and effectively. How do we address feelings correctly? By hearing, understanding, and accurately validating the emotional message sent. We validate emotions when we correctly label them. If we mislabel the emotional message sent to us, the sender will correct us. If we get it right, we validate them, and we can move on to the next stage of problem-solving-answering the unfulfilled need. When we empathize correctly (remember empathy does not mean agreement, rather it demonstrates understanding), it allows us to deal with the emotional part of the problem. After resolving the emotional aspect of the complex problem, we can resolve the unfulfilled need. When we validate the emotional message, we turn a complex problem into a simple problem. Once it is a simple problem, we can address it like any other simple problem – fulfill the unfulfilled need.

I witnessed Leticia, a sales clerk at Lowes, resolve a complex problem with an irate customer. When the customer came into the store, Leticia was working in the customer return department. There was only one customer in the line in front of him, whose simple problem took a few minutes to solve. As the angry customer waited, he uttered loud comments, which Leticia heard. When he stepped up to the counter, he loudly cursed the store, stating that he regretted ever having bought anything from this "second-rate loser outfit." He had a few more negative things to say before his emotions declined and ceased for a moment; this pause gave Leticia a chance to validate his emotional message.

Their dialogue went something like this:

Leticia: "Wow, I can see that you are really angry."
Customer: "Oh, you can!?"
Leticia: "Yes, I can."
Customer: "I am pissed because I bought a junk lawnmower here, and it stopped working. I have no way to mow my lawn now, and I am not going to pay some kid $50 to mow it!"
Leticia: "So you are upset because you bought a mower from us that stopped working, and now you don't have a way to take care of your lawn. That is creating real issues and is causing stress for you?"
Customer: "I don't have time to keep messing with this ****!"
Leticia: "So this is inconveniencing you a lot, which adds to your frustration?"
Customer: "I bought a top-of-the-line mower from you people, and it is a piece of junk!"
Leticia: "So you were expecting a super mower, and it didn't turn out that way. So, you feel cheated?"

Customer: "Yeah, I'm sorry for yelling and being miserable. I am just so irritated. Can you help me?"

Leticia: "I'm sure I can. What would you like to happen?"

Customer: "I just want a new mower that works, so I don't have to come in here again."

Leticia: "I can help you do that. I see that a warranty covers the mower you bought. Do you want the same model or a different one to replace the one that stopped working?"

Customer: "I definitely want a different model."

Leticia: "Great, let's fill out the return paperwork; then we will have a sales clerk in that area help you get what you want."

Customer: "Hey, thanks, you have been so helpful. What is your name?"

Notice that Leticia didn't take his yelling personally, and she just kept validating his emotions until he felt understood. As soon as he felt completely understood, the emotional issues disappeared, and he was ready to resolve his mower problem. After validating his emotions, she was able to hook his adult mode and solve the simple problem. She would not have been successful if she had tried to solve the unfulfilled need before dealing with the emotions because he was not ready for a simple solution. The solution would have been the same, but they would probably never have gotten to the answer without a battle if Letitia hadn't effectively addressed his emotions first. By the way, Leticia was so good at dealing with difficult customers that they made her the "go-to person" for pain-in-the-butt customers.

Understand that people with complex problems don't necessarily stay at the same level of emotion; they can get even more emotional if we don't recognize and validate their feelings. We can turn complex problems into more complex problems if we don't take the time to validate their current emotions. I know that many companies teach their customer service people to try and resolve emotional customer issues first before offering a simple solution. The trouble is that most teach their people to deflate emotions by saying something trite like: "I understand" or "I understand that you are frustrated." Then they try to move on to provide a simple solution. It seldom works as they hope because customers know they don't understand; it is simply a tactic to fast-track the problem-solving process. There is no way to fast-track understanding someone's emotions; you need to hear, understand, and validate each emotional message until they feel understood. Until they confirm emotional messages, they have not understood and can't effectively solve the simple problem until validating the emotional part of the complex ones.

Dr. Bob Carkhuff taught us at the University of Toronto to never say "I understand" as a way to validate emotions. He explained that if we say we understand, people will believe we understand until we later demonstrate that we don't understand. As soon as they realize that we didn't understand them, they will feel lied to, and trust will disappear. He taught us that rather than saying, "I understand," validate what you think you understand with the person. If you are correct, they will be validated and know that you understand. If you are incorrect, they will correct you until you get it right. Dr. Bob taught us that saying, "I understand," is a garbage statement.

I recently experienced the "I understand" tactic when I went to a Verizon store to resolve a multi-occurring monthly payment problem. I had been dealing with the payment issue for five months. Every month I was assured that they had fixed the billing error and no further problems would happen. They did not fix it, and it happened again every month. I started going to the local store to have one of their technicians enter the information to ensure the payment was correct. On the fourth visit, I met with the store manager and explained my frustration and problem. After my first sentence, he replied, "I understand. How can we fix the problem?" I knew that he didn't understand my emotions or my unresolved problem. So instead of letting him move on to solving the simple problem that his people had previously not solved, I ask him, "What do you understand." He looked a little taken back and said, "I understand that you have a problem with your phone and that you are frustrated." I took it further by asking, "What level of frustration am I feeling, and what is my phone problem?" He said, "I don't know." I said, "If you don't understand then, please don't tell me that you do; that only irritates me more." I then requested that he try and understand my emotions before he attempted to solve the telephone issue. We had a ten-minute conversation about teaching his staff to validate customers' emotions before solving a simple problem. He said that everyone who deals with customers at Verizon should get this message. I agree.

While talking about customer service, I want to share my second most significant issue, which constitutes poor customer service. When I bring my problem to the attention of a person who is supposed to help me, the first thing they do is make an excuse or say that it is not their fault. That bugs me because I don't want an excuse, nor do I want to know that it is not their fault. I want a simple solution to my problem. Giving me an excuse or telling me that it is not their fault turns a simple problem into a complex one. I try not to let it hook my parent mode or child mode, but I am not always successful. When my adult mode or child mode is hooked, I behave in ways that hook their parent mode or child mode, becoming an adversarial confrontation. I admit, I know better and shouldn't let that happen. The trouble is that I am competitive and want to win when someone avoids helping me or dodges responsibility for an issue they should own and fix. (Can you see how I just justified a behavioral addiction?)

We frequently turn simple problems into complex ones when we over-analyze simple requests for a solution to a simple problem. For example, it would probably drive us crazy if someone came to us and asked us where our pet Fido is, and we respond by saying, "Tell me why you want to know where Fido is because if I understand your motive, then I can better help you." With simple questions or problems, provide straightforward answers or solutions. When we do more than that, we risk adding emotions to an unfulfilled need (to know where Fido is) where previously no feelings existed. We just created a complex problem. There are many ways to add emotions to simple problems, like giving advice, criticizing, judging, giving unsolicited advice, or condescending problem-solving.

But why do people give complex answers to simple questions? Not sure I know all of the why's, but the following may offer some reasons for it:

1. They want to demonstrate their affection for the person they care about and love.
2. A simple answer doesn't satisfy deep unfulfilled needs to feel helpful and important.
3. They are projecting their own experiences to the person they are trying to help.
4. They view life as having no simple problems.
5. They need to feel validated as being intelligent, thoughtful, and wise.
6. They need to reaffirm their position as one of importance, power, and control.

Notice that all these reasons focus on oneself rather than the person they are trying to help.

When your children come to you with a complex problem and are emotional, don't say, "I understand," and then try to offer a solution. Take the time to hear, understand, and validate their emotions until they feel understood. Doing so will show your love and concern, creating a loving connection between you. When they feel understood, then you can discuss ways to make their problem seem more manageable and less severe than they thought it was when they first came to you.

The bottom line is that we become much more effective problem solvers when we reduce complex problems to become simple problems by first validating the emotional part.

Primary and Secondary Needs of "Helpees" and Helpers" in the problem-solving process

Most of us in America are "premature problem solvers." That means we try to solve problems before the conditions are right. This problem relates to complex problems because it is appropriate to solve simple problems with a quick and easy solution. When an issue includes emotions, it is a complex problem, and we shouldn't attempt to problem-solve until we have validated the emotions. Remember, emotions are the first thing that needs addressing with complex problems. The desire to try and solve problems is part of being a caring, helpful person.

Men are driven to problem-solve because we are hunters and warriors. We are always on the lookout for a lurking problem that we can stalk, stab and eliminate. We take problems personally, especially the concerns of people we care about and love. As many women know, when they bring up an issue, from work or about anything causing them discomfort, their significant other tunes right in and starts trying to problem-solve. They give women unsolicited advice and recommendations about solving their problem (or volunteer to handle the situation themselves). The women cry that they don't want help to fix the problem; they just want to be listened to and heard. This elicits a little defensiveness in her man, who responds with something like, "I was just trying to help you." He then dejectedly steps out of the helping process. Thousands upon thousands of such conversations take place every day.

Ladies, it is not just a male predilection to problem solve prematurely. I have found that women are premature problem solvers as well. They are different than men in that before women start to problem solve, they listen, hear, and validate until they can personally relate to the feelings or circumstances that the other person is sharing with them. As soon as they can personally relate to the issue, they become like men, offering insight, suggestions, and advice about what they should do. At least in the case of women problem solvers, the person advised has received a little bit of empathy before problem-solving starts.

So why do most of us tend to be premature problem solvers? Is it a bad thing to help solve people's problems? The first question is easy to answer: We problem solve because we have an internal urge to help people; we need to problem-solve. It is in our nature to do so. The answer to the second question is also easy, but with an added qualifier. No, it is a beautiful thing to try and help people solve their problems. The qualifier is: Providing we help them. We should get an A grade for our intentions, but most fail to provide authentic, substantial, and lasting help fixing other people's problems, especially when the issues are complex.

People don't solve complex problems as effectively as they think. When a complex problem continues, it is good evidence that the Helper didn't solve it. If we are solving problems and the person we are helping is still trying to be heard, understood, and validated, we are out of sync with her needs, and we won't be effective, even if we have a great solution. To become someone who can help others problem solve, we need to know two things:

First, we need to know the primary and secondary needs of "Helpees" (the person needing a problem solved) and "Helpers" (the person wanting to aid the Helpee). The primary and secondary needs are different between Helpers and Helpees. But they can be aligned with one another by aligning our needs with their needs. If we match our needs to their needs, our actions will fill both our needs.

Second, we need to learn how to coach people to understand their problems and know how to resolve them. Of course, we can always inherit their problems, which will lift the burden from their shoulders, but now we have them on our shoulders. It is still a problem needing resolution. To help people, we need to be the person who helps people deal with their issues. We help them deal with their issues as a problem-solving coach rather than an advice-giver. Ultimately, the best and most effective problem-solving happens when people resolve their issues.

The model below illustrates the primary and secondary needs of helpees and helpers. Please keep in mind that problem solving requires that we align the primary and secondary needs of Helpees and Helpers.

	Helpee	Helper
Primary need	To be heard, understood, and validated	To solve the problem, fix it, make it go away
Secondary need	To be helped	To be appreciated for solving the problem and helping

In the model above, note that the primary needs of Helpees and Helpers don't match up with one another. That misalignment can cause problems when a Helper is trying to solve the Helpee's problems.

While living in Chicago, an elderly lady missionary came to visit me for personal counseling. (I was the bishop of the church unit that she and her husband attended.) She and her husband had been married for well over 60 years. He was a retired university professor, and she was a homemaker. She said she loved her husband, but she didn't like him much. He was so controlling and dominant that she just couldn't stand it anymore. She felt that he was constantly telling her what to do and giving advice not asked for. She told me that she would leave him if she were 30 years younger. She poured her heart out. Eventually, when she felt heard, understood, and validated, she asked me what she should do. I politely asked if she ever had a similar discussion with her husband that she had with me. She said she had told him to, "Just shut up!" or made similar remarks occasionally. She confessed that usually, she just sat and stewed. I explained that before I could try to help, I needed to meet with her husband. That concerned her. I promised that I would keep our conversation private, other than to tell him that she had come to visit me. She consented.

When I met with the professor, I expected a brash, forceful, and controlling General Patton. I was surprised when the fellow that showed up was soft-spoken and almost shy. He appeared to be just the opposite of the picture she had painted of him. After visiting with him for a couple of hours, I could not see a dominant bone in his body or any controlling aspect in his personality. I liked the guy; he seemed humble, kind, and caring.

I met with his wife again and explained my conundrum to her. At this point, I suggested that all three of us meet together. I promised that I would help her clarify her issues with her husband. When we met a couple of days later, I asked her to explain to her husband the purpose of her visit with me. She had not said fifty words until her husband jumped in and attempted to interpret her message and offer helpful advice. I requested that he let her talk and explain her issues. Shortly after she started to describe her feelings, he again interrupted with advice that he felt would solve the problem. She exploded and said, "Do you see what I mean?! I can't get in a word without him taking control and trying to fix me!" I asked if this was the type of behavior driving her crazy, and she confirmed it. He looked concerned and explained that he loved his wife and was just trying to help.

As you can see, he was not trying to be controlling or hurtful; he was just trying to help the woman he loved by offering solutions. I might add premature solutions. His wife's primary need was to be heard, understood, and validated. His primary need was to solve problems – her problems. Their primary needs did not align, and he was operating from his primary need, not hers. Their misaligned needs meant that no one's needs were being satisfied. It never dawned on him that his actions should align with his wife's needs and that he could defer fulfilling his primary need until he met her primary need.

We talked about how both of their primary and secondary needs were misaligned. The professor consistently tried to solve his wife's problems instead of hearing, listening and validating her expressed messages. I helped him see that he consistently focused on her secondary need "to be helped," which he couldn't accomplish until he met her primary need of being heard, understood, and validated. I explained why he would never be appreciated, by her, for his help because he was irritating her rather than helping her. I further explained that he could be helpful if he satisfied her primary need and waited for her to ask for his help. I cautioned him that there is a likelihood that she never would ask and that he should learn that he is supporting his wife and showing love by just validating her messages. Before the evening ended, they both had a better understanding of what was happening. They understood that he was creating them by trying to solve her problems. We agreed that he needed to stop problem-solving and start hearing, understanding, and validating where she was coming from and refrain from problem-solving until she asked for his help. I provided some communication sessions with them, which cooled the flames until they had a better foundation in interpersonal connections and communications.

They both audited my relationship class at the graduate school and told me that it changed their lives. They expressed frustration that they had lived for nearly 90 years without ever being taught these simple concepts, principles, and skills. They said that one of their great desires was for their kids, grandkids, and great-grandkids to be exposed to these teachings soon. That summer, they flew me to Denver for their family reunion to share some of their newly found discoveries with their posterity. It was a little disconcerting to see their children in their 60s and 70s. Their grandkids were in their 30s and 40s, and their great-grandchildren were babes in arms or grade-schoolers.

As you can see, the professors' good intentions to help his wife were driving her nuts, to the point that she started seeing him as the personification of a controlling and uncaring husband. He loved her deeply and tried to show his love by helping her. She had a tremendous unfulfilled need to be heard, understood, and validated, especially by him. That was her primary unfulfilled need. She didn't want him to solve her problems; she wanted him to listen to her, understand her, and validate what she was feeling and saying. He was her problem. His primary need was to fix her problems and satisfy all her needs, expressed and unexpressed, but in doing so, he focused on his own needs and not her needs. The disconnection happened because of a misalignment between his primary need to fix the problem (or prevent one) and her primary need to be heard, understood, and validated.

It took a while, but when both of them understood what was happening, things got better because they knew why it was happening and its consequences. With understanding came a level of forgiveness from the wife and a sense of guilt from him, where he felt a great need to explain and an even greater need to justify his previous attempts to show his love by "helping" her. We spent a good deal of time helping her learn how to give feedback appropriately and helping him learn how to listen better, hear, understand, and validate her messages. They audited the whole 15 weeks of my relationships graduate class and were an excellent addition to the group; they added unique insights and experiences that the students, over 50 years younger than they, could never have imagined. I noticed that she no longer tolerated his attempts to speak for her, interpret what she was saying, or problem-solve for her. She even became an excellent coach at helping him hear, understand, and validate her messages. He almost reached 100 years of age, and she made it past that extraordinary milestone.

Below is an expanded model that illustrates how to align actions with the needs of helpers and helpees.

	Helpee	Helper
Align the actions of the helper with the primary needs of the helpee	Helpee's primary need is to be heard, understood, and validated.	Aligned helper action would be to hear, understand, validate the helpee's message.
The primary need of the helper satisfies the Secondary need of the helpee	The secondary need of the helpee is to be helped after the helpee's first need is satisfied	The primary need of the helper to solve the problem has to be delayed until the primary need of the helpee is met.
The secondary need of the helper is satisfied when the helpee expresses appreciation to the helper	The helpee thanks the helper for helping her to solve her problem which satisfies the secondary need of the helper.	The helpers secondary need to be appreciated for solving the problem is satisfied when the helpee shows appreciation for the helpers help.

Helpers need to stay focused on hearing, understanding, and validating the messages sent by the person they want to help. They need to stay focused on the Helpee's primary needs until they are satisfied. That may take a while, especially if they have a lot of emotional layers that need to be validated. Once all the emotional messages are validated, the Helpee will ask for help if it is wanted. Frequently the Helpee just wants to be heard, understood, and validated and never wants to be helped or have their problems solved for them. As a result, the Helper's primary need to solve the problem or to fix it may never get satisfied through their direct actions. Usually, the Helpee themselves will address the issues, and the Helper could take satisfaction in making that happen. Fortunately, the Helper's secondary need to be appreciated will be satisfied by the person who will undoubtedly appreciate their attentiveness to hearing, understanding, and validating their messages.

If you require a refresher on hearing, understanding, and validating messages, go back to the section on Peeling the Onion.

Coaching

After we have successfully peeled a person's onion, they will be in a place where they will trust us and would likely follow any advice, we would offer them. But giving advice is not the best alternative to help them because then the solution would have come from us, and they would be dependent upon us. Even if we have the right solutions, our solutions aren't the best option to solve their problems. Providing our solutions is not providing them with a long-term skill set for self-reliant problem-solving. They need to be in charge, own their problems, and take responsibility for solving them. That is the only way to become strong and independent, and to solve their problems. In short, it is not good for them to comply with our suggestions to solve their problems.

When we find ourselves in a place where people want our help to solve their problems, we enter the realm of problem-solving. In this book, we are not getting deeply into the general science, approaches, and methodologies for problem-solving. That is a vast and fascinating subject, as broad as there are different kinds of problems or areas of specialized technical knowledge. Nevertheless, we will address how we can help people help themselves to solve their problems through a specific coaching process.

People must own their problems and take responsibility for resolving them. When we inherit their problems or take responsibility for solving them, they become our problems. The person from whom we inherited them learns little about solving their problems except how to unload them onto others or seek us out to take responsibility for solving them constantly. We have done little to help them if they remain dependent on us or others to solve or deal with their unfulfilled needs. Coaching is a way to help them own their problems, understand why they have them, know how they contribute to their problems, and discover alternative ways to resolve their issues. The R.E.A.C.H. coaching model is a realistic, step-by-step way to find and execute solutions to their problems.

Our R.E.A.C.H. coaching concept and process help others help themselves. The acronym stands for Results, Evaluation, Alternatives,

Choose, and How. It is a five-step coaching process that is simple to learn and use. Coaches can apply it to modest problems and complicated ones. The first thing about learning the R.E.A.C.H. coaching process is understanding the meaning behind each acronym letter and word.

- The letter **R** and **Results** stand for determining the **desired results** that the person coached wants to achieve. It signifies a description of where they want to be at the end of the process.
- The letter **E** and **Evaluate** stand for the **evaluation process** that explains the Helpee's status and why. It includes them taking responsibility for the part they contributed to the problem.
- The letter **A** and **Alternatives** signifies the process of identifying the **available alternatives** for resolving the problem and getting to where they want to end up.
- The letter **C** and **Choose** signifies the process of **choosing the best alternative**, or a combination of other options, that would get them to where they want to end up.
- The letter **H** and **How** signifies the process for deciding **how they will plan and execute their choice** for getting to where they want to end up. It is a step-by-step process.

It is important to understand, upfront, that we do effective coaching by skillful questioning to help the Coachee make discoveries (and come to conclusions) rather than by teaching or telling people the answers.

The first step in the coaching process focuses on defining the desired outcome or **results**.

Results: Determine the desired outcome or where they want to be at the end of the process

Coaching Tips
- Ask questions such as:
  - "Could you describe what your most desirable outcome would look like?"
  - "What are the results you want to achieve?"
  - "How will you define success?"

- Be prepared to hear, understand, and validate.
- Establish outcomes that meet the SMART criteria before pro-ceeding to the second component in the coaching process.

The First Coaching Process Step	The Coach's Job
Determine precisely the Results the helpee wants to achieve.	Assist the helpee in clarifying the desired outcome to meet the SMART criteria for well-defined objectives$?. The SMART outcome would cover all these elements: Specific-clear, detailed results Measurable- quantifiable or observable Achievable- possible to achieve Rewarding - fulfilling, meriting self-recognition Timed reasonably - achievable time schedule to achieve results

In the first step of the coaching process, realize that people often state their fantasy objective. For example: "I want to become a million-aire by playing in a famous rock band." We have to get past this to a SMART objective. We can usually get past this and to a realistic goal by asking questions, such as:

"Do you think that this is a realistic goal to plan for at this time?"

"Would you agree that it is better to focus on something that we can make happen within the next six months?"

When they come up with the desired Result, check it against the SMART criteria.

"Do you feel that this objective is clear and specific enough for you to know if you are heading there?"

"Have you included how you will measure your progress?"

"Is this achievable? If so, how will you know it is?"

"How will you feel when you achieve this goal?"

Or "How will you reward or recognize yourself for achieving it?"

"How long will it take you to get there? Have you included your time frame in the objective?"

The following is an example of the coaching process done with a teen-age female volleyball player named Lily. I will share examples as we go through each stage of the coaching process. She wasn't currently playing on my team but came to me because she previously played on one of my teams, and we had developed a great relationship. She came to me for advice. I peeled her onion for a little over an hour and got to the core, where she revealed that she felt like a volleyball failure and was thinking about quitting the sport. She tearfully expressed that she loved volleyball and was disappointed that she was not excelling as much as she had hoped. She did tell me that she wanted to continue playing volleyball. I'll begin sharing our coaching experience from this point.

Result: Determining the desired outcome

Me: "Lily, we now know that you want to keep playing volleyball, but I'd appreciate knowing more specifically what your volleyball goals are, the level at which you want to be playing, and how you will know when you have gotten there."

Lily: "First, I want to be a starter who plays all the rotations."

Me: "OK, now I know you want to stay on the court. But stay on the court with what team and at what level?"

Lily: "I want to play at an elite level which means that I am good enough to play on a Division I college team. And I want to be a varsity starter on my high school volleyball team."

Me: "That's the kind of information that I am looking for. You are a sophomore now. When do you want to be a starter on your high school varsity team?"

Lily: "Next year, my junior year."

Me: "And how close are you now to being able to be a starter on your varsity team?"

Lily: "Not very close."

Me: "How will you know when you are qualified?"

Lily: "When I start practicing with the varsity girls. And when the coach gives me a varsity jersey."

Me: "That will tell you that you will be a starter?"

Lily: "No, but it opens the door to prove myself and shows that I should be a starter."

Me: "Yeah, OK. What team were you playing on at your high school this year?"

Lily: "The sophomore team, but sometimes I played in the Junior Varsity matches."

Me: "How well did you play in the JV matches?"

Lily: "I played OK."

Me: "Based on your high school play thus far, do you think it is reasonable to become a starting varsity player next year?"

Lily: "It may seem crazy, but I think that I have the potential to be a varsity player right now. So, yes, I think it is reasonable to become a starting varsity player next year."

The second step in the coaching process focuses on **evaluating** why the situation exists.

Evaluate: Assist the Coachee in clarifying and understanding the current situation – what is happening, why, and accepting personal responsibility for their contribution to the situation.

Coachees must understand their part in the situation; otherwise, they tend to see themselves as victims with no control over their current situation and no ability to control their future. People in "Victim Mode" are likely to transfer responsibility for problem resolution to others and remain dependent on them to resolve the problem for them. Ironically, they come to believe that their unfortunate situation is someone else's responsibility to fix. (*"When is the government going to give me enough to live on properly?!"*) If the Coachee doesn't own the problem, they often get resentful, waiting for "somebody" to change the world to make them happy. In short, the person with the unfulfilled expectation (problem) must lead the way in getting the expectation met and not wait for, nor expect, others to solve it for them.

Worse still is when a Coachee expects you, as the Coach, to change others to meet their expectations. A wise tip for a coach is not to inherit the Coachee's problems but to help them resolve their problems.

Coaching Tips

Ask questions, such as:

"How would you describe what has been happening?"

"What have you tried to resolve the problem? What were the results?"

"What challenges have you experienced in this situation?"

"What is your role in this situation?"

"In what ways have you contributed to this?"

Ensure that the Coachee understands their contribution to the situation before progressing to the next step. Be sensitive not to offend, but you may need to be candid to get beyond this step. Consider asking questions such as:

"What changes will you need to make?"

"How are you going to behave differently, compared to the past, to change this situation?"

The Second Coaching Process Step	The Coach's Job
Evaluate current situation	Assist the helpee, in understanding why this situation exists and how they contribute or allow the problem to happen or continue. This step is essential because nothing that happens after this point is reality-based if they don't have a realistic understanding of their situation and the part they are contributing to making or allowing it to happen. Alternatives, choices, and action plans have to be reality-based to achieve the desired outcome they wish for or have described.

The following dialogue focuses on the second step of the R.E.A.C.H. coaching process: **Evaluation.**

Evaluation of reality clarifies where she is today and the part she contributes to making it that way.

Me: "To determine what needs to happen to make your desires come true, please summarize for me where you are and why you are here."

Lily: "I am currently not getting the playing time on my current club team that I need to improve. Maybe I should probably go to a different club team."

Me: "Before we talk about solutions, like going to a different team, let's figure out why you are not getting the playing time you feel you need. OK?"

Lily: "I don't think the coach likes me very much."

Me: "So you believe you are not playing more because of the coach? Really? If you were the coach, would you play you more?"

Lily: "Well, probably not."

Me: "Why is that?"

Lily: "Because I haven't played well. I make many passing and serving errors."

Me: "And why is that happening?"

Lily: "It's happening because I miss a lot of practices and don't focus enough on my volleyball skills."

Me: "Can you change the level and improve the skills of the volleyball you are playing?"

Lily: "I guess."

Me: "We agree then that what happens in volleyball depends on you?"

Lily: "Yeah, I guess so."

Me: "I don't want you to guess. Who controls your volleyball future and your volleyball opportunities?"

Lily: "I do."

The third step in the coaching process focuses on developing **alternatives** or possible solutions.

Alternatives: Identify the available options to achieve the desired outcome.

In this step, have the Coachee list all the alternatives they can think of to deal with their problem. It won't take long because they seldom have many solutions. If you feel that their options are not good enough or there aren't an adequate number of good alternatives from which to choose, then offer more by asking questions rather than by submitting your ideas. You might ask:

"Would you like any suggestions from me? (They always say "yes")

Then ask questions like:

"Have you thought about....?"

"Have you considered ....?"

"What would happen if....?"

"Imagine if...."

Coaching Tips

- Ask a question, such as: "If you could do anything to get the results you want, what would you do?"

- Remember not to throw out ideas. If you want the Coachee to consider other ideas, put them forth as questions so that they assess them and can accept them as their own.

The Third Coaching Process Step	Coach's Job
Develop a list of alternatives that will enable the person being coached to reach the desired outcome.	Assist the helpee in identifying alternatives to get them to their desired outcome and evaluating their usefulness to achieve desired results Use questions rather than opinions or personal judgments in evaluating alternatives. Remember, these need to be the helpee's alternatives, not yours. The helpee has to own them and be responsible for them.

Once the Coachee has a good list of viable alternatives, then move on to selecting the best alternative or combination of alternatives that will get them to where they want to be.

The following dialogue focuses on the third step of the R.E.A.C.H. coaching process: **Alternatives.**

Alternatives: Have Lily identify the available options to achieve her desired outcome.

Me: "You threw out an alternative to me early in our conversation. It was to switch to another team. Is that still an acceptable alternative for you?"

Lily: "I don't know."

Me: "Can you think of other alternatives to help you achieve your goals? Let's write them down."

Lily: "Well, I could get on Matt's or Reed's team and get the kind of coaching that would take me there."

Me: "You believe that Matt or Reed could be the magic coaches that would transform you to be a top player?"

Lily: "I think so."

Me: "Matt and Reed only coach girls your age who are already on track to be Division I college players. Do you think that you could play well enough right now to get on one of their teams? Be honest."

Lily: "Not really."

Me: "What other ways that you control could get you there?"

Lily: "I could come to all the practices and focus hard on improving my volleyball skills."

Me: "Good! What else?"

Lily: "Maybe I could come to extra practices with other teams."

Me: "Great! What else?"

Lily: "I can't think of anything else."

Me: "Would you like any suggestions from me?"

Lily: "Yes!"

Me: "What would you think about getting private lessons to help you specifically with your serving and passing skills?"

Lily: "I think that would be a good thing for me to do. Some of my friends who are on the varsity team take private lessons."

The fourth step of the R.E.A.C.H. coaching process focuses on selecting the best solution to achieve the desired result: **Choose.**

Choose: Have the Coachee select the best alternative, or combination of alternatives, to achieve their desired outcome.

Coaching Tips

- Eliminate obvious poor choices or fantasy alternatives.
- Evaluate the pros and cons of each alternative.
- Ensure that the alternatives support the desired outcome.
- Consider combinations of alternatives.
- Ask questions, such as: "Which alternative is most likely to help you achieve the results you want?"
- Assure that the Coachee chooses and commits to a viable way forward.

The Fourth Coaching Process Step	Coach's Job
Combination of alternative for achieving the desired outcome.	Assist the helpee in determining their best alternative for achieving the desired outcome.
	Have them justify why they believe it is the best alternative going forward. "Why do you believe this is the best alternative to achieve your desired outcome?"

The following narrative focuses on the fourth step of the R.E.A.C.H. coaching process: **Choose.**

Choose: Help Lily select the best alternative, or a combination of alternatives, to achieve her desired outcome.

Me: "When you look at all the options available to you, which one, or ones, seems the best to help you become a varsity starter next year and to prepare you to play Division I volleyball?"

Lily: "I want to come to all the practices and participate in extra practices with other teams. I also want to start taking private lessons with coach Diana to help with my passing and serving skills."

Me: "Anything missing?"

Lily: "I can't think of anything else."

Me: "Imagine for a minute what you could do during your regular practices to help you achieve your goals."

Lily: "I need to come to all the practices and really focus and work hard to improve."

Me: "I like that! Anything else you can do to make your coach want to help you more?"

Lily: "I guess I should meet with my coach and tell him that I am sorry for not working hard and not coming to all his practices and ask him to help me become a better volleyball player."

Me: "He will appreciate that! I am impressed with your choices and your attitude to do these things. Do you think doing these things will enable you to get where you want to be?"

Lily: "I do!"

Me: "It is up to you to make it happen. Are you ready to implement your choices?"

Lily: "I am ready. How do I start?"

The fifth step in the R. E. A. C. H. coaching process is laying out **how** to implement the solutions.

How:

- **Establish a plan to implement the chosen alternative.**
- **Anticipate potential obstacles and identify ways to address them.**
- **Envision what life will be like when the desired outcome happens.**

Assist the Coachee in implementing and executing the choices made thus far. The hardest part for many Coachees is knowing where to start. They often need help determining how to begin the process to achieve the desired outcome once they make the best choice. Once they lay out the first step, it becomes easier to execute the rest. Implementation planning defines the planned sequential stages step-by-step until a complete path to the desired outcome is clear. Successful execution then becomes following the plan.

The motivation to implement the plan unfolds by envisioning what life and feelings will be like once the plan is executed successfully. The coach's job is to walk the Coachee through the steps and to help them start implementing the plan. Great coaches continue to provide support until they reach the desired outcome. Then the Coachee will decide if the coach will remain a part of her life. Don't feel bad if she doesn't; it shows that she has moved on and is no longer dependent.

Coaching Tips

- Assist the Coachee in developing a step-by-step action plan for implementing the chosen alternative. Start with the first step before trying to define all of the steps. Ask questions such as:
  - "What would be your first step to get started?"
  - "Where do you think you should begin?"
  - "What is your starting point?"
- Help the Coachee identify potential obstacles they might encounter at the first step and list possible ways to resolve them. Ask questions such as:
  - "What obstacles do you think you might encounter here?"

- – "How will you overcome them?"
- – "What would be the next step?"
- Repeat this process on each subsequent step until there are no more steps.
- Test the implementation plan (the plan for all the steps) against the desired result to ensure that the action plan meets the S.M.A.R.T. model criteria. Ask questions such as: "If you were to implement these steps, will you achieve the outcome you desire?"
- Identify a realistic start date for the first step.

The Fifth Coaching Process Step	Coach's Job
Layout a plan to effectively implement the chosen alternative for achieving the desired outcome.	Assist the helpee in developing an action plan that anticipates potential obstacles and paves the way to the desired outcome. Help them envision what they will experience at each step. Help them envision their life and what they will feel when they get to their desired outcome. Encourage them to start immediately.

The following dialogue focuses on the fifth step of the R.E.A.C.H. coaching process: **How.**

How:

1. **Help Lily to Establish a plan to implement the chosen alternatives.**
2. **Help her anticipate potential obstacles and identify ways to address them.**
3. **Help her envision what life will be like when she achieves her desired outcome.**

Me: "Let's decide on the first step that you can do to get the ball rolling. What do you think is the most productive thing you could do right now?"

Lily: "I think it would be good to talk with my coach and explain things to him."

Me: "I think that is a super idea. What are you going to talk about?"

Lily: "I want to apologize for missing practices and tell him that I want to become a great volleyball player and that I need him to help me know how to do it."

Me: "I think that will almost make him cry. I'm not sure about the crying part, but I know he will appreciate you coming to him and apologizing and asking for his help. Do you anticipate any obstacles or rough patches in that conversation?"

Lily: "He may not believe me because he knows that my mom has been criticizing him to some other mothers."

Me: "How will you deal with that if he doesn't believe you?"

Lily: "I will admit that my mom and I were wrong and that we will apologize to the other parents if he wants us to."

Me: "Any other bumps in the road that you might expect?"

Lily: "He will watch me a lot closer to see if I am serious during practices."

Me: "I'm sure he will. It is an opportunity to show him that you are serious. Right?"

Lily: "Yes."

Me: "What would be your next step?"

Lily: "Setting up private lessons with Diana."

Me: "Do you anticipate any issues with Diana?"

Lily: "Only getting the time that fits both of our schedules."

Me: "How will you deal with that?'

Lily: "My mom and I will work it out with Diana."

Me: "What about making to all the practices?"

Lily: "I can make it to all the practices; it was my fault when I used to miss them."

Me: "Anticipate any problems?"

Lily: "If I get sick, I might miss some."

Me: "What will you do if that happens?"

Lily: "I'll call my coach and find a way to make up for the missed practice."

Me: "If you do everything we've talked about, do you think you can become a starting varsity player next year?"

Lily: "I do, but I will have to work really, really hard to make it happen."

Me: "Lily, your future is in your hands now. I would like you to ponder what your life will be like if you successfully do all of these things for a few moments. How do you think you would feel?"

Lily: "My life would be absolutely fabulous; my dreams would come true, and I would feel proud of myself."

Me: "Are you ready to pay the price to make it happen?"

Lily: "I am."

Me: "What time will you meet with your coach to take the first step?"

Lily: "I'll call him today and set up a time to meet with him before or after practice tomorrow."

Me: "Your call is the first step to demonstrating seriousness."

Lily: "I know. I will do it, I promise."

I would estimate that the total time to peel Lily's onion and to go through the coaching process took a little over two hours. We can coach many issues in much less time. Coaching employees to help them solve a work problem or perform a specific work duty can take 10 or 15 minutes, maybe less. If you take the time to coach them, they will feel empowered and feel that they are implementing their plan to fix a problem or do their job better.

Extreme situations can take a long period just to get through the first two stages of coaching. When people have no vision of anything being different than it already is, it takes time and patience to help them see a new and better future. Others have great difficulty seeing reality and their part in creating it. People who can never accept responsibility for their contribution to their current situation can't take responsibility for a future that they must make.

Parents, please practice coaching with your children. You will find that children love the attention that they receive from you. As you take the time to walk them through the coaching steps, you establish a model in their minds of how to help other people. Children have minds like sponges. What requires a lot of time and repeated practice for us to master, they can grasp and conquer in just a few coaching lessons. I have had parents tell me how difficult it is to communicate with their teenagers. I don't seem to have the same problem with their teenagers.

Maybe it is because when I talk with them, they are looking for an adult who will listen, hear, understand and validate what they want someone to understand and validate. I laugh when someone I have taught how to coach corrects me when I fail to do it as I have taught them to do it. Don't be surprised if your children start helping you coach them correctly.

We explored some problem-solving competencies that are valuable in helping others solve their problems. Here is a mini-reminder of four helpful problem-solving concepts.

Simple versus Complex Problems

We must align our problem-solving approach with the nature of the problem. Simple problems require a simple solution because they involve few or no emotions. Complex problems have two parts, an emotional component and a contextual component. We must deal with the emotional component before resolving the contextual element. We deal with the emotional component by labeling it correctly. After we resolve the emotional component, the complex problem becomes a simple problem that we can fix by providing an answer to the problem.

Peeling the Onion

People with complex problems are like an onion with many layers. The layers are defenses put in place to protect their emotionally naked core. The outer layers are messages about others, while the core is always about their emotionally defenseless self. To help them, we must hear, listen, understand, and validate each message sent to us so that we are trustworthy to gain access to their core. Using the skills of hearing, listening, understanding, and validating, we call Deep Listening. Once we reach their core, without judging them, evaluating them, or seeking new information, they will feel understood and desire our help.

Four of the characteristics of Deep Listening that ensure we are effectively peeling the onion are:

1. Keeping the **spotlight** on the person whose onion we are peeling
2. Staying **now**, in the present moment

3. Using their **reference** as the focus of the discussion
4. **Validating** each message sent

The primary and secondary needs of Helpees and Helpers

The primary and secondary of Helpees and Helpers don't align with one another naturally; the Helpee's primary need is to be heard, understood, and validated, while the primary need of Helpers is to solve the problem. If the Helper acts on the need to fix the problem before satisfying the primary need of the Helpee to be heard, understood, and validated, neither's needs will be fulfilled. The Helper must delay satisfaction of the need to problem-solve until the Helpee's primary needs are satisfied. Once we fill the Helpee's primary need, the Helpee will welcome the Helper's problem-solving. When the Helper solves the Helpee's problems, the Helpee will express appreciation for the Helper's help which will satisfy the Helper's secondary need to be appreciated for providing the solution to the problem.

The R.E.A.C.H. Coaching Process

When a person is ready to be helped, the best way to help them is to coach rather than provide suggestions or inherit their problem. Coaching offers a way to aid people in solving their problems. It makes them responsible and accountable for fixing the problem while still providing the necessary assistance. The R.E.A.C.H. coaching model is a five-step process. The first step is to help them define their desired **results**. The second step is to **evaluate** where they are currently, why they are there, and their part. The third step is determining the **alternatives** to resolve the problem. The fourth step is to **choose** the best option to reach their desired outcome. The fifth step is planning **how** to implement the choices they have made.

Summary of the Tensegrus Touchpoints Competencies

Emotional States Competencies

*   We can learn to manage and control our emotions.
*   We can learn to develop desired relationships through managing our emotional states.

- We can increase our emotional vocabulary to understand ourselves better and validate others.
- We can learn to hear, listen, understand, and validate others to connect with them deeply.
- We can peel the onion with people who need help to deal with deeply concealed core issues.
- We can apply the four characteristics of Deep Listening: spotlight, now, reference, and validation.

Operating Mode Competencies

- We can use our understanding of Parent mode, Child mode, and Adult mode to understand and manage ourselves and our interactions with others.
- We can learn to engage our Adult mode as our personal change agent for personal learning, growth, and development.
- We can analyze the transactions of others and understand what is happening.

Personal Boundary Competencies

- We can protect our personal boundaries and respect other people's boundaries, enabling us to develop synergistic relationships.
- We can protect ourselves from "Stompers."
- We can understand and help "Stompees."
- We can avoid and prevent Adversarial and Enemy relationships.
- We can provide feedback instead of criticism when our boundaries are infringed or violated.
- We can learn to say "no" when we have a more important "yes."
- We can stop others from playing games with us.
- We can shelter our time, body, mind, emotions, possessions, information, and self-identity.

Power Competencies

- We can combine Synergistic power with all Circumstantial powers to benefit ourselves and others.
- We can shield ourselves from others who combine Dominant power with Circumstantial powers to benefit themselves at our expense.

Values Competencies

- We can define our core moral and ethical values.
- We can be value-based people who use unconditional values as the basis for all our decisions and actions.
- We can operate far above the rule-based cultures that aim for compliance to minimum acceptable standards.

Commitment Level Competencies

- We can learn, grow, change, and be better than now.
- We can help others learn, grow, change, and be better than they are now.
- We can be "why" people, so people engage willingly and understand why they want to do something.
- We can be catalysts for people to operate from internalized commitment.
- We can take a stand against coerced obedience which motivates disobedience and rebellion.

Competencies to Help Others

- We can decipher between simple and complex problems and manage them accordingly.
- We know how to align our responses to Helpee's and Helper's primary and secondary needs.
- We can coach people to help them get from where they are to where they want to be using the five-step R.E.A.C.H coaching process.

50

The Whole Kit and Caboodle of Tensegrus

A relationship simply describes a type of interpersonal connection that exists between people. When we describe a relationship using the current status of the Relationship Touchpoints, we are describing a Tensegrus Relationship. We have explored five categories of Tensegrus Relationships: Synergistic, Associative, Command and Control, Mutually Destructive, and Indifferent. Within each category, we have described different types of relationships. For example, in the Synergistic category, we have Soulmate, Tribe Member, Friend, Partner, and Advocate relationships. Within the Associative category, we have Associate and Colleague relationships. The Command and Control category has Stompers and Stompees. The Mutually Destructive category has Adversaries and Enemies, and the Indifferent category has no relationships.

Each type of relationship can be profiled by the status of the Relationship Touchpoints. For example, look at a profile of Synergistic relationships in the model below.

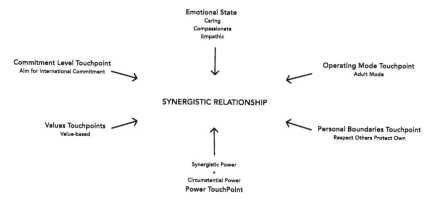

Notice how the status of each Relationship Touchpoint contributes to the Synergistic Relationship. Of particular note is that every touchpoint is connected to and works symbiotically with the other touchpoints. All the relationship touchpoints support one another – they work as a team.

If we were to change the nature of one touchpoint, it would change the nature of all the touchpoints. For example, if we changed from Adult mode to Parent mode in the Operating Mode Touchpoint, it would cause a change in all the other touchpoints; Personal Boundaries would change from respecting other's boundaries and protecting one's own to protecting one's own and disrespecting other's boundaries. The Power Touchpoint would shift from Synergistic Power to Dominance Power. The Values Touchpoint would move from value-based to rule-based. The Commitment Level Touchpoint would change to aiming for compliance rather than internalized commitment. And the Emotional State would shift from empathic and caring to fearful and distrusting. These changes would change the relationship from a Synergistic Relationship to a Command and Control Relationship.

The profile below exemplifies how changing the Touchpoint characteristics changes the relationship.

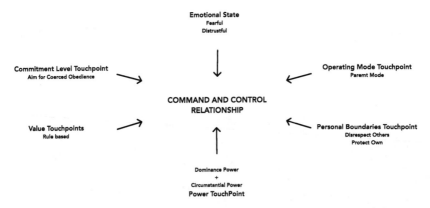

Every Relationship Touchpoint exists on a positive to negative continuum. The positive characteristics of a Touchpoint connect with and reinforce every other positive characteristic of the other Touchpoints. Likewise, the negative characteristic of a Touchpoint connects with and supports every other negative characteristic of a Touchpoint. This interconnectedness leads us to several conclusions.

One is that we can change a positive relationship to a negative relationship by moving from a positive to a negative characteristic of a Touchpoint. Take, for instance, changing from applying a positive characteristic of the Power Touchpoint (using Synergistic Power) to applying a negative characteristic of the Power Touchpoint (using Dominance Power). You can see that shift alone would change the relationship from a Synergistic relationship to a Command and Control relationship. We can do the opposite by changing from a negative characteristic of a Touchpoint to a positive characteristic.

A second conclusion is that each Touchpoint can be an entry point for a new relationship or an exit point from a current relationship. By changing one Touchpoint characteristic, we will positively or negatively impact all the other Touchpoints, depending on the kind of change we choose to make. The good thing to remember is that we can change unhealthy relationships to healthy ones by choosing to apply the positive characteristics of a Touchpoint and make it easier to capture the positive characteristics of all the other Touchpoints.

The third conclusion is that we can choose to have Synergistic Relationships by aligning ourselves with the positive characteristics of each Relationship Touchpoint.

One of the great things about Tensegrus: Touchpoints of Relationships concepts is that we can use our understanding of the types of relationships and how they are formed by the Relationship Touchpoints to diagnose our current relationships. By doing a "check-up from the neck up" and evaluating how we are applying each Relationship Touchpoint, we can see why we have the relationship we have (good or bad).

The model below is an example of a self-diagnosis by a person with a bitter relationship with his brother-in-law. After he listed the characteristics he was applying from each Relationship Touchpoint, it was easy to see that he had an enemy relationship and why it was so bitter between them.

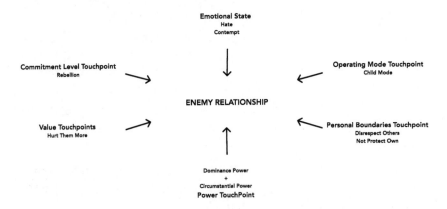

In this relationship, he did not want to change the relationship with his brother-in-law; he wanted to destroy him. They decided that the best thing was to put a lot of distance between them, both physically and emotionally.

The last model illustrates how we can use our knowledge of Tensegrus Relationships and Relationship Touchpoints as a tool to create Synergistic Relationships or to repair unhealthy ones. Please note that fixing unhealthy relationships happens by choosing and applying the healthy characteristics of each Relationship Touchpoint. In the model below, we suggest changing from an Enemy relationship to a Friend relationship by changing the Relationship Touchpoint characteristics. Please notice that it does not imply that you change the other person. You will change the relationship by changing how you operate. What the other party does is their choice.

But remember, it will be hard for them to treat you like an enemy when you treat them like a friend.

To apply the Relationship Touchpoints effectively to develop and sustain Synergistic relationships, we need to understand relationships and the Relationship Touchpoints. We also need to know how to use the competencies associated with the Relationship Touchpoints effectively. There is a lot of information about all of these subjects contained in this book. Please review the information when needed.

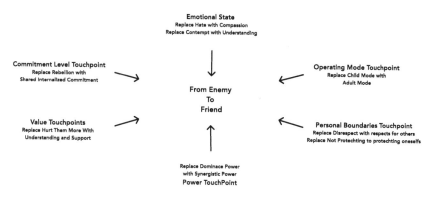

HOW TO CHANGE RELATIONSHIPS
FROM AN ENEMY TO A FRIEND

Emotional State
Replace Hate with Compassion
Replace Contempt with Understanding

Commitment Level Touchpoint
Replace Rebellion with
Shared Internalized Commitment

Operating Mode Touchpoint
Replace Child Mode with
Adult Mode

From Enemy
To
Friend

Value Touchpoints
Replace Hurt Them More With
Understanding and Support

Personal Boundaries Touchpoint
Replace Disrespect with respects for others
Replace Not Protechting to protechting oneselfs

Replace Dominace Power
with Synergistic Power
Power TouchPoint

A little personal application

We add new relationships to our lives as we live and interact with people. Sometimes these quickly become Synergistic relationships; other times, we struggle to get there. I have new associations with parents and players this year due to coaching volleyball again. Some of the relationships haven't become as Synergistic as I had hoped. These new associations allow me to apply the concepts we have been sharing with you and see if I can change a new and important relationship that I need to change. The relationship is with a young lady on our 15-year-old club volleyball team. Nicki (not her real name) is a respectful girl, laid back, but not shy. She is intelligent, has friends, but is not part of the popular group at school. She wants to play on her high school volleyball team and has joined our club to help her prepare to play there.

She is not a skillful volleyball player. She is somewhat athletic, but her volleyball skills don't match her athletic ability. She has three principal weaknesses in her game: First, her passing is poor. She is inconsistent and frequently shanks balls when receiving serves or passing to the setter. Her passing angles are misaligned and set up too late. Second, her four-step approach to the net and arm swing when attacking the ball are screwy. She takes three steps, stops, and jumps while bringing her heels to her butt. Her arm swing is low and looks like a rubber spatula slapping at the ball. Third, she doesn't remember where she is supposed to be on rotational changes, offensively or defensively.

The relationship with Nicki is important; her parents are paying me to coach her and help her play volleyball well. I am not satisfied with how our relationship is progressing. I am pretty sure that she isn't either. It's late to do this, but it is time for me to do a "check-up from the neck up" and make an honest evaluation of my contribution to this disappointing connection. I will assess myself against each Relationship Touchpoint and use the results to determine the Tensegrus Relationship I am creating with Nicki. I will see what changes I need to make to have a Synergistic Relationship with her. I have to be honest with myself, or it will do no good to go through the process; I'll end up justifying myself by blaming her. Here goes my self-assessment of each Relationship Touchpoint.

My Emotional State Touchpoint with Nicki is disappointment and frustration.

My Operating Mode Touchpoint is Critical Parent.

My Personal Boundary Touchpoint is to manage the situation to protect my boundaries at the expense of hers.

My Power Touchpoint has two: I have position power, being the coach. I have knowledge power as I know volleyball much better than she does. Unfortunately, I am applying "Big Boss Power" and "Manipulator Power" to improve her. I am trying to use dominance power to change her, and it isn't working.

My Value Touchpoint is being a "Do" coach; I operate from my volleyball "should's" and "ought to's" rules. I am judging her on what she does ineffectively. I am focused on where I want her to be rather than where she is.

My Commitment Level Touchpoint is aiming for compliance to my expectations and advice.

The result of how I am applying the Relationship Touchpoints leads me to accept that I am playing the part of a **Stomper** or maybe an **Adversary** in this Relationship. It is sobering to take responsibility for what I

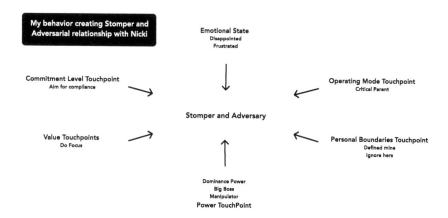

am doing. It would be much easier to blame her for the Emotional State of our relationship. I need to own this relationship. It is not an acceptable relationship for me; I want to have Synergistic Relationships with Nicki that include being Partners and Team Members. I need to change my behavior within each Relationship Touchpoint for that to happen. Here is what I need to change in each Touchpoint.

The Emotional State needs to be understanding and empathic rather than disappointment and frustration.

The Operating Mode needs to be a Nurturing Parent rather than a Critical Parent.

The Personal Boundaries behavior needs to respect her boundaries rather than defend mine.

The Power used needs to be Synergistic Power, specifically, Lifter Power and Radiant Power, rather than "Big Boss" and "Manipulator Power."

The Values need to focus on "Be" values rather than "Do" skill rules.

The Commitment Level behavior needs to focus on internalized commitment rather than compliance.

There are Touchpoint changes that I need to make to change our relationship. I need to apply the positive characteristics with each

Relationship Touchpoint. Here are the changes I have decided to make.

With the Emotional State Touchpoint, I need to manage my feelings. I can do that because I now recognize the unwelcome guests I have let move in on me. My feelings are an extension of me, not me as an extension of my feelings. I won't allow myself to succumb to making a Fundamental Attribution Error and aligning my perception of reality to emotions spawned from unfulfilled expectations.

With the Operating Mode Touchpoint, I need to engage my adult mode reasoning. I need to understand what is happening and why. I will figure that out. Then I will work with her to help her become the kind of volleyball player she wants to be.

With the Personal Boundaries Touchpoint, I need to hear, listen, understand, and validate her perspectives, so she feels understood and supported in her self-improvement journey rather than feeling judged. My goal here is to help her feel energized and motivated rather than powerless and discouraged.

With the Power Touchpoint, I need to use Lifter Power to understand her, support her, and coach her. I need to use Radiant Power to bathe her in knowledge in a way that she explores and discovers what she needs to know and to do to play as she hopes to play.

With the Values Touchpoint, I need to stay focused on who she is rather than what she does poorly.

With the Commitment Level Touchpoint, I need to help her climb up the commitment level spectrum by coaching in a way that inspires her to aim for effective volleyball skills willingly, so the results validate her efforts. Then use those validated results to become converted to skillful playing so that she becomes internally committed to the game of volleyball.

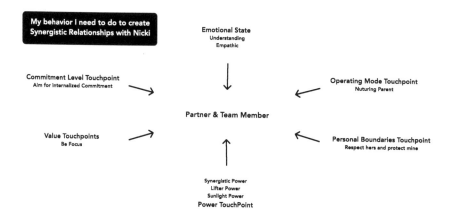

I don't know if I will successfully change my relationship with Nicki. Having gone through this "check-up from the neck up,"[58] I have a much better chance of making it happen. I take responsibility for the current relationship. I have changed my perspective. I now see our relationship from an adult mode perspective rather than from parent and child modes. I will operate in adult mode, and I'll bet Nicki will appreciate the difference.

Our Sendoff Message

We trust that you have found some new and helpful information about relationships and the Touchpoints that define them. When we experience something new, we are different after that experience than before. Once we see or experience something new, we are forever somehow changed. We hope you have experienced something new that will positively change your life and help you have quality, important relationships that will provide you with a high-quality life.

---

58 Morris Massey, "What You Are Is What You Were When" (YouTube, Enterprise Media Video, 2014).

About the Authors

V. Wayne Carlson

I'm not certain that anything in this book is completely an original thought, considering the unimageable combined output of everyone that has contributed to the behavioral sciences and from whom I have learned so much. However, this book is the culmination of a lifetime of study, learning, observation, and experience. Over the years, through interactions as a business executive, consultant, adjunct professor, church leader, father, entrepreneur, spouse, life-time student, consumer, etc., I have observed a lot and have formed many opinions and drawn many conclusions. This book is a distillation of many of those opinions and conclusions that I have formed specifically about relationships. My opinions may be no better than anyone else's, but I stand by them and think that I can show them to be reasonable, defendable, and useful.

As long as I can remember, I've been a people observer. With observation, there has always been a deep-rooted question of "Why?" This book is my answer to some of the why's about people's behavior within the context of relationships and interpersonal connections.

I started my career as a salesman for McNeil Pharmaceutical, a division of Johnson & Johnson. I worked for J&J companies for 18 years, the final ten years as a Vice President of Human Resources and Organizational Development for Janssen Pharmaceutica. I then worked at a different corporation called Amersham for five years, where I was VP of Administration and Organizational Development for four USA divisions and General Manager of the Diagnostic Division. Kodak purchased the Diagnostic Division and shortly thereafter offered me the opportunity to head up the newly combined Kodak Diagnostic Division as an outside consultant. Apparently, I wasn't part of the sale and Amersham told Kodak that they had other plans for me at Amersham Corporate. As a result, Kodak offered to set me up as an independent consulting firm to secure my services to manage that part of their business. As it turned out, Amersham offered me the opportunity to be a board member and the corporate director of Human Resources for the corporation, provided that we establish permanent residence in England. Ultimately, I declined, not because we would have to live in England (we love England!), but because the job itself was not my cup of tea. A few months later, Amersham (having learned that Kodak had offered me an opportunity to start my own consulting business) actually set me up in my own consulting business and licensed my consulting services for five years, provided I would give them at least 50% of my time. I consulted for Amersham for eight years, until they sold the USA business to Pharmacia.

A few years later, I teamed up with an old college colleague, Dale Karren, where he had his own consulting firm based in Utah. We incorporated a consulting business called Petrous. It turned out to be a perfect match; he provided expertise in developing operational strategy and I helped with the implementation, specifically in leadership, performance, and relationship management. He has been an extraordinary source of life learnings and created countless opportunities to apply the principles contained in this book in the companies with whom we consulted.

We lived near Chicago for ten years before returning to Utah. For the last six years of those years, I agreed to be an adjunct professor at the Lake Forest Graduate School of Management. Predictably I taught courses in performance, leadership, and relationship management. During those six years, I received four Teaching Excellence awards and the last year was chosen by the students as the Outstanding Professor (Professor of the Year). My relationship course was reportedly the most sought-after course in the MBA program. Because of student desires to attend my class, I always accepted, at least, double the number of students attending a normal graduate class. Even so, there was a waiting list of students seeking to participate in the course. I mention that because the information in the relationship class was reported, by the students, to be some of the most useful information that they would get in their graduate studies. As I mentioned in the Introduction, the graduate students often remarked that the content of my course was just common sense and they were frustrated that this "common sense" hadn't been shared with them in grade school, junior high school, high school, or undergraduate college. Why was their first in-depth exposure to common sense relationship concepts and skills delayed until graduate school? I think it is still a very good question and needs to be answered by people who can do something about it.

After consulting, I worked for Maverik as the Exccutive Director of Organizational Development and Training, which I did for seven years, until the owner of Flying J purchased Maverik. I then retired and have been working with youth, specifically as a volleyball coach and officiator since 2012.

Church has always been important to me and I have served in multiple positions, on a local and regional level. Church positions have provided me with opportunities for thousands of hours to counsel with individuals and families.

During my last year of college, I developed a great interest in clinical and child psychology. From the psychological masters, I took the parts I agreed with, and thought that I understood; the rest I discarded. Ultimately, I became a great fan of Reality Therapy, Rogerian Therapy, Logotherapy, and Transactional Analysis. I love studying all the behavioral sciences. Yet, I could never narrow my focus to just one specialty area. If I could live two hundred years, I would specialize in all areas of the behavioral sciences. You could call me a behavioral science geek; I do. Also, I am addicted to studying history because history is a linear laboratory of the behavioral sciences. History is a Petri dish of life. We can take any point in time and see how people got there by tracing the sequence of events prior to that time. History provides a perspective of people at their best and worst. And, history provides the perfect vehicle for analysis and insight about "why." Aside from the flow of circumstances, good historical writers offer us insight into who the key players were, what they did, and why they did what they did. History provides a never-ending opportunity to observe, study, and analyze people, through their circumstances, decisions, behaviors, relationships, and interpersonal connections.

My relationship and interpersonal connection concepts have been instilled within me from lifetime study and from association with students, executives, academics, friends, family, and life contacts. I have learned much from those I have helped and from those who have helped me. The concepts presented in this book are distilled from my conclusions of the information I have gleaned from my unstructured study of the behavioral sciences – principally: psychology, sociology, adult learning, counseling, etc. To me, at some point all behavioral sciences intertwine and become one.

When the disciplines connect and intertwine, does it really matter what label it carries? What really matters is how the information becomes useful tools for developing beautiful relationships and healthy interpersonal connections. Whoever planted the ideas in my mind and heart to observe and validate these concepts, I am forever grateful. If I have made errors or misrepresentations of other people's ideas, I apologize for that; it is just my interpretation of their concepts insofar as they fit into our message. If you disagree with what is written here, or think that I'm really off base, I respect your opinion; I am responsible for the content, right or wrong, but I believe in the messages herein contained. I am not a licensed counselor or therapist, but I do believe in and support the good ones. Please, do not accept my opinion as absolute truth. If you can take my stuff apart and disprove it, or improve it, please do so. I hope you will share your thoughts with me and others.

If it were not for my talented and brilliant son Matt, this book wouldn't have happened. Working month after month with him has been a lifetime highpoint which means more to me than I can express. Oh, that you could see his majesty as I do.

Matthew James Carlson

Matthew J Carlson has a BS in Finance from the University of Utah and an MBA with an emphasis on Entrepreneurship from Westminster College in Salt Lake City, UT. He is currently the CEO of Club V Sports, Inc which is one of the largest youth volleyball & basketball organizations in the United States. He co-founded Club V with his brother, Reed Carlson. Club V is currently considered one of the top 50 volleyball organizations in the US. Matthew is obsessed with learning, specifically on psychology and behavioral sciences. He has a wife, to whom he has been married 16 years, and a beautiful daughter.

Made in the USA
Middletown, DE
13 September 2022

10327835R10426